THE CRUSADES
ISLAMIC PERSPECTIVES

Carole Hillenbrand

EDINBURGH
University Press

© Carole Hillenbrand, 1999

Edinburgh University Press Ltd.
22 George Square, Edinburgh

Typeset in Trump Mediaeval
by Pioneer Associates, Perthshire, and
printed and bound in Great Britain by
The Bath Press

A CIP record for this book is available from
the British Library

ISBN 0 7486 0905 9 (hardback)
ISBN 0 7486 0630 0 (paperback)

To Margaret and Ruth

Contents

vii

Expanded Contents List

CHAPTER 3: *Jihad* in the Period 493–569/1100–1174

CHAPTER 4: *Jihad* in the Period from the Death of Nur al-Din until the Fall of Acre (569–690/1174–1291)

**CHAPTER 5: How the Muslims Saw the Franks: Ethnic and
               Religious Stereotypes**

CHAPTER 6: Aspects of Life in the Levant in the Crusading Period

CHAPTER 7: Armies, Arms, Armour and Fortifications

CHAPTER 8: The Conduct of War

CHAPTER 9: Epilogue: The Heritage of the Crusades

List of Plates

Half tone Plates

List of Figures

Preface

THIS BOOK on the Crusades is a timely and welcome addition to a burgeoning modern scholarship on the subject in the West. Its publication coincides with the 900th anniversary of the occupation of Jerusalem by the Crusading armies, but it is not written to celebrate this event or to lend support to the ideology which brought it about. On the contrary, the author has as her primary aim the scholarly objective of balancing the skewed picture of the Crusades in Western scholarship. She does so by interrogating the Arabic sources on the subject in a way which throws fresh light on a formative and, for the most part, antagonistic period in the history of Arabo-Islamic and Euro-Christian relations.

Methodologically, this is a tricky task to perform because of the double 'otherness' it invokes. Here we have a scholar who, in post-colonial terms, is attempting to write about a subject not from her position of perceived 'otherness' in relation to the Arabo-Islamic tradition, but from that of the neglected 'otherness' of this tradition as defined by Western discourses on the subject. Her task is made all the more tricky by the symbolic power of the Crusades in the contemporary Arab and Muslim worlds as a boundless source of meanings which straddle history, politics, culture, religious beliefs and a lot more. Within the modern currents which permeate the life of the contemporary Arab world in particular, the Crusades are one of the most important and live undercurrents, not least because they involve momentous happenings which evoke the painful realities and tortured hopes of a present deeply steeped in the pastness of its past.

A project of this nature demands many skills, in addition to the usual ones of sound methodological training and the ability to generalise in an empirically valid manner across a diverse terrain of extremely varied and, sometimes, recalcitrant data. To begin with, this project demands discerning powers in critical self-awareness, on both the intellectual and personal level, to ensure that its scholarly integrity emerges intact. By subjectivising or problematising the author, this project further demands a nuanced and deliberate use of language to convey the subtle and slippery meanings of events, practices and competing conceptualisations in a way which ensures that the narrative remains true to its original aim. A project of this kind also demands an extensive and linguistically competent reading of varied source materials in Arabic, hardly any of which is specifically dedicated to the subject *per se*. To make things even more difficult, the author aims her book at a wide readership consisting of general readers, students and specialists who would be approaching it with mixed agendas of wanting to find out, learn, evaluate or, even, criticise.

Carole Hillenbrand's book meets all these challenges. It is scholarly without being stuffy, and accessible without being patronising. It articulates issues of immense importance to the historian who is less interested in chronology – although there is more than enough of that between its two covers – than the societal institutions which animate the progress of history. It covers themes of interest to the student of theology, and to those who wish to delve into the nature of warfare or to examine how the past so clearly and decisively informs the present. It deals with stereotypes and counter-stereotypes. And it does so in a lively style, permeated by the authoritative voice of the author as a self-aware interpreter who, intentionally, paints with a broad brush to define the main parameters of her subject. The fact that this author is a very close friend and a highly respected colleague makes the task of recommending this book to the reader a great pleasure and a privilege.

Yasir Suleiman
Edinburgh, 1 January 1999

Acknowledgements

I HAVE RECEIVED much help in the writing of this book from various institutions and friends. In particular, I am extremely grateful to the British Academy for granting me a Readership during which I was able to conduct some of the research for this book. I should also like to give my wholehearted thanks to the University of Edinburgh, Faculty of Arts, for their additional financial support during my research leave and for contributing to the costs of producing this book. I am also indebted to the Carnegie Trust for the Universities of Scotland for enabling me to visit Crusader sites in Syria.

Many friends and colleagues have given advice, help and encouragement – Nasra Affara, Dionysius Agius, James Allan, Michael Angold, Julia Ashtiany-Bray, Sylvia Auld, Edmund Bosworth, Michael Broome, Eileen Broughton, Alistair Duncan, Anne-Marie Eddé, Teresa Fitzherbert, Barry Flood, Tariq al-Janabi, David Kerr, Remke Kruk, Paul Lalor, Nancy Lambton, David McDowall, Bernadette Martel-Thoumian, John Mattock, Julie Meisami, Françoise Micheau, May Mi'marbashi, Ibrahim Muhawi, Ian Netton, David Nicolle, Andrew Petersen, Jonathan Phillips, Louis Pouzet, Denys Pringle, John Richardson, Lutz Richter-Bernburg, Joe Rock, Michael Rogers, Abdallah al-Sayed, Lesley Scobie, Avinoam Shalem, Jacqueline Sublet, and Urbain Vermeulen. I am very grateful to them all.

I should like to make special mention of 'Adil Jader who managed, seemingly against all odds, to obtain for me a photocopy of al-Sulami's manuscript, just before the completion of this book. I also wish to thank Donald Richards for his enthusiastic and erudite teaching on the Crusades many years ago, which first aroused my interest in this subject.

I also owe a special debt of gratitude to my good friend and esteemed colleague Yasir Suleiman, Professor of Arabic at the University of Edinburgh, for writing the preface to this book. His encouragement and support have been absolutely invaluable in recent years.

Special thanks go to Campbell Purton for providing the index, Jane Gough for typing the various drafts of this book, always with skill, cheerfulness, enthusiasm and interest, and Rita Winter for her meticulous work and for her exemplary tact and patience in the long task of copy-editing. I wish also to express my gratitude to all the staff of Edinburgh University Press who have shown such interest in this work – and in particular to Archie Turnbull (who persuaded me to write the book in the first place), Vivian Bone, Jane Feore (who made me finish it), Timothy Wright, Jackie Jones, Nicola Carr, Richard Allen, James Dale, and Ian Davidson who guided it towards publication. I should like to express my appreciation and admiration for the work of Lesley Parker and Janet Dunn, who brought flair and ingenuity to the challenging task of designing this book. I count myself fortunate to have worked with them.

I should also like to thank all those who executed the drawings for this book: Hamish Auld, Nicola Burns, Jenny Capon, Anne Cunningham, Victoria Lamb and Jessica Wallwork.

ACKNOWLEDGEMENTS

Lastly, I would like to thank my daughters Margaret and Ruth for their loving interest and support. My debt to my husband, Robert, cannot be adequately expressed in words. More photographs in this book come from him than from any other source except the Creswell archive. He has read all the drafts of this book, giving many helpful criticisms and suggestions. He has also taught me the value of looking closely at art-historical material and from his own scholarly knowledge of Islamic art and architecture he has laboriously chosen or guided me in choosing all the illustrations for this book. Above all, he has never failed to give me much-needed support and encouragement.

Note on Transliteration and Translations

In view of the length and costs of this book, a decision was made to dispense with any system of transliteration for the Arabic, Persian and Turkish names and terms used in the main body of the text. However, the properly transliterated forms of such words will be found in the index. Throughout the book the words Ibn and b. are used interchangeably.

The Arabic translations in this book are mine, except when otherwise indicated in the notes. When good translations already exist in other languages, I have retranslated them into English.

Note on the Illustrations

The decision to illustrate this book lavishly was taken for several reasons. First, and most important, was the desire to set the text within a visual context that would invoke the medieval Levant. Hence the many illustrations that depict everyday objects in common use in Muslim society, from coins to clothing, or show Muslims enjoying themselves in a variety of leisure pursuits, or reflect the many faces of war. Special care has been taken to evoke the world of the court, its ceremonies and hierarchies, and conversely the many ways in which the religion of Islam found visual expression: mosques, *madrasa*s, the tombs of saints and warriors for the faith, embellished with their resounding titles, and even the very pulpits from which *jihad* was preached. Where possible the photographic plates depict the Levant as it was before the full onset of the modern age – for example, the mosques of Hims and Hama are shown as they were before their respective rebuilding and destruction.

Second, the illustrations are intended to fill the multiple gaps left by the medieval Islamic sources. The authors of those sources were not writing for a modern audience and they saw no reason to comment on what to them was obvious or everyday. Very few of them had a visual sense and they rarely mention the visual arts. The illustrations, then, function as a kind of sub-text so as to make good this deficiency and to tell a somewhat different story. Very occasionally material from before or after the eleventh to fourteenth centuries is used, for example in Chapter 9, which in any case deals with the aftermath of the Crusades.

Third, these visual arts are, by and large, devoid of the bias which almost inevitably afflicts those who write about the past from the viewpoint of the present. Chronicles are often later and thus flawed interpretations of what happened – and sometimes happened long ago. The works of art of the eleventh to fourteenth centuries which are depicted here, however, are for the most part unselfconsciously contemporary. They rarely have an axe to grind. Accordingly they can shed unexpected sidelights on historical events, whether they tell us how a castle was built, what weapons a warrior carried or how a ruler sat in state and enjoyed himself. Occasionally, too, as in the statue of Saladin erected in 1992, they tell us something about modern Muslim attitudes to this particular past.

These illustrations, then, are intended to flesh out the sometimes over-terse or rhetorical accounts by the Muslim historians of the Wars of the Cross, and to show in detail how the other half lived. True to the focus of this book, a deliberate decision was taken to exclude all Crusader illustrative material, apart from a few Crusader artefacts that have been Islamised – such as coins, or elements of architecture reused in an Islamic context. Now and again, too, artefacts made by Oriental Christians feature among the illustrations; these Christians, after all, were not an intrusive presence like the Franks but had been a permanent feature of local society since the Muslim invasions. Perhaps the most notable feature of these illustrations is the absence of Muslim depictions of the Franks (with the possible exception of colour plate 13), whereas

Frankish representations of Muslims are frequently encountered. Perhaps the dearth of twelfth-century book painting has something to do with this; but the fact remains that the Crusaders made no visual impact on any Islamic figural art that survives from the medieval period. This is indeed food for thought.

Some account of the *raison d'être* of the placing of the illustrative material in this book may be helpful. Some illustrations are intended to complement a specific passage in the text. These are identified by cross-references within the text itself. Others are more generally relevant to the material in a given sub-section. These are listed immediately after the relevant sub-heading, but there will be no further reference to them in the text. Yet others are intended to function in a still more general fashion, as an evocation of medieval Islamic society in the Middle East. These are scattered throughout the book. All illustrations can be tracked down by the list of captions on pages xv–xxxv.

Glossary of Islamic Terms

Abu: father (of), used in many Muslim names in combination with the name of the first-born son.

amir: commander, prince.

atabeg: guardian of a prince; often a governor.

b.:   son of (Arabic *ibn*, *bin*).

caliph: the name given to leaders of the Muslim community (from Arabic *khalifa*, 'successor' – to Muhammad).

caravansarai: lodging place for travellers, merchants and their goods; often fortified and situated on a trade route.

dhimma: a covenant made between the Islamic state and the adherents of other revealed religions living under Islamic rule. The *dhimma* gives them protection on condition that they pay the *jizya*.

dhimmi: a member of a protected religious community.

dinar: gold coin.

dirham: silver coin (later copper).

diwan: government office or ministry; royal reception chamber; collection of poems.

fals: copper coin.

fatwa: a ruling or opinion based on Islamic law delivered by a qualified legal scholar.

ghazi: warrior for the faith.

hadith: collective body of traditions relating to Muhammad and his Companions; they constitute one of the sources of guidance for Muslims.

hajj: the pilgrimage to Mecca.

hammam: steam baths; bathing establishment for the public.

haram: that which is forbidden or sacrosanct. This term applies especially in this book to the area of the Islamic sanctuaries in Jerusalem.

hijra (hegira): Muhammad's emigration from Mecca to Medina in 622, the date which marks the beginning of the Muslim calendar.

ibn: *see* b.

imam: a prayer leader; the sovereign head of the Islamic community; the spiritual leader of the Shi'ites.

Islam: submitting oneself to the will of Allah.

Isma'ilis or   members of the Shi'ite group who believe that the legitimate succession
Seveners: of *imam*s includes the seventh *imam* Isma'il, son of the *imam* Ja'far al-Sadiq.

jami':   the great mosque in which the communal Friday prayer takes place and the Friday sermon is preached.

jihad: holy war against unbelievers.

jizya: the poll-tax paid by the protected religious groups within the Islamic state, cf. *dhimma*.

khan: lodging place for travellers and merchants; lord, prince.

khassakiyya: personal military entourage of a sultan.

khutba: bidding prayer or sermon delivered in the mosque at midday prayers on Fridays.

madhhab: school of law.

madrasa: an institution for the study of law and other Islamic sciences.

Maghrib: the Muslim world in North Africa west of and including Tunisia.

maqsura: a special section of the mosque reserved for the ruler.

maristan: hospital.

maslaha: the principle of what is beneficial to the common good.

maydan: open public square or plaza, central ceremonial space.

mamluk: slave (often also used of manumitted slave).

mihrab: arched niche, usually concave but sometimes flat, indicating the direction of Mecca (the *qibla*) and thus of prayer.

mina'i: pottery in which colours are applied both under and over the glaze.

minaret: the tower of a mosque from which the faithful are called to prayer.

minbar: stepped pulpit in a mosque, used for the pronouncement of the *khutba*.

mi'raj: the ascent of the Prophet Muhammad into heaven.

mosque: a place where Muslims worship.

mujahid: one who strives in the path of God; one who fights *jihad*.

muqarnas: honeycomb or stalactite vaulting made up of individual cells or small arches.

Muslim: a person who follows the religion of Islam.

nafs: soul.

qadi: a judge, usually in matters of civil law.

qasr: castle or palace; fort.

qibla: direction of prayer, that is to the Ka'ba in Mecca.

qubba: dome.

Qur'an: God's Word revealed to the Prophet Muhammad.

ratl: a unit of weight corresponding in Syria to c. 3.202 kilos.

ribat: a fortified Muslim monastery or frontier post.

sahn: interior court, usually of a mosque.

Seveners: see Isma'ilis.

shahid: a martyr in the path of God.

Shari'a: Islamic law.

Shi'a: (hence Shi'ite) generic term for a series of 'sects' not regarded as part of orthodox Islam; they all recognise 'Ali (cousin and son-in-law of the Prophet) as the first legitimate caliph.

Sufi: Islamic mystic.

sultan: ruler, king.

Sunni: orthodox Muslim.

sura: chapter of the Qur'an.

tiraz: inscribed fabrics made in a state workshop.

'ulama': those who possess knowledge, scholars of Islamic theology and law; the learned class.

umma: the Islamic community.

vizier: minister.

Glossary of Arabic Military Terms

amir:	army commander.
'amud:	mace, club.
'arrada:	ballista, that is a type of mangonel used for throwing stones over long distances.
'ayn:	spy.
bahriyya:	navy.
burj:	siege tower.
dabbaba:	wooden tower used in siege warfare for the protection of soldiers.
dar al-sina'a:	arsenal.
daraqa:	wooden shield, covered with leather.
dir':	coat of mail.
faris:	horseman, cavalryman.
farr:	withdraw or run.
ghazw:	raid.
hasak:	caltrop.
hisar:	siege.
hisn:	fortress.
jawshan:	coat of mail, protecting the front part of the warrior's body only.
kabsh:	ram.
kamin:	ambush.
karr:	attack or hit, return to attack.
khanjar:	dagger.
khayl:	cavalry.
liwa':	banner.
manjaniq:	mangonel.
maymana:	the right flank of the army.
maysara:	the left flank of the army.
mighfar:	a helmet covering the head and the whole of the face except the eyes.
mutatawwi'a:	volunteers.
naft:	Greek fire.
naqb:	mine.
qalb:	the centre column of the army.
qaws:	bow.
raya:	flag, standard.
sabigha:	a long-sleeved coat of mail.
sayf:	sword.
tabar:	axe.
tariqa:	cuirass.
turs:	shield.

Chronological List of Major Medieval Islamic Authors Mentioned in the Text

Al-Sulami (d. early 6th/12th century)
Al-'Azimi (d. c. 555/1160)
Ibn al-Qalanisi (d. 555/1160)
Usama b. Munqidh (d. 584/1188)
Al-Qadi al-Fadil (d. 596/1200)
Ibn al-Jawzi (d. 597/1200)
'Imad al-Din al-Isfahani (d. 597/1201)
Ibn Jubayr (d. 614/1217)
Ibn Zafir (d. 613/1216 or 623/1226)
Ibn Abi Tayyi' (d. 630/1233)
Ibn al-Athir (d. 630/1233)
Baha' al-Din Ibn Shaddad (d. 632/1234)
Sibt b. al-Jawzi (d. 654/1257)
Ibn al-'Adim (d. 660/1262)
Abu Shama (d. 665/1267)
Ibn Muyassar (d. 677/1278)
Ibn Khallikan (d. 681/1282)
'Izz al-Din Ibn Shaddad (d. 684/1285)
Ibn 'Abd al-Zahir (d. 692/1292)
Ibn Wasil (d. 697/1298)
Al-Yunini (d. 726/1326)
Ibn Taymiyya (d. 728/1328)
Al-Nuwayri (d. 732/1332)
Shafi' b. 'Ali (d. 750/1349)
Ibn al-Furat (d. 807/1405)
Ibn Khaldun (d. 808/1406)
Al-Qalqashandi (d. 821/1418)
Al-Maqrizi (d. 845/1441)
Ibn Taghribirdi (d. 874/1470)

Chronological Table of Important Events until the Fall of Acre in 690/1291

1189–92 The Third Crusade
1190 (10 June) Drowning of the Emperor Frederick I in Cilicia
1191 (12 July) Richard I of England and Philip II of France received capitulation of Acre
(7 Sept.) Battle of Arsuf
1192 (2 Sept.) Treaty of Jaffa
1193 Death of Saladin
1198 (Aug.) Pope Innocent III proclaimed the Fourth Crusade
1202–4 The Fourth Crusade
1204 (12–15 Apr.) Constantinople sacked by the Franks
1213 (Apr) Pope Innocent III proclaimed the Fifth Crusade
1217–29 The Fifth Crusade
1218 (27 May–5 Nov. 1219) Siege of Damietta
1221 (30 Aug.) Franks in Egypt defeated at al-Mansura
1228–9 Crusade of the Emperor Frederick II of Sicily (last part of the Fifth Crusade)
1229 (18 Feb.) Jerusalem restored to Franks by treaty with the Ayyubids
1244 (11 July–23 Aug.) Khwarazmians sacked Jerusalem
(17 Oct.) Battle of La Forbie
1250 (8 Feb.) Franks in Egypt defeated at al-Mansura
1250–4 St Louis in the Holy Land
1258 (19 Feb.) Mongols sacked Baghdad and killed the 'Abbasid caliph
1260 (3 Sept.) Battle of 'Ayn Jalut – Mamluks defeated depleted Mongol army
(23 Oct.) Baybars became sultan of Egypt
1268 (18 May) Baybars took Jaffa, Belfort and Antioch
1270 Death of St Louis
1271 Baybars took Krak des Chevaliers and Montfort
1277 Death of Baybars
1289 (26 Apr.) Qalawun took Tripoli
1291 (18 May) Mamluks under al-Ashraf Khalil took Acre
(July) Sidon and Beirut fell to Mamluks

Dynastic Tables

The Fatimids (Egypt and Syria)

365/975	Al-'Aziz
386/996	Al-Hakim
411/1021	Al-Zahir
427/1036	Al-Mustansir
487/1094	Al-Musta'li
495/1101	Al-Amir
525/1131	Al-Hafiz
544/1149	Al-Zafir
549/1154	Al-Fa'iz
555–67/1160–71	Al-'Adid

The Seljuqs

*Great Seljuqs, 431–590/1040–1194
(Iraq and Persia)*

431/1040	Tughril
455/1063	Alp Arslan
465/1072	Malikshah
485/1092	Mahmud
487/1094	Barkyaruq
498/1105	Muhammad
511–22/1118–57	Sanjar (ruler in eastern Persia)
after 511/1118	supreme Sultan of the Seljuq family

The Seljuqs in Iraq and western Persia only

511/1118	Mahmud
525/1131	Da'ud
526/1132	Tughril II
529/1134	Mas'ud
547/1152	Malik-Shah III
548/1153	Muhammad II
555/1160	Sulayman Shah
556/1161	Arslan
571–90/1176–94	Tughril III

The Seljuqs in Syria

471/1078	Tutush
488–507/1095–1113	Ridwan (in Aleppo)
488–97/1095–1104	Duqaq (in Damascus)

The Zengids (Jazira and Syria)

521/1127	Zengi
541/1146	Nur al-Din

(Some branches of the dynasty lasted until the middle of the thirteenth century)

The Ayyubids (Egypt, Syria, Diyarbakr, Yemen)

The Ayyubids in Egypt

564/1169	al-Malik al-Nasir I Salah al-Din (Saladin)
589/1193	al-Malik al-'Aziz 'Imad al-Din
595/1198	al-Malik al-Mansur Nasir al-Din
596/1200	al-Malik al-'Adil I Sayf al-Din
615/1218	al-Malik al-Kamil I Nasir al-Din
635/1238	al-Malik al-'Adil II Sayf al-Din
637/1240	al-Malik al-Salih Najm al-Din Ayyub
647/1249	al-Malik al-Mu'azzam Turan-Shah
648–50/1250–2	al-Malik al-Ashraf II Muzaffar al-Din

The Ayyubids in Damascus

582/1186	al-Malik al-Afdal Nur al-Din ʿAli
592/1196	al-Malik al-ʿAdil I Sayf al-Din
615/1218	al-Malik al-Muʿazzam Sharaf al-Din
624/1227	al-Malik al-Nasir Salah al-Din Daʾud
626/1229	al-Malik al-Ashraf I Muzaffar al-Din
634/1237	al-Malik al-Salih ʿImad al-Din (*first reign*)
635/1238	al-Malik al-Kamil I Nasir al-Din
636/1239	al-Malik al-Salih Najm al-Din Ayyub (*first reign*)
637/1239	al-Malik al-Salih ʿImad al-Din (*second reign*)
643/1245	al-Malik al-Salih Najm al-Din Ayyub (*second reign*)
647/1249	al-Malik al-Muʿazzam Turan-Shah (with Egypt)
648–58/1250–60	al-Malik al-Nasir II Salah al-Din

The Mamluks, 648–922/1250–1517 (Egypt and Syria) – up to the fall of Acre

648/1250	Shajarat al-Durr
648/1250	al-Muʿizz ʿIzz al-Din Aybak
655/1257	al-Mansur Nur al-Din ʿAli
657/1259	al-Muzaffar Sayf al-Din Qutuz
658/1260	al-Zahir Rukn al-Din Baybars I al-Bunduqdari
676/1277	al-Saʿid Nasir al-Din Baraka (or Berke) Khan
678/1279	al-ʿAdil Badr al-Din Salamish
678/1279	al-Mansur Sayf al-Din Qalawun al-Alfi
689/1290	al-Ashraf Salah al-Din Khalil
693/1294	al-Nasir Nasir al-Din Muhammad (*first reign*)

Note: These tables have been simplified. They do not include all the short-lived rulers in the period covered by this book. For full details, cf. C. E. Bosworth, *The new Islamic dynasties*, Edinburgh, 1996.

Key to Abbreviations Used in the Text

Abu Shama = Abu Shama, *Kitab al-rawdatayn*, ed. M. H. M. Ahmad, Cairo, 1954.

Abu Shama, *RHC* = Abu Shama, *Kitab al-rawdatayn*, *RHC*, IV.

Al-Ansari, trans. Scanlon = Al-Ansari, *Tafrij al-kurub fi tadbir al-hurub*, trans. G. T. Scanlon as *A Muslim Manual of War*, Cairo, 1961.

Al-'Azimi = Al-'Azimi, 'La chronique abrégée d'al-'Azimi', ed. C. Cahen, *JA*, 230 (1938), 353–448.

Al-Harawi, ed. Sourdel-Thomine = Al-Harawi, *Al-tadhkira al-harawiyya fi'l-hiyal al-har-biyya*, trans. J. Sourdel-Thomine, *BEO*, 17 (1962), 105–268.

Al-Harawi, trans. Sourdel-Thomine, *Guide* = Al-Harawi, *Kitab al-ziyarat*, trans. J. Sourdel-Thomine as *Guide des lieux de pèlerinage*, Damascus, 1957.

Al-Maqrizi, *Itti'az* = Al-Maqrizi, *Itti'az al-hunafa'*, II, ed. M. H. M. Ahmad, Cairo, 1971.

Al-Maqrizi, trans. Broadhurst = Al-Maqrizi, *Kitab al-suluk*, trans. R. J. C. Broadhurst as *History of Ayyubids and Mamluks*, Boston, 1980.

Al-Nuwayri = Al-Nuwayri, *Nihayat al-arab fi funun al-adab*, XXVIII, ed. S. A. al-Nuri, Cairo, 1992.

Al-'Umari, Lundquist = Al-'Umari, *Masalik al-absar*, partial trans. E. R. Lundquist as *Saladin and Richard the Lionhearted*, Lund, 1996.

Al-Yunini = Al-Yunini, *Dhayl mir'at al-zaman*, 4 vols, Hyderabad, 1954–61.

Atabegs = Ibn al-Athir, *Al-tarikh al-bahir fi'l-dawlat al-atabakiyya*, ed. A. A. Tulaymat, Cairo, 1963.

BEO = *Bulletin des Études Orientales*

BIFAO = *Bulletin de l'Institut Français d'Archéologie Orientale du Caire*

BSOAS = *Bulletin of the School of Oriental and African Studies*

Bughya = Ibn al-'Adim, *Bughyat al-talab*, partial ed. A. Sevim, Ankara, 1976.

Bughya, Zakkar = Ibn al-'Adim, *Bughyat al-talab*, ed. S. Zakkar, Damascus, 1988.

EI[1] = *Encyclopaedia of Islam*, first edition.

EI[2] = *Encyclopaedia of Islam*, second edition.

Gabrieli = F. Gabrieli, *Arab Historians of the Crusades*, London, 1969.

Ibn 'Abd al-Zahir, *Rawd* = Ibn 'Abd al-Zahir, *Al-rawd al-zahir*, ed. A. A. al-Khuwaytir, Riyadh, 1976.

Ibn 'Abd al-Zahir, *Tashrif* = Ibn 'Abd al-Zahir, *Tashrif al-ayyam wa'l-'usur*, ed. M. Kamil and M. A. al-Najjar, Cairo, 1961.

Ibn al-'Adim, *Zubda* = Ibn al-'Adim, *Zubdat al-halab min tarikh Halab*, ed. S. Zakkar, Damascus, 1997.

Ibn al-'Adim, *Zubda*, Dahan = Ibn al-'Adim, *Zubdat al-halab*, ed. S. Dahan, Damascus, 1954.

Ibn al-'Adim, *Zubda*, *RHC*, III = Ibn al-'Adim, *Zubdat al-halab min tarikh Halab*, *RHC*, III.

Ibn al-Athir, *Atabegs*, *RHC* = Ibn al-Athir, *Al-tarikh al-bahir fi'l-dawlat al-atabakiyya*, *RHC*, III.

Ibn al-Athir, *Kamil* = Ibn al-Athir, *Al-Kamil fi'l-tarikh*, ed. C. J. Tornberg, Leiden and Uppsala, 1851–76.

Ibn al-Athir, *RHC, Kamil* = Ibn al-Athir, *Kamil* in *Recueil des historiens des Croisades*, I.

Ibn al-Dawadari = Ibn al-Dawadari, *Kanz al-durar*, VI, ed. S. al-Munajjid, Cairo, 1961.

Ibn al-Furat, Lyons = Ibn al-Furat, *Tarikh al-duwal wa'l-muluk*, ed. and trans. U. and M. C. Lyons as *Ayyubids, Mamlukes and Crusaders*, Cambridge, 1971.

Ibn al-Furat, Shayyal = Ibn al-Furat, *Tarikh al-duwal wa'l-muluk*, partial ed. M. F. El-Shayyal, unpublished Ph.D. thesis, University of Edinburgh, 1986.

Ibn al-Jawzi = Ibn al-Jawzi, *Al-muntazam fi tarikh al-muluk wa'l-umam*, X, Hyderabad, 1940.

Ibn al-Qalanisi, Gibb = Ibn al-Qalanisi, *Dhayl tarikh Dimishq*, trans. H. A. R. Gibb as *The Damascus Chronicle of the Crusades*, London, 1932.

Ibn al-Qalanisi, Le Tourneau = Ibn al-Qalanisi, *Dhayl tarikh Dimishq*, trans. R. Le Tourneau as *Damas de 1075 à 1154*, Damascus, 1952.

Ibn Jubayr, Broadhurst = Ibn Jubayr, *The Travels of Ibn Jubayr*, trans. R. J. C. Broadhurst, London, 1952.

Ibn Khallikan, de Slane = Ibn Khallikan, *Wafayat al-a'yan*, 4 vols, trans. W. M. de Slane as *Ibn Khallikan's Biographical Dictionary*, Paris, 1843-71.

Ibn Muyassar = Ibn Muyassar, *Akhbar Misr*, ed. H. Massé, Cairo, 1919.

Ibn Shaddad, *RHC* = Ibn Shaddad, *Al-nawadir al-sultaniyya*, RHC, III.

Ibn Shaddad, Eddé = Ibn Shaddad, 'Izz al-Din, *Al-a'laq al-khatira*, trans. A.-M. Eddé as *Description de la Syrie du Nord*, Damascus, 1984.

Ibn Shaddad, *Nawadir* = Ibn Shaddad, *Al-nawadir al-sultaniyya*, ed. J. El-Shayyal, Cairo, 1964.

Ibn Taghribirdi, *Nujum* = Ibn Taghribirdi, *Nujum al-zahira*, Cairo, 1939.

Ibn Wasil = Ibn Wasil, *Mufarrij al-kurub*, ed. J. al-Shayyal, Cairo, 1953–7.

Ibn Zafir = Ibn Zafir, *Akhbar al-duwal al-munqati'a*, ed. A. Ferré, Cairo, 1972.

IJMES = International Journal of Middle Eastern Studies

'Imad al-Din, *Kharida* = 'Imad al-Din, *Kharidat al-qasr*, Cairo, 1951; Baghdad, 1955; Tunis, 1966.

'Imad al-Din, *Sana* = 'Imad al-Din al-Isfahani, *Sana al-barq al-shami*, ed. F. al-Nabarawi, Cairo, 1979.

IOS = Israel Oriental Studies

IQ = Islamic Quarterly

JA = Journal Asiatique

JAOS = Journal of the American Oriental Society

JESHO = Journal of the Economic and Social History of the Orient

JRAS = Journal of the Royal Asiatic Society

JSS = Journal of Semitic Studies

Köhler = M. A. Köhler, *Allianzen und Verträge zwischen frankischen und islamischen Herrschern im Vorderen Orient*, Berlin and New York, 1991.

Lewis, Islam = B. Lewis, *Islam from the Prophet Muhammad to the Capture of Constantinople*, New York, 1974.

Mémoires = C. Cahen, 'Les mémoires de Sa'd al-Din Ibn Hamawiya Djuwayni', in *Les peuples musulmans dans l'histoire médiévale*, Damascus, 1977, 457–82.

MW = Muslim World

Nasir-i Khusraw, Schefer = Nasir-i Khusraw, *Safarnama*, trans. C. Schefer, Paris, 1881.

Quatremère = Al-Maqrizi, *Kitab al-suluk*, trans. E. Quatremère as *Histoire des Sultans Mamlouks de l'Égypte*, Paris, 1837-45.

RCEA = Répertoire Chronologique d'Épigraphie Arabe, Cairo, 1931 onwards.

REI = Revue des Études Islamiques

RHC = *Recueil des Historiens des Croisades: Historiens Orientaux*, I–V, Paris, 1872–1906.

Runciman = S. Runciman, *A History of the Crusades*, Cambridge, 1951–4.

Sibt = Sibt b. al-Jawzi, *Mir'at al-zaman*, Hyderabad, 1951.

Sibt, Jewett = Sibt b. al-Jawzi, *Mir'at al-zaman*, facsimile edn by J. R. Jewett, Chicago, 1907.

Sivan, *L'Islam* = E. Sivan, *L'Islam et la Croisade*, Paris, 1968.

Sivan, 'Modern Arab historiography' = E. Sivan, 'The Crusaders described by modern Arab historiography', *Asian and African Studies*, 8 (1972), 104–49.

Usama, Hitti = Usama b. Munqidh, *Kitab al-i'tibar*, trans. P. K. Hitti as *Memoirs of an Arab-Syrian Gentleman*, Beirut, 1964.

WZKM = *Wiener Zeitschrift für die Kunde des Morgenlandes*

SOURCES FOR THE ILLUSTRATIONS

Sauvaget, J., *La Mosquée Omeyyade de Médine. Etude sur les origines architecturales de la mosquée et de la basilique* (Paris 1947): ill. 3.8

Sauvaget, J., in *Syria* XI (1930): ills. 5.16–20, 7.57–8

Sauvaget, J., *La poste aux chevaux dans l'empire des Mameloukes* (Paris 1941): ills. 4.33, 8.24, 8.26

Schlumberger, G., et al., *Lashkari Bazar: Une résidence royale ghaznévide et ghoride. 1A. L'architecture* (Paris 1978): ill. 7.47

Schmid, H., *Die Madrasa des Kalifen al-Mustansir in Baghdad* (Mainz 1980): ills. 4.9–10, 4.12

Schneider, M., *Mubarak al-Makki: An Arabic Lapicide of the Third/Ninth Century* (Manchester 1986): ill. 5.27

Schulz, P. W. *Die persisch–islamische Miniaturmalerei: Ein Beitrag zur Kunstgeschichte Irans* (Leipzig 1914): ill. 5.15

Sotheby's, *Oriental Manuscripts and Miniatures: London, Wednesday 29 April 1998* (London 1998): ill. 8.38

Spengler, W. F. and Sayles, W. G., *Turkoman Figural Bronze Coins and Their Iconography* (Lodi, Wis. 1996): ills. 2.27, 8.5

Sublet, J., *Les Trois Vies du Sultan Baïbars* (Paris 1992): ills. 1.1, 2.23, 6.35, 6.63, 7.11, 7.18–19, 7.21–4, 7.26, 7.28, 7.30, 7.43, 8.3, 8.9

Tabbaa, Y. in Goss, V. P. (ed.), *The Meeting of Two Worlds* (Kalamazoo 1986): ills. 3.21, 3.36, 4.3

Tantum, G., in Elgood, R. (ed.), *Islamic Arms and Armour* (London 1979): ills. 7.23, 7.28, 8.8

Tate, G., trans. L. Frankel, *The Crusades and the Holy Land* (London 1996): ills. 2.20, 7.5–7, 7.33–4, 8.10, 8.12, 8.42

Walther, W., trans. C. S. V. Salt, *Woman in Islam* (London 1981): ill. 1.25

Wellesz, E., in *Ars Orientalis* III (1959): ill. 8.49

Wilson, E., *Islamic Designs* (London 1988): ills. 4.4, 6.8, 6.16, 6.22, 6.36, 6.70, 8.17

CHAPTER ONE

Prologue

The history of the Middle Ages has no more imposing spectacle than the wars undertaken for the conquest of the Holy Land.[1] (Michaud)

General Introduction

THE CRUSADES, as the Western viewpoint sees them, were a series of campaigns – at least eight of them – motivated by the desire on the part of western European Christians to bring the holy places of Christendom and, above all, Jerusalem under their protection. In the West the Crusades are thought to have lasted from 1095, when Pope Urban II made his famous call to arms, until the fifteenth century and even later, although many pinpoint the fall of Acre in 1291 as the termination of serious Crusader activity against the Muslim Levant.

From the outset, the Crusades formed important chapters in two distinct but interconnected histories, Occidental and Oriental. In the first, they were part of the evolution of medieval western Europe. Their significance has long been recognised and studied by many generations of Western scholars. Indeed, the Crusades are an undeniably fashionable area of Western medieval studies – this is hardly surprising in view of the fact that they were a Western phenomenon.[2] In the Muslim East, the Crusades played a transient but unforgettable role which has left its impact on the Islamic consciousness until the present day; but it must be emphasised that the body of scholarship produced on them in the Middle East is incomparably less. The Muslim world has approached the subject less globally and in more piecemeal fashion. The full, composite story of the Crusades needs, of course, the drawing together of evidence from both sides of the divide to illuminate each other. Such a task needs to be redone in each generation. But it will be helped without doubt by a fuller understanding of the Muslim perspective.

This book is the first full-length monographic treatment of the Crusades as seen by the Muslims – a study devoted not to establishing the bare chronological facts, vital though they are, but rather to evoking the detailed response of the Muslims to the Crusader presence. As a pioneering venture, it cannot hope to do more than sketch an outline for future research.

Figure 1.1 *Horseman, enamelled glass beaker, c. 1260, Aleppo, Syria*

I

The Approach of This Study

Figure 1.2
(above and opposite)
*Signs of the zodiac on the
Wade Cup (a: Taurus,
b: Cancer, c: Virgo, d: Scorpio,
e: Capricorn, f: Pisces),
inlaid brass, c. 1230, Iran*

This book is intended primarily for students and the general public, although it is hoped that specialists will also find something of interest in it. As its title suggests, only Islamic perspectives of the Crusades will be discussed. Through the evidence of Islamic sources only, an attempt is made to enter the mind-set of the medieval Muslims who suffered the impact of the Crusades and to tease out from the sources some hints at least of how the Muslims felt and how they reacted to the unprecedented experience of western European intervention in their lands and in their lives. It may seem an affectation, an exaggeratedly one-sided stance, to view the phenomenon of the Crusades from a solely Muslim perspective. Yet such a stance is timely, since so much of the scholarship on the Crusades has been unabashedly Eurocentric and has been penned by scholars of the medieval West. This study hopes to redress the balance. Such a focus should yield new insights into a phenomenon which left an indelible mark on the Muslim Near East psychologically and ideologically, even if the actual military occupation of the Crusaders touched only a small area of the Islamic world.

No aspect of Mediterranean history has been studied more thoroughly than the Crusades, and given their Western origins it is natural that they should have generated so much scholarship in the West. Yet on the Muslim side too, although medieval writers did not view them as being so momentous – coupling them jointly with the Mongol scourge as hated interventions into the Islamic world by infidel outsiders from outside – there is still much to be said. Beyond the establishment of chronologies and events, the background and context of Syria and Egypt in the twelfth and thirteenth centuries need further study. Moreover, although lip-service is paid to the phenomenon of Muslim–Crusader cross-cultural relations, there is still more to be done in this area.

What is the justification for presenting, or attempting to present, just the Muslim side? A few words of introductory background are needed. For the non-Muslim reader living in a so-called secular age in different parts of the world at the end of the twentieth century – indeed on the eve of the 900th anniversary of the capture of Jerusalem by the Crusading armies – there is great benefit to be derived from an examination of the way in which one medieval religious ideology shaped history by confronting another similarly deep-felt religious ideology. It is also salutary for the heirs to the Judaeo-Christian tradition in the West to view the Crusades through the eyes of the Muslims who were the victims of this onslaught on their territories from a completely unexpected quarter. Nowadays, when Christian 'fanaticism' is normally regarded as the preserve of extreme sects whose activities are given sensationalist treatment by the media, and with Muslim movements declaring *jihad* and a return to fundamental Islamic principles frequently in the headlines and represented negatively, it is worth returning to the period of the Crusades to see what lessons can be learned and what insights gleaned.

The Crusades shaped western European perceptions of the Muslim world just as decisively as they formed Muslim views of the West. These stereotypical images of the old 'enemy' are deeply entrenched and need to be aired and scrutinised in order to be understood and modified. It is undoubtedly time to balance the western European view with the Islamic perspective. Riley-Smith rightly identifies the problem when he writes that the history of the Latin East would be transformed if Islamic studies were given the prominence they deserve: 'It is curious how peripheral they have so far proved to be – how many Crusade historians have bothered to learn Arabic?'[3] Riley-Smith then also criticises the attitude of Islamicists themselves, 'to most of whom the Crusades and the Latin settlements are of marginal significance'.

d

So both sides need to be better informed. Indeed, there is much to be gained by modern scholars of the Islamic Middle Ages studying the period of the Crusades. Such research throws light on a range of historical issues and themes – military history, politico-religious ideologies and the evolution of border societies. Over and above all this is the moulding of socio-cultural attitudes between the Middle East and the West which have survived until the present day.

The intention is that this book will be of interest not only to non-Muslims but also to the many Muslims who cannot read Arabic. Both groups may find some of their preconceptions about the Crusades modified by the evidence presented. Muslims may well be surprised at the way in which their medieval counterparts co-existed, indeed on occasion collaborated with the invading Franks, whilst non-Muslims will have cause to ponder on the ideological heritage which the Crusades have left in the Near East. This book does not aim to be especially radical, original or comprehensive. It attempts, instead, to present some ideas and themes for those who wish to pursue this fascinating topic in greater depth, having acquired a clearer idea of the neglected side of the question.

e

In a way this book needs no justification. So many popular books have been written about the Crusades from the Western side that any new general work which highlights the Muslim viewpoint, so sadly under-represented, should be a welcome addition to our knowledge of the subject. In Britain the popularity of Terry Jones's television series *Crusades* (early 1990s) and book on the Crusades (in which he stressed to a wide audience the high level of Islamic civilisation at the time of the Crusades) points to considerable interest in this subject.[4]

f

There are many different but complementary perspectives which together cast fresh light on the phenomenon of the Crusades. At the basic level the political and military story needs to be told. The ideology and motivation of both sides need to be examined. The social and economic interaction between Crusader and Muslim also provides more nuanced insights into the reality of life in the twelfth- and

3

thirteenth-century Levant. Last but by no means least – indeed perhaps the most important theme of all – is the nature of warfare in this period, since the advent of the Crusaders in Muslim territory involved wars which they first won and then lost.

It is, of course, vital to avoid viewing Islamic history, or for that matter any other kind of history, exclusively from the Western perspective. Even Orientalists who know Arabic and are knowledgeable about Islam have often been rightly criticised in the past for having a colonialist agenda and for being unable to represent honestly the views of the indigenous peoples of the Middle East. Thus it might be argued that the writing of the Islamic view of the Crusades should be left on the whole to Muslim scholars themselves. This is, of course, a reasonable point of view and the fact that this book is the work of a Western scholar does not imply disagreement with such a view. But there has been no spate of books written from the Islamic side about the Crusades by internationally respected contemporary Muslim scholars themselves. It is a sad fact that the best Muslim historians have, as it happens, specialised in other areas.

But just as it is important for the history of the Christian West to be studied and written about by scholars of non-Western origins, so too there is benefit in Western scholars writing about aspects of medieval Islamic history. What matters is the methodology used: a careful reading of a wide range of sources and an awareness of how to evaluate historiographical evidence in the light of recent researches in medieval history, both Western and Oriental.

Recent Arab Scholarly Approaches to the Crusades

Not surprisingly, since the Crusader attacks from Europe afflicted what is now perceived quite rightly as being part of the Arab world – Syria, Egypt and Palestine – the Crusades have been viewed in the Muslim writings of the twentieth century as an *Arab* phenomenon, as will be seen in greater detail in the last chapter of this book, and the lessons of the Crusades have been embraced most ardently by the Arabs. Some contemporary Arab and Muslim scholars evaluate and reinterpret the Crusading phenomenon in the light of recent experiences such as colonialism, Arab nationalism, the establishment of the state of Israel, the liberation of Palestine and the rise of 'Islamic fundamentalism'.

A typical example of recent Muslim writing on the Crusades is a work in Arabic by 'Ashur, published in 1995, entitled *The Islamic Jihad against the Crusaders and Mongols in the Mamluk Period*.[5] The author is concerned not to give a scholarly historical account of his subject but wishes rather to use Mamluk history as a rallying cry for *jihad* against present-day governments in the Middle East, especially in Egypt. This is an illustration of 'late twentieth-century Islamist history' which is characterised by moralising and an explicit political agenda.[6]

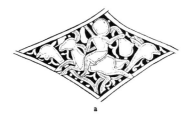

Figure 1.3
(above and opposite)
Signs of the zodiac on the Wade Cup (a: Aries, b: Gemini, c: Leo, d: Libra, e: Sagittarius, f: Aquarius), inlaid brass, c. 1230, Iran

Whilst this interpretation has obvious validity in nineteenth- and twentieth-century terms, it is by no means the whole picture. Above all, despite its intense fascination in modern political and sociological terms, it can scarcely claim to reflect medieval realities, and such works are often marred by emotional rhetoric. Others write histories of the Crusades more in the Western 'mode'; they rely very heavily on European scholarship in the Crusades, notably Runciman, to provide what turns out disappointingly to be yet another straight chronological narrative of the Crusades, not notably enriched by the use of hitherto unexploited Arabic sources. A typical example of the latter approach is the Syrian scholar Zakkar, who published a two-part work entitled *The Crusading Wars* (*Al-hurub al-salibiyya*).[7] This is a disappointing book which contains long narrative passages and little interpretation of events. The reading of a similar work by al-Matwi, with the same title, published in Tunis in 1954, yields little benefit. It has to be said that precisely those historians whose native language is Arabic have done very little indeed to provide a properly documented counterweight, based on Arabic materials, of the accounts of the Crusades produced by modern historians of the medieval West.

d

e

Whilst anachronistic nationalist labels should be avoided in the study of medieval history, there is no doubt that recent Muslim writing has underplayed the role of the Turks in the Crusading period. The study of the Muslim response to the coming of the Crusades needs to be undertaken within the wider context of the role played by the eastern Islamic world in general, and especially taking into account the military and ideological role played by the newly Islamicised Turks and the continuing heritage of the Seljuq empire in Syria and Palestine. Although there is no doubt in the minds of Arab Muslims today that almost all the great fighters of *jihad* (*mujahidun*) who finally defeated the Crusaders – Zengi, Nur al-Din, Baybars – were Turks, this has been inadequately recognised, perhaps because of several centuries of Ottoman Turkish rule which followed the end of the Crusades. Traditionally, this period has been regarded by the Arabs of the Levant with loathing, and this is perhaps the reason for modern neglect of the Turkish achievement in the medieval context. It is noteworthy that non-Arab scholars from the Muslim world – Turks, Kurds, Persians, Pakistanis and others – have not worked seriously on the topic of medieval Muslim reactions to the Crusades. The modern Muslim interest, then, is a resolutely Arab one (cf. plates 1.1 and 1.2).

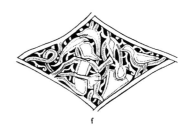

f

Some of the Limitations of This Book

The material presented in this book excludes the views and attitudes of Near Eastern Christians – Coptic, Syriac, Armenian and others[8] – whose experiences are also an integral part, together with the Byzantine and Jewish perspectives, of the total truth about the phenomenon

Plate 1.1 *Statue of Saladin,
1992, Damascus, Syria*

Plate 1.2 *Statue of Saladin,*
foot soldier, 1992, Damascus,
Syria

of the Crusades (plate 1.3). These facets of Crusading history deserve
full treatment of their own, a task which is beyond the remit of the
current book.

This study does not set out to give a full and detailed chronological
account of the Crusades in the Levant as presented in the Muslim
sources – a good deal of this work has been done already. Nor will it
deal in any detail with aspects of the Crusades in Spain – a growth
industry in modern scholarship – and Sicily. Instead, it attempts much
more to adopt a thematic approach which addresses the broader ideological and socio-cultural issues raised by the Crusader occupation
of the Muslim Levant. In spite of periods of peaceful co-existence and

Plate 1.3 *Ayyubid canteen
with Christian scenes, back,
inlaid brass, c. 1250, Syria*

of rather murky *Realpolitik* in which groups of Crusaders and Muslims allied with each other against other such factions, the Crusaders were undoubtedly a pernicious foreign body which eventually had to be removed from the 'House of Islam' by force; much of this book, therefore, inevitably focuses on military aspects of the Muslim–Crusader confrontation. But it also deals with religious and social themes which fit into the wider context of the medieval Islamic world. Finally, it traces the heritage of the Crusades into modern times – for the Crusades have had a remarkable afterlife spanning many centuries, and their impact is still strong at the end of the twentieth century.

It is, of course, impossible for Western scholars to divest themselves totally of preconceived opinions and prejudices. Nevertheless, the textual and artistic evidence presented in this book is based entirely on Muslim sources, which to some extent tell their own story. The selection and interpretation of them may be relatively subjective, but at least the technique of presenting them on their own will encourage the debate to progress and more material will thus be made accessible. An audience with interests wider than those of Crusader specialists will thereby be in a position to make an informed judgement about the Muslim response to the Crusades.

Figure 1.4 Tent, Cappella Palatina, ceiling, c. 1140, Palermo, Sicily

The Nature of Medieval Muslim Sources

The Muslims themselves amply recorded the history of the two hundred years or so which witnessed western European Christian intervention in territory which had been ruled by Muslims since the seventh century. But their treatment of the subject of the Crusades is by no means easy to analyse – the concept of 'Crusade' is a Western one. It has no particular resonance for Islamic ears and the Muslim historians are not concerned with it. For them, these are simply wars with an enemy – in this case, the Franks, as distinct, say, from the Fatimids. Accordingly, their reflections on the events of the Crusading period have to be pieced together like a jigsaw from stray references, anecdotes and comments tucked away in universal or dynastic histories of the Islamic world and the chronicles of cities – in other words, works with quite other emphases and historiographical aims. The Crusades were not treated in any extant Islamic work as an isolated topic. Nevertheless, much varied information on Muslim responses to the Franks can be found in the Arabic annals, biographical dictionaries and other literary works of the twelfth to the fifteenth century. Major problems arise, however, when one tries to evaluate and interpret such snippets of information so many centuries later.

It will be clear from all this how important it is not to cherish unrealistic expectations of what may be found in these primary sources. They have serious limitations, as of course do Western medieval Christian sources themselves. They are couched in rigidly ideological terms where the enemy is irrevocably the enemy and

Figure 1.5 Seated ruler, Cappella Palatina, ceiling, c. 1140, Palermo, Sicily

9

where God is on the Muslim side, guiding the faithful towards the inevitable victory preordained by Him. War, even if fought against fellow-Muslims, is described as *jihad*. Altogether, the Muslim sources show little interest in the activities and motivations of the other side. There is disappointingly little information about social contacts between Crusaders and Muslims. The information which does exist is of interest, of course, but its importance must not be exaggerated or distorted simply because it exists in the first place.

The Accessibility of Medieval Muslim Sources

A number of medieval Arabic sources still remain only in manuscript form. It is to be hoped that Middle Eastern scholars in Damascus, Cairo, Istanbul and other centres of scholarship will continue the slow but vital task of publishing them in edited form.

On the Western side, those who write about the Crusades and who do not read Arabic (which is the vast majority of scholars) depend for their knowledge of the Muslim sources on translations which cover the field in a patchy and unsatisfactory way. Many important works remain inaccessible to them. Their image of the Muslim perspective is therefore incomplete and is skewed by the availability of those sources which have actually been translated. It is also unfortunate to find that all too frequently Islamic specialists, for their part, rather than daring to branch out into the unknown and translate a new source, prefer the safer option of retranslating a work: thus we find two translations of the chronicle of Ibn al-Qalanisi[9] and several of Usama's memoirs in different European languages,[10] whilst other key works, such as most of Ibn al-Athir's *Universal History*,[11] remain inaccessible to those who cannot read Arabic. If more scholars of medieval Islamic history would devote more time to translating such sources into English or other European languages, the great divide between Western and Islamic perceptions of the Crusades would be substantially narrowed to the benefit of scholarship on both sides.[12]

Books in European Languages about the Muslim Side of the Crusades

This discussion will be limited to a selection of useful books about the Muslim side of the Crusades; those who wish to delve more deeply into the subject should as a starting point consult the bibliographies provided by the authors mentioned below, as well as various works discussed in different chapters of this book and listed in the Bibliography.

A number of general books and scholarly monographs have been written about aspects of the Muslim side of the Crusades. The interested reader will find P. M. Holt, *The Age of the Crusades: The Near East from the Eleventh Century to 1517*, London and New York, 1986, a short but very lucid historical overview of the subject. A

much earlier work of scholarship, W. B. Stevenson, *The Crusaders in the East*, Cambridge, 1907, is still very readable and gives a detailed narrative account based on the medieval Arabic sources accessible to the author at that time. It has to be said, though, that Stevenson, for all his emphasis on the Arabic side, does not try to present events from that viewpoint alone, for he also uses Western sources; nor does he try to evoke in detail the way that the Muslims and Crusaders co-existed in the Levant. There are also some very useful chapters on Muslim aspects of the Crusades in K. M. Setton and M. W. Baldwin (eds), *A History of the Crusades*, 6 vols, Madison, Wis., 1969–89. Finally, two very helpful historical monographs on major dynasties may be cited here: one on the Ayyubids (S. Humphreys, *From Saladin to the Mongols: The Ayyubids of Damascus 1193–1260*, Albany, 1977) and the other on the Mamluks (R. Irwin, *The Middle East in*

Figure 1.6 *Animated inscription on cup made for Khalaf al-Julaki, inlaid metal, c. 1230, Syria(?)*

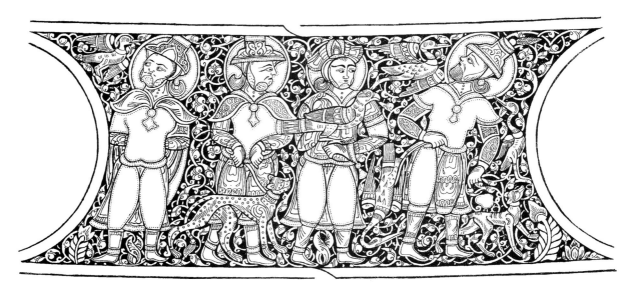

Figure 1.7 *Servants, inlaid brass basin known as the 'Baptistère de St Louis', c. 1300 or earlier, Syria*

the Middle Ages: The Early Mamluk Sultanate 1250–1382, London and Sydney, 1986).

A. Maalouf's book *The Crusades through Arab Eyes*, London, 1984, came as a breath of fresh air into this field; it is lively and always popular with students. Moreover, the book lives up to its title. Its drawbacks are that it is unashamedly general in its approach, is not comprehensive or academic, and furnishes little new information.

Amongst individual Muslim leaders of the Counter-Crusade, Saladin takes pride of place in modern scholarly biographies. There is a wide spectrum of scholarly opinion on him, ranging from the eulogies of Gibb and others to the more realistic appraisal of Ehrenkreutz. A very balanced and well-documented view of Saladin is given by M. C. Lyons and D. E. P. Jackson in their book *Saladin: The Politics of the Holy War*, Cambridge, 1982. Regrettably the other great Muslim leaders at the time of the Crusades have not received the same thorough treatment as Saladin. Zengi, the conqueror of Edessa, for example, remains unjustifiably neglected, as do many other important Muslim figures of the Crusader period. As for Nur al-Din, N. Elisseeff wrote a three-volume monograph in French entitled *Nur al-Din: un grand prince musulman de Syrie au temps des Croisades*, 3 vols, Damascus, 1967. Whilst being undoubtedly scholarly, this work strangely does not provide a full assessment of this key figure of the Counter-Crusade. That task remains to be attempted. The later period is well served by P. Thorau who provides good biographical coverage of Baybars in *The Lion of Egypt: Sultan Baybars I and the Near East in the Thirteenth Century*, trans. P. M. Holt, London and New York, 1992. Still worthy of particular mention is the work in French of E. Sivan, *L'Islam et la Croisade: Idéologie et propagande dans les reactions musulmanes aux Croisades*, Paris, 1968. This important book bases itself firmly on Islamic sources and analyses the evolution of the *jihad* phenomenon at the time of the Crusades.

All this bibliography should, of course, be balanced by a thorough reading of the much more extensive body of work done on the Western side of the Crusades: an excellent starting point is still S. Runciman, *A History of the Crusades*, 3 vols, Cambridge, 1951–4, but this should now be complemented by the more recent works of J. S. C. Riley-Smith written for the general reader, such as *The Crusades: A Short History*, London and New Haven, 1987, and *What Were the Crusades?*, London, 1992; and by the composite book *The Oxford Illustrated History of the Crusades*, ed. J. Riley-Smith, Oxford, 1995.

Translations of Primary Arabic Sources

As already mentioned, a major problem for Crusader historians in modern times has been the relative lack of translations of Islamic sources into European languages. Those works which *are* translated are indeed used, but the remainder remain inaccessible; and they are so numerous that the whole historiographical picture of an event or a reign from the Islamic side cannot be grasped. It should be added that sometimes the translations that have been made are faulty, although of course it can be argued that 'half a loaf is better than no bread'. It is sobering to see how often in the few existing books on the Crusades from the Muslim side the same limited number of Islamic sources have been used again and again. It makes a reconsideration of the primary sources all the more imperative.

Figure 1.8 Mounted archer, inlaid brass basin known as the 'Baptistère de St Louis', c. 1300 or earlier, Syria

Figure 1.9 *Enthroned ruler, inlaid brass basin known as the 'Baptistère de St Louis', c. 1300 or earlier, Syria. Note the artist's signature on the throne*

It is therefore incumbent on those who can read the Islamic sources, and especially modern historians in the Middle East itself, to produce thoughtful, careful editions, translations and analyses of the texts and thus enable a wider public to understand more profoundly the Muslim perspectives on the events of the period of the Crusades. The Mamluk period is particularly rich in historiographical materials which often contain excerpts from earlier lost chronicles.

A useful starting point for sampling the Arabic chronicles is F. Gabrieli, *Arab Historians of the Crusades*, London, 1969. However, its excerpts were translated from Arabic into Italian and then into English and are thus some way from the original. Moreover, they often seem more like summaries of the original texts than actual translations. On the basis that any translation is better than none, the much criticised *Recueil des historiens des Croisades: Historiens orientaux I–V*, Paris, 1872–1906 (Arabic excerpts with French translations) is still of use for those who cannot read Arabic but can read French, despite its frequent faults of editing and its mistranslations. The reader will find a fuller list of other primary Arabic sources which have been translated into European languages in the Bibliography at the end of this book.

The Crusades: A Short Historical Overview

The short historical overview which follows is intended to provide a broad chronological framework within which to place the thematic chapters which form the heart of this book. Much more detailed discussions on these events will occur at appropriate places within the book.

Introduction: The Pre-Crusading Period

Europe's first encounter with Islam was the result of the expansionist policies of the new Muslim state, established after the death of the Prophet Muhammad in 632. A century later, the Muslims had crossed the Pyrenees and conquered lands extending from northern India to southern France. For the next two hundred years, the balance of power between Europe and the Islamic world remained decisively in the hands of the Muslims, who enjoyed massive economic growth and whose culture flowered in spectacular fashion. From 750 onwards the 'Abbasid state was moulded by Perso-Islamic culture and government and increasingly sustained by the military support of Turkish slave armies.

By the tenth and eleventh centuries, however, the political fragmentation of the great 'Abbasid empire centred on Baghdad was well under way; the situation favoured the reappearance of Europeans in the eastern Mediterranean and the beginnings of the revival of Christian power in Spain. Trading links were followed up by maritime successes against the Muslims. The Normans took Sicily from the Muslims and the Christians of northern Spain reconquered Toledo and began an inexorable advance southwards. The close neighbour of the Islamic world, Byzantium, had conducted successful raids into northern Syria in the late tenth century and briefly held towns there.

During the first centuries of Muslim rule, Christian pilgrims from Europe had usually been able to visit the sacred places associated with their faith in Jerusalem and the Holy Land; they travelled overland via the Balkans, Anatolia and Syria or took the sea route to Egypt or Palestine. Thus news came back to Europe of the sophisticated way of life and high cultural achievements of the Islamic world; in the eleventh century, the Pope and European monarchs were also told of the weakening and decentralisation of Muslim political and military power. However, rumours of the notoriety of one particular Islamic ruler – the sixth Fatimid caliph, al-Hakim – had also reached Europe (figures 1.11, 1.12). His persecution of the Christians within his realm, which extended to Syria and Palestine, culminated in the destruction

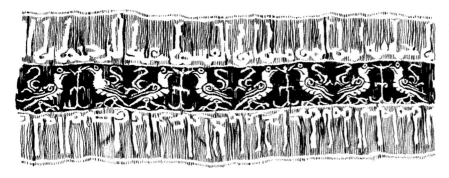

Figure 1.10 Border of a robe of honour made for the Fatimid caliph al-Hakim (386–411/996–1021), Egypt

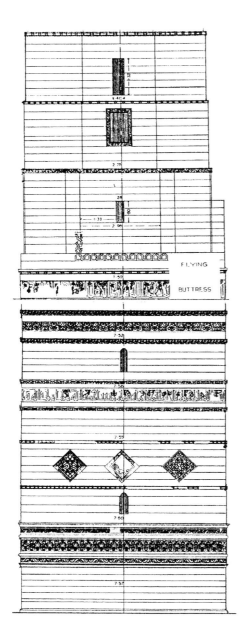

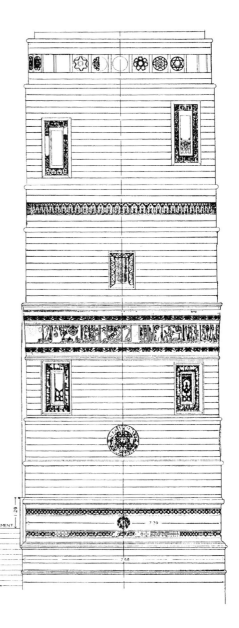

Figure 1.11 (above)
Western minaret, Mosque of al-Hakim, 380–93/990–1003, Cairo, Egypt

Figure 1.12 (right)
Northern minaret, Mosque of al-Hakim, 393/1003, Cairo, Egypt

Figure 1.13 *Fatimid carved wooden frieze, eleventh century, Egypt*

of the Church of the Holy Sepulcre in Jerusalem in 1009–10.[13] Al-Hakim's actions are usually considered to have been a contributing factor to the gradual evolution of the desire in Christian Europe to launch the First Crusade and to rescue what were perceived as the endangered holy places of Christendom.

In the second half of the eleventh century Syria and Palestine became the arena for a fierce conflict between the Seljuq Turks who ruled the eastern Islamic world and the Fatimid empire centred on Egypt. The Fatimids, who were Isma'ili (Sevener) Shi'ites, espoused an ideology which was anathema to Sunni Muslims, especially since Fatimid ideology – dynamic and expansionist in aim – threatened at one point to overthrow the Sunni 'Abbasid caliphate in Baghdad. The Seljuq Turks, recent converts to Islam, presented themselves as supporters of the 'Abbasid caliph and Sunni Islam, and embarked on protracted military engagements against the Fatimids.

The Seljuq leadership were still reliant on their nomadic kinsmen for military support. The Turkish nomads lived in an uneasy relationship with the cities of the Near East. Their chiefs mulcted the cities for taxes, and through this contact were often attracted into assuming some at least of the trappings of settled rulers. The attitude of the urban population towards the nomads was ambivalent: they often needed them for military protection but they found their alien ways irksome and disruptive. On balance, the recent influx of nomadic Turks in large numbers was probably regarded as a necessary evil within the Islamic body politic because of their unrivalled military skills and religious zeal. The famous Muslim intellectual al-Ghazali (d. 1111) argues:

Figure 1.14 *Monolithic funerary statues depicting Turkic princes, c. ninth century, southern Siberia*

> In this age of ours, from amongst the [various] kinds of human beings it is the Turks who possess force . . . If there should be an insurrection in any region of the earth against this resplendent

Figure 1.15 *Seljuq inscription on city walls, 484/1091–2, Diyarbakr, Turkey*

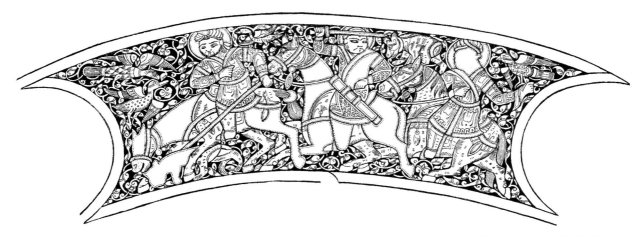

Figure 1.16 *Mounted hunters, inlaid brass basin known as the 'Baptistère de St Louis', c. 1300 or earlier, Syria*

state [the Seljuqs] there is not one among them [the Turks] who on seeing strife beyond its frontiers would not fight in the way of God waging *jihad* against the infidels.[14]

The reality of the nomadic Turkish presence was, however, often hard to bear and the cities and countryside of Syria and Palestine, soon to receive the impact of Crusader attacks, had already suffered much at the hands of the Turcomans (i.e. nomadic Turks) and had served too as the arena for the lengthy military engagements between Seljuq and Fatimid forces.

The political situation in nearby Anatolia (nowadays Turkey) was also destabilised at this time, with Byzantium losing to the Seljuq Turks its buffer territories to the east, formerly under Armenian control. The Byzantine empire suffered a devastating blow to its prestige; it was defeated by the Seljuq Turks under sultan Alp Arslan at the battle of Manzikert (sometimes known as Malazgird) in 1071. This famous confrontation is usually taken by historians as the point after which waves of nomadic Turks, loosely affiliated to the Seljuq empire further east or sometimes completely independent of it, accelerated a process begun earlier in the century of infiltrating and occupying Armenian and Byzantine territory (plate 1.4). One group of Turks under the leadership of Sulayman b. Qutlumush, a scion of the Seljuq family, established a small state, first at Nicaea (Iznik) and later at Iconium (Konya), which was to develop into the Seljuq sultanate of Rum (the Muslim name for Byzantium). This polity ruled parts of Anatolia until the coming of the Mongols and beyond. Other Turkish groups, most notably the Danishmendids, vied with the Seljuqs of Rum in Anatolia and incidentally made the land journey from Constantinople to Syria and the Holy Land, which passed through their territory, precarious.

Figure 1.17 *Peacock, Seljuq underglaze tile, thirteenth century, Kubadabad, Turkey*

As the next chapter will show in greater detail, the last decade of the eleventh century saw ever greater Muslim political weakness, instability and disunity. The deaths in quick succession of the Seljuq

Plate 1.4 Horseman, stone tympanum, twelfth century, Daghestan, eastern Caucasus

chief minister (*wazir*) Nizam al-Mulk and the Seljuq sultan Malik-shah in 1092, followed by those of the 'Abbasid caliph al-Muqtadi and the Fatimid caliph al-Mustansir in 1094, left an enormous political vacuum. Internal strife and jockeying for power in both the eastern Islamic world and Egypt ensued. Fratricidal struggles amongst the Seljuqs deprived the Sunni Muslims of any effective leadership and led to further decentralisation in Syria and to the emergence of small, often mutually hostile city-states. Further west in Egypt, the Fatimid empire was never again to exert the supremacy it had enjoyed in the first half of the eleventh century and became introverted and strife-ridden. The Islamic world was thus in no position to fend off the utterly unexpected and indeed unprecedented attacks from western

Figure 1.18 Seljuq double-headed eagle on city wall, thirteenth century, Konya, Turkey

19

Europe which were about to occur. Appeals for European help from Byzantium had begun after the battle of Manzikert in 1071 when the Byzantine emperor begged for military support on his eastern border against the Seljuq Turks. In the 1090s the Byzantine emperor Alexius Comnenus once again appealed to Europe which was moved by what it heard of Seljuq oppression of Near Eastern Christians. The Papacy itself had its own reasons for wishing to move against the Muslims. Pope Urban II pronounced a momentous sermon on 27 November 1095 at Clermont, calling on Christians to set out to liberate the holy city of Jerusalem from Muslim oppression. By 1097 a mixed Christian army under various leaders from different parts of western Europe had reached Constantinople and had embarked on the land journey across Anatolia towards Jerusalem.

Thus began the series of military campaigns spearheaded from western Europe against the Islamic Near East which have come to be known as the Crusades.

The First Crusade

The First Crusade, despite its mixed leadership, which included Raymond of Toulouse, Bohemond of Sicily and Godfrey of Bouillon, achieved significant military successes whilst still *en route* through Anatolia. The Franks conquered the Seljuq capital at Iznik in June 1097 and inflicted a heavy defeat on the Seljuq army under Sultan Qilij Arslan at the battle of Dorylaeum in July of the same year. On reaching Antioch in northern Syria, the Crusader forces laid siege to it in October 1097. A splinter group of Crusader forces under Baldwin of Boulogne crossed to the Christian Armenian city of Edessa and conquered it on 10 March 1098, thereby establishing the first Crusader state in the Near East (usually known as the County of Edessa).

Antioch fell to the Crusaders in June 1098 and in January of the following year the Principality of Antioch was inaugurated under the leadership of the Norman ruler Bohemond of Sicily. The ultimate prize – Jerusalem – was gained on 15 July 1099 and Godfrey of Bouillon became its first ruler. The final Crusader state, the County of Tripoli, was established when that city fell to the Franks in 1109. Thus four Crusader principalities were created in the Near East: Jerusalem, Edessa, Antioch and Tripoli. It is noticeable, however, that even in the first flush of success the Crusaders were unable to capture either of the two major cities in the region, namely Aleppo or Damascus.

The Muslim Response to the Crusaders: The First Phases

The Muslim response to the coming of the Crusades was initially one of apathy, compromise and preoccupation with internal problems. The early decades of the twelfth century were a period of great Muslim disunity; there was little military reaction to the ever more

Figure 1.19 Blazons on Mamluk coins, thirteenth–fifteenth centuries, Egypt and Syria

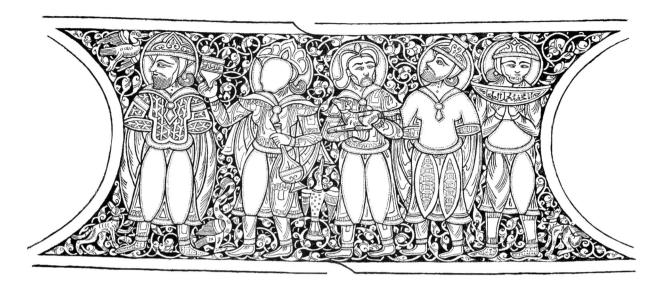

pressing danger of Frankish expansionism and no substantial Muslim gains in territory were achieved. Instead of fending off the Crusader threat, the disunited petty Muslim rulers of Syria made truces with the Franks and were perennially engaged in small territorial struggles, often within a framework of Muslim–Crusader alliances. Against a fragmented, weakened Muslim world, the Franks, by contrast, showed themselves during these years to be strong and determined, vibrant with fanaticism and highly motivated to build structures of defence which would ensure their continuing presence in the Levant.

The first decade of the twelfth century saw the Franks taking most of the Levantine seaports, thus ensuring that they would be able to receive reinforcements of men and equipment by sea. The territory henceforward occupied by the Crusaders was a long, narrow strip of land along the Mediterranean. When they tried to expand eastwards they were less successful; only distant Edessa penetrated the Euphrates and Tigris valleys; significantly too Edessa was the first Crusader state to be extinguished. As already noted, the Crusaders never possessed the key cities of Aleppo and Damascus and never controlled Syria.

There were some intermittent but uncoordinated Muslim attempts to combat the Crusaders in the early twelfth century. Several expeditions were launched from the east under the command of the ruler of Mosul, Mawdud, and the sponsorship of the Seljuq sultan Muhammad (in 1108, 1111 and 1113). These received little support from the rulers of Aleppo and Damascus, who did not welcome Seljuq interference. Indeed, a further expeditionary army sent by Muhammad into Syria in 1115 was routed by a combined Crusader–Muslim army at the battle of Danith. The Artuqid Turcoman ruler of distant Mardin, called upon by the people of

Figure 1.20 Servants, inlaid brass basin known as the 'Baptistère de St Louis', c. 1300 or earlier, Syria

Figure 1.21 Enthroned ruler and attendants, painted ivory casket, thirteenth century, Sicily

Aleppo to defend them against the Franks, defeated Roger of Antioch at the battle of Balat (also known as the Field of Blood) in June 1119; this was a great but isolated Muslim victory and was not followed up. The first major signs of Muslim recovery may be seen in the career of the redoubtable Zengi (d. 1146) whose efforts were directed, at least partly, towards fighting the Franks. It was he who succeeded in conquering the first of the Crusader states for Islam, when he took Edessa in 1144. The fall of Edessa may be seen as the first major landmark in the Muslim recovery. Zengi was murdered by a slave in 1146; there can be little doubt that his removal from the scene was a major reprieve for the Crusaders.

Nur al-Din and the Second Crusade

During the next phase of Muslim recovery, Zengi's son, Nur al-Din (d 1174), combined strong-arm politics with very skilful religious propaganda. Within the context of his ambitions for himself and for his family, he worked slowly towards the unification of Egypt and Syria and the encirclement of the remaining Frankish states, beginning with Antioch.

Figure 1.22 Horseman with a banner, lustre dish, tenth century, Samarra, Iraq

The loss of Edessa and the vulnerability of Antioch provoked the preaching and sending of the Second Crusade in 1147–8 under the command of Conrad III, the German emperor, and Louis VII, the French king. This Crusade was a fiasco. It made for Damascus, then under the control of the city's governor Ünür, and conducted an unsuccessful siege of the city (which had an alliance at that time with Crusader Jerusalem). The Crusade then fizzled out, without recapturing Edessa or stemming the mounting power of Nur al-Din.

Nur al-Din conquered Damascus in 1154 and made himself supreme Muslim ruler in Syria. Both Nur al-Din and the Crusaders then turned their attention to Egypt and the ailing Fatimid caliphate, which was wracked with internal dissension and weakness. Ascalon had fallen to the Franks in 1153 and some factions at the Fatimid court favoured accommodation with them; others asked Nur al-Din for help. A Muslim army sent under the command of the Kurdish soldier Shirkuh in 1168–9 prevented the Crusaders from conquering Egypt. Salah al-Din (Saladin) b. Ayyub, Shirkuh's nephew, took over the leadership of the Muslim army in Egypt in March 1169 on the death of his uncle. Acting officially as the lieutenant of Nur al-Din, Saladin took control of the Fatimid caliphate which he abolished in 1171. Nur al-Din had laid the foundations of Muslim reunification and reaffirmed the sole legitimacy of the Sunni Abbasid caliphate. A rift between Saladin and Nur al-Din, which was clearly on the cards, was prevented by the death of Nur al-Din in 1174.

Saladin, 569–589/1174–1193

Saladin became the next and most famous of the Muslim Counter-Crusade leaders (plate 1.5). He promoted himself as the rightful successor of Nur al-Din. In the years 1174 to 1187 many of Saladin's efforts were directed at subjugating his Muslim rivals and creating a united front in Egypt and Syria against the Crusaders. Finally in

Plate 1.5 Fals *of Saladin, copper, 578/1182–3, Nisibin, Turkey*

1187 he fought the Crusaders under the command of King Guy of Lusignan in the key battle of Hattin on 4 July and inflicted a famous victory on them. The reconquest of important Crusader possessions, such as Acre, followed. Saladin's triumph was crowned with the retaking of Jerusalem on 2 October 1187. By the end of 1187, only a few parts of the Latin kingdom of Jerusalem remained in Crusader hands, notably Tyre. Saladin had created a system of collective family rule, delegating to his relations control of the major cities and territories which he conquered, thereby creating a loose confederation of states with himself at the head. This system continued under his successors, the Ayyubids, his own family dynasty.

The Third and Fourth Crusades

The defeat at Hattin and the fall of Jerusalem triggered a new Crusading enterprise: the three most powerful monarchs of western Europe, Frederick Barbarossa of the Holy Roman Empire, Philip of France and Richard the Lionheart, embarked on the Third Crusade. This began in earnest with a Crusader attack against Acre which finally capitulated to the Crusaders in 1191. Despite this and other Crusader victories over Saladin, the Third Crusade ended with a truce in 1192; it was agreed that the Franks should hold most of the coastal strip whilst Jerusalem remained in Muslim hands. A year later, Saladin died. Although he had won at Hattin, regained Jerusalem for Islam and kept Egypt united with the rest of the Muslim Levant, he had failed to take Tyre and to rid the Levant of the Crusaders. His success in abolishing the Fatimid Shi'ite caliphate of Cairo removed the ancient Sunni–Shi'ite feud between the Egyptian government on the one hand and the Sunni rulers of Syria on the other – a rift from which the Crusaders had benefited. From 1193 onwards, the Crusaders focused much more attention on attacking Egypt, believing that it held the key to reconquering Jerusalem. Egypt was the ostensible target of the Fourth Crusade in 1202, led by Boniface de Montferrat and Baldwin IX of Flanders. However, this notorious Crusade did not fight Muslims but instead ended with the conquest of Constantinople in April 1204 and the establishment of the Latin empire of Constantinople (1204–61).

The Ayyubids, Saladin's Family Dynasty, 589–648/1193–1250

At the death of Saladin, the Muslims still had the upper hand and the Crusader states were seriously weakened. The latter possessed a few ports and a narrow strip of the hinterland. Yet, despite the Muslims' advantages, they did not press them home.[15] They preferred to treat the Franks as rulers with whom to make political alliances and commercial treaties. The Kurdish Ayyubids, members of Saladin's family, succeeded to his territories in Egypt, Syria and Mesopotamia. Their government traditions were based on those of the Seljuqs and

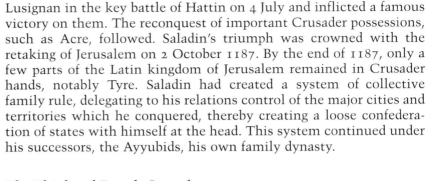

Figure 1.23 Bronze coin of the Seljuq prince Rukn al-Din Sulayman (reigned 592–600/1195–1204), Turkey

Figure 1.24 Astrological image (the moon?) on copper coin, 626/1228–9, Mosul, Iraq

Figure 1.25 *Dinar of the only female Mamluk ruler, Shajarat al-Durr ('Tree of Pearls'), 648/1250–1, Cairo, Egypt*

they were also heirs to the Fatimid administration in Egypt. Individual Ayyubid rulers governed as a confederacy rather than a centralised polity, thereby ensuring the continued survival of the Crusader states. The Ayyubid princes expended their energies in capturing cities and fortresses from each other rather than in prosecuting *jihad* against the Franks. They were usually concerned with *détente* with the Crusader settlements on the Syrian coast rather than overt hostilities so that they could reap the economic advantages of maintaining trade routes across Frankish territory to the sea. In the second half of the Ayyubid period family conflicts abounded and political equilibrium was rare.[16]

Subsequent Crusades in the Ayyubid period were sent against Egypt; at a time when the Mongols from the east posed an even greater threat to the Islamic world, some Christian monarchs sought alliances with the Mongols against the Muslims (cf. colour plate 4). Saladin's brother, al-ʿAdil, was still sultan of Egypt when the Fifth Crusade began to arrive in 1218 on the Nile Delta and took Damietta the following year. Al-ʿAdil died the same year and his son, al-Kamil, who succeeded him, regained Damietta in 1221.

Figure 1.26 *Mounted hunters, mina'i tile in relief, early thirteenth century, probably Kashan, Iran*

In 1228 Frederick II of Sicily arrived on Crusade in Palestine. The Ayyubid sultan al-Kamil, threatened by internal family strife, preferred negotiation to war and concluded a treaty with Frederick a year later, surrendering Jerusalem, Bethlehem, Nazareth and other districts to the Crusaders. This capitulation over Jerusalem brought al-Kamil widespread Muslim criticism. A devastating blow was dealt to Jerusalem in 1244 when soldiers from distant Khwarazm in Central Asia, displaced by the Mongol invasions and moving westwards on the rampage, took advantage of the weakness of the city, which they conquered and sacked. Thereafter Jerusalem reverted to Islamic rule. Frankish decline continued, despite the Crusade of Louis IV of France who captured Damietta in 1249 and then advanced on Cairo. He was cornered in al-Mansura and forced to surrender.

It was in the Ayyubid period, especially in the 1240s, that the Franks reached their greatest territorial expansion of the thirteenth century. It was at this point that it was most apparent how fully integrated the Franks had become in the political map of the Near East; they were one of a number of quasi-indigenous groups vying for power in the area and treated as such by their Muslim neighbours. The Franks might still rely on Europe for men and equipment but politically they were part of the Near Eastern political jigsaw; the Franks in the Ayyubid period, lodged as they were between the intensive campaigns of the last years of Saladin's career and the uncompromising attempts to destroy them which were to come from the Mamluks in the second half of the thirteenth century, enjoyed a short intermezzo in which they seem to have been in some ways just another warring faction in Middle Eastern politics.

The Mamluks: The Expulsion of the Franks from the Levant

With the overthrow of the Ayyubids and the accession of a new dynasty, the militant Mamluks of Egypt, in 1250, the Islamic Counter-Crusade was revitalised and the steps necessary to remove

Figure 1.27 *Inscription on the minaret of the Great Mosque with the name of the craftsman and the date 483/1090, Aleppo, Syria*

Figure 1.28 Qasr al-Ablaq, citadel (palace of al-Nasir Muhammad), plan and interior view, 713–14/1313–15, Cairo, Egypt

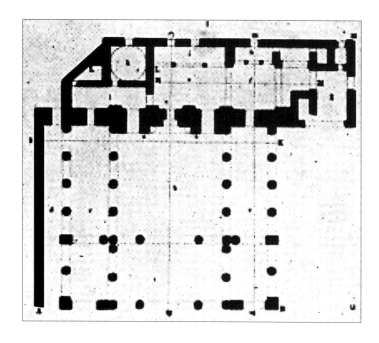

Plate 1.6 Silver dirham, obverse, struck 667/1268 in Cairo

the Crusaders permanently from the Near East could be set in train. The Mamluk sultans were interested in the public face of religion and readily donned the mantle of the leaders of the Sunni world. Pressures from a new enemy, the Mongols, and the continuing presence of the Franks formed a powerful focus to channel the energies of the new dynasty. Although the Mongol army under Hülegü set out with the express aims of abolishing the 'Abbasid caliphate, destroying the Assassins of Alamut and advancing on Egypt, the last of these objectives was never achieved. Concerned with the Mongol threat, the Mamluk sultans nevertheless made the extirpation of the Crusader presence a major priority, especially after their famous victory over the hitherto invincible Mongols at the battle of Goliath's Well ('Ayn Jalut) in 1260.

Figure 1.29 Transcription of coin of Baybars, late thirteenth century, Egypt

The General State of the Islamic World on the Eve of the First Crusade

It is a familiar tenet of Crusader history that the warriors of the First Crusade succeeded because of Muslim disunity and weakness. Had the First Crusade arrived even ten years earlier, it would have met strong, unified resistance from the state then ruled by Malikshah, the last of the three so-called Great Seljuq sultans. His western domains included Iraq, Syria and Palestine. Yet previous scholarly discussions of the overall Muslim position in 488/1095 have not gone far enough in emphasising to what extent the Islamic world was bereft of unity and catastrophically weakened both by a complete lack of powerful leadership and by religious schism.

The Devastating Events of the Years 485–487/1092–1094

In the space of less than two years, beginning in 485/1092, there was a clean sweep of *all* the major political leaders of the Islamic world from Egypt eastwards. In 485/1092 the greatest figure of Seljuq history, the vizier Nizam al-Mulk, the *de facto* ruler of the Seljuq empire for over thirty years, was murdered. A month later, Malikshah, the third Seljuq sultan, died in suspicious circumstances, after a successful twenty-year reign, followed closely by his wife, grandson and other powerful political figures. The Muslim sources view the year 487/1094 as even more doom-laden, for in this year yet another era was brought to an end with the death of the Fatimid caliph of Egypt, al-Mustansir, the arch-enemy of the Seljuqs, who had ruled for fifty-eight years. His death was closely followed by that of *his* vizier, Badr al-Jamali, builder of the city wall of Cairo (plates 2.1–2.3, 2.4–2.6). Also in 487/1094 the ʿAbbasid Sunni caliph al-Muqtadi died. As the Mamluk historian Ibn Taghribirdi puts it: 'This year is called the year of the death of caliphs and commanders.'[10]

Figure 2.2 Quarter dinar minted by the Fatimid caliph al-Mustansir (427–87/1036–94), Sicily

This succession of deaths in both the key power centres of the Islamic world, namely the Seljuq and Fatimid empires, occurring at exactly the same time, must have had the same impact as the disintegration of the Iron Curtain from 1989 onwards: familiar political entities gave way to disorientation and anarchy. The timing of the First Crusade simply could not have been more propitious. Had the Europeans somehow been briefed that *this* was the perfect moment to pounce? Unfortunately there is little evidence on this in the Islamic sources, but seldom has the arm of coincidence been longer.

The Debilitating Effects of Religious Schism

Religious schism permeated Islamic life at every level of society. As 'good Sunni Islamic rulers' the Seljuqs had pursued a vigorous foreign policy in the period 1063–92, the main thrust of which had been to wage war not against Byzantium or the Christian kingdoms of the Caucasus, although such initiatives did occur, but against fellow

Plate 2.1 Bab al-Futuh,
480/1087, Cairo, Egypt

(Creswell Photographic Archive, Ashmolean Museum, Oxford, neg. C. 3623)

(Creswell Photographic Archive, Ashmolean Museum, Oxford, neg. C. 3614)

Plate 2.2 Bab al-Futuh,
bastions, 480/1087, Cairo, Egypt

35

Plate 2.3 *Bab al-Futuh,*
480/1087, Cairo, Egypt

(Creswell Photographic Archive,
Ashmolean Museum, Oxford,
neg. C. 163)

Muslims – the 'heretical' Fatimid Shi'ite caliphate of Cairo – and a protracted struggle was fought out in Syria and Palestine. The ideological and political enmity between Fatimid Isma'ili Shi'ites and Seljuq Sunnis was deeply entrenched and in practice it was almost unthinkable for them to form a united Islamic front against the external enemy, the Crusaders.

The Spirit of the Times

The loss of all effective leadership and the rampant sectarian suspicion and hostility within the bosom of Islam provoked disorientation and angst. The Muslims were living through exceptionally turbulent times. A new Islamic century – the sixth – was imminent (it would begin on 2 September 1106) and many awaited it with fear, especially after the year 492/1099 had witnessed the fall of Jerusalem. Perhaps some of them believed the Final Day was coming; others hoped that the new century would, like preceding centuries, bring a 'renewer' (*mujaddid*) of the Islamic faith. Indeed, many thought that al-Ghazali was that figure. During the years leading up to the new century, the fragmented Muslim world, torn apart by schism, wars and nomadic invasions, must have felt doom-laden. But even so, the last thing that the Muslims had expected was invasion from western Europe. After the initial onslaught had hit them, perhaps they thought that other even more cataclysmic events would follow. Medieval Muslims were acquainted with astrological phenomena – comets, meteors, the movement of the stars – and were accustomed to deriving omens and foreseeing the future from them. The Syrian chronicler al-'Azimi, who incorporates only brief snippets of historical information in his work, takes the trouble to report for the year 489/1096 that when the Franks first appear 'Saturn was in Virgo'.[11] His readers would be able to interpret this account as being highly inauspicious and alarming. As the Muslim encyclopaedist al-Qazwini, writes: 'the astrologers call Saturn the largest star of misfortune . . . and they ascribe to it devastation, ruin, grief and cares'.[12]

The incidence of plague, mentioned for Egypt in the years

Plate 2.4 *Bab al-Nasr, 480/1087, Cairo, Egypt*

(Creswell Photographic Archive, Ashmolean Museum, Oxford, neg. C. 1429)

Figure 2.3 *Signs of the zodiac, mirror of Artuq Shah, cast bronze, between 631/1233 and 660/1262, Turkey*

490/1097 and 493/1099–1100, must have deepened the atmosphere of gloom.[13] This disaster alone must have played its part in preventing the Fatimids from getting more closely involved than they did in the battles of the First Crusade and retaining their new-won control of Jerusalem and Palestine.

The Eastern Perspective – Seljuq Disunity, 485–492/1092–1099

After the deaths of Nizam al-Mulk and Malikshah in 485/1092, the Seljuqs, and especially two sons of Malikshah, Barkyaruq and Muhammad, were locked in a protracted military conflict which lasted until Barkyaruq's death in 498/1105. This conflict gobbled up almost all the available military resources. It was fought out in western Iran, but its repercussions were felt in Iraq, the traditional

38

Figure 2.4 Signs of the zodiac, Vaso del Rota, inlaid metal, late twelfth century, Iran

Plate 2.5 *Bab al-Nasr from within, 480/1087, Cairo, Egypt*

(Creswell Photographic Archive, Ashmolean Museum, Oxford, neg. C. 151)

seat of the Sunni caliph, in eastern Iran and Central Asia, and, by default, in distant Syria and Palestine, earlier centres of Seljuq activity. The Seljuq princes in the east had no time or motivation to concern themselves with events in the Levant and left Jerusalem to its fate.

Anatolia in the Late Eleventh Century

The same disunity characterised other areas of the Islamic world. The nomadic Turks of Anatolia were the first Muslim foe to be encountered by the Crusaders after they left Constantinople. As already mentioned, the battle of Manzikert in 463/1071 is usually taken as a convenient date to symbolise the beginning of a gradual but steady process by which diverse groups of nomadic Turks infiltrated the Byzantine empire, pursuing their time-honoured lifestyle of pastoralism and raiding. We do not know how numerous these groups were: some were authorised to raid by the Seljuq sultans, others progressed unchecked by any allegiance, even nominal, to a supra-tribal authority. The Seljuq ruler of western Asia Minor, Qilij Arslan (ruled 485–500/1092–1107), called 'sultan' retrospectively in the sources, came from a renegade branch of the great Seljuq family, and even though he was far from Iran he was still attached emotionally to his tribal heritage in the east. In the political instability of the post-485/1092 period he interfered whenever possible in the affairs of

Figure 2.5 Sign of Libra, Mamluk bowl, inlaid metal, fourteenth century, Syria(?)

Figure 2.6 Apotropaic door-knocker for a mosque, cast bronze, c. 1200, Jazirat ibn 'Umar (Cizre), Turkey

the Seljuq sultanate in the east, to exploit its weakness and to gain territory for himself. This was of far greater moment to him than embarking on campaigns across the mountains into Syria and Palestine to fight the Crusaders. Even within Anatolia there was no semblance of overall political unity between the disparate nomadic Turkish groups vying for territory there in the aftermath of the battle of Manzikert.[14] The Danishmendids, who held sway in central Anatolia between Sivas and Malatya, did, it is true, form a temporary alliance with the Seljuqs of western Anatolia for the battle of Dorylaeum (July 1097), but such alliances were always ephemeral. Any concerted Turcoman initiative into Palestine or Syria was inconceivable.[15]

Figure 2.7 Harpy, stone relief on city wall, early thirteenth century, Konya, Turkey

Figure 2.8 The sun as an astrological image, inlaid bronze basin, c. 1250, Mosul, Iraq

بعمله والإنفاق عليه من ماله مولانا

Figure 2.9 *Inscription on city walls, late twelfth century, Diyarbakr, Turkey*

The Turks of Anatolia, although fierce and effective fighters, were few in number. They could not prevail in fixed encounters, where superior numerical forces were bound to win. But they could harass their enemies by firing arrows from horseback and they caused much hardship to the incoming Crusader armies. What they could not do, however, was stop the progress of the Franks *en bloc* across Asia Minor. Unfortunately, being nomads, they did not leave behind written records of their achievements; more especially, there are no accounts of the First Crusade from the perspective of these nomads of Anatolia.

The Egyptian Perspective 487–492/1094–1099

The Fatimid rulers of Egypt are portrayed most unfavourably by the great Sunni historians of the Islamic Middle Ages, for they had begun life as a secretive, esoteric, extremist Isma'ili Shi'ite sect and in the second half of the eleventh century they became the major enemies of the Seljuqs, who presented themselves as the 'defenders of Sunni Islam'. On the eve of the First Crusade, the Fatimids were experiencing difficulties. Their 'aberrant' religious persuasion usually cut them off altogether from alliances with neighbouring Sunni Muslim powers in Syria and Palestine. Their *de facto* rulers, the viziers Badr al-Jamali (d 488/1095) and then his son, al-Afdal (d 515/1121), chose to rule through young puppet caliphs. The great medieval Muslim

Figure 2.10 *Seljuq inscription on city walls, 476/1083–4, Diyarbakr, Turkey*

AMIDA ·476·AH شهور في الواحد ابن عباس محمد

Plate 2.6 Bab al-Nasr,
480/1087, Cairo, Egypt

(Creswell Photographic Archive,
Ashmolean Museum, Oxford,
neg. C. 3430)

biographer Ibn Khallikan (d 681/1282) believes Fatimid decline to
have been under way as early as the year 466/1074: 'the authority of
al-Mustansir had been greatly enfeebled and the affairs of the empire
had fallen into disorder'.[16]

Events within the Fatimid empire and initiatives launched by
its leaders into Palestine and Syria played an important part in the
build-up to the coming of the First Crusade. All too often, it must be
said, Fatimid activity in this period has been sadly neglected.

The Nizari Schism

In 487/1094 the death of the Fatimid caliph al-Mustansir provoked a
major succession crisis: his eldest son, Nizar, was passed over in
favour of another son, al-Musta'li. Nizar fled to Alexandria where he
was killed, and al-Musta'li came to the throne. This so-called Nizari
schism split the Isma'ilis once again. The heart went out of the

Fatimid ideology in Cairo. It was around this time, in 483/1090, that the Persian Isma'ilis, who under the charismatic leadership of Hasan-i Sabbah had made the remote citadel of Alamut in north-west Iran their headquarters, espoused the claims of Nizar and broke away from Cairo. Henceforth the missionary zeal and revolutionary dynamism of the Isma'ilis were vested in this breakaway group – popularly known, amongst other derogatory titles, as the Assassins (*Hashishiyya*). In the twelfth century they were to play a significant part in the rich tapestry of Levantine and Crusader political life and intrigues.

Fatimid Involvement in Syria and Palestine

Figure 2.11 *Hare, Fatimid lustre dish, eleventh century, Egypt*

In the year 491/1097–8, during the early stages of the First Crusade, the Fatimid army under the personal leadership of al-Afdal, the vizier and *de facto* ruler of the empire, made a pre-emptive strike on Palestine and seized Jerusalem. The city had been left in the hands of two Seljuq vassals, Turcoman chiefs of the Artuqid family: Sukman and his brother, Il-Ghazi.[17] A year later the Crusaders took Jerusalem and routed an army under al-Afdal at Ascalon.[18] The sudden move by al-Afdal on Jerusalem, with its extraordinary timing, requires an explanation which scholars on the Islamic side do not give. Why did al-Afdal make this move? Was he acting because he had prior knowledge of the Crusaders' plans? If so, did he take the city *on behalf* of the Crusaders, with whom he may have made an alliance beforehand, or did he do it *to stop* the Crusaders capturing Jerusalem? These are important historical questions to which one might expect to find answers in the Islamic sources. The evidence is very scanty indeed but is worth examining here,[19] since, as the German scholar Köhler observes, scholarly discussions on this question tend to ignore the Islamic evidence.

What do the Muslim chroniclers say about all this? The Aleppan chronicler al-'Azimi relates for the year 489/1095–6 that the Byzantine emperor 'wrote to the Muslims informing them of the appearance of the Franks'.[20] This is a very early date for the Muslims to have known of the Franks' plans. It is not clear which Muslims are meant here, but it could well have been the Fatimids, and the information, which incidentally could be interpreted to put the Byzantine emperor in a bad light, might well have sparked off al-Afdal's decision to take Jerusalem. Alternatively, this snippet of information may have been included so as to suggest that the Byzantine emperor was party to an agreement with both the Crusaders *and* the 'Muslims' and that he was just telling the latter when to expect the Crusaders' arrival. Or again, the Byzantine emperor may have been threatening the Muslims. The fact that no other source mentions this letter could mean that it is a fabrication or that other Muslim chroniclers omitted it because it puts some of their co-religionists (whoever they may be) in a bad light.

Figure 2.12 Horsemen in combat, Cappella Palatina, ceiling, c. 1140, Palermo, Sicily

All these interpretations suggest that one group of Muslims knew about the coming of the Crusade in good time but that possibly they had their own reasons for not spreading the information and trying to defend Islamic territory more effectively.

A second piece of evidence from another chronicle should now be mentioned. The chronicle of Ibn Zafir (d. 613/1216) is the earliest surviving account of the last century of Fatimid rule. When speaking of the Franks' seizure of Jerusalem from the Fatimids, Ibn Zafir writes: 'nobody there had the strength to resist the Franks. If it [Jerusalem] had been left in the hands of the Artuqids [i.e. Sukman and Il-Ghazi] it would have been better for the Muslims.' For al-Afdal, Ibn Zafir goes on to say, it was better that the Franks should occupy the Syrian ports, 'so that they could prevent the spread of the influence of the Turks to the lands of Egypt'.[21]

This strongly suggests that initially at least al-Afdal was adopting a policy of favouring the Crusaders rather than the Seljuq Turks, whom he viewed as his greater enemy; and that he hoped that the Crusaders would form a buffer between Egypt and the Turks. The invasion of Syria by the Turcomans under Atsiz in the 1070s was still a traumatic memory for the Fatimids.[22]

Why then do we read that the Franks routed al-Afdal and the Fatimid army who had attacked them while they were besieging Jerusalem? It may well be that al-Afdal thought that the Franks would allow him to keep Jerusalem as part of a pre-arranged agreement and that he then found out too late that the Franks had their own sights on the city. So he broke with them. Certainly the Franks' siege of Jerusalem seems to have prompted al-Afdal to move against the Franks, as is suggested by Ibn Muyassar: 'In Rajab [492] the Franks laid siege to Jerusalem . . . al-Afdal went out to them with his troops. When the Franks heard about his departure [from Cairo] they persisted in besieging it until they took possession of it on Friday 22 Sha'ban.'[23] After the city had fallen, according to Ibn Muyassar:

'Al-Afdal came to Ascalon on 14 Ramadan. He sent an envoy to the Franks rebuking them for what they had done.'[24]

The Frankish response, such as it was, menaced al-Afdal with references to their great numbers of men. They then attacked al-Afdal's army. He fled to Ascalon which the Franks then besieged. They departed and al-Afdal departed by sea for Cairo.[25]

The reasons for the timing of al-Afdal's attack on Jerusalem are also perhaps hinted at by the Damascus chronicler Ibn al-Qalanisi. Immediately after his account of the fall of Antioch to the Crusaders in the month of Jumada I 491/June 1098, he launches into an account of al-Afdal's conquest of Jerusalem the very next month.[26] We may infer from this timing that for al-Afdal the fall of Antioch was perhaps a turning point, and that he felt he could not trust the Franks not to move south. If there ever had been an agreement between the Franks and the Fatimids to divide up the Levant, it certainly seems to have collapsed after Antioch. On the Muslim side the preceding evidence seems to be all that has come to light so far but it is enough to suggest initial Fatimid–Crusader collaboration, followed by Fatimid disillusionment. It is difficult to assess how much of this is anti-Fatimid propaganda on the part of later Sunni historians, but on balance – and especially bearing in mind the testimony of al-'Azimi – the evidence is very telling.[27]

The chronicler Ibn al-Athir (d. 630/1233), speaking of the genesis of the First Crusade, includes an account which lays the blame squarely on the Fatimids:

> It was said that the 'Alid rulers of Egypt, when they saw the power of the Seljuq state and their strength and their conquering of the lands of Syria as far as Gaza, there remaining between them and Egypt no province to hold them back, and [when they saw too] Atsiz [a Seljuq commander] entering Egypt and blockading it, they were afraid and they sent messages to the Franks inviting them to go out to Syria to conquer it so that they [the Franks] would be between them [the Fatimids] and the Muslims.[28]

Incidentally, the writer's prejudices against the Fatimids are clear here as he is speaking of two distinct groups, the Fatimids and the Muslims.

From the above accounts, we can see that unlike most other medieval Islamic sources which gloss over the Fatimids' activities in the period immediately before and after the coming of the Franks, there are some clues here that the Fatimids were more interested in defending their own territories against their traditional enemy, the Turks, than in staving off the threat from western Europe. Long familiarity with the Christian Byzantine empire may even have led to an agreement with Byzantium to collaborate with the Crusaders when they came. Possibly, too, al-Afdal viewed the Crusaders as working for the Byzantines, with whom he was well acquainted.

Whatever the fuller truth may be,[29] the Fatimids clearly underestimated the objectives of the Franks and discovered them too late. We see here too the strong possibility that even before the fall of Jerusalem and the establishment of the Crusader states in the Levant, Muslim politicians were prepared to collaborate with the new 'enemy' against their traditional rivals, even though the latter were fellow-Muslims. This trend was to increase in the early decades of the twelfth century and to persist as a feature of Crusader–Muslim relations right up to the end of the Crusader presence in the Near East.

A Summary of the State of the Islamic Lands on the Eve of the First Crusade

It has frequently been said that the initial success of the Crusaders was due to their unity and to Muslim disunity. This disunity has just been dissected and re-emphasised. The Muslim world – to put it succinctly – was bereft of major leaders in all the areas which were to receive the impact of the Frankish invasions. Nor was there strong Muslim leadership in neighbouring countries. Previous scholarship on the Muslim world has also not adequately stressed the crippling effects of religious schisms. The 'heretical' Fatimid Isma'ili Shi'ite caliphate had set itself up in the tenth century in direct opposition to the 'Abbasid Sunni caliphate centred on Baghdad. In the eleventh century the resultant rivalry manifested itself in military confrontation between the Fatimids and the Seljuqs. Indeed, the Seljuqs, despite being famous for their victory in 463/1071 under Alp Arslan over the Byzantine army under the emperor Romanus Diogenes IV at the battle of Manzikert, were in fact far more zealous in their prosecution of *jihad* against the 'heretical' Fatimids than in following up their success in Asia Minor. In making this choice of priorities the Seljuqs were merely conforming to the pattern of settled introversion which was so characteristic of much of the Muslim world in the Middle Ages. The close focus on the conflicts within the *Dar al-Islam* or Islamic community entailed a reciprocal neglect of threats from the outside world. The initial response to the Mongol invasions a little over a century later told the same story.

The Seljuq military commanders and princes who ruled a series of city-states centred on places such as Aleppo, Damascus and Mosul at the turn of the eleventh century might well be mutually hostile and in a state of almost constant war with each other but these were, so to speak, family squabbles. The vast majority of these leaders had inherited a deep-rooted reluctance to make alliances with Fatimid Egypt, the old enemy Shi'ite superpower. Therein lay their downfall. For such a supra-sectarian Muslim alliance – uniting the Fatimids, who still had access to the sea along the Egyptian coast, with the Turkish armies of the Muslim cities of Syria and Palestine – could have contained and even eradicated the Crusader threat before it was

Figure 2.13 *Epigraphic roundel on a brass basin made for Hugh de Lusignan, King of Jerusalem and Cyprus (1324–59), the only Islamic vessel which bears the name and titles of a non-Muslim ruler; probably Egypt or Syria*

too late and before the Franks had seized and fortified the Syrian ports and gone on to establish four Crusader states in the area – Jerusalem, Edessa, Antioch and Tripoli.

Syria and Palestine on the Eve of the First Crusade

The religious identity of the Muslims of Syria and Palestine, the areas about to be affected most directly by the First Crusade, was not uniform. These lands were probably mostly Sunni but they also contained some Shi'ite communities, such as in Tripoli and other cities which had periodically been under the suzerainty of the Fatimids, as well as in Aleppo and Damascus. There were also long-established Christian and Jewish communities in the area. The Christians had widely varying affiliations – the Maronites, Armenians, Jacobites, Nestorians and Melkites were all represented – whilst in Egypt the Copts were a powerful minority, especially in the administration.

Some evidence as to Muslim attitudes to Christians in the eleventh century can be found in the work of the Muslim writer al-Wasiti, a Shafi'ite preacher in the Aqsa mosque in Jerusalem. He composed a work on the Merits of Jerusalem (*Fada'il al-Quds*) no later than 410/1019–20 and it is important to note that in it there is an unmistakable tone of hostility towards Christianity. Indeed, he warns Muslim pilgrims to Jerusalem not to enter the churches there.[30] Perhaps this is a reflection of the atmosphere which may well have prevailed after the persecutions of al-Hakim. Those persecutions had of course culminated in the destruction of the Church of the Holy Sepulcre itself on 4 Safar 400/28 September 1009.[31]

Figure 2.14 Foot soldier, glazed ceramic bowl, ninth–tenth centuries, Iran

However, at least in the view of some observers, the situation had improved by the middle of the century. For example, the Persian Isma'ili traveller Nasir-i Khusraw, who visited the Holy Land and Jerusalem in 438/1046, gives a much more neutral account. He records that Jerusalem was a centre of pilgrimage for those who could not make the journey to Mecca; in some years, more than 20,000 people assembled there.[32] He also mentions the presence of Christians and Jews: 'The Christians and Jews come there too in a great number from the provinces of the Byzantine empire and other countries to visit the Church and the Temple.'[33]

As well as a very detailed description of Jerusalem and its Islamic monuments, Nasir-i Khusraw describes the Church of the Holy Sepulchre: 'The Christians possess in Jerusalem a big church which bears the name of the Church of Refuse (*Bi'at al-Qumama*) and they revere it greatly. Every year people come in large numbers from the Byzantine lands to make pilgrimage to it.'[34] The derogatory pun, well known in Crusader times, on the name of the Church of the Holy Sepulchre, known to the eastern Christians as *Bi'at* (or *Kanisat*) *al-Qiyama* – the Church of the Resurrection – was obviously in use by the 1040s.

Nasir-i Khusraw is full of admiration for the church, which he describes as holding up to 8,000 people. His very detailed description is straightforward and free from religious rhetoric, and, unlike later Muslim writers, he does not pass judgement on the images that he sees displayed in this Christian place of worship: 'One sees there in several places pictures representing Jesus mounted upon an ass; one also notices portraits of the prophets Abraham, Ishmael, Isaac, Jacob and his sons.'[35] These portraits were varnished and covered with glass which was polished every day. He ends up with the admiring words: 'This church is such that one could not see any other like it in any other place in the world.'[36]

What of life in the Holy Land itself and in the sacred city of Jerusalem in particular, in the 1090s? A solitary Muslim source has survived from the period immediately preceding the First Crusade and this sheds light on certain aspects of life in the Holy Land in the last decade of the eleventh century. It is an account of a journey made to the east from Spain by a Muslim *hadith* scholar, Ibn al-'Arabi (not the celebrated mystic of the same name), who set out with his father in Rabi'I 485/April 1092.[37] The motives for this journey may have been to escape from political persecution, but Ibn al-'Arabi, like many a Muslim scholar of al-Andalus before and after him, says that he went east in search of knowledge: 'I was desirous of seeking knowledge in the utmost extremities [of the earth].'[38] Father and son survived a shipwreck off the North African coast when the boat on which they were travelling broke into pieces near Barqa.

Figure 2.15 *Foot soldiers, cauldron, inlaid metal, early fourteenth century, probably Iraq*

Whilst his father went on to perform the pilgrimage to Mecca, Ibn al-'Arabi opted to stay on in the Holy Land and to imbibe the religious knowledge which he saw all around him. His account of the religious milieu in Palestine indicates that it was 'teeming with scholars',[39] both inhabitants of the area itself and those who had come from other regions of the Islamic world. Faced with such an opportunity, he felt impelled to postpone the pilgrimage.[40] In Jerusalem, Ibn al-'Arabi found thriving *madrasa*s for the Shafi'ites and the Hanafites, and he lists the names of prominent scholars who met to study and to engage in scholarly disputations there.[41] Perhaps the most famous figure whom Ibn al-'Arabi met in Jerusalem was al-Tartushi, who had also come from distant Spain and was staying in a part of the Aqsa mosque. This holy monument also housed religious scholars from Khurasan in eastern Iran.[42] Ibn al-'Arabi is fired with enthusiasm for what he saw: 'We entered the Holy Land and reached the Aqsa mosque. The full moon of knowledge shone for me and I was illuminated by it for more than three years.'[43]

Incidentally, it was around the end of Ibn al-'Arabi's stay in Jerusalem that the most famous medieval Islamic scholar of all, al-Ghazali, underwent his spiritual crisis in Baghdad in 488/1095 and came for a while to Jerusalem to meditate daily in the Dome of the Rock.[44] Ibn al-'Arabi stresses that Jerusalem was the meeting place for religious scholars of all three faiths – Islam, Christianity and Judaism.[45]

49

Ibn al-'Arabi does not suggest that the local Christians were suffering from oppression on the part of their Muslim overlords; nor were the Jews, for that matter. Commenting on Jerusalem as a whole, he remarks that the Christians cultivated its estates and kept its churches in good repair.[46] When he moved to Ascalon, Ibn al-'Arabi found a similarly thriving scholarly atmosphere, describing it as a 'sea of culture'.[47]

It is, of course, dangerous to generalise on the basis of an isolated account of one traveller, Ibn al-'Arabi, who visited the Holy Land, stayed for only a short time there and wrote up his experiences ten years later when he arrived back in Spain. Nevertheless, his testimony, dated as it is to the very eve of the First Crusade, does give some information on the Islamic religious milieu of Jerusalem and the Holy Land just before the Franks came. According to Ibn al-'Arabi at least, Jerusalem was a religious centre for believers in all three monotheistic faiths, Muslims, Christians and Jews. There is no suggestion here that Christian pilgrims, either from Byzantium or western Europe, were being prevented from visiting the Holy Places of Jerusalem.

However, the rosy picture given to us by Ibn al-'Arabi should be counterbalanced by an interesting observation recorded by al-'Azimi for the year 486/1093–4: 'The people of the Syrian ports (al-Sawahil) prevented Frankish and Byzantine pilgrims from crossing to Jerusalem. Those of them who survived spread the news about that to their country. So they prepared themselves for military invasion (*ghaza*).'[48]

Here is a clear statement – but only in a single source – that Muslims had harassed Christian pilgrims and that not all of them had survived to tell the tale.[49]

Why Did the First Crusade Come? – Muslim Interpretations

We shall now look in chronological order at what was said by some of the Muslim chroniclers themselves in the centuries immediately following the First Crusade and at how much they understood of this unexpected invasion of the House of Islam. It was common practice for each successive generation of chroniclers to copy the historiographical material of their predecessors – there was no ignominy attached to such plagiarism which was seen as the continuation of a long tradition to be safeguarded. Thus there is much similarity between many of the Muslim accounts of the First Crusade which date from different periods and many of them relate the events without comment or interpretation. The excerpts given here have been chosen because they say something of special interest which makes them stand out from the usual narratives. The Islamic chroniclers do not seem to link the arrival of the western Europeans with the distant event of al-Hakim's destruction of the Church of the Holy Sepulchre nor with the appeals by Byzantium to Europe for help against the Turkish threat on its eastern borders. Nor do the Muslim sources present sophisticated analyses of historical events – their horizons are narrowly Islamic – but some of them at least drop revealing hints.

The earliest surviving sources – Ibn al-Qalanisi and al-'Azimi – both write about the coming of the First Crusade, but Ibn al-Qalanisi does not say why the Franks have come. Instead, he just launches straight into the story.[50] Moreover, al-'Azimi, as already noted, is the only writer to mention as an immediate *casus belli* that Christian pilgrims were prevented from visiting Jerusalem in the year 486/1093–4 and he links this event with the Crusaders coming to the Levant.

Al-'Azimi's chronicle has survived in very fragmentary form: his work often looks like draft notes for (or from) a longer history. Despite the brevity of his account, he implies that there is a pattern of Crusader movement southwards which extends from Spain through North Africa to the Levant. He sees the link between the fall of Toledo to the Christians of Muslim Spain in 461/1068,[51] the taking of al-Mahdiyya in North Africa by the Normans of Sicily in 479/1086,[52] and the coming of the Crusaders to the Levant.

Figure 2.16 *Mosque of al-Hakim, perspectival view, 380–403/990–1013, Cairo, Egypt*

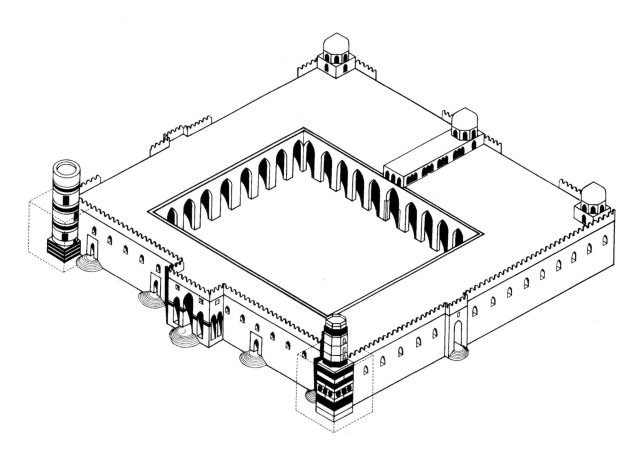

Figure 2.17 Mosque of
al-Hakim, inscription band,
*380–403/990–1013, Cairo,
Egypt*

These rudimentary hints of al-'Azimi – which, for all their brevity, reveal a remarkable grasp of the geopolitical situation – are followed up by a later Muslim historian, the great Ibn al-Athir (d. 630/1233) in his *Universal History*. For the year 491/1097–8 he writes:

The beginning of the appearance of the state (*dawla*) of the Franks and the intensification of their activity and their departure to the lands of Islam and their conquest of some of them was the year 478 (1085–6). They took the city of Toledo and other parts of al-Andalus [Muslim Spain] as already mentioned. Then they attacked in the year 484 the island of Sicily and conquered it, and I have already mentioned that too, and they turned to the coasts of North Africa and conquered part of that. . . .[53]

Ibn al-Athir then begins his account of the Franks in Syria and Palestine. Thus we see that he too grasps the significance of the whole sweep of Christian conquests southwards in the wider Mediterranean world. However, he does not seem to see any specific religious motivation behind the Crusaders' arrival in the Holy Land, or for that matter in their conquests in Spain, Sicily or North Africa.

Reporting for the year 490/1097 an imaginary correspondence between a certain Baldwin and Roger of Sicily, Ibn al-Athir represents Roger as singularly reluctant to join forces with Baldwin in conquering the African coast (where he has allies for the moment and for which he has his own plans for conquest). Instead, Roger deflects the European offensive eastwards, telling Baldwin's messenger: 'If you have decided to make war on the Muslims, the best thing would be to conquer Jerusalem and to liberate it from their hands; and the glory will be yours.'[54]

We have already noted that one strand of the Muslim historical tradition blamed the Fatimids for inviting the Crusaders to come and attack Syria and Palestine in order to protect Egypt from the Seljuqs. With his usual breadth of vision, Ibn al-Athir gives both interpretations for the coming of the First Crusade, ending with the usual cautionary

Figure 2.18 *Signs of the zodiac, Vaso Vescovali, c. 1200, Iran*

Figure 2.19 (above and overleaf) *Signs of the zodiac in their respective* domicilia; *ewer made for a Shi'ite patron, c. 1350, probably Syria*

Figure 2.20 (opposite) *Map of the route of the First Crusade*

statement 'God knows best'.[55] He does not see it as his job to adjudicate between these contradictory versions of events.

A later account by the Mamluk historian al-Nuwayri (d. 733/1333) also reflects on wider aspects of the coming of the First Crusade. Under the title of 'What the Franks took of the coasts of Syria in 491 and afterwards', al-Nuwayri speaks at some length, and with unusual breadth of vision, about Spain:

> The beginning of their appearing, expanding and penetrating into the Islamic lands was in 478. This came about in the following way. When the kings of the lands of Spain became divided after the Umayyads and each area fell into the hand of one king and the soul of each one disdained to be led by the other and to enter into obedience to anyone else, they were like the Party Kings in Persian times.[56]

Al-Nuwayri writes that this fragmentation of Muslim Spain: 'led to the disturbance of conditions and the conquering of Islamic countries by enemies. The first place they conquered was the city of Toledo in al-Andalus as we have related under the year 478'.[57] He then, like Ibn al-Athir before him, mentions the conquest of Sicily by the Normans in 484/1091 and their infiltration into parts of the North African coast.[58]

The Course of the First Crusade: Muslim Accounts

The First Crusade is poorly documented on the Muslim side in comparison with the relative wealth of documentation in the Crusader sources. Nevertheless, the Muslim sources, such as they are, do give some interesting insights into the campaign.[59] Muslim chroniclers have a clear idea of the sequence of the events, battles and conquests of the First Crusade, and they know its main landmarks. They are aware that many of the Crusaders assembled first in Constantinople and that they proceeded across Anatolia towards Syria. The alliance between the Crusaders and the Byzantine emperor, and the subsequent estrangement between the two parties, are well understood. As al-'Azimi writes for the year 490/1097 (with the usual exaggeration over numbers):

> The fleets of the Franks appeared at the port of Constantinople with 300,000 men and their kings were six. They swore oaths to the king of Byzantium that they would hand over to him the first fortress which they conquered but they did not keep faith about that.[60]

The Muslim sources mention the harassment of the Crusader army by the Turks as it crossed Anatolia. Ibn al-Qalanisi mentions the efforts of Qilij Arslan I to halt the Crusaders' progress: 'He

54

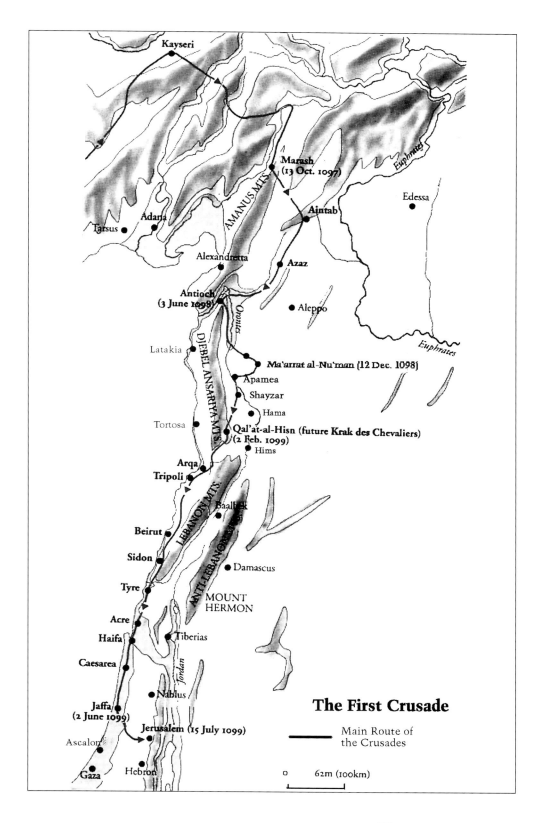

Kayseri

Marash
(13 Oct. 1097)

Edessa

Euphrates

AMANUS MTS.

Aintab

Adana

Tarsus

Alexandretta

Azaz

Aleppo

Antioch
(3 June 1098)

Orontes

Latakia

DJEBEL ANSARIYA MTS.

Ma'arrat al-Nu'man (12 Dec. 1098)

Apamea

Euphrates

Shayzar

Hama

Tortosa

Qal'at-al-Hisn (future Krak des Chevaliers)
(2 Feb. 1099)

Hims

Arqa

Tripoli

LEBANON MTS.

Baalbek

Beirut

ANTI-LEBANON MTS.

Sidon

Damascus

Tyre

MOUNT
HERMON

Acre

Haifa

Tiberias

Caesarea

Jordan

Nablus

Jaffa
(2 June 1099)

Jerusalem (15 July 1099)

Ascalon

The First Crusade

——— Main Route of
the Crusades

Gaza

Hebron

o   62m (100km)

55

marched out to the fords, tracks and roads by which the Franks must pass, and showed no mercy to all of them who fell into his hands.'[61]

Al-'Azimi reports that the Turks burned the Crusader fleets and blocked the watering-places, and he mentions the fall of Nicaea (Iznik) very briefly.[62]

In July 1097 the Crusaders defeated the Seljuq sultan Qilij Arslan I at the battle of Dorylaeum on the edge of the Anatolian plateau. The early history of the nomadic Turks of Anatolia is, as already mentioned, very poorly documented; so we should perhaps not read too much into the neglect of this battle in the Islamic sources. Ibn al-Qalanisi does mention the battle, dating it to 20 Rajab 490/4 July 1097 and stating clearly that the Turks were soundly defeated.[63] Ibn al-Athir, normally so comprehensive in his coverage, skates over the disaster in a single phrase: 'they [the Franks] fought him [Qilij Arslan] and they routed him in Rajab [4]90'.[64]

Events in distant Anatolia perhaps deserved little attention in the eyes of the Islamic chroniclers; but as the Crusader threat loomed nearer and nearer to Syria and Palestine and thus to areas of greater concern to them, the historiographical coverage becomes fuller. The Muslim chroniclers spare no effort to relate the disasters which ensued – and especially at Antioch, Ma'arrat al-Nu'man and, as the final catastrophe, at Jerusalem. Edessa (al-Ruha), the first of the Crusader states in the Near East, which was held by an Armenian lord named Toros, fell to Baldwin of Boulogne in March 1098. This is almost completely ignored by the Muslim chroniclers who in later years simply speak without explanation of the 'Franks of Edessa'.[65] Ibn al-Athir, as is often the case, is the exception: he does not place the fall of Edessa in its correct chronological slot but instead, under the year 494/1100–1, he writes: 'The Franks had taken the city of Edessa through correspondence [letters] from its population because the majority of them were Armenians and there were only a few Muslims there.'[66]

This lack of interest in Edessa – doubtless due to its happening to be in Christian hands already at the time of the First Crusade – is in sharp contrast to the loud historiographical fanfares which understandably greeted the Islamic reconquest of Edessa by Zengi in 539/1144.

The Fall of Antioch

The loss of Antioch, on the other hand, is viewed with some attention by the Muslim chroniclers. This was a much bigger city and it had a greater strategic importance than Edessa. The city underwent a protracted siege (from October 1097 to June 1098). The governor, Yaghisiyan, was killed in flight. A relieving army under the command of the ruler of Mosul, Kirbogha, met the Crusaders in battle but was defeated. The citadel then surrendered and became the centre of the second Crusader state, the Principality of Antioch, under the rule of

Bohemond. Ibn al-Qalanisi gives a detailed report of events at Antioch. He relates that on the news of the approach of the Franks, Yaghisiyan fortified the city and expelled its Christian population. He also sent pleas for reinforcements to the rulers of Syria.[67] Ibn al-Qalanisi gives few details about the actual siege, except to point out that oil, salt and other necessities became hard to find but that so much was smuggled into the city that they became cheap again.[68] He also mentions that the Franks dug a trench between themselves and the city because of the frequent attacks made on them by the army of Antioch (for a different account, see p. 68 below).

The fall of Antioch was, according to Ibn al-Qalanisi, precipitated by the treachery of some of the armourers in Yaghisiyan's retinue who harboured a grudge against him. They conspired with the Franks and agreed to hand over the city to them. The traitors seized one of the bastions of the city, sold it to the Franks and then let them into the city at night.[69] Later on in his narrative Ibn al-Qalanisi blames only one armourer, an Armenian called Firuz, for handing Antioch over to the Franks.[70] Yaghisiyan fled, fell from his horse repeatedly and died. But the departure of the city's governor was not the end of the siege. Although many of the population were killed or taken prisoner, some three thousand men fortified themselves in the citadel of Antioch and refused to move.[71]

The account of Ibn al-Qalanisi of the actual battle of Antioch (26 Rajab 491/29 June 1098), when the Muslims came to recapture the city, is vague and inadequate. The relieving army of Syria besieged the Franks until 'they were reduced to eating carrion'. His narrative then continues:

> Thereafter the Franks, though they were in the extremity of weakness, advanced in battle order against the armies of Islam, which were at the height of strength and numbers, and they broke the ranks of the Muslims and scattered their multitudes.[72]

We are given no account of the actual course of the battle and no reason for Crusader victory, although the chronicler is honest enough to admit that the Muslims were numerically superior and that the Franks were weak with hunger.

Al-'Azimi, the contemporary of Ibn al-Qalanisi, blames the Muslims squarely for the defeat at Antioch: 'The Franks went out to them. They [the Franks] were extremely weak and the Muslims were strong. The Muslims were defeated, because of the evil of their intentions.'[73]

What of the version of Ibn al-Athir, whose account of the First Crusade the Italian scholar Gabrieli describes as 'the most complete and convincing, if not the most strongly factual'?[74] His narrative is fuller than that of Ibn al-Qalanisi.[75] Ibn al-Athir stresses too that the Franks were weak and short of food.[76] They had nothing to eat for twelve days; so the rich ate their horses and the poor ate carrion and leaves from the trees. Kirbogha's army contained contingents who

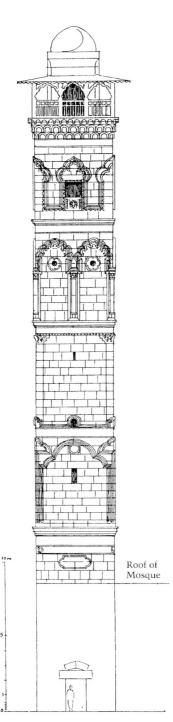

Roof of Mosque

had rallied to him from many quarters but, according to Ibn al-Athir, he lacked the necessary leadership skills and alienated the other army chiefs by his pride and ill-treatment.[77] Indeed, 'they [the other Muslim commanders] plotted in secret anger to betray him and desert him in the heat of battle'. When the Franks asked Kirbogha for safe-conduct he would not allow them it, declaring instead that they would have to fight their way out.

Ibn al-Athir mentions the names of some of the Crusader leaders – Baldwin, (Raymond of) St. Gilles, Godfrey (of Bouillon) and Bohemond whom he describes as their leader. He also includes the story of Christ's lance, which is discussed in Chapter 5.

As for the actual battle of Antioch, its contours are extremely blurred in the account of Ibn al-Athir. He explains that the Franks came out of Antioch in small groups and that the Muslims wanted to pick them off as they emerged. Kirbogha forbade this, preferring instead to wait for all the Franks to have left the city. The battle is minimised; the Muslim defeat is not in a military encounter:

> When a good quantity of the Franks had come out and not one of them was left behind in Antioch, they attacked strongly, and the Muslims turned and fled . . . They were completely defeated without any of them striking a single blow with the sword or a single spear being thrown or a single arrow being fired . . . There had not even been any fighting from which to flee.[78]

A small valiant band from the Holy Land stood firm and fought. The Franks killed them by the thousand.

How could the Muslim army at Antioch ever have gained the victory in a period of such fragmentation, decentralisation and disunity? The fact was that there was no real corporate will to make the union effective, even in a single offensive against a common foe, the Franks outside Antioch. Such a motley combination of Janah al-Dawla of Hims, Tughtegin of Damascus, the Artuqid Sulayman from Mardin, and others, had no hope of working together amicably, especially under the leadership of Kirbogha, the ruler of distant Mosul, whose motives were no doubt questioned by the rest of the Muslim commanders. Disunity and infighting underlay this Muslim defeat, against all expectations and against distinctly underwhelming odds, outside Antioch. This much is suggested implicitly by the account of Ibn al-Athir, but on this occasion he certainly attempts to whitewash this ignominious defeat for the Muslims. The earlier and less detailed version of al-'Azimi, on the other hand, does not shirk the responsibility of blaming the Muslims for the evil of their intentions, no doubt a reference to their mutual rancour, suspicion and hostility, and their lack of commitment to *jihad*. The geographer of northern Syria, Ibn Shaddad (d. 684/1285) mentions discord in the ranks of the Muslim army at Antioch, speaking of mutual suspicion between the commanders and discord between the Turks and Arabs.[79]

58

Ibn Taghribirdi (d. 874/1469–70) makes the Fatimids a scapegoat for the Muslim defeat at Antioch and specifically blames al-Afdal, the vizier of Egypt, for not sending out the Fatimid armies to join the Syrian commanders: 'I do not know the reason for his not sending them out, [what] with his strength in money and men.'[80] He repeats this sentiment at the very end of his account of the defeat at Antioch: 'All this and still the armies of Egypt did not prepare to leave.'[81] Thus he sidesteps the real reason for the Muslims' ignominious and unnecessary defeat.

The real significance of the battle of Antioch for the Muslim world has to be teased out of the chronicles. Ibn al-Athir dismisses the significance of the finding of Christ's lance, which Crusader sources say gave the Crusader morale a tremendous psychological boost: for him this is mere superstition. The real reason for the Crusader victory at Antioch is much more prosaic. Behind the bland statements that the Crusaders were hungry and weak and that the Muslims were numerically strong but that the Crusaders won the day is the unpalatable truth that this was probably *the* turning-point of the First Crusade. The Muslim commanders of Syria came together to relieve Antioch but in the decentralised political climate of the day they were unable even to stay together long enough to achieve victory. After Antioch, the way to Jerusalem lay open to the Crusaders.

The Fall of Ma'arrat al-Nu'man

In Muharram 492/December 1098 the Syrian city of Ma'arrat al-Nu'man (plates 2.7–2.8, 2.9, 2.10,–2.11; cf. plates 5.2 and 5.4), situated between Aleppo and Hama, fell to the Crusaders. The city was never of any substantial size or importance, but these facts were overshadowed by the psychological effect of what happened there. The Muslim sources dwell on the fall of Ma'arrat al-Nu'man because of the dreadful massacre of the city's population, which they recount in some detail. Ibn al-Qalanisi reports soberly that the Franks had made overtures for the peaceful handover of the city, promising security for lives and property, but that the citizens could not agree among themselves to accept these terms.[82] Again, the theme of Muslim disunity is prominent. So the Franks took the city (by force) and 'a great number from both sides were killed'.[83] Thereafter, the Franks behaved treacherously to the citizens after promising them safety and plundered everything that they found.[84]

Ibn al-Athir, whose narratives are normally so detailed, has only a brief account of the fall of Ma'arrat al-Nu'man. He comments: 'For three days the Franks placed the sword among them: they killed more than 100,000 men and took many prisoners.'

His version of events stresses, however, that the citizens were not prepared to surrender peacefully.[85] So the Franks prepared to attack by force, as was customary in their rules of war for a city which offered resistance. The numbers cited by Ibn al-Athir are of course absurdly

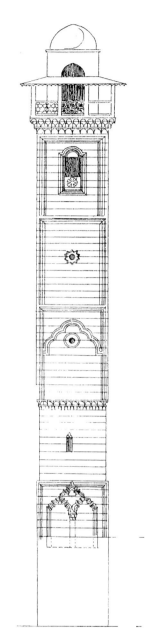

Figure 2.21
(above and opposite)
Great Mosque, minaret, elevation, 483–7/1090–5, Aleppo, Syria (left); Great Mosque, minaret, elevation, c. 1170, Ma'arrat al-Nu'man, Syria

Plate 2.7 *Minaret and courtyard, Great Mosque, twelfth century, Ma'arrat al-Nu'man, Syria*

Plate 2.8 Minaret, detail, Great Mosque, c. 1170, Ma'arrat al-Nu'man, Syria

Plate 2.9 *Treasury, Great Mosque, twelfth century(?) but using pre-Islamic spolia, Ma'arrat al-Nu'man, Syria*

Plate 2.10 Courtyard and sanctuary, Great Mosque, twelfth century, Ma'arrat al-Nu'man, Syria

(Creswell Photographic Archive, Ashmolean Museum, Oxford, neg. C. 6039)

inflated – they imply, if taken at face value, that Ma'arrat al-Nu'man was one of the great metropolises of the Near East. It may be that this inflation of the figures of the victims – the number of people killed is given as being the same as at Jerusalem, as we shall see – is the result of the surge of indignation felt by later generations of Muslim chroniclers.

The most detailed Muslim account of the fall of Ma'arrat al-Nu'man is that of the chronicler of nearby Aleppo, Ibn al-'Adim (d. 660/1262). He emphasises the carnage and devastation caused in the town:

> They [the Franks] killed a great number under torture. They extorted people's treasures. They prevented people from [getting] water, and sold it to them. Most of the people died of thirst . . . No treasure remained there that was not extorted by them. They destroyed the walls of the town, burned its mosques and houses and broke the *minbars*.[86]

The Conquest of Jerusalem

Predictably, the fall of Jerusalem in 492/1099 receives full coverage in the Muslim sources – even the earliest extant works were written

Plate 2.11 *Courtyard and sanctuary, mosque, twelfth century, Ma'arrat al-Nu'man, Syria*

(Creswell Photographic Archive, Ashmolean Museum, Oxford, neg. C. 6034)

by authors who had had time to assess the significance of this event and many later Muslim authors knew well the importance that Saladin had attached to regaining the Holy City (plate 2.12).

Under the year 492/1099 al-'Azimi's narrative is very brief. 'Then they turned to Jerusalem and conquered it from the hands of the Egyptians. Godfrey took it. They burned the Church of the Jews (*Kanisat al-Yahud*).'[87] This 'church' was presumably the principal Jewish synagogue.

Ibn al-Qalanisi's account is longer and is sober and restrained. On the news that al-Afdal was on his way with a large army against the Franks, they renewed their attempts to take Jerusalem:

The Franks stormed the town and gained possession of it. A number of the townsfolk fled to the sanctuary and a great host were killed. The Jews assembled in the synagogue, and the Franks burned it over their heads. The sanctuary was surrendered to them on guarantee of safety on 22 Sha'ban [14 July] of this year, and they destroyed the shrines and the tomb of Abraham.[88]

By the time of Ibn al-Jawzi (d. 597/1200), however, the story of the fall of Jerusalem has become embroidered with new details about massacre and pillage:

Among the events in this year was the taking of Jerusalem by the Franks on Friday 13 Sha'ban [5 July]. They killed more than 70,000 Muslims there. They took forty-odd silver candelabra from the Dome of the Rock, each one worth 360,000 *dirham*s. They took a silver lamp weighing forty Syrian *ratl*s. They took twenty-odd gold lamps, innumerable items of clothing and other things.[89]

Plate 2.12 Southern stairway to the upper platform, Haram al-Sharif, undated but medieval, Jerusalem

(Creswell Photographic Archive, Ashmolean Museum, Oxford, neg. C. 4980)

The account of Ibn Muyassar (d. 677/1278) contains some of these details, adding that the Franks burned copies of the Qur'an.[90]

As for Ibn al-Athir (d. 630/1233), he includes in his account similar information about candelabra and lamps but he includes a new detail, emphasising the killing of Muslim holy men:

> The Franks killed more than 70,000 people in the Aqsa mosque, among them a large group of Muslim imams, religious scholars, devout men and ascetics from amongst those who had left their homelands and lived in the vicinity of that Holy Place.[91]

By the time of Ibn Taghribirdi, the story has become even more elaborated. The Muslims are killed in both the Aqsa mosque (plate 2.13) and the Dome of the Rock and the number of those killed has increased to 100,000, including the old and the sick.[92] Even the lower figure of 70,000 dead is, as we have shown, not mentioned in the earliest extant Muslim sources and is obviously exaggerated. However, the city must have contained a sizeable population at the time of the Crusader siege, since, as well as its own inhabitants, it probably also housed refugees from other towns and villages who had sought asylum behind its walls.

In addition to the general carnage in Jerusalem which is mentioned in all the Islamic sources, the Franks on occasion targeted individual religious figures. The tale of al-Rumayli, a prominent religious scholar, is very poignant. He was taken captive by the Franks who said they would set him free in return for a ransom of a thousand dinars. Since the required sum was not produced they stoned him to death on 12 Shawwal 492/1 December 1099.[93]

In all these Muslim accounts of the fall of Jerusalem there is no recognition of the motivation – religious or military – for the coming of the Franks. They simply turn up out of the blue and wreak havoc among the Muslims. The conquest of the city is a disastrous event recorded with great sadness but without reflection; it is an event to be suffered and from which lessons are to be learned.

The Treatment of the Jews in the First Crusade

For the medieval Muslims, the Jews were 'People of the Book' and as such entitled to religious tolerance and protection within the Islamic community under the covenant (*dhimma*). According to the Muslim sources, there were Jews living in Jerusalem at the time of the First Crusade and they shared the same terrible fate as the Muslims when the city fell to the Franks. As already mentioned, al-'Azimi reports that they burned the 'Church of the Jews'.[94] Ibn Taghribirdi is more detailed: 'They collected the Jews in the "church" and burnt it down with them in it. They destroyed shrines and the tomb of Abraham – on him be peace – and they took the *mihrab* of David peacefully'.[95]

Not surprisingly, the Muslim chroniclers do not view the Jews

Plate 2.13 Aqsa Mosque,
interior, Umayyad period
(seventh century) onwards,
Jerusalem

67

with the same suspicion as that which they harboured on occasion towards the Oriental Christians who might, rightly or wrongly, have been expected to side with their co-religionists, the Crusaders. The subsequent fate of the Jews of Palestine during the Frankish occupation is not dealt with in the Islamic sources.

The Oriental Christians at the Time of the First Crusade

As already mentioned, the demography of Syria and Palestine at this period was very complex in ethnic and religious terms. A number of different groups of Christians lived in the area. Ibn al-Athir singles out the ruler of Antioch, Yaghisiyan, for special praise for his treatment of the local Christian population of the city at the time of the siege of Antioch in 491/1098.[96] Ibn al-Athir points out first that Yaghisiyan was afraid of the Christians who were in Antioch. So he made the Muslims and then the Christians build the trench outside the city. When the Christians wanted to go home at the end of the day he would not let them:

> He said to them: 'Antioch belongs to you. Give it to me so that I can see what will become of us and the Franks.' They said to him: 'Who will look after our children and our wives?' He said to them: 'I swear to you about them.' So they kept away and stayed in the Frankish camp. They [the Franks] besieged it for nine months.[97]

Ibn al-Athir concludes: 'Yaghisiyan protected the Christian population of Antioch whom he had sent away and prevented hands from reaching them.'[98]

This is an interesting narrative. Obviously Yaghisiyan, as a Muslim Turkish overlord, was worried how the local Christian population would respond to the Western Christian invaders – would they side with the Christian newcomers or remain loyal to the local Muslims with whom they lived? What the general mass of the Christian male citizens of Antioch thought as the siege progressed is not clear. However, as already noted, according to some sources – and this is a recurring theme in other chapters of the Crusades as told by the Muslims – it was a Christian who handed over Antioch to the Crusaders. As mentioned earlier, al-'Azimi calls him Firuz and states that he was an Armenian, and some later sources continue this story.[99]

The Role of the Byzantine Emperor in the First Crusade and its Aftermath – The Muslim Version

The shadowy but important part played in the drama of the First Crusade by the Byzantine emperor Alexius Comnenus is a crucial dimension which is mentioned occasionally in the Islamic sources. There are hints that he conducted a clever diplomatic game, involving many of the players in the ensuing drama.[100]

We have already mentioned that, according to al-'Azimi, the Byzantine emperor wrote to the Muslims in 489/1096 informing them of the arrival of the Franks.[101] It seems likely that it was the Fatimids who are meant here by the term 'Muslims' since they had long-standing links with Byzantium. Whether Alexius' motives were to inform or to threaten is not explained by al-'Azimi. As we saw earlier, Alexius' involvement with the Crusader leaders when they arrived in Constantinople is also mentioned by al-'Azimi. According to his testimony, they swore oaths to the king of Byzantium that they would hand over to him the first fortress which they conquered, but they did not keep faith in this matter.[102]

Al-'Azimi also suggests that the king of Byzantium was still active in northern Syria in 496/1102–3, mentioning that he took Lattakia in that year.[103] In Jumada II 504/December 1110–January 1111, the Byzantine emperor, labelled the upstart king (*mutamallik*), sent an envoy to the Seljuq sultan asking for help against the Franks, urging him to fight them and drive them out of the Muslim lands. Ibn al-Qalanisi reports a very convoluted message which is a mixture of cajolement and threat:

> He [the Byzantine emperor] stated that he had prevented them [the Franks] from traversing his dominions to the lands of the Muslims and had gone to war with them, but if their ambitious designs upon the land of Islam led to a constant succession of their armies and reinforcements proceeding hereto, he would be impelled by imperious necessities to come to terms with them and to give them free passage and assistance with their aims and objects.[104]

Muslim Reactions to the First Crusade and the Establishment of the Frankish States in the Levant

Hitti speaks of the Crusaders as 'a strange and unexpected enemy'.[105] This is a good description of the initial reaction of the Muslims most in the firing line of the First Crusade. Waves of shock, fear and incomprehension spread from the areas most affected across the Islamic world. But the impact of the catastrophe diminished the further afield the news of it spread.

Our knowledge of the immediate Muslim reactions to the impact of the First Crusade is based on two contemporary sources, Arabic poetry and the work entitled the *Book of Holy War* written by al-Sulami. Some Arabic poems written by contemporary poets – al-Abiwardi (d. 507/1113), Ibn al-Khayyat (d. in the 1120s) and others – have survived.

Perhaps al-Abiwardi,[106] who spent much of his life in Baghdad, was present when one or more of the delegations from Syria visited Baghdad to tell of the tribulations they had undergone at the hands of the Crusaders and to implore the Seljuq leadership and the caliph to send military help against them. At all events, he composed some

Figure 2.22 *Lance of the Mamluk sultan Tuman Ba'i, early sixteenth century, Cairo, Egypt*

very moving and passionate lines lamenting the fall of Jerusalem and the lack of wider Islamic response to it:

> How can the eye sleep between the lids at a time of disasters
>   that would waken any sleeper?
> While your Syrian brothers can only sleep on the backs of their
>   chargers, or in vultures' bellies! . . .
> This is war, and the infidel's sword is naked in his hand, ready
>   to be sheathed again in men's necks and skulls.
> This is war, and he who lies in the tomb at Medina [i.e. the
>   Prophet himself] seems to raise his voice and cry: 'O sons
>   of Hashim!'[107]

A second poet, Ibn al-Khayyat, had worked for the rulers of Tripoli before the coming of the First Crusade and kept in touch with them after he moved to Damascus.[108] Perhaps his memories of life in Tripoli made him more aware of the Frankish threat than many of his contemporaries. Some of the verses he wrote for his patron, a military commander in Damascus called 'Adb al-Dawla (d. 502–3/1109), are concerned with the need to wage *jihad* against the Franks.[109] He stresses first the enormous size and unrelenting succession of the Crusading armies:

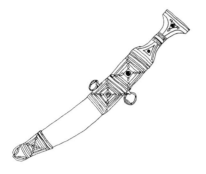

Figure 2.23 Parade dagger, ninth–eleventh centuries, Syria

> The polytheists have swelled in a torrent of terrifying extent.
>   How long will this continue?
> Armies like mountains, coming again and again, have ranged
>   forth from the lands of the Franks.

Those who have tried to fight the Franks have been annihilated or bought off:

> They [the Franks] push violently into the mire those who ven-
>   ture forth [against them].
> And those who would fight they make them forget with money.

He refers elliptically to the evil effect of grudges harboured by Muslim princes against each other; indeed, they have become worse with the presence of the Franks:

> The evil of grudges [continues] whilst grudges have become
>   inflamed by unbelief.

Warming now to his major theme, Ibn al-Khayyat rises to a climax of outraged grief and indignation against the massacres perpetrated by the Franks and urges immediate action against them:

> The heads of the polytheists have already ripened,
> So do not neglect them as a vintage and a harvest!

The cutting edge of their sword must be blunted
  And their pillar must be demolished.

Finally, the poet invokes the name of the great Seljuq sultan Alp Arslan who won the famous victory at Manzikert against the Byzantines in 463/1071.

A third poet whose identity remains unknown has moving words preserved in the history of the Mamluk historian Ibn Taghribirdi.[110] He takes a traditional form – the panegyric ode (*qasida*), normally addressed by the poet to his patron – and, stung by the disasters of the First Crusade, transforms it into an eloquent outburst against the Muslims who have allowed these catastrophes to happen:

Do you not owe an obligation to God and Islam, defending
  thereby young men and old?
Respond to God! Woe to you! Respond![111]

Other poets also dwell on the anguish and fear caused by the Crusader onslaught. One such poet, gazing on his house after the carnage at Ma'arrat al-Nu'man, declares:

I do not know whether it is a pasturing place for wild beasts or
  my house, my native residence . . .
I turned towards it and asked, my voice choked with tears, my
  heart torn with affliction and love.
'O house, why has destiny pronounced such an unjust
  sentence on us?'[112]

A merchant from Ma'arrat Misrin relates a similar tale of lamentation and pain: 'I am from a city which God has condemned, my friend, to be destroyed. They have killed all its inhabitants, putting old men and children to the sword.'[113]

Apart from the poetry, the other surviving testimony which dates from shortly after the first coming of the Crusaders is the *Book of Holy War*, apparently completed around 498/1105 by al-Sulami, a Damascus legal scholar and preacher at the famous Umayyad mosque. If this represents the true date of the composition of this treatise, we have here an extraordinarily far-sighted and illuminating work, showing an understanding, probably unique at this early stage of the Crusades, of what the Franks were planning to do and of how the Muslims should respond.[114]

Al-Sulami has a clear idea of the difference between Frank and Byzantine. He calls the newcomers *Ifranj*, a term previously used, for example by al-Mas'udi, to denote the inhabitants of the Carolingian empire. The Islamic world had long been used to Byzantium as its neighbour, and parts of northern Syria in particular had been ruled intermittently from Constantinople in the period immediately preceding the Crusade (Antioch, for example, had been Byzantine for

Figure 2.24
(above and opposite)
Leisure pursuits and animals,
Fatimid carved ivory plaques
(from a book-cover?),
eleventh–twelfth centuries,
Egypt

over a century until 1084). It is understandable, therefore, that initially at least there might have been confusion as to the identity of the Christian invaders who took Jerusalem. Al-Abiwardi, for example, in his lament on the fall of Jerusalem, calls the invaders *al-Rum*, the usual term for the Byzantines,[115] and Ibn Shaddad also confuses Byzantines and Franks in his geography of northern Syria.[116] But al-Sulami is not confused. He sees the Franks' aims all too clearly.

His work is a legal treatise about Holy War (*jihad*), and it will be discussed in that context in Chapter 3. However, as well as providing rules for the conduct of *jihad*, al-Sulami also adds his personal comments in the margin, linking what he is saying in the main body of his text with what is *actually* happening in his own time. In particular, in the introduction to the second part of his work, al-Sulami explains why he wrote it, and he gives a detailed description of the political situation in Syria after the Frankish invasion. Al-Sulami has a wide view of the Crusader enterprise, seeing the whole sweep of the western European Christian advances southwards: 'A group [of Franks] pounced on the island of Sicily at a moment of discord and mutual rivalry and they conquered in like fashion one town after another in Spain.'[117] He is in no doubt that the reason for Crusader success in his own time in different parts of the world is the lacklustre attitude on the Muslims' part towards the observances of their religion:

> This interruption [in waging *jihad*] combined with the negligence of the Muslims towards the prescribed regulations [of Islam] . . . has inevitably meant that God has made Muslims rise up one against another, has placed violent hostility and hatred amongst them and has incited their enemies to seize their territories.[118]

Turning to his own land, al-Sulami also blames the Frankish success on the disturbed political conditions whose result was that 'the rulers hated and fought each other'. Clearly the Franks knew the situation in advance:

> Examining the country of Syria, they [the Franks] confirmed that the states there were involved one with another, their opinions diverged, their relationships rested on secret desires for vengeance. Their [the Franks'] greed was thereby reinforced, encouraging them to apply themselves [to the attack].[119]

The Muslims only had themselves to blame for 'manifesting a lack of energy and unity in war, each trying to leave the task to the others'.[120]

It is important to stress that al-Sulami certainly understands what the Franks are after: 'Jerusalem was the goal of their desires.'[121] Writing only a few years after the loss of the Holy City, al-Sulami sees all too clearly that the Franks have further expansionist aims which must be stopped at all costs by Muslim reunification:

> Even now they are continuing the effort to enlarge their territory; their greed is constantly growing as they see the cowardice of their enemies who are happy to live away from danger. Moreover, they hope now for sure to make themselves masters of the whole country and to take its inhabitants captive. Would to God that, in His goodness, He would frustrate them in their aspirations by re-establishing the unity of the community.[122]

It should be noted here that in 498/1105 a number of the Syrian ports – Ascalon, Tyre, Tripoli and others – were still in Muslim hands. Al-Sulami's jeremiad is uncannily prescient; but, like many a prophet of doom, he was without honour in his own country. He was born at least a generation too early.

In a prophetic statement, al-Sulami foresees what would happen later in the century when Nur al-Din and Saladin worked towards the encirclement of the Crusader state of Jerusalem and in particular the unification of Syria and Egypt, divided politically and ideologically since the tenth century:

> The sovereign ... must devote himself to his relations with the sovereigns of other countries, Syria, the Jazira, Egypt and adjacent regions, for terror [of the Franks] can reconcile the old hatreds and secret hostilities of the inhabitants of these countries as well as turn them away from their rivalries and mutual jealousies.[123]

Al-Sulami stresses the need for urgent action in the defence of the Syrian coastline before it is too late. Although a religious lawyer, he seems to have penetrating insights into the military and political vulnerability of the Franks: 'One knows for sure their weakness, the small amount of cavalry and equipment they have at their disposal and the distance from which their reinforcements come . . . It is an opportunity which must be seized quickly.'[124]

Sadly, these warnings were to remain unheard for over half a century. Instead, the Franks duly took the Syrian coastline and fortified the ports, thus facilitating the continuing traffic of men, arms and equipment from Europe; as al-'Azimi writes without elaboration for the year 497/1104: 'The Franks built up the coastal towns because all of them were broken down.'[125]

An Overview of the Years 492–504/1099–1110

By 1110 the Franks had established four states in the Near East – Jerusalem, Edessa, Antioch and Tripoli. They had also kept the Fatimids of Egypt at bay, although the latter still held the port of Ascalon with its garrison. Very quickly indeed, the Franks had built up a strong coastal base, ensuring free and easy access for supplies and soldiers to be sent from western Europe. Apart from Edessa in the north and Jerusalem in the south, all the Frankish possessions were along the coast, a location which immediately halved the defensive measures necessary to protect them. They did not, however, possess Aleppo or Damascus with their much greater financial resources, thereby allowing these cities to remain foci for Muslim retrenchment and revitalisation. Nor did they own any bases in Egypt itself. They were still very much a beleaguered minority. A united Muslim onslaught by land and sea could have finished them off then and there. But this was, of course, an unrealisable ideal. The Muslims were disunited, disorganised and dispirited on land, and incompetent in maritime matters. They were also motivated by considerations of *Realpolitik*, as we shall see later in this chapter. The Franks too on occasion proved themselves to be shrewd diplomats, as the Muslim sources make clear; but they were also actuated, again as the Muslim sources reveal, although it took them some time to realise it, by religious fervour of a kind that the Muslims were not yet ready to match. Moreover, they were fully aware that they were far from home and that they lacked speedy military backup – this is the implication of al-Sulami's exhortation to the Muslims to control the Levantine ports – which must have given an edge of desperation to their courage. Thus it came to pass that the Franks, in spite of their limited territorial possessions and obvious numerical inferiority, were able to fortify themselves and to continue to receive reinforcements from western Europe. Even if these took some time to arrive, their route to the Near East was relatively secure from harassment.

Displacement of the Muslim Population

As well as the vicissitudes of war, foreign occupation, famine and disease,[126] those fortunate enough to survive the initial Crusader onslaught had the option of flight. It seems that some chose this

Figure 2.25 Soldier wearing Mongol armour, Rashid al-Din, Jami' al-Tawarikh ('World History'), 714/1314, Tabriz, Iran

option. Ibn Muyassar mentions for the year 493/1100: 'Many people from the Syrian territories came to Egypt fleeing from the Franks and famine.'[127]

Certain famous individuals are known to have moved because of the First Crusade – a typical example is the poet Ibn al-Qaysarani ('the man from Caesarea') who was forced to flee from that town after the Franks seized the Levantine coasts.[128]

Panic and fear must have been rife as some of the population moved to safer refuges whilst the Franks continued their victorious wave of campaigns. People were afraid for their property and their venerated objects. Those possessions that were portable were moved to more secure locations; Ibn al-Dawadari (in the early fourteenth century) records that after the sack of Ma'arrat al-Nu'man the Muslims took the 'Uthmanic Qur'an from there to Damascus.[129] Such precautions would have been unnecessary in intra-Muslim squabbles and merely underline how alien an enemy the Franks were to the Muslims of the Near East.

There is also some evidence for larger-scale refugee movements in Syria and Palestine in the wake of the Crusader onslaught.[130] The demographic exodus of Muslims from lands occupied by Crusaders began in 491/1098 with the conquest of Antioch and continued in tandem with the setting-up of the remaining Crusader states, which culminated in the taking of Tyre in 518/1124.

Many Muslims fled massacres perpetrated by the Crusaders when they entered cities by force or even cities which had capitulated and been promised terms of truce but where the army leaders were unable to impose their authority on their troops. Refugees fled, according to the sources, from terrible carnage, as for example at Saruj in 494/1101. According to Ibn al-Qalanisi: 'The Franks then advanced to Saruj, recaptured it, and killed and enslaved its inhabitants, *except those of them who escaped by flight.*'[131]

In the case of Arsuf, also captured that year, the same source mentions that the Franks drove out its inhabitants.[132] This process must have been repeated many times over as the Franks continued to expand in the period 493–518/1099–1124. Thereafter, the situation changed as a *modus vivendi* was often established between Frankish overlord and Muslim subject.

Sometimes the inhabitants of towns that had capitulated or certain sections of the population of a city were able to leave because the Crusaders honoured their promises to save their lives. Such was the case with the governor of 'Arqa and some of the troops who were allowed to depart after the conquest of the town in 502/1109.[133]

On other occasions desperate populations abandoned their cities *en masse*, as in the case of Ramla in 492/1099 where 'The people fled in panic from their abodes',[134] fearing that a Frankish attack was imminent and taking refuge in towns which were considered safe havens. According to the Syrian chronicler Ibn Abi Tayyi', many Aleppans fled to the Jazira and Iraq on hearing of the fall of Tripoli in 502/1109.[135]

Because of the scanty documentation it is not possible to establish whether similar demographic movements affected the Syro-Palestinian countryside but it seems likely that the exodus from the cities must have continued – though less dramatically – throughout the twelfth century and that it may have affected villages too.

Crusader Expansionism and Muslim Disunity, 491–518/1099–1124

The Islamic chroniclers are well aware of the dismal catalogue of continuing Crusader conquests and Muslim failures which followed in the wake of the fall of Jerusalem. Of the subsequent territorial gains, Tripoli eventually succumbed to become the fourth of the Crusader states in the Levant and the sources devote detailed coverage to its protracted siege by the Franks. Geographical factors influenced the spread of their conquests. They were able to occupy the Syrian coastline, but when they tried to expand eastwards they were less successful. Nevertheless, their achievements were impressive, especially in view of their small numbers and unfamiliarity with the terrain. As we have seen, the Islamic sources do not point this out, stressing instead Muslim disunity and lack of concerted response to the Franks.

The case of the Assassins typifies this disunity. As already mentioned, the Assassins had formed a breakaway Isma'ili group in Iran after the death of al-Mustansir in 487/1094. They soon adopted a policy of murdering prominent political and religious figures in Iran and began to exploit the weakness and instability of Syria. Hasan-i Sabbah, the Assassin leader based in Alamut in north-western Iran, decided around the beginning of the twelfth century to send missionaries to spread their secret doctrines in Syria. This timing was of course disastrous to the Muslim war effort against the Franks. Although their numbers were very small, the Assassins were able eventually to seize a number of mountain citadels and to entrench themselves there. But during the early decades of the twelfth century they operated from Aleppo and Damascus. They added to the complexity of the fragmented political landscape and came to be used on both sides, Muslim and Frankish, as the century progressed.

There were, of course, serious efforts on the part of the Muslims to stop the Frankish threat and it is now time to examine these. Three possible areas might have provided armies with which to stem the rising tide of Crusader expansionism in this period – Fatimid Egypt, the Seljuqs in the east and the local rulers of Syria. Even better than a single one of these would have been a coalition of two or more of them. In the event, all Muslim attempts to stop the Franks failed.

The Egyptian Response

Despite the negative judgements voiced in the Islamic sources, Fatimid

Egypt responded, and responded early, to the Crusader threat. Soon after the fall of Jerusalem in 492/1099, as we have already noted, al-Afdal, the Fatimid vizier, went in person to Palestine where the Franks inflicted a heavy defeat on his army. He then retreated to Cairo.[136] Ibn Zafir records reproachfully: 'He had given up hope of the Syrian coastline remaining in Muslim hands and he did not personally wage war against them after that.'[137]

However, Fatimid activities in northern Syria and Palestine did not cease altogether, although, as Ibn Zafir mentions: 'Most of the cities of Syria and the country were divided up between the Turks and the Franks (may God curse them).'[138]

In fact several other attempts were made against the Franks from Egypt by land and sea. In 503/1109, for example, after the Franks had finally taken Tripoli, the Egyptian fleet arrived – eight days too late to defend it. Al-Afdal also tried on two occasions to enlist help from Damascus against the Franks. In 498/1104–5 a combined Egyptian–Damascene force met the Franks between Jaffa and Ascalon, but the outcome of this encounter was inconclusive.[139] Further campaigns were spearheaded from Ascalon by the Fatimids, in 499/1105–6, 505/1111–12 and 506/1112–13, but they became increasingly infrequent as more and more of the coastline fell to the Franks.

As a result of these easy victories, the Franks even felt bold enough to attack Egypt itself. Baldwin, the king of Jerusalem, reached al-Farama and Tinnis in 511/1117. Ibn Zafir records this campaign by Baldwin, mentioning that he burned the main mosque and other mosques in al-Farama, as well as the town's gates. Baldwin died on his way back to Palestine. Thereafter, the Fatimids withdrew within their borders and interfered little in the affairs of the Levant.

In modern scholarship as in the medieval period, it has been customary to blame Fatimid Egypt for its lack of effort against the Franks. The years under discussion in this chapter – so the argument goes – would have offered during this vital period of Frankish expansion, especially on the coast, the prime opportunity for the Fatimids (who still had access to their own ports) to have nipped the Frankish threat in the bud. Moreover, at this time the Fatimids could have reconquered some of the territories they had lost to the Seljuqs in the second half of the eleventh century. But the dynamic impetus of the Fatimid state was a thing of the past and, as Brett points out, the establishment of the Frankish Kingdom of Jerusalem put an end to any territorial ambitions in Syria that the Fatimids may have had and ushered in a long period of Egyptian isolationism.[140] However, another interpretation of Fatimid activities has been given recently by the German scholar Köhler. Following the line presented in some of the Islamic sources, he argues that the Fatimids did not *want* to have the Turkish rulers of Syria as their direct neighbours and that they preferred on the whole to maintain a buffer area between them and the Turks. So Fatimid attacks on the Franks were directed mainly at defending the Syrian ports, where their direct interests as a notionally

Figure 2.26 *Fatimid carved wooden panel, twelfth century, Egypt*

maritime power were at stake. In other respects their efforts against the Franks may well have been deliberately perfunctory. Whatever the truth may be, the Fatimid army and navy could do little against the Franks.

The Seljuq Response

In sharp contrast to the treatment of the Shi'ite Fatimids in the Sunni historical sources, the Seljuqs' efforts against the Crusaders in this period are inflated by Muslim authors and the Seljuqs' notable lack of success minimised. In particular, sultan Muhammad (d. 511/1118) is praised in the sources as a great *jihad* fighter, although the evidence for this image of him is singularly meagre. Despite praise for the Seljuqs' campaigns against the Franks, it is clear from the sources that the many cries for help from dispossessed Levantine rulers and terrified citizens did not strike a very responsive chord in distant Baghdad and beyond. It was entirely understandable that appeals should be made to the Sunni rulers of the east by the Sunnis of Syria. Writing from Baghdad, the historian Ibn al-Jawzi (d. 597/1200) notes in his record for the year 491/1097–8, that is before the fall of Jerusalem: 'There were many calls to go out and fight against the Franks and complaints multiplied in every place.'[141] He mentioned that, on the orders of the Seljuq sultan Barkyaruq, commanders assembled: 'But then this resoluteness fizzled out.'[142]

Barkyaruq himself, locked in a struggle for succession with his brother Muhammad, had, of course, other concerns on his mind. It is unlikely that he put his personal authority behind the drive to send help to Syria. The following year, after Jerusalem was taken, Ibn al-Jawzi records mournfully:

> Those from Syria seeking help arrived [from Baghdad] and told what had happened to the Muslims. The *qadi* Abu Sa'id al-Harawi, the *qadi of Damascus, stood up in the diwan* [my italics] and delivered a speech which made those present weep. Someone was delegated from the *diwan* to go to the troops to inform them about this disaster. The people remained aloof.[143]

Figure 2.27
(above, opposite and overleaf)
Coins of various Turcoman principalities,
twelfth–thirteenth centuries,
Turkey and Iraq

So we see that nobody was willing to help the beleaguered Syrians.

In the immediately following years, increased Crusader expansion, and in particular the activities of Tancred in northern Syria, prompted further appeals to Baghdad. Some prominent citizens from Aleppo made the long journey across the desert in 504/1111 to plead personally for help against the constant threat and pillaging of the Franks. On the first Friday of their visit in Sha'ban 504/February 1111 they publicly called for assistance in the sultan's mosque. According to Ibn al-'Adim (and other sources), they completely disrupted the performance of the Friday prayers: 'They prevented the preachers from giving the sermon, crying out for Islamic troops against the Franks,

78

and they broke some of the pulpits.'[144] Ibn al-Qalanisi writes in similar vein: 'They drove the preacher from the pulpit and broke it into pieces, clamouring and weeping for the misfortunes that had befallen Islam at the hands of the Franks, the slaughter of men, and enslavement of women.'[145]

In view of the close connection in Islamic ritual between the pulpit and the reigning political authority, the breaking of the pulpit was no mere act of random vandalism but an unmistakable challenge to the sultan himself.

A week later there was a similar disturbance in the caliph's mosque. This suggests the deliberate orchestration of a campaign designed to shame into action both the titular and the *de facto* rulers of the Islamic state. The caliph, al-Mustazhir, was not amused; the timing of the Aleppan visit clashed with the arrival of his new bride from Isfahan who entered Baghdad amidst much pomp and ceremony. Al-Mustazhir was held back by the sultan from punishing those who had created all the commotion and the sultan agreed to send out an army to Syria.[146]

There were in fact some tangible results of this and other earlier protest visits to Baghdad. A few armies were set out in the course of the next few years into Syria with the publicly declared aim of fighting the Franks. These armies were headed by successive governors of Mosul who were working under the auspices of sultan Muhammad. Their achievements were singularly unimpressive. Mawdud, governor of Mosul, had led the first campaign, sponsored by the Seljuq sultan Muhammad, against the Franks in 503/1110; it was directed specifically at Edessa. Mawdud was joined by two Turcoman leaders who held power in what is now eastern Turkey, Sukman al-Qutbi of Akhlat and Najm al-Din Il-Ghazi of Mardin. This campaign was abortive.

Muhammad then sponsored an army in 505/1111–12 to return to Syria, again under the command of Mawdud, together with the contingents of a number of other commanders from different Seljuq territories.[147] This campaign was a total fiasco. The Seljuq prince Ridwan invited the army to come to Aleppo but when its members actually reached the walls of the city, they were incredulous as Ridwan closed its gates in their faces.[148] Their incredulity soon turned to anger as the gates remained closed for seventeen nights. Rampage and pillaging in the territory around Aleppo then followed. Thus a great Muslim campaign, sponsored by the Seljuq sultan, fizzled out ignominiously and without any tangible successes, with wasted time and resources. Indeed, it positively weakened the position of the Syrians.

Clearly it is easy to use Ridwan, who is often castigated in the sources for having 'Shi'ite leanings', as a scapegoat and to accuse him of vacillation and lack of loyalty to a higher Muslim cause. In an unusually scathing attack on him, Ibn al-'Adim, who wrote a biography of him, notes:

Ridwan's situation became weak and he began to favour the Batiniyya [the Isma'ilis] and their sect appeared in Aleppo. Ridwan took their side and they established a missionary house (*dar al-da'wa*) in Aleppo. The kings of Islam wrote to him about them but he paid no attention.[149]

However, the evidence of the sources does not indicate that Ridwan alone was to blame for this military disaster. The commanders in the sultan's army do not seem to have made much effort to win Ridwan over. Perhaps, at the last minute, he was afraid that the goal of the army sent by this relative from the east was to erode his personal authority at Aleppo.

Sultan Muhammad sent another campaign into Syria in 509/1115. On this occasion the rulers of Aleppo and Damascus actually sided with the Crusader leader Roger of Antioch, and the sultan's army was soundly defeated in Rabi' II 509/September 1115 by Roger at the battle of Danith.[150] This marked the end of the Seljuq offensive from the east against the Franks. It had foundered because of internal political factors within the Seljuq sphere of influence. Seljuq motivation was always mistrusted by local Muslim rulers in Syria who feared interference from Baghdad and Isfahan in their affairs, and these rulers would not generally give the Seljuq armies their support. And it could well have been the case that what the pro-Seljuq sources present as campaigns against the Franks in Syria were indeed efforts on the part of the Seljuqs of the east to reimpose the more centralised authority which had once existed under the Great Seljuqs before 485/1092. Whatever the motivation for these campaigns may have been – spearheaded from Mosul and nominally at least under the sponsorship of the Seljuq sultan Muhammad – they were a signal failure. One must also take into account the possibility that the missions dispatched from Syria to Baghdad to seek help against the Franks were popular in nature and did not always enjoy the support of the rulers themselves. Hence when help was sent, it was not accepted and the prospective saviours of Syria were reduced to attacking the very Muslims they had ostensibly come to help.

As already mentioned, most Sunni Islamic sources try to whitewash Seljuq indifference to the loss of Jerusalem and the Syrian ports and they point to these campaigns which were actually sent out under the auspices of the Seljuq sultan to wage *jihad* against the Crusaders. However, no matter how biased they are in favour of the Seljuqs, these accounts cannot disguise the fact that Crusader expansionist aims were not stopped as a result of any of these military efforts. The Franks slotted easily into the atmosphere of small territorial units with ephemeral alliances and changing priorities which prevailed in Syria in the first decade of their presence in the area, and they exploited this labile situation to their full advantage. Had the Seljuqs from the east focused on the Franks and sent a unified army under the leadership of the sultan himself, things might have ended differently. It has

often been pointed out that it was the Turkish warriors, not the Fatimid armies, who posed a real military threat to the Crusaders. Only the Seljuq armies could seriously have arrested Latin Christian expansion in the Levant. Whilst the Seljuq sultan paid lip service to the cause and sent some armies to fight the Franks, he did not take the field himself at the head of an army in Syria, as Alp Arslan had done against the Byzantine emperor at the battle of Manzikert in 463/1071. Muhammad did not dare to leave his power base in the east undefended.

And that was the territory that counted for him, not Syria. The fate of Jerusalem and the Syrian ports was sealed, therefore, in distant Isfahan. This geopolitical reality is often overlooked in accounts of the First Crusade and its immediate aftermath. As we shall see in Chapter 7, the disparate nature of the Seljuq army – composed as it was of the standing troops, provincial contingents under local commanders, and groups of nomadic Turcomans organised on tribal lines – necessitated strong military leadership, epitomised in the figure of the sultan. Otherwise, and this proved the case in this crucial period of Crusader consolidation in the region, there was dissension, defection and defeat on the Muslim side.

The Local Syrian Response to the Frankish Presence

Henceforward, if there was to be resistance to the Franks it would have to come from those who lived closest to them. The Turcoman Artuqid ruler of Mardin, Il-Ghazi, who held Aleppo for a while, showed the way with a resounding victory in 513/1119 over Roger of Antioch in a battle which came to be known as the battle of Balat or the Field of Blood. Roger was killed.[151] This was the first major Muslim victory against the Franks and significantly it had been achieved without help of outside armies from the east. But it was an isolated success and Il-Ghazi did not follow it up by moving on Antioch. Ibn al-Qalanisi rises to unusual heights of eloquence in his description of this victory:

> The Franks were on the ground, one prostrate mass, horsemen and footmen alike, with their horses and their weapons, so that not one man of them escaped to tell the tale, and their leader Roger was found stretched out among the dead. A number of the eye witnesses of this battle . . . saw some of the horses stretched out on the ground like hedgehogs because of the quantities of arrows sticking into them. This victory was one of the finest of victories, and such plenitude of divine aid was never granted to Islam in all its past ages.[152]

After the First Crusade and in the year immediately following it, the power of the local Muslim rulers in Syria and Palestine was gradually eroded and their lands were first pillaged and then captured by the Franks. Instead of uniting against a common enemy, the Muslims tended to make unilateral agreements with the Franks and pay tribute to them. Lacking a strong overall leadership, such as could have been provided by the Seljuq sultan to the east, and still cut off by religious differences from the Shi'ite government of Fatimid Egypt, the local Muslim rulers of Syria and Palestine could and did form ephemeral alliances with each other against the Franks, but these were extremely fragile and were broken at the least provocation.

Far from uniting against a common enemy, local rulers in Syria with their power centred on a single city, such as Aleppo or Damascus, had no intention whatsoever of sacrificing their own political interests for the sake of some nebulous ideal of Islamic solidarity. It was precisely in this period of the early Crusader presence that the political and military alliances mentioned above were frequently established between Muslims and Franks in which their shared local interests in Syria were paramount.[153]

Figure 2.28 *Soldier wearing Mongol armour, Rashid al-Din, Jami' al-Tawarikh ('World History'), 714/1314, Tabriz, Iran*

Two episodes illustrate this very clearly. Aleppo under Ridwan and Antioch under Tancred formed an alliance against what they perceived as military interference in their affairs by the ruler of Mosul, Jawali Saqao, Ridwan's main political rival. Accordingly, Ridwan wrote to Tancred saying that it would be right for the two of them to unite against Jawali in order to drive him from their territories.[154] Such alliances as these were, of course, opportunistic and short-lived. After Tancred's death in 506/1112, Ridwan allied himself with Tughtegin of Damascus. Such readiness to become involved in the pragmatic politics of survival and co-existence characterises this period.

Similar arrangements were made between the Crusader Kingdom of Jerusalem and the Fatimid governor of Ascalon. According to Ibn al-Qalanisi, the governor, Shams al-Khilafa, bought a truce from Baldwin. Al-Afdal, the Fatimid vizier of Egypt, was not at all happy about this and he sent an army to Ascalon in 504/1111 to have the governor removed. Shams al-Khilafa got in touch with Baldwin, who agreed to send him supplies of men and fodder. The Fatimid garrison was driven out of Ascalon as Shams al-Khilafa suspected them of being on the Fatimid side. The episode ended with Shams al-Khilafa being conveniently killed and Ascalon reverting to Fatimid control.[155] In the case of Ascalon, concern to leave trade undisturbed played an important part in the decision of Shams al-Khilafa to side with the Franks: 'Now Shams al-Khilafa was more desirous of trading than of fighting, and returned to peaceful and friendly relations and the securing of the safety of travellers.'[156]

Thus we see how frequently in this period a mutually acceptable *modus vivendi* was established between Frank and Muslim across the ideological divide; this realism could even survive military skirmishes and raids between the two sides. As Baldwin said to Tughtegin after Tughtegin had been defeated in battle in Sha'ban 502/March

1108: 'Do not think that I am breaking the truce which has been con-cluded with you because of this defeat.'[157]

Behind these opportunistic alliances made between Muslim and Frank lay two principal factors: pan-Syrian solidarity against the out-siders – 'We do not want anybody from the east' was the cry of the local Syrian rulers – and the particular ambitions of the local rulers to maintain their own power intact. According to the chronicler of the city, Ibn al-'Adim, the political elite of Aleppo were in favour of the continuing existence of the Franks in Syria, because it helped them to perpetuate the independent status of their city.[158] Similarly Ibn al-Qalanisi, the local historian of Damascus, describes Tughtegin as acting more as a local territorial ruler than a far-sighted *jihad* fighter.[159]

Tailpiece

It is worth highlighting at this point some of the themes discussed in the preceding pages. Overall, Muslim disunity meant the dominance of local interests. Muslim rivalries which had existed before the First Crusade continued after it. The Crusader states slotted into the polit-ical map of Syria and Palestine and both Fatimids and Turks were able and willing to use Frankish power creatively in their own inter-ests. On both sides these seem to have favoured the continuation of buffer territory between the Isma'ili Shi'ite Fatimid state and the Sunni Turkish rulers of Syria and further east.[160]

Summarising his mournful catalogue of Muslim defeats, Ibn al-Athir is in no doubt as to why the Franks achieved such resounding suc-cesses in the First Crusade: 'The sultans disagreed, as we shall relate, and the Franks seized the lands.'[161] This thought is elaborated by Abu Shama (d. 665/1258) who, speaking about Seljuq internecine strife in the period 487–498/1094–1105, writes:

> Malikshah's [two] sons, Barkyaruq and Muhammad, fought each other and the wars between them lasted for around twelve years until Barkyaruq died and the sultanate became established for Muhammad. In the period of these wars the Franks appeared on the Syrian coast [the *Sahil*] and took possession first of Antioch and then of other parts of the country.[162]

This chapter has focused closely on the impact and repercussions of the First Crusade in particular. It is clear that although other Crusades were to follow, they did not result in *major* territorial gains nor in the establishment of new Frankish states. Just as no Crusade was as glorious in Western eyes as this one, so too its effects were more profoundly felt by the Islamic world than any other subsequent attacks. As time went on, like it or not, the Muslims became accus-tomed to the Crusader presence in their midst and in a sense they came to expect further invasions from the West. But the years

1099–1109 were the period in which the Muslims of the Levant had to learn to adjust to these unexpected and powerful invaders who did not go away but stayed to put down roots in what was traditionally Islamic territory.

Notes

1. Ibn al-Athir, *Kamil*, X, 256.
2. L. and J. Riley-Smith, *The Crusades: Idea and Reality 1095–1274*, London, 1981, 1.
3. Al-ʿAzimi, 'La chronique abrégée d'al-ʿAzimi', ed. C. Cahen, *JA*, 230, (1938), 353–448; new edn as *Tarikh Halab*, ed. I. Zaʿrur, Damascus, 1984.
4. Hamdan b. ʿAbd al-Rahim al-Atharibi. For more discussion about this author, cf. Ibn Muyassar, 70. Cf. also F. Rosenthal, *A History of Muslim Historiography*, Leiden, 1968, 62 and 466.
5. For example, Ibn Taghribirdi, *Nujum al-zahira*, Cairo, 1939.
6. Al-Abiwardi, *Diwan*, ed. U. al-Asʿad, Damascus, 1974–5; Ibn al-Khayyat, *Diwan*, ed. H. Mardam Bek, Damascus, 1958.
7. For a discussion of this work, cf. Chapter 3. A photocopy of one of the manuscripts in Damascus was consulted during the final stages of writing this book thanks to the perseverance and generosity of my friend Dr ʿAdil Jadir.
8. Ibn al-Athir, *Al-Kamil fi'l-tarikh*, ed. C. J. Tornberg, Leiden and Uppsala, 1851–6.
9. Ibn al-ʿAdim, *Zubdat al-halab*, ed. S. Dahan, Damascus, 1954.
10. Ibn Taghribirdi, *Nujum*, V, 139.
11. Al-ʿAzimi, 371.
12. *EI*[1]: Zuhal.
13. Al-Maqrizi, *Ittiʿaz*, 283–4.
14. *EI*[2]: Malazgird.
15. *EI*[2]: Kilidj Arslan.
16. Ibn Khallikan, de Slane, I, 612.
17. Al-Nuwayri, 246–7; Ibn Khallikan, de Slane, I, 160; Ibn al-Dawadari, VI, 450; al-ʿAzimi, 373; Ibn Zafir, 82; Ibn Muyassar, 38.
18. Al-Nuwayri, 258; al-ʿAzimi, 373; Ibn Taghribirdi, *Nujum*, V, 149–50.
19. For a modern analysis of this issue, cf. M.A.Köhler, 'Al-Afdal und Jerusalem – was versprach sich Ägypten vom ersten Kreuzzug?', *Saeculum*, 37 (1986), 228–39.
20. Al-ʿAzimi, 371.
21. Ibn Zafir, 82.
22. *EI*[2]: Atsiz.
23. Ibn Muyassar, 39.
24. Ibn Muyassar, 39.
25. Ibn Muyassar, 39.
26. Ibn al-Qalanisi, Gibb, 45.
27. Crusader sources point clearly to the Fatimids and the Franks being in contact at Antioch.
28. Ibn al-Athir, *Kamil*, X, 186.
29. Here, of course, recourse to Western Crusader sources is essential in establishing a balanced historical assessment of the truth. The aim here has been to highlight hints in the Islamic sources which have been rather neglected in modern scholarship. The Crusader sources

clearly point to Fatimid/Crusader contacts and to collaboration between them. Cf. the discussion in Köhler, 'Al-Afdal und Jerusalem', 228–39.

30. E. Sivan, 'The beginnings of the Fada'il al-Quds literature', *Israel Oriental Studies*, 1 (1971), 263–72.

31. Al-Maqrizi, *Itti'az*, 81.

32. Nasir-i Khusraw, Schefer, 66.

33. Nasir-i Khusraw, Schefer, 66–7.

34. Nasir-i Khusraw, Schefer, 106–7.

35. Nasir-i Khusraw, Schefer, 108.

36. Nasir-i Khusraw, Schefer, 108.

37. I. 'Abbas, 'Rihlat Ibn al-'Arabi ila al-mashriq kama sawwaraha "Qanun al-ta'wil"', *Al-Abhath*, 21/1 (1968), 59–92, hereafter mentioned as *Rihla*; id., 'Al-janib al-siyasi min rihlat Ibn al-'Arabi ila al-mashriq', Al-abhath, 12/2 (1963), 217–36.

38. *Rihla*, 73.

39. *Rihla*, 64.

40. *Rihla*, 64.

41. *Rihla*, 64–5.

42. *Rihla*, 82.

43. *Rihla*, 79.

44. *Al-munqidh min al-dalal*, trans. R. McCarthy as *Freedom and fulfillment*, Boston, 1980, 93.

45. *Rihla*, 65.

46. *Rihla*, 81; the text is a little ambiguous – *yu'ammiruna kana'isah* could mean 'to build', 'rebuild' or 'keep in good repair'. The last possibility seems the most reasonable.

47. *Rihla*, 66 and 84.

48. Al-'Azimi, 369. The word *ghaza* means a military raid or expedition and often implies conquest.

49. In his commentary on his edition of al-'Azimi, Cahen (430, n. 3) wonders whether this even relates to a real event or whether it is a reflection of later Crusader lore.

50. Ibn al-Qalanisi, Gibb, 41–4.

51. Al-'Azimi, 358.

52. Al-'Azimi, 366.

53. Ibn al-Athir, *Kamil*, X, 185.

54. Ibn al-Athir, *Kamil*, X, 186.

55. Ibn al-Athir, *Kamil*, X, 186.

56. Al-Nuwayri, 248.

57. Al-Nuwayri, 248.

58. Al-Nuwayri, 248.

59. The reader is recommended to read the book by J. France on the First Crusade – *Victory in the East*, Cambridge, 1995.

60. Al-'Azimi, 372.

61. Ibn al-Qalanisi, Gibb, 42.

62. Nicaea was reintegrated into the Byzantine empire in June 1097. Cf. P. M. Holt, *The Age of the Crusades*, London, 1986, 21.

63. Ibn al-Qalanisi, Gibb, 42.

64. Ibn al-Athir, *Kamil*, X, 187.

65. As, for example, Ibn al-Qalanisi, Gibb, 50.

66. Ibn al-Athir, *Kamil*, X, 222.

67. Ibn al-Qalanisi, Gibb, 42.

68. Ibn al-Qalanisi, Gibb, 43.

69. Ibn al-Qalanisi, Gibb, 44.

70. Ibn al-Qalanisi, Gibb, 45; there is a similar account in al-'Azimi, 373.
71. Ibn al-Qalanisi, Gibb, 44.
72. Ibn al-Qalanisi, Gibb, 46.
73. Al-'Azimi, 373.
74. F. Gabrieli, *Arab Historians of the Crusades*, London, 1969, 3.
75. Ibn al-Athir, *Kamil*, X, 187–90.
76. Ibn al-Athir, *Kamil*, X, 188.
77. Ibn al-Athir, *Kamil*, X, 188–9.
78. Ibn al-Athir, *Kamil*, X, 189–90.
79. Ibn Shaddad, Eddé, 248.
80. Ibn Taghribirdi, *Nujum*, V, 147.
81. Ibn Taghribirdi, *Nujum*, V, 148.
82. Ibn al-Qalanisi, Gibb, 47.
83. Ibn al-Qalanisi, Gibb, 47.
84. Ibn al-Qalanisi, Gibb, 47.
85. Ibn al-Athir, *Kamil*, X, 190.
86. Ibn al-'Adim, *Zubda*, I, 356.
87. Al-'Azimi, 373.
88. Ibn al-Qalanisi, Gibb, 48.
89. Ibn al-Jawzi, IX, 108.
90. Ibn Muyassar, 39.
91. Ibn al-Athir, *Kamil*, X, 192.
92. Ibn Taghribirdi, *Nujum*, V, 149.
93. Cf. the discussion in B. Kedar, 'The subjected Muslims of the Levant', in *Muslims under Latin Rule 1100–1300*, ed. J. M. Powell, Princeton, 1990, 144.
94. Al-'Azimi, 373.
95. Ibn Taghribirdi, *Nujum*, V, 150.
96. Cf. also Ibn Shaddad, Eddé, 34.
97. Ibn al-Athir, *Kamil*, X, 187.
98. Ibn al-Athir, *Kamil*, X, 187.
99. Al-'Azimi, 373; Ibn al-'Adim, *Zubda*; Ibn Shaddad, Eddé, 247.
100. For a recent analysis from the Byzantine side, cf. J. Shepard, 'Cross-purposes: Alexius Comnenus and the First Crusade', in *The First Crusade: Origins and Impact*, ed. J. Phillips, Manchester, 1997, 107–29.
101. Al-'Azimi, 370–1.
102. Al-'Azimi, 371–2.
103. Al-'Azimi, 376.
104. Ibn al-Qalanisi, Gibb, 112.
105. P. K. Hitti, *History of Syria*, London, 1951, 589.
106. Cf. *EI²*: Al-Abiwardi.
107. This ode is quoted more fully by Ibn al-Jawzi, IX, 108, Ibn al-Athir, *Kamil*, X, 192–3 and Ibn Taghribirdi, *Nujum*, V, 151; it is partly translated by Gabrieli, 12.
108. Sivan, *L'Islam*, 32.
109. Ibn al-Khayyat, *Diwan*, ed. H. Mardam Bek, Damascus, 1958, 184–6; Sivan discusses the importance of this poetry, *L'Islam*, 18, 24, 32, 36.
110. H. Dajani-Shakeel, 'Jihad in twelfth-century Arabic poetry', *Muslim World*, 66 (1976), 96–113; C. Hillenbrand, 'The First Crusade: the Muslim perspective', in *The First Crusade: Origins and Impact*, ed. J. Phillips, Manchester, 1997, 137–8.
111. Ibn Taghribirdi, *Nujum*, V, 152.
112. E. Sivan, 'Réfugiés syro-palestiniens au temps des Croisades', *REI*, 35 (1965), 140; 'Imad al-Din, *Kharidat al-qasr*, Damascus, 1959, vol. II, 57.

113. 'Imad al-Din, *Kharida*, II, 101.
114. Cf. E. Sivan, 'La genèse de la contre-Croisade: un traité damasquin du début du XIIe siècle', *JA* 254 (1966), 197–224. This article contains an edition of selected passages of the surviving text, together with a translation of them. The references to al-Sulami which follow will be based on Sivan's article. Cf. also al-Maqrizi, *Muqaffa'*, 154–5.
115. Ibn al-Athir, *Kamil*, X, 193.
116. Ibn Shaddad, Eddé, 270. In the Arabic popular epics the Franks often appear as staunch allies of the Byzantine emperor. Cf. P. Heath, *The Thirsty Sword. Sirat 'Antar and the Arabic Popular Epic*, Salt Lake City, 1996, 29.
117. Fol. 174a; French trans., 215.
118. Fol. 174a; French trans., 215.
119. Fol. 174a–b; French trans., 215.
120. Ibid.
121. Ibid.
122. Ibid., 216.
123. Fols 188b–189a; French trans., 220.
124. Fols 189b; French trans., 221.
125. Al-'Azimi, 377.
126. Ibn Muyassar records famine for the years 490/1096–7 and 493/1099–1100; Ibn Muyassar, 37 and 39.
127. Ibn Muyassar, 39.
128. 'Imad al–Din, *Kharida*, I, 96.
129. Ibn al-Dawadari, 451; cf. also al-Harawi, Sourdel-Thomine, 15.
130. This has been analysed by Sivan. Cf. Sivan, 'Réfugiés syro-palestiniens, 135–47.
131. Ibn al-Qalanisi, Gibb, 51 (my italics).
132. Ibn al-Qalanisi, Gibb, 51.
133. Ibn al-Qalanisi, Gibb, 90.
134. Ibn al-Qalanisi, Gibb, 47.
135. According to Ibn al-Furat, *Tarikh*, Vienna ms. vol. 1, fol. 39a; cited by Sivan, *L'Islam*, 137.
136. Al-Maqrizi, *Itti'az*, 283.
137. Ibn Zafir, 82.
138. Ibn Zafir, 102; cf. also al-Maqrizi, *Itti'az*, 284.
139. Ibn Muyassar, 41.
140. Brett, 'Ramla', 20.
141. Ibn al-Jawzi, IX, 105.
142. Ibn al-Jawzi, IX, 105.
143. Ibn al-Jawzi, IX, 108.
144. *Bughya*, 146.
145. Ibn al-Qalanisi, Gibb, 111.
146. Ibn al-Qalanisi, Gibb, 111–12.
147. *Bughya*, 147.
148. *Bughya*, Zakkar, VIII, 3664; Ibn al-'Adim, *Zubda*, I, 369.
149. *Bughya*, Zakkar, VIII, 3661.
150. Al-'Azimi, 383.
151. Ibn al-'Adim, *Zubda*, Dahan, II, 187–90.
152. Ibn al-Qalanisi, Gibb, 160–1.
153. These alliances are analysed in some detail by Köhler.
154. The evidence of Ibn al-Athir is quoted by Köhler, 83.
155. Ibn al-Qalanisi, Gibb, 109–10; Ibn al-Athir, *Kamil*, X, 337–8.
156. Ibn al-Qalanisi, Gibb, 109.
157. Ibn al-Athir, *Kamil*, X, 328–9.

158. *Zubda*, Dahan, II, 173.
159. Ibn al-Qalanisi, *Dhayl tarikh Dimishq*, ed. H. F. Amedroz, Leiden, 1908, 216–17.
160. Abu Shama, I, 26.
161. Ibn al-Athir, *Kamil*, X, 192; cf. also al-Nuwayri, 258.
162. Abu Shama, I, 26.

CHAPTER THREE

Jihad in the Period 493–569/1100–1174

Among men there are those who battle, just as the Companions of the Prophet used to battle, for the hope of Paradise and not in order to satisfy a desire or win a reputation.[1] (Usama)

Introduction: Aims and Structure of the Chapter

IN A RECENT BOOK devoted to the subject of war in the Middle East with contributions from a number of specialists, it is interesting to note that there was no chapter on the ideological aspects of warfare, namely *jihad*, Holy War in Islam.[2] Moreover, one of the contributors, Rustow, repeats the view generally held in the West that 'Islam is the most martial of the world's great religions'.[3]

The Crusades seem to be the very epitome of the phrase 'wars of religion'. The motives that propelled the Franks towards the Holy Land were of course multifarious. But Western scholarship has shown that there is no doubt that religion played a large part in the whole enterprise. There is no doubt also that the tools of religious propaganda and the symbols evoked in speeches and tracts of the Franks were those of the Christian faith – above all, the Cross, Jerusalem and Holy War.

This chapter and the next examine from the Muslim side some of the religious aspects of the conflict between the Islamic world and Christian Europe. They will focus on the evolution of the Islamic concept of *jihad* (Holy War) during the Crusading period and will highlight the role which religious propaganda – including religious architecture (plates 3.1, 3.2, 3.3–5; cf. plates 3.6 and 3.7) – played in the conflict.

Figure 3.1 *Mounted warrior, stone mould, eleventh–twelfth centuries, Iran*

Definition of *Jihad*: Its Roots in the Qur'an and the *Hadith*

Religious war is a concept deeply embedded in Islamic belief. Indeed, *jihad* has often been called the sixth pillar (*rukn*) of Islam; it denotes struggle on the part of Muslims. The Revelation itself, the Qur'an,

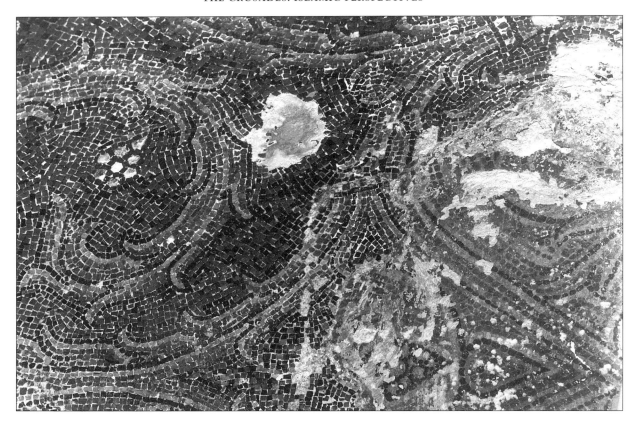

Plate 3.1 *Great Mosque of Nur al-Din, mosaic decoration in* mihrab, *thirteenth century, Hims, Syria*

contains plentiful imagery of struggle and fighting, and this has formed the foundation of the theory of *jihad*. Although a number of Qur'anic chapters (*sura*s) mention the concept of struggle (the Arabic root j h d), the most important chapter in this context is chapter 9, the *sura* of repentance (*al-Tawba*). It is incidentally the only chapter of the Qur'an which omits the opening formula 'In the name of Allah, the Merciful, the Compassionate', the formula stressing the Creator's infinite and constant mercy to His creation. The omission

Figure 3.2 *Silver dirham of Rukn al-Din Sulayman Shah; its reverse quotes Sura 9: 33 which has* jihad *associations. 592/1195–6, Kayseri, Turkey*

of this formula is generally believed to have been caused by the presence within chapter 9 of fierce commandments about idolaters and the steps which should be taken against them. Verse 14, for example, enjoins the Muslims as follows: 'Fight them! Allah will chastise them at your hands, and He will lay them low and give you victory over them.' Verse 36 declares: 'Fight the polytheists totally as they fight you totally.' In verses 88–9 this chapter also promises Paradise for those that strive (j h d) in the path of God:

But the messenger and those who believe with him strive with their wealth and their lives. Such are they for whom are the good things. Such are they who are the successful. Allah hath made ready for them Gardens underneath which rivers flow, wherein they will reside. That is the supreme triumph.[4]

Plate 3.2 *Great Mosque of Nur al-Din, sanctuary showing minbar and mihrab, twelfth–thirteenth centuries, Hims, Syria*

(Creswell Photographic Archive, Ashmolean Museum, Oxford, neg. C. 5904)

Plate 3.3 *Great Mosque of Nur al-Din, courtyard, twelfth–thirteenth centuries, Hims, Syria*

(Creswell Photographic Archive, Ashmolean Museum, Oxford, neg. C. 5907)

The second canonical source in Islam, the *hadith*, the corpus of sayings attributed to the Prophet Muhammad, also contains many references to *jihad*. One such *hadith* declares: 'A morning or an evening expedition in God's path is better than the world and what it contains, and for one of you to remain in the line of battle is better than his prayers for sixty years.'[5]

The *hadith* also stress repeatedly that those who fight *jihad* are given God's promise that they will enter Paradise: 'The gates of Paradise are under the shadow of the swords.'[6]

Jihad in the Early Islamic Period

There is no doubt that there was a religious motivation to the early Muslim conquests of the seventh century, especially amongst the elite of the Muslim community (*umma*) who had been closest to the

Prophet and who had experienced his charismatic personality and the power of the Islamic revelation. Indeed, the religious impetus played a crucial part in the phenomenon which allowed the Arabs to establish an empire which by the beginning of the eighth century stretched from Spain in the west to northern India and Central Asia in the east.

In the eighth century the Arabs made several unsuccessful attempts by land and sea to take Constantinople. Their failure marked a watershed. Thereafter, the great surge of conquest receded in the lands which bordered Christian territory: the Byzantine empire on the one hand and the kingdoms of northern Spain on the other. The Muslim rulers opted for consolidation rather than expansion. On the Byzantine–Islamic borders, both Christians and Muslims continued to be active, and lines of defensive forts were built or rebuilt to strengthen the frontiers. It became the practice for both empires to engage in annual campaigns, described in the Islamic sources as *jihad*, but these gradually became a ritual, important for the image of the caliph and emperor, rather than being motivated by a vigorous desire to conquer new territories for their respective faiths. The boundaries between the Islamic and Christian worlds remained more or less stabilised and from the later eighth century onwards it was deemed more important to defend existing frontiers than to extend them.

Plate 3.4 *Great Mosque of Nur al-Din, courtyard, twelfth–thirteenth centuries, Hims, Syria*

(Creswell Photographic Archive, Ashmolean Museum, Oxford, neg. C. 5896)

Plate 3.5 Masjid al-Hasanayn, exterior, rebuilt after 552/1157 by Nur al-Din, Hama, Syria

Moreover, the tenth century saw the emergence of a major ideological rival to the 'Abbasid caliphs of Baghdad – namely the Shi'ite Isma'ili Fatimid *imam*s who moved from North Africa to Egypt and established a new dynamic Mediterranean state. Both Sunni and Shi'ite became locked in an internal battle for supremacy within the Islamic world and much less effort was expended on prosecuting *jihad* against the outside world of the infidel.

The Elaboration of the Classical Islamic Theory of *Jihad*

It was during the 'Abbasid period (from 750 onwards) that Islamic law was definitively formulated although its practice had been evolving since the earliest days of the Muslim empire. It is important to stress that the classical theory of *jihad* is an entirely Islamic phenomenon. It is a hermetically sealed tradition and does not appear to have been influenced by Christian notions of Holy War, although both religions use similar sets of images for fighting on God's side and stress the aspect of spiritual renewal and personal struggle in God's path. Muslim legists were motivated by a deep religious concern to provide and uphold an ideal framework within which the Islamic state might flourish, and it was in their books of Islamic law that the classical theory of *jihad* was elaborated.

94

The classical works of Islamic law (*Shari'a*), such as that of al-Shafi'i (d. 204/820), usually contain a chapter on *jihad*. This follows a predictable layout. First, the evidence for *jihad* in the Qur'an and the *hadith* is presented and interpreted. As we have seen, the theory of *jihad* has a sound Qur'anic basis and many verses from the Qur'an are cited in the legal books in support of *jihad*. The conventional chapter on *jihad* in the law books also draws very fully on the *hadith*. From the evidence provided by the Qur'an and the *hadith*,

Plate 3.6 *Great Mosque of Nur al-Din,* minbar *portal, twelfth–thirteenth centuries, Hims, Syria*

95

Plate 3.7 *Great Mosque of*
Nur al-Din, mihrab,
twelfth–thirteenth centuries,
Hims, Syria

(Creswell Photographic Archive, Ashmolean Museum, Oxford, neg. C. 5903)

Figure 3.7 *Craftsman's signature on a brass ewer dated 627/1229, probably Mosul, Iraq*

to strict religio-military rules and in a constant state of military readiness. It was these *jihad* fighters who made regular forays into nomadic Turkish territory and converted many of the tribesmen to Islam.

The Muslim Frontier with Byzantium

Another early blueprint for *jihad* activity, as noted above, was the tenth-century Shiʿite dynasty of the Hamdanids. Under its most famous ruler, Sayf al-Dawla (ruled 333–56/944–67) it became famous throughout the Islamic world for its annual campaigns of *jihad* against the Byzantine Christians. This was, it should be stressed, in response to renewed expansionism on the Byzantine side. The efforts of the Hamdanids became so well known that thousands of volunteer *mujahidun* or *ghazi*s from far-away Central Asia travelled vast distances to join in these wars. Here proselytism was not in question. This *jihad* was waged in response to perceived external aggression on the part of the Christians.

According to the tenth-century writer al-Tarsusi, a judge (*qadi*) in Maʿarrat al-Nuʿman and Kafartab who wrote a work (now lost) entitled *Ways of Life along the Frontiers* (*Siyar al-thughur*), in 290/903 the town of Tarsus on the Muslim–Byzantine border contained many houses for the lodging of Muslim warriors for the faith (*ghazi*s) who had come from all parts of the Islamic world. The warriors were supported by the charitable donations of the pious and rulers.[15]

The propaganda for *jihad* developed by the Hamdanids showed the beginnings of a much more sophisticated approach. Dating from the Hamdanid period are the famous, if little studied, *jihad* sermons of Ibn Nubata al-Fariqi (d. 374/984–5) of Mayyafariqin in present-day Turkey. These are written in very elaborate and resonant rhymed prose. They were intended to exhort the people of Mayyafariqin and Aleppo to fight *jihad* against the Byzantines. These sermons display a careful symmetry of balanced couplets and a clever exploitation of the long-established and cherished Arab tradition of oratory. They utilise alliteration, assonance, repetition and similar devices in a manner which recalls to Western ears the Old Testament or Ciceronian prose. To their Muslim hearers the language of these sermons was impregnated with Qur'anic echoes and allusions and would have moved them to tears – and to action (cf. colour plate 2). Indeed, the elevated style of Ibn Nubata's sermons was itself part of a deliberate attempt to arouse the faithful; he is known to have preached both before military campaigns and afterwards to celebrate victory in battle. In one such sermon Ibn Nubata praises Sayf al-Dawla for taming heretics and encouraging *jihad* fighters.[16] In another sermon delivered in 352/963 to *jihad* volunteers who had come from distant Khurasan to Mayyafariqin Ibn Nubata exhorts the people to rouse themselves from their comfortable beds and to fight like lions in the path of *jihad*.[17] The sermon reaches its climax when Ibn Nubata explicitly mentions the victory of Islam over Christianity: 'God has graciously bestowed on us and on you His near victory and He has made the people of monotheism victorious over the servants of the Cross.'[18]

A particularly rousing sermon was the one delivered on the conquest of Aleppo in 351/962. Having praised God and His manifold attributes, Ibn Nubata rises to heights of eloquence:

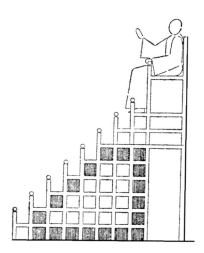

Figure 3.8 *Diagram illustrating function of* minbar

> Do you think that He will forsake you whilst you are assisting Him or do you imagine that He will desert you whilst you are steadfast in His path? Certainly not! Indeed, no tyranny is left unpunished by Him and no trivial offence escapes Him . . . So put on – may God have mercy on you – for the *jihad* the coat of mail of the faithful and equip yourselves with the armour of those who trust [in God].[19]

Not surprisingly, these sermons have become models of Arab oratory. They also laid the foundations for the sermons of preachers in the armies of Nur al-Din and Saladin, when fighting against the Franks.

Panegyric verse about the exploits of Sayf al-Dawla was composed by the most honoured of all classical Arabic poets, al-Mutanabbi. Such poetry was a forum for the expression of pride in the achievements of *jihad*. Al-Mutanabbi produced a famous panegyric after the conquest by Sayf al-Dawla of the border fortress, al-Hadath. The piece includes the following lines:

> You were not a king routing an equal, but *monotheism routing polytheism*
>   We put our hope in you and your refuge Islam,
> Why should merciful God not guard it when through you
>   He cleaves the unbeliever asunder?

Popular epics echoed the *jihad* spirit of the high literature written for the Hamdanid court. The epic usually known as *Sirat Dhat al-Himma* has an alternative title, *Sirat al-mujahidin* (*The Way of the* jihad

Fighters). It mirrors the Muslim–Byzantine conflicts from the Umay-yad period onwards and is full of expressions of the *jihad* spirit. At the beginning the anonymous story-teller declares: 'Jihad is God's solid link and the *jihad* warriors occupy a high position near Him in the seventh Heaven.'[20]

The campaigns of Sayf al-Dawla were prosecuted in a limited geographical area of the Muslim world and were not followed up by his successors. His highly effective *jihad* propaganda died with him, although, as we shall see, its lessons were not lost on those responsible for the Muslim Counter-Crusade two hundred years later. Indeed, the fusion of the life of personal asceticism of the *ghazi*s of Central Asia, Spain and Anatolia with the fight against unbelievers was a paradigm for the Muslims of Syria and Palestine to remember and emulate in their war against the Franks.

The Lack of *Jihad* Spirit in Syria and Palestine

Writing in the latter half of the tenth century, the Arab geographer Ibn Hawqal, whose Spanish origins no doubt sharpened his concern, deplores the fact that *jihad* has ceased.[21] This criticism is reiterated by the even more famous Arab writer al-Muqaddasi who, speaking about the province of Syria, complains that: 'The inhabitants have no enthusiasm for *jihad* and no energy in the struggle against the enemy'.[22]

When the Crusaders approached the Holy Land in 1099 the dis-united and strife-ridden Muslim world had, it seems, buried the idea of *jihad* deep into the recesses of its mind. Indeed, it was the Crusaders who possessed the ideological edge over the Muslims.

The Evolution of the Phenomenon of *Jihad* in Crusader Times

Modern knowledge of the development of the *jihad* theme in the Muslim world at the time of the Crusades was considerably enlarged with the appearance in 1968 of the very important pioneering book in French on this subject by Emmanuel Sivan: *L'Islam*. In it he analyses by very close reference to a wide range of medieval Arabic literary sources the evolution of *jihad* as an ideology and as a propaganda campaign, and its role in the Muslim response to the Crusades. Much of Sivan's argument still holds good, although inevitably scholars may wish to take issue with him on some points and indeed, as we shall see later, to stress the gulf between propaganda and polit-ical realities. As Humphreys says of *jihad*: 'The concept of *jihad* is a plastic one, which can be deployed in widely varying ways for vary-ing ends.'[23]

Sivan argues that the serious mobilisation of *jihad* as an instrument in the war against the Crusaders began in the time of Zengi (d 539/1144), and this is undoubtedly true.[24] It is important, however,

Figure 3.9 *Armour for hand and arm, Firdawsi,* Shahnama *('Book of Kings'), leaves mounted in albums, c. 1370–80, Iran*

to look closely at the earliest response of the religious classes in Syria and Palestine to the incoming Crusader threat, since it would be wrong to assume that there were no stirrings of *jihad* feelings in the period between the fall of Jerusalem in 482/1099 and the Muslim reconquest of Edessa in 539/1144. Indeed, it is probably true to say that amongst the *religious* classes feelings against the Franks and the desire to promote *jihad* always ran high; the problem was to find a way of infusing Islamic fervour into the *military* leaders of the time. The political situation in Syria and Palestine in the early decades of the twelfth century was not conducive to Muslim solidarity and overall military unity. Instead, this was a period of decentralised power in which Turkish commanders and Frankish rulers alike sought to establish themselves in the urban centres. Periodically, they would come together across the religious divide when the territories of Syria and Palestine were threatened from outside. Religious ideology played no part in these ephemeral and pragmatic alliances to defend local territorial interests.

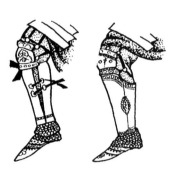

Figure 3.10 *Armour for leg and foot, Firdawsi,* Shahnama *('Book of Kings'), leaves mounted in albums, c. 1370–80, Iran*

At the time of the First Crusade the first focus for any call to *jihad* was the Sunni caliph in Baghdad; it was certainly he who was expected to be involved in a *jihad* and it was he who had the legitimate right to promote *jihad* against the Franks.[25] This is the clear implication of the various delegations that made their way to Baghdad in the wake of the First Crusade, as we have already noted in Chapter 1. Although the Seljuq sultans restricted the caliphs' movements, preferring them to be mere figureheads and not to meddle in the politics of the time, the Syrian religious leaders who went to Baghdad to summon support against the Franks seem to have believed that the caliphs were their principal recourse. Despite these expectations, there were no independent military undertakings sponsored by the caliphs, although the sources make it clear that some of the caliphs, such as al-Mustarshid and al-Rashid, did take the field with their own armies.[26]

So who else could promote *jihad* against the Franks? Certainly, in strict interpretation of Islamic law, the military barons who ruled Syria in the twelfth century were not bound to fight *jihad*. None of them were legitimate rulers. They had usurped power. Put simply, they could fight *jihad* but they did not have to do so.[27] The major emphasis of *jihad* seems to have been a personal undertaking and the personal reward which every Muslim would receive from God for his meritorious struggle.[28] Possibly when the sources mention terms such as *mutatawwi'a* ('volunteers'), they are referring to the kind of warriors who in previous eras frequented the *ribat*s on the frontiers of Islam and who waged *jihad* against the infidel at their own personal costs. Certainly the presence of such volunteers (*mujahidun*) is mentioned at the fall of Antioch in 491/1098 when they fought 'for divine reward and seeking martyrdom'.[29]

We have already seen that there were only a few isolated voices which spoke out in consternation at the loss of Jerusalem. Still fewer

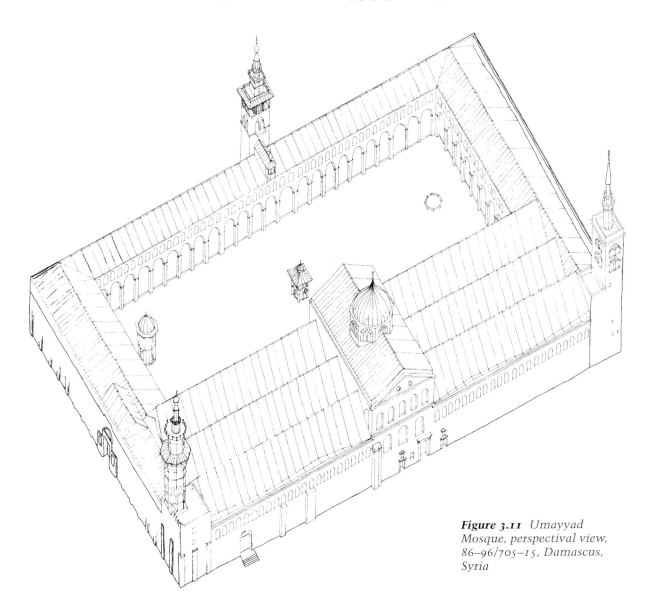

Figure 3.11 *Umayyad Mosque, perspectival view, 86–96/705–15, Damascus, Syria*

drew any moral lessons from this loss. The outstanding exception to this lethargy and lack of concern was the Syrian legist al-Sulami, who preached in the Umayyad mosque in Damascus in the early years after the fall of Jerusalem that Muslims should rally against their enemy, the Crusaders. Muslim defeat – argues al-Sulami – was God's punishment for the abandoning of their religious duties and, above all, for their neglect of *jihad*.

It is important to remember that al-Sulami's extant work is called the *Book of Holy War* (figure 3.12), and indeed the concept of *jihad*

سمع جميع هذا الأمر السيد الأجل الأوحد عبد الرحمن أحمد علي جامع الإسلام
أسد الدولة عبد الله وكان له الأمير الأجل السيد بأبي بكر عبد الله السيد عبد السلام
وسمع من أولاد الأمير محمد عباد والعلماء دعا لهم بدوام العز والطاعة وتمام
محمد عبد الغني القيم وكذا في الترين العليم الحلم السعيد القسم أحمد السيد بن أحمد العز
والله وسمع من وكذا كما في الترين الحلم السعيد القسم أحمد السيد بن أحمد العز

الجزء الثاني من كتاب الجهاد المشتمل
على الحث عليه والترغيب فيه وكشف عيبه وجوبه وما
يتعلق به من أسباره وإحكامه وعمّا وبعض
مما بقّا لفضائل الشام والثغور وغير ذلك من الكتاب
والأمور والتفسير والتعريف ذلك من غريب المعاني والألفاظ
ما يغمغم معه ونسأل الله فيه علينا طا من يوم جميع السلف تقبل الله
وجعله خالصًا لوجهه
وقف أبو يسر من محمد بن منصور الهلالي

سمع جميع هذا الأمر من الفظ السيد الأجل الأوحد السيد علي بن طاهر بن عز المسلم من أربعة نسخ
الشرفاء أبو محمد عبد الرحمن بن أحمد بن كتاب بن صائن بن الإسلام وحسان بن أحمد بن علي الدار وكان بن
الأشعث أحمد بن عبد الدائم الحسن المقدسي ويل الخلائع بهيأة بيها ومحمد بن عطاء بن سيد عثمان
وله عن إبراهيم بن أربع عاما والجهاد لهم وعمال أن عليهم بدوام مجدهم والدوام دار وسلم سلام عليهم

سمع جميع هذا الأمر من أوله إلى آخره الذهبي لمقصيه الشيخ الأجل الأمير العالم
على باطن وجهم الإسلام من عبد الملك بن إبراهيم الله رجاله من الظاهر
المنهاج والسيد المحبوب العالم بمن العدو وكاتبه وكاتب الأمير السلام
سلامته ويحيى كما في أواخر ربيع الأول بسنة وتسعة ذو العزة ذو العزيز مادة

lies at the heart of all that he says. He protests strongly that it is the Muslims' indifference to the Frankish presence and their neglect of the religious duty of *jihad* that have caused the Crusaders to triumph. According to al-Sulami, the neglect of *jihad* which he so deplores is not a phenomenon peculiar to his own time nor just to Syria. It has existed since the caliphs first began to neglect their religious duty to conduct at least one campaign a year into infidel territory. In his view this forms part of a wider religious and moral decline amongst Muslims, which, he argues, has resulted in the fragmentation of Islam and has encouraged the enemies of Islam to take the offensive and seize Muslim territories.

Al-Sulami's solution to this dire predicament lies first in moral rearmament to end this process of Muslim spiritual decline. The Crusader attacks are a punishment as well as a Divine warning to Muslims to return to the 'right path'. According to al-Sulami, conducting *jihad* against the infidel is a hollow sham if it is not preceded by the greater *jihad* (*al-jihad al-akbar*) over one's baser self and he stresses that the latter must be accomplished if the former is to be successful. And he calls on Muslim rulers to lead the way. Thus, personal spiritual struggle is an absolute requirement before conducting war against the Franks.[30]

Plate 3.8 *Great Mosque, minbar, detail, 548/1153, 'Amadiyya, Iraq*

Al-Sulami's words proclaimed in the mosque from the *minbar* (cf. plate 3.8) and preserved in his *Book of Holy War* do not seem to have had a widespread effect on his fellow Muslims at large, nor did they strike a chord with Muslim rulers and commanders at the time of maximum Crusader expansionism in the early twelfth century. The concept of *jihad* remained alive within the circles frequented by religious scholars, but it had yet to be harnessed to full-scale military activity under vigorous Muslim leadership: the alliance between the religious classes and the military had yet to be forged.

It may well be that al-Sulami's challenge did not go completely unheeded and that after him other preachers continued to shout vociferously from the pulpits. The sources are unhelpful on developments within the period 1100–1130, but even if there was a strong local reaction amongst some of the religious classes it was not backed up by the *political* or military will to act in concerted fashion on the part of the leaders of the time. Even if the circles of the religious scholars in the time of al-Sulami propagated the essential idea of *jihad* it does not mean necessarily that their words and writings were heeded by the military leaders of the period. Nor did rousing poems in the cause of *jihad* written after the shock of the First Crusade necessarily imply that those to whom they were addressed rose up and obeyed the eloquent calls made by the poets. For *jihad* propaganda to be a really effective weapon a tight and meaningful alliance was necessary between the religious classes and the army leaders. This did not prove viable until later in the twelfth century.

It is not appropriate to give the title *jihad* to the series of campaigns (as, for example, those of Mawdud of Mosul during the years 503–7/ 1110–13) launched from the Seljuq east under Turkish commanders into Syria in the first two decades of the twelfth century, nor were these pan-Islamic activities. They were ill-assorted, heterogeneous, ephemeral alliances of rival princelings and military barons – not true coalition forces – and as such destined, on the whole, to fail and disperse. Freeing Jerusalem had no significance to such rulers in this period.

The First Tentative Steps towards the Revival of *Jihad*

As already mentioned, Sivan believes that the turning point in Muslim attitudes came with the fall of Edessa in 539/1144. But the tide was probably beginning to turn in the preceding decades. Indeed, the process of the reawakening of *jihad* must have been slow and gradual and in some part at least it must have come as a direct response to Crusader fanaticism, witnessed first-hand.

There are isolated signs of this early Muslim reawakening and the battle of Balat might be seen as a tentative turning-point. An early model for the active participation of the religious classes in the fight against the Franks seems to have been the *qadi* Abu'l Fadl b. al-Khashshab of Aleppo. Not content to sit back in the mosque or *madrasa* and to preach and teach *jihad*, Ibn al-Khashshab was also closely involved in the running of affairs in Aleppo at a time when the city was extremely vulnerable to external attacks. Indeed, in the early twelfth century the Aleppan notables had sought military support from Baghdad against the Franks, before turning in desperation to the Turcoman ruler of Mardin, Il-Ghazi. In these negotiations Ibn al-Khashshab was prominent. According to the town chronicler of Aleppo, Ibn al-ʿAdim, Ibn al-Khashshab was responsible for the defence of the city and for taking care of its interests. In difficult and anarchical times it is noteworthy that prominent religious figures were ready to shoulder administrative duties and assume civic leadership.[31]

There is no evidence that al-Sulami had personally involved himself in actual fighting, although he was well known as a preacher. Ibn al-Khashshab (d. 528/1133–4), on the other hand, is known to have been present amongst the troops just before the battle of Balat in 513/1119, preaching to them. At this stage, however, his presence was obviously not welcome to everybody. As Ibn al-ʿAdim writes:

Figure 3.13 Mounted archer, silk and linen textile, second half of the eleventh century, Egypt

The qadi Abuʾl Fadl b. al-Khashshab came, spurring the people on to fight, riding on a mare and with a spear in his hand. One of the troops saw him and belittled him saying: ʾ[So] we have come from our lands only to follow this man in a turban!ʾ He [Ibn al-Khashshab] went up to the people and amongst the ranks preached them an eloquent sermon in which he awakened their resolutions and sharpened their resolves. He made the people weep and there was agony in their eyes.[32]

Thus we see a man of religion, clearly identifiable by his turban, standing out by his choice of riding-animal, and flourishing both a lance and the weapons of his rhetoric. He clearly swayed the emotions and won the day.

Just as on the Byzantine frontier Ibn Nubata had preached *jihad* in an earlier period, so too here we see an example, albeit an isolated one, of the potential of *jihad* as a stimulus before battle and of the emotional impact which the presence of the religious classes had in the midst of the soldiers themselves. The author of this account, Ibn al-ʿAdim, may well be viewing this battle through the eyes of thirteenth-century Syria, when people were long-used to *jihad* against the Franks, but he does not write in this way about any of the other military encounters between Muslims and Crusaders in the early twelfth century. We can reasonably believe, therefore, that this episode was rather unusual for its time. Ibn al-ʿAdim does not labour his point; but it is of course significant that this battle, the battle of the Field of Blood, was a major victory for the Muslims under the Artuqid military leader Il-Ghazi, a battle, moreover, in which a major Crusader leader, Roger of Antioch, was slain. Il-Ghazi emerges from the sources as an erratic, uncoordinated adventurer who was unable to follow up this victory because of his prolonged alcoholic celebration of it, which lasted a week. He was not a man with staying power or political vision. As a Turcoman nomad, his attitude to Islam was probably pragmatic too. Whilst he too may well have been swayed by the eloquence of Ibn al-Khashshab, he did not have the personality around which other Muslim military commanders could congregate under the banner of *jihad*. So his victory at Balat remained an isolated one. But Ibn al-Khashshab had shown the way.[33]

Another legal activist was the Hanbalite preacher 'Abd al-Wahhab al-Shirazi who was sent with a group of merchants to Baghdad to beg for help in 523/1129, after the Franks had appeared outside the very gate of Damascus. The delegation was on the point of breaking the *minbar* when the people in Baghdad promised to get in touch with the sultan about sending the Syrians help against the Franks.[34]

Il-Ghazi's nephew, Balak, is also worthy of mention in a *jihad* context. He became a much-feared opponent of the Crusaders, displaying tremendous vigour in a number of small-scale encounters against them. He was killed outside Manbij in 518/1124 and buried in a tomb at Aleppo. The inscription on his tomb is a key piece of evidence in any discussion of the evolution of the concept of *jihad* in Syria in the early Crusading period. It is worth setting the scene a little here. Within the period 482–541/1099–1146, right across the Muslim world from Spain to Central Asia, there are *no* surviving inscriptions which mention *jihad* except those in Syria. Even in Spain, the other theatre of war with the Crusaders, none have survived. This makes the few examples in Syria stand out all the more; indeed, it suggests that they may have had something to do with the proximity of the Crusaders and their invasion of the Muslim heartlands.[35]

In his funerary inscription Balak is called 'sword of those who fight the Holy War, leader of the armies of the Muslims, vanquisher of the infidels and the polytheists'.[36] We find here, then, a whole sequence of resonant titles reflecting a clear concern with *jihad* against the Crusaders, and Balak is extolled as a Muslim champion in the wars against the unbelievers. In addition he is also called 'martyr' (*shahid*). There are also two very telling Qur'anic quotations on Balak's tomb. The first is chapter 3, verse 169: 'Think not of those who are slain in the way of Allah as dead. Nay, they are living. With their Lord they have provision.' The second, chapter 9, verse 21, says: 'Their Lord giveth them good tidings of mercy from Him, and acceptance, and Gardens where enduring pleasure will be theirs.'

Both these Qur'anic verses show Balak clearly as a *jihad* warrior who has been martyred in the way of God and for whom Paradise is the reward.[37] Had he lived, Balak might have inspired a Muslim response to the Franks much earlier.

Zengi's victory at Edessa in 539/1144 singles him out as the first major player in the Muslim recovery against the Franks. However, he was a warrior with sprawling ambitions that straddled both the arena of Crusader activity in Syria and Palestine and also Seljuq power

Figure 3.14 *Horseman and foot soldier, stone tympanum, twelfth century, Daghestan, eastern Caucasus*

politics further east in Baghdad and Mosul. But clearly his capture of Edessa was a key turning-point for the Muslims; indeed, it prompted the Second Crusade. He too is described in contemporary inscriptions in terms of *jihad*, even before his victory at Edessa. For example, in an inscription at Aleppo dated Muharram 537/August 1142 he is called 'tamer of the infidels and the polytheists, leader of those who fight the Holy War, helper of the armies, protector of the territory of the Muslims'.[38]

Why the emphasis here on these Islamic monumental inscriptions? Their value lies in their very contemporaneity: they are dated to the period of early Crusader presence in the Near East and show that, unlike elsewhere in the Islamic world at this time, monuments in the area right next to the Franks were proclaiming the virtues of those who fought *jihad*. This is surely not a coincidence, but rather the beginning of a stirring of *jihad* spirit amongst at least some of the lacklustre and disunited Muslim leaders of Syria. The timing of the first appearance of *jihad* titles on public buildings coincides with the first modest military victories of the Muslims against the Crusaders. The evidence of these inscriptions shows that the Muslims were beginning at last to interpret these victories in the light of *jihad*. It was the Muslim jurists who preached and wrote about *jihad* and it was also they who probably composed the wording of inscriptions, who were the leaders of public opinion in the mosque and the market place and who provided the bridge between the common people and their military overlords. The modest beginning of an alliance between the Turkish commanders and princes and the religious classes can be seen in these monumental records of Muslim victories in the period before the fall of Edessa.

But the Muslim world still lacked a really charismatic leader who could unite the conflicting factions and realise the full potential of the weapon of *jihad* propaganda in the task of unifying the lands bordering the Franks.

Zengi and the Fall of Edessa

The fall of Edessa marked a significant turning-point in Muslim fortunes. Edessa was the first of the Crusader states to be regained for Islam, and although the Second Crusade was launched shortly after-wards as a direct consequence of Zengi's victory, this new initiative from Europe achieved little. Was 'Imad al-Din Zengi the long-needed Muslim leader, the *jihad* fighter who could unite the Islamic world and rid it of the Frankish presence? Certainly, Ibn al-Athir, the court chronicler of the Zengid dynasty in the thirteenth century, was in no doubt that the good fortune of the Muslim world in its struggle against the Franks began with the achievements of Zengi.[39] Deploring the great weakness of the Islamic lands and the vast extent of Frankish power before the coming of Zengi, Ibn al-Athir launches into a panegyrical passage about Zengi's achievements in revivifying Islam:

> When Almighty God saw the princes of the Islamic lands and the commanders of the Hanafite creed and how unable they were to support the [true] religion and their inability to defend those who believe in the One God and He saw their subjugation by their enemy and the severity of their despotism . . . He then wished to set over the Franks someone who could requite the evil of their deeds and to send to the devils of the crosses stones from Him to destroy and annihilate them [the crosses]. He looked at the roster of valiants among His helpers and of those possessed of judgement, support and sagacity amongst His friends and He did not see in it (the roster) anyone more capable of that command, more solid as regards inclination, stronger of purpose and more penetrating than the lord, the martyr (*al-shahid*) 'Imad al-Din.[40]

Such inflated claims in respect of Zengi by Ibn al-Athir are hard to reconcile with the detailed facts of his career as an opportunistic and ruthless military commander who ruled his territories with a rod of iron.

Zengi was in a different class from the Muslim military leaders of the early twelfth century – such as Il-Ghazi or Tughtegin – who had preceded him and had fought the Franks in rather desultory fashion. Zengi's death in 1146 – so soon after his famous conquest of Edessa two years earlier – prevents us from assessing whether he would have been presented in the Islamic sources as a true fighter of *jihad*. But brilliant leadership qualities he certainly did have. He is shown in the majority of the sources as a despot of chillingly ruthless personality who literally inspired terror in his army and subjects alike. His cruelty and iron grip on affairs were legendary.

'Imad al-Din al-Isfahani launches into a diatribe against Zengi of a ferocity usually kept for his descriptions of the Franks:

> Zengi was tyrannical and he would strike with indiscriminate recklessness. He was like a leopard in character, like a lion in fury, not renouncing any severity, not knowing any kindness . . . He was feared for his sudden attacking, shunned for his roughness, aggressive, insolent, death to enemies and citizens.[41]

Fear is the word most often associated with Zengi in the Islamic sources. Like Baybars after him, Zengi was a zealous upholder of public morals, especially those of his soldiers' wives.[42] In a manner reminiscent of the Mongol commanders, Zengi kept cast-iron discipline amongst his troops. The chronicler of Aleppo, Ibn al-'Adim, writes as follows: 'When Zengi was on horseback, the troops used to walk behind him as if they were between two threads, out of fear that they would trample on the crops . . . If anyone transgressed, he was crucified.'[43]

Side by side with these fear-inspiring qualities, Zengi possessed undoubted military and political skills. He came from a family long used to military service and to rulership and is praised in the sources for his excellent government. His career lies on the cusp of Muslim fortunes

Figure 3.15 Huntsman, inlaid brass basin known as the 'Baptistère de St Louis', c. 1300 or earlier, Syria

against the Franks. In the eyes of posterity Zengi was remembered principally for his taking of Edessa. Even those sources which dwell on his despotic qualities are prepared to forget them because of Edessa. All his misdeeds are pardoned by this one act. Towards the end of his life, Zengi is portrayed in the Muslim sources as a real hero of Islam. He is generally called *shahid* (martyr) in the sources, although he was killed in a drunken stupor in his tent by a slave.

Zengi did not patronise the religious classes as assiduously as his son Nur al-Din was to do. Two years before his death and after a long career of frenetic and wide-ranging military activity, the fall of Edessa was of course Zengi's passport to fame and Ibn al-Athir exploits this victory to the full: 'This was truly the victory of victories and the one of them most similar in truth to Badr: those who witnessed it were devoted to *jihad* with the firmest conviction.'

Thus Zengi's conquest of Edessa is likened to the Prophet Muhammad's famous victory at Badr. Ibn al-Athir then goes on to say that Zengi's conquests of other places in the area were achieved whilst he had his eye all the time on Edessa. The whole event of Edessa is described in a rosy religious aura, although Ibn al-Athir spends many pages cataloguing Zengi's other activities which have nothing to do with *jihad* against the Franks: 'Islam became like the full moon after it had been obscured [as at the end of the lunar month] and the suns of the faith became illuminated after their lights had been obliterated.'[44]

Ibn al-Athir's partiality towards Zengi and his dynastic successors has clouded his normally sound judgement here.

It is doubtful whether the foundations for a true Muslim recovery against the Franks were in place during Zengi's career. Indeed, it was only in the last few years of Zengi's lifetime that he came to be viewed in the sources as a *mujahid*. It is, of course, difficult to evaluate the actual military activities of Zengi against the panegyrics of those who wished to create him in the image of a champion of *jihad*. Two poets who had escaped the Frankish conquest of the Syrian coast, Ibn al-Qaysarani (from Caesarea) and Ibn Munir (from Tripoli), eventually joined Zengi's entourage. The bitter experience of being wrenched from their homes must have added an extra dimension to the calls for *jihad* in their poetry addressed to their patron Zengi.[45]

Whilst no doubt motivated by the desire for remuneration (the life of court poets was always precarious), Ibn al-Qaysarani and Ibn Munir, after the fall of Edessa, pointed out how the Counter-Crusade should proceed,[46] and they eloquently urged Zengi along that way. Ibn al-Qaysarani stressed the need for the Muslims to make the reconquest of the whole Syrian coastline (the *Sahil*) the principal aim of *jihad*: 'Tell the infidel rulers to surrender after it [Edessa] all their territories, for it is his [Zengi's] country.'[47]

As Sivan argues persuasively, the fall of Edessa allowed the Muslims to shift from a predominantly defensive stance to an offensive one. Apart from the views of al-Sulami and perhaps other

Figure 3.16 *Mounted hunter, inlaid brass basin known as the 'Baptistère de St Louis', c. 1300 or earlier, Syria*

members of the religio-legal elite in Syria, before the fall of Edessa *jihad* as a motivating factor had been erratic, piecemeal and rather unfocused. After the fall of Edessa, these two poets helped to crystallise *jihad* around the concept of the reconquest of Jerusalem. As Ibn Munir writes: 'He [Zengi] will turn tomorrow towards Jerusalem.'[48] Ibn al-Qaysarani joins him in this emphasis on Jerusalem: 'If the conquest of Edessa is the high sea, Jerusalem and the *Sahil* are its shore.'[49]

Whether or not Zengi himself accepted this mantle of true *mujahid*, it is important to stress that contemporary poets viewed him in this light; and it is surely plausible to argue that his victory at Edessa must have raised Muslim hopes concerning him and also shaped his own self-image *vis-à-vis* the Franks.

Certainly it is possible that Zengi would have gone on to take Damascus and unite Muslim Syria under his iron fist. An alliance with the religious classes could then have followed and he could have been presented as a true *jihad* leader of the Muslims in a propaganda campaign of mounting intensity focused on Jerusalem. The caliph of Baghdad had already paved the way by congratulating Zengi after his conquest of Edessa with a string of honorific titles stressing his Islamic credentials: according to Ibn Wasil, he was called *inter alia* 'The adornment of Islam, the king helped by God, the helper of the believers'.[50]

Instead, Zengi was murdered in Rabi' I 541/September 1146 and it was his son Nur al-Din who was to achieve the reputation in the Muslim sources of the real architect of the Muslim Counter-Crusade. But Zengi had paved the way, presenting a model of ruthless military government which his son was to emulate.

The Muslim response to the Franks, which involved skilful use of the weapons of *jihad* propaganda, may be seen as gradual and cumulative, each generation building on and developing the experiences of the previous one. Yet the fall of Edessa may be picked out as a decisive moment in propelling the movement of *jihad* forward. This was the easternmost Frankish possession, the only one across the Euphrates, and thus the one that most directly threatened the seat of Zengid power, Mosul. Henceforth the Franks were confined to the Levant proper. It would be left to Zengi's son, Nur al-Din, to take over the struggle against the Franks and to move inexorably towards their encirclement and the acquisition of the city of Jerusalem.

So much, then, for the development of the idea of *jihad* in religious, political, military and ideological terms up to the fall of Edessa in 1144 and the advent of the Second Crusade. The rest of this chapter will seek to illuminate the further development of *jihad* through the study of its role in the career of one of the key personalities of the Near East in the second half of the twelfth century, namely Nur al-Din.

The Coming of the Second Crusade in 543/1148 – a Turning-Point in the *Jihad*

We have seen in Chapter 2 that the Muslim rulers of Syria in the early decades of the twelfth century pursued a policy of collaboration with the Franks when their territories were threatened from outside by armies sponsored by the Seljuq sultans or the governors of Mosul. Such military help ostensibly against the Franks was viewed as interference by princes 'of the east' and met with opposition in the form of city gates being closed in the faces of the incoming Muslim army, as with Aleppo under Ridwan in 505/1111–12, or a Frankish–local Muslim coalition army. This hostility to the Muslim east was an important factor in Zengi's failure to capture Damascus on several occasions in the 1130s.

As is well known, the Second Crusade proved to be a fiasco, as the Franks decided to mount a massive attack on Damascus, rather than recapturing Edessa or taking Aleppo. Despite the size of the Frankish army sent to Damascus, it was repelled and the enterprise fizzled out thereafter. As a result of the Frankish siege of Damascus in 543/1148 the mood within Damascus and thereafter elsewhere in Syria seems to have changed. Not since the humiliating experiences of the First Crusade and, above all, the Frankish conquest of Jerusalem had the inhabitants of a major Muslim city seen and felt *first-hand* the presence of the Franks within their walls, pillaging and killing. It is made

(Creswell Photographic Archive, Ashmolean Museum, Oxford, neg. C. 5673)

Plate 3.11 Funerary madrasa of Nur al-Din, 567/1172, door, Damascus, Syria

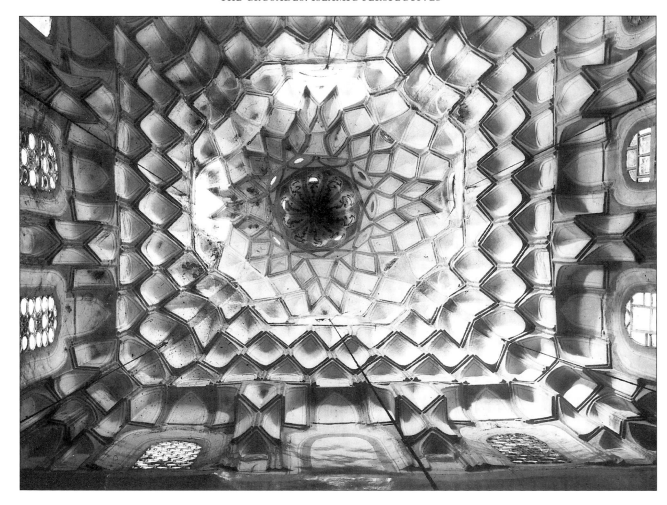

Plate 3.12 *Funerary* madrasa *of Nur al-Din,* 567/1172, *interior of* muqarnas *dome, Damascus, Syria*

(Creswell Photographic Archive, Ashmolean Museum, Oxford, neg. C. 5502)

to fight in the ranks.[54] Also in the ranks were other figures – prayer leaders, Qur'an readers, preachers, judges – who enhanced the religious dimension of the military conflict.

In his turn Nur al-Din gave generous sponsorship to the religious classes with his patronage of religious monuments as part of his aim to revitalise Sunni Islam in his territories and to stimulate popular piety and *jihad*. Such monuments, because they are often dated precisely by their inscriptions, provide invaluable first-hand historical evidence. Some texts were colossal in size: the inscription in the name of Nur al-Din on the Jami' al-Nuri in Hama, for example, is more than seven metres long (plates 3.13, 3.14, 3.15 and figure 3.21). It should be emphasised that these inscriptions, with their grandiose titulature in the name of Nur al-Din, were all in public buildings, so that his claims to be a *mujahid* (a fighter for *jihad*) had a proclamatory quality, a marked public dimension which could be seen by all.

The monuments of Nur al-Din have been studied very closely in recent years by Tabbaa who is in no doubt of their propagandistic significance in the *jihad* campaign against the Crusaders. He is at pains to link monuments and inscriptions in this context. Beginning with the second inscription in the name of Nur al-Din, on the Madrasa al-Halawiyya, dated Shawwal 544/February–March 1149, the titles given to him, in sharp contrast to the Persian and Turkish ones recorded for his father Zengi, emphasise his dedication to *jihad* and the upholding of Sunni Islam.[55] Indeed, nearly half of the thirty-eight preserved inscriptions of Nur al-Din call him the fighter of *jihad* (*al-mujahid*). This noteworthy shift in the kind of titles used to describe Nur al-Din reflects his successes against the Franks in the preceding years, the first four of his rule (1146–50).[56] The titles accorded to him reflect a close and harmonious relationship with the Sunni caliph at

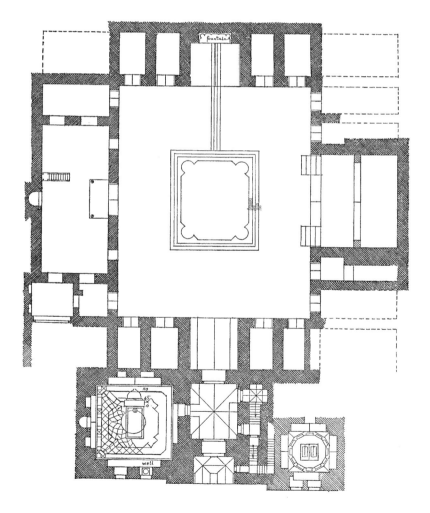

Figure 3.18 *Funerary* madrasa *of Nur al-Din, plan, 567/1172, Damascus, Syria*

Figure 3.19 *Funerary* madrasa *of Nur al-Din,* muqarnas *dome, 567/1172, Damascus, Syria*

Figure 3.20 *Jami' al-Nuri,* alabaster *mihrab* in courtyard, *early thirteenth century, Mosul, Iraq*

124

Plate 3.13 *Jami' al-Nuri,
inscription on outer north wall,
after 552/1157, probably
558/1162–3 and later, Hama, Syria*

Plate 3.14
*Jami' al-Nuri,
inscription on
outer north
wall, detail
with the name
of Nur al-Din,
after 552/1157,
probably
558/1162–3
and later,
Hama, Syria*

Plate 3.15 *Jami' al-Nuri, inscription on outer north wall, detail with the date, after 552/1157, probably 558/1162–3 and later, Hama, Syria*

لمولانا الملك العادل العالم العا
لكفة والمشركنز مصفر لها

Figure 3.21 *Jami' al-Nuri, exterior, inscription on north wall, detail, probably 558/1162–3 and later, Hama, Syria*

Baghdad. They also reveal his desire to be a good Muslim ruler and to be viewed as such – by his dispensing of Islamic justice, by his personal piety and by his prosecution of *jihad* against the enemies of Islam.

One facet of the ideological revival in the time of Nur al-Din was his establishment of a 'House of Justice' (*Dar al-'adl*) in Damascus around the year 1163. Others like it were constructed later, for example in Aleppo by one of Saladin's sons and in Cairo by Saladin's brother, al-Kamil; but the timing of this particular building was not a coincidence. Indeed, this monument was part of the prevailing atmosphere of the Counter-Crusade in which the ruler used a range of propaganda tools to gain popular support and approbation. As Rabbat argues, the struggle between Muslims and Crusaders generated 'a combative reaction among the religious intelligentsia in the Islamic Orient' and it made rulers aware of their religious obligations. Thus, in the House of Justice, Nur al-Din, or one of his appointed deputies, would preside over sessions in which his subjects could bring their grievances to be redressed.[57] According to Ibn al-Athir: 'He [Nur al-Din] used to sit [in the House of Justice] two days a week, with the judge and legists.'[58]

Indeed, a veritable spate of religious monuments was erected in the middle of the twelfth century in Syria – the Jami' al-Nuri in Hama, dated 558/1162–3, teaching colleges such as the Madrasa al-Shu'aybiyya created in 545/1159 in Aleppo (forty-two were built in the time of Nur al-Din, half of them sponsored by him personally), Sufi cloisters, a hospital (the famous Bimaristan Nur al-Din dated 549/1154–5) (plates 3.16, 3.17, 3.18, 3.19, 3.20 and colour plate 14) the *Dar al-hadith* (the House of Hadith Scholarship) (figure 3.29) – and together they testify to a profound Sunni revival during the rule of Nur al-Din. It was typical that Nur al-Din took the trouble to attend sessions in the *Dar al-hadith* in person. This building was created in 566/1170 to enhance his own credentials as a pious Sunni ruler.[59]

Figure 3.22 Jami' al-Nuri, mihrab *with frieze depicting real and fabulous creatures, early thirteenth century, Hama, Syria*

Figure 3.23 *Funerary* madrasa
of Nur al-Din, section of the
muqarnas *dome, 567/1172,*
Damascus, Syria

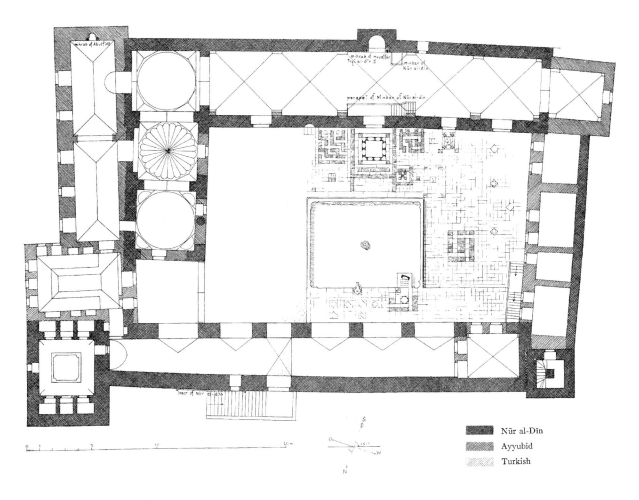

Figure 3.24 Jami' al-Nuri, plan, from 558/1162–3, Hama, Syria

Nūr al-Dīn

Ayyubid

Turkish

Between 560/1165 and 566/1170 Nur al-Din sponsored the building of a number of minarets in Syria – in Damascus and al-Raqqa amongst other places (cf. plate 3.21) – and in Iraq (cf. plate 5.1). These monuments, towering over the cities and fortresses, had a strong propaganda message testifying to the triumph of Islam. Several serious earthquakes in Syria had damaged or destroyed its buildings. Nur al-Din saw it as his duty to rebuild them, taking seriously the public duty of the ruler to build in the name of Islam, despite the great costs that such a building programme must have incurred.

Thus we see from the sheer number of religious monuments built under the patronage of Nur al-Din, and by the nature of the monumental inscriptions carved in his name by the local craftsmen under the guidance of the '*ulama*', that already in his own lifetime Nur al-Din was perceived (or was keen to be perceived) as a warrior for *jihad* and a model Sunni Muslim ruler. Ibn al-Athir sums up the building activities of Nur al-Din, mentioning that he built the walls 'of all

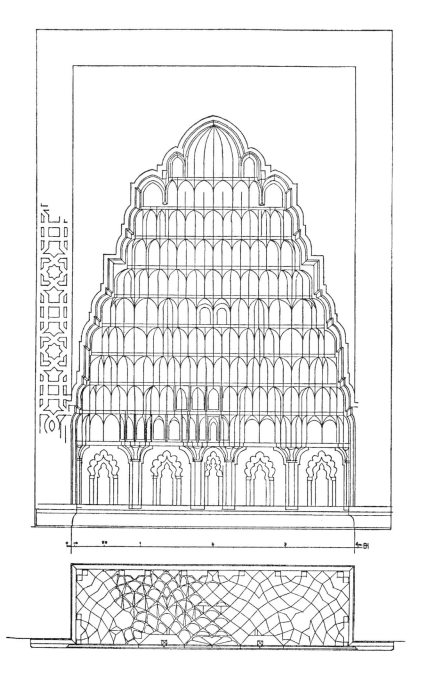

Figure 3.25 Maristan
(hospital) of Nur al-Din,
section of portal dome,
549/1154, Damascus, Syria

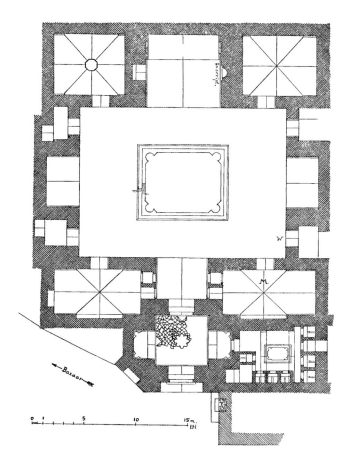

Figure 3.26 Maristan (hospital) of Nur al-Din, plan, 549/1154, Damascus, Syria

the cities and citadels of Syria', mosques, hospitals, caravanserais, towers, Sufi cloisters and orphanages.[60] Nur al-Din visited Medina in 556/1161 on the pilgrimage and on that occasion he rebuilt its walls.[61]

Unlike monumental epigraphy, the titles which appear in coinage must perforce be brief since the space available is very small. It is all the more noteworthy therefore that many of the extant coins which bear the name of Nur al-Din give him the title 'the just prince' (*al-malik al-ʿadil*) (figure 3.27).[62] Unlike monumental inscriptions which are *in situ*, those coins often travelled far and wide, carrying with them the reputation of Nur al-Din as a ruler who above all else dispensed Islamic justice.

It was during the career of Nur al-Din, then, the first major Muslim leader against the Franks, that the concept of *jihad* as a rallying-cry for the Muslims gathered real momentum and that the alliance between the religious classes and the military leadership became meaningful. It is during his rule that the key elements in Muslim *jihad* propaganda can be clearly identified. Ideally, spiritual and

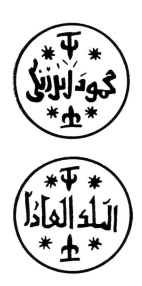

Figure 3.27 Coin of Nur al-Din, twelfth century, Syria

131

Plate 3.16 Maristan *of Nur al-Din, exterior of* muqarnas *dome, 549/1154, Damascus, Syria*

public *jihad* combine in the person of the ruler, and this is certainly the way in which Nur al-Din is presented in the Islamic sources. But the problem of the historical veracity of this image cannot really be resolved satisfactorily.

The Image of Nur al-Din in the Written Sources

According to Elisseeff, whose three-volume work on Nur al-Din is widely regarded as a major scholarly contribution, the first years of the career of Nur al-Din were devoted to the unification of Syria and only when he had achieved this did he turn his attention to the Franks.[63] This gives a favourable interpretation of the military activities of Nur al-Din and suggests that from the outset he had an overall strategy in mind, consisting of Muslim unification followed by *jihad* against the Franks.

Such an interpretation is, however, too pat. It is far more likely that Nur al-Din began his career (and maybe even continued it) by playing the same game of power politics in the Near East as his ruthless father, Zengi, had done. Yet the Islamic sources give the activities of Nur al-Din far more of an Islamic coating than those of his father and it is naturally difficult to determine how valid this interpretation is. Are the Islamic historians, who of course write with hindsight, being swayed in the very presentation of events by their knowledge of what was to come?

Various landmarks in the career of Nur al-Din are invested with didactic significance in the Muslim sources as he is shown as changing from a military warlord to a pious Sunni Muslim ruler. The same image is given of Saladin, as we shall see, and so this process may well be stereotypical and a stock theme of Muslim historiography.

How, then, do the sources handle this issue? According to them, signs of God's favour could be discerned in the early stages of the career of Nur al-Din and the contemporary Damascene chronicler Ibn al-Qalanisi attributes to Nur al-Din lofty religious motives for his actions:

> I seek nothing but the good of the Muslims and to make war against the Franks . . . If . . . we aid one another in waging the Holy War, and matters are arranged harmoniously and with a single eye to the good, my desire and purpose will be fully achieved.[64]

Of course, Ibn al-Qalanisi may well be guilty of partiality, but he writes here with an ardour notably absent from his descriptions of the activities of Zengi. A key moment may well have been the

Plate 3.17 Maristan *of Nur al-Din, interior, painted inscription, 549/1154, Damascus, Syria*

Plate 3.18 Maristan *of Nur al-Din, interior, detail of* muqarnas *vaulting in arch, 549/1154, Damascus, Syria*

victory of Nur al-Din against Raymond of Antioch at the battle of Inab in Safar 544/June 1149. According to Elisseeff, after his capture of Damascus in 549/1154, Nur al-Din took each step 'in the name of *jihad* against the Crusaders and to help the revitalisation of Sunni Islam'.[65] This reverential tone is taken directly from the chroniclers themselves. Ibn al-'Adim remarks, probably more out of piety than conviction, that 'from this point on Nur al-Din dedicated himself to *jihad*'.[66]

But adversity, not success, was to prove a far more skilful instructor for Nur al-Din on his path to personal religious piety and to acceptance by the religious classes as a good Sunni ruler. Two bouts of serious illness, in Ramadan 552/October 1157 and Dhu'l-hijja 553/January 1159, may well have caused Nur al-Din to think about the religious dimension of his political activities as well as the salvation of his own soul. Significantly, he took time off in 556/1161 to perform the Pilgrimage to Mecca. But the most important turning-point in the religious development of Nur al-Din seems to have been the humiliating defeat he suffered at the hands of the Franks in 558/1163

134

on the plain of al-Buqay'a. This defeat had a profound effect, according to the sources, on the personal life and policies of Nur al-Din. Henceforth, he adopted a life of piety and asceticism, a stance which was to gain him the staunch respect of the religious classes in Syria and the loyalty of the population. Ibn al-'Adim mentions an episode which seems to have sharpened his religious resolve still further.[67] A man called Burhan al-Din al-Balkhi said to Nur al-Din: 'Do you want to celebrate victory whilst in your camp there are intoxicating drinks and drums and wind-instruments? No, by God!' (cf. figure 3.28)

According to the story, Nur al-Din was deeply affected by these reproaches and he vowed repentance. He changed his grand clothing for the rough garments of the Sufi, he let it be known that he would henceforth combine a desire to undertake personal spiritual *jihad* with prosecuting public *jihad* against the Franks and he summoned other Muslim princes to rally to him in support of *jihad*. Such didactic stories are common in medieval Islamic historical writings: intoxicating drinks and musical instruments denote laxity in religious observances (figures 6.31, 6.69). But the timing of this anecdote in Ibn al-'Adim's account may be significant.

Saladin's future adviser and friend, 'Imad al-Din al-Isfahani arrived

Figure 3.28 Man holding a wind instrument, ink drawing on paper, twelfth century, Egypt

Plate 3.19 Maristan *of Nur al-Din, detail of portal, 549/1154, Damascus, Syria*

Plate 3.20 Maristan *of*
Nur al-Din, portal, 549/1154,
Damascus, Syria

(Creswell Photographic Archive, Ashmolean Museum, Oxford, neg. C. 5497)

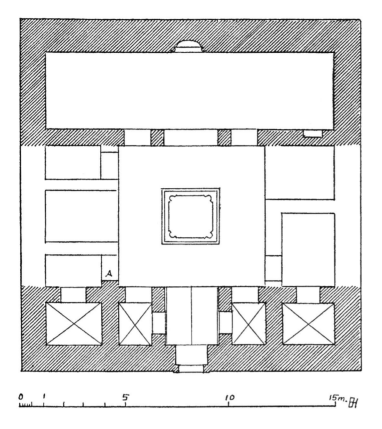

Figure 3.29 *Dar al-Hadith al-Nuriyya, plan, before 569/1174, Damascus, Syria*

in Damascus and joined the service of Nur al-Din in 562/1166–7. He describes his new master as 'the most chaste, pious, sagacious, pure and virtuous of kings' and he praises him for restoring 'the splendour of Islam to the land of Syria'.[68] Ibn al-Athir writes a very lengthy obituary of Nur al-Din in his history of the Zengid dynasty, entitled the *History of the Atabegs of Mosul*.[69] It is unashamedly panegyrical in tone:

> I have read the histories of early kings before Islam, and in Islam until these time of ours, and I have not seen after the Rightly Guided caliphs and 'Umar b. 'Abd al-'Aziz a king of better conduct than the just king Nur al-Din.[70]

Such high praise, likening Nur al-Din to those held in Islam to have been the most pious and just caliphs, is followed up in the obituary by an enumeration of the virtues of Nur al-Din. It is noteworthy, too, that in conformity with the practice of contemporary public inscriptions, he chooses, from all possible adjectives, the epithet 'just' (*'adil*) to sum up Nur al-Din.

The same laudatory stance towards Nur al-Din is shown by the

137

Figure 3.30 *Fatimid textile with addorsed lions, eleventh century, Egypt*

later writer Abu Shama (d. 665/1258). He describes Nur al-Din as the most zealous in raiding against the Franks,[71] and he stresses his orthodoxy, his justice, his devotion to *jihad* and his personal piety:

> He displayed religious orthodoxy (*sunna*) in Aleppo and changed the innovation (*bid'a*) which they had in the call to prayer and he tamed the heretics there and built there religious colleges, established endowments and dispensed justice . . . In war he was steadfast in going forward, good at shooting, hard in striking . . . he would run the risk of martyrdom . . . he had a good handwriting [and] he often studied religious books.[72]

It is certainly possible to 'demythologise' this picture of Nur al-Din and this was done recently by the German scholar Köhler. He argues that the efforts made by Nur al-Din in the service of *jihad* in the first half of his career were not impressive, and he cites the evidence of the Fatimid vizier Tala'i' b. Ruzzik, who reproaches Nur al-Din very sharply some time after 549/1154 for not fighting against the Franks

138

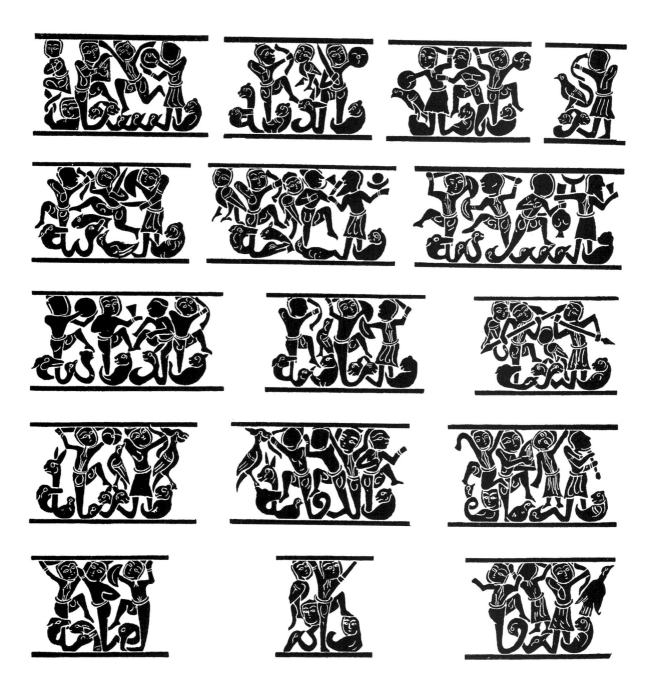

Figure 3.31 *Individual words of the animated inscription on the Wade Cup, inlaid brass, c. 1230, north-west Iran*

Plate 3.21 *Jami' al-Nuri,*
minaret, probably after
552/1157, Hama, Syria

(Creswell Photographic Archive,
Ashmolean Museum, Oxford,
neg. C. 1516)

and for tolerating their continuing rule in Palestine: 'Tell him: how
long will you delay [the wiping out of the blame] with regard to
the unbelievers? . . . Go to Jerusalem! . . . Leave your penchant for the
Franks!'[73]

This clearly indicates that, according at least to Abu Shama, who
was himself not an Isma'ili and therefore not predisposed to favour
the Fatimids, it was not Nur al-Din but the 'hated' Fatimids who

were pressing for *jihad* against the Franks. Contrary to the expressed desire of his poets, Köhler argues, Nur al-Din did not embark on *jihad* against the Franks after he had taken Damascus. He preferred instead to consolidate his power in Syria. Köhler puts the turning-point for Nur al-Din and the use of *jihad* propaganda at 553/1157.

But even in the struggle between Nur al-Din and the Franks for supremacy in Egypt (553–569/1157–1174), Köhler argues,[74] Nur al-Din used *jihad* propaganda simply as an instrument of his power politics. Indeed, despite the numerous *jihad* inscriptions which bear his name from 553/1157, he was doing nothing – so Köhler argues – to merit such grandiose titles. In fact, he was only behaving as his father Zengi had done. *Jihad* propaganda, for him, was only a means of acquiring caliphal legitimacy and recognition of his suzerainty over neighbouring Islamic states.[75]

The exact balance of motives which propelled Nur al-Din at different stages in his career must remain a matter of speculation. What can be known and assessed is what he achieved, the religious atmosphere in Syria within which he operated and the religious buildings and inscriptions which were erected in his name (e.g. plates 3.22, 3.23–3.24; cf. plate 3.25). These all point forcefully to the view that in the eyes of his contemporaries he was perceived to be a fighter of *jihad* in a propaganda movement of mounting conviction and success.

It is now time to turn to Jerusalem which seems to have played a key role in this propaganda movement.

The General Status of Jerusalem in the Medieval Islamic World

It has to be admitted that the status of Jerusalem fluctuated in the medieval Islamic world. Its religious importance as a centre for the other two great monotheistic faiths, Judaism and Christianity, made it vulnerable in the view of some Muslim thinkers, notably Ibn Taymiyya and other Hanbalite legists, to the criticism that the Islamic sanctity of Jerusalem was tainted by the influence of Judaeo-Christian traditions and 'innovations'. Mecca and Medina, on the other hand, were the true foci of Islamic sanctity (figures 3.32, 3.33).

Here is not the place to discuss the ambivalent reputation of Jerusalem from the very beginning of Islam. What *is* important in the context of the Crusades (and of course, at the end of the 1990s, when the city is under Israeli rule) is to stress that Jerusalem *can become* the focus of intense religious yearning on the part of Muslims, and that there is more than sufficient basis on which to argue that Islam can take a share in the city's sanctity. The Muslims of the twelfth century longed with increasing intensity to repossess Jerusalem, and the city came to be the focal point for a highly successful campaign of *jihad* propaganda, culminating in its reconquest by Saladin in 583/1187.

The Fatimids had paved the way for Jerusalem's seminal importance

Plate 3.22 *Great Mosque,*
central aisle from the west,
rebuilt by Nur al-Din after
565/1169–70, Aleppo, Syria

(Creswell Photographic Archive, Ashmolean Museum, Oxford, neg. C. 5648)

(Creswell Photographic Archive, Ashmolean Museum, Oxford, neg. C. 5646)

Plate 3.23 *Great Mosque,*
aerial view of marble
patterning in courtyard, after
565/1169–70, Aleppo, Syria

Plate 3.24 *Great Mosque,* *minaret, 483–7/1090–5,* *Aleppo, Syria*

(Creswell Photographic Archive, Ashmolean Museum, Oxford, neg. C. 5653)

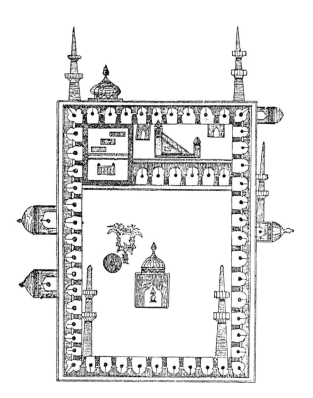

Figure 3.32 *The Mosque of the Prophet, Madina, painting on paper, fifteenth century, Egypt*

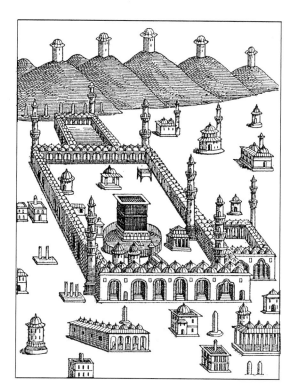

Figure 3.33 *The Ka'ba, painting on paper, fifteenth century, Egypt*

Plate 3.25 *Great Mosque,* mihrab *and* minbar, *after 565/1169–70, Aleppo, Syria*

(Creswell Photographic Archive, Ashmolean Museum, Oxford, neg. C. 5651)

in the twelfth century; indeed, it is clear that for their own political and religious motives they had aimed at enhancing the city's sanctity in the eleventh century. Perhaps al-Hakim's destruction of the Holy Sepulchre in 1009 should be placed in this context, though whether this action was so intended at the time or helped to trigger renewed awareness of the specifically Muslim sanctity of Jerusalem is a matter for debate. But within a very short time of al-Hakim's act, the policy of the Fatimids towards Jerusalem had crystallised. They rebuilt the Aqsa mosque in the reign of al-Zahir (d. 427/1036) (plate 3.26); its imperial mosaic inscription is the first one in Jerusalem to begin with the Qur'anic verse which Muslims believe refers to Muhammad's ascent into the Heavens (17:1). Al-Zahir also restored the Dome of the Rock in 413/1022–3 and its mosaics in 418/1027–8.[76] The Persian scholar and traveller Nasir-i Khusraw visited Jerusalem in 439/1047

Plate 3.26 *Aqsa Mosque, interior,* qibla *arch with Fatimid mosaics dated 426/1035, Jerusalem*

(Creswell Photographic Archive, Ashmolean Museum, Oxford, neg. C. 524)

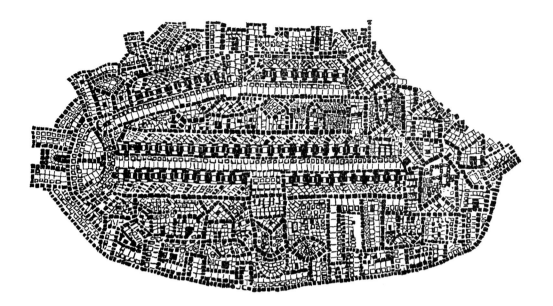

Figure 3.34 Floor mosaic with map of Jerusalem, sixth century, Madaba, Jordan

and notes that those in Palestine who could not perform the *hajj* assembled in Jerusalem and carried out certain of the ceremonies there:

> The people of these provinces, if they are unable to make the pilgrimage, will go up at the appointed season to Jerusalem and there perform their rites and upon the feast day slay the sacrifice as is customary to do (at Mecca). There are years when as many as 20,000 people will be present at Jerusalem during the first days of the month of Dhu'l-hijja.[77]

The mystics (Sufis) of Islam such as Sufyan al-Thawri and Ibrahim b. Adham had also venerated Jerusalem greatly and groups of them came there in increasing numbers in the eleventh century; the great scholar al-Ghazali meditated there in the late 1090s after his spiritual crisis had compelled him to leave Baghdad.

Thus it would appear that by the end of the eleventh century, that is on the eve of the Crusades, the key elements in the sanctity of Jerusalem were in place. They could therefore be exploited to the full in the forthcoming struggle with the Franks and utilised very effectively in *jihad* propaganda. The modern Arab historian Duri is in no doubt on this point:

> The Crusades probably added a new dimension to the significance of the *Bayt al-muqaddas* [Jerusalem]. But it was the great sanctity the city attained by the eleventh century that made it the symbol of the Jihad against the invaders.[78]

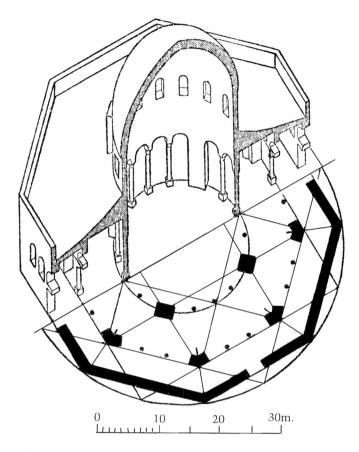

0   10   20   30m.

Figure 3.35 Dome of the Rock,
cut-away perspectival view,
72/691–2, Jerusalem

As well as the actual physical presence of the Dome of the Rock and the Aqsa mosque within Jerusalem, and the meritorious qualities attributed to prayer and pilgrimage there, Muslims believed that the Prophet Muhammad had made his Night Journey into the Heavens from Jerusalem, and that Jerusalem would be the site on which the Resurrection would take place on the Last Day.

As already mentioned, there have been conflicting views amongst Muslim scholars over the centuries on the relative merits of the Holy Cities of Mecca and Medina as opposed to Jerusalem, but the Palestinian writer al-Muqaddasi (d. 387/997), speaking with pride of his native city, sums up the pro-Jerusalem viewpoint: 'The province of Syria is in the first rank, the Land of the Prophets, the dwelling-place of the saints, the first *qibla*; the site of the Night Journey and the Gathering.'[79] Then he turns to Jerusalem itself: 'Mecca and Medina derive their high position from the Ka'ba and the Prophet, but on the Day of Judgement they will both be brought to Jerusalem.'[80]

The connection of Jerusalem with the Prophet's Night Journey is found in the work of the early eleventh-century preacher al-Wasiti,

149

who writes, in a passage redolent with Qur'anic echoes: 'Glorified be He who carried His servant by night from the Invincible Place of Worship to the Far Distant Place of Worship (al-masjid al-aqsa), the neighbourhood whereof We have blessed.'[81]

There is then sufficient basis here on which the religious scholars in the twelfth century could build a propaganda campaign extolling the virtues of *jihad* and focused on Jerusalem.

The Role of Jerusalem in the Propaganda of the Counter-Crusade

It is difficult to pinpoint precisely when Muslim military leaders began to focus on the reconquest of Jerusalem as an integral or even central part of their ambitions. As we have already mentioned, apart from the Fatimid initiative immediately after the Frankish conquest of Jerusalem in 492/1099, the loss of the city did not prompt any further attempts on the part of the Muslims to recapture it. On the contrary, there seems to have been little reaction until the fall of Edessa in 539/1144. This victory by Zengi seems to mark a turning-point, a moment when Muslim morale began to rise. Certainly, as we have seen, there are hints to this effect in the panegyric poetry commemorating Zengi's conquest of Edessa.

Sivan argues that Jerusalem began to loom in the Muslim consciousness as a focus for *jihad* against the Franks in the last years of Zengi's life. However, the momentum for the recapture of the city was considerably intensified during the career of his son, Nur al-Din, as Jerusalem became a major theme of the programme of *jihad* propaganda emanating from the cities of Syria and above all Damascus.

Indeed, Jerusalem became the focus of a cleverly orchestrated ideological campaign which played on its loss to the Crusaders. The yearning for Jerusalem could be exploited to the full by Muslim propagandists, who dwelt on the pain and humiliation of seeing Jerusalem become a Christian city, with mosques and Muslim shrines being turned into churches or secular buildings.

It appears likely that at some point in his career Nur al-Din's ambitions became focused on Jerusalem, although it is not clear exactly when this happened. Successive military victories, personal piety and his increasingly close relationship with the religious classes in Syria (his power base) – cf. plate 3.27 and colour plate 16 – enabled Nur al-Din to develop a most effective religious propaganda programme. It emphasised Muslim unification and a call to *jihad*, and was focused on the sanctity of Palestine and more especially of Jerusalem. This process can be traced in the Arabic chronicles and it is alluded to in the religious poetry of the period itself. The poet Ibn Munir urges Nur al-Din to fight against the Crusaders, 'until you see Jesus fleeing from Jerusalem'.[82]

Ibn al-Qaysarani reiterates the centrality of Jerusalem and in particular the Aqsa mosque in the ambitions of Nur al-Din:

May it, the city of Jerusalem, be purified by the shedding of
    blood
The decision of Nur al-Din is as strong as ever and the iron of
    his lance is directed at the Aqsa.[83]

Plate 3.27 *Jami' al-Nuri,
riparian facade, after 552/1157,
probably 558/1162–3 and later,
Hama, Syria*

Jerusalem may well have been in the minds of the poets before it had
become implanted in the heart of Nur al-Din.[84]

The Arab historian Abu Shama quotes the text of a letter from
Nur al-Din to the caliph in which Nur al-Din stresses the urgent
need to recapture Jerusalem, stating that his main aim is 'to banish the
worshippers of the Cross from the Aqsa mosque'.[85]

All this might smack of pious attempts by Muslim chroniclers
to remake Nur al-Din *after* the event into a perfect *jihad* fighter and
Sunni leader, instead of one who fought and won the game of Muslim
power politics in Syria in his own time. Yet their image of Nur al-Din
is reinforced, as we have seen, by the contemporary testimony of
the inscriptions on the monuments he founded and above all by the
evidence of an elaborate pulpit (*minbar*) which was ordered by Nur
al-Din and intended by him to be placed in the Aqsa mosque when
he had conquered Jerusalem. Much scholarly work has been done on
this topic; basic research carried out by Max van Berchem has been
supplemented by recent studies by Yasser Tabbaa and Sylvia Auld.

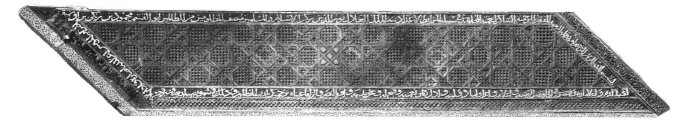

Plate 3.28 *Aqsa Mosque,* minbar *of Nur al-Din, detail of main inscription, 564/1168, Jerusalem*

(Creswell Photographic Archive, Ashmolean Museum, Oxford, neg. C. 5006)

It is worth examining in some detail (plates 3.28–3.29, 3.30; cf. plate 3.31 and colour plate 10).

One of the inscriptions on the *minbar* stated that it had been commissioned by Nur al-Din in 564/1168–9. It was first used in the Great Mosque of Aleppo and was eventually brought to Jerusalem – after Nur al-Din's death – at Saladin's request. The *minbar* remained in the Aqsa mosque until it was destroyed by an Australian fanatic in 1969. In the context of the importance in the Counter-Crusade of the role of Jerusalem, the *minbar* plays a key role.

Nur al-Din's *minbar* is an eloquent statement of *jihad*, as the main inscription once testified. It is, according to Tabbaa, 'the richest of all Nur al-Din's inscriptions in proclamations of the victory of Islam and defeat of the infidels'.[86] The beginning of the inscription, which is dated 564 (equivalent to 1168–9) reads as follows:

> Its construction has been ordered by the slave,[87] the one needful of His mercy, the one thankful for His grace, the fighter of *jihad* in His path, the one who defends [the frontiers] against the enemies of His religion, the just king, Nur al-Din, the pillar of Islam and the Muslims, the dispenser of justice to those who are oppressed in the face of the oppressors, Abu'l-Qasim Mahmud b. Zengi b. Aqsunqur, the helper of the Commander of the Faithful.[88]

Later on, the text of the inscription seems even to be requesting God to grant him the personal favour of conquering Jerusalem himself: 'May He grant conquest to him [Nur al-Din] and at his own hands.'[89] Tabbaa finds, quite rightly, that the *minbar* inscription is very unusual, both in length and in its emotional invocations to God.[90]

Supporting evidence for the commissioning of this *minbar* by Nur al-Din for Jerusalem, even though the city was still in Frankish hands, is provided in the writings of the Muslim chroniclers. 'Imad al-Din al-Isfahani records that after the conquest of Jerusalem, when Saladin wanted a more splendid *minbar* for the Aqsa mosque, he recalled that Nur al-Din had commissioned one for Jerusalem more than twenty years before the conquest of the city. Saladin therefore wrote to Aleppo to have the *minbar* brought and installed in Jerusalem. 'Imad al-Din, perhaps twisting the story to please his master Saladin, then claims retrospectively that Nur al-Din knew

152

(Creswell Photographic Archive, Ashmolean Museum, Oxford, neg. C. 5011)

Plate 3.29 *Aqsa Mosque,* minbar *of Nur al-Din, detail showing craftsman's signature, 564/1168, Jerusalem*

Plate 3.30 *Aqsa Mosque,*
minbar *of Nur al-Din,*
564/1168, Jerusalem

God would not grant him the conquest of Jerusalem. There is strict adherence to truth, however, in the statement that the *minbar* was built by an outstanding carpenter called al-Akharini whose name actually appeared on the inscriptions of the *minbar* together with four other signatures.[91]

In his summary of another work of 'Imad al-din, *Sana al-barq al-shami*, the later chronicler al-Bundari includes a slightly different account of the *minbar*:

Plate 3.31 *Aqsa Mosque,* minbar *of Nur al-Din, detail showing doors, 564/1168, Jerusalem*

(Creswell Photographic Archive, Ashmolean Museum, Oxford, neg. C. 5008)

By the light of his discernment the just prince Nur al-Din Mahmud b. Zengi had known in his time about the conquest of Jerusalem after him. So he commissioned in Aleppo the making of a *minbar* for Jerusalem; carpenters, craftsmen and architects laboured on it for years and they made it outstanding in its solidness and decoration. That *minbar* remained installed in the mosque of Aleppo, sheathed like a sword in the scabbard of protection until the sultan [Saladin] in this age ordered the fulfilment of the Nurid vow and the *minbar* was brought to its place in Jerusalem.[92]

Here too we see 'Imad al-Din claiming that Nur al-Din knew that Jerusalem would be conquered but not in his own time. Strikingly, the *minbar* is likened here to a sword in its scabbard, awaiting its unsheathing as a weapon of religious propaganda in its final destination, Jerusalem.

The account of Ibn al-Athir concerning the *minbar* is more prosaic. He describes the making and transporting of the *minbar* as follows:

He [Saladin] ordered that a *minbar* should be made for him. So he was told that Nur al-Din Mahmud had made a *minbar* in Aleppo. He ordered craftsmen to go to great lengths to fashion it beautifully and to perfect it and he said 'We have made it to be erected in Jerusalem'. So carpenters made it in a number of years; nothing like it was made in Islam.

So he [Saladin] ordered that it should be brought and it was carried from Aleppo and erected in Jerusalem. Between the making of the *minbar* and its being carried [to Jerusalem] was more than twenty years. This was one of the blessings and good intentions of Nur al-Din, may God have mercy on him.[93]

Clearly, there is good reason to assume that towards the end of his career Nur al-Din had his eyes set on the goal of Jerusalem and that the *minbar* he had commissioned was intended to record for posterity his own role in such an enterprise. The *minbar* may be viewed, on a much loftier level, as a forerunner of the gigantic monument of intersecting scimitars erected by Saddam Husain in 1985 to celebrate his coming victory in the Iraq–Iran war – a victory he too was never to see. The Aqsa *minbar* was a palpable and lasting symbol of the Muslim Counter-Crusade; it was in effect a piece of sympathetic magic. The inscriptions which Nur al-Din chose for his *minbar* concern the Day of Resurrection (Sura 16: 92–5), the fulfilling of solemn oaths taken and the Sura of Light (probably used also – as in his *minbar* in the Jami' al-Nuri at Hama [plates 3.32–3.33 and figure 3.36; cf. plate 3.34] – as a play on words with his own name, which means 'light of religion').

One senses in some of the sources at least that Muslim chroniclers would have liked Nur al-Din rather than Saladin to have won the prize of Jerusalem. As Ibn al-Jawzi (d. 597/1200) writes: 'He was resolved to conquer Jerusalem, but fate overtook him' (plate 3.35).[94] Certainly, until the dawn of the modern era, it was Nur al-Din, rather than Saladin, who was taken by later Muslim writers as the prototype of the *mujahid*, the model *jihad* fighter. Saladin, as we shall see in Chapter 8, became popular in the Muslim world initially – and paradoxically – as a result of his glowing reputation in Christian Europe.

Plate 3.32 Jami' al-Nuri, minbar (now in Hama Museum), with a Qur'anic inscription (25: 62–3) perhaps punning on the associations with light (nur) in the title 'Nur al-Din': 'Blessed be He that fixed to the firmament the constellations, who hung the lamp, and the moon that shines. He has made night and day . . .', 559/1164, Hama, Syria

Plate 3.33 *Jami' al-Nuri,* minbar *(now in Hama Museum), upper section, 559/1164, Hama, Syria*

(Creswell Photographic Archive, Ashmolean Museum, Oxford, neg. C. 6079)

Abu Shama (d. 665/1258) relates how the *minbar* was transported to Jerusalem and stresses the role of Nur al-Din in the ultimate conquest of the city as well as his vow to see the *minbar* taken to its rightful destination:

As it happened, the blessing which he [Nur al-Din] received from God was extended to Islam after him and sealed by the conquest

لا اله الا الله
محمد رسول الله

Figure 3.36 Jami' al-Nuri, minbar, *inscription at the rear with the* shahada *(the Muslim confession of faith),* 559/1164, Hama, Syria

Plate 3.34 Jami' al-Nuri, minbar *(now in Hama Museum), upper section with dome,* 559/1164, Hama, Syria

(Creswell Photographic Archive, Ashmolean Museum, Oxford, neg. C. 6078)

Plate 3.35 *Funerary* madrasa
of Nur al-Din, 567/1172,
undated cenotaph,
Damascus, Syria

of Saladin . . . The *minbar* had stayed in its place in the great
Mosque of Aleppo . . . until the present day, when Saladin ordered
the fulfilment of the vow of Nur al-Din and had the *minbar* transported to the place for which it was destined in Jerusalem.[95]

Ibn Jubayr saw the *minbar* in 1182 when it was in Aleppo and
writes: 'I have not seen in any other country a *minbar* which resembles its shape and the uniqueness of its manufacture . . . It rises like
an enormous crown above the *mihrab* until it reaches the ceiling.'[96]
Another tantalising snippet of evidence testifying to the preoccupation of Nur al-Din with Jerusalem is an inscription from the Nuri
mosque in Mosul. The monument was founded by Nur al-Din on his
taking possession of the town in 1171,[97] in other words, shortly
before his death. It suggests that the recapture of Jerusalem was still
very much on his mind and that he wished to announce in faraway
Mosul the *jihad* message which he had exploited so successfully in
Syria. The damaged inscription (plate 3.36), now in the Museum in
Baghdad but once part of the Nuri mosque,[98] includes a portion of a
verse from the Sura of the Cow: in this context the crucial words
from it are as follows: 'And whencesoever thou comest forth turn thy
face toward the Inviolable Place of Worship.'[99]
The choice of this inscription in the mosque founded by Nur al-Din
in Mosul is deliberate; it is an allusion to Jerusalem since the preceding

'Asakir's works glorifying Jerusalem were read out publicly to large audiences in Damascus from 1160 onwards. Such public meetings no doubt intensified popular awareness of the sanctity of Jerusalem and built up the expectation that the Holy City would be recaptured.

Jihad *Prayers and Sermons*

The text of a little-known *jihad* prayer of invocation made after a Friday sermon and allegedly dating from the late eleventh century has survived in at least two later works. Written by a scholar called Ibn al-Mawsilaya, the prayer is very revealing of the type of propaganda used to arouse the faithful to *jihad*.[113] The Arabic is highly rhetorical in style, interspersed with suitable Qur'anic quotations. It lacks the stylistic felicities and elegance of the rhymed couplets used in the classic sermons of Ibn Nubata, the famous tenth-century preacher who has already been mentioned; indeed, the style of the prayer is baroque in its piling up of hyperbole, word-plays and esoteric vocabulary. When read aloud, however, its rousing resonances make up for its linguistic flaws and it reflects the deep-rooted Near Eastern belief in the effective value of the spoken word. The following lines come from this prayer:

> O God, raise the banner of Islam and its helper and refute polytheism by wounding its back and cutting its ropes. Help those who fight *jihad* for your sake and who in obedience to you have sacrificed themselves and sold their souls to you.

The prayer ends powerfully: 'Because they persist in going astray, may the eyeball of the proponents of polytheism become blind to the paths of righteousness.'[114]

There must have been many *jihad* sermons, no doubt modelled on those of Ibn Nubata which expressed the same rousing emotions, but their texts have not survived.

Special Books on Jihad

We have already referred to the *Book of Holy War* composed by al-Sulami at the beginning of the twelfth century. This fitted into a genre of writing which dates from the eighth century; the first such work was written by Ibn al-Mubarak (d. 181/797).[115] Such books flourished above all in the second half of the twelfth century, precisely at the time of Nur al-Din and Saladin; these works served as weapons in the armoury of *jihad* propaganda, alongside inspiring sermons, eloquent poetry and *Fada'il al-Quds* literature. The book of *jihad* contained a compilation of selected *hadith* which evoked the memory of the wars at the beginning of Islam and the promise of Paradise to those who fought *jihad*.

There was a direct link in the chroniclers' minds between such

Figure 3.39 *Foot soldier, inlaid metal vase made by 'Ali ibn Hamud al-Mawsili, 657/1259, Mosul(?), Iraq*

literature and military action. Indeed, a relative of the famous Muslim writer Usama, namely 'Ali b. Munqidh, was taught a *Book of Holy War* by Ibn 'Asakir. Thus inspired, 'Ali went to defend Ascalon in 546/1151 against the Franks and perished in the battle.[116] Amongst those who compiled books on *jihad* was Ibn Shaddad, Saladin's biographer (d. 623/1234), who presented a work, now no longer extant, entitled *The Merits of* Jihad, to Saladin when the latter was besieging the castle of Krac des Chevaliers in 580/1184. This book allegedly gathered together all the *hadith* of the Prophet on the subject of Holy War.

Poetry Extolling the Virtues of Jihad

Perhaps the most rousing literary vehicle for *jihad* was the poetry written by contemporary poets to their patrons, the princes and commanders of the time, and especially to Nur al-Din. Such poetry would be read out publicly at court and would greatly affect those listening to it. As already mentioned, enthusiastic poetic claims were made for Zengi after the conquest of Edessa by poets such as Ibn Munir and Ibn al-Qaysarani.[117] After 'Imad al-Din al-Isfahani joined the service of Nur al-Din, he too wrote poetry in praise of his master's pursuit of *jihad*. He writes:

> Nur al-Din asked me to write a two-line poem on his tongue about the meaning of *jihad*, so I said:

> 'My zeal is for campaigning and my delight is in it. I do not have any other wish in life except it.
> The successful outcome of seeking is by striving and by *jihad*.
> Freedom from care is dependent on exertion [in the path of God]'.[118]

In another poetic snippet, 'Imad al-Din puts the following lines into the mouth of Nur al-Din:

> I have no wish except *jihad*
> Repose in anything other than it is exertion for me.
> Seeking achieves nothing except by striving.
> Life without the striving of *jihad* is an [idle] pastime.[119]

Predictably, full-blown rhetorical claims are made for Nur al-Din in his funeral elegy, also written by 'Imad al-Din:

> Religion is in darkness because of the absence of his light [this is a pun on the name of Nur al-Din – the light of religion]
> The age is in grief because of the loss of its commander.
> Let Islam mourn the defender of its people
> And Syria [mourn] the protector of its Kingdom and its borders.[120]

Yet, such claims may well have been justified in the case of this charismatic leader, whose career has been unjustly neglected in the West.

Notes

1. Usama, Hitti, 124.
2. *War, Technology and Society in the Middle East*, ed. V. J. Parry and M. E. Yapp, London, 1975.
3. Ibid., 386.
4. Cf. also Qur'an 2: 186–9, 2: 190–3, 47: 4–5.
5. Al-Tibrizi, *Mishkat al-masabih*, trans. J. Robson as *Mishkat*, Lahore, 1972, vol. III, 817.
6. Ibid., III, 817.
7. Al-Shafi'i, *Risala*, trans. M. Khadduri as *Islamic Jurisprudence*, Baltimore, 1961, 84.
8. Such as al-Shafi'i, and al-Mawardi. Cf. *EI²: Dar al-'ahd*.
9. Ibn Qudama, *Al-'Umda*, trans. H. Laoust as *Le précis de droit d'Ibn Qudama*, Beirut, 1950, 280.
10. C. Imber, *Ebu's-Su'ud: The Islamic Legal Tradition*, Edinburgh, 1997.
11. Ibid., 67–8.
12. Ibid., 68–9.
13. Th. W. Juynboll, *Handbuch des islamischen Gesetzes nach der Lehre der schafi'itischen Schule*, Leiden and Leipzig, 1910, 339.
14. B. Lewis, 'Politics and war', in *idem, Studies in Classical and Ottoman Islam (7th–16th Centuries)*, London, 1976, I, 176.
15. C. E. Bosworth, 'The city of Tarsus and the Arab–Byzantine frontiers in early and middle 'Abbasid times', *Oriens*, 33 (1992), 271, 280–1.
16. Arabic text in M. Canard, *Sayf al-Dawla: recueil des textes*, Algiers, 1934, 261.
17. Ibid., 168–9.
18. Ibid., 172–3.
19. Ibid., 156–7.
20. Sivan, *L'Islam*, 195, citing Paris ms. 4958, fol. 16.
21. Quoted by Sivan, *L'Islam*, 13.
22. Sivan, *L'Islam*, 13.
23. R. S. Humphreys, 'Ayyubids, Mamluks, and the Latin East in the thirteenth century', *Mamluk Studies Review*, 2 (1998), 4.
24. Sivan, *L'Islam*, 44.
25. Cf. the discussion in A. Noth, 'Heiliger Kampf (Gihad) gegen die "Franken": Zur Position der Kreuzzüge im Rahmen der Islamgeschichte', *Saeculum*, 37 (1986), 243.
26. *EI²*: Al-Mustarshid.
27. Cf. Noth, 'Heiliger Kampf', 250.
28. Ibid., 251–2.
29. Ibn al-Athir, *Kamil*, X, 190.
30. E. Sivan, 'La genèse de la contre-croisade', *JA*, 254 (1966), 199–204.
31. Ibn al-'Adim, *Zubda*, Dahan, II, 185.
32. Ibn al-'Adim, *Zubda*, Dahan, II, 188–9.
33. C. Hillenbrand, 'The career of Najm al-Din Il-Ghazi', *Der Islam*, 58/2 (1981), 250–92.
34. Ibn al-Jawzi, X, 13.
35. C. Hillenbrand, 'Jihad propaganda in Syria from the time of the First Crusade until the death of Zengi: the evidence of monumental

inscriptions', in *The Frankish Wars and Their Influence on Palestine*, ed. K. Athamina and R. Heacock, Birzeit, 1994, 60–9.

36. J. Sauvaget, 'La tombe de l'Ortokide Balak', *Ars Islamica*, 5/2 (1938), 207–15.

37. The example of Balak's tomb was followed up by an inscription dated 524/1130 on a religious college (*madrasa*) in Damascus founded by Mu'in al-Din Ünür, a freedman of Tughtegin. The latter was one of Balak's contemporaries and the ruler of Damascus. Unur's inscription describes his master, who had died a year earlier, in a series of *jihad* titles, 'the prince, the one who fights the Holy War, the one who perseveres assiduously on the frontier (against the enemy), the warrior' (*RCEA*, VIII, inscription no. 3033, 165).

38. *RCEA*, VIII, inscription no. 3112, 229–30.

39. *Atabegs*, 33–4.

40. *Atabegs*, 33–4.

41. Al-Bundari, *Zubdat al-nusra*, ed. M. T. Houtsma, Leiden, 1889, 205.

42. Ibn al-Athir, *Kamil*, XI, 73.

43. Ibn al-'Adim, *Zubda, RHC*, III, 689.

44. *Atabegs*, 34.

45. Abu Shama, I, 32, 34.

46. Sivan, 'Réfugiés', 142.

47. 'Imad al-Din, *Kharida*, I, 155.

48. 'Imad al-Din, *Kharida*, I, 110; Ibn Munir, according to Abu Shama, I, 40.

49. Abu Shama, I, 39.

50. Inscriptions from the late 1130s in Zengi's name also include such grandiloquent titles. Cf. *RCEA*, VIII, inscription no. 3093, 213–14.

51. *Atabegs*, 160, 162; Usama, Hitti, 124; Abu Shama, *RHC*, IV, 56; Ibn al-Athir, *Kamil, RHC*, I, 468, 470; Ibn al-Qalanisi, Gibb, 284; cf. also J.-M. Mouton, *Damas et sa principauté sous les Saljoukides et les Bourides 468–549/1076–1154*, Cairo, 1994, 60, n. 44.

52. For the activities of Nur al-Din in Egypt, cf. Ibn Zafir, 114.

53. H. Laoust, *La profession de foi d'Ibn Batta*, Damascus, 1958.

54. N. Elisséeff, *Nur al-Din: un grand prince musulman de Syrie au temps des Croisades*, Damascus, 1967, vol. III, 735.

55. Y. Tabbaa, 'Monuments with a message: Propagation of Jihad under Nur al-Din', in *The Meeting of Two Worlds*, ed. V. P. Goss, Kalamazoo, 1986, 224–6.

56. Elisséeff, *Nur al-Din*, III, 394–423.

57. N. O. Rabbat, 'The ideological significance of the Dar al-Adl in the medieval Islamic Orient', *IJMES*, 27 (1995), 3–28, especially 19.

58. *Atabegs*, 168.

59. Cf. T. Allen, *A Classical Revival in Islamic Architecture*, Wiesbaden, 1986, ix and 1–6.

60. *Atabegs*, 170–2; 'Imad al-Din, *Sana*, 16.

61. Elisséeff, *Nur al-Din*, II, 559.

62. Elisséeff, *Nur al-Din*, III, 821.

63. Elisséeff, *Nur al-Din*, II, 400.

64. Ibn al-Qalanisi, Gibb, 303.

65. Elisséeff, *Nur al-Din*, II, 426.

66. Ibn al-'Adim, *Zubda*, Dahan, II, 291.

67. Ibn al-'Adim, *Zubda*, Dahan, II, 315; Elisséeff, *Nur al-Din*, II, 577.

68. 'Imad al-Din, *Sana*, 16.

69. *Atabegs*, 163–75.

70. *Atabegs*, 163.

71. Abu Shama, I, 175.

72. Abu Shama, I, 5.
73. Abu Shama, I, 293–4, 297–8.
74. Köhler, 239.
75. Köhler, 277.
76. K. A. C. Creswell, *Muslim Architecture of Egypt*, Oxford, 1959, I/1, 94–5.
77. According to G. Le Strange, *Palestine under the Moslems*, Beirut, 1965, 88.
78. A. A. Duri, 'Bait al-Maqdis in Islam', *Studies in the History and Archaeology of Jordan*, I, ed. A. Hadidi, Amman, 1982, 355.
79. Al-Muqaddasi, trans. Miquel, 145.
80. Ibid., 187.
81. Al-Wasiti, *Fada'il al-bait al-muqaddas*, ed. A. Hasson, Jerusalem, 1979.
82. Quoted by Sivan, *L'Islam*, 62.
83. Ibn al-Qaysarani, quoted by Sivan, *L'Islam*, 62.
84. Cf. also *Atabegs*, 103, when Ibn al-Athir quotes celebratory verses of Ibn al-Qaysarani on the capture of Joscelin by Nur al-Din.
85. Quoted by Sivan, *L'Islam*, 63.
86. Tabbaa, 'Monuments with a message', in *The Meeting of Two Worlds*, ed. V. P. Goss, Kalamazoo, 1986, 233.
87. Lit.: There has ordered its construction the slave. . .
88. *RCEA*, IX, inscription no. 3281, 56–7; N. Elisséef, 'La titulature de Nur al-Din d'après ses inscriptions', *BEO*, 14 (1952–4), 163.
89. Tabbaa, 'Monuments', 233; M. van Berchem, *Matériaux pour un corpus inscriptionum arabicarum*, II: *Syrie du Sud, Jérusalem* [II: Haram] (Mémoires publiés par les membres de l'IFAO du Caire, XLIV/1–2), Cairo, 1925–7, 401.
90. Tabbaa, 'Monuments', 233.
91. M. van Berchem, *Corpus inscriptionum arabicarum: Jerusalem Haram*, Cairo, 1920–7, vol. III, 398–400.
92. *Sana*, 314–15. Al-Bundari's date of death is not known. He was working for the Ayyubid ruler al-Mu'azzam 'Isa in the 1220s.
93. Ibn al-Athir, *Kamil*, XI, 365.
94. Ibn al-Jawzi, X, 249.
95. In a letter written in 565/1169–70.
96. Ibn Jubayr, according to Tabbaa, 'Monuments', 232.
97. Ibn al-Athir, *Atabegs*, *RHC*, II, 278.
98. The photograph of this inscription clearly shows the words: 'Turn thy face toward the Inviolable Place of Worship'. I am deeply indebted to Dr Tariq al-Janabi for lending me a photograph of this inscription.
99. Sura 2: 149.
100. Abu Shama, I, 215; Sivan, *L'Islam*, 63; cf. also al-Maqrizi, trans. Broadhurst, 85.
101. Abu Shama, I, 18.
102. E. Baden, 'Die sufik nach 'Ammar al-Bidlisi', *Oriens*, 33 (1992), 91.
103. Abu Shama, I, 18.
104. Anon., *The Sea of Precious Virtues*, trans. J. S. Meisami, Salt Lake City, 1991, viii.
105. Elisseeff, *Nur al-Din*, II, 461–2; *The Sea*, trans. Meisami, x.
106. Ibid., 25 and 27–8.
107. Ibn Jubayr, trans. Broadhurst, 273.
108. Ibn al-Murajja compiled a work on the Merits of Jerusalem in the 1130s. Cf. Ibn al-Murajja, *Fada'il Bayt al-Maqdis*, ed. O. Livre-Kafri, Shfaram, 1995.

109. It is even conceivable that al-Wasiti, who was a preacher at the Aqsa mosque, had a particular purpose in writing and reciting his work when he did. A severe earthquake had hit Palestine in 1016, damaging both the Aqsa mosque and the Dome of the Rock. Inscriptions in both buildings record that they were subsequently repaired by order of the Fatimid caliph al-Zahir; the Dome of the Rock in 1022 and 1027 and the Aqsa mosque in 1034. It is likely that the appearance of the first Merits of Jerusalem treatise at this time was related in some way to this restoration work. It is even possible that al-Wasiti's compilation was read out publicly when these restorations were complete, perhaps as a stimulus to encourage the faithful to contribute to the costs.

110. E. Sivan, 'The beginnings of the Fada'il al-Quds literature', *Israel Oriental Studies*, 1 (1971), 264.

111. Al-Sakhawi, *I'lan*, trans. Rosenthal, 464: 'he compiled the history and praise of Jerusalem but did not complete it [the work]'.

112. Al-Wasiti, *Fada'il al-bayt al-muqaddas*, ed. A. Hasson, Jerusalem, 1979, 93.

113. For details of this man, cf. Ibn al-Jawzi, IX, 80; Ibn al-Athir, *Kamil*, X, 259.

114. Al-Husayni, *Akhbar al-dawla al-saljuqiyya*, ed. M. Iqbal, Lahore, 1933, 47–8. Ibn al-'Adim also quotes it in his biographical dictionary.

115. Ibn al-Mubarak, *Kitab al-jihad*, ed. N. al-Hammad, Tunis, 1972.

116. Mouton, *Damas*, 61, n. 46.

117. Sivan, *L'Islam*, 46–7.

118. *Kharida*, 43; *Sana*, 104; Abu Shama, I, 528.

119. Abu Shama, I, 625; *Kharida*, 72.

120. Abu Shama, I, 528; *Kharida*, 42.

CHAPTER FOUR

Jihad in the Period from the Death of Nur al-Din until the Fall of Acre (569–690/1174–1291)

The spirit of the jihad, *in the final analysis, is only a military fiction, a source of energy and enthusiasm at the outset, an ideal mobilization of defensive reflexes in the second Islamic period.*[1] (Djait)

THIS CHAPTER considers first the importance of *jihad* in the time of Saladin and his successors, the Ayyubids. It then discusses the *jihad* context of the Mamluk state which finally uprooted the Crusaders from the Levant at the end of the thirteenth century.

The Career of Saladin: The Basic Framework

As with the career of Nur al-Din, the achievements of his more famous successor, Salah al-Din (Saladin), were recorded with admiration and piety by the Muslim chroniclers. Before assessing the *jihad* context of Saladin's career, it is important to cast a brief eye on its major landmarks. The sources for Saladin's career are unusually rich since two of his close advisers, 'Imad al-Din al-Isfahani (d. 597/1201) and Baha' al-Din ibn Shaddad (d. 632/1234), actually wrote biographical accounts of him – a most rare historiographical occurrence up to this period. Other chroniclers, such as Ibn al-Athir (d. 630/1233) and Abu Shama (d. 665/1258), give Saladin's career very detailed coverage. Another close adviser of Saladin's, al-Qadi al-Fadil, left a number of letters which are also a valuable and contemporary source for our knowledge of Saladin's activities and which were quoted at some length by Lyons and Jackson in their book *Saladin: The Politics of the Holy War.*

Figure 4.1 Coin of Saladin, late twelfth century, Turkey

The first phase of Saladin's rise to prominence, as already mentioned, had occurred during the lifetime of Nur al-Din, when Saladin was engaged in a complicated struggle for power in Egypt, as the lieutenant of Nur al-Din. The death of Nur al-Din in 569/1174 probably prevented a serious rift erupting between them.[2]

After 569/1174 Saladin's major concern was to gain credibility as

Plate 4.1 Fals *of Saladin,*
copper, 586/1190–1,
Turkey or Iraq

the successor to Nur al-Din, in the face of the hostility of the latter's family who aspired to rule his territories. Just like Nur al-Din, Saladin spent his first decade in power fighting fellow Muslims in order to achieve a unified base, and engaged only intermittently in combat with the Franks. Like Nur al-Din he spent many years subjugating his Muslim rivals and he made truces with the Franks. By 579/1183, with his capture of Aleppo, he had united Syria and Egypt under his rule. It was at this point that he turned his attention seriously to the Franks. The inflammatory actions of Reynald of Chatillon in the Red Sea, threatening the Holy Cities, prompted Saladin to attack Reynald's fortress of al-Karak in 579/1183 and 580/1184: these attempts proved unsuccessful.[3]

The following year (581/1185–6) Saladin fell seriously ill and he spent a considerable time recuperating.[4] Soon after his recovery he summoned his allies from the surrounding territories and in 583/1187 launched a major campaign against the Franks. The Frankish town of Antioch was specifically excluded because he had made a truce with its ruler. He met the Franks at Hattin on Saturday 24 Rabi' II 583/4 July 1187 and gained a great victory. Acre capitulated five days later, and by the middle of Jumada II/early September the southern Levantine coast from Gaza to Jubayl (with the exception of Tyre) was in Saladin's hands. He then advanced on Jerusalem which surrendered on 27 Rajab/2 October.

Jerusalem may well have been the psychological climax to Saladin's career but it still left the Franks in possession of 350 miles of the Syrian coastline and a number of key ports. Saladin followed up the reconquest of Jerusalem by taking more strongholds in northern Syria in 584/1188, but he failed to take Tyre. The advent of the Third Crusade saw the investing of Acre by the Crusaders and its eventual surrender to them in Jumada II/July 1191, followed by a truce between Saladin and the Franks in Sha'ban 588/September 1192. Saladin died on Wednesday 27 Safar 589/3 March 1193.

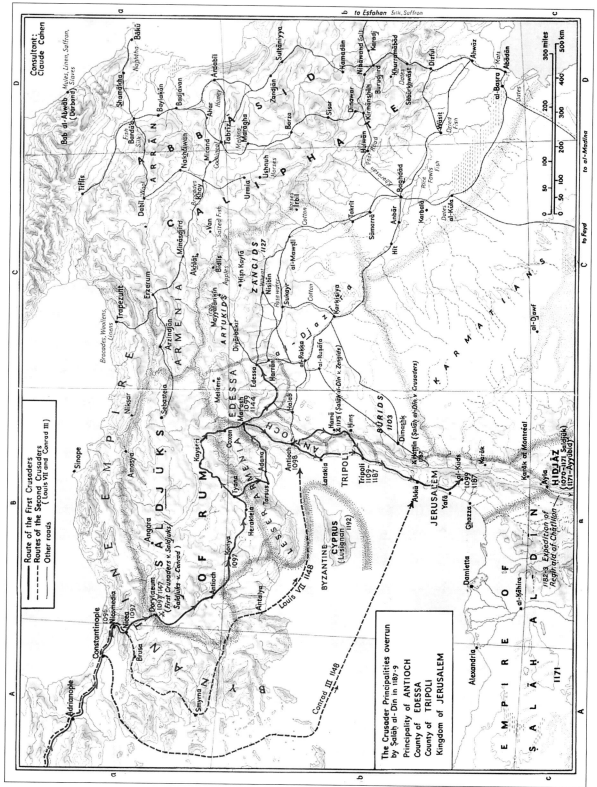

Figure 4.2 Map of the Near East in the twelfth century

The Heritage of Nur al-Din

As Lyons and Jackson explain clearly in their biography of Saladin, family dynasties such as those of the Turkish military commanders in Syria in the twelfth century felt the need to justify the power they had usurped; for this they required the support of the religious classes, as well as public ratification of their military activities by the caliph.[5] Their religious propaganda, including architecture (plates 4.2–4.5, 4.6; cf. plates 5.7, 3.36 and 5.8; figure 4.3), had the same aim of justifying their authority. We have seen how Nur al-Din's entourage harnessed his aims in personal and familial expansionist terms to the concept of Holy War and how Nur al-Din himself is portrayed in the sources – certainly in the latter part of his career – as combining personal and public *jihad*. Saladin could build on the bases of moral unity left by Nur al-Din and like his illustrious predecessor, whose empire he usurped, he could present himself as the defender of Sunni Islam and the promoter of *jihad* against the Franks.

Plate 4.2 Jami' al-Nuri, exterior view (photograph taken before 1940 rebuilding), 566–8/1170–3, Mosul, Iraq

Plate 4.3 Jami' al-Nuri, window-frame in sanctuary, 566–8/1170–3, Mosul, Iraq

Jihad Propaganda in the Time of Saladin

When Saladin succeeded Nur al-Din as the supreme *jihad* warrior and the architect of Muslim unity he continued to exploit the wide range of propaganda methods which had proved so successful in the time of Nur al-Din. The early Merits of Jerusalem work of al-Raba'i was read out in public in April 1187,[6] at the time when Saladin's forces were preparing for the campaign which culminated in their taking Jerusalem. This is a clear indication of the emotional impact which the Merits of Jerusalem works now exerted on their audience.

Saladin's triumphant capture of Jerusalem, the climax of his career,

Plate 4.4 *Jami' al-Nuri,*
mihrab, *566–8/1170–3, Mosul,*
Iraq

Plate 4.5 *Jami' al-Nuri, dome over* mihrab *(photograph taken before 1940 rebuilding),* mihrab *of 566–8/1170–3, dome rebuilt thereafter, Mosul, Iraq*

Plate 4.6 Jami' al-Nuri, dark blue marble columns in sanctuary. The octagonal columns date from 566–8/1170–3; the composite columns with lyre-shaped capitals were probably incorporated from an earlier building but at a later date. Mosul, Iraq

Figure 4.3 *Jami' al-Nuri,
inscriptions on columns,
566–8/1170–3, Mosul, Iraq*

was not heralded by jubilation in Palestine and Syria alone. For once, a writer not in the immediate vicinity of Palestine was moved to compose a Merits of Jerusalem work. The famous Baghdad preacher, lawyer and historian Ibn al-Jawzi (d. 597/1200) wrote such a work, in which the shame of the Crusaders' conquest of Jerusalem is emphasised and the glory of Saladin's crowning achievement in recapturing it is extolled.[7]

Saladin was accompanied on campaign by prominent representatives of the *'ulama'* class. The Hanbalite legist Ibn Qudama (d. 620/1223), for example, was with Saladin when he made his triumphal entry into Jerusalem and he and his cousin 'Abd al-Ghani had been in Saladin's army in the campaigns of the 1180s. The work entitled *The Profession of Faith* of the Hanbalite scholar Ibn Batta was read out publicly by Ibn Qudama in 582/1186 on the eve of Saladin's decisive campaign against the Franks.[8] In the time of Saladin, 'Abd al-Ghani wrote a work praising *jihad* which was read out in Damascene religious circles.[9]

As in the time of Nur al-Din, the poets in Saladin's entourage also emphasised the religious aspects of his career, stressing his prosecution of *jihad* and his role as an ideal Sunni ruler. The poet Ibn Sana' al-Mulk (d. 608/1211) addressed a rapturous panegyric to Saladin after his glorious victory at Hattin in 583/1187:[10]

> You took possession of Paradises (*jinan*) palace by palace, when
> you conquered Syria fortress by fortress.
> Indeed, the religion of Islam has spread its blessings over
> created beings.
> But it is you who have glorified it . . .
> You have risen up in the darkness of the battle like the moon
> when it climbs slowly in the night.
> You have never shown yourself in battles without appearing,
> o Joseph, as beautiful as Joseph [in the Qur'an].

> They attacked *en masse* like mountains, but the assaults of
> your chivalry have turned them into wool . . .
> Syria is not the only object of the congratulations addressed to
> you, but it is also every region and country.
> You have possessed the lands from east to west.
> You have embraced the horizons, plain and steppe . . .
> God has said: Obey him;
> We have heard Our Lord and obeyed.[11]

These lines are permeated with Qur'anic allusions, not only from
Sura 12 which tells the story of Joseph (a pun on one of Saladin's own
names) but also Sura 70: 9 ('And the hills became as flakes of wool').[12]
Above all, these lines demonstrate how Saladin is viewed as the
favoured one of God who is carrying out His divine will and purpose.

Saladin's Islamic credentials are fully recognised on a surviving
gold coin, minted in his name in Syria and dated 583/1187. On this
coin, which may well be celebrating Saladin's victories at Hattin and
Jerusalem, he is called 'the sultan of Islam and the Muslims'. Here is
a piece of irrefutably contemporary evidence: a small but expensive
coin on whose limited space the title chosen to describe Saladin is a
triumphantly Islamic one.[13] Given the high value of gold, it was used
for the minting of coins on important commemorative occasions: the
climax of Saladin's career in religious terms is thus recorded at the
very time it happened in the most precious metal available.[14]

Saladin's *Jihad*: The Evidence of the Medieval Muslim Chroniclers

The Muslim sources expend much energy in presenting Saladin as a
model Muslim, the champion of the faith. A typical example is the
biography of Ibn Shaddad, which is worth analysing in some detail.
As Holt points out, this work is divided into three distinct parts, by
far the largest part (c. 83 per cent) being devoted to the enumeration
of Saladin's merits and an account of the last six years of his life.[15]
This is clearly, then, a deliberate tilting of the evidence towards the
last phase of Saladin's career with a view to presenting him at the
peak of his achievements as the ideal *mujahid*. Conversely, it glosses
over his rise to power in the wake of what might be viewed by a less
laudatory commentator as a series of extremely opportune deaths –
notably those of his uncle Shirkuh, of the Fatimid caliph, and even
those of Nur al-Din himself and his son al-Malik al-Salih.

Ibn Shaddad was writing his biography of Saladin in the afterglow
of the victories at Hattin and Jerusalem: indeed, he entered Saladin's
service in 584/1188 and remained with his master until his death five
years later. Understandably, his work is infused with exultant pride
in Saladin's achievements. He does not only wish to praise his patron
– which is, of course, the task of any court biographer – but he aims

Figure 4.4 *Combatants,*
Blacas ewer, inlaid brass,
629/1232, Mosul, Iraq

also to expatiate on the reconquest of Jerusalem and the victory of
Islam over Christianity.

There are various events in Saladin's career which are taken by Ibn
Shaddad as significant milestones in Saladin's spiritual evolution into
an ideal *mujahid*. As early as his seizure of power in Egypt after the
death of Shirkuh in 564/1168, Saladin 'gave up wine and renounced
pastimes, putting on the garment of serious endeavour'.[16] Saladin has
re-established Sunni Islam in Egypt and is now ready to fight the
Franks. Ibn Shaddad does not mention Saladin's truces with the Franks
and he interprets Saladin's efforts to seize the lands of Nur al-Din
from the latter's family as part of his devotion to *jihad*. He thus puts
the best possible construction on manœuvres which a more impartial
historian might describe as opportunistic.

Similarly, Ibn Shaddad gives a warm, adulatory account of his
master's religious merits: 'Saladin was a man of firm faith, one who
often had God's name on his lips.'[17]

Saladin's religious orthodoxy is stressed and we are assured that
'speculation never led him into any theological error or heresy'.[18] The
fact that Saladin left an empty treasury when he died is attributed by
Ibn Shaddad to the fact that he had given away his wealth, dying with
only forty-seven Nasirite *dirhams* and a single piece of Tyrian gold
in his treasury.[19] Thus Saladin's lack of care with money, a target of
criticism by others, is turned into a pious virtue by his devoted
admirer Ibn Shaddad. The two of them, Saladin and Ibn Shaddad,
prayed together when they heard that the Franks intended to besiege
Jerusalem and shortly afterwards 'came the joyful news that they had
withdrawn and were returning to the region of al-Ramla'.[20]

Saladin's prayers had been answered. So, in his personal life, which
was seen by only a small handful of followers, Saladin is shown to be

pious and God-fearing. These virtues are then extended by Ibn Shaddad into his role as ruler, the dispenser of justice: 'He never turned away anyone who had suffered injustice.'[21]

Saladin's role as army general and supreme *mujahid* is of course given pride of place. He would make himself known to the rank and file of the soldiers in his army, creating bonds of loyalty and solidarity and enhancing corporate morale: 'He would traverse the whole army from the right wing to the left, creating a sense of unity and urging them to advance and stand firm at the right time.'[22]

Sections of the *hadith* were read out by the '*ulama*' to the army 'while we were all in the saddle'.[23] No doubt these were the *hadith* that had to do specifically with *jihad* and the rewards of martyrdom in the path of God.[24]

Ibn Shaddad also points out that he himself was one of those who wrote a work on *jihad* for Saladin, to whom he presented it in 584/1188–9: 'I had collected for him a book on *jihad* in Damascus during my stay there, with all its [*jihad*] precepts and etiquette. I presented it to him and he liked it and used to study it constantly.'[25] As for Saladin's zeal in the pursuance of Holy War, he was, according to Ibn Shaddad, 'more assiduous and zealous in this than in anything else'.[26] In his description of Saladin's qualities as a *mujahid*, Ibn Shaddad indulges in full-blown hyperbole: 'For love of the Holy War and on God's path he left his family and his sons, his homeland, his home and all his estates, and chose out of all the world to live in the shade of his tent.'[27]

Saladin's other contemporary biographer, 'Imad al-Din al-Isfahani, also writes about him in laudatory terms in his work entitled *The Eloquent Exposition of the Conquest of Jerusalem (Al-fath al-qussi fi'l-fath al-Qudsi)*. Recent research has suggested that the work was written in Saladin's lifetime and that part of it was actually read out to him in 588/1192.[28] It is scarcely surprising, therefore, that the work has a tone of such high rhetoric and that in its introduction Saladin's conquest of Jerusalem is likened to the Prophet's *hijra* to Medina in the year 1/622.[29]

In these circumstances, the evidence of the pro-Zengid Ibn al-Athir, often a stern critic of Saladin, is of especial value as a corrective to the heights of panegyric reached by Saladin's two contemporary biographers. Yet even Ibn al-Athir sees Saladin as being full of zeal for waging *jihad*, and when describing Saladin on his death praises him: 'He was much given to good deeds and fine actions, a mighty warrior of the *jihad* against the infidels.'[30]

There is also value in the contemporary account of Saladin given by Ibn Jubayr, an outsider from Spain. He describes the pious foundations established by Saladin in Alexandria – colleges, hostels, baths and a hospital.[31] He also praises Saladin for his just administration of the taxes. He sums up Saladin's achievements as follows: 'The memorable acts of the Sultan, his efforts for justice, and his stands in defence of Islamic lands are too numerous to count.'[32] Ibn Jubayr

never fails to eulogise Saladin, speaking of 'his memorable deeds in the affairs of the world and of religion, and his zeal in waging holy war against the enemies of God'.[33]

Even though Ibn Jubayr stayed only a short while in the Levant, he must have heard such favourable views of Saladin as these from the people whom he met there. Thus the testimony of outsiders satisfactorily corroborates the statements of those close to Saladin.

Figure 4.5 Riders, one on a barded horse, the other shooting a cross-bow, inlaid bronze flask, early thirteenth century, Iraq

Saladin's Personal *Jihad*

Like Nur al-Din, Saladin is presented in the sources as having undergone a moment of religious awakening after which he prosecuted *jihad* with a genuine sense of purpose, *personally* as well as publicly. However, as already mentioned, such presentations of Muslim rulers were clichés in the writings of the chroniclers; Saladin's son, al-Afdal, is also recorded as having a change of heart after Saladin's death.[34]

Yet there is some justification for the belief that Saladin did undergo a genuine religious conversion. Certain disturbing experiences may well have exercised a deep impact on Saladin's own personal religious stance. First, in the years immediately following the death of Nur al-Din, Saladin survived two attacks from the Assassins,[35] one in 571/1175–6 and another in 581/1185. He also fell seriously ill and must have had time then to reflect on the fragility of human affairs. His adviser and biographer, 'Imad al-Din al-Isfahani, certainly views Saladin's illness as a key moment in his religious development and this seems a much more plausible interpretation than Saladin's alleged moral transformation whilst still in Egypt in the early 1170s. During his illness Saladin is said to have vowed that he would devote himself to taking Jerusalem whatever the cost. According to 'Imad al-Din, the illness was sent by God to Saladin 'to wake him from the sleep of forgetfulness'.[36]

During Saladin's convalescence 'Imad al-Din took the opportunity to arrange for preachers and lawyers to speak to Saladin during Ramadan.[37] Another close adviser of his, al-Qadi al-Fadil, also tried to make Saladin take a vow that he would never fight against fellow Muslims again and that he would devote himself to the *jihad*.[38] Saladin's illness came soon after Reynald's audacious and offensive campaigns in the Red Sea which seem to have affected Saladin personally in a

183

way which the conventional and familiar warfare with the Franks in Palestine and Syria did not. Thus, behind the rhetoric and panegyric of his biographers, one may detect key events in Saladin's life which may well have influenced him spiritually and thus have made his *jihad* a more meaningful personal one.

Despite the evidence cited so far, the sources leave little doubt that even in his own time or shortly thereafter Saladin was not immune from criticism. According to some, his policy of expansionism (1174–86), called *jihad* in the sources, was directed at creating a personal power base strong enough to take on the Franks. To this end he fought fellow Muslims in Syria and Mesopotamia (not merely Shi'ite 'heretics' but rival princes and commanders who would not submit to his overlordship) and he turned away for long periods from attacking the Franks.

Even his devoted scribe, the Qadi al-Fadil, reproached him, saying: 'How shall we turn aside to fight with Muslims, which is forbidden, when we are called to war against the people of war?'[39]

Saladin's ambitions could, with a more critical eye, be viewed as those of an empire-builder with aspirations far beyond the confines of Jerusalem, the Holy Land and Syria. Jerusalem was not the unique focus of Saladin's efforts in the 1170s and the early 1180s. After the death of al-Malik al-Salih, the son of Nur al-Din, in 1181, Saladin is revealed as having a grand design of expansionism which embraced – as he writes in a letter to the caliph at Baghdad – Mosul, Jerusalem, Constantinople, Georgia and the lands of the Almohads in the west. This design is seen in the light of the ultimate triumph of Islam and more especially the 'Abbasid caliphate, whose servant Saladin allegedly is. Even if the undeniable rhetoric is ignored, the underlying grandiose military design is apparent and it is in marked contrast to the more modest and focused designs of Nur al-Din.

Saladin's expansionist plans *eastwards*, which are reported only by Ibn al-Athir, also reflect personal and family territorial ambitions and cannot be construed as *jihad*. In a conversation between Saladin, his son al-Afdal and his brother al-'Adil, shortly before Saladin's death, he is reported to have said: 'We have now finished with the Franks and have nothing to do in this country. In which direction shall we turn?'[40] After some discussion, Saladin proceeds as follows:

> You [al-'Adil] take some of my sons and a part of the army and attack Akhlat [in present-day eastern Turkey], and when I have finished with the land of Rum [Byzantium], I will come to you and we will press on from there into Azarbayjan. Then we will have access to the land of Persia. There is nobody there who could prevent us from it.[41]

This may well be, of course, an attempt by Ibn al-Athir (with his known bias towards Nur al-Din) to besmirch Saladin's reputation as a *jihad* fighter in Palestine and Syria, especially since he places this conversation in his obituary notice of Saladin. But this could also be a true reflection of the importance of what Saladin and his contemporaries still felt to be the *real* centre of Muslim power, Iraq and Iran, and the influence which those lands still exerted on the Seljuq successor-states in Syria and Palestine. Clearly, according to Ibn al-Athir at least, the Franks were only one part of Saladin's grandiose design for himself and his family. It must be remembered in this context that Saladin came of Kurdish, not of Syrian or Palestinian stock, and he had begun life further east. That heritage would naturally have predisposed him to focus on the Jazira, eastern Anatolia and Iran.

Saladin and *Jihad* in Modern Scholarship

A very favourable attitude to Saladin, based on the accounts of 'Imad al-Din, his private secretary, and Ibn Shaddad, his army judge, was adopted by the Western Orientalist scholars Lane-Poole and Gibb, who view Saladin as imbued with high moral standards and motivated by a desire to restore the *Shari'a* and to act in obedience to the caliph.[42]

As Gibb writes: 'For a brief but decisive moment, by sheer goodness and firmness of character, he raised Islam out of the rut of political demoralization.'[43]

A critical stance towards Saladin's *jihad* has also been adopted very vigorously by some modern scholars. They too point to the fact that many of Saladin's military activities were directed against rival fellow Muslims, not all of whom were 'heretics', although Saladin's propagandists might label them as such. Ehrenkreutz, for example, asks rhetorically whether Saladin would have been remembered for anything other than 'a record of unscrupulous schemes and campaigns aimed at personal and family aggrandizement', if he had died from his serious illness in 581/1185?[44]

Lyons and Jackson share this view and they point out that if Saladin had died he would have been remembered as 'a dynast who used Islam for his own purposes'.[45]

Köhler also cuts a swathe through the aura of ideological probity surrounding Saladin's activities. He stresses that Saladin made a number of treaties with the Christian states of Europe and the Levant.[46] Saladin and his official advisers used *jihad* propaganda to legitimise his power and to present their opponents as allies of infidels. In reality, Saladin had just as few scruples as Zengi or Nur al-Din about making alliances with the Franks. This contrasts markedly with Saladin's *jihad* claims which are proclaimed at length in letters written for him by his advisers and addressed to the caliph, as well as in monumental inscriptions.[47] Heavily loaded epithets of religious abuse are levelled against Saladin's political opponents (even though they are fellow Muslims). Al-Qadi al-Fadil, Saladin's scribe, labels them rebels and hypocrites.[48] Köhler concludes with the rhetorical flourish that the longer Saladin undertook nothing of significance

Figure 4.6 *Horse with crouching groom, inlaid metal ewer, thirteenth century, probably Iraq*

against the Franks, the more he depicted his struggles against his fellow Muslims as *jihad*. Köhler's interpretation of Saladin's career is shared to some extent at least by another German scholar, Möhring, who concludes that *jihad* was not the driving force in Saladin's career and that his ultimate objective was not the reconquest of Jerusalem but the revival of the entire Islamic empire under his leadership.[49]

Perhaps one can go too far in the demythologisation of Saladin as a true warrior of Islam. In the years leading up to Hattin and the recapture of Jerusalem, Saladin's rather low-key attempts at *jihad* against the Franks could be viewed as being a more prudent policy than an all-out attempt to crush them, since this could well have provoked a dangerous new major Crusading effort from Europe. It is, moreover, perhaps unfair to criticise Saladin for not devoting all his efforts after Hattin and the recapture of Jerusalem to the expulsion of the Franks. Saladin not only experienced the inevitable anti-climax which follows the attainment of a long-cherished goal – in his case, the conquest of Jerusalem – but had also to suffer the impact of the Third Crusade; thus his capture of the Holy City paradoxically brought him his greatest glory as well as many difficulties in the last and disappointing years of his life.

In any case, what mattered, after all, in the context of the revitalisation of the *jihad* ideal in the Levant was the *public* stance of the ruler. Here Saladin built on the foundations laid by Nur al-Din. Each step on Saladin's path towards the goal of recapturing Jerusalem was ratified retrospectively by the Sunni caliph at Baghdad. This was a 'legal fiction', yet Saladin punctiliously asked for the caliph's 'diploma of investiture' after each new conquest. After his capture of Hims in Syria from fellow Sunni Muslims he attempts to justify this as part of his progress in a just cause: 'Our move was not made in order to snatch a kingdom for ourselves but to set up the standard of *jihad*. These men had become enemies, preventing the accomplishment of our purpose with regard to this war.'[50]

Thus, whatever his personal motives may have been, and they almost certainly included personal and family aggrandisement, the importance of Saladin to a discussion of *jihad* propaganda is that every inch of the way he is shown as justifying his actions retrospectively in terms of *jihad*. The truth of Saladin's motivation can never be assessed and this is probably an irrelevant consideration anyway. What mattered was how his contemporaries – his fellow military commanders, his personal advisers and the religious classes – saw him and reacted to him. Thus it was possible for Saladin to evolve into a charismatic and highly successful *jihad* leader and to sustain the propaganda campaign which underpinned his two great successes, at Hattin and Jerusalem. One of his contemporaries, 'Abd al-Latif, sums up most eloquently Saladin's undoubted charisma: 'Men grieved for him as they grieve for prophets. I have seen no other ruler for whose death the people mourned, for he was loved by good and bad, Muslim and unbeliever alike.' (plate 4.7 and figure 4.7)[51]

Plate 4.7 *Mausoleum of
Saladin, medieval and
modern cenotaphs, Damascus,
Syria*

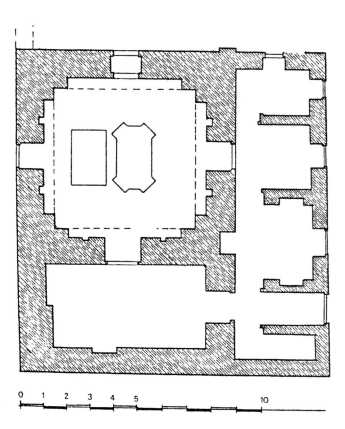

Figure 4.7 *Mausoleum of Saladin, plan, late twelfth century, Damascus, Syria*

Saladin and Jerusalem

The sources point clearly to the reconquest of Jerusalem by Saladin as the pinnacle of his career. This reconquest is portrayed as the realisation of a burning personal ambition on his part. By the time that Saladin had actually taken Jerusalem he retrospectively describes all his actions leading up to the event as having been entirely directed towards that end. It would appear too that public opinion had been so successfully mobilised by this point that only the capture of Jerusalem would be the ultimate proof both of his success and of his sincerity. Jerusalem was not strategically important but it had become the focus of Saladin's somewhat tardily launched *jihad* campaign, and the Holy City simply *had* to be taken.

A tone of profound emotional intensity and longing for Jerusalem is exploited to the full by Saladin's entourage and by the religious classes who gave him their wholehearted support. With Saladin's capture of the city in 583/1187, the theme of Jerusalem reaches its peak. Some sixty letters, a dozen poems and several sermons (*khutba*s) are dedicated to this triumphal moment. A celebratory ode (*qasida*) sent to

188

Saladin in Jerusalem from Cairo after his conquest of the Holy City proclaims:

> You have revivified the religion of Muhammad and its
>   props . . .
> You have kept in firm order the office of Holy War (*diwan
>   al-jihad*).[52]

Thus we see that this military conquest is invested with its full quota of religious significance; God's will has been done and the right religion has been reinstated in His Holy City.

The deep impact of the recapture of Jerusalem on the Muslim population of the Levant was recorded joyfully by contemporary chroniclers. According to 'Imad al-Din and Ibn Shaddad, Muslims gathered to witness Saladin's ceremonial entry into Jerusalem, to participate in the festivities and to start the *hajj* from there. Maximum propaganda benefit was derived from the chosen moment of entry into the city. Always astute and aware of the profound impact which his victorious entry into Jerusalem would make, Saladin waited to take possession of the city until Friday 27 Rajab 583/2 October 1187, the anniversary of the Prophet's Night Journey into Heaven. Ibn Shaddad exults in this felicitous timing: 'What a wonderful coincidence! God allowed the Muslims to take the city as a celebration of the anniversary of their Holy Prophet's Night Journey.'[53] This event was the climax of Saladin's career. At long last the paramount aim of his *jihad* had been achieved.

The role of Jerusalem in the Muslim Counter-Crusade, and the multifaceted image which Muslims by now had of the Holy City, is epitomised in the sermon (*khutba*) delivered by Ibn al-Zaki (d. 588/1192), a Shafi'ite preacher from Damascus, on the occasion of Saladin's entry into Jerusalem. Ibn al-Zaki was selected after a fierce competition as the best preacher amongst many to proclaim the victory sermon.[54] A lengthy quotation from the actual sermon is given by the medieval biographer Ibn Khallikan in his obituary notice of Ibn al-Zaki: 'Praise be unto God by whose aid Islam hath been exalted, and by whose might polytheism hath been humbled. . . . '[55]

Ibn Zaki reminds his hearers of the importance to the Muslims of Jerusalem, which has returned to the fold of Islam after being 'abused by the polytheists for nearly one hundred years'.[56]

In this sermon we see the encapsulation of the Muslim view of Jerusalem in the twelfth century. We can also identify here the elements which constituted the composite Islamic sanctity of the Holy City and which were already to be found in the Merits of Jerusalem literature:

> It was the dwelling-place of your father Abraham; the spot from which your blessed Prophet Muhammad mounted to Heaven; the *qibla* towards which you turned to pray at the commencement of

Islam, the abode of the prophets; the place visited by the saints; the cemetery of the apostles . . . it is the country where mankind will be assembled for judgement; the ground where the resurrection will take place. . . .[57]

According to Ibn al-Zaki, then, Jerusalem is the home of Abraham, the place of the ascension (*mi'raj*) of the Prophet Muhammad from the Dome of the Rock (plate 4.8) into the Heavens, the first *qibla* of Islam; thus the city possesses important connotations associated with the foundation of Islam. It is also the place where mankind will assemble to be judged on the Last Day.

In full-blown panegyric, Saladin's victories are compared by Ibn al-Zaki to the Prophet's achievements at Badr and the glorious days of the first conquests of Islam. Saladin is labelled amongst other lofty epithets 'the champion and protector of thy [God's] holy land' and the

Plate 4.8 *Dome of the Rock, exterior, 72/691–2 onwards, Jerusalem*

(Creswell Photographic Archive, Ashmolean Museum, Oxford, neg. C. 1406)

one 'who vanquished the adorers of the Cross'.[58] Indeed, Saladin is placed on the same level as the first caliphs of Islam who established an empire stretching from Spain to India. Speaking of Saladin, Ibn al-Zaki proclaims:

> You have renewed for Islam the glorious days of al-Qadisiyya, the battle of al-Yarmuk, the siege of Khaybar, and the impetuous attacks of Khalid b. al-Walid. May God grant you His best reward for the service you have rendered to His blessed Prophet Muhammad.[59]

Official letters, sent to the caliph and other rulers, celebrated the glorious victory in Jerusalem. 'Imad al-Din quotes part of a celebratory letter on Saladin's entry into the city, in which the importance of Jerusalem is explained:

> Jerusalem (al-Bayt al-Muqaddas), which God has exalted and ennobled and has made sacrosanct as He made His sanctuary sacrosanct and holy (at Mecca), is the dwelling place of the prophets who have been sent, the settlement of the saints and the righteous, the place of the heavenly ascent (*mi'raj*) of the chief of the prophets and the apostle of 'the Lord of the worlds'.[60]

Of course, the letters and sermons from this period are highly rhetorical in nature; they make inflated claims and are full of clichés and word-plays. What is the truth which lies beneath them? Clearly Saladin should be judged by his actions. Strategically Jerusalem was much less important than the coastline, but emotionally its significance was paramount. It had to be taken for Islam and Saladin became increasingly determined to take it. His biographers show him as being genuinely devoted to *jihad*. The importance of the *jihad* propaganda was that it served as a rallying cry, as a force for unification and religious commitment both for the public and in the ranks of the armies and military leaders. It was the ideal focus for a joint purpose which animated ruler, troops, *'ulama'* and the population at large, all of whom were infused with the shared aim of taking back Jerusalem from the infidel. Indeed, it is true to say that by 1187 the Muslims had acquired an ideological edge over the Franks, an edge which the Muslims had long lacked. Their armies were now regularly accompanied by the *'ulama'* who read to them and preached to them, and Saladin is presented as being personally and publicly committed to *jihad*. Once again, Islam had shown itself able to revitalise itself from within.

The importance of Jerusalem to Saladin is enshrined in a monumental inscription dated 587/1191 in his name on the Dome of Joseph (Qubbat Yusuf) on the Haram esplanade: 'the victorious king, the probity of this world and of [true] religion, the Sultan of Islam and of the Muslims, the servant of the two noble sanctuaries and of Jerusalem'.[61]

During the course of the Third Crusade, Saladin and Richard the Lionheart negotiated over Jerusalem. Richard vowed that he would never give up Jerusalem, to which Saladin's response was unequivocal:

> Jerusalem is to us as it is to you. It is even more important for us, since it is the site of our Prophet's nocturnal journey and the place where the people will assemble on the Day of Judgement. Do not imagine therefore that we can waver in this regard.[62]

Saladin's devotion to Jerusalem is epitomised in the sources by their accounts of his personal and practical involvement in building up its fortifications (plates 4.9–4.10):

> He was then (589/1193) concerned with building walls and digging trenches round Jerusalem. He took charge of it himself and even carried stones on his own shoulders, so that all, rich and poor, strong and weak, followed his example, including even the scribe 'Imad al-Din and the Qadi al-Fadil.[63]

Plate 4.9 City walls from within, various periods from antiquity onwards, Jerusalem

(Creswell Photographic Archive, Ashmolean Museum, Oxford, neg. C. 4969)

Nur al-Din and Saladin – a Comparison

Both Nur al-Din and Saladin are treated as exemplary models by medieval Muslim historians,[64] but even in Saladin's own time a comparison was made between him and his illustrious predecessor, Nur al-Din. According to 'Imad al-Din al-Isfahani, Nur al-Din and Saladin were both meritorious and he views Saladin as the true heir of Nur al-Din. In his judgement, however, Saladin, is the greater of the two: 'He modelled himself on all the qualities of Nur al-Din . . . He studied from him the principles of virtue, and then in his own days surpassed him in them.'[65]

Writing in the Ayyubid period, Abu Shama (d. 665/1258) yearns for a rediscovery of religious unity and *jihad*. His historical work is entitled *The Book of the Two Gardens* (*Kitab al-rawdatayn*); this romantic title is a reference to the two reigns of Nur al-Din and Saladin. Whilst he values both these great men, he also pronounces that 'Saladin was greater in *jihad*'.[66] The word *rawda*, especially in this highly charged religious atmosphere, also has paradisal connotations, and these may be deliberately alluded to here. Abu Shama underlines Saladin's

Plate 4.10 *City walls, exterior with view of the snow-covered city behind, various periods from antiquity onwards, Jerusalem*

(Creswell Photographic Archive, Ashmolean Museum, Oxford, neg. C. 1456)

superiority over Nur al-Din by stressing that Saladin ruled more territories, and above all that it was he who conquered the Holy Land.[67]

Recent research suggests that it is possible that the other contemporary biographer of Saladin, Ibn Shaddad, may have written his biography of Saladin as a response to a work of Ibn al-Athir, entitled *The Splendid Chronicle of the Atabegs of Mosul (Al-bahir fi tarikh atabakat al-Mawsil)*, half of which is devoted to eulogising the deeds of Nur al-Din. Nur al-Din is shown in this work as the ideal ruler and *mujahid*, ascetic, pious and just. Holt argues that Ibn Shaddad in his turn, when writing his biography of Saladin, was doing so not just to gratify his Ayyubid patrons, the family of Saladin, but also to better the achievements of Ibn al-Athir. Furthermore, he wished to legitimise his master's usurpation of the territories of the family of Nur al-Din and the continuation of Ayyubid rule after Saladin's death in 1193.[68]

Regardless of the competitive aspect in the composition of the biographies of Nur al-Din and Saladin, so shrewdly analysed by Holt, it remains indisputable that both these leaders were military chiefs with no Islamic right to rule. They had come to power through their military strength. Neither of them, then, fitted the requirements of the Shari'a. Both felt the need for legitimisation from the caliph for their seizure of territories held by other Muslim princes. It is, moreover, significant that their rival biographers make great efforts to portray their masters as pious prosecutors of the *jihad* and as embodying the virtues of the ideal *mujahid*, even when the evidence points unmistakably in rather different directions.

In general, when dealing with the Islamic sources, it is difficult to speak with confidence about the *motives* of the protagonists in the Counter-Crusade. The sources were often written later than the events they describe and they display obvious partiality. This is true of Nur al-Din, who is regularly eulogised in the Islamic sources, and even more so of Saladin. As Richards points out, ambition, both personal and familial, can co-exist with a moral and religious purpose.[69] Certainly it is worth mentioning that, unlike Saladin, Nur al-Din did not have the obvious advantages of two contemporary image-makers to mould his career in the way they wished to present it. Ibn al-Athir, writing two generations or so later for the court circle of the successors of Nur al-Din, is the writer whose role most resembles that of a panegyrical biographer for Nur al-Din. Nevertheless, he is in some respects at a critical disadvantage because of the time lapse between himself and his subject.

Saladin's biographers, for their part, make it clear underneath their rhetoric that their master was, in their eyes at least, capable of inspiring great loyalty amongst his advisers and soldiers, many of whom would have given their lives for him, and their accounts of his charismatic personal qualities, chivalry and generosity are echoed in the Western Crusader chronicles, which lie outside the remit of this

Figure 4.8 *Rabi' ibn 'Adnan making a night attack,* Varqa va Gulshah *('Varqa and Gulshah'), c. 1250, Turkey*

book. Together, they formed the basis of the legend of Saladin in later medieval Europe which the Muslims were eventually to reclaim as their own in the nineteenth and twentieth centuries. Saladin's moral superiority over his contemporary peers, both Muslim and Christian, was acknowledged in his own lifetime by his enemies, the Crusaders; his image, even amidst the anti-Muslim bigotry of the European Middle Ages, remained unsullied, even romanticised, and that at a time when Europe's attitude towards Islam was a sorry mixture of ignorance and hostility.

As for Nur al-Din, he was deprived of the ultimate prize of Jerusalem. Without it his achievements remain less dramatic than those of Saladin; but it was through the career of Nur al-Din that the foundations of a fully-fledged *jihad* programme were established. Saladin would not have attained his successes had Nur al-Din not prepared the way.

Confronted by the Crusaders, and by the ideological challenge which they represented, the Muslims of the twelfth century were able gradually to restore the notion of *jihad* from the state of somnolence into which it had fallen and thus to permit it to assume to the full the role that the theoreticians of Islamic law had given it in their books. The real turning-point was the careers of Nur al-Din and Saladin. The one cannot be divorced from the other; they form a continuum in this respect. During their periods in power, Syria and an increasing number of the territories around it were held under strong one-man rule for nearly fifty years. This crucial half-century enabled the Muslims to enjoy a much greater sense of cohesion and unity and to regain Jerusalem from the Franks, who noticeably lacked such continuity of leadership.

Clearly, Muslim military leaders and their entourage learned in this crucial period how to use a full range of propaganda tools in order to work towards Muslim reunification and Muslim corporate effort against the Franks. Jerusalem in these decades became the supreme focus of Muslim efforts and its *Muslim* identity was elaborated and appreciated to the full. After the conquest of Jerusalem, it is perhaps understandable that Saladin's emotional commitment to *jihad* faltered. Ibn Zaki urges the faithful to continue to prosecute the *jihad*, and to take back the rest of the Holy Land: 'Maintain the Holy War; it is the best means which you have of serving God, the most noble occupation of your lives.'[70] But no comparable focus for the emotions generated by *jihad* presented itself to Saladin after Jerusalem.

A Historical Introduction to the Ayyubid Period, 589–647/1193–1249

In a recent overview, the American scholar Humphreys describes the relations between the Muslim rulers of the Levant and the Crusader states after the death of Saladin as 'something of a puzzle'. Certainly he and others have done much to solve this puzzle,[71] as well as to

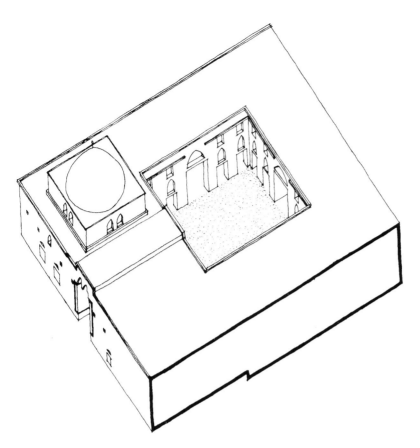

Figure 4.9 *Madrasa al-'Adiliyya, perspectival view, 619/1223, Damascus, Syria*

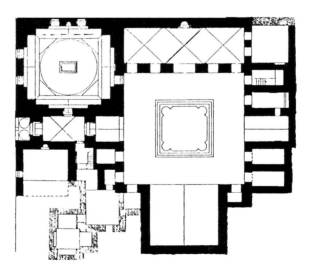

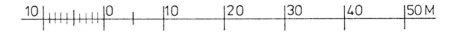

196

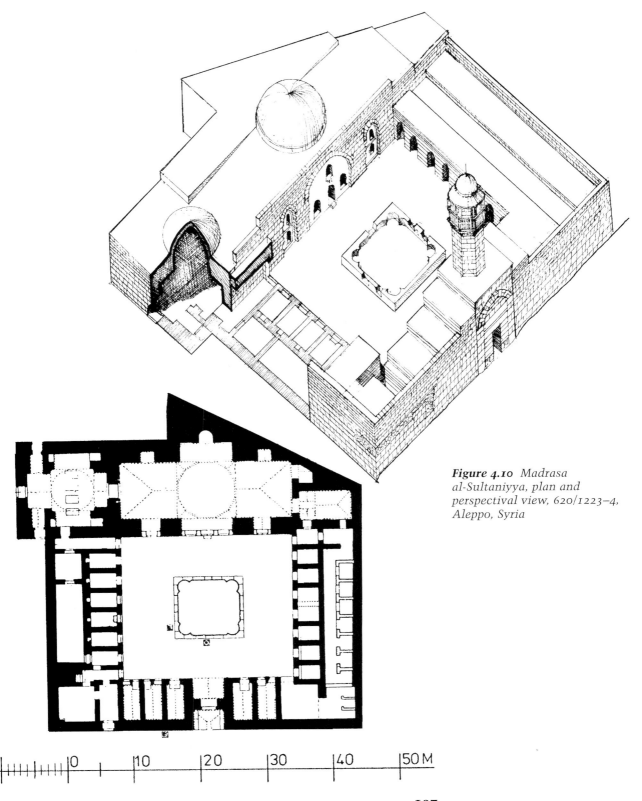

Figure 4.10 Madrasa
al-Sultaniyya, plan and
perspectival view, 620/1223–4,
Aleppo, Syria

|0 |0 |10 |20 |30 |40 |50 M

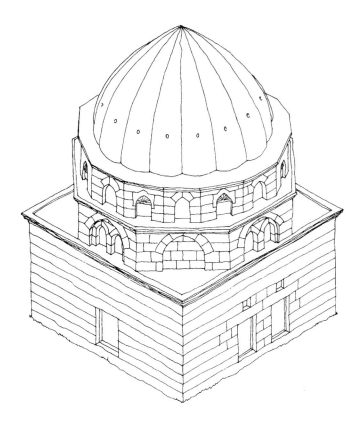

Figure 4.11 *Madrasa al-Rukniyya* extra muros, *plan and perspectival view, 621/1224–5, Damascus, Syria*

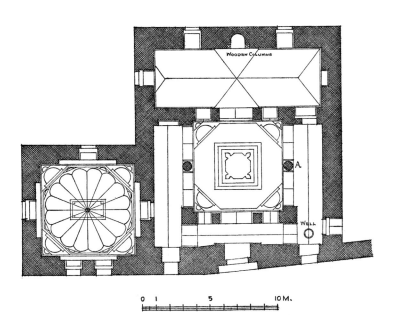

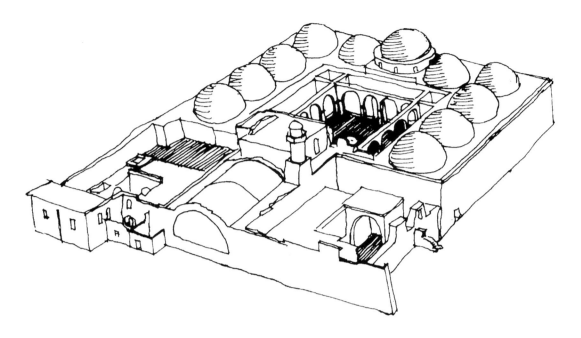

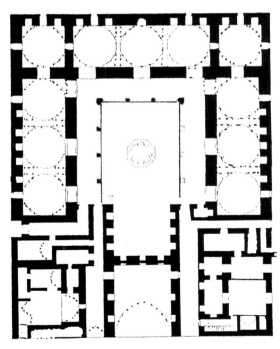

Figure 4.12 Complex of
al-Firdaws, plan and
perspectival sketch,
633/1235–6, Aleppo, Syria

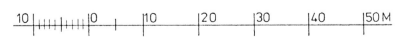

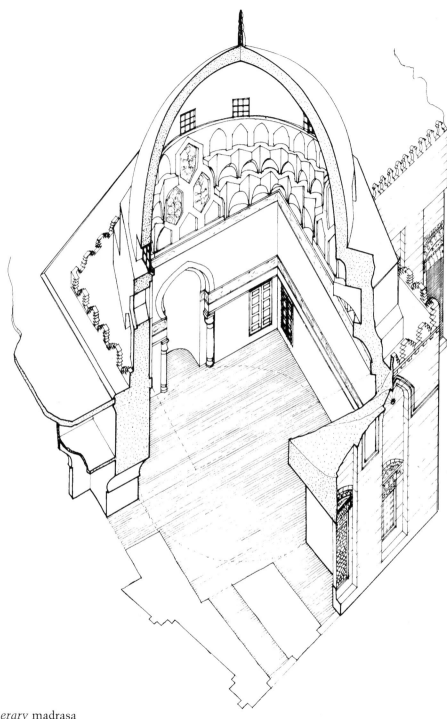

Figure 4.13 *Funerary* madrasa
*of al-Salih Najm al-Din
Ayyub, perspectival view,
641–8/1243–50, Cairo, Egypt*

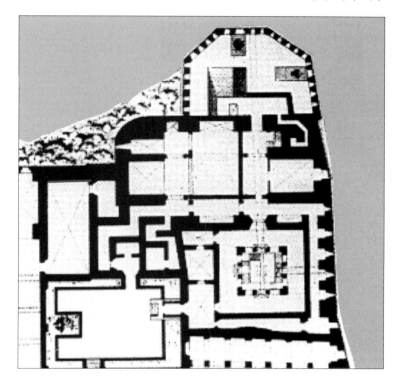

Figure 4.14 *Palace of al-Salih Najm al-Din Ayyub, plan, 638/1240–1, Cairo, Egypt*

cast light on the 'apparently vacillating, shifting Muslim policies towards the Crusader states during the decades between 1193 and 1291'.[72]

After Saladin's death in 589/1193 his territories were ruled by members of his own family, a dynasty which has come to be known as the Ayyubids. Ayyubid rule, which lasted until the *coup d'état* by the Mamluks in 647/1249, witnessed great dissension within the Ayyubid family and often prolonged periods of peace with the Franks. The Ayyubid 'state' can be described rather as 'a confederation of autonomous appanages or principalities'.[73]

Internally, Saladin's successors followed the age-old principle of division of territories and confederate rule which had prevailed further east under their predecessors, the Buyids and the Seljuqs. For most of the period from 1193 to 1250 there were six Ayyubid principalities. Three Ayyubid rulers – al-'Adil, Saladin's brother (596–615/1200–18), al-Kamil (615–35/1218–38) and al-Salih (637–47/1240–9) – stand out as having succeeded in imposing their control over their relatives as senior family members. Otherwise, the individual Ayyubid rulers held small parcels of territory in Syria, the Jazira (plates 4.11, 4.12) and Egypt and were frequently in conflict with each other over the ownership of these territories. As Holt points out, Saladin was an exception in the Ayyubid family with his ability to hold his relatives together and to create corporate loyalty amongst them.[74]

Plate 4.11 Unidentified building,
throne niche of stone with
representations of the royal khassakiyya
corps, the personal mamluks of the
Ayyubid ruler, c. 1220–30,
Gu'-Kummet, Sinjar, Iraq

Plate 4.12 Unidentified building, throne niche of stone with representations of the royal khassakiyya *corps, the personal* mamluks *of the Ayyubid ruler, c. 1220-30, Gu'-Kummet, Sinjar, Iraq*

In their relations with the Franks, individual members of the Ayyubid family sought peace rather than war. The Ayyubid period witnessed the full integration of the Franks as local Levantine rulers. The Ayyubid rulers made alliances with them, or fought both against them and on their side.

In the 1240s the Ayyubid ruler al-Salih Isma'il handed over to the Franks a number of the castles in Galilee and southern Lebanon which Saladin had conquered: this initiative on the part of al-Salih Isma'il was prompted by his desire for Frankish support against his nephew al-Salih Ayyub. The Ayyubids strove to build up commercial links with the Italian maritime states to make money – and peace. Great wealth came to the Ayyubids from Levantine ports, such as Jaffa, Acre and Tyre. They feared that any serious disturbance in the 'Levantine peace' could provoke the launching of yet another Crusade from western Europe. Conciliation with the Franks was therefore preferable to confrontation. A typical example of this approach was al-Kamil's opting for a treaty with the Franks in 618/1221 rather than conquering Damietta. The contemporary chronicler Ibn Wasil mentions that al-Kamil realised that if the kings of the Franks in Europe and the Pope should come to hear of any aggression on his part, even stronger Frankish reinforcements would be sent against Egypt.[75] Humphreys argues convincingly that the Ayyubids were terrified of the Franks who 'just kept coming back'.[76]

Thus the Ayyubids allowed the emotionally charged atmosphere which had peaked with the conquest of Jerusalem to relax in favour of *détente* with the Franks, and whilst religious rhetoric still spoke in grandiose terms about *jihad*, this Islamic discourse bore little relation to the political realities of the Ayyubid period.

In this period Jerusalem was even handed back to the Franks for a while – a political accommodation unthinkable in the time of Saladin – and later sacked by the Khwarazmians from Central Asia, who were at least nominally Muslims. These two events, following relatively close on each other within a bare half-century of Saladin's recapture of Jerusalem, are a silent commentary on the ephemeral nature of extreme religious fervour.

Jihad in the Ayyubid Period: A Hollow Sham?

Ibn al-Athir complains bitterly that *jihad* has disappeared in his own time:

> Amongst the rulers of Islam we see not one who desires to wage *jihad* or aid . . . religion. Each one devotes himself to his pastimes and amusements and to wronging his flock. This is more dreadful to me than the enemy.[77]

Certainly the evidence points to the *Zeitgeist* of the post-Saladin era as being one of *détente* rather than *jihad*; indeed, the Islamic sources which catalogue the events of this period dwell much more on inter-familial Ayyubid strife than on the conflict with the Franks. This suggests that the lack of interest in *jihad* may even have extended to some members of the learned classes.

The old alliance between the religious classes and the military leadership which had been forged so successfully under Nur al-Din and Saladin was in fact still present in certain cities in Syria in the Ayyubid period (see plates 4.13, 4.14, 4.15, 4.16); but it had lost its edge. Whilst the propagandists and poets of the Ayyubids honoured them with *jihad* titles, their commitment to *jihad* against the Franks

Plate 4.13 *Great Mosque, minaret, originally dated 529/1134–5, rebuilt after its destruction in 1982, Hama, Syria*

Plate 4.16 *Great Mosque, interior arcades and vaults (1923 photograph), probably twelfth–thirteenth centuries, Hama, Syria*

(Creswell Photographic Archive, Ashmolean Museum, Oxford, neg. C. 6066)

Plate 4.17 Unidentified
building, marble intarsia
work, twelfth century, Mosul,
Iraq

Plate 4.18 *Unidentified building, marble intarsia work, twelfth century, Mosul, Iraq*

Figure 4.15 Ruler and two dragons, apotropaic sculpture, Talisman Gate, 618/1221, Baghdad, Iraq

But *jihad* could and was interpreted more widely than fighting the infidel on the borders of Islam (figure 4.15). We have already stressed the spiritual dimensions of *jihad* for individual Muslims and especially the military leaders. There were other activities too which formed part of the overall *jihad* impulse from the period of Nur al-Din onwards. It was understood that the ruler who fought *jihad* did so within his realm as well as outside it: it was his pious duty to combat heresy and laxity of religious practice and to promote 'sound religion' and Islamic justice. In this respect, the Ayyubid princes' record is more impressive. They were responsible for the founding of sixty-three religious colleges (*madrasa*s) in Damascus alone (figures 4.9–4.12, 4.16). The Jazira too saw an outburst of building activity in this period (plates 4.17–4.25; cf. plates 4.2–4.6, 4.11–4.12 and figure 4.3).[84]

The Fate of Jerusalem in the Ayyubid Period

The fate of Jerusalem in the Ayyubid period is a clear illustration of the dynasty's pragmatic attitude to the Franks, and despite their loud protestations the religious classes could do nothing.

Some of the Ayyubid rulers seem to have shared Saladin's reverence for Jerusalem and its sacred places and his desire to contribute towards its religious life by endowing Islamic monuments. Saladin's son, al-Afdal (d. 622/1225), endowed a religious college (*al-Madrasa*

Plate 4.19 *Jami' al-Nuri, inscription on* mihrab *capital with the name of Taqi al-Din Mahmud, Ayyubid prince of Hama between 626/1228 and 642/1243, Hama, Syria*

Plate 4.24 City gate, between
631/1233–4 and 657/1259,
'Amadiyya, Iraq

Plate 4.25 *Mashhad 'Awn al-Din, carved alabaster portal, between 631/1233–4 and 657/1259, Mosul, Iraq*

The fact of the matter was that strategically Jerusalem was not crucial to Ayyubid rulers whose power base was in Egypt or Syria. Jerusalem always had its political price so long as the Franks still desired to possess it. However much individual Ayyubid rulers may have embellished the city of Jerusalem with new monuments and pious foundations, in the end this counted for less than political expediency.

Predictably there was widespread indignation and outrage amongst Muslims at al-Kamil's handing over of Jerusalem to Frederick. For the year 626/1229, the chronicler Sibt b. al-Jawzi writes: 'In it [this year] al-Kamil gave Jerusalem to the emperor... The news of the handing over of Jerusalem to the Franks arrived and all hell broke loose in all the lands of Islam.'[92]

Sibt b. al-Jawzi, himself a renowned preacher, then reports that the

Plate 4.26 *Aqsa Mosque, facade showing both the central gable (formerly bearing Fatimid inscription, second half of eleventh century), and Ayyubid porch (note incorporation of Frankish elements, perhaps as references to Muslim victory), 615/1218–19, Jerusalem*

(Creswell Photographic Archive, Ashmolean Museum, Oxford, neg. C. 4993)

Ayyubid ruler of Damascus, al-Malik Da'ud, asked him to speak in the Great Mosque about what had happened to Jerusalem and he waxed lyrical about the recent indignities the city had suffered.[93] Apart from this chronicler and Ibn Wasil, another contemporary witness, the other Islamic sources (probably out of justified feelings of corporate shame) tend to gloss over this rather ignominious episode.[94]

The fortunes of Jerusalem went from bad to worse. The city remained in Frankish hands until after al-Kamil's death in 635/1238. It then reverted briefly to Ayyubid control in 636/1239 under al-Nasir Da'ud, the ruler of Kerak, but again as a result of internal rivalries amongst the Ayyubids it was handed back to the Franks in 641/1243–4 in exchange for the promise of Frankish help to al-Nasir Da'ud and his allies against the Ayyubid ruler in Egypt, al-Malik al-Salih Ayyub.[95] Thus once again the Muslim world suffered the humiliation of the Dome of the Rock being in the possession of the Franks.[96] Truly Saladin and his propagandists must have turned in their graves at this betrayal.

Jerusalem's fortunes reached their lowest ebb in 642/1244. In order to destroy his enemies, the Ayyubid sultan Najm al-Din Ayyub called in the Khwarazmians, dispossessed nomadic troops (originally Kipchak Turks) who had been forced westwards from their Central Asian homeland, displaced by the invasions of the Mongols. The Khwarazmians fell upon Syria and Palestine and sacked Jerusalem in Rabi' I 642/August 1244,[97] slaughtering the Christians and desecrating the Holy Sepulcre and other Christian churches. Thereafter, in an alliance typical of the time, in Jumada I 642/October 1244, the Khwarazmians and the Egyptian Ayyubids fought at Harbiyya against the Syrian Ayyubids who had joined forces with the Crusaders, an encounter in which the Khwarazmian–Ayyubid coalition emerged victorious.

Sibt b. al-Jawzi is outraged by this Muslim–Frankish collaboration and yearns for the halcyon days of Islamic unity. Bemoaning the fact that Muslim troops fought under the banners of the Franks, with crosses over their heads, ministered to by Christian priests, he continues: 'It was a calamitous day, the like of which had not happened in [early] Islam nor in the time of Nur al-Din and Saladin.'[98]

Jerusalem henceforth was to be ruled from Egypt.[99] The hard-headed attitude of the later Ayyubids towards Jerusalem and their preference for Egypt as a power base continued until the very end of the dynasty. Indeed, al-Salih Ayyub advised his son Turanshah, the last Ayyubid sultan of Egypt: 'If they [the Franks] demand the coast and Jerusalem from you, give them these places without delay on condition that they have no foothold in Egypt.'[100]

This dismal picture of Ayyubid *Realpolitik* coupled with indifference to *jihad* and the fate of Jerusalem was occasionally modified by individual Ayyubid rulers in Syria. The alliance between the religious classes in the Ayyubid period and the military leadership remained stronger there than in Palestine. The modern scholars Sivan and

Figure 4.18
(above and opposite)
Foot soldiers, stone relief,
Bab al-'Amadiyya, between
631/1233 and 657/1259, Iraq

Pouzet argue that two Ayyubid princes, al-Mu'azzam 'Isa and his son al-Nasir Da'ud, showed a real spirit of *jihad*, thus salvaging the reputation of the dynasty at least to some extent.[101] The city of Damascus and especially its Hanbalite quarter, al-Salihiyya, remained a milieu impregnated with the spirit of *jihad*. Here were produced at least two treaties on *jihad* in the Ayyubid period, one by Ibn Qudama (d. 620/1223) and the other by Diya' al-Din al-Maqdisi (d. 643/1245).

Generally speaking, however, the impulse of the religious classes towards the propagation of *jihad* against the Franks, which had sustained and strengthened Saladin's activities – certainly in the years immediately preceding the reconquest of Jerusalem – was an embarrassment rather than a stimulus to these sultans. They preferred pragmatism to piety and worked towards an accommodation with the Franks. Occasionally the sources refer to explicit pressure from the religious classes aimed at making the ruler prosecute *jihad*. One example is an episode which occurred as early as 601/1204, when Ibn Qudama openly accused the Ayyubid sultan al-'Adil of occupying himself with wars against his fellow Muslims and of neglecting the fight against the infidel.[102]

The Power of the Preacher to Rouse the Populace to *Jihad*

The contemporary chronicler Sibt b. al-Jawzi describes the prelude to a military campaign conducted by the Ayyubid prince al-Mu'azzam 'Isa in the year 607/1210–11. The author himself was one of the greatest preachers of the day and he used his skills to mobilise the population on behalf of the ruler:

> I sat in the congregational mosque on Saturday 5 Rabi 'I and the [throng of] people stretched from the gate of the shrine of Zayn al-'Abidin to the gate of al-Natifanin and the gate of the clocks. The [number of people] standing in the courtyard[103] was more than what would fill the Damascus mosque [for the Friday prayer]. They estimated 30,000 [people] and it was a day the like of which had not been seen in Damascus or anywhere else.

Such was his fame as a preacher that he had drawn crowds more numerous than those who came to pray on Fridays: certainly, the Great Mosque in Damascus could house a vast number of worshippers.[104]

Sibt b. al-Jawzi relates that many strands of hair had come into his possession and he recalled a story of a woman who had cut her hair and sent it to him, saying: 'Make it into a hobble for your horse in the path of God.'

This example of devotional piety shows women's participation in the corporate *jihad* activities of the community and is used to powerful effect in the rest of the story told by Sibt b. al-Jawzi:

> So I made fetters and hobbles for the horses of the *jihad* warriors

(*mujahidun*) from the hairs which had come into my possession. When I climbed into the pulpit, I ordered them to be brought and they were put round the men's necks. There were 300 fetters. When the people saw them they let out a great cry and cut [their hair] likewise.[105]

Scenes like this demonstrate the power of the eloquent preacher to move the citizens to join the *jihad*.

Occasionally in the Ayyubid period a serious external crisis could cause the rulers to act in concert against the Franks. The fall of Damietta in 616/1219 was one such rare occurrence when the Ayyubids showed solidarity. On this occasion Sibt b. al-Jawzi read out in the Great Mosque in Damascus a letter which al-Mu'azzam 'Isa had written to him with the aim of rousing the people to fight *jihad*.[106]

An Overview of *Jihad* in the Ayyubid Period

The conflicting pressures of political expediency and *jihad* against the Franks, so apparent in the Ayyubid period, had, of course, manifested themselves since the very beginning of the Crusades. Yet the conduct of the Ayyubids – their lacklustre performance in *jihad* and their handing back of Jerusalem to the Franks – was castigated at the time and has since been roundly condemned as a betrayal of the aims and achievements of their illustrious predecessor Saladin.

It is worth examining whether this is a just assessment. The emphasis on *jihad* which was the hallmark of Saladin's later years until he captured Jerusalem should probably be viewed as an exception, a rare emotional peak for the Muslims, even within the context of his own career. For most of his adult life Saladin operated within the usual contemporary framework of shifting alliances, truces and petty territorial warfare, as other rulers and military barons did. This *modus operandi* was consistently the norm for the later Ayyubids too. As we have seen, it was in Saladin's career, and perhaps partially also as a result of his charismatic personality, that the religious classes managed to carry with them the military leadership and the populace at large in a rare and focused campaign against the Franks. For a brief while *jihad* transcended the rhetoric of the propagandists and realised its full potential for the Muslims of Syria and Palestine in the conquest of Jerusalem. For the later Ayyubids, however, Jerusalem was a dispensable commodity: occasionally it could be the focus of displays of public piety on their part but more frequently it would fall victim to their hard-headed military realism.

Various factors contributed to the lack of a single-minded focus by the Ayyubids on *jihad* against the Franks. They were enthusiastic about the benefits of trade with the Franks and the wider world, using the Frankish ports. A common interest in the local defence of Syria and Palestine no doubt motivated both Ayyubids and Franks to

Figure 4.19 *Horseman, glazed ceramic bowl, thirteenth century, Aleppo region, Syria*

unite on occasion against external aggressors, be they the Khwarazmians, Franks from Europe or even Ayyubid rivals from Egypt. Certainly, in the early Ayyubid period, in the years immediately following Saladin's death, there must have been an inevitable emotional anticlimax after the recapture of Jerusalem. Once Saladin, the charismatic military leader, had gone and the perfect focus provided for *jihad* in Saladin's time, namely that of the recapture of Jerusalem, had disappeared, there was no longer a common will amongst the Ayyubid elite to finish off the job and remove the Franks definitively. Each Ayyubid ruler within the confederacy could adopt his own negotiating position with the Franks.[107] In the time-honoured way of their ancestors the individual Ayyubids defended their portion of territory against all comers, Muslim or Frank, and united against outsiders with other local rulers in times of external crisis.[108]

The Mamluk Period until the Fall of Acre, 648–690/1250–1291

Saladin did not, of course, oust the Crusaders definitively from the Near East. Acre and most of the Syrian coast remained in Crusader hands for another century and it was left to the Mamluk dynasty of Egypt, carrying on the traditions of Saladin's family, to achieve the fall of Acre in 690/1291 and thereby to remove the Crusader presence once and for all from Muslim territory. *Jihad* played an important part in underpinning and inspiring the Mamluk military achievement.

With the accession of the Mamluks in 648/1250 a new dynasty was established which was to survive until the Ottoman conquest of Egypt in 922/1516–17. The new rulers, the commanders of Mamluk regiments, were well equipped for the difficult decades ahead. Indeed, the early Mamluk period witnessed the last great Mongol attacks on the Middle East as well as continuing Crusading activity and occupation. The Mongol forces under Hülegü swept through Syria and threatened Egypt. The Mamluk army under the command of the future sultan Baybars confronted a depleted Mongol army now led by Kitbogha Noyan and defeated them at the battle of ʿAyn Jalut in Ramadan 658/September 1260. Shortly afterwards, in a bloody *coup*

Figure 4.20 Animated inscription on candlestick of Kitbugha, inlaid metal, early 1290s, probably Egypt

225

d'état which put an end to the early instability at the heart of the Mamluk state, Baybars claimed the sultanate for himself. Under the firm hand of Baybars, the Mamluk state wiped out the Ayyubids in Egypt, extended its power towards Syria and continued to tackle the much-dreaded Mongols from the east. The Mamluks' military successes against the Mongols went side by side with vigorous attempts to remove the Franks from Muslim soil. Unlike their predecessors the Ayyubids, the Mamluk sultans had to contend with the Mongols on their very doorstep and this moulded their international policies in a very significant way. As Berkey argues:

> The European Crusaders were in some ways the least of the problems faced by contemporary Muslims: more threatening to the social and political order were the repeated waves of Turkic and Mongol invasion and settlement, culminating in the continual stream of immigrating Mamluks themselves.[109]

An enthusiastic and romanticised view of the Mamluks is given by the famous North African Muslim historian Ibn Khaldun (d. 808/1406) who describes them as possessing:

> the firm resolve of true believers and yet with nomadic virtues unsullied by debased nature, unadulterated with the filth of pleasure, undefiled by the ways of civilized living, and with their ardour unbroken by the profusion of luxury.[110]

Despite this romanticisation of 'nomadic peoples', presaging the ideal of the Noble Savage, Ibn Khaldun's praise for the way in which the Mamluks revitalised the Islamic Near East is in many ways justified. Ruling from Cairo rather than Syria and holding themselves formally aloof from the indigenous peoples whom they ruled, the Mamluks formed a highly centralised state, normally known in the Arabic sources as the 'state of the Turks' (*dawlat al-Atrak*), which showed remarkable cohesion and could mount a unified front against the Crusaders. Although they had usurped power, their victories against both Mongols and Franks enhanced their prestige.

Under Baybars, the Mamluk state inaugurated an era of 'increasing aggression' against the Franks.[111] The religious classes who wrote their history present a curiously impenetrable, uniform and generally favourable image of this dynasty. But this favourable image seems to hold true. Abroad, the Mamluk sultans were seen as the supreme warriors of *jihad*, whilst inside the state they dispensed true justice and eradicated rebellion and heresy. They were interested in the public face of religion and readily donned the mantle of leaders of the Sunni world. They patronised the religious classes, performed the pilgrimage and built many monuments in the service of Islam, not just for political reasons but out of genuine interest and piety (plate 4.27). Many members of the Mamluk military cadres were

Figure 4.21 *Blazons on Mamluk coins, thirteenth–fifteenth centuries, Egypt and Syria*

actually religious scholars in their own right. Berkey argues convincingly that Islam had never been a static and monolithic entity and that the Mamluks helped to mould from within the Islam of their own day[112] – religion, civilisation and society – more than has previously been recognised.

The Mamluks were at pains to have their activities legitimised and prosecuted *jihad* with a public display of vigour and determination. Some of the spiritual inheritance of the 'Abbasid caliphate of Baghdad which had been snuffed out by the Mongols in 656/1258 was revived by the establishment of a puppet 'Abbasid caliphate in Cairo in 659/1261. This move was typical of the ostentatious piety of the new dynasty, as was the reinvigorated ideal of *jihad*, with a greater emphasis on the military aspects of that concept – war against the infidel.

Baybars was the key figure who began the process of finally eradicating the Frankish presence from the Near East. He began a series of successful campaigns in the 1260s. Pressures from the new enemy, the Mongols, and the continuing presence of the Franks formed a powerful focus for channelling the energies of the new dynasty.

The Career of Baybars, 648–676/1260–1277

Whilst Baybars' military skills were undoubtedly remarkable, he was also favoured by unusually good luck in the timing of his accession. The Mongols were disunited after their withdrawal from Syria in 1260 and in his wars against the Franks he was able to utilise the numerous Muslim refugees who poured into Syria and Egypt from Iraq, still held by the Mongols. Nevertheless Baybars was a brilliant and ruthless sultan and an unusually energetic military leader who stayed in power for a long time. His numerous campaigns were extremely well planned. Before taking on the Franks, Baybars aimed at extinguishing all remaining opposition to his overall authority on the part of the Ayyubid princes. In other words, in a familiar pattern, he wished to achieve Muslim unity in Egypt and Syria and to secure his power base.

In 663/1265 he began a series of offensives against the Franks which continued until 670/1271. In these years important Frankish citadels fell into Muslim hands and Antioch, which had been ruled uninterruptedly by the Franks since 1097, was also conquered. At the same time Baybars fought against the pagan Mongols,[113] Christians in Little Armenia, fellow Muslims in Anatolia and Isma'ili 'heretics'. Out of a total of thirty-eight campaigns which he led into Syria, however, twenty-one were conducted against the Franks, and by the time of his death in 676/1277 he had inflicted very serious damage on them. His aim may be seen primarily as defensive – to secure the frontiers of the Mamluk state against the infidels from both east and west. His activities against the Franks formed a key part of the image created of him by his propagandists, that of a mighty warrior of *jihad*

Figure 4.22 *Blazons on Mamluk coins, thirteenth–fifteenth centuries, Egypt and Syria*

Figure 4.23 Part of a militantly Shi'ite verse inscription, Mamluk silver-inlaid bowl, probably early fourteenth century, Syria (?)

(Creswell Photographic Archive, Ashmolean Museum, Oxford, neg. C. 6067)

Plate 4.27 *Great Mosque, Mamluk minaret (1923 photograph), probably fourteenth century, Hama, Syria*

and defender of the Islamic world. His legendary exploits lived on in the popular folk epic *Sirat Baybars*.

The *Jihad* Titulature of the Mamluks – Evidence of Monumental Inscriptions and Chancellery Documents

Predictably enough, the Mamluk sultans, with their military achievements against the infidel, Christian Frank and pagan Mongol alike, were accorded grandiloquent *jihad* titles by their epigraphers and chroniclers.

In three inscriptions dated Dhu'l-hijja 664/September 1266 on a mausoleum in Hims in Syria, Baybars is described in the most glowing terms as a supreme *jihad* warrior. One of them calls him:

> The sultan, the victorious prince, the pillar of the world and religion, the sultan of Islam and the Muslims, the killer of infidels and polytheists, the tamer of rebels and heretics, the reviver of justice in the two worlds, the possessor of the two seas, the lord of the two *qibla*s, the servant of the two noble sanctuaries, the heir of the kingdom, the sultan of the Arabs and the Persians and the Turks, the Alexander of the age, the lord of the fortunate conjunction, Baybars al-Salihi, the associate of the Commander of the Faithful.[114]

The inscription also records that it was engraved 'on the occasion of his [Baybars] passing through [Hims] to fight (*ghaza*) in the land of Sis [Armenia]'.[115]

This inscription is a valuable contemporary historical document. The occasion is right: Baybars is on his way to conduct *jihad* against the Christians of Armenia. The titulature is elaborate; in it Baybars is accorded the role of defender of Islam, just ruler and fighter against the infidel. The careful antithetical patterning of the words and the use of such devices as antiphonal pairing of words, or rhymed endings, adds a formal and sonorous note to these ceremonial, proclamatory words. Baybars is shown to be the defender of the most holy sanctuaries of Islam in the Hijaz. Like Tamerlane after him, Baybars is called the Alexander of the age, the one favoured by auspicious astrological signs to lead the whole Muslim world – Arab, Persian, Turk. Such fanciful rhetoric (the Mamluks did not and never would rule in the east) is accompanied by a clear view of the publicity value of the location of the inscription. This is no ordinary monument on which to carve an inscription as Baybars and his army passed through Hims. After all, this is the mausoleum of the most famous of all Arab Muslim generals, 'the Sword of Islam, the Companion of the Messenger of God, Khalid b. al-Walid', the great architect of the first Muslim conquests in the seventh century. Thus Baybars is seen by his propagandists as forging a lasting link between the glorious days of Islam and his own achievements on behalf of the faith.

Figure 4.24 Soldiers wearing Mongol armour, Rashid al-Din, Jami' al-Tawarikh ('World History'), 714/1314, Tabriz, Iran

Figure 4.25 *Kufic inscription stating 'this is the mosque of Khalid ibn al-Walid, the Companion of the Prophet, blessings' and quoting Qur'an 2: 256 and 3: 17. Shrine of Khalid ibn al-Walid, eleventh century, Hims, Syria*

A more explicit association with the Franks is made in an extant inscription in the name of Baybars on the citadel of Safad dated 666/1267–8:

> He ordered the renovation of this citadel and its fortification and the completion of its building and its embellishment after he had delivered it from the hands of the accursed Franks and he gave it back to the hand of the Muslims after having removed it from the possession of the Templars to the possession of the Muslims.

This inscription praises Baybars' efforts in the *jihad*: 'He made efforts and struggled (*jahada*) until he exchanged unbelief for faith, church bell for the call to prayer, and the Gospel for the Qur'an.'[116] This inscription rejoices in Baybars' recapture of Safad which Ibn al-Furat graphically describes as 'an obstruction in the throat of Syria and a blockage in the chest of Islam'.[117]

The practice of recording the glorious achievements of the Mamluk sultans in monumental inscriptions continued apace throughout their rule. In the first fifty years of the dynasty the emphasis on *jihad* and related themes is marked. A revealing example of such Mamluk titulature is an inscription on the citadel of Aleppo dated 691/1292 in the name of Khalil b. Qalawun, who is called:

> tamer of the worshippers of crosses, the Alexander of the age, . . . the ruler of the armies of the Franks, the Armenians and the Tartars, the destroyer of Acre and the coastal regions, the reviver of the illustrious 'Abbasid state.[118]

This is a more elaborate and ambitious set of titles than ever Nur al-Din had enjoyed in an earlier period. The inscription encapsulates the triumphant Mamluk achievement against the Franks. It specifically highlights the Franks in the pejorative term 'worshippers of crosses' (which is unusual phrasing on a monument) and refers clearly to the Mamluk policy of razing the Levantine ports to the ground in the phrase 'the destroyer of Acre and the coastal regions'. The inscription then places the Mamluk realm firmly under the banner of Sunni Islam with the reminder that it is they who have revived the fortunes of the ʿAbbasid caliphate.

Quoting an earlier work by al-ʿUmari (d. 749/1349), the chancellery manual of al-Qalqashandi (d. 821/1418), in which scribes are told of appropriate modes of address, lists among the noble titles which should be given to the Mamluk sultan:

> the warrior of *jihad*, the one who dwells in a *ribat*, the defender of the frontier, . . . the sultan of Islam and the Muslims, the reviver of justice in the two worlds, the one who dispenses equity to those who have been wronged by wrongdoers, . . . the sultan of the Arabs and Persians and Turks . . . the Alexander of the age . . . the prince of the two seas, . . . the servant of the two noble sanctuaries . . . the one who is close to the Commander of the Faithful.[119]

These titles are very similar indeed to those attributed to Baybars on the mausoleum of Khalid b. al-Walid. Obviously, by the time of al-ʿUmari they were already enshrined in government practice as the official titles of the Mamluk sultan to be used on chancellery documents. It was these grandiloquent protocols, strings of titles emphasising again and again the religious credentials of the sultan, which were transferred on to selected monuments in inscriptions carved at key moments of Mamluk victory against the Franks, Armenians or Mongols. No doubt it was the government clerks who gave the precise instructions to the engravers as to what should be carved on the monuments.

After the conquest of Arsuf in 663/1265, Baybars distributed decrees to his commanders authorising them to own some of the conquered lands. Each commander was issued with a certificate of ownership, the text of which is quoted by the chronicler Ibn al-Furat. It is an example of panegyrical chancellery prose in praise of Baybars' achievements so far. Baybars' reign, according to these texts, compares most favourably to that of the Ayyubid dynasty:

> The best favour is that which follows despair, coming after a period when kings have been feeble and the people negligent. How excellent a favour it was to the religion of Mohammad which brought it unity, opening the doors to conquest when the two enemies, Frank and Tartar, were routed.[120]

The document rises to a climax in praise of Baybars, and describes him in the following terms:

> All this has been achieved by one appointed by God, to whom He gave a drawn sword with which he struck. The winds of divine aid were made to serve him and bore up his stirrup as he travelled to the home of Victory, journeying day and night. After seeing him in

Figure 4.26 *Mosque of Baybars, south-west porch, 665–7/1266–9, Cairo, Egypt*

her court, Fortune made him King: extolling him, she exclaimed: 'This is no mortal'.[121]

Thus we see Baybars' court scribes depicting him as the chosen one of God, the conqueror of Mongol and Frank, the munificent sultan who shares his conquered territories with those who have helped him towards his God-ordained victories.

Al-Maqrizi (d. 845/1442) quotes from the diploma written by the chief secretary of the chancellery, Ibn Lukman, solemnising the ceremony of the investiture of Baybars as sultan by the puppet caliph whom Baybars himself had installed. In the course of this high-flown text, proclaimed before his assembled courtiers, Baybars is described as having shown unparalleled zeal in the defence of religion (plates 4.28–4.29 and figures 4.26–4.27).[122] Turning specifically to the *jihad*, Ibn Lukman declares:

As regards Holy War, you have distinguished yourself by brilliant deeds . . . Through you God has protected the ramparts of Islam and

Plate 4.28 *Mosque of Baybars, detail of portal, 665–7/1266–9, Cairo, Egypt*

(Creswell Photographic Archive, Ashmolean Museum, Oxford, neg. C. 2586)

has preserved them from the profanations of the enemy; your courage has maintained for the Muslims the integrity of their empire.[123]

Baybars and *Jihad*: The Evidence of the Chroniclers

Baybars' highly successful career is recorded by a number of contemporary and near-contemporary biographers. Ibn ʿAbd al-Zahir, who states that he actually accompanied the Sultan on his various campaigns,[124] (d. 692/1292) presents Baybars as the spiritual heir of the last Ayyubid sultan (although Baybars was a first-generation convert to Islam, recruited from the Kipchak Turks) and his acts of murder and usurpation are glossed over.[125] The warrior from the steppes with blood on

Plate 4.29 *Mosque of Baybars, portal, 665–7/1266–9, Cairo, Egypt*

(Creswell Photographic Archive, Ashmolean Museum, Oxford, neg. C. 4503)

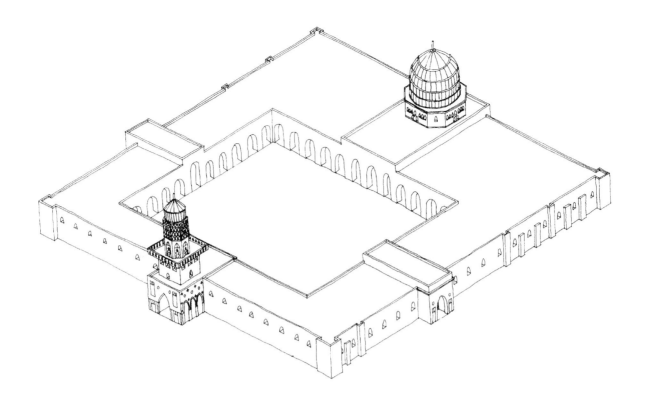

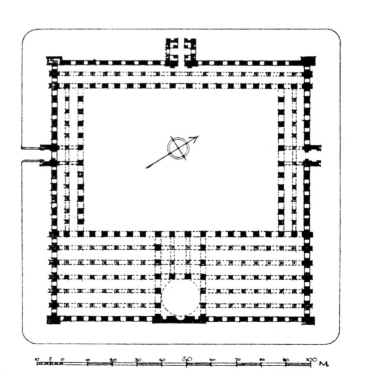

Figure 4.27 *Mosque of Baybars, plan and perspectival view, 665–7/1266–9, Cairo, Egypt*

his hands is transformed by the pen of his panegyrist into the ideal *mujahid*, repelling the pagan Mongols and continuing with distinction the *jihad* against the Franks: 'He prosecuted the *jihad* with the utmost zeal and fought against the unbelievers, for which God rewarded him.'[126]

Ibn 'Abd al-Zahir made strenuous attempts to portray his master as a worthy successor to Saladin: indeed, in his view, Baybars outdid Saladin. As Holt points out in his book on the Crusades, Baybars was a better soldier than Saladin and more single-minded in his military aims.[127] Thus there was a good basis on which to build up the image of Baybars as an ideal *mujahid*. The nephew of Ibn 'Abd al-Zahir, Shafi' b. 'Ali al-'Asqalani (d. 730/1330), wrote a somewhat revisionist biography of Baybars after the deaths of both the sultan and his own uncle.[128] Nevertheless, as Holt remarks, the Baybars of Shafi' is still an impressive figure with great achievements.[129] Another contemporary biographer of Baybars, Ibn Shaddad (d. 684/1285), also sees Baybars as the real hero of the Islamic reconquest of Frankish lands.[130]

As early as 663/1265 Shafi' b. 'Ali proclaims that his master Baybars will fight 'until no more Franks remain on the surface of the earth'.[131] This war is a reconquest depicted as 'a lost ewe which is brought back to the flock of Islam'.[132] Baybars is depicted as a puritanical and uncompromising Muslim general. The texts mention that he imposed the strictest discipline on his troops. According to Ibn al-Furat, 'The army brought no wine in its train nor were there any lewd practices: there were only virtuous women who brought the soldiers water to drink in the middle of the fighting'.[133] At the siege of Safad in 664/1265–6 Baybars went so far as to proclaim that any-one in the army who brought in and drank wine would be hanged.[134]

Through the panegyrics of his contemporary chroniclers and the works of later medieval historians Baybars emerges as a truly formidable figure, full of hatred towards those who dared to attack the House of Islam, uncompromisingly severe on malefactors, razing monuments to the ground with a barely suppressed zeal and anger of a kind seldom shown by Saladin (except in the latter's treatment of Reynald of Chatillon). As Thorau points out, Baybars was an exceptional military commander who managed to convey to his subordinates 'a sense of his omnipresence'.[135] Baybars' army was obviously controlled by a reign of terror and an iron discipline reminiscent of the extraordinary cohesion of the Mongol troops under Genghis Khan. Baybars would on occasion move around his territories incognito to pick up information on the conduct of his officials.[136] The Muslim world had indeed found in Baybars a worthy leader to protect it against all comers.

The Attitude to *Jihad* amongst the Military and Religious Classes in the Early Mamluk Period

The public attitude to *jihad* displayed by the Mamluk sultans is also mirrored in the enthusiasm for it shown by the Mamluk military commanders who fought under them. Baybars al-Mansuri (d. 725/1325), a well-known chronicler who served as governor of Kerak for a while and was an active participant in military campaigns, declares: 'My soul had a strong desire for *jihad*, a desire for it like the earth thirsts for delivering rain.' He wrote to the sultan asking for permission to participate in the siege of Acre in 690/1291 and when he received a favourable response, he explains: 'I was like one who has had the happiness of seeing his hopes realised and for whom the night has dissipated before the dawn.'[137]

The links of the religious classes with the Mamluk ruling elite seem to have been unusually close. Indeed, Sivan goes as far as to say that without the support of the religious classes, the Mamluks would not have been able to maintain themselves in power for so long.[138] Members of the Sufi orders and the *'ulama'* are mentioned as being on campaign with the sultans. At the conquest of Beaufort (Shaqif Arnun) in 666/1268, for example, Ibn al-Furat mentions that pious shaykhs and *'ulama'* were present: 'Each one of them did his best to fight in God's cause as far as his circumstances allowed.'[139]

Two Merits of Jerusalem works date from the early Mamluk period, written by al-Miknasi and al-Kanji, thus testifying to continuing religious interest in the Holy City.[140] The Mamluks sponsored religious building programmes elsewhere in their empire, established pious bequests (*waqf*s) and provided support for the Pilgrimage. In return, the religious classes underpinned Mamluk military initiatives with their writings on *jihad* and their personal presence on campaign.[141]

Jihad and the Fall of Acre, 690/1291

A modern scholar of the Mamluks, Donald Little, has recently analysed in some detail the campaign of the Mamluk sultan al-Ashraf in 690/1291, which culminated in the fall of Acre. It is clear that the religious context of this campaign was extremely important to those participating in it. About a week before embarking on the campaign in Safar 690/February 1291, al-Ashraf assembled Qur'an reciters, *'ulama'*, *qadi*s and other notables in the tomb chamber of his father Qalawun in Cairo.[142] There a complete recitation of the Qur'an took place. This was followed by the sultan's distribution of largesse to the poor and to those who lived in religious establishments.[143] The involvement of the religious classes continued during the month-long campaign – a public recitation of the *Sahih* of al-Bukhari in the presence of the religious notables of Damascus was attended by a large crowd and helped to fire up public enthusiasm.[144]

It is interesting to note that the Damascus manuscript copy of the collection of the sermons of Ibn Nubata dates from this very time,[145] thus indicating that perhaps they too had performed a role in arousing public emotion for the proposed attack on Acre.[146] According to Ibn Taghribirdi, more volunteers than regular troops assembled for this campaign, surely an indication of the effectiveness of the religious ceremonies and enhanced public awareness which had preceded it.[147]

As for the triumphal entry of the victorious sultan into Damascus in Jumada II 690/June 1291 after Acre had fallen, this was a splendid occasion in which everyone was involved:

The entire city had been decorated, and sheets of satin had been laid along his triumphal path through the city leading to the

Figure 4.28 Mosque lamp, pierced metal, mosque in complex of Qalawun, 683–4/1284–5, Cairo, Egypt

viceregal palace. The regal Sultan was preceded by 280 fettered prisoners. One bore a reversed Frankish banner; another carried a banner and spear from which hair of slain comrades was suspended. Al-Ashraf was greeted by the whole population of Damascus and of the surrounding countryside lining the route: 'ulama', mosque officials, Sufi shaykhs, Christians, and Jews, all holding candles, even though the parade took place before noon.[148]

Al-Ashraf ended his campaign where it had begun – giving thanks at his father's tomb in Cairo. In the eyes of Muslim historians, then,[149] it is clear that this was a successful and splendidly orchestrated campaign, culminating in the final removal of the Franks from Muslim soil. Its religious dimensions were stressed at every stage of the way.

A triumphal panegyric to al-Ashraf praises him for his victory over the Franks, but much more than that it celebrates the removal of the infidel from Muslim soil and the triumph of Islam over Christianity:

> Because of you no town is left in which unbelief can repair, no hope for the Christian religion! Through al-Ashraf the Lord Sultan, we are delivered from the Trinity, and Unity rejoices in the struggle!
> Praise be to God, the nation of the Cross has fallen; through the Turks the religion of the chosen Arab has triumphed![150]

Other poets addressed the enemy thus:

> O you yellow-faced Christians (Banu Asfar),[151] the vengeance of God has come down upon you! O you 'images' which decorate churches . . . too long have proud chieftains been seen prostrating themselves before you.[152]

It was surely no coincidence that one of the honorific titles borne by al-Ashraf was Salah al-Din (Saladin).[153] After the fall of Acre, Ibn al-Furat writes: 'Full of anger you have avenged Saladin, thanks to this secret which God had concealed in this title.'[154] Literally the title means 'Probity of religion' but no doubt what is being suggested here is that al-Ashraf Khalil, an inexperienced Mamluk sultan who had just come to the throne, could acquire some of the blessing (*baraka*) and religious credentials of his charismatic predecessor, Saladin (Salah al-Din) by adopting this title.

Figure 4.29
(above and opposite)
*Helmets, album paintings,
early fourteenth century,
Tabriz, Iran*

The panegyrics of the chroniclers writing long after the event are confirmed by contemporary evidence solidly dated to the time of the fall of Acre itself. Two coins minted in the name of al-Ashraf Khalil link him with Saladin. The first is an undated gold coin which calls him Salah al-dunya wa'l-din (the probity of this world and of religion) – the identical title used of Saladin in the inscription dated 587/1191 on the Qubbat Yusuf.[155] The second is an undated silver coin which gives him the title Salah al-Din (Saladin) 'the helper of the Muhammadan community, the reviver of the 'Abbasid state'.[156]

Two extant inscriptions call al-Ashraf Khalil by such a title in 690/1291. The first calls him Salah al-Din.[157] The second, recorded on the citadel of Baalbek in Syria, dated Sha'ban 690/August 1291 (two months after the fall of Acre), declares triumphantly that he is 'the probity of this world and religion . . . the subjugator of the worshippers of crosses, the conqueror of the coastal marches, the revivifier of the 'Abbasid state'.[158]

Thus we see that the wider historical significance of the fall of Acre and the expulsion of the Franks was not lost on Muslim contemporaries. But this event is clearly not viewed as the end of the story – how could it be, since *jihad* against the House of War is continuous? Immediately after the conquest of Acre, al-Ashraf declared the Armenian Kingdom of Cilicia and the Mongols as his next targets: the struggle must continue.

Ibn Taymiyya and *Jihad*

Although Ibn Taymiyya (d. 728/1328) lived and wrote beyond the fall of Acre in 690/1291, he was such an influential figure in Mamluk religious circles and public life that his views are included here. A recent study of his influence by Morabia calls Ibn Taymiyya 'the last great theoretician of medieval *jihad*'.[159]

The period through which Ibn Taymiyya lived had experienced not only the expulsion of the Crusaders but also the continuing Mongol threat on the borders of Islam. As we have seen earlier, the dreaded Mongols, with their apparent favouring of Shi'ites and Christians in Iran, sharpened the resolve of the Mamluks to present themselves as the champions of Sunni Islamic orthodoxy and the implacable opponents of heretics and infidels. We have also seen how under the Mamluks there was a close alliance between the religious classes and the military. The Hanbalites, to whose *madhhab* Ibn Taymiyya belonged, with their traditionalist approach and emphasis on pure Islam uncontaminated by innovations, were especially well suited to promote intense religious feeling amongst the Mamluks who faced the Crusader and Mongol threat.[160]

But Ibn Taymiyya was also heeded by those outside the confines of his own legal school and especially by other leading *'ulama'* in Damascus. He was a truly charismatic figure; indeed, some Mamluk amirs said that they were his 'disciples'. He also commanded tremendous popular support, especially when he preached against the Christians. Attitudes had hardened since the advent of the Crusaders. Ibn Taymiyya was often very useful to the Mamluk regime when he and the ruling elite shared the same aims – such as, for example, the waging of *jihad* against Christians, heretics and Mongols. On other occasions, he was viewed as difficult and uncooperative, and indeed he spent considerable periods of his life in prison. One thing was always certain: he could never be ignored and his uncompromising views earned him the respect of his supporters and opponents alike.

241

Figure 4.30 Helmet, Dioscorides, De Materia Medica, c. 1225, Iraq

Figure 4.31
(above and opposite)
Warriors wearing a 'corset cuirass' with lamellar and laminated armour. Above, Rashid al-Din, Jami' al-Tawarikh *('World History'), 714/1314, Tabriz, Iran; opposite, Firdawsi,* Shahnama *('Book of Kings' – the Great Mongol* Shahnama*), c. 1330, Tabriz, Iran*

Ibn Taymiyya advocated a 'fundamentalist' approach in religion, a 'back to basics' stance which stripped Islam of all polluting innovations and concentrated exclusively on the pristine values of the Qur'an and the Sunna.

What is the difference between the *jihad* envisaged by Ibn Taymiyya and the propaganda campaign utilised so effectively under Nur al-Din and Saladin? Certainly there were many similarities. The familiar alliance was forged between the 'men of the sword' and the men of religion, with each supporting the other. There was the same spate of *jihad* literature, renewing the old ideas of classical *jihad* theory. Many *jihad* sermons were written and the sultans were accompanied on campaign by an entourage of clerics, Sufis, Qur'an reciters and preachers. The sultans in turn sponsored a massive building programme of religious monuments in which officially approved Sunni Islam was taught. These monuments often bore titles with a distinct flavour of *jihad*.

So what is new in the Mamluk situation and in the role of Ibn Taymiyya? A few significant episodes in his turbulent career may be illuminating here. Ibn Taymiyya's first public appearance of note was after the fall of Acre. Ibn Taymiyya never forgot, however, the spectre of the Crusaders and the Muslim disunity which in the early twelfth century had allowed these outsiders to gain territory in the Islamic world. He was invited in 692/1293 to give a *fatwa* on a Christian who had been accused of insulting the Prophet. Ibn Taymiyya decreed the death penalty for him. In 696/1297 the Mamluk sultan Lajin asked Ibn Taymiyya to arouse the people to fight *jihad* against the Christian Armenians of Cilicia. In 699/1300 Ibn Taymiyya participated personally in a campaign waged by the Mamluk sultan in the Lebanese mountains against Shi'ites who were accused of collaboration with Christians and Mongols. In 702/1303 he was again present personally on campaign with the Mamluk army. On this occasion he pronounced a *fatwa*, in which he allowed the soldiers to be excused the Ramadan fast so that they would be able to fight the Mongols more effectively. Ibn Taymiyya argued that 'fasting weakened the *mujahidun* and compromised the success of the *jihad* for the triumph of the True Religion'.[161]

There was in the Mamluk period a greater fanaticism, a profound conviction that the world of Sunni Islam must be rid of 'infidel contamination' altogether. It was Ibn Taymiyya who best articulated this change of approach. Ibn Taymiyya was a figure with a high public profile whose words were often heeded and never ignored. There had been no comparable man of religion in the twelfth century whose views became synonymous with *jihad* propaganda. In Ibn Taymiyya's time, there was no longer an overriding preoccupation with recapturing the Holy City of Jerusalem. *Jihad* now went deeper and had much wider implications. For him *jihad* is defensive – to purge the Sunni world both of the infidel presence and of Muslim heresy. Both these aspects are important in his views on *jihad*. His anti-rationalist faith and traditionalist approach were ideally suited to his aims. He is not an advocate of military aggression into the 'House of War' (*Dar al-harb*) but he argues that Muslims should strive to put their own house in order first. Thus he favours the moral rearmament of the Muslims within their own lands and strong resistance to any external intervention. His implacable diatribes against all kinds of innovations in Islam – against mystical practices, philosophy, theology, the veneration of tombs – are all motivated by his desire that the True Religion should not resemble in any way the practices of non-Muslims.

For him, *jihad*, both spiritual and physical, is a force within Islam which can create a society dedicated to God's service. With Ibn Taymiyya, *jihad* to Jerusalem is replaced by an internal movement within the *Dar al-Islam* ('House of Islam') itself, both spiritual and physical. Hence Ibn Taymiyya lays great emphasis on the greater *jihad*, the spiritual dimensions of which he outlines in his *fatwa*s on *jihad*. At the same time, whilst stressing the prototypical religious importance of the Prophet's career for those who wish to wage *jihad*, Ibn Taymiyya is sufficiently a man of his own age to draw parallels between Muhammad's time and contemporary events. Ibn Taymiyya sees the Muslim world assailed by external enemies of all kinds [162] and the only solution is to fight *jihad* so that 'the whole of religion may belong to God'.[163]

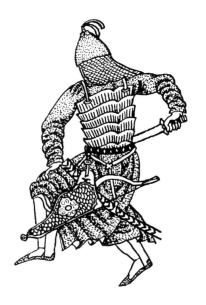

It is small wonder that Ibn Taymiyya's ideas have been embraced enthusiastically by modern Islamic reform movements. What is less well known are the formative influences which moulded his uncompromising stance. The spectre of the Franks in Muslim territory exacerbated his deep-rooted hatred of infidels and heretics and his strong desire to purify Islam and Islamic territory from all extraneous intrusion and corruption. And while the Franks were plainly a spent force by the later thirteenth century, the Mongols were the exact opposite – the most fearsome enemy that the world of Islam had ever encountered, an alien force that had taken over most of the eastern Islamic world and seemed poised to extend its conquests to the Levant. No wonder that Ibn Taymiyya saw it as his responsibility to galvanise the forces of the Islamic faith against such perils.

Mamluks and *Jihad*: An Overview

It is clear that *jihad* as a propaganda weapon and as a rallying cry uniting the Muslims became revitalised under the Mamluk sultans. These tough military men, relative newcomers to the Near East and to Islam, were ideally suited to the promotion of clear-cut and uncompromising Sunni beliefs and to the hammering of those who opposed them – be they external infidels (Mongol, Armenian or Frank), or internal 'heretics' such as Isma'ilis. As Sivan remarks, the Mamluks revitalised in dramatic fashion the *jihad* tradition which had flourished in the last part of the twelfth century.[164] Indeed, the

Figure 4.32 *Mosque of*
al-Nasir Muhammad, citadel,
minaret, 735/1334–5, Cairo,
Egypt

Figure 4.33 *Mamluk*
epigraphic disc: 'Glory to our
lord the sultan', personal
blazon of Sultan al-Nasir
Muhammad, early fourteenth
century, Egypt

Mamluks saw themselves as heirs to Saladin's achievements. The propaganda benefits of contrasting themselves with the *laissez-faire* attitude of their Ayyubid predecessors was also no minor consideration.

Historical events exacerbated Mamluk xenophobia and hostility to those who followed other faiths. Above all, the dreaded Mongol threat loomed over the early Mamluk period and enhanced the urgency of the need to defend the state against this formidable foe. Victory over the Mongol army at 'Ayn Jalut in 658/1260 gave the Mamluks great prestige and they readily donned the mantle of protectors of the 'House of Islam'. Clearly Mamluk *jihad* efforts were directed first and foremost against the Mongols (cf. figures 4.24 and 4.31), but in moments of respite on the Mongol front they turned their attention to the Franks. The Mamluks were all too aware of the possibility of further Crusades coming from Europe to the Syrian coast. Hence their determined efforts to raze many of the ports and fortifications to the ground.[165]

Although the Mamluk sultans, especially Baybars and Qalawun, were at pains to patronise the building of religious monuments in Jerusalem, the Holy City now in Muslim hands could of course no longer form the focus of an anti-Frankish *jihad* campaign as it had done to such great effect under Nur al-Din and Saladin. New targets had to be found. Hence *jihad* against the Franks formed part of the defence of the House of Islam against a wide range of infidels from without – Franks, Armenians and Mongols – and all kinds of heresy and innovation from within. The interpretation of *jihad* propounded by Ibn Taymiyya, who had himself lived through the Mongol assaults, epitomises this need to rid the House of Islam of all extraneous elements and to return to what was perceived as the pristine religion practised by the early Muslims. As we shall see in Chapters 5 and 6, anti-Christian polemical writing and anti-Christian political measures characterised the early Mamluk period. Nur al-Din and Saladin, and their Ayyubid successors, had grown up in the multi-confessional atmosphere of the Near East and did not generally penalise the Oriental Christians within their territories. The situation with the

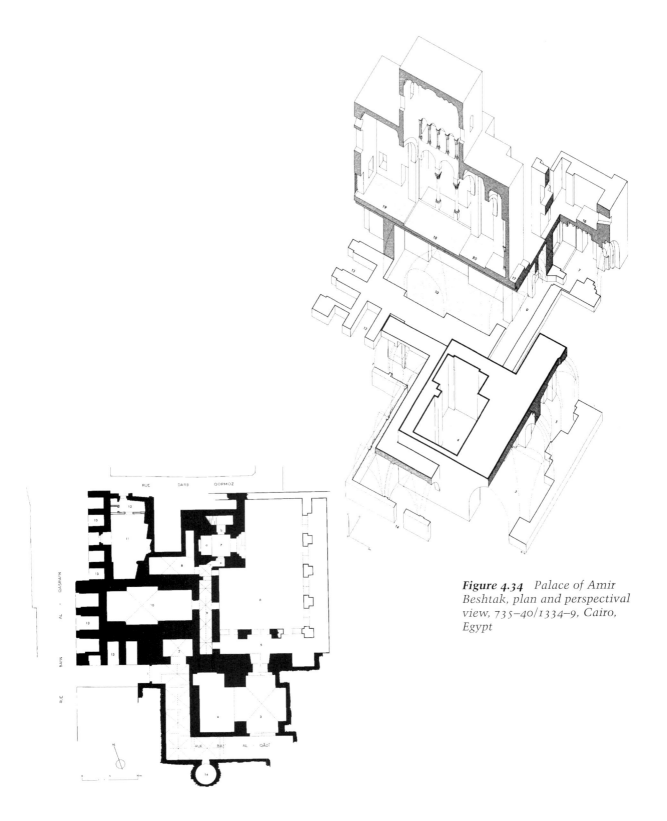

Figure 4.34 *Palace of Amir Beshtak, plan and perspectival view, 735–40/1334–9, Cairo, Egypt*

245

Mamluks was fundamentally different. The Mamluks' recent conversion to Islam, their aloofness from the indigenous population and their narrowly focused military education predisposed them to a much harsher approach to non-Muslims. The massive crisis brought to the Islamic world by the Mongols, and their destruction of Baghdad and the caliphate in 1258, can only have sharpened these attitudes.

A true interpretation of *jihad*, however, should have gone hand in hand with the honouring of the covenant (*dhimma*) with the 'People of the Book' within their lands. This long-cherished principle seems to have been threatened in the Mamluk period, even though it was enshrined in Islamic law. Whether the Franks had contributed to this rise in hostile feelings towards Oriental Christians (and Jews) within the Mamluk empire will be discussed in Chapter 6.

General Reflections

We have seen how highly successful campaigns of *jihad* propaganda harnessed to charismatic leadership reached two climaxes within the Crusading period: the first in 1187, when Saladin reconquered Jerusalem, and the second in the drive which culminated in the Mamluk expulsion of the Franks from the Levant in 1291.

It is clear from the evidence presented here that the full exploitation of an extremely effective and multifaceted *jihad* propaganda machine was the key factor for the revitalisation and reunification of those Muslim territories contiguous with the Crusader states and for the Muslim reconquest of areas snatched from them by the Crusaders. The propaganda was given an extra emotional dimension, lacking in early manifestations of *jihad* movements, such as the Hamdanids' struggles on the Byzantine frontier, by the increased focus on Jerusalem as a tangible goal linked to the general aims of *jihad*. Subsequent *jihad* propaganda did without the symbol of Jerusalem. In Ibn Taymiyya's time there was no overriding preoccupation with recapturing the Holy City of Jerusalem. His *jihad* was *defensive* – to purge the Sunni world of the infidel presence and of Muslim heresy.

It will also be apparent that neither in the example of the *jihad* waged by Nur al-Din and Saladin nor in the *jihad* propaganda of the Mamluks and Ibn Taymiyya was there any question of *jihad* being taken to mean 'waging war' so as to *convert* the infidel. *Jihad* was waged as a *reaction* to perceived aggression from outside. All this is a far cry from the stereotyped image of Islam as the religion of the sword.

It is tempting in view of the preceding discussion to put the primary emphasis on religious motivation and ideological considerations. After all, the actions of the great Muslim warriors against the Franks, such as Nur al-Din, Saladin and Baybars, are depicted in the sources as an expression of *jihad*, and there is a marked crescendo in ideological fervour at the time of Saladin's capture of Jerusalem and in the descriptions of Baybars' activities after the arrival of the dreaded

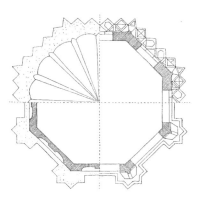

Figure 4.35 Northern minaret, Mosque of al-Hakim, upper part, plan and elevation, 703/1303–4, Cairo, Egypt

Mongols. As already mentioned, Saladin is shown by his biographers as seeking to justify every act on his way to Jerusalem as taken in the 'path of God' (*fi sabil Allah*). Baybars' biographers too portray him as waging *jihad* against both Frank and Mongol and they rise to heights of exaggerated ideological rhetoric in a way strongly reminiscent of Saladin's panegyrists.

Taken as a whole, the period of Frankish presence in the Near East – 1099–1291 – is characterised by two main surges of *jihad* fervour. The first built up to the battle of Hattin and the second occurred after the accession of Baybars and the deep shock experienced by the Muslim world with the horrific invasions of the Mongols. This certainly had its repercussions on Muslim determination to rid their

Figure 4.36 Funerary complex of Sultan Qalawun, perspectival view, 683–4/1284–5, Cairo, Egypt

247

territories of the unwanted presence of aggressive infidels from both east and west, and led ultimately to the definitive removal of the Franks from Muslim soil.

Yet the *jihad* card must not be overplayed. It is clear that in the first fifty years of Frankish occupation the Muslims learned quickly to co-exist with their unexpected neighbours from Europe; they traded with them, they signed truces and they formed military alliances with them. The same atmosphere of *détente* and petty local politics is apparent in the period between Saladin's death and the establishment of the Mamluk sultanate in 1260. The descendants of Saladin, the Ayyubids, were far too preoccupied with internal dissensions and rivalries amongst themselves to wage *jihad* in a concerted effort to build on Saladin's achievements and to oust the Franks. They were too weak to wage such a war. The Near East in the Ayyubid period was indeed a jigsaw of small territorial entities, sometimes at war with each other, on other occasions in a state of truce, with constantly shifting alliances; amongst them the Franks were so well established and familiar by this stage that they took their full part in the local internecine squabbles and were almost just another 'indigenous' group in the area, together with the Ayyubid princes, the Isma'ilis and others.

There was, moreover, even in the times when an atmosphere of heightened *jihad* prevailed, a gulf between the public written postures of the scribes seeking to justify and eulogise their masters, and the political and military reality. Nur al-Din, Saladin and Baybars had to move slowly towards their goals, and this often involved even these great figures, portrayed in the sources as *mujahidun*, in temporary truces and such pragmatic concerns as trading with the Franks and exchanging diplomatic missions with them. Saladin clearly lost his focused motivation after the fall of Jerusalem. The Mamluk sultans, often portrayed as the great prosecutors of *jihad* who hounded the Franks out of the Levant, can also be seen in reality to have moved cautiously and by degrees towards their goals.

The Theories of Sivan and Köhler

Was the Counter-Crusade ideological? Sivan argues that it was, and he provides powerful evidence to support his argument. Yet even he stresses in his conclusions that care should be taken not to accord the *jihad* element too decisive or exclusive a weight in the Muslim wars against the Crusaders. The *jihad* element always operated in parallel with many others – expansionism, politico-military imperatives, xenophobia, economic factors and fear of attacks from Europe.[166]

Köhler goes even further.[167] Indeed he challenges the whole sweep of Sivan's book – the apparent hardening of attitudes towards *jihad*, the psychological changes in the motivation of the Muslim forces and the grand climax of the *jihad* campaign, namely the reconquest of Jerusalem. And there is much evidence from the sources to

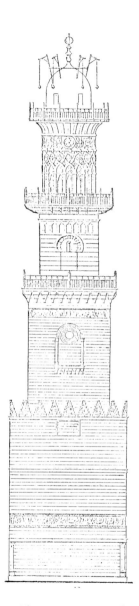

Figure 4.37 *Complex of Qalawun, minaret, 683–4/1284–5, Cairo, Egypt*

Figure 4.38 *Carved wooden panel*, maristan *(hospital), complex of Qalawun, 683–4/1284–5, Cairo, Egypt*

support Köhler's ideas – above all, the clear picture of a much more complex web of relationships, peace treaties between Muslims and Franks, 'jihad' waged against fellow Muslims and the 'cynical' use of *jihad* propaganda for the legitimation of usurped personal and family power on the part of Zengi, Nur al-Din and Saladin.

There are many ways of looking at the chronology of the Crusading period. It can easily be divided into sections of weakness, strength, demoralisation, revival, first steps, climaxes. To some extent such a process of demarcation is arbitrary and is imposed retrospectively by scholars wishing to establish order and to see historical patterns. Sivan, who espoused so firmly and persuasively the idea of the awakening of *jihad* amongst the Muslims of the Levant in the twelfth century, not surprisingly fixes on Saladin's reconquest of Jerusalem in 1187 as a glorious climax, the culmination of a carefully orchestrated programme of public *jihad* focused on the Holy City. At first sight this makes good sense, and the argument has a satisfactory shape to it.

Yet it is clear that such high points did not change social and political realities overnight – if they did so at all. Unfortunately for the Muslims, the victories at Hattin and Jerusalem did not turn out to mean the removal of the Franks. Unfortunately for the neatness of Sivan's theory there was a so-called 'relaxation' in the heightened atmosphere of *jihad* in the period after Saladin's death. His immediate successors spoke about *jihad* but actually embraced *détente*. Two of the Ayyubids were actually prepared after negotiating with the Franks to hand back Jerusalem to them. It would be possible to argue that the political expediency of using *jihad* had been temporarily buried again in favour of collaboration, co-existence and co-operation with the Franks and that the particular concatenation of circumstances which surrounded the build-up to Saladin's conquest of Jerusalem was peculiar, even unique. But the situation was much more complicated: indeed, it seems that the two strands, one of pragmatic co-operation or at least a state of truce with the Franks and the other of military confrontation with them, co-existed for the majority of the time. Certainly the year 1187 can be seen as a high point for the exploitation of religio-political rhetoric. Moreover, the last campaigns of the Mamluk sultans sprang from a heightened xenophobic atmosphere given extra edge by the much greater Mongol menace and they culminated in the final expulsion of the Franks from the Near East. But interspersed with these particular 'moments' when *jihad* feelings were especially aroused, there were prolonged periods of treaties, truces, commercial relations and military alliances. So the role of religion should not be overplayed.

Whilst there is much to commend Köhler's arguments – and Chapter 6 of this book deals in some detail with the social relationship between Muslims and Crusaders – ultimately the exact weighting of the interplay between *jihad* and *détente* must remain a matter of scholarly debate and of varying interpretations of the primary sources, both Islamic and Crusader. Therein lies the continuing interest and fascination of the history of the Crusades.

Jihad in More Recent Times

Throughout Islamic history there have been numerous reform movements, missionary activities and frontier struggles conducted under the banner of *jihad* – the Almohads in Spain and the Ghaznavids and Ghurids in Muslim India, to mention but two examples. It is, however, in the Muslim response to the Crusades in the twelfth and thirteenth centuries that we find perhaps the most seminal expression of *jihad*. This came in response to the irruption of the Crusaders from western Europe into the heart of the Islamic Near East and their seizure of Muslim territories and, above all, Jerusalem. The *jihad* programme which developed in Syria and the Holy Land in reaction to this unheralded external aggression from western Europe has become the model for subsequent manifestations of the spirit of *jihad*.[168]

The legal theory of *jihad*, as enshrined in the Shari'a, has been the mainspring of important movements of conquest, proselytism and defence throughout Islamic history. The special emphasis placed in this chapter on *jihad* in the Crusading period is not without its relevance to the modern Arab and modern Muslim consciousness. The Crusades are viewed by some Muslims as the first attempt by the West at colonisation of the 'House of Islam'. It was, moreover, the successful exploitation of the *jihad* ideal which removed the alien presence of the Crusaders from Muslim soil. There are lessons here for our own age. To many Muslims in the 1990s Israel is the new Crusader state against which *jihad* must now be waged. The enduring value of the *jihad* concept is thus vividly illustrated. The legal intricacies of *jihad* are not understood by many Muslims today; for them, *jihad* is nothing but a rhetorical term, a rallying, unifying cry which appeals to the emotions but for which there is no clear programme. Awkward legal questions are not asked in such an atmosphere. The term *jihad* is bandied about by modern heads of state who do not

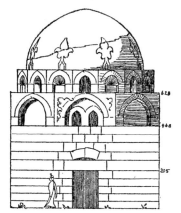

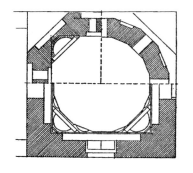

Figure 4.39 Madrasa al-Shibliyya, mausoleum, plan and elevation, early thirteenth century, Damascus, Syria

have the supporting system of lawyers, tract-writers and preachers who underpinned the claims of a Nur al-Din or a Saladin to be waging Holy War, and who carefully defined the implications and targets of *jihad*. But, at the end of the twentieth century, Jerusalem is as much on the scene as it was in Crusader times.

Notes

1. H. Djait, *Europe and Islam*, London, 1985, 70.
2. For the estrangement between Nur al-Din and Saladin, cf. Ibn al-Athir, *Kamil*, XI, 150; Ibn al-Furat, *Tarikh al-duwal wa'l-muluk*, ed. H. al-Shamma, Basra, 1967–9, 184–6.
3. 'Imad al-Din, *Sana*, 289; al-Maqrizi, trans. Broadhurst, 63, 70, 81.
4. Al-Maqrizi, trans. Broadhurst, 79–80.
5. M. C. Lyons and D. E. P. Jackson, *Saladin: The Politics of the Holy War*, Cambridge, 1982, 41.
6. Al-Raba'i, *Fada'il al-Sham wa Dimishq*, ed. S. al-Munajjid, Damascus, 1950.
7. Ibn al-Jawzi, *Fada'il al-Quds al-sharif*, ms. Princeton, Garrett, Arabic 586, mentioned in Sivan, *L'Islam*, 117.
8. Sivan, *L'Islam*, 143.
9. Entitled *Tuhfat al-talibin fi'l-jihad wa'l-mujahidin*; cf. Sibt, VIII, 520.
10. J. Rikabi, *La poésie profane sous les Ayyoubides*, Paris, 1949, 75–6; 293–4.
11. Ibid., 75–6; 293–4.
12. Cf. also Sura 101: 5, 'And the mountains will become as carded wool.'
13. Cf. P. Balog, *The Coinage of the Ayyubids*, London, 1980, 77.
14. Cf. the huge gold coins minted by the Ghurids and the Almohads.
15. 532/1137–87–558/1163 (1 page), 558/1163–583/1187 (40 pages), 583/1187–589/1193 (170 pages); P. M. Holt, 'The sultan as ideal ruler: Ayyubid and Mamluk prototypes', in *Suleyman the Magnificent and His Age*, ed. M. Kunt and C. Woodhead, Harrow, 1995, 124, page nos. from Ibn Shaddad, *Al-nawadir al-sultaniyya*, ed. J. El-Shayyal, Cairo, 1964.
16. Ibn Shaddad, *Nawadir*, 40; al-Maqrizi makes the same point: 'Repenting past wine-bibbing, he renounced drink and shunned frivolous pleasures' (trans. Broadhurst, 37).
17. Quoted by Gabrieli, 87.
18. Gabrieli, 88. Indeed in 1191 he put to death the Sufi al-Suhrawardi for alleged heretical beliefs (Illuminationism – *ishraqiyya*).
19. Al-Maqrizi, trans. Broadhurst, 99.
20. Ibn Shaddad, quoted by Gabrieli, 93.
21. Gabrieli, 93.
22. Gabrieli, 98.
23. Gabrieli, 98.
24. *Fi sabil Allah*, a common Qur'anic phrase.
25. Ibn Shaddad, *RHC*, III, 106.
26. Gabrieli, 99.
27. Gabrieli, 100.
28. D. S. Richards, 'A consideration of two sources for the life of Saladin', *JSS*, 25/1 (1980), 46–65.
29. Holt, 'The sultan', 126.

30. Ibn al-Athir, *Kamil*, XII, 63.
31. Ibn Jubayr, Broadhurst, 33.
32. Ibn Jubayr, Broadhurst, 35.
33. Ibn Jubayr, Broadhurst, 311.
34. Al-Maqrizi, trans. Broadhurst, 105.
35. 'Imad al-Din, *Sana*, 100; al-Maqrizi, trans. Broadhurst, 54.
36. Abu Shama, II, 65.
37. *Sana*, 328, according to Lyons and Jackson, *Saladin*, 246.
38. *Sana*, 331, according to Lyons and Jackson, *Saladin*, 246.
39. Abu Shama, II, 70; according to Lyons and Jackson, *Saladin*, 245.
40. Ibn al-Athir, *Kamil*, XII, 62.
41. Ibn al-Athir, *Kamil*, XII, 62.
42. S. Lane-Poole, *Saladin and the Fall of the Kingdom of Jerusalem*, London, 1985.
43. H. A. R. Gibb, 'The achievement of Saladin', in *Saladin: Studies in Islamic history*, ed. Y. Ibish, Beirut, 1972, 176.
44. A. S. Ehrenkreutz, *Saladin*, Albany, 1972, 237.
45. Lyons and Jackson, *Saladin*, 240.
46. Köhler, 316.
47. Cf. G. Wiet, 'Les inscriptions de Saladin', *Syria*, 3 (1922), 307–28.
48. Köhler, 320, n. 382, citing ms. Bibl. nat. arabe 6/24, fol. 10r.
49. H. Möhring, 'Der andere Islam: Zum Bild vom toleranten Sultan Saladin' in *Die Begegnung des Westens mit dem Osten*, ed. O. Engels and P. Schreiner, Sigmaringen, 1991, 140.
50. Al-Qadi al-Fadil, quoted by Lyons and Jackson, *Saladin*, 85.
51. Cited by Lewis, *Islam*, I, 67.
52. *RHC*, IV, 336. Cf. also the text of a letter written by al-Qadi al-Fadil on Saladin's behalf to the caliph al-Nasir, in al-Qalqashandi, *Subh al-a'sha*, ed. M. A. Ibrahim, Cairo, 1913–20, vol. VIII, 282–9.
53. Ibn Shaddad, *RHC*, III, 100–1.
54. Ibn Khallikan, de Slane, II, 633–42; 'Imad al-Din, *Sana*, 314.
55. Ibn Khallikan, de Slane, II, 635.
56. Ibn Khallikan, de Slane, II, 636.
57. Ibn Khallikan, de Slane, II, 636–7.
58. Ibn Khallikan, de Slane, II, 640.
59. Ibn Khallikan, de Slane, II, 637.
60. 'Imad al-Din al-Isfahani, *Kitab al-fath al-qussi fi'l-fath al-qudsi*, ed. C. Landberg, Leiden, 1888, 413.
61. *RCEA*, IX, inscription no. 3447, 174–5, quoted by Lewis, *Islam*, I, 65–6.
62. Ibn Shaddad, *RHC*, III, 265; D. Little, 'Jerusalem under the Ayyubids and Mamluks 1197–1516 AD', in *Jerusalem in History*, ed. K. J. Asali, London, 1989, 179.
63. 'Abd al-Latif, quoted in Ibn Abi Usaybi'a, *'Uyun al-anba'*, II, 206, quoted by Lewis, *Islam*, I, 66.
64. Cf. H. Daiber, 'Die Kreuzzüge im Licht islamischer Theologie', in A. Zimmermann and I. Craemer-Ruegensberg, *Orientalische Kultur und europäisches Mittelalter*, Berlin and New York, 1985, 77–85.
65. 'Imad al-Din, *Sana*, 52 and 56.
66. Abu Shama, *RHC*, IV, 12.
67. Abu Shama, *RHC*, IV, 12.
68. Holt, 'The sultan as ideal ruler', 128.
69. *EI²*: Salah al-Din.
70. Ibn Khallikan, de Slane, II, 639.
71. Cf. R. S. Humphreys, 'Ayyubids, Mamluks and the Latin East in the thirteenth century', *Mamluk Studies Review*, 2 (1998), 1.

72. Ibid., 4.
73. Ibid., 5.
74. P. M. Holt, *The Age of the Crusades*, London, 1986, 61.
75. Ibn Wasil, IV, 97.
76. Humphreys, 'Ayyubids, Mamluks', 10.
77. Ibn al-Athir, *Kamil*, XII, 497, quoted by D. S. Richards, 'Ibn al-Athir and the later parts of the *Kamil*', in *Medieval Historical Writing in the Christian and Islamic Worlds*, ed. D. O. Morgan, London, 1982, 97; cf. also a similar view expressed by Ibn 'Abd al-Zahir, *Rawd*, 46.
78. Balog, *Coinage*, 45.
79. Cf. L. Atrache, *Die Politik der Ayyubiden*, Münster, 1996, 236.
80. D. Sourdel and J. Sourdel-Thomine, 'Un texte d'invocation en faveur de deux princes Ayyubides', *Near Eastern Numismatics, Iconography, Epigraphy and History. Studies in Honor of George C. Miles*, ed. D. K. Kouymjian, Beirut, 1974, 349.
81. Qur'an 3: 200.
82. M. van Berchem, 'Eine arabische Inschrift aus dem Ostjordanlande', in van Berchem, *Opera Minora*, Geneva, 1978, vol. I, 539. Another inscription dated 627/1229–30 is in the name of 'Uthman b. al-Malik al-'Adil – *al-mujahid al-murabit al-ghazi al-shahid*: M. van Berchem, 'Le château de Bâniâs et ses inscriptions', in van Berchem, *Opera Minora*, 282–3.
83. Sibt b. al-Jawzi calls this Ayyubid prince 'a *jihad* fighter in the path of God' in his obituary, VIII/2, 644.
84. R. S. Humphreys, 'Politics and architectural patronage in Ayyubid Damascus', in *The Islamic World from Classical to Modern Times*, ed. C. E. Bosworth et al., Princeton, 1989, 157–74.
85. Little, 'Jerusalem', 180.
86. Ibid., 181.
87. Sibt, VIII/2, 601.
88. Sibt, VIII/2, 601.
89. For a record of the contacts between al-Kamil and Frederick, cf. Ibn Wasil, IV, 242 and 244–5; Ibn Nazif, 176–7.
90. Ibn Wasil, IV, 243–4; cf. also al-Maqrizi, trans. Broadhurst, 26; quoted by Little, 'Jerusalem', 184.
91. Little, 'Jerusalem', 184.
92. Sibt, VIII/2, 653.
93. Sibt, VIII/2, 654; Ibn Wasil, IV, 245.
94. L. Pouzet, *Damas au VIIe/XIIe siècle*, Beirut, 1988, 140, n. 159.
95. Ibn al-Furat, Lyons, 1; al-Maqrizi, trans. Broadhurst, 272.
96. Al-Maqrizi, trans. Broadhurst, 272; Ibn al-Furat, Lyons, 1; Little, 'Jerusalem', 185.
97. Al-Maqrizi, trans. Broadhurst, 274.
98. Sibt, VIII/2, 746; cf. also Ibn al-Furat, Lyons, 5.
99. Except for a short period in 647/1249.
100. C. Cahen and I. Chabbouh, 'Le testament d'al-Malik as-Salih Ayyub', *Mélanges Laoust, BEO*, 29 (1977), 100.
101. Pouzet, *Damas*, 284–5; Sivan, *L'Islam*, 136, 140.
102. Sivan, *L'Islam*, 144.
103. The reading *sahn* (courtyard) makes better sense than *hisn* (citadel) here.
104. There was an acceptable density of people needed to perform the prayer properly. That density involves a certain distance between worshippers so that they can accomplish the movements of prayer. But since this was a Saturday, the body of people in the mosque could have

been much more tightly packed since it appears that they were there to hear Sibt b. al-Jawzi address them and could therefore sit much more closely together.

105. Sibt, VIII/2, 544–5.
106. Sibt, VIII/2, 604.
107. Humphreys, 'Ayyubids, Mamluks', 7.
108. For a recent assessment of *jihad* in the Ayyubid period, cf. Atrache, *Die Politik*, 234–5.
109. J. P. Berkey, 'The Mamluks as Muslims: the military elite and the construction of Islam in medieval Egypt', in *The Mamluks in Egyptian Politics and Society*, ed. T. Philipp and U. Haarmann, Cambridge, 1998, 167.
110. Quoted by Lewis, *Islam*, I, 98.
111. Holt, *The Age of the Crusades*, 95.
112. An excellent summary can be found in Berkey, 'The Mamluks as Muslims', 163–5.
113. For a recent analysis of Mamluk–Mongol relations, cf. R. Amitai-Preiss, *Mongols and Mamluks: The Mamluk-Ilkhanid War, 1260–1281*, Cambridge, 1995.
114. *RCEA*, XII, inscription no. 4556, 104. There are echoes of this in the Mamluk sultan Qalawun's inscription over the entrance to the gatehouse of the Aleppo citadel. Cf. Irwin, 'Islam and the Crusades, 1096–1699', 225.
115. *RCEA*, XII, inscription no. 4556, 104–5.
116. *RCEA*, XII, inscription no. 4589, 125–6.
117. Ibn al-Furat, Lyons, 89.
118. E. Herzfeld, *Matériaux pour un corpus inscriptionum arabicarum: Deuxième partie: Syrie du Nord*, vol. I/1, Cairo, 1955, 90, inscription no. 40.
119. Al-Qalqashandi, *Subh al-a'sha fi sina'at al-insha'*, ed. M. A. Ibrahim, Cairo, 1913–20, VII, 378–9.
120. Ibn al-Furat, Lyons, 78.
121. Ibn al-Furat, Lyons, 78–9.
122. Quatremère, I, 152.
123. Quatremère, I, 156.
124. *Rawd*, 76.
125. Holt, 'The sultan as ideal ruler', 131; Ibn 'Abd al-Zahir, *Al-rawd al zahir fi sirat al-Malik al-Zahir*, ed. A. A. Al-Khuwaytir, Riyadh, 1976.
126. *Rawd*, 77–8.
127. Holt, *The Age of the Crusades*, 97.
128. It is entitled *Husn al-manaqib al-sirriyya al-muntaza'* and was finished in 716/1316.
129. Holt, 'The sultan as ideal ruler', 136–7.
130. 'Izz al-Din Ibn Shaddad, author of the geographical work *Al-a'laq al-khatira*, wrote a biography of Baybars called *Al-rawd al-zahir fi sirat al-Malik al-Zahir*. The part before 670/1271 is lost but the rest is extant. Cf. Ibn Shaddad, Eddé, xiii.
131. Sivan, *L'Islam*, 172; citing Shafi' b. 'Ali, *Husn al-manaqib*, ms. Paris arabe 1707, fol. 89a. The work was edited by A. A. Al-Khuwaytir, Riyadh, 1976.
132. Sivan, *L'Islam*, 172, citing Shafi', fol. 103a.
133. Ibn al-Furat, Lyons, 75.
134. Ibn al-Furat, Lyons, 92.
135. P. Thorau, *The Lion of Egypt*, trans. P. M. Holt, London, 1992, 254.

136. Baybars wandered around the province of al-Gharbiyya, for example, to collect information on its governor; cf. Quatremère, I, 231.

137. Baybars al-Mansuri, *Zubdat al-fikra*, 278.

138. Sivan, *L'Islam*, 178.

139. Ibn al-Furat, Lyons, 110.

140. Sivan, *L'Islam*, 173.

141. Cf. M. Burgoyne, *Mamluk Jerusalem*, London, 1987.

142. Qalawun is also presented by Shafi' b. 'Ali and other Mamluk sources as a great *mujahid* against the Mongols and the Franks.

143. D. P. Little, 'The fall of 'Akka in 690/1291: the Muslim version', in *Studies in Islamic History and Civilisation in Honour of Professor David Ayalon*, ed. M. Sharon, Jerusalem, 1986, 170.

144. Ibid., 178; Sivan, *L'Islam*, 183.

145. Cf. Chapter 3, 101–2.

146. Sivan, *L'Islam*, 183.

147. Cited by Sivan, *L'Islam*, 183.

148. Little, ''Akka', 179.

149. Ibid., 179.

150. Ibid., 181; cf. also Sivan, *L'Islam*, 183–4.

151. The root in Arabic has pejorative connotations: 'may God turn your face yellow' is what was said if a person wished ill on someone. The origin of the term used here, 'Banu'l-Asfar' is disputed. According to Dozy, it was used for the Byzantines and Christians more generally. 'His blood is yellow' means 'he is a coward'. This whole root in Arabic has meanings associated with pallor, jaundice, bile, etc. R. Dozy, *Supplément aux dictionnaires arabes*, Leiden, 1881, vol. I, 835–6.

152. Sivan, *L'Islam*, 183.

153. Already as Qalawun's heir-apparent he had been given such a title: Salah al-Dunya wa'l-Din (the probity of this world and religion) in 689/1290, perhaps as a pious spur for him to emulate Saladin. Cf. *RCEA*, XIII, inscription no. 4927, 87.

154. Sivan, *L'Islam*, 165; Baybars al-Mansuri, *Tuhfa*, 127.

155. Balog, *Coinage*, 121.

156. Ibid., 122.

157. *RCEA*, XIII, inscription no. 4946, 98–9: the inscription is on the Khan Ayyah in Damascus.

158. *RCEA*, XIII, inscription no. 4947, 100–1.

159. A. Morabia, 'Ibn Taymiyya, dernier grand théoricien du jihad médiéval', *BEO*, XXX/2, 1978, 85–99; cf. also A. Morabia, *Le gihad dans l'islam médiéval*, Paris, 1983.

160. *EI*²: Hanabila.

161. For the views of Ibn Taymiyya on *jihad*, cf. the works of A. Morabia; H. Laoust, *Essai sur les doctrines sociales et politiques d'Ibn Taymiyya*, Cairo, 1939, 360–70.

162. Ibn Taymiyya, *Majmu' fatawa Shaykh al-Islam Ahmad b. Taymiyya*, Riyadh, 1383, vol. XXVIII, 441–4.

163. Ibid., 442.

164. Sivan, *L'Islam*, 165.

165. Cf. Chapter 5.

166. Sivan, *L'Islam*, 205–6.

167. Köhler, *Allianzen*.

168. For a more extended discussion cf. Chapter 9.

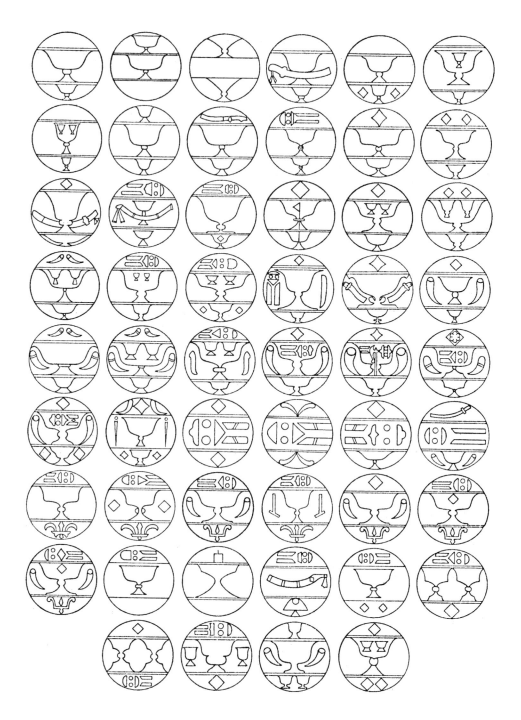

Figure 5.3 Composite Mamluk blazons, thirteenth–fifteenth centuries, Egypt and Syria

the truth might be stretched a little, or more than a little. So it would perhaps be fair to regard many of Usama's stories about the Franks as reflections of stereotypes, revealing the exaggerated and often comic behaviour of the newcomers with whom the Muslims were forced into unwanted and unexpected proximity, and about whom they would tell tall stories and saucy jokes. It is, after all, a common enough response to unwanted military occupation in any age to debunk the intruders by snide suggestions as to their uncouth behaviour and lack of culture and breeding. This was the case with the Persians after the Arab conquest of their ancient land in the seventh century.

But in spite of all these warnings, Usama's work, if interpreted with caution, is a rich source on the socio-cultural life of the twelfth century in Syria and the Holy Land. It has, however, been over-exploited, often rather too simplistically, by scholars, as if it is always appropriate to take it at its face value and as if no other evidence were available in the Islamic sources.

The other contemporary Muslim source, the travelogue of Ibn Jubayr, contains valuable insights into life in the Levant at the time of the Crusades, although it should be emphasised that its author was only one individual speaking of his personal impressions in certain areas of the Levant at one specific time. Ibn Jubayr was a Spaniard, used to close contact with Christians in Muslim al-Andalus and perhaps able to see the Frankish occupation of Syria and Palestine with greater objectivity than those who were experiencing it at first-hand; at any rate, he brought to the situation the perspective of one single Muslim from a different area of the Islamic world, an area which was nevertheless experiencing on its northern frontiers similar aggression from Christian Europe. Like Usama, Ibn Jubayr aimed to divert and inform his audience, and his evidence too should be approached cautiously. Perhaps his view might have been regarded by some of his more cosmopolitan contemporaries as positively provincial. As was common practice, the performance of the pilgrimage to Mecca (*hajj*) allowed those who made the journey from distant parts of the Muslim world to take the opportunity of seeing different lands and recording their experiences. Ibn Jubayr kept a diary and his first-hand evidence, dating to the 1180s, is of great interest. However, a word of warning should be sounded here. Travel literature is vulnerable to error. It can be based on the inaccurate or biased testimony of local guides, and it draws on notes made on journeys and often written up later, subject to faults of human memory, once the traveller has returned home. There was, of course, no photographic evidence from which to check retrospectively the veracity of information. Ibn Jubayr's account is susceptible to these very faults.

Usama's evidence, too, in so far as it is autobiographical, belongs to a category of medieval Islamic literature which is certainly vulnerable to similar criticisms of unreliability and inaccuracy. Autobiography as a literary genre was frowned upon in the Islamic world because it

Figure 5.4
(above and opposite)
*Wooden door and metal table
from the complex of Sultan
Qalawun, 683–4/1284–5,
Cairo, Egypt*

was outside the bounds of the verification process which was the hallmark of works written in the various fields of the religious sciences. In the classical period of Islam, in the heyday of the 'Abbasid empire (the eighth to the tenth centuries), books on law, *hadith* and even history had long been subjected to a complex system of determining the authenticity of the information they contained, and every snippet was scrupulously examined before inclusion. The memoirs of a single person would be viewed as an anarchical and individualistic type of literature and thus it occurred only very rarely. And how could the veracity of such information be checked? Despite all these reservations, however, the works of Usama and Ibn Jubayr should be used by scholars of the Crusades since they provide two authentic Muslim voices from the very period of Crusader occupation. As such, they cannot be ignored.

The Value of Popular Folk Literature

At the end of his important work on *jihad* published in 1968, Sivan wisely pointed to the importance of conducting future research on what he described as the Islamic epic literature which seems to have been popular at the time of the Crusades (figure 5.5).[12] As in other areas of medieval history, a major gap in our knowledge of the social aspects of the Crusades is the perspective of the ordinary people. Of course, their lives rarely come under the scrutiny of the chroniclers, who are almost exclusively concerned with the narrowly defined ruling echelons of society – the court, the military and the religious classes. It is true that from time to time the writers of annalistic chronicles mention at the end of each year unusual events – famines, earthquakes, bizarre births, Nile floodings – but such details are rarely elaborated and the background to them is sadly lost to us. It is therefore necessary to investigate other spheres of Islamic culture in order to try to find more information about how the ordinary people felt about the Crusades. Such a task of 'literary archaeology' is difficult and still experimental, but it has already yielded some interesting results.

Until the 1970s the great works of popular Arabic literature – the traditional equivalent of today's soap operas – had received inadequate scholarly attention and were looked down on by Arab intellectuals. Yet such works played an important part in traditional Arab life, and one of them, the *Arabian Nights*, is probably the best-known work of Arabic literature in the West.[13] With their colourful reworking of familiar themes and motifs, these works reveal the taste of traditional Arab audiences. Sometimes too they may offer 'a glimpse of the secret wishes, taboos and fears harboured by such audiences'.[14]

These works do not conform to the literary and linguistic standards of the Arabic literary elite. Part of this narrative corpus consists of some long heroic cycles focusing on a central hero, usually a historical

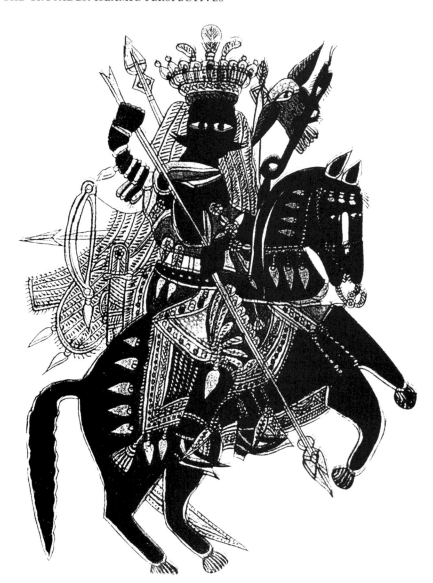

Figure 5.5 Muslim folk hero,
under-glass painting,
twentieth century, Tunisia

figure who has acquired legendary status and has been turned into a fictional personality. One such epic cycle concerns Sultan Baybars.[15] In the skilful hands of scholars such as Lyons, Irwin, Kruk and others, this fruitful area of research is beginning to open up. Many of these popular folk epics have their foundations in Islamic history but do not, of course, lend themselves easily to historical analysis. With their stock themes, standard ingredients and their basis in a long-established but fluid oral tradition, they make good story-telling material, but they lack proper chronology and historical accuracy. Nevertheless, it is worth while to focus on such pseudo-historical

Figure 5.6 *L'la Yamina seated, under-glass painting, twentieth century, Tunisia*

material and to try to identify strands and themes which shed particular light on the Crusading period or, to use Lyons's archaeological image, to find evidence of a 'Crusading stratum'. The legendary exploits of Saladin and Baybars are a case in point. Historians eager to use this material to enrich the information in the chronicles will be disappointed – for the charismatic names of these warrior sultans are merely pegs on which to hang adventures of a comic-strip type. What the use of these names does prove, of course, is that these Muslim heroes had a vigorous afterlife in the popular imagination.

For the Crusades do lurk in the shadows of some of this popular literature from the Middle Ages. Chronology, as noted above, has little or no significance in the sequence of events as they unfold in folk epics – a personage may be killed at one part in the narrative only to appear alive and active in the later part of the story. Characters from the seventh to the tenth centuries are juxtaposed with figures who have obviously Frankish names such as Bohemond. One episode in the popular folk epic *Sirat Dhat al-Himma* concerns the Frankish king Malis, son of Bulus (Paul). Jesus appears to him in a dream and

***Figure* 5.7** '*Antar and Abla,
under-glass painting,
twentieth century, Tunisia*

tells him to go east through Byzantium 'to deliver the [Church of the] Garbage (*al-Qumama*) [i.e. the Church of the Holy Sepulchre] and Jerusalem from the hands of the Muslims'.[16] Whilst some glimpses of historical memory may be seen here, the tale assumes the contours of an Islamic legend, as Malis, having appealed to all the Frankish countries and assembled a great army, passes through Constantinople on his way to Syria where he is defeated and killed by the heroine of the epic, Dhat al-Himma, 'the mother of the warriors of the faith and the defender of the religion of Muhammad'. Later Dhat al-Himma is praised for saving Jerusalem from the infidel threat. She is by no means an isolated example of legendary female warriors in the Islamic folk tradition who perform marvellous feats.[17]

As in a modern soap opera, persons in Islamic popular epics can be resurrected in the plot without any justification being needed. It is therefore difficult to evaluate such material in historical terms. What is clear, however, is that this literature is a vast and largely untapped source of popular attitudes, beliefs and stories which helped to create Muslim stereotypes of the Franks. Specific references to this material will be made at intervals in the rest of this chapter.

Muslim Stereotypes of the Franks: The Formation of an Image before the Crusades

Western Europe held few attractions to the medieval Muslims; from their perspective their own culture was so obviously more sophisticated and advanced. The medieval Muslim felt superiority and condescension towards Christians. For him it was indisputable that Christianity, an incomplete and imperfect revelation, had been superseded and perfected by Islam, the final Revelation, and that the Prophet Muhammad was the seal of the prophets. Such supreme

Figure 5.8 '*Abdallah ibn Ja'far and L'la Yamina, daughter of the Great King of Tunis, under-glass painting by Mahmud al-Feriani, c. 1890, Sfax, Tunisia*

267

Figure 5.9 *The princess Abla, wife of 'Antar, and the princess Zubayda, wife of Harun al-Rashid, under-glass painting, twentieth century, Tunisia*

confidence in the values that were based on this Revelation did not engender great intellectual curiosity in peoples of other faiths which were by definition wrong or incomplete. The Muslims showed little interest in Christianity, whether it was the Latin Christianity of the barbarians of western Europe, the eastern Christianity of their great enemy and neighbour, Byzantium, or the Oriental Christian communities who had lived under Muslim rule since the Arab conquests in the seventh century. The Muslims knew little and cared less about Europe; it just did not impinge much on their world view. They knew a certain amount about Christianity from the Christian communities in the Middle East, but even to these familiar groups they gave scant attention.

Before the coming of the First Crusade at the end of the eleventh century, the Muslims had heard of the Franks and formed opinions about them. These opinions were based on travel accounts,[18] oral narratives from prisoners of war,[19] pilgrims, merchants and diplomats, geographical works and popular stories. These opinions were sharpened, moreover, by the natural tendency of those of one race or religion to form stereotypical images of the 'other'.

Many of the earliest Muslim perceptions of the geography of western Europe and its inhabitants were based on the writing of the

268

second-century Greek scholar of Alexandria, Ptolemy, which came into the Islamic world through the work of the tenth-century Muslim scholar al-Khwarazmi and others. Indeed, the Ptolemaic heritage

Plate 5.1 *Jami' al-Nuri, minaret, probably 566–8/1170–3, Mosul, Iraq*

269

remained intact for many centuries of Islamic history, with few new ideas being added by Muslim authors.

Accordingly, medieval Muslim geographers divided the world into seven latitudinal zones or 'climes'; the position of a given race in a particular clime predisposed them to the possession of certain attributes. The greatest harmony and balance lay in the third and fourth zones which comprised the central lands of the Arab world (cf. colour plate 5), North Africa, Iran and parts of China. The Franks, on the other hand, dwelt in the sixth clime. Like the Slavs and Turks who also inhabited this zone, the Franks pursued the arts of war and the chase, were of melancholic temperament and prone to savagery. They were also filthy and treacherous.

The great 'Abbasid writer al-Mas'udi (d. 345/956) has unusually wide horizons within an Islamic context. In two of his works he includes a list of the kings of the Franks from Clovis to Louis IV.[20] This was, on his own admission, based on a book written in 328/939 by a Frankish bishop for the future Umayyad Spanish ruler al-Hakam. According to al-Mas'udi, the Franks are descended from Japhet (the son of Noah); they are 'a numerous, courageous, well-organised and well-disciplined people, with a vast and unified realm'.[21]

Al-Mas'udi goes on to describe the land of the Franks as follows:

As regards the people of the northern quadrant, they are the ones for whom the sun is distant from the zenith, those who penetrate to the North, such as the Slavs, the Franks, and those nations that are their neighbors. The power of the sun is weak among them because of their distance from it; cold and damp prevail in their regions, and snow and ice follow one another in endless succession. The warm humor is lacking among them; their bodies are large, their natures gross, their manners harsh, their understanding dull, and their tongues heavy. Their color is so excessively white that it passes from white to blue; their skin is thin and their flesh thick. Their eyes are also blue, matching the character of their coloring; their hair is lank and reddish because of the prevalence of damp mists. Their religious beliefs lack solidity, and this is because of the nature of cold and the lack of warmth.[22]

The above account emphasises the excessive cold and dampness of the clime within which the Franks reside: it is these climatic characteristics that render the inhabitants dull of understanding, gross of nature, lumbering in stature and coarse in manners. These negative qualities became rooted in the Muslim mind in relation to the Franks. Indeed, they reappear, for example, in a work on the categories of the nations, written in 1068 by a Muslim judge in Toledo, Sa'id b. Ahmad. He describes the barbarians who live in the north (that is, Europe) as more like beasts than men and he continues in the following terms: 'their temperaments are therefore frigid, their humours raw, their bellies gross, their colour pale, their hair long and

lank. Thus they lack keenness of understanding and clarity of intelligence and are overcome by ignorance and apathy, lack of discernment and stupidity.'[23]

Figure 5.10 Types of Mamluk pen-box blazon, thirteenth–fifteenth centuries, Egypt and Syria

Other Spanish Muslim writers depict western Europe as a vast, cold, fertile land and they stress once again that the Franks are doughty fighters but unhygienic in their habits.[24]

The Dutch scholar Remke Kruk has recently studied the work of Ibn Abi'l-Ash'ath, a Persian physician who lived in Mosul and died around the year 360/970.[25] In his *Book of Animals* (*Kitab al-hayawan*) Ibn Abi'l-Ash'ath gives a systematic survey of animate beings, including man.[26] Speaking of those who dwell in the intemperate zones of the world, Ibn Abi'l-Ash'ath writes that they have no wisdom (*hikma* – the 'knowledge of the two opposites').[27] Since they are deficient in this attribute, they are like animals in that they have only generic characteristics and they lack individuality.[28] He declares confidently that the inhabitants of the intemperate cold regions shed their hair annually as animals do.[29]

Later Medieval Views of the Franks in the Cosmographical and Geographical Literature

During the Crusading period, the Muslim writer al-Idrisi (died c. 560/1165), living under Norman Christian rule in Sicily, completed his geographical work normally known by the short title the *Book of Roger* in 1154. He relies in this work on informants from western Europe as well as the usual earlier geographical writers, and he has an unusually wide outlook and range of information.

His description of France in the sixth clime is precise enough to include details of place-names and distances, but it perpetuates the image of the swirling gloom of the northern regions of the world. Speaking of the Sea of Darkness, al-Idrisi writes: 'The waters of this sea are thick and dark in colour; the waves rise up in frightening manner: its depth is considerable; darkness prevails there continually.'[30]

England in the seventh clime fares a little better: it is described as a large island shaped like an ostrich's head: 'Its inhabitants are courageous, vigorous and enterprising but a continual winter prevails there.'[31]

An important source for Muslim views of the Franks is the work of the cosmographer and geographer al-Qazwini (d. 682/1283) (cf. colour plate 6). In his geographical work entitled *The Monuments of the Countries and the History of the Inhabitants* (*Athar al-bilad wa-akhbar al-'ibad*) he borrows extensively from a number of earlier sources.[32] Indeed, this work of al-Qazwini is far from being one of original scholarship, but it is a very learned compilation and synthesis of existing knowledge. He draws, for example, on the geography of al-Udhri, the works of al-Mas'udi, as well as Ibn Fadlan's account of his journey to southern Russia in the 920s. Al-Qazwini builds, then, on the corpus of 'information' about western Europe which had circulated in the Islamic world for centuries. There is little that is new in his details about the Franks and his account, the usual mixture of the exotic, the real and the imaginary, is intended, as were other works of 'marvels' (*'aja'ib*) literature, to titillate and entertain audiences. He describes the Franks and their country as follows:

> Frank-land, a mighty land and a broad kingdom in the realms of the Christians. Its cold is very great, and its air is thick because of the extreme cold. It is full of good things and fruits and crops, rich in rivers, plentiful of produce, possessing tillage and cattle, trees and honey. There is a wide variety of game there and also silver mines. They forge very sharp swords there, and the swords of Frank-land are keener than the swords of India.
>
> Its people are Christians, and they have a king possessing courage, great numbers, and power to rule. He has two or three cities on the shore of the sea on this side, in the midst of the lands of Islam, and he protects them from his side. Whenever the Muslims send forces to them to capture them, he sends forces from his side to defend them. His soldiers are of mighty courage and in the hour of combat do not even think of flight, rather preferring death. But you shall see none more filthy than they. They are a people of perfidy and mean character. They do not cleanse or bathe themselves more than once or twice a year, and then in cold water, and they do not wash their garments from the time they put them on until they fall to pieces. They shave their beards, and after shaving they sprout only a revolting stubble. One of them was asked as to the shaving of the beard, and he said, 'Hair is a superfluity. You remove it from your private parts, so why should we leave it on our faces?'[33]

There is an emphasis here on the cold climate of the land of the Franks but there is little concrete information and no supplementary details which might have filtered through to the author through obvious knowledge acquired about the Franks during their presence on Muslim soil for two centuries. It is, however, important to stress that al-Qazwini mentions once again the moral baseness and the lack of personal hygiene of the Franks. As we have already seen, these characteristics stem inevitably from their geographical position in the world. As in earlier accounts, the Franks are praised for their courage in war.

The Muslim geographer al-Dimishqi (d. 727/1327) also deals with the Franks in his erudite compilation entitled *The Selection of Time amongst the Marvels of Land and Sea* (*Nukhbat al-dahr fi 'aja'ib al-barr wa'l-bahr*).[34] In the sixth clime he places the Franks as well as the Turks and the Khazars: 'The sixth [clime] is most extreme in cold, dryness and distance from the sun, together with a preponderance of dampness too.' In his view the Franks are white and like wild beasts. They are concerned with nothing but wars, fighting and hunting.[35]

The Portrayal of the Franks in Popular Folk Literature

As well as the vague and stereotyped descriptions of the Franks and Frankland perpetuated throughout the early centuries of Islam in the genres of 'high literature' such as historical chronicles, cosmographical works and diverse geographical writings, there is a further dimension to be considered: the depiction of the Franks in popular folk literature already mentioned above.

As Lyons, Kruk and others have shown recently, the popular epics knew of areas of the world beyond Byzantium, kingdoms and islands inhabited by 'Franks'. Lyons describes the Franks as 'silhouettes' on the historical horizon of this kind of literature.[36] They are 'huge, clean-shaven men'; 'they carry lances or spears of tempered steel, with broad heads; their archers never miss, and their shafts pierce mail. In their armies, rider, horse and armour form a single whole'.[37] Such descriptions reflect cultural attitudes over many centuries but are often too imprecise to be evaluated as proper historical evidence, although we can see here a repetition of the clear emphasis on the military skills of the Franks, stressed as early as the time of al-Mas'udi, as well as comments on their size and lack of facial hair.

Such popular literature is a vast and largely untapped source of popular attitudes, beliefs and stories which helped to create Muslim stereotypes of the Franks. Such works help to show the development of the Muslim perception of the 'enemy' and the constituent parts of that perception – the portrayal of the Franks as dirty, deceitful and lacking in marital jealousy, and of Frankish women as sexually loose. Clearly, then, the stylised anecdotes and jokes about the Franks in Usama's memoirs which have been taken as 'historical truth' by some scholars need to be seen as being a reflection of shared attitudes and prejudices about the Franks which were already deeply ingrained by Usama's own time.

Figure 5.11 Mihrab, *Mosque of al-'Ayni, 814/1411, Cairo, Egypt*

An Overview of Muslim Attitudes to the Franks before 492/1099

The preceding discussion points to entrenched Muslim attitudes towards the Franks which had been moulded long before the coming of the First Crusade. An awareness of these attitudes is essential for an understanding of the comments and themes found in Muslim writings about the Franks of the twelfth and thirteenth centuries in the Near East. We can thus understand the horizons of Muslim expectation about the Franks and realise that there was little likelihood of genuinely deep understanding of the attitudes and beliefs of the other side. An awareness of the Muslim attitudes to the Franks which were widespread before 1100 helps towards a truer evaluation of Usama's testimony in particular, and allows us to make a more accurate assessment of the major themes which the Muslim writers of the Crusading period continue to discuss in relation to the Franks. As we shall see shortly, there is collusion between Usama and his readers when he writes knowingly about the curious antics of the Franks. Usama is unashamedly exploiting a range of preconceptions and prejudices about the Franks, knowing that his audience shares these views and will enjoy his stories which illustrate them. He begins his discussion of the idiosyncrasies and customs of the Franks with a typical flourish:

> Mysterious are the works of the Creator, the author of all things! When one comes to recount cases regarding the Franks, he cannot but glorify Allah (exalted is He!) and sanctify him, for he sees them as animals (*baha'im*) possessing the virtues of courage and fighting, nothing else; just as animals have only the virtues of strength and carrying loads.[38]

As we have seen, other medieval Muslim writers display the same prejudices.

By the time of the Crusades therefore there was a whole repertoire of stereotyped images of the Franks, long embedded in the Muslim psyche, and repeated over time with little variation in cosmographical, historical and other literary genres.[39] The Franks did not follow civilised pursuits. They were filthy in their personal habits, lacking in sexual morality and proper marital jealousy, but courageous and redoubtable in war.

Arabic ethnographic writings which formed an integral part of *adab* literature, urban secular writing for a sophisticate elite, fostered a clear sense of a common cultural identity. Outside this identity lay 'barbarism' in its many manifestations. Such internal cohesion was nurtured by a feeling of Muslim exclusivity, 'consolidating their differences from outsiders'.[40] Closer acquaintance with the Franks was to enhance such feelings of Muslim exclusivity rather than modify this rigid edifice of preconceived and vague opinions and prejudices.

Two Stereotypical Frankish Characteristics: Lack of Hygiene and Sexual Laxity

We have seen how the filth of the inhabitants of northern Europe was a cliché of Muslim ethnographic literature long before the coming of

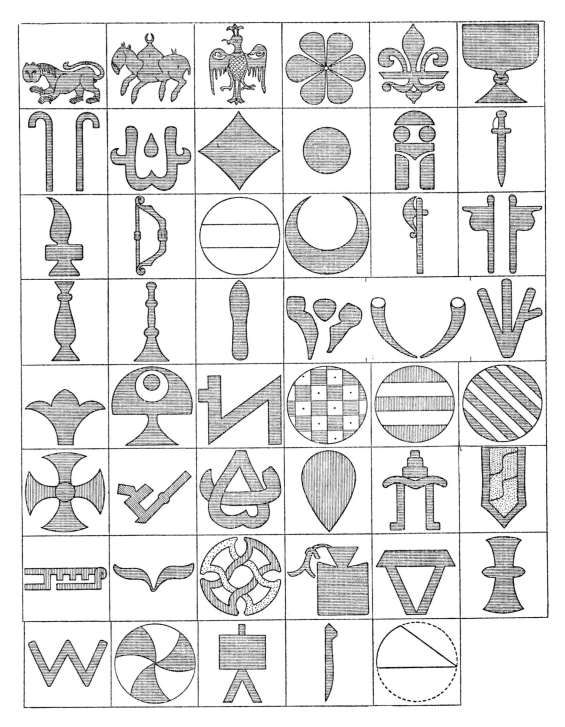

Figure 5.12 *Simple Mamluk charges, thirteenth–fifteenth centuries, Egypt and Syria*

275

the Crusades. It is interesting to speculate on the extent to which living in the Middle East might modify both the Franks' own attitudes to hygiene and washing habits, and the Muslims' unfavourable view of them in this respect. A difference in climate could exert an influence in this sphere of human activity, as too would the practices of the Muslims, who visited the public bathhouses regularly and for whom ablutions were an integral part of daily religious worship.

On his travels through the Holy Land Ibn Jubayr speaks of the Franks' 'absence of cleanliness'.[41] He is particularly scathing in his description of Crusader Acre: 'it stinks and is filthy, being full of refuse and excrement'.[42]

On his journey eastwards Ibn Jubayr expresses little concern about having to travel in ships controlled by Christian sailors. Perhaps as a result of his experiences of the Franks in the Near East and what he has heard from fellow Muslims during his stay there, he is, however, happy on his return journey from Acre to find that Muslim passengers are placed in separate quarters from the Frankish travellers. Ibn Jubayr hopes and prays that the two thousand Christian pilgrims on the ship will soon leave it.[43] Kedar points out that the attitude of Ibn Jubayr towards the Crusaders in the Levant is harsher than towards the Christians of Sicily.[44]

The testimony of Usama seems to suggest that some of the Franks, especially the knightly classes, began to go regularly to the public bathhouse, once they became settled in the Near East. Their comportment there, however, allows Usama a wonderful opportunity to debunk them. Usama's famous account of a visit to a bathhouse has been quoted many times in books on the Crusades. The story is put

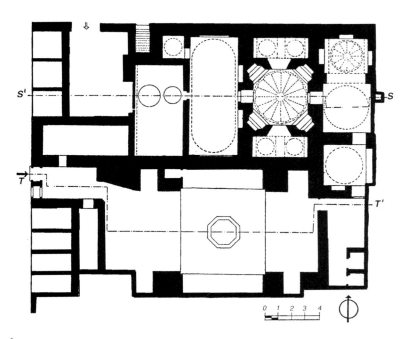

Figure 5.13 Hammam al-Bazuriyya (also known as Hammam Nur al-Din), plan, founded between 549/1154–5 and 568/1172–3, with Ottoman additions, Damascus, Syria

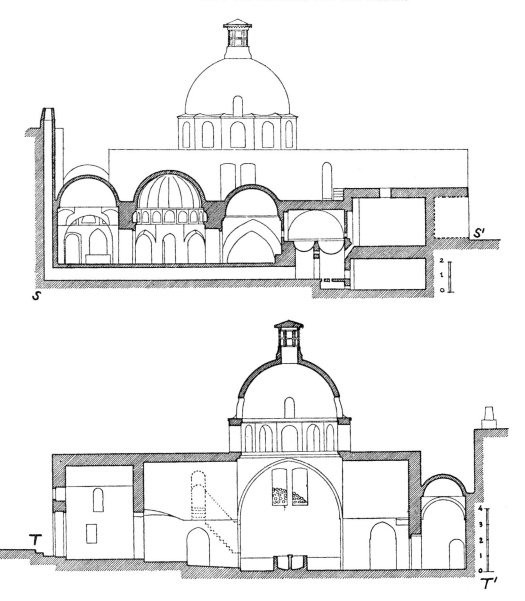

Figure 5.14 Hammam al-Bazuriyya (also known as Hammam Nur al-Din), sections, founded between 549/1154–5 and 568/1172–3, with Ottoman additions, Damascus, Syria

into the mouth of an attendant called Salim from the town of Ma'arrat al-Nu'man who was working in one of Usama's father's bathhouses:

I once opened a bath in al-Ma'arra in order to earn my living. To this bath there came a Frankish knight. The Franks disapprove of girding a cover around one's waist while in the bath. So this Frank stretched out his arm and pulled off my cover from my waist and threw it away. He looked and saw that I had recently shaved off my pubes. So he shouted, 'Salim!' As I drew near him he stretched his

Figure 5.15 Hammam *scene, sketch, Nizami, Khamsa ('Quintet'), 915–34/1507–27, Iran*

hand over my pubes and said, 'Salim, good! By the truth of my religion, do the same for me.' Saying this, he lay on his back and I found that in that place the hair was like his beard. So I shaved it off. Then he passed his hand over the place and, finding it smooth, he said, 'Salim, by the truth of my religion, do that same to madame (*al-dama*)' (*al-dama* in their language means the lady), referring to his wife. He then said to a servant of his, 'Tell madame to come here.' Accordingly the servant went and brought her and made her enter the bath. She also lay on her back. The knight repeated, 'Do what thou hast done to me.' So I shaved all that hair while her husband was sitting looking at me. At last he thanked me and handed me the pay for my service.

Consider now this great contradiction! They have neither jealousy nor zeal but they have great courage, although courage is nothing but the product of zeal and of ambition to be above ill repute.[45]

278

This anecdote about the Franks encapsulates the Muslim perception of them as boorish, ill-bred and lacking in proper pride towards their womenfolk. The Crusader knight in question suggests with alacrity and enthusiasm that his own wife should expose herself in a public bathhouse to the bath attendant who then shaves her pubic hair. Each detail of this story is carefully selected to put down the Franks. The Frankish knight behaves with a marked lack of decorum and etiquette from the moment he enters the bathhouse, and Usama makes the most of the comic potential of the situation. We are told that in conformity with Islamic custom the Frankish knight does not wear the usual loin cloth (of knotted towels) around his waist and thereby exhibited his private parts for all to see on his arrival. He then rips off the loin cloth of the bath attendant and displays a naive admiration for Salim's shaved pubic hair, whilst his own is 'as long as his beard'.

Usama then takes his story further into the realm of farce by having the knight's wife brought to the bathhouse where she too is shaved publicly, whilst her husband stands by with total equanimity. This part of the story touches on the essential difference perceived by Muslims between their own society and that of the Franks. In a society where women were protected by their menfolk, not allowed to reveal their unveiled faces except to a prescribed number of close

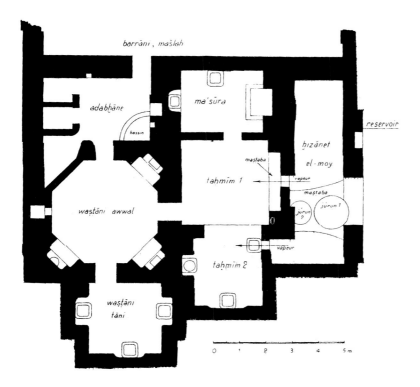

Figure 5.16 Hammam al-Sami, plan, thirteenth century, Damascus, Syria

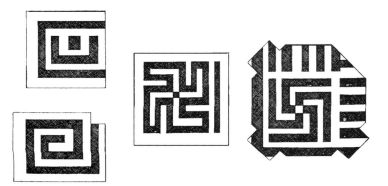

Figure 5.17 Hammam
al-Sami, decorative marble
patterning of the floor,
thirteenth century, Damascus,
Syria

male relations, the conduct of the Frankish knight and his wife, as
portrayed in this edifying anecdote, both castigates Frankish
immorality and lack of 'proper' marital jealousy and also reinforces
the values of Muslim society.

A further disreputable element of this story is the very presence
of a woman in the bathhouse on a day when it was obviously being
used by men rather than women. It was standard Islamic custom to
set aside certain times or days when the bathhouse was reserved for
one sex only. Here too, then, the Crusader knight blunders dismally,
flouting Muslim custom, and his behaviour is both ludicrous and
shocking. Usama's readers must have smiled with condescension at
the absurdities of the Frankish knight's behaviour, which are heightened by his attempts to ape Muslim ways. The anti-hero of this story

Figure 5.18 Hammam
al-Sami, domes inlaid with
crown glass, thirteenth
century, Damascus, Syria

belongs to the higher echelons of Crusader society to whom Usama
does attribute at the end of the story some chivalric values; but even
he cannot behave properly in the bathhouse.

Whereas Muslims, following Roman practice, went to the bathhouse for relaxation as well as for purposes of hygiene, there is no
suggestion that this was the motive of the Crusader knight. Usama
does not comment on the interesting fact that the Franks have taken
to the practice of frequenting the bathhouse since their arrival in
the Levant – this improvement in the hygienic habits of the filthy
Franks from the sixth clime of the earth may well have been due to

Figure 5.19 Hammam
al-Sami, transverse section,
thirteenth century, Damascus,
Syria

Figure 5.20 Hammam
al-Sami, section of tepidarium,
thirteenth century, Damascus,
Syria

of the Holy Sepulchre in 400/1009–10, at the behest of the Fatimid caliph al-Hakim. It was, of course, a great blessing that the Franks did not go so far as to destroy either the Dome of the Rock or the Aqsa mosque in retaliation for al-Hakim's action. Although such an act would never have been forgiven, the infidels' defiling and occupying of Islamic monuments, second only to those of Mecca and Medina in the veneration with which they are viewed by Muslims, must have been almost as hard to bear. For eighty-eight years, the gilded dome of the Dome of the Rock was surmounted by a cross and the monument became the Templum Domini. The Aqsa mosque was occupied by the Knights Templar (figure 5.24).

These familiar and much-loved monuments in Jerusalem underwent structural and visual changes. In the Aqsa mosque, the Templars added large sections, mainly in the front of the building, and they refurbished the facade. In the Dome of the Rock the Christian presence was announced externally by the crowning cross, and internally by a grille (plate 5.3) and an altar which was erected on the rock itself.

The Dome of the Rock, which had been built in 72/691 as a triumphant statement of the superiority of Islam over other faiths, especially Christianity, displays a careful selection of Qur'anic inscriptions which tilt at the Trinity and the Incarnation. Islam's uncompromising monotheism is emphasised in a long band of inscriptions measuring around 240 metres in length: the message is unambiguous: 'There is no god but the One God and He has no partner.'[55]

The irony of this very monument in the heart of Jerusalem being

Figure 5.24 Aqsa Mosque, *perspectival view, seventh–eleventh centuries, Jerusalem*

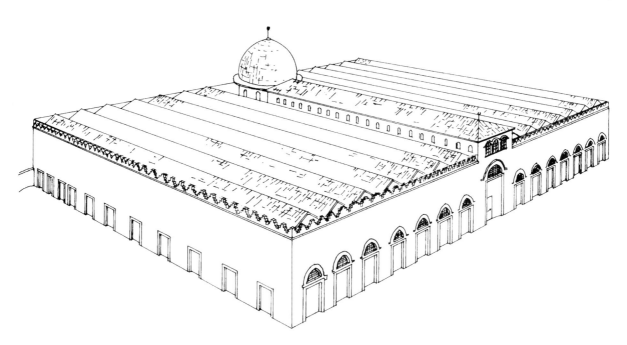

Plate 5.3 *Dome of the Rock, interior showing the Crusader grille around the Rock, 72/691–2 onwards, Jerusalem*

(Creswell Photographic Archive, Ashmolean Museum, Oxford, neg. C. 60)

topped with a cross could not have been lost on the Muslims. Indeed, the removal of that cross was the first aim of the companions of Saladin in 583/1187:

> There was on the top of the Dome of the Rock a large golden cross. When the Muslims entered the city on the Friday a group of them scaled up to the top of the dome to remove the cross. When they reached the top all the people cried out with one voice.[56]

'Imad al-Din al-Isfahani describes the changes wrought on the Dome of the Rock by the Franks in some detail:

> As for the Dome of the Rock, the Franks had built on it a church and an altar . . . They had adorned it with pictures and statues and they had appointed in it places for monks and a place for the Gospel . . . They put in it over the place of the [Prophet's] foot a small gilded dome with raised marble pillars and they said it was the place of the Messiah's foot . . . In it were pictures of grazing animals fixed in marble and I saw amongst those depictions the likenesses of pigs.[57]

It is in the highest degree unlikely that 'Imad al-Din saw any pigs in the Christian decoration of the Dome of the Rock. Perhaps his biased eye was too ready to interpret sheep – a common feature in Christian paradisal iconography – as pigs. He is of course unlikely to have been challenged by his readers. As with Usama, one suspects him of playing to the gallery. The excessively artificial literary devices, such as alliteration, internal rhyme, parallelism, antithesis and repetition, of which he is so fond, point in the same direction.

The Dome of the Rock is portrayed as being 'wounded' by the Franks:

> The Franks had cut pieces from the Rock and carried some of them to Constantinople and some of them to Sicily. It was said that they had sold them for their weight in gold . . . When it [the Rock] was brought to light, its places [where it had been cut] became visible and hearts were cut because of its cuts which became manifest.[58]

The eyewitness account of the 'vagabond ascetic' 'Ali b. Abi Bakr al-Harawi (d. 611/1215),[59] who visited Jerusalem under Frankish rule in 569/1173, is especially valuable. He entered the Dome of the Rock and saw 'on an iron door a representation of the Messiah in gold encrusted with precious stones'.[60]

An anecdote given in Usama's memoirs suggests that the Franks had hung a painting of the Madonna and Child in the Dome of the Rock:

> I saw one of the Franks come to al-Amir Mu'in al-Din when he was in the Dome of the Rock,[61] and say to him, 'Dost thou want to see God as a child?' Mu'in al-Din said, 'Yes'. The Frank walked ahead of us until he showed us the picture of Mary with Christ (may peace be upon him!) as an infant in her lap. He then said, 'This is God as a child'. But Allah is exalted far above what the infidels say about him![62]

Usama's comment reveals the traditional and deep-seated Muslim horror of Christian anthropomorphism.

During the Franks' reoccupation of Jerusalem in the thirteenth century the Muslims felt the same deep outrage at what they saw as a public display of infidelity (kufr).[63] The Ayyubid chronicler Ibn

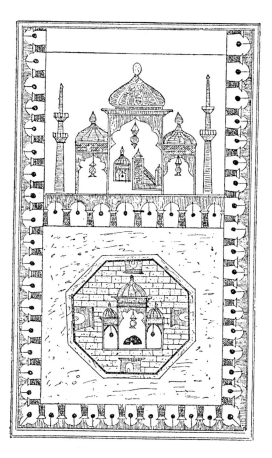

Figure 5.25 Dome of the Rock, manuscript painting, fifteenth century, Egypt

Wasil describes the situation first-hand: 'I entered Jerusalem and I saw monks and priests in charge of the Sacred Rock . . . I saw on it bottles of wine for the ceremony of the mass. I entered the Aqsa mosque and in it a bell was suspended.'[64] He then bemoans the way in which the call to prayer in the holy sanctuary (*al-haram al-sharif*) has been rendered invalid.

The Frankish Threat to the Pilgrimage and to the Holy Cities of Arabia, Mecca and Medina

To perform the Pilgrimage (*hajj*) once in a lifetime is one of the five Pillars of Islam. To many medieval Muslims this occasion of profound religious significance involved enormous expense and hardship. Over the centuries the safety of the routes leading to the Hijaz were threatened by marauding Bedouin, keen to plunder the wealth of the caravans passing through their territory. Now, however, with the advent of the Franks, the threat to the traditional pilgrimage routes was intensified.

The castle of Karak to the east of the Dead Sea had been built in

1142; together with Shawbak, it was intended to threaten the main routes leading from Syria to Egypt and down into Arabia. One of the major assembly points for the *hajj* was Damascus. Crossing the territory policed by these and other Crusader castles in the area required the making of treaties with the Franks; otherwise, the Muslims wishing to perform the *hajj* had to travel by more circuitous and dangerous routes. In the 1180s Ibn Jubayr describes Karak as 'lying astride the Hejaz road and hindering the overland passage of the Muslims'.[65]

Figure 5.26 *Departure of the pilgrimage caravan with the* mahmal *(ceremonial litter), al-Hariri,* al-Maqamat *('The Assemblies'), 634/1237, probably Baghdad, Iraq*

Figure 5.27 *Tombstone with Kufic inscription, undated but probably tenth century, Hijaz, Arabia*

The extreme attitudes and actions of Reynald of Chatillon, the Crusader lord of Karak, should be seen against this background. In 580/1184–5 he broke a treaty and attacked a particularly well-laden caravan (figure 5.26). 'Imad al-Din states that he was in league with an 'evil-intentioned bunch' who were positioned on the pilgrimage route to the Hijaz, hinting thereby that Reynauld had joined up with some local Bedouin tribesmen.[66] Earlier, in 578/1182–3 Reynald had undertaken the enterprise which had gained him widespread opprobrium in the Islamic world. He had gone down the Red Sea by ship and threatened to attack the Holy Cities themselves.[67] (figure 5.27) These two incidents, aimed at the very heart of the Islamic world, were viewed as a hideous outrage against its revered sanctuaries.[68]

Popular Muslim Views of Frankish Filth and Contamination

The perception that the Franks had not only invaded but – far worse – polluted Islamic territory was pervasive. It was not just theological: it did not spring only from the academic circles of those who engaged in polemical writing to prove the superiority of Islam over Christianity. It was the concern of all Muslims who every single moment of their lives tried to adhere to the strict rituals of purity enshrined in Islamic law. It was also a deeply felt perception which manifested itself as clichés and jokes about the 'other side', pitched at a crude and comic level.

We have already referred to Ibn Jubayr's description of Crusader Acre as stinking of excrement and refuse. This perception is reinforced in popular literature. *The Tale of 'Umar b. Nu'man* in the *Thousand and One Nights* contains revealing passages about underlying Muslim perceptions of Christianity. The story, like many others in the collection, seems to conflate Muslim struggles against the Byzantines in the ninth and tenth centuries with *jihad* in the twelfth and thirteenth centuries against the Franks.

> To tell you something of the supreme incense of patriarchal excrements: When the High Patriarch of the Christians in Constantinople made a motion, the priests would diligently collect it in squares of silk and dry it in the sun. They then would mix it with musk, amber and benzoin, and, when it was quite dry, powder it and put it in little gold boxes. These boxes were sent to all Christian kings and churches, and the powder was used as the holiest incense for the sanctification of Christians on all solemn occasions, to bless the bride, to fumigate the newly born, and to purify a priest on ordination. As the genuine excrements of the High Patriarch could hardly suffice for ten provinces, much less for all Christian lands, the priests used to forge the powder by mixing less holy matters with it, that is to say, the excrements of lesser patriarchs and even of the priests themselves. This imposture was not easy to detect. These Greek swine valued the powder for other virtues; they used it as a salve for sore eyes and as a medicine for the stomach and bowels. But only kings and queens and the very rich could obtain these cures, since, owing to the limited quantity of raw materials, a dirham-weight of the powder used to be sold for a thousand dinars in gold. So much for it.[69]

The story concentrates further on the juxtaposition of crosses and excrement:

> In the morning King Afridun assembled the captains and lieutenants of his army and, making them kiss a great cross of wood, fumigated them with the incense described above. On this occasion there could be no doubt as to the genuineness of the powder as it smelt terribly and would have killed any elephant in the Muslim armies.

In the single combat that follows, the Christian protagonist Luka b. Shamlut, grotesquely described as an ass, ape and a cross between a toad and a serpent, 'had stolen his colouring from night and his breath from old latrines. For these reasons he was known as the Sword of Christ.'[70] We see here details which would no doubt entertain and amuse a popular audience assembled on street-corners or at public festivities.

Disease and filth are associated with the Franks: the unfortunate Baldwin IV, the Crusader leper king, is spared no sympathy in the tirade of the Qadi al-Fadil who describes him amongst other epithets as a 'blue-eyed, freckled, leprous evil-doer'.[71] 'Imad al-Din also refers to the Franks as 'a swarm of flies',[72] 'grasshoppers without wings',[73]

Figure 5.28 Part of a militantly Shi'ite verse inscription, Mamluk silver-inlaid bowl, probably early fourteenth century, Syria (?)

and 'howling, savage dogs'. Ibn al-Furat writes that in a raid against the Franks in 530/1136 the *shihna* of Aleppo killed 'innumerable pigs'.[74] Whether he means this literally or metaphorically is not clear. Ibn Jubayr, on the other hand, unambiguously calls Agnes of Courtenay, the mother of Baldwin IV, 'the sow known as Queen who is the mother of the pig who is the Lord of Acre'.[75]

Speaking of a portable tent church used by the Franks, Usama says scathingly:

> The patriarch pitched a huge tent which he used as a church in which they hold their prayers. The church services were conducted by an old deacon who had covered its floor with bulrushes and grass, which resulted in a pest of fleas.[76]

Ibn Jubayr is deeply concerned for the religious health of those Muslims, especially the masses, whose faith will become contaminated by proximity to the Franks: 'There can be no excuse in the eyes of God for a Muslim to stay in any infidel country, save when passing through it, while the way lies clear to Muslim lands.'[77] In particular, the Muslims will face the pains and terrors of

> the hearing of what will distress the heart in the reviling of him [Muhammad] whose memory God has sanctified, and whose rank He has exalted; there is also the absence of cleanliness, the mixing with the pigs, and all the other prohibited matters too numerous to be related or enumerated.[78]

Beneath the scatological humour of the *Tale of 'Umar b. Nu'man* and the concerns of Ibn Jubayr, the deep Muslim revulsion for Christian defilement comes through. Such feelings must have been especially deep in respect of Crusader presence in Muslim territory and Crusader occupation of Muslim religious monuments, such as the Dome of the Rock and the Aqsa mosque. These were, after all, not ordinary religious buildings but the jewels in the crown of Jerusalem, the third holiest city of Islam and the First Qibla of the faith. The grossly offensive antics of the fanatical Crusader buccaneer Reynald of Chatillon on the Red Sea, when he publicly threatened the two Holy Cities of Mecca and Medina, must have sent profound shock waves around the Muslim world since the sanctity of the Ka'ba itself was in jeopardy.

The Muslims were long used to seeing Oriental Christians practising their faith in the Near East and not adhering to the requirements of Islamic purity. But the Franks had transgressed Islamic sacred space. The Muslim population in Syria and Palestine were also well used to the damage wrought by foreign invaders – Turks, Byzantines, Persians – but their reaction to the Crusader newcomers' adorning the Dome of the Rock with crosses and statues and to the

1. *Youthful rider*

(Joe Rock and A. K. Sutherland)

(above and opposite)
2. *Abu Zayd preaching, al-Hariri,* al-Maqamat *('The Assemblies'), 634/1237, probably Baghdad, Iraq*

(Courtesy of the Bibliothèque Nationale de France)

3. *Two men on camels*

(Joe Rock and A. K. Sutherland)

4. *Extract of a letter in Mongol script sent in 705/1305 by the Mongol ruler of Iran, Öljeitü, to King Philip of France, recalling the ancient ties of friendship between the house of Genghis Khan and the French court*

(Courtesy of Archives Nationales, Paris)

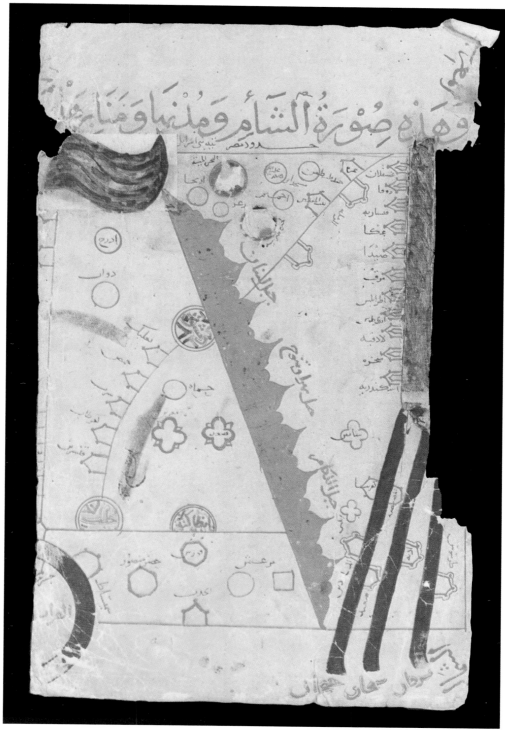

*5. Thirteenth-century Arab map of
the coast of the Levant*

(Courtesy of Ahuan Ltd.)

6. *Image of the world, al-Qazwini,*
ʿAjaʾib al-makhluqat, 790/1388

(Courtesy of the Bibliothèque
Nationale de France)

7. *The Golden Dome (i.e. the Holy Sepulchre) in Jerusalem, al-Qazwini, ʿAjaʾib al-makhluqat, 790/1388*

(Courtesy of the Bibliothèque Nationale de France)

8. *Iskandar (Alexander) fighting the Amazons, al-Qazwini, ʿAjaʾib al-makhluqat, 790/1388*
(Courtesy of the Bibliothèque Nationale de France)

9. *A high-ranking military officer (amir), inlaid brass basin known as the 'Baptistère de St Louis', c. 1300 or earlier, Syria*

(Courtesy of the Louvre, Paris)

10. *Aqsa Mosque,* minbar *of Nur al-Din,* *564/1168 (now destroyed); in the* *background, the* mihrab *restored by* *Saladin after 583/1187–8, Jerusalem*

(Alistair Duncan)

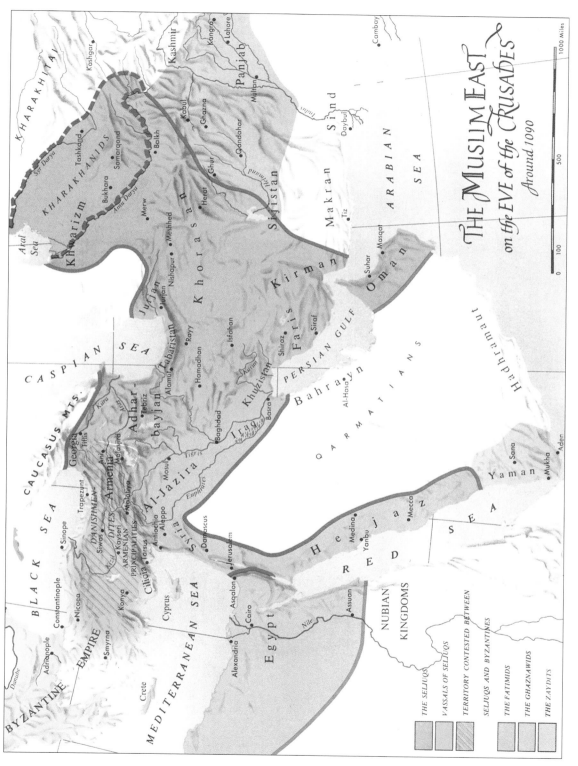

11. Map of the Muslim East on the eve of the Crusades

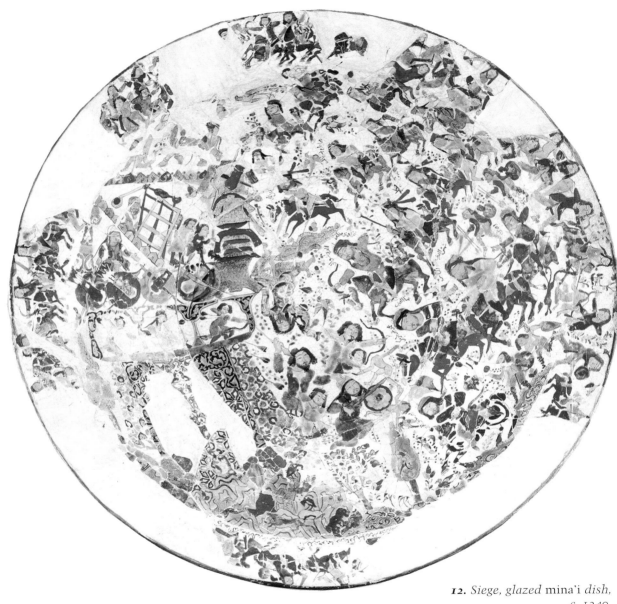

12. *Siege, glazed* mina'i *dish,*
c. 1240,
probably Kashan, Iran
(Courtesy of the Freer Gallery of Art,
Smithsonian Institution, Washington DC
(Accession number 45.8))

(above) *13. Siege, Fatimid drawing with added colour, twelfth century, Fustat, Egypt*

(© The British Museum)

(below) *14. Maristan (hospital) of Nur al-Din, interior view of portal dome, 549/1154, Damascus, Syria*

(Robert Hillenbrand)

(above) **15.** *Citadel, tower, thirteenth century, with modern political poster depicting President Asad, Damascus, Syria*

(Robert Hillenbrand)

(below) **16.** *Jami' al-Nuri, courtyard and sanctuary, after 552/1157, probably 558/1163 and later, Hama, Syria*

(Robert Hillenbrand)

17. *Dome of the Rock, exterior,
72/691–2 and later, Jerusalem*

(Robert Hillenbrand)

Templars' lodging in the Aqsa mosque must have been profound atavistic disgust.

Plate 5.4 Fountain, Great Mosque, twelfth century(?) but using pre-Islamic spolia, Ma'arrat al-Nu'man, Syria

The Evidence of Contemporary Muslim Poetry

Poetry, in many ways the quintessential Arabic literary achievement and renowned in Arab lands for its power to move the hearts of its hearers, is a powerful vehicle in the Crusading period. Contemporary poetry is replete with the symbolism of pollution and purity. The brutal irruption of the Franks in the First Crusade provides an ideal locus for these themes. An anonymous poet of the time writes these moving words:

> The unbelief of the infidels has declared it lawful to inflict harm
> on Islam,
>   Causing prolonged lamentation for the faith.
> What is right is null and void and what is forbidden is (now)
> made licit.
>   The sword is cutting and blood is spilt.

How many Muslim men have become booty (*salib*)
And how many Muslim women's inviolability has been
    plundered (*salib*)?
How many a mosque have they made into a church!
The cross (*salib*) has been set up in the *mihrab*.
    The blood of the pig is suitable for it.
Qur'ans have been burned under the guise of incense.[79]

There is a clear perception in these lines of Muslim spatial consciousness; it is obvious that sacred space has been invaded and polluted. This invasion is both physical and psychological. The Crusaders are portrayed as polluters, invaders, and eaters of unclean meat, and the poet dwells on the word-play between *salib* (booty) and *ṣalib* (cross).

The poet Ibn al-Khayyat suggests in powerful imagery the terror of Muslim women normally protected by the walls of the *harim*:

How many young girls have begun to beat their throats and
    necks out of fear of them [the Franks]?
How many nubile girls have not known the heat [of the day] nor
    felt the cold at night [until now]?
They are almost wasting away with fear and dying of grief and
    agitation.[80]

This imagery of rape is being used at the time of the First Crusade; the Crusaders are jeopardising that most sacred pillar of Islamic society, the sanctity of the womenfolk.

The Purification of Islamic Space

With so much emphasis on the defilement of the Franks, it is not at all surprising that Islamic victories are described with the antithetical symbolism of purification. Describing the surrender of Damietta to the Muslims in 648/1250, Ibn Wasil declares: 'God purified Egypt of them [the Franks]'.[81] The fall of Acre in 690/1291 is heralded by Abu'l-Fida in similar terms: 'Thus the whole of Syria and the coastal areas were purified of the Franks.'[82]

However, the main emphasis on purification in the Islamic sources is reserved – not surprisingly – for the Holy City itself, Jerusalem, and its twin foci, the Aqsa mosque and the Dome of the Rock. The desecration of these two monuments provides an ideal opportunity to draw telling parallels between Islam and Christianity, to express long-suppressed outrage and to reclaim publicly and corporately these holy places which belong to Islam.

The testimony of 'Imad al-Din al-Isfahani, who was present at the conquest of Jerusalem, is particularly important, and he exults in the central role played by his master Saladin in the re-Islamisation of the city. Once the city had been captured, the most urgent task was

Figure 5.29 Muqarnas *squinch, fourteenth century, Cairo, Egypt*

the restoring of the Dome of the Rock and the Aqsa mosque to a state in which they were fit again for Islamic worship. The actions taken by Saladin and his followers were not mere ceremonies of reappropriation of Muslim religious buildings: these centres of Islamic sanctity needed to be cleansed and purified of Frankish pollution. The occasion was recorded on the Dome of the Rock itself. When Frederick II of Sicily entered Jerusalem and visited the Dome of the Rock he saw an inscription which had been engraved on the dome; it read: 'Saladin has purified this sacred house from the polytheists.'[83]

Saladin's nephew, Taqi al-Din 'Umar, was in charge of the actual process of purification. Rose-water was poured over the walls and floors of the two buildings which were then perfumed with incense. Before valid Islamic worship could take place, the Dome of the Rock had to be denuded of all the Christian trappings placed on it during the Crusader occupation.

299

Ibn al-Athir remarks soberly that once Jerusalem had been taken and the infidels had departed, Saladin 'ordered the purification (*tathir*) of the [Aqsa] mosque and the [Dome of the] Rock of the filths (*aqdhar*) and impurities (*anjas*) and it was all done'.[84]

'Imad al-Din is more fulsome in his language. After the re-Islamicisation of the building, the Dome of the Rock emerged like 'a young bride'.[85] This simile was often applied to the Ka'ba in medieval Islamic poetry, and the allusion would not have been lost on his hearers. The implied equation of the Dome of the Rock with the Ka'ba itself is a measure of the sanctity which surrounded the Jerusalem shrine. The description of 'Imad al-Din pinpoints those features which were abhorrent to the Muslims in this, their holy sanctuary, their *haram*: images, statues, monks – these constituted the hallmarks of Christianity in the Muslim popular imagination.

Similar changes were necessary in the Aqsa mosque (plates 5.5–5.6). The niche (*mihrab*) had to be uncovered again since it had been concealed by a wall built by the Knights Templar, who had made the building into a granary, or, in the version of 'Imad al-Din, into a lavatory. He dwells on the defiled state of the Aqsa mosque:

Plate 5.5 *Aqsa Mosque, Ayyubid* mihrab *with glass mosaic ornament restored by Saladin, 583/1187–8, Jerusalem*

(Creswell Photographic Archive, Ashmolean Museum, Oxford, neg. C. 5002)

The Aqsa mosque, especially its *mihrab*, was full of pigs and obscene language, replete with the excrement they had dropped in the building,[86] inhabited by those who have professed unbelief, have erred and strayed, acted unjustly and perpetrated offences, overflowing with impurities. Slackness in purifying it is forbidden to us.[87]

Once again one may feel that 'Imad al-Din's pen is running away with him, and once again it is hard to believe that 'the Aqsa mosque, especially its *mihrab*, was full of pigs and . . . excrement'. But this invective, a kind of performance art, fulfils its purpose in maintaining the mood of abhorrence for the spiritual defilement of the Christians.

'Imad al-Din speaks of 'the driving away (*iqsa'*) of those whom God had driven away (*aqsa'*) with His curse from the Aqsa'.[88] Church bells have been silenced by the call to prayer and the faith has been purified 'from the pollutions (*anjas*) of those races (*ajnas*) and the filths of the lowest people (*adnas adna al-nas*)'.[89]

'Imad al-Din uses this remarkable verbal dexterity and erudition to give expression to the long-suppressed indignation at the occupation of the Islamic monuments, the Dome of the Rock and the Aqsa mosque, by the infidel Franks. The Christianity of the Franks is identified by the hated bells of the church towers and reviled at a much deeper level by their invasion of the Islamic sacred space which has been contaminated by their pollution and filth. The conquest of Jerusalem is viewed as Islam's triumph over Christianity.

In the sermon preached on the reconquest of Jerusalem, Ibn Zaki stresses the theme of purification at regular intervals: 'I praise Him . . . for his cleansing of His Holy House from the filth of polytheism and its pollutions.'[90] He speaks of the 'perfume of sanctification and glorification' in the mosque and calls on the faithful to 'purify the rest of the land from this filth which hath angered God and His Apostle'.[91]

In a letter to the caliph, 'Imad al-Din allows himself the literary device of replacing rose-water with the believers' tears: 'The Rock has been cleansed of the filth of the infidels by the tears of the pious.'[92]

The Holy Land Itself

Muslim sources usually speak of Jerusalem as 'al-Quds', 'Bayt al-Muqaddas' or 'Bayt al-Maqdis'. All these names stress the sanctity (q d s in Arabic means 'to be holy') of the city. They also speak of *al-ard al-muqaddasa* (the Holy Land), referring to the wider area around Jerusalem which is replete with shrines and memories of prophets and saints. With Saladin's conquest of Jerusalem, the Muslim sources extend the images of purification to include the Holy Land itself and they play on the similarity between the names *al-Quds* and *al-muqaddas*.

This theme is highlighted by Ibn Jubayr who addresses a victory ode in this vein to Saladin:

> You have conquered the sacred part (*al-muqaddas*) of His earth. It has become pure (*tahir*) again.[93]

Not just Jerusalem but its hallowed environs, the home of saints and prophets, has also become pure again. The Qur'an proclaims:

> They question thee concerning menstruation. Say: It is an illness, so let women alone at such times and go not in unto them till they are cleansed. And when they have purified themselves, then go in unto them.[94]

Such a deep-rooted taboo is echoed in the powerful language used by Saladin's scribe, the Qadi al-Fadil, in his triumphal letter to the caliph in Baghdad announcing Saladin's conquest of Jerusalem: 'It has become the sacred, pure land, when once it was the menstruating (*tamitha*) one.' Not just Jerusalem but the Holy Land itself are included here.[95]

The Image of 'the Other': What's in a Name?

Cultures define themselves as different from other cultures by using a variety of interconnecting criteria. The terminology by which they exclude groups and individuals may also vary.

When they arrived in the Near East, the Crusaders began to be called *Ifranj* or *Firanj* by the medieval Muslims. Originally, this term probably signified the inhabitants of Charlemagne's empire, but at a later stage it was widened to embrace people from western Europe in general. The country of the Franks, that is those Christian European territories situated beyond the Pyrenees, was known as *Ifranja* by the Arabs and *Firanjistan* by the Persians and the Turks.[96] Incidentally, in modern Arabic the verb *tafarnaja*, derived from the root *Ifranj*, means 'to become Europeanised', whilst the term *al-ifranji* has been used as one of the words for syphilis. As well as these terms, the Crusaders were known by a variety of stereotyped pejorative and abusive epithets: devils, dogs, pigs and other beasts.

Religious differences are particularly highlighted in some of the titles given to the Franks. Muslim writers were long used to branding heretics as 'accursed' (*la'in*). The Isma'ilis, in particular, were given such a label,[97] and it was easy to shift it to the Franks.[98] Exactly when the Muslim chroniclers began to use such formulae when writing about the Franks is difficult to pinpoint, especially since, as already noted, the earliest surviving sources date from the middle of the twelfth century only. Perhaps as a result of experiencing first-hand the Franks' attack on his home town of Damascus and the heightened atmosphere of *jihad* during the reign of Nur al-Din in Syria, Ibn al-Qalanisi adds for the first time the formula 'God forsake them' when referring to the Franks in his account of the year 553/1158–9.[99] Thereafter it becomes standard practice amongst the chroniclers.

According to Lewis, the term 'infidel' (*kafir*) is the term of ultimate exclusion from the Islamic community, defining the difference between Muslims and the rest of the world. Certainly the term *kafir* (with its plural *kuffar*) is frequently used of the Franks. The term is accompanied in the sources by standard phrases of abuse addressed to either groups or individuals, such as 'May God curse them', 'May God send them to perdition'. Whether such maledictions were deeply meant or perfunctory is hard to say, but at key moments of religious intensity and political triumph they are clearly meaningful. As with other groups of Christians, the Franks are called 'polytheists' (*mushrikun*) and the 'enemies of God'. Sibt b. al-Jawzi labels them 'people of stubbornness' whilst Ibn al-Dawadari derides them as 'worshippers of crosses'.[100] They are also described as 'the people of the Trinity' (ahl al-tathlith),[101] 'the servants of the Messiah',[102] and 'polytheist dogs'.[103]

The Christian Symbol of the Cross

There is no doubt that the symbol of the cross epitomised Christianity for the Muslims. In the popular Muslim mind Christianity was clearly identified by the cross. A Christian king in one of the folk epics is given the trumped-up name 'Abd al-Salib (slave of the cross),[104] a name modelled on the plethora of Muslim names which involve the use of 'Abd in conjunction with one of the ninety-nine beautiful names of God (such as 'Abd al-Wahhab) but which in a Christian context has pejorative undertones.

Whilst the Muslims had long been used to the presence of the Oriental Christians in the Near East, the arrival of the Franks brought new experiences in which the cross played a much more prominent role than hitherto. Clearly there was a marked difference between the cross as a symbol of the faith of the indigenous Oriental Christians who were a tolerated minority under majority Islamic rule and the cross as a symbol of the conquests and occupation of a foreign invader, the Franks.

Whilst the Muslim sources do not mention the cross being worn by individual Frankish soldiers as part of their martial garments, it is clear from many references that the cross became a more visible symbol after the arrival of the Crusaders. Once a town had been

Figure 5.30 The arms of Jerusalem ('arg. a cross potent between four crosslets or') on a brass basin made by an Arab craftsman for Hugh de Lusignan, King of Jerusalem and Cyprus (1324–59); probably Egypt or Syria

taken by the Franks, it was often Christianised by the conversion of Muslim buildings into Christian ones and by the erection of new churches. Ibn al-Qalanisi remarks that after the conquest of Ma'arrat al-Nu'man by the Franks in 492/1099 'they erected crosses over the town'.[105]

For their part the Muslims heralded their victory by gaining possession of their enemy's emotional focus. A typical example occurred after the victory of Mawdud and Tughtegin over the Franks in 506/1113 near the bridge of al-Sannabra, when the Muslims triumphantly seized the tent-church of the Franks.[106] Both sides felt the overwhelming need to destroy the symbols of the other's faith.[107] Breaking crosses was a symbolic act in which Christianity was defeated and Islam triumphant. Saladin is praised in Ibn Jubayr's victory ode for breaking 'their cross by force' at Hattin.[108] Ibn Abi Tayyi' describes the cross captured at Hattin: 'Saladin brought back as booty the cross of crosses, which is a piece of wood covered with gold and encrusted with precious stones on which, they allege, their God was crucified.'[109] The gilded cross on the Dome of the Rock was not pulled down gently. Ibn Shaddad makes it clear that it was hurled to the ground, despite its immense size.[110]

After the fall of Jerusalem, Saladin sent the caliph in Baghdad important trophies of his great victory. The crowning piece was the cross on top of the Dome of the Rock in Jerusalem: 'The cross which was of copper and coated with gold was buried beneath the Nubian gate [in Baghdad] and thus was trodden upon.'[111]

The Contrasting Symbols of the Cross and the Qur'an

Ibn al-Jawzi (d. 597/1200) and his grandson use the highly charged emotional atmosphere of the siege of Damascus by the Franks in 543/1148 as an opportunity to score propaganda points. Here the Cross and the Qur'an are used as palpable symbols of the opposing faiths.

These two sources highlight the way in which the most potent Islamic religious symbol, the Qur'an, could sustain morale and build up faith in adversity. Its triumph is inevitable. On the occasion of the siege of Damascus the Syrian 'Uthmanic Qur'an – an object of the first importance, indeed a much-treasured relic – was used as a rallying force in the Great Mosque. As Sibt b. al-Jawzi writes: 'The people assembled in the mosque, the men, women and young boys, and they opened the 'Uthmanic Qur'an.[112] They scattered ashes on their heads and wept and abased themselves. God answered them.'[113]

[Incidentally, Ibn al-Dawadari mentions that when the Franks had captured Ma'arrat al-Nu'man in 492/1098 the Muslims took the 'Uthmanic Qur'an for safe-keeping to Damascus.] Both chroniclers also insert the following story immediately afterwards:

> There was with the Franks a tall priest with a long beard who gave
> them guidance . . . He mounted his donkey and hung a cross round

his neck and put two crosses in his hands and hung a cross round the neck of his donkey. He placed in front of him the Gospels and [more] crosses [and the Holy Scriptures].

He then said [to the army] 'The Messiah has promised me that I will be victorious today.'

Predictably, this figure, absurdly encumbered with crosses, and his donkey (also wearing a cross), came to a sticky end. Ibn al-Jawzi writes: 'When the Muslims saw him they displayed zeal for Islam and they all attacked him and killed him and the donkey. They took the crosses and burned them.'[114]

The message is clear and the juxtaposition of these two anecdotes is quite deliberate.

On other occasions the antithesis of the Cross and the minaret is used. The Ayyubid poet Ibn al-Nabih writes of al-'Adil as follows: 'Through him God has destroyed the Cross and its followers. Through him the minaret of the community of Islam is lifted.'[115]

The Cross as a Symbol of Misfortune for Muslims

As the prime outward symbol of Christianity, the cross carried with it misfortune to Muslims who became associated with it. Muslims who fought under it were inevitably doomed to defeat. The chroniclers make great play of this at the infamous battle of Gaza in 642/1244 when the Muslim armies of Damascus and Hims fought under the banners of the Franks against the Khwarazmians and the Egyptian forces. This whole episode is recorded mournfully by Sibt b. al-Jawzi:

Crosses were above their heads and priests with the battalions were making the sign of the cross over the Muslims and offering them the sacrament. In their hand were chalices and drinking vessels from which they gave them to drink ... As for the lord of Hims ... he began to weep, saying 'I knew when we departed under the crosses of the Franks that we would not prosper'.[116]

In the Mamluk period, Baybars' ill-fated naval attack on Cyprus in 670/1271 is seen by some chroniclers as divine retribution for the Muslims' having resorted to the trick of putting the cross on the ships' flags.[117]

The Central Importance of the Cross

Describing the King of Jerusalem, the Qadi al-Fadil realises the central importance of the cross, both to the King and his followers:

Their despot was taken prisoner, bearing in his hand the object in which he placed his utmost confidence, the strongest bond by which he held to his religion, namely, the cross of the Crucifixion, by which were led to battle the people of arrogance.[118]

The Qadi continues: 'They did not ever go forward into a danger without having it in their midst; they would fly around it like moths around the light.'[119]

It is incidentally noteworthy that in this Muslim rhetoric the Islamic counterweight to the Christian cross is either the Qur'an or the minaret. It is not, as it was much later to become, the crescent, although as early as the eleventh century, when the Armenian cathedral of Ani in eastern Anatolia was converted into a mosque, the cross on its dome was taken down and replaced by a silver crescent.[120]

Plate 5.7 *Jami' al-Nuri, window-frame in sanctuary, 566–8/1170–3, Mosul, Iraq*

Christianity's Use of Images

There is frequent mention in Islamic sources of the pictures and statues of the Christians which were used in their worship. The stance of Muslim writers towards such pictures is almost uniformly hostile. A contrast is drawn between the constituent parts of the mosque and what is found in a church.

Ibn al-Nabih declares of the Ayyubid prince al-Ashraf:

> You have purified its [Damietta's] high *mihrab* and *minbar* from their filth after its feet [the *minbar's*] had trembled.
>   And you have begun to destroy the statue of the Messiah on it in spite of those who kiss it as if it were a deity.[121]

In the popular epic *Sirat al-amira Dhat al-Himma* a Muslim hero enters a church where a picture drops tears on to the Gospel.[122]

Al-'Umari mentions the power of Christian religious pictures to move and persuade. He relates under the year 585/1189 that the Franks at Tyre had sent to Europe asking for reinforcements: 'They had drawn a picture of the Messiah and an Arab beating the Messiah who had made him bleed. They said: "this is the Prophet of the Arabs beating the Messiah".'[123]

Al-'Umari does not say whether this picture was sent as part of the message to Europe to muster support or whether it was for local consumption. Apocryphal as this story may well be, it is an indication of Muslim views on the pernicious power of visual images and the gullibility of the Christians in believing in their powers.

In 665/1266–7 Baybars went up to the citadel of Safad to pray in a tower. As Ibn al-Furat relates, Baybars saw there a large idol which, according to the Franks, protected the citadel. They called it Abu Jurj (George's father): 'He ordered that it should be torn out and smashed, and the place was purified of it, its site being turned into a *mihrab*.'[124]

Figure 5.31
(above and opposite)
Shields, Firdawsi, Shahnama ('Book of Kings') manuscripts, c. 1330–45, Shiraz, Iran

What the Muslims Knew about Christianity

Despite Islamic conviction that theirs was the one true faith, Muslims at the time of the Crusades had some knowledge of the tenets of Christianity and the Church. Ibn al-Athir mentions the different ecclesiastical centres of the Oriental Christians. When mentioning the conquest of Edessa, he writes:

> This Edessa is one of the noblest and most admired cities for the Christians. It is one of the ecclesiastical sees for them: for the noblest of them is Jerusalem, then Antioch, then Rome and Constantinople and Edessa.[125]

Al-Harawi knows that Bethlehem is the place of Jesus' birth.[126] Ibn Wasil in his account of his visit as Baybars' envoy to Manfred of Sicily in Ramadan 659/1261 shows considerable interest in the Papacy and tries to explain it to his Muslim readers:

> The Pope in Rome is for them [the Franks] the caliph of Christ, taking his place. To him belongs the declaring of what is forbidden and what is licit, the cutting and the separating [i.e. the power to excommunicate]. He it is who puts the crowns of royalty on kings and appoints them. Nothing is established for them in their law except by him. He is celibate and when he dies someone takes his place who is also characterised by the attribute of celibacy.[127]

In his little-known work, the Book of the Stick (*Kitab al-'asa*), described by Irwin as a 'rhabdophilist's anthology',[128] Usama praises the piety of Christian monks of the Chapter of St John whom he saw praying in a church near the tomb of John the Baptist in Sebastea in the province of Nablus:

> After saying my prayers, I came out into the square that was bounded on one side by the Holy Precinct. I found a half-closed gate, opened it and entered a church. Inside were about ten old men, their bare heads as white as combed cotton. They were facing the east, and wore (embroidered?) on their breasts staves ending in crossbars turned up like the rear of a saddle. They took their oath on this sign, and gave hospitality to those who needed it. The sight of their piety touched my heart, but at the same time it displeased and saddened me, for I had never seen such zeal and devotion among the Muslims.[129]

As usual, however, Usama's comments about 'the other side' are never unstinting in their praise. He goes on to mention Sufis whose number and degree of devotion far exceed those of the Christian monks:

> For the moment I thought there was no one there. Then I saw about a hundred prayer-mats, and on each a Sufi, his face expressing peaceful serenity, and his body humble devotion. This was a reassuring sight, and I gave thanks to Almighty God that there were among the Muslims men of even more zealous devotion than those Christian priests. Before this I had never seen Sufis in their monastery, and was ignorant of the way they lived.[130]

Once again Usama cannot resist the temptation to make a telling and damaging comparison which asserts the superiority of Islam.

There can be little doubt that, by Saladin's time at least, the Muslims knew that the Franks were fighting a religious war just as they were. As Ibn Shaddad writes: 'Each of the two enemies sold his life for the delights of the next life, preferring eternal life to that of this world.'[131]

Al-Qalqashandi, quoting a letter dated 1190, speaks of the Franks: 'Everyone summoned himself [to the *jihad*] before being called.'[132]

When the Franks first arrived in the Near East, it seems very clear that the Muslims had little idea of why they had come. As we have seen, certain clearly identifiable visual elements associated with the Franks are often mentioned in the sources, such as crosses, gospels and priests. Gradually, however, Muslim knowledge of the enemy's views seems to have become greater and based on more solid information. By the time of Saladin's reconquest of Jerusalem, the Franks' perception of the conflict is used by Muslim writers as a linchpin in their propaganda of the 1180s.[133] The alleged text of a letter from Richard the Lionheart himself to Saladin is recorded by Ibn Shaddad:

> The sole topic here is Jerusalem, the Cross and the Land. As for Jerusalem, it is our belief that we will not give it up even if we are down to our last man.[134] As for the Land, it will be returned to us from here until the other side of the Jordan. As for the Cross, for you it is a piece of wood of no value. For us it is important, so let the sultan graciously restore it to us and we will feel at peace and be at rest from this constant toil.[135]

The Muslim propagandists acknowledge that the Franks possess true religious fervour. In 585/1189–90 'Imad al-Din quotes a letter which was written to rouse the Muslim faithful to *jihad*. In it he presents the Franks' zeal for their faith as a model for the flagging morale of the Muslims. He praises them for realising their goals, for displaying courage, and for spending their wealth in the cause of religion:

> There has remained no king in their countries and islands, no ruler or great man, who has not kept pace with his neighbour in the area of troops and has not outstripped his peer in endeavour and effort. They have put at nought the sacrifice of their hearts' blood and lives in the safeguarding of their religion . . . They did what they did and they sacrificed what they sacrificed purely and simply to defend him whom they worship and to honour their belief.[136]

When the Muslims seized 'the True Cross' in 583/1187 it seems that its role as a focus for the Franks in battle was understood, at least by important Muslims such as al-Qadi al-Fadil and 'Imad al-Din. Calling it the Cross of the Crucifixion (*salib al-salbut*), 'Imad al-Din says: 'They fight beneath that Cross most stubbornly and faithfully and they see it as a covenant on which they build the strongest and surest of contracts.'[137]

Muslim Polemic and Propaganda about Frankish Christianity

There was a well-established tradition of interfaith public debate and

Figure 5.32 Page of Qur'an made for the Mamluk sultan Sha'ban, c. 1370, Cairo, Egypt

of Muslim writings against Christianity long before the coming of the Franks, from the Umayyad period onwards. Indeed, the inscriptions of the Dome of the Rock, dated 72/691, attack the Christian doctrines of the Incarnation and the Trinity. Muslim writers, using the Qur'anic revelation, had focused in particular on the Christian doctrines of the divinity of Jesus and the Trinity as the basis for their polemical tracts.[138]

The attitudes of Muslim writers in the period of the Crusades had been moulded by this tradition, but it is important to examine to what extent these pre-existing views formed on the basis of long acquaintance with Oriental Christianity were modified by prolonged co-existence with the Crusader newcomers.

The Muslim polemical writings against Christianity should not, however, be viewed in isolation, as a separate propaganda initiative so to speak. The Mamluk period in particular witnessed a spate of treatises condemning innovations in Islamic beliefs and practices.[139] There was deep concern to define the identity of Islam in the wake of the Turkish and Mongol invasions and the presence of the parvenu Mamluks in Egypt and Syria. Treatises were composed condemning popular religious practices, theosophical Sufism, philosophy, heresies and innovations. Indeed, Ibn Taymiyya, the central figure in this debate, attacked all these with his customary vigour. Above all, he was convinced that 'right religion' was essential for the spiritual welfare and social stability of the Islamic community. The attacks on Christianity formed part of this ongoing debate about the nature of true Islam and the defence of it against all comers. The Mamluk period may well have brought with it substantial numbers of Coptic converts to Islam who carried over Christian practices and modes of thought into their new religious life as Muslims: the Muslim view was that such trends should be eschewed at all costs.[140]

Ibn Taymiyya's tract against Christianity called *The Right Answer to Those who Alter the Religion of the Messiah* is massive and may be viewed as the most comprehensive work of its kind.[141] It fits into his overall defence of the True Faith. Ibn Taymiyya lived through the double catastrophe of the Crusades and the Mongol onslaught on the Islamic world, and his attacks on Christianity, on its doctrines and practitioners alike, are uncompromisingly hostile. Writing about Christianity he declares:

> They have divided up into sects on the subject of the Trinity and of the union [of the divinity and humanity of Christ]; they have separated on things that no intelligent [individual] could believe and that no tradition reports.[142]

Ibn Taymiyya castigates priests and monks, including patriarchs, metropolitans and bishops, for their hypocrisy towards kings.[143] The charlatanism of monks comes under particular fire.[144] A trick allegedly practised by the Christians was the putting of *kohl* on the Virgin's eyes for tears: 'They put *kohl* in water moving with a very slight movement, which then flowed slowly so that it ran down the picture of the Virgin and came out of her eyes. People thought it was tears.'[145]

Interesting evidence is also found in a work entitled *An Answer to the Dhimmis and to Those who Follow Them*, written by the late thirteenth-century or early fourteenth-century writer Ghazi b. al-Wasiti.[146] In the medieval Islamic world, polemical treatises abound in which medieval Muslim or Christian scholars engage in a refutation of their opponents' beliefs. But this work of al-Wasiti is significant because it was written just after the expulsion of the Crusaders. Predictably, the work aims to prove the superiority of Islam, and this is done mainly through illustrative anecdotes dating back to early periods of Islamic history but also set in the author's own time. The work is vehemently hostile to the Copts.

On the first page of his tract, the author establishes a clear link between the Oriental Christians and the Crusaders. He states that he wishes to bring to light the harm the Christians have caused Islam: 'desiring to cleanse the days of the exalted [Mamluk] sultanate of their [the Christians'] filthiness, just as it has blotted out their strong, well-defended kingdoms and their lofty, towering fortifications'.[147]

Ghazi, who comments sharply on the ubiquitous Copt who can be seen 'at the buzzing of every fly',[148] accuses the Christians of 'being spies of the un-eyelashed Tartars' (that is, the Mongols) and of paying the ransoms for Crusader captives – royal princes, rich women and notables – from Tripoli.[149] The whole tone of this work is vituperative and strongly anti-Christian. Anecdote after anecdote proclaims the duplicity and perfidy of the Copts, culminating in the final invective: 'In the polytheist [i.e. Christian] are four attributes: lack of religion, abundance of treachery, deceiving of Muslims and alienating people of (true) faith.'[150] But the anti-Christian polemic did not just emerge in apologetic works written by religious lawyers. There is valuable evidence in other literary genres.

The Sufi and legal circles of Aleppo at the time of Nur al-Din, where there was a heightening awareness of *jihad*, included the Persian author of the *Sea of Precious Virtues*, and he devotes a complete section to a refutation of the Byzantines and the Franks. In chapter 1 of this section, entitled 'On the iniquities of the Christians', the anonymous author writes:

> The most amazing thing in the world is that the Christians say that Jesus is divine, that He is God, and then say that the Jews seized him and crucified him. How then can a God who cannot protect himself protect others?[151]

This kind of argumentation is nothing new in Islamic polemic against Christianity, but the fact that it is placed in a work of spiritual guidance to the ruler, the genre of Mirrors for Princes, is unusual and must be a result of direct confrontation with the Franks, who are mentioned specifically and grouped with the Byzantines.

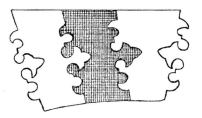

Figure 5.33 *Mamluk joggled voussoirs, fourteenth century, Cairo, Egypt*

The demolition of the doctrine of the divinity of Christ is nothing short of vitriolic: 'Anyone who believes that his God came out of a woman's privates is quite mad; he should not be spoken to, and he has neither intelligence nor faith.' It sounds too as if the author has either visited a particular Christian church or heard about it: 'In a church they have painted a picture of Jesus hanging from a cross, and chained it to a wall in prison and another similar picture in a church that has numerous pictures in it.'[152]

This work contains stereotypical allegations of loose living amongst Christian women, reminiscent of the stories of Usama. The author accuses the Christians of allowing a woman without a husband to indulge in fornication, alleging that the Christians say: 'A woman knows best about her own affairs; her private parts are hers; if she wishes, she can guard them, and if she wishes she can bestow them.'[153]

Christian judges fix the rate for copulation and lust as follows: 'four *fils* for each act of coition and one *fils* for each ejaculation'.[154] The author also accuses Christian women of fornicating with priests at night and of not veiling their faces. These passages reveal a deep revulsion for the Christians and a contempt for both their absurd doctrines and the immoral ways which come from a false revelation.

The Religious Gullibility of the Franks

The chronicles too contain many illuminating anecdotes. Even a Frankish victory can be used for scoring propaganda points with the hindsight of later Muslim reunification and successes. The famous story of the Holy Lance at the siege of Antioch in 491/1098 is exploited by some Muslim chroniclers who use the legend as an example of Christian gullibility. The lance, which according to Crusader sources served as a powerful emotional focus for the dispirited Franks in their victory at Antioch, is shown by Ibn al-Athir (d. 630/1233) to be the cynical trick of a Christian monk. He had buried the lance in St Peter's Church in Antioch beforehand, promised the Franks victory if they found it, and then led them to the place where they could uncover it.[155]

Later on, Ibn Taghribirdi (d. 874/1470) tells a similar story of the same incident but he involves the Frankish leader, St Gilles, in the trickery:

St Gilles, the leader of the Franks, was cunning and sly and he arranged a ruse with a monk, saying: 'Go and bury this lance in such-and-such a place. Then tell the Franks after that: "I saw the Messiah in a dream saying 'In such-and-such a place there is a lance buried, so go and look for it, for if you find it the victory is yours. It is my lance'"'.' So they fasted for three days and prayed and gave alms. Then he [the monk] went up to the place and the Franks were with him and they searched for it. The lance appeared. They shouted and fasted and gave alms and went out to the Muslims and they fought them until they drove them out of the town.[156]

Unlike Ibn al-Athir, who makes no comment on the ultimate Frankish victory which seems to be linked with a trick, Ibn Taghribirdi comments more honestly:

The amazing thing was that the Franks when they sallied forth against the Muslims were extremely weak from hunger and lack of food so that they ate carrion, and the forces of Islam were extremely strong and plentiful; and [yet] they defeated the Muslims.[157]

The Intensification of anti-Christian Propaganda in Saladin's Time

Questions of doctrine became more prominent during Saladin's time: the arguments focused as usual on two key themes, the divinity of

Plate 5.8 Jami' al-Nuri, dark blue marble columns in sanctuary. The octagonal columns date from 566–8/1170–3; the composite columns with lyre-shaped capitals were probably incorporated from an earlier building but at a later date. Mosul, Iraq

Jesus and the Trinity. In the first sermon pronounced in the newly conquered Jerusalem Ibn Zaki quoted selected Qur'anic verses which emphasise God's Oneness[158] – 'Praise be to Allah, who hath not taken unto Himself a son, and who hath no partner in the Sovereignty'[159] – and the Sura of Unity itself, the very heart of the Qur'anic message:

Say: He is Allah, the One!
Allah, the eternally Besought of all!
He begetted not nor was begotten.
And there is none comparable unto Him.[160]

These quotations are precisely the ones with which the Umayyad caliph had adorned the interior of the Dome of the Rock in 72/691. It is likely enough that Ibn Zaki's sermon, which was delivered at the Aqsa mosque, near the Dome of the Rock, deliberately evoked these echoes and that some of his audience would have noted them.

Later in the sermon Ibn Zaki returns to his attack on Christianity. Describing Jesus as an honoured prophet, he nevertheless roundly denies his divinity: 'They are surely infidels who say: Verily God is Christ, the son of Mary.'[161]

The contrasting symbols of Islam and Christianity are used to powerful effect in the Qadi al-Fadil's letter to the caliph. Speaking of Saladin, he writes:

> From their places of prayer he cast down the cross and set up the call to prayer. The altars were replaced by *minbar*s and the churches converted into mosques; the people of the Qur'an succeeded to the people of the cross.[162]

The Propaganda Value of Saladin's Magnanimity

The Muslims had a long memory. The events of 1099 were alive in their minds eighty-eight years later when Saladin entered Jerusalem in triumph. The temptation for vengeance, to obliterate the collective memory of the horror and shame of the Frankish conquest, must have been very strong. Three or four generations of Muslims would have heard about this event and its significance would have been buried deep in their minds, not as a mere political and military fact but as a shame and violation of two of the most Holy Places of Islam.

Saladin is presented by Ibn al-Athir as wanting initially to exact vengeance on the Franks:

> They [the Franks] agreed to ask for peace terms and to hand over Jerusalem to Saladin, so they sent a group of their notables and leaders to ask for peace. When they mentioned that to the sultan he refrained from concurring with them and said: 'I shall deal with you only in the way you dealt with its inhabitants when you conquered it in the year 492 with killing and taking prisoners and other similar offences'.[163]

Yet for Ibn al-Athir and other Muslim chroniclers of this event, the propaganda value of the bloodless conquest of Jerusalem by Saladin counts for much more than the temptation, soon overcome, to exact vengeance. For them it is important to display the subsequent magnanimity of Saladin's conduct not just as a personal characteristic of his but also as a demonstration of the superiority of Muslim conduct over Christian conduct, of Islamic values over Christian values.

Thus Saladin is shown to have honoured his assurances of safety to the Franks and to have granted safe-conduct to high-ranking

Crusader ladies. He is shown to be the epitome of chivalry and Muslim honour:[164]

> When the great patriarch of the Franks left with only God knows what from the churches, including the Rock and the Aqsa and the Refuse,[165] and he [personally] had an equivalent amount of money, Saladin did not put any obstacle in his way. He [Saladin] was told to take what he [the patriarch] had with him in order to strengthen the Muslims thereby and he said: 'I will not act treacherously towards him'.

The Importance of the Church of the Holy Sepulchre

The old word play on the name of this church – called the Church of the Resurrection (*kanisat al-qiyama*) in Arabic (colour plate 7) but satirised by the Muslims since the seventh century as the Church of Refuse (*kanisat al-qumama*) – was fully exploited to debunk the Franks in the twelfth and thirteenth centuries.[166]

Al-Harawi visited Jerusalem in 569/1173 and writes about this church:

> As for the places of pilgrimage of the Christians, the most important of them is the Church of Refuse . . . For the Christians the tomb is situated there which they call the tomb of the Resurrection (*qiyama*) because they locate in this place the resurrection of the Messiah; in reality the site was Refuse (*qumama*), the place of refuse because the sweepings of the area were thrown there; it was a place outside the city where the hands of malefactors were cut off and thieves were crucified: that is what the Gospel says. And God alone knows the truth.[167]

Saladin's adviser, the Qadi al-Fadil, knew the religious purpose of the Franks' coming to Jerusalem. In his famous triumphal letter to the caliph on Saladin's behalf he speaks of 'kings bearing crosses, groups from across the sea, throngs of different kinds of infidels'; their aim was to 'liberate the Tomb and restore the [Church of] Refuse (*qumama*)'.[168]

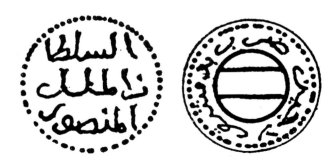

Figure 5.34 Coin of the Mamluk sultan Lajin, 1290s, Cairo, Egypt

Saladin decided not to destroy the Church of the Holy Sepulchre in 583/1187 although some Muslims more zealous than he pressed for him to do so. In his usual hyperbolic rhymed prose 'Imad al-Din al-Isfahani records:

> He [Saladin] parleyed with the people with him about it [the Church of the Holy Sepulchre]. Amongst them were those who advised that its structures should be demolished, its traces should be blotted out, the way to visiting it should be blinded, its statues should be removed, its errors should be obliterated, its candelabras should be extinguished, its Gospels should be destroyed, its seductions should be removed and its pronouncements should be exposed as lies.[169]

These advisers went on to say that with the actual building destroyed it would no longer be the focus for Christian visitation and pilgrimage: 'The Franks will stop wanting to make pilgrimage there and thus we will finally succeed in being at peace in respect to them.'[170]

However, Saladin was obviously swayed by those who said that the church should be kept intact, arguing that it would not be possible to stop the Franks coming to Jerusalem 'since what they adore is the sanctity of Jerusalem of which the Refuse is only the noblest place'.[171]

'Imad al-Din is well aware of the importance of this church to the Franks. He puts the following words into the mouths of the Franks defending the Church of the Holy Sepulchre: 'They said: "We will die beneath the tomb of our Lord and we will pass away out of fear that it will pass from us. We will defend it and we will fight for it. We have no alternative but to fight."'[172] During the actual fighting the Franks express the same sentiments.[173] The church is a symbol for which they are fighting:

> Each of us is worth twenty... We shall bring about the end of the world in defence of the [Church of the] Resurrection [qiyama].[174]

'Imad al-Din then goes further. Under a special section entitled 'The account of the Church of Refuse', he launches into his views on Frankish Christianity. He is fully aware that the Franks too are ready and willing to shed their own blood in defence of their faith and this, their holy monument. Indeed, Frankish honour is bound up with the protection of the Church of the Holy Sepulchre. In it, he says, is the place of the Crucifixion; in it there are many pictures and sculptures:

> In it are the pictures of the Apostles talking, holy men informing, monks in their cells, priests in their congregations, the Magi with

Figure 5.35 *Mamluk coin, 701/1301, Aleppo, Syria*

their ropes,[175] priests and their delusion; the image of the Lady and the Lord, the Temple and the Birthplace, the Table and the Fishes . . . the Disciple and the Teacher, the Cradle and the Child speaking, the picture of the ram and the ass, Paradise and the Fire, the [church] bells and the laws. They said, in it [Jerusalem] the Messiah was crucified, the sacrificial victim was slaughtered, divinity became incarnate and humanity became deified.[176]

To Christians this concatenation of details about Christianity will be viewed as a mishmash of truths, half-truths and misconceptions: but it is in fact an excellent depiction of what twelfth-century Muslims probably believed about the religion of the enemy. This passage shows Christianity and Christians through the prism of Muslim popular beliefs. This dazzling display of details about Christianity does not, as Gabrieli suggests, betray 'the Muslim author's lack of real information'.[177] Rather, it is a view of Christianity which is based on the Qur'anic revelation (Jesus speaking from the cradle, the Magi with their ropes), overlaid with strongly held Muslim popular prejudices against Christian practices – epitomised by images in churches, monkery and church bells.

Muslim Views on the Papacy and the Superiority of the Caliphate

Ibn Wasil records an alleged conversation between Frederick II and a Muslim dignitary called Fakhr al-Din b. al-Shaykh. This is a perfect opportunity for Ibn Wasil to make an unfavourable comparison between the Pope and the caliph and to put it into the mouth of a Frankish ruler. Frederick asks about the caliph and Fakhr al-din replies:

He is the son of the uncle of our Prophet [peace and blessings be upon him]. He [the Caliph] took the caliphate from his father, and his father took it from his father and the caliphate has been continuous in the house of Prophethood (i.e. the Prophet's family), not leaving them.[178]

Frederick's response is to attack the traditions of the Papacy and to extol the virtues of the caliphal system:

> The emperor said: 'What a good thing that [the caliphate] is! But those people of limited intelligence – meaning the Franks – take an ignorant and dull-witted man from the dunghill – there is no relationship or link between him and the Messiah – [and] they make him caliph over them, taking the position of the Messiah over them, whilst your caliph is the scion of the uncle of your Prophet and he is the person most worthy of his position.'[179]

There is no need to interpret this passage as recording the exact words of Frederick II, and indeed it is very doubtful that he would have said this. Ibn al-Furat, drawing on the evidence of Ibn Wasil, is also concerned to discuss the role of the Pope:

> You must know that amongst the Franks the Pope is the caliph of the Messiah, in whose place he stands. He has the power to make things unlawful and lawful. . . . It is he who crowns and establishes the kings, and, according to Frankish law, it is through him alone that they can be properly appointed.[180]

The value of these passages rests rather in the light which they shed on Muslim attitudes to the Papacy.

Figure 5.36 Marble panel, Mosque of al-Mu'ayyad, 818–23/1415–20, Cairo, Egypt

The Propaganda Value of the Correspondence of Muslim Rulers

We have already seen the importance of official letters composed in Saladin's name and sent to the caliph, the kings of the Franks and other potentates. Many similar letters have survived from the Mamluk period in which great emphasis was placed on chancellery skills. Baybars made a speciality of sending taunting letters to his opponents. In 666/1268 he wrote a letter to Bohemond VI announcing his intentions towards Antioch. Part of its fiery rhetoric touches on the fabric of Christianity:

> If you had seen your churches destroyed, your crosses sawn asunder, the pages of the lying Gospels exposed, the tombs of the Patriarchs collapsed, if you had seen your enemy the Muslim trampling the sanctuary, with the monk, the priest, the deacon sacrificed on the altar . . . the Churches of St Paul and St Peter pulled down and destroyed, you would have said 'Would to God that I were transformed to dust[181] or would to God that I had not received the letter which tells me of this sad catastrophe.'[182]

91. Ibid.
92. Sibt, VIII/1, 397. In his turn, Baybars attached great importance to the Dome of the Rock, refurbishing it and engraving his name in lapis lazuli blue and gold on the dome; cf. al-Maqrizi, *Suluk*, I, 445; Ibn ʿAbd al-Zahir, *Rawd*, 89.
93. Ibn Jubayr, *Rihlat Ibn Jubayr*, ed. W. Wright and M. J. de Goeje, Leiden and London, 1907, 29.
94. Qurʾan 2: 222.
95. *RHC*, III, 416; the translator misses this point completely. Cf. also Ibn Khallikan's biography of Saladin.
96. Syphilis is called the 'Frankish chancre'.
97. Ibn al-Furat, Shayyal, 18.
98. Ibn al-Furat, Shayyal, 18–19. Leaders such as Guillaume de Bures and Baldwin 'Lord of Jerusalem' were given such titles.
99. Ibn al-Qalanisi, Gibb, 344.
100. Ibn al-Dawadari, cited by Atrache, *Die Politik*, 198.
101. ʿImad al-Din, *Fath*, 103.
102. Ibn ʿAbd al-Zahir, *Tashrif*, 80.
103. Ibn al-Furat, Lyons, 23.
104. Lyons, *Arabian Epic*, III, 419.
105. Ibn al-Qalanisi, Gibb, 47.
106. Ibn al-Qalanisi, Gibb, 135–6.
107. Mouton, *Damas*, 90.
108. Ibn Jubayr, Broadhurst, 29.
109. Quoted by Ibn Shaddad, Eddé, 254.
110. Cited by Ibn Khallikan, de Slane, IV, 529.
111. Al-Maqrizi, trans. Broadhurst, 89–90.
112. Presumably this refers to one of the early Qurʾans sent to the provinces of the Islamic empire after ʿUthman's recension, which is generally dated to 656.
113. Sibt, VIII/1, 198.
114. Ibn al-Jawzi, X, 131.
115. Ibn al-Nabih, *Diwan*, 202.
116. Sibt, VIII/2, 746–7.
117. Cf. Thorau, *The Lion*, 207.
118. Ibn Khallikan, de Slane, IV, 523; for another reference to the Franks' reliance on the cross, cf. Abu Shama, *RHC*, IV, 264.
119. Quoted by M. Michaud, *Histoire des Croisades*, Paris, 1829, II, 481.
120. Cf. *EI²*: hilal.
121. Ibn al-Nabih, *Diwan*, 458.
122. Lyons, *The Arabian Epic*, III, 372.
123. Al-ʿUmari, Lundquist, 34.
124. Ibn al-Furat, Lyons, 105.
125. *Atabegs*, 66–7.
126. Al-Harawi, trans. Sourdel-Thomine, *Guide*, 69.
127. Ibn Wasil, IV, 249.
128. *Encyclopedia of Arabic Literature*, II, art.: Usama ibn Munqidh, 797.
129. Quoted in Gabrieli, 84; citing the text from H. Derenbourg, *Ousama ibn Mounkidh, un émir syrien au premier siècle des Croisades*, Paris, 1889, vol. I, 528–9.
130. Gabrieli, 84.
131. According to Sivan, *L'Islam*, 114.
132. Al-Qalqashandi, *Subh*, VI, 528.
133. Cf. Sivan, *L'Islam*, 112.
134. Lit.: even if only one man of us remains.

135. Ibn Shaddad, *RHC*, III, 275.
136. Quoted by Abu Shama, *RHC*, III, 429–30.
137. Al-Qalqashandi, *Subh*, 6, 500; quoting 'Imad al-Din.
138. For an excellent review of this apologetic literature, cf. F.-E. Wilms, *Al-Ghazalis Schrift wider die Gottheit Jesu*, Leiden, 1996, 216 ff.
139. Cf. Berkey, 'The Mamluks as Muslims', 166–7; M. Fierro, 'The treatises against innovations (kutub al-bida')', *Der Islam*, 69 (1992), 204–46.
140. Berkey, 'The Mamluks as Muslims', 168; D. Little, 'Coptic conversion to Islam under the Bahri Mamluks, 692–755/1293–1354', *BSOAS*, 39 (1976), 552–69.
141. Ibn Taymiyya, *Al-jawab al-sahih li-man baddal din al-Masih*, Cairo, 1322.
142. Ibn Taymiyya, *Lettre à un roi croisé*, trans. J. R. Michot, Louvain, 1995, 142.
143. Ibid., 145.
144. Indeed, they are a *topos* of anti-Christian polemical writing, as for example in the work of al-Jawbari, a Damascene dervish and alchemist who flourished in the first half of the thirteenth century and whose writings may well have been read by Ibn Taymiyya (ibid., 147).
145. T. F. Michel, *A Muslim theologian's response to Christianity*, New York, 1984, 206.
146. R. Gottheil, 'An answer to the Dhimmis', *JAOS*, 41 (1921), 383–487.
147. Ibid., 386.
148. Ibid., 439.
149. Ibid., 451.
150. Ibid., 415.
151. *Sea of Precious Virtues*, 231.
152. Ibid.
153. Ibid.
154. Ibid.
155. Called al-Qusyan in Arabic after the man whose son was raised from the dead by St Peter. Cf. Gabrieli, 8.
156. Ibn Taghribirdi, *Nujum*, V, 147–8.
157. Ibn Taghribirdi, *Nujum*, V, 148.
158. Ibn Khallikan, de Slane, II, 635–6.
159. Sura 17: 111.
160. Sura 112.
161. Ibn Khallikan, de Slane, IV, 637.
162. Ibn Khallikan, de Slane, IV, 524.
163. Ibn al-Athir, *Kamil*, XI, 362.
164. Ibn al-Athir, *Kamil*, XI, 364.
165. Cf. the discussion below.
166. Cf. Sivan, *L'Islam*, 128, n. 162.
167. Al-Harawi, trans. Sourdel-Thomine, *Guide*, 68–9.
168. Quoted by al-Qalqashandi, *Subh*, VII, 128.
169. *Fath*, 69.
170. Cf. Sivan, *L'Islam*, 128, 168, citing Sibt b. al-Jawzi, *Mir'at*, Paris ms. 5866, fol. 237a.
171. Ibid.
172. 'Imad al-Din, *Fath*, 49.
173. 'Imad al-Din, *Fath*, 52.
174. 'Imad al-Din, *Fath*, quoted by Gabrieli, 154.
175. Gabrieli, 148; Qur'an 20: 60.
176. *Fath*, 48–9.
177. Gabrieli, 149.

178. Ibn Wasil, IV, 251.
179. Ibn Wasil, IV, 251.
180. Ibn al-Furat, Lyons, 9.
181. Sura 78: 40.
182. J. Sublet, *Sultan Baibars*, Paris, 1992, 138; Quatremère's translation of Baybars' letter came from the chronicler al-Nuwayri. Cf. Quatremère, I, 190–4, esp. 193; cf. also Ibn al-Furat, Lyons, 124.
183. Sivan, *L'Islam*, 205–6.
184. *Al-durr al-thamin fi manaqib al-muslimin wa mathalib al-mushrikin.*
185. Sivan, *L'Islam*, 107.
186. Sivan, *L'Islam*, 205–6.
187. Usama b. Munqidh, *Kitab al-i'tibar*, ed. P. Hitti, Princeton, 1930, 132: *yahujja.*
188. M. G. S. Hodgson, *Rethinking World History*, ed. E. Burke III, Cambridge, 1993, 14.

CHAPTER SIX

Aspects of Life in the Levant in the Crusading Period

Peace was not, however, the favourite subject of the Muslim historians – nor perhaps of any historian.[1] (Gabrieli)

Introduction

IN THE PERIOD before 1100 there had been two major frontier areas where Christians and Muslims could and did exert influence on each other's society: the frontier between Muslim al-Andalus and the Christian kingdoms of northern Spain, and the frontier between Muslim Sicily and Christian Italy. An interesting frontier society would soon also develop between Muslim Anatolia and Christian Byzantium. In such border areas a chivalric code developed in which both sides often respected the other during protracted periods of mutual warfare.

The Crusading situation was different. Despite being linked by sea with Europe, the Crusader states were set amidst a Muslim world

Figure 6.1 Mounted hunter and groom carrying game, Cappella Palatina, ceiling, c. 1140, Palermo, Sicily

whose population vastly outnumbered theirs. Crusaders from northern Europe who arrived in Syria and Palestine in 1099 represented a novel phenomenon. They brought a kind of war which was markedly different from the often almost stylised skirmishes on the long-established frontiers of Islam in Spain, eastern Anatolia and southern Italy. The First Crusade crashed into the very heartlands of Islam, and the establishment of four Crusader states in the Levant therefore presents the historian with an opportunity to study the socio-cultural interplay between the Muslims and the 'barbarians' from Europe over a period of two centuries. How were these European, Christian, feudal 'proto-colonies' going to co-exist with the Muslims who almost literally surrounded them and against whom they were numerically a tiny force? And how did the Muslims, their 'victims', view them close up, as opposed to their preconceptions of the denizens of the frozen, barbarian lands of the north?

The Crusades brought the Muslims of the Middle East into an enforced and close proximity to the Franks from western Europe. It might therefore be expected that these new circumstances would have given the Muslims more accurate and detailed information about their enemy.[2] This chapter will examine to what extent this was so. We have already examined the stereotypical Muslim images of the Franks in Chapter 5. Yet despite the pervasiveness of these stereotypes, it is worth analysing the Franks as a social phenomenon, both as individuals and groups, in order to see if the Muslims gradually developed a more nuanced view of them.

Figure 6.2 *Groom carrying game, Cappella Palatina, ceiling, c. 1140, Palermo, Sicily*

The Visual Landscape of Frankish Occupation

The Islamic sources are generally silent about the visual impact made by the Frankish presence in the Near East, but it takes only a little effort of the imagination to reconstruct the Muslim reaction, even if only speculatively. There is surprisingly little mention of the physical appearance of the Franks, the colour of their skin and hair, the strange clothing they wore before some of them at least adopted Islamic dress, and a host of other external features that must have marked them out immediately from the Muslims or indeed the indigenous Christian groups of the Near East. The different colouring of hair and skin of the Franks in the Levant is barely mentioned in the Islamic sources. Occasionally the colour of their eyes attracts attention as in earlier writings (see Chapter 5). 'Imad al-Din, for example, refers to the Franks as the 'blue-eyed enemy'.[3] As already mentioned, Muslim folk literature speaks of the Franks' clean-shaven faces.[4]

Figure 6.3 *Silk cloth with lions and harpies, c. 1100, Muslim Spain*

All kinds of visible signs must have acted as a constant reminder to the Muslims in Frankish-held territory that they were under occupation, although there is little comment made in the sources about this. Such signs may well have included markers on the roads in what chroniclers describe as 'Frankish script' and shop fronts with similar alien words written on them. The religious architecture of the Franks, as evidenced by the cathedral of Tartus (cf. figure 6.43) and the church of St Anne in Jerusalem, would also have looked dramatically intrusive in an urban landscape in which the Oriental Christian churches blended modestly. In secular architecture, too, the advent of the Franks brought some rude surprises.

Of course, the Muslims were well used to seeing towers, castles and fortifications, but not on the same scale as quickly became apparent after the Frankish conquests. As an embattled minority seeking to establish themselves in an alien landscape the Franks took over existing structures as well as building many new castles – in the countryside, on strategic routes, near and even on occasion in the sea – in their efforts to defend themselves. The plethora of Frankish defensive structures, built in the western European style all over their territories, must have been a constant reminder of their presence to the Muslims. These buildings must have appeared, initially at least, until the Muslims became more accustomed to the Franks, as unwelcome excrescences on the Muslim landscape – tangible symbols of foreign, infidel occupation.

The Language Barrier

The Islamic sources suggest that very few Muslims were concerned to learn the languages of the Crusaders. In fact, although there is some awareness of their ethnic diversity on the part of the Muslim chroniclers – English (*Inkitar*), French (*Faransis*), Germans (*Alman*), Venetians (*Banadiqa*) and others are mentioned – there seems to be no perception that there was more than one 'Frankish language'. Usama writes dismissively: 'These people speak nothing but Frankish; we do not understand what they say.'[5] On another occasion he declares: 'A Frankish women hung on to me, prattling in their language, and I did not understand what she was saying.'[6]

Figure 6.4 *Cock-fight, Cappella Palatina, ceiling, c. 1140, Palermo, Sicily*

The Muslim chroniclers, however, make some effort to produce the names of the Crusader leaders: St Louis, for example, is known as 'Raidafrans' which al-Maqrizi explains as 'a term in the language of the Franks signifying "King of the Franks"'.[7]

Whilst it is understandable that the Muslims would not wish to speak the language of the 'accursed Franks', it is less impressive that there does not seem to be much mention of the Arab knights learning Turkish, the language of their military overlords, nor that the Turks learned much Arabic. Usama is unabashed in admitting that he cannot understand either Frankish or Turkish.[8] In view of all this, it is perhaps not surprising that there is a certain lack of veracity in the conversations recorded in the Islamic sources. Dialogues in high-sounding Arabic which could never have actually taken place are put into the mouths of Turkish commanders and sultans.

On the Crusader side, however, there is mention from time to time in the Islamic sources of Frankish leaders who had taken the

Figure 6.5 *Dancer, Fatimid ivory carving, eleventh century, Egypt*

trouble to learn Arabic. Such knowledge could prove very useful, as in the story of Richard the Lionheart who was saved by one of his companions, William de Pratelles, when they had fallen into a Muslim ambush. William shouted out that he was the king (*malik*) and was taken prisoner whilst Richard got away.[9] There is, however, no information on whether the Franks, for their part, were aware of the linguistic range of the local Muslim military classes with whom they were in contact, and who often spoke Turkish and Kurdish rather than Arabic.

332

It seems likely that the Franks used local dragomans (interpreters) for official encounters at a high level with Muslim princes and generals. These dragomans were often local Oriental Christians who must have mastered a number of languages. Baybars is reported to have used an interpreter who knew how 'to write in Frankish script'.[10] The 'Old Man of the Mountain', the Syrian leader of the Assassins, had taught two of his followers how to speak the Frankish language.[11]

The Franks needed expertise in Arabic both to ensure their survival and to promote their commercial aims. Their leaders needed to know about enemy movements and their merchants wanted to find out about trading possibilities and conditions. No wonder, then, that the officials at the customs house in Acre spoke and wrote Arabic.[12] Nor were warfare and commerce the only incentives for acquiring the local language. Captivity, too, often enabled the Franks to learn Arabic. Raymond of Tripoli, for example, had languished in a Muslim jail long enough to learn Arabic. And while information on mixed marriages is scarce, there can be little doubt that this was another factor that encouraged some Franks, at least, to become proficient in Arabic. To judge by the laconic references to such matters in the sources, however, the Muslim historians did not regard it as important that the Franks should be able to communicate efficiently in Arabic. All this merely confirms that strong sense of the otherness of the Franks which the Muslims felt.

Figure 6.6 *Seated ruler, Cappella Palatina, ceiling, c. 1140, Palermo, Sicily*

Differences between the Franks

It is unrealistic to expect the medieval Islamic chroniclers to give us detailed portraits of individual Franks: even their descriptions of Muslims are stereotyped. But it is interesting to note that the Islamic sources begin to draw a distinction between those Franks who have lived for some time in the Levant and those who have recently arrived from Europe.

Usama makes such a distinction between Orientalised and Western Franks in a much-quoted passage of his *Memoirs*: 'Everyone who is a fresh emigrant from the Frankish lands is ruder in character than those who have become acclimatized and have held long association with the Moslems.'[13]

This is an interesting remark since it suggests clearly that the Franks who have lived for one or two generations in the Muslim world have been influenced and, above all, improved by their environment and their association with Muslims. In the story which Usama then gives to illustrate the truth of his general statement, a Frank recently arrived from Europe reprimands Usama for not praying to the east and forcibly tries to turn Usama's face towards the Christian direction of prayer. It is the Templars, long used to Muslim ways and whom Usama describes as his friends, who rush to pull Usama's assailant away from him, apologising that this man is 'a stranger who has arrived in these days from the country of the Franks'.[14]

The Muslim awareness of this difference between the Franks played an important role in the events of the Second Crusade, when – for the first time since the fall of Jerusalem – significantly large armies of Franks came from Europe to the Near East. Indeed, in 543/1148 they slaughtered and pillaged within Damascus itself before the Muslims gained the upper hand. A distinction is drawn on this occasion, and frequently thereafter, between two different groups of Franks: the 'coastal Franks' (al-faranj al-sahiliyyun) and the 'western Franks' (al-faranj al-ghuraba').

The governor of Damascus, Mu'in al-Din Ünür, is mentioned as persuading the 'Syrian Franks' to lift the siege of Damascus. Clearly, therefore, he knew how to drive a wedge between the Orientalised and Western Franks. One of the chief reasons for the failure of the Second Crusade has been shown to be the difference in outlook and aims between the two kinds of Franks,[15] and despite the very incomplete picture of the Second Crusade given in the Muslim sources, this aspect of affairs is clearly understood on the Muslim side.[16]

This whole episode is recorded in some detail by Ibn al-Athir, who writes as follows:

> Mu'in al-Din contacted the Western Franks saying to them: 'The prince of the East [meaning Sayf al-Din Ghazi, Zengi's son] has come. If you retreat [well and good]. If not, I will hand over the town to him and then you will rue the day'. He [also] contacted the Franks of Syria saying to them: 'Why are you helping these people [meaning the Western Franks] against us when you know that if they take Damascus they will take what coastal territories are in your hands . . .' The coastal Franks met the King of the Germans [Alman] and made him afraid of Sayf al-Din and the multitude of his troops and the continuous supply of reinforcements coming to him . . . They [the Syrian Franks] kept on like this until he [Conrad] retreated from the town.[17]

Perhaps predictably, the Muslims tended to feel a greater rapport with, or at least to show more willingness to negotiate and ally with, the Orientalised Franks with whom they were more familiar. Such a policy was used on occasion both to strengthen different rival groups of Muslims and to cause internal divisions among the Franks.

A similar distinction between the Franks continues to be made in the Ayyubid period. The 'Western Franks' are sometimes seen as conducting different policies from the 'Oriental Franks'. According to Ibn Nazif al-Hamawi, the 'Western Franks' restored the port of Sidon in the year 625/1227–8 without the consent of the 'coastal Franks'.[18]

Muslim Views on the Crusader Religious Orders

The Muslim sources single out the Hospitallers (Isbitariyya[19]) and the Templars (Dawiyya[20]). Other military orders established in the

Figure 6.8 Musicians, Blacas ewer, inlaid brass, 629/1232, Mosul, Iraq

Levant pass without comment. It is not clear when the Muslims first picked out the Hospitallers and Templars as two separate groups within the Frankish armies. Usama mentions without an exact date the Templars residing in the Aqsa mosque.[21] Ibn al-Qalanisi records under the year 557/1157 that a Frankish squadron sent to Banyas included 'seven hundred horsemen of the bravest of the Hospitallers, the serjeantry and the Templars'.[22] He does not, however, explain who they were or how long they had been in Syria. This lack of specific comment may indicate an assumption that his readers were by now well used to the sight of these knightly orders (the Hospitallers, for example, had established themselves in Krak des Chevaliers in 539/1144) or it could spring from the usual lack of Muslim curiosity about the differences between the Frankish invaders.

Saladin treated the Templars and Hospitallers especially severely after the battle of Hattin in 583/1187;[23] indeed, during Saladin's time they are mentioned more frequently in the Islamic sources. Ibn al-Athir remarks in his account of the massacre of the prisoners: 'These were singled out to be killed only because they fought more fiercely than all the [other] Franks'. On a later occasion he refers to them as the 'firebrand (*jumra*) of the Franks'.[24]

'Imad al-Din, Saladin's close companion, rises to baroque heights of long-winded exultation after Hattin. Amongst the many images of the dismembered Frankish corpses he declares: 'The faces of the Templars were glowering and their heads were beneath the soles of our feet.'[25] Saladin himself said of the Hospitallers and Templars:

I will purify the earth of these two filthy races (*jins*). For their custom has no use and they will certainly not desist from aggression and they will not serve in captivity. They are the most wicked of all the infidels.[26]

In the Ayyubid period Ibn Wasil reveals an awareness of the Hospitallers as a distinct order, speaking of 'the Hospitallers' House'[27] (*bayt al-istibar*) and 'brothers'[28] (*al-ikhwa*). As Humphreys suggests, such remarks show 'a rising level of knowledge and sophistication' about the Franks amongst the Muslims.[29] These two orders continue

335

to be mentioned occasionally in the Mamluk period until the fall of Acre.

Muslim Views of the Frankish Leadership

The official nature of many medieval Islamic historical sources – chronicles and biographical dictionaries alike – presents obituaries and biographies of prominent Muslim figures in a very stereotyped way as if they are the heroes in a shadowy epic rather than people with individual characteristics. So it is not surprising that on the occasions when Crusader leaders receive a special mention in the Islamic sources they appear as even more wooden figures. Nevertheless some of them *are* discussed, and it is worth analysing how and why.

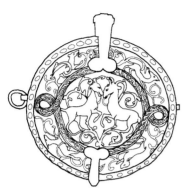

Figure 6.9 Roundel on ivory box, twelfth century, Sicily or Spain

Frankish Leaders who are Praised by Medieval Muslim Writers

Baldwin the Little

The death of 'Baldwin the Little, King of the Franks and lord of Jerusalem' is reported by Ibn al-Qalanisi under the year 526/1131–2. The account is almost sympathetic and certainly shows respect for Baldwin's abilities:

> He was an old man whom time had worn down with its hardships, and who had suffered many rigours of fortune from its vicissitudes and calamities. On many occasions he fell into the hands of the Muslims as a prisoner, in times both of war and of peace, but he always escaped from them through his famous devices and historic stratagems. After him there was none left amongst them possessed of sound judgement and capacity to govern.[30]

Richard the Lionheart

Warm praise is showered by Muslim authors on Richard the Lionheart. Under the year 587 Ibn al-Athir writes: 'He was the man of his age as regards courage, shrewdness, endurance and forbearance and because of him the Muslims were sorely tested by unprecedented disaster.'[31]

Thus Richard is portrayed as a redoubtable opponent, and a worthy foe for the likes of Saladin. The same respect for Richard is shown by Ibn Shaddad, who speaks of him as follows: 'He possessed judgement, experience, audacity and astuteness. His arrival aroused apprehension and fear in the hearts of the Muslims.'[32]

St Louis

King Louis IX of France (Raidafrans – roi de France),[33] St Louis, whom Ibn Wasil describes as 'one of the greatest princes of the West' and 'a very devout observer of the Christian faith',[34] receives many plaudits in the Islamic sources. He is especially praised for his conduct when he was taken prisoner in 648/1250–1 since he opted to share the fate of his men when he could have escaped.[35] Sa'd al-Din Juwayni, in his fragmentary eyewitness memoirs, writes: 'If the Frenchman [Louis] had wanted to escape, he could have done so but he remained in the heart of the mêlée, to protect his men.'[36]

According to Juwayni, Louis refused to don a robe of honour offered to him by a sovereign whose realm was less strong and extensive than his own and he also declined to attend a banquet where he would have been the butt of ridicule.[37] Juwayni describes Louis as endowed with 'judgement, firmness, religion in the Frankish sense [of the term]; they [the Franks] had great trust in him, and he [had] a fine physical bearing'.[38]

This positive opinion is shared by Ibn al-Furat who describes Louis as 'an extremely intelligent, sensible and alert man'.[39]

Figure 6.10 *Panel from Umayyad ivory casket, early eleventh century, Spain*

The French scholar Anne-Marie Eddé gives a detailed picture of how St Louis is presented in the Islamic sources. He is a powerful and courageous king, with deep Christian convictions: 'This Frenchman is the most powerful of the princes of the West; a zealous faith animates him.' Thus Frederick II is said to have described him to the sultan al-Salih to warn him about the arrival of the Seventh Crusade.[40]

Frederick II

The rulers of Sicily attract praise and admiration from the Muslim chroniclers.[41] Notable among them was Frederick II of Hohenstaufen,

Figure 6.11 *Scenes of courtly life, Cappella Palatina, ceiling, c. 1140, Palermo, Sicily*

the Holy Roman Emperor, King of Jerusalem, a fascinating and enigmatic Crusader ruler, who has had much ink spilt about him and is given great prominence in Islamic sources. Having been brought up in Sicily, he had a widely cosmopolitan outlook and was openly interested in Arabic and Islam, to such an extent that he was accused of being pro-Muslim.

Ibn Wasil, who served as a Mamluk envoy to Frederick's son, Manfred of Sicily, and who was proud of his experience and knowledge of Europe, has left some first-hand impressions of how the Muslims viewed Frederick when he arrived in Acre in Shawwal 625/September 1228. He writes as follows:

> Amongst the kings of the Franks the Emperor was outstanding; a lover of wisdom, logic and medicine, inclining towards the Muslims because his place of origin and upbringing was the land of Sicily and he and his father and his grandfather were its kings and the majority of that island are Muslims.[42]

Figure 6.12 Musician, Cappella Palatina, ceiling, c. 1140, Palermo, Sicily

Figure 6.13 Board game players, Cappella Palatina, ceiling, c. 1140, Palermo, Sicily

Ibn Wasil dwells on Frederick's intellectual prowess and his relationship with the Ayyubid sultan al-Malik al-Kamil. He relates how Frederick sent mathematical problems to al-Malik al-Kamil which took a whole team of Muslim scholars to solve.

> Dialogues used to take place between the two of them on diverse topics. In the course of that the Emperor sent al-Malik al-Kamil complicated philosophical, geometrical and mathematical problems by which he might test the learned men he [al-Malik al-Kamil] had with him. Al-Malik al-Kamil showed the mathematical problems he had received to Shaykh ['Alam al-Din] Qaysar b. Abi'l-Qasim, the leading proponent of this art, and he showed the rest to a group of learned men and they answered everything.[43]

Presumably we are to infer from this that Frederick himself was able to answer the knotty questions he had sent. Indeed, al-Maqrizi also stresses the emperor's own personal intellectual powers in this particular field: 'This king was knowledgeable, penetrating deeply into the science of geometry, arithmetic and mathematics.'[44] Ibn Wasil also stresses that Frederick was unusually interested in Islam. Ibn al-Furat reports on the rift between Frederick and the Pope (Innocent IV) and on an assassination attempt allegedly instigated by the Pope on Frederick because 'the Emperor had abandoned Christianity and favoured the Muslims'.[45]

Figure 6.14 Wrestlers,
Cappella Palatina, ceiling,
c. 1140, Palermo, Sicily

Frederick's upbringing in Sicily, of course, naturally predisposed him in the Muslim view to a higher level of civilisation than other Frankish leaders. So much attention is devoted to him in Muslim sources precisely because he is a Frankish leader deeply immersed in *Islamic* culture, a 'Mozarab' so to speak, the next best thing to a Muslim himself. Indeed, Ibn al-Furat remarks that the rumours were that Frederick was 'a secret Muslim'.[46] The geographical 'accident' (of being raised in Sicily) had allowed him to acquire some of the attributes of a more favourable 'clime',[47] in the same way as the second and third generations of 'Orientalised' Franks referred to by Usama were 'better' than the ones newly arrived from Europe.[48]

Manfred

Manfred of Hohenstaufen, Frederick II's bastard son and successor, shared many of his father's attitudes, as well as his intellectual brilliance, and he maintained friendly contact with Egypt. In Ramadan 659/August 1261, Baybars sent Ibn Wasil to Manfred. Ibn Wasil shows a lively interest in the affairs of Sicily and the relationship between its idiosyncratic rulers and the Pope: 'All these [the Sicilian rulers] were loathed by the Pope, the caliph of the Franks, the lord of Rome, because of their inclination towards the Muslims.'[49] Ibn Wasil writes of his visit as follows: 'I stayed with him [Manfred] and was honourably treated. I met him several times and found him to be

340

distinguished, liking the rational sciences, memorising ten articles from the book of Euclid on geometry.'[50]

Ibn Wasil is impressed that Manfred has begun to build a 'house of knowledge' in which to study the exact sciences.[51] Perhaps Ibn Wasil made a connection between this enterprise and the storied 'House of Wisdom' (*Dar al-hikma*) founded by the 'Abbasid caliphs in Baghdad.

What is fascinating here is that the singular achievements of both Manfred and his father seem to have some sub-conscious link in Ibn Wasil's mind with their natural inclinations towards Islam and their contact with Muslims. He remarks in the same breath that many of Manfred's attendants were Muslims and that the call to prayer and the prayer itself took place openly in the ranks of Manfred's own army.[52]

Frankish Leaders about whom Muslim Writers give Neutral or Inconclusive Evidence

Baldwin I

Al-Maqrizi, in his voluminous biographical dictionary the *Kitab al-muqaffa'*, actually devotes an entry to Baldwin, King of Jerusalem. It contains no assessment of the character or achievements of this important Frankish leader. One suspects that the obituary is included by al-Maqrizi because Baldwin fought against the Fatimids and actually died in Egyptian territory. In particular, al-Maqrizi tells two well-known anecdotes about Baldwin's exploits: his battle against the Fatimid army in 495/1101, in which he was routed, and his flight to a reed thicket from which he managed to escape, although the Muslims set fire to the thicket and he received burns to his body. He is thus presented as a redoubtable foe. Later, in 512/1118, Baldwin raided Egypt again but died on the way home. His entrails, and his reputation with them, lingered on in local Egyptian folklore for long afterwards:

Figure 6.15 *Hunter with dog, lid of ivory casket, eleventh–twelfth centuries, Muslim work from south Italy*

> The Franks were afraid of publicising his death and so they concealed it. They took him [away to Palestine] after they had torn open his belly and stuffed it with straw. They buried what was in his belly in a swamp . . . The common people called it Baldwin's swamp and the place of his grave is marked with a stone.[53]

Bohemond VI

Also typical of the rather unsatisfactory, even inconsequential nature of the information provided by Muslim medieval writers on the Crusader leaders are two obituaries given by the chronicler al-Yunini (d. 1326). The first concerns Bohemond VI, prince of Antioch and count of Tripoli. According to al-Yunini, Bohemond died during the first ten days of Ramadan 673/February–March 1275 and was buried in the church in Tripoli. Al-Yunini continues: 'He was good-looking and pleasant in appearance. I myself saw him in Ba'albakk in the year 658/1260.'[54]

Perhaps the clue to the inclusion of this information at all is the fact that the author had actually seen Bohemond in person and was proud of it. He is certainly prepared to comment favourably on his physical appearance. Al-Yunini then adds that when the Mamluk sultan Qalawun captured Tripoli in 688/1289, Bohemond's bones were dug up and strewn around the streets of the city.[55]

Guy II

Al-Yunini also wrote an obituary of Guy II, the lord of Jubayl (d. 681/1282). The actual notice does not shed much light on the personality involved. The stereotypical phrases give very little away: 'He was one of the famous knights amongst the Franks, beloved of them for his courage and generosity. He was one of the revered knights in Tripoli.'[56]

Such reports as these are lacklustre and lifeless; but beneath the surface there is a lack of active hostility and even grudging praise for the elite of the enemy's knightly classes.

Raymond of Tripoli

Orientalised Franks were often branded as treacherous by both sides. One such example was Raymond of Tripoli (d. 1187), whom Ibn Shaddad describes as intelligent and perspicacious.[57] According to 'Imad al-Din, Raymond took refuge in 580/1184–5 with Saladin, offered him help against the people of his own religion (*milla*) and became one of the sultan's followers. 'Imad al-Din then adds: 'His sincere intentions towards the Muslims strengthened to such an extent that were it not for fear of his co-religionists he would have become a Muslim.'[58]

Figure 6.16 *Seated prince, lustre dish, twelfth century, Syria*

Ibn Jubayr praises Raymond's skills in government. He remarks that Baldwin IV, the leper, lived in seclusion, having delegated the administration of his government to his uncle, the Count (Raymond) who 'supervises all with firmness and authority'.[59] Ibn Jubayr then sums up Raymond's character as follows:

> The most considerable amongst the accursed Franks is the accursed Count, the lord of Tripoli and Tiberias. He has authority and position among them. He is qualified to be king, and indeed is a candidate for the office. He is described as being shrewd and crafty.[60]

High praise indeed for an infidel. Yet the Qadi al-Fadil roundly condemns Raymond at Hattin: 'He fled [the battle of Hattin] for fear of being struck by lances and swords. Then God took him in his hands and killed him according to his promise and sent him to the kingdom of death in hell.'[61]

Reynald of Sidon

Reynald of Sidon, the lord of Shaqif, is mentioned in the Muslim sources as being another Crusader who had taken the trouble to learn about the culture in which he was living. Under the year 585/1189–90 Abu Shama mentions that Reynald of Sidon went to see Saladin personally to conciliate him in order to buy time to rebuild the defences of his fortress. This he managed to do by impressing Saladin and his entourage, and in spite of the Muslims' subsequent discovery of this man's devious motives in visiting Saladin, Abu Shama is still sufficiently laudatory about Reynald's abilities:

> He was one of the great ones and most intelligent of the Franks. He knew Arabic and he had some acquaintance with histories and traditions. He had a Muslim with him who used to read to him and make him understand and he had perseverance. He used to debate with us on the rightness of his religion and we would argue its falsity. He was good to be with, cultivated in his speech.[62]

Here then was a Frank who had succeeded in achieving a certain mastery of Arabic.

Crusader Leaders who are Reviled in the Muslim Sources

Conrad of Montferrat

Conrad of Montferrat, the lord of Tyre, is known as 'the Marquis' and is singled out in the Islamic sources for special condemnation and invective. Under the year 583/1187–8, Ibn al-Athir writes soberly of Conrad's achievements in rallying the Franks against Saladin: 'He [Conrad] had ruled them [the people of Tyre] well and gone to great extremes to fortify the town. He was a human devil, good at administration and defence, and he had great courage.'[63]

Figure 6.17 *Seated prince, inlaid brass basin signed by Ibn al-Zayn, c. 1300, Syria*

Figure 6.18 *Sign of Libra, Mamluk mirror, inlaid metal, fourteenth century, Syria(?)*

343

Ibn Shaddad shares these views, calling him 'the most intrepid and the most powerful of them [the Franks] in war and the most proven of them in administration'.[64]

Abu Shama, on the other hand, fulminates virulently against Conrad, most probably because it was he who saved Tyre from Saladin's attacks and thereby caused the Muslims a very serious reverse. In an outburst of venom and rhetorical floridness he writes:

> Tyre exchanged [masters] from the count to the marquis, like exchanging the Devil for Satan . . . The marquis was one of the greatest tempters of unbelief and the most seductive of its devils, the most rapacious of its wolves, the most vicious of its jackals, the most unclean of its dogs; he is the epitome of the wily tyrant. It was for him and the likes of him that the Inferno was created.[65]

Reynald of Chatillon

By far the greatest acrimony and hatred are reserved for the arch-villain of the Crusading ruling class, Reynald of Chatillon, known in the Arabic sources as Arnat. Reynald, the lord of Karak and al-Shawbak, earned undying notoriety and opprobrium amongst Muslims for his lack of the chivalric values recognised by both sides and above all for his activities in the Red Sea where he threatened the very heart of the Islamic world, the two Holy Cities of Mecca and Medina.

Saladin's biographer, Ibn Shaddad, describes Reynald as 'an infidel, tyrannical, powerful and violent',[66] whilst Ibn al-Athir, usually restrained in his judgements, calls him 'one of the devils and defiant ones amongst the Franks and the most hostile of them towards the Muslims'.[67] One of the two episodes on which the Muslim chroniclers dwell with shock and horror is Reynald's seizing of a caravan from Egypt during a period of truce between Crusaders and Muslims. According to Ibn Shaddad, when Reynald had seized those travelling with the caravan, Ibn Shaddad writes:

Figure 6.19 Terracotta stamps for bread, eleventh–thirteenth centuries, Egypt

> He [Reynald] maltreated them, tortured them and put them in underground storehouses and narrow prison cells. They mentioned the truce to him and he said: 'Tell your Muhammad to set you free'. When that [news] reached him [Saladin] he vowed that when Almighty God should give him victory over him [Reynald] he would kill him himself.[68]

Thus Reynald's sins of breaking truces and maltreating prisoners are compounded in Muslim historiography by his being seen as mocking Islam and its Prophet. Moreover, a vow to God seals Saladin's personal commitment to Reynald's downfall and death.

An even more infamous incident concerns Reynald's plans to

threaten the Holy Cities themselves. In 578/1182–3 he built a fleet in Karak and carried the ships in pieces to the Red Sea coast where they were quickly assembled and dispatched.[69] Ibn al-Athir describes the aims of this campaign as follows: 'They were resolved to enter the Hijaz, Mecca and Medina, may Almighty God protect them, to take the pilgrims and to prevent them from [entering] the *Bayt al-haram* and to go after that into Yemen.'[70]

Small wonder that the Muslim chroniclers reserved their most virulent epithets for Reynald. Reynald's subsequent raids down the Red Sea were foiled by a Muslim fleet under the leadership of Husam al-Din Lu'lu'. Reynald escaped capture but some of his men were seized. Their punishment was terrible: 'He sent some of them to Mina [near Mecca] in order that they should have their throats cut as a punishment to those who had alarmed the sacred sanctuary of Almighty God.'[71] Yet, Reynald, the instigator of this act which threatened Islam's holiest places, had avoided punishment.

The well-known story of Saladin's capture of high-ranking Crusader prisoners at the battle of Hattin in 583/1187 is given great prominence in the Islamic sources. In the various accounts Saladin makes a very sharp distinction between the treatment which he normally accorded to captured Crusader rulers and the punishment which he decides personally to inflict on Reynald of Chatillon, who has flouted every honourable code. Saladin gave an iced drink to the king of the Franks (that is, Guy) who then passed it to Reynald. Ibn al-Athir's account continues:

> Reynald also drank of Saladin's iced water, so Saladin said: 'This accursed one did not drink the water with my permission and so is excluded from my safe-conduct'. Then he spoke to the prince [Reynald], upraided him for his sins and enumerated to him his treacherous acts. He himself rose up against him and executed him.[72]

Figure 6.20 *'Hedwig' glass beaker, twelfth century, Egypt(?)*

After Saladin had killed Reynald, his body was trailed ignominiously along the ground and out of Saladin's tent, no doubt a prelude to being dragged by the forelock into the fires of Hell. Abu Shama's account of the episode recalls Reynald's earlier taunting of his Muslim prisoners:

> He [Saladin] summoned prince Reynald and reminded him of what he had said. [Then] he said to him: '*I am* the one who will take vengeance for Muhammad on *you*!' . . . God took his spirit speedily to the Fire.[73]

Honour had been satisfied; as Saladin is reported to have written in a letter recorded by 'Imad al-Din: 'It is important to recall that we had vowed to execute the prince, the lord of Karak, the perfidious one, the infidel of infidels.'[74]

General Comments on Muslim Views of Frankish Leadership

This evidence demonstrates of course all too clearly that medieval Muslim chroniclers were not interested in the wellsprings of the Franks' behaviour. As far as they were concerned, an inscrutable – and malign – destiny had foisted these foreigners on them, and it was their duty as pious Muslims to defend the Dar al-Islam and send them packing. They were not concerned to probe the religious or for that matter the economic motivation of their foes.

It often occurs in the sources that when a Frank shows signs of interest in Islam, reciprocal interest is shown in him, though that Frank's intellectual leanings, especially in so far as these encroach on things Islamic, mark the limits of the enquiry. Conversely, the most severe opprobrium is reserved for Reynald because he had the idea of attacking the Holy Cities.

Reviewing some of the information presented here, one cannot help being struck by the random and sometimes even trivial nature of some of the comments made on the Crusader leaders by Muslim writers. It is possible to discern certain general Muslim opinions about the Franks. In addition to the qualities which arose directly from their nature as western European 'barbarians' and 'infidels', the Franks as a group, in Muslim eyes, possessed certain characteristics. They are frequently labelled as being contentious and untrustworthy, but they are also, on occasion, capable of exciting respect. Under the year 587/1191–2, Ibn Shaddad remarks of the Franks: 'Look at the endurance (sabr) of these people in arduous tasks.'[75] The Franks' valour in battle is not disputed. To Nur al-Din himself is attributed the

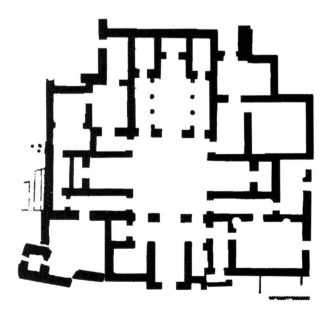

Figure 6.21 Qasr al-Banat, palace, plan, twelfth century, Raqqa, Syria

following statement which seems to reflect a general Muslim perception: 'I have struggled only with the most courageous of people, the Franks.'[76] Yet such comments tell us little of the Franks' personalities or of what brought them to the Levant. The Muslim chroniclers remain too anchored in their own culture to develop a sense of these wider horizons. None of the Muslim chroniclers was sufficiently interested or well informed to draw up a *general* assessment of the Crusader leadership as a group. There is little evidence that they sought corroboration or extra information from other Christians on what might be called in Western terms the 'phenomenon' of the Crusaders.

Frankish women

Young Frankish women

Not surprisingly in a society which had long prized the lighter-coloured skin of Circassian female slaves, the physical attributes of Crusader women, so rarely seen in the Levant before the First Crusade, must have caused many a Muslim man and woman to turn and stare in the street. The Muslim poet Ibn al-Qaysarani, who had fled the Syrian coast after the advent of the First Crusade and who laments in plainest tones the devastation caused by the newcomers from Europe, can nevertheless appreciate the alien beauty of the Frankish women whom he espied in Antioch in 540/1145–6. Saladin's scribe and biographer 'Imad al-Din, who collected chosen extracts from the work of Muslim poets in the twelfth century, remarks that Ibn al-Qaysarani was much taken with the 'blue-eyed' beauty of a Frankish woman and he then quotes the following poetic lines of Ibn al-Qaysarani:

> A Frankish woman has captivated me.
> The breeze of fragrance lingers on her.
> In her clothing there is a soft branch
> And in her crown is a radiant[77] moon.[78]

We have already seen in the bathhouse story of Usama that Frankish women were regarded as having loose sexual morals. Under the year 585/1189–90, Abu Shama quoting 'Imad al-Din continues this theme: he describes the arrival by sea of 'three hundred beautiful Frankish women from the islands'. In flowery rhyming prose he rises to great heights of invective against their sexual profligacy, stating that they had come to offer relief to any Franks who wanted their services, and that the priests themselves condoned this conduct.[79]

Another well-known tall story of Usama's also illustrates the Frankish male's lack of an appropriate marital jealousy (*ghayra*) and the Frankish female's licentiousness. Usama remarks as follows:

The Franks are without any vestige of a sense of honour and jealousy. If one of them goes along the street with his wife and meets a friend, this man will take the woman's hand and lead her aside to talk, while the husband stands by waiting until she has finished her conversation. If she takes too long about it he leaves her with the other man and goes on his way.

This kind of vague generalisation is applied to the Franks as a group but Usama then goes on to illustrate it with a particularly salacious incident which he alleges comes from his own personal experience:

> While I was in Nablus I stayed with a man called Mu'izz, whose house served as an inn for Muslim travellers. Its windows overlooked the street. On the other side of the road lived a Frank who sold wine for the merchants.

Usama is thus careful to cast a slur on the cuckolded husband from the beginning by noting that he is a wine-seller.

> Now this man returned home one day and found a man in bed with his wife. 'What are you doing here with my wife?' he demanded. 'I was tired', replied the man, 'and so I came in to rest.' 'And how do you come to be in my bed?' 'I found the bed made up, and lay down to sleep.' 'And this woman slept with you, I suppose?' 'The bed,' he replied, 'is hers. How could I prevent her getting into her own bed?' 'I swear if you do it again I shall take you to court!' – and this was his only reaction, the height of his outburst of jealousy![80]

Figure 6.22 *Archer shooting birds, Blacas ewer, inlaid brass, 629/1232, Mosul, Iraq*

This is a cleverly constructed apocryphal tale which plays shamelessly on the prejudices of Usama's readers.

As already mentioned, Baybars enforced strict discipline, morality and religious orthodoxy on his realm. He forbade all taverns and wine-presses, and the cultivation and consumption of hashish, although the state lost much revenue thereby.[81] Whilst in Alexandria in 661/1262 he ordered the city to be purged of 'Frankish' prostitutes.[82] Incidentally, in Jumada II 667/February 1269 Baybars forbade prostitution in Cairo and the whole of his realm and stipulated that prostitutes should marry and be locked up.[83]

Frankish Women Warriors

'Imad al-Din finds the phenomenon of Frankish female warriors interesting enough to discuss at some length:

> Amongst the Franks are women knights (*fawaris*). They have coats of mail and helmets. They are in men's garb and they are prominent in the thick of the fray. They act in the manner of those endowed with intellect [i.e. men] although they are ladies.[84]

In battle they are indeed indistinguishable from men:

> On the day of the battle some of them come forth in the same way as the (male) knights. Despite their softness there is hardness (*qaswa*) in them. They have no clothing (*kiswa*) other than coats of mail. They have not been recognised [as women] until they are stripped and laid bare. A number of them have been enslaved and sold.[85]

Such Frankish women undoubtedly possessed military skills. Ibn al-Athir mentions that at Saladin's siege of Burzay in 584/1188 there was 'a woman shooting from the citadel by means of the mangonel and it was she who put the Muslims' mangonel out of action'.[86]

Ibn Shaddad records the testimony of an old man who was present at the Muslim siege of Acre in 587/1191:

> Inside their walls was a woman wearing a green coat (*milwata*). She kept on shooting at us with a wooden bow, so much so that she wounded a group of us. We overpowered her and killed her and took her bow, carrying it to the sultan, who was very amazed about that.[87]

'Imad al-Din draws a moral on the occasion of visiting the Frankish corpses on the battlefield before Acre in 586/1190: 'We saw a woman slain because of her being a warrior.'[88]

Frankish Women Travelling in an Independent Fashion

Having railed against the morals of the 300 Frankish prostitutes, 'Imad al-Din allows himself to discuss other kinds of Frankish women. Under the same year of 585/1189–90 he mentions that a wealthy Frankish woman of high status arrived by sea, accompanied by 500 horsemen with their horses and retinues. She supplied all their provisions and paid the expenses of the ship. The purpose of this aristocratic Frankish woman's visit to the Levant is not stated.

Figure 6.23 *Animated inscriptions on inlaid brass container ('the Bobrinski bucket'), 559/1163, Herat, Afghanistan*

Maybe she was joining her husband who was already there – only the highest echelons of Frankish society could have afforded the expenses of such a trip from Europe. Alternatively, she may have been a female Frankish warrior, one of a category which 'Imad al-Din then goes on to describe.

In an Islamic context it was not unheard of for high-class ladies to travel unaccompanied by their male relations (cf. figure 6.36) but it occasioned comment and seems perhaps to have been a practice amongst ladies of the Turcoman dynasties who may have been more used to an independent lifestyle. Ibn Jubayr mentions several examples of such women, including the daughter of the Saljuq sultan of Konya, Qilij Arslan II;[89] her activities he describes as 'among the strange affairs that are discussed and listened to by men'.[90]

Old Frankish Women

Old Frankish women are specifically mentioned by 'Imad al-Din. Such an age group in medieval Islamic culture is often regarded as redoubtable and wise. A typical example is an old female slave, Burayka, who is mentioned by Usama, and above all Usama's beloved grandmother.[91] 'Imad al-Din describes some of their Frankish counterparts as follows: 'As for old women ('aja'iz), the military posts are full of them. Sometimes they are harsh and sometimes they are soft. They stir up and inflame [the warriors].'[92]

Usama tells a cruelly comic story of a Frankish festivity which he himself witnessed in Tiberias:

> The cavaliers went out to exercise with lances. With them went out two decrepit, aged women whom they stationed at one end of the race course. At the other end of the field they left a pig which they had scalded and laid on a rock. They then made the two aged women run a race while each one of them was accompanied by a detachment of horsemen urging her on. At every step they took, the women would fall down and rise again, while the spectators would laugh. Finally one of them got ahead of the other and won that pig for a prize.[93]

Again the story is a caricature: the juxtaposition of two aged women and a pig is bound to lead to laughter for a Muslim audience.

Marriage

It is very probable that those Franks who came on Crusade and stayed on in the Levant intermarried for the most part with Oriental Christian women. However, some Franks must also have married Muslim women or have taken Muslim concubines. Unfortunately, confirmation of this is hard to find in the sources. Marriages between Crusaders and Oriental Christians would not merit a mention in

Figure 6.24 Dome inscription, mausoleum of Sitta Nafisa, before 683/1284, Cairo, Egypt

Islamic sources but occasional comments suggest – not surprisingly in view of the relatively small number of Crusader women who must have come out to the Levant – that Crusader–Muslim marriages, especially in the lower echelons of society, must have occurred.

When well-born Frankish women fell into Muslim hands as an inevitable result of the vicissitudes of war, they may well have been spared enslavement if they were young and pretty. Badran b. Malik, a scion of the ʿUqaylids, a Bedouin Arab dynasty which held Qalʿat Jaʿbar for several generations, was the son of the union between his father and a beautiful Frankish girl who had been taken prisoner on a pilgrimage to Afamiyya and was sent to Malik as a present by Usama's father.[94]

Usama tells the story of a Muslim woman from Nablus who was married to a Crusader. She killed her husband and made a practice of assassinating travelling Frankish pilgrims.[95] Unfortunately, there are no more details about this woman and we are left in the dark as to the reasons why she married her Crusader husband, why she killed him and why she embarked on her career as a highwaywoman.

Ibn Jubayr, whose impressions of Crusader Tyre are much more positive than of Acre, includes a detailed account of a Crusader wedding procession near the town which he witnessed personally. He describes the event as 'an alluring worldly spectacle deserving of record'.[96] The bride was clad most elegantly,

> in a beautiful dress from which trailed, according to their traditional style, a long train of golden silk. On her head she wore a golden diadem covered by a net of woven gold, and on her breast was a like arrangement.

Figure 6.25 Lady at her toilette *attended by her maid, Blacas ewer, inlaid brass, 629/1232, Mosul, Iraq*

Her 'alluring' attractions move Ibn Jubayr to write: 'Proud she was in her ornaments and dress, walking with little steps of half a span, like a dove, or in the manner of a wisp of cloud.'.[97] Ibn Jubayr then protects himself as usual from the dangers of praising the Franks, adding carefully and sententiously: 'God protect us from the seductions of the sight.'[98] The procession involved many of the town's wealthy people and was watched by Muslims and Christians alike.[99]

Education

The Muslims felt themselves to be far advanced *vis-à-vis* the Crusaders in education. Usama made friends with a Crusader knight who offered to take Usama's son back to Europe to learn of the arts of politics and chivalry. The Crusader knight then added that on his return home Usama's son would be a truly cultivated man. Usama comments caustically: 'A truly cultivated man would never be guilty of such a suggestion; my son might just as well be taken prisoner as go off into the land of the Franks.'[100]

Medicine

The skills of Arab doctors are apparent in various places in Usama's narrative. They are proficient in diagnosis and in finding cures, in bone-setting,[101] in stitching,[102] dressing wounds,[103] diet, bloodletting,[104] and cauterisation. Usama had a great personal interest in medicine. In a section about noteworthy cures, he mentions remedies for hernia, dropsy, colic and the common cold.[105]

He speaks in a tone of ironic superiority about the level of Crusader medical knowledge which lagged far behind the great medieval tradition of Arab medicine. He relates how an Oriental Christian doctor went to look at a Crusader knight with an abscess on his leg and a woman with consumption.[106] The story is worth retelling in full:

Figure 6.26 *Leather binding of a volume of al-Hamawi,* Thubut al-Hujja, *fifteenth century, Egypt*

They brought before me a knight in whose leg an abscess had grown; and a woman afflicted with imbecility. To the knight I applied a small poultice until the abscess opened and became well; and the woman I put on a diet and made her humor wet. Then a Frankish physician came to them and said, 'This man knows nothing about treating them'. He then said to the knight, 'Which wouldst thou prefer, living with one leg or dying with two?' The latter replied, 'Living with one leg'. The physician said, 'Bring me a strong knight and a sharp axe.' A knight came with the axe. And I was standing by. Then the physician laid the leg of the patient on a block of wood and bade the knight strike his leg with the ax and chop it off at one blow. Accordingly he struck it – while I was looking on – one blow, but the leg was not severed. He dealt another blow, upon which the marrow of the leg flowed out and the patient died on the spot. He then examined the woman and said, 'This is a woman in whose head there is a devil which has possessed her. Shave off her hair.' Accordingly they shaved it off and the woman began once more to eat their ordinary diet – garlic and mustard. Her imbecility took a turn for the worse. The physician then said, 'The devil has penetrated through her head.' He therefore took a razor, made a deep cruciform incision on it, peeled off the skin at the middle of the incision until the bone of the skull was exposed and rubbed it with salt. The woman also expired instantly. Thereupon I asked them whether my services

Figure 6.27 *Muslim surgical instruments (scrapers, scalpels, hooks and forceps),* *al-Zahrawi,* Kitab al-Tasrif *('Book of Explanation'),* *670/1271–2, Egypt(?)*

were needed any longer, and when they replied in the negative I returned home, having learned of their medicine what I knew not before.[107]

On the other hand, Usama can on occasion praise the efficacity of Frankish medicine. The Crusader leader Fulk had a treasurer, a knight called Bernard, who was kicked by a horse; his infected leg was cured by a Frankish doctor with very strong vinegar. 'He was cured and stood up (again) like the devil'.[108] In another story, illustrating their curious medicine, Usama speaks of a cure for a Muslim boy suffering from scrofula on his neck. An unnamed Frank (not mentioned as a doctor) gives the boy's father the 'recipe' for a cure consisting first of an application of burnt glasswort leaves, olive oil and sharp vinegar and then of burnt lead soaked in clarified butter. The boy was cured.[109] Usama himself used the same method successfully on others afflicted with scrofula.

The Franks themselves recognised the skills of the local Arab

Figure 6.28
(above, below and opposite)
Animated inscription on the Wade Cup, inlaid brass, c. 1230, north-west Iran

doctors. In his biographical dictionary of doctors, Ibn Abi Usaybi'a (d. 1270) mentions Abu Sulayman Da'ud.[110]

Abu Sulayman Da'ud, born of Christian parents in Jerusalem under Frankish occupation, had entered the service of the Shi'ite Fatimid caliph in Egypt. When the Crusader leader Amalric came to Egypt he was much taken with Abu Sulayman's medical knowledge and he took him (and his five children) back with him to Jerusalem. There Abu Sulayman prepared a suitable treatment for Amalric's leprous son. Abu Sulayman's sons were also involved in Amalric's affairs – one of them, al-Muhadhdhab Abu Sa'id, took over from his father as Amalric's physician. Another son, Abu'l-Khayr, was given the care of Amalric's leprous son and taught him riding. After Saladin's conquest of Jerusalem, this talented family joined the service of Saladin and his successors.[111]

Such biographies cross ideological divides and show the greater flexibility of everyday life (and man's continuing need for good doctors, whatever their religious persuasion or ethnic origin).

Was the Frankish Lifestyle Influenced by the Muslims?

Usama states clearly that some Franks had adopted a Muslim lifestyle: 'Amongst the Franks there is a group who have become acclimatised and have associated with Muslims.'[112] But these, he declares, are an exception.

Usama describes the lifestyle of one Orientalised Frank who was visited in his house by 'a friend' of Usama's. The friend goes on to say:

I went with him and we came to the house of one of the old knights who had come out in the Franks' first expedition [i.e. the First Crusade]. He had been removed from the register and [military] service and had a property in Antioch from which he lived. He brought out a fine table and extremely clean and excellent food. He saw me refraining from eating and said: 'Eat, set your mind at

rest, for I don't eat the Franks' food. I have Egyptian women cooks. I eat only what they have cooked and no pork enters my house.' So I ate, albeit warily, and we left.[113]

Shared Chivalric Values between Muslim and Frankish Knights

An awareness of the common religious purpose and knightly qualities of the Franks occasionally emerges from the Muslim commentators. The poet al-'Unayn writes of the Franks in 618/1221–2: 'A host of Christians beyond count . . . had assembled, one in idea, religion, ardour and resolve.'[114]

We have already seen that the Islamic sources reveal a grudging admiration for the military skills of the Frankish leaders, some of whom they view as worthy adversaries. This admiration is limited: the Muslim chroniclers rarely, for example, praise the magnanimity of the Frankish leaders towards their captives in war. An exception is Baldwin the Leper who is singled out by Ibn al-Athir for his chivalrous treatment of 160 Muslim prisoners from the countryside of Aleppo, releasing them, and giving them clothes before sending them home.[115] Saladin's honourable treatment of Crusader ladies in Jerusalem in 1187 receives high praise,[116] but there is nothing comparable mentioned in connection with Frankish victories.

Usama calls the Templars his friends,[117] and mentions several instances of contact between himself and the upper echelons of Frankish society. Usama is open about his friendship with one particular knight:

There was in the army of King Fulk son of Fulk a modest knight who had come from their country to go on pilgrimage and return home. He got on friendly terms with me, became my constant companion and used to call me 'my brother' and there was between us love and companionship.[118]

This story is very difficult to take literally since the knight was obviously only on a short visit to the Holy Land and Usama states elsewhere that he does not understand the Frankish language at all. So how can this friendship have developed at all? Of course it is necessary for Usama to claim first-hand intimacy with some Franks in order to 'know' their ways and satirise them. Even when his narratives begin with favourable comments about the Franks this is merely

355

Figure 6.29 *Hunting scene, glazed ceramic dish, early thirteenth century, Rusafa(?), Syria*

setting the scene for a cleverly constructed story which debunks them. In the case of the knight in Fulk's army, for example, Usama goes on to make disparaging comments about the level of Frankish education in Europe.

Usama believes that the Franks are courageous and that they rate their knights highly and place them in the counsels of kings:

> The Franks (may Allah render them helpless!) possess none of the virtues of men except courage, consider no precedence or high rank except that of the knights, and have nobody that counts except the knights. These are the men on whose counsel they rely, and the ones who make legal decisions and judgements.[119]

Usama complained to Fulk V, count of Anjou, that the Frankish lord of Banyas had stolen some sheep of his during a period of truce and that, when the sheep gave birth, the lambs died and the remainder were then returned to him. Fulk referred the case to six or seven of his knights who withdrew to consider what to do. They then returned, pronouncing that the lord of Banyas should pay a fine for the damage caused. Usama accordingly accepted a sum of 400 dinars. He then reflects: 'Such a judgement, after having been pronounced by the knights, not even the king nor any of the chieftains of the Franks can alter or revoke. Thus the knight is something great in their esteem.'[120]

Usama is impressed by the valour of the Frankish knight Badrhawa who routs four Muslim warriors, but he cannot allow him to remain a hero in his narrative. Whilst he is at pains to emphasise that the four Muslim warriors learned their lesson and 'now became imbued with valour', Badrhawa has to come to a sticky end. On his way to Antioch, or so Usama's story goes: 'a lion fell upon him from a forest in al-Ruj, snatched him off his mule and carried him into the forest where he devoured him – may Allah's mercy not rest upon his soul'.[121]

356

Cultural and religious pride cannot allow the Frankish knight to have the last word in this tall story: the Muslim warriors learn from their experience and the Frankish knight, though valorous, falls mightily and meets his appointed death in comic retribution. It is perhaps not a coincidence that the Crusader hero, Badrhawa, is riding a mule, not the animal associated with chivalry, a horse.

Yet the Frankish knight at whose table Usama had eaten, as already mentioned, was able later in an explosive scene in the market to save Usama's life: 'The effect of that eating together was my escape from being killed.'[122]

According to Usama, the Franks were able in their turn to recognise valour in a Muslim enemy. Tancred, who succeeded Bohemond as lord of Antioch in 1104, made peace with Usama's uncle who at Tancred's request sent him a fine horse, mounted by a young Kurdish cavalier called Hasanun. The Franks recognised in him a valiant cavalier and Tancred gave him a robe of honour.[123] A year later, however, once the truce had expired, Hasanun was taken prisoner and tortured by those selfsame Franks and his right eye was gouged out.[124] Such, notes Usama, are the vicissitudes of peace and war and the untrustworthiness of the Franks.

The Ridiculous Side of Frankish Chivalry

Usama tells the following tall story about a leopard. Every day at noon a leopard would come and jump up to the window of the church of Hunak (40 cubits high), where it would sleep all day. The Frankish knight, Sir Adam, who owned the castle of Hunak, heard about the leopard and

> put on his coat of mail, mounted his horse, took his shield and lance and came to the church . . . As soon as the leopard saw him, it jumped from the window upon him while he was on his horse, broke his back and killed him. It then went away. The peasants of Hunak used to call that leopard, 'the leopard that takes part in the holy war (al-namir al-mujahid)'.[125]

Usama's story makes the Frankish knight seem mildly ridiculous as all his defensive measures were of no avail against the speed and strength of the leopard. It is also significant that just before this story Usama has related how he and some companions had managed to kill a leopard.[126] Similarly no sympathy is shown for the accidental drowning of the mighty monarch Frederick I Barbarossa in 586/1190. He is presented by 'Imad al-Din in two differing versions of the story as an ignorant fool for venturing at all into the River Calycadnus.[127]

The Fate of Muslims under Crusader Rule

Frankish rule over Levantine Muslims was much shorter than Muslim

Figure 6.30 *Inlaid brass pen-case with the titles of Abu'l-Fida Isma'il, ruler of Hama (d. 732/1331), Syria*

rule over the Christians of Spain. In Spain a slow acculturation process was possible over several centuries and in the Granada area for considerably longer. Some of the Frankish states were of very short duration (Jerusalem for the periods 1099–1187 and 1229–44); other areas with Muslim populations were ruled by the Franks for much longer (Antioch, for example, from 1098 to 1268 and Tyre from 1124 to 1291).

When searching for information about the Muslim perspective on Frankish rule, one is confronted by the problem that all but one of the Muslim chroniclers lived outside the Frankish states themselves. The work of the sole Muslim writer who did live under Frankish rule, Hamdan b. ʿAbd al-Rahim al-Atharibi, as already mentioned, has unfortunately not survived. In general, therefore, it is difficult to make firm statements about how Muslims fared under Crusader rule since the evidence is scanty, is not of local origin and comes from different periods of time.

Refugee Movements

From the very beginning of the Frankish occupation, refugees from the coastal cities of Syria and Palestine fled to Damascus and Aleppo as well as Egypt and Iraq. Damascus was especially affected because it was close and the refugees often wanted to go back out of a deep ancestral attachment to their land. The movement of refugees was most acute in the first years – from 492/1099 until the fall of Tyre in 518/1124. Nevertheless, it continued at least until the middle of the twelfth century. The sources – which as a rule only mention rulers and the scholarly elite – do not allow one to quantify the number of refugees. But it seems reasonable to conjecture that the common people are unlikely to have moved; only the relatively wealthy would have been able to do so.[128] Amongst such refugees were city governors, notables and poets. Some of those who fled, for example from Tyre, travelled with absolutely nothing, with no riding-beasts and only what they had on their backs.[129] The Shiʿite governors of Acre and Tripoli fled to their co-religionists in Egypt.[130] The poets who fled, such as Ibn Munir and Ibn al-Qaysarani, wrote elegies lamenting their lost homes.[131]

Yet on the basis of the sources, it would seem that such demographic disruption was the exception rather than the rule and that the majority of the Muslims living in territories conquered by the Franks remained where they were. It should be remembered that Greater Syria had been subjected throughout the second half of the eleventh century to frequent changes of government and military conflicts which caused damage and disruption to both villages and towns. Peasants, the old and the sick were predictably the ones who had to stay while the higher stratum of a village or town had more chance to leave. According to Ibn al-Qalanisi, the only Muslims in Tyre who stayed on after the conquest of the town in 1124 were those who were too weak to travel.[132] 'Imad al-Din remarks that the subjected Muslims in Sidon, Beirut and Jubayl were the poor.[133]

Kedar rightly raises the possibility that Muslim writers may have wished to minimise the size of the Muslim population who opted to remain under Frankish rule. On balance, it seems that the ordinary Muslims of Syria and Palestine endured foreign rule – this time, as it happens, from western Europe – with their customary passivity. When Muslim armies came occasionally from the east to fight the Franks in the early decades of the twelfth century, the local Muslim population must have helped their co-religionists, as for example during Mawdud's campaign in 506/1113. Ibn al-Qalanisi reports that there was considerable Muslim reaction to Mawdud's arrival:

> There was not a Muslim left in the land of the Franks who did not send to the atabek [i.e. Mawdud] begging that he should guarantee him security and confirm him in the possession of his property and a part of the revenue of Nablus was brought to him.[134]

But generally speaking, the Muslims under Crusader rule must have acquiesced, in realistic acknowledgement that submission was more sensible than conflict, however much tensions might smoulder under the surface. It seems likely that for the mass of the Muslim population the Frankish conquest did not bring about any profound transformation. Their lot remained much the same, whoever their overlords.[135]

One important, though short, Muslim source which bears on these matters has recently come to light. A sixteenth-century chronicler of Damascus, Ibn Tulun, describes the exodus of a number of Hanbali families from villages to the south-west of Nablus in the year 551/1156–7.[136] His source is Diya' al-Din al-Muqaddasi (d. 1245) who was a second-generation descendant of the original refugees who had settled after their emigration to a new quarter of Damascus, al-Salihiyya. Diya' al-Din describes Frankish rule in general as tyrannical:

> The Muslims came under the rule of the Franks in the lands of Jerusalem and its environs and they used to work the land for

Figure 6.31 Musicians,
Fatimid ivory carving,
eleventh century, Egypt

them. They [the Franks] used to harm them and imprison them and take something from them like the poll-tax (*jizya*).[137]

But the tyranny of one Crusader ruler is singled out for particular condemnation, that of Ibn Barzan (Baldwin of Ibelin, lord of Mirabel) who owned a number of the villages to the south-west of Nablus:

> When the infidels used to take from every man under their rule one dinar, he [Baldwin] (may God curse him!) used to take from each of them four dinars and he used to cut off their feet. There was not among the Franks anyone more arrogant or proud than he was (may God put him to shame!).[138]

Baldwin's ire was directed especially at a Hanbalite legal scholar, Ahmad b. Muhammad b. Qudama, who hailed from the village of Jamma'il and was the grandfather of the narrator, Diya' al-Din al-Muqaddasi. Ibn Qudama used to read the Qur'an to the villagers and preach to them on Fridays, and people from the surrounding villages would flock to hear him. Baldwin, to whom these activities were reported as 'distracting the peasants from their work', spoke about killing him.[139] Thereupon Ahmad decided to flee to Damascus 'because of his fear for himself and his inability to practise his religion publicly'.[140] Ibn Qudama's secret departure was followed by that of the members of his own family and related families who escaped in small groups to Damascus; their exodus encouraged the inhabitants of at least eight villages in the area to leave and reside in the Damascus suburb of al-Salihiyya, where Ibn Qudama and his followers had settled.

Despite the poignancy of this account, it seems probable that most Muslims in the Latin east did not leave their homes and emigrate to nearby Islamic territory. Attachment to their land and to their property and lack of the resources necessary for travel prevailed over whatever religious, political or fiscal difficulties they may have experienced. The Nablus area seems to have remained a hotbed of resentment against the Crusaders. In 583/1187–8 Muslim peasants attacked the Franks, forcing them to take refuge in their castles even before the arrival of Saladin's army. As 'Imad al-Din writes:

> When they [the Franks] learned of their defeat and that they could not hope to rectify their situation, they were afraid of living closely with the Muslims and they dispersed. The people of the estates attacked them in the houses and quarters and plundered what stores and goods they found and they attacked their weak ones and blockaded the citadels to the disadvantage of their strong ones.[141]

The Neglect of Muslim Cemeteries

It seems that demoralisation or restrictions – or perhaps just the advanced age and lowly social status of those Muslims who did stay

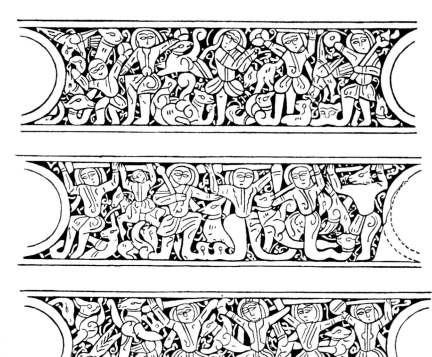

Figure 6.32
(above and opposite)
Animated inscription on the
Fano Cup, inlaid metal,
c. 1250, Syria

on in the Kingdom of Jerusalem – discouraged the upkeep of ceme-
teries and tombs. 'Ali al-Harawi, who visited the area in the early
1180s and wrote a guide to the pilgrimage sites there, suggests that
neglect and ignorance had set in.[142] He writes that in the cemetery at
Ascalon as well as Gaza, Acre, Tyre, Sidon and the whole coastal
region there are many tombs of holy men whose identity is no longer
known. The same criticism is addressed to the upkeep of the tombs
near the walls of Jerusalem.[143]

Muslims under Frankish Rule: Better to stay or Better to Leave?

The Christian reconquest of the eleventh century, in Sicily, Spain
and the Levant, created a new problem for the Muslim lawyers whose
system was predicated on the basis that Islam was society's predominant faith. Instead, steadily in Sicily and Spain and suddenly in
the Levant, long-established Muslim populations found themselves
under Christian rulers. This was a disturbing experience.[144] Should
they leave for Muslim lands or should they stay, and if so, on what
basis?[145]

362

Sometimes the Franks made efforts to induce the Muslims back to their homes. According to Ibn al-ʿAdim, at Atharib in northern Syria, shortly after the surrender of Sidon, Tancred tried to persuade Muslims to stay and organised the return of their wives who had fled to Aleppo.[146]

As usual, Ibn Jubayr offers comments but, as Kedar points out, his evidence is flawed by the disadvantage that he stayed only thirty-two days in the Kingdom of Jerusalem, of which thirteen were spent on a ship in the harbour at Acre, waiting for a favourable wind.[147]

At the time of conquest, flight was often the favoured Muslim option. However, the pull of the homeland would be strong, as Ibn Jubayr points out: 'But there were some whose love of native land impelled them to return and, under the conditions of a safeguard which was written for them, to live amongst the infidels.'[148] Ibn Jubayr, the traveller from distant Spain, is uncomprehendingly judgemental about such Levantine Muslims: 'There can be no excuse in the eyes of God for a Muslim to stay in any infidel country, save when passing through it while the way lies clear in Muslim lands.'[149]

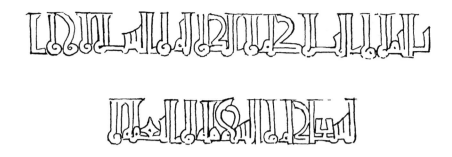

Figure 6.33 Brass casket with benedictory Kufic inscription, late twelfth century, Iran

Muslim Views of Frankish Government

Ibn Jubayr's verdict on Crusader Tyre is relatively favourable:

> Its roads and streets are cleaner than those of Acre. Its people are by disposition less stubborn in their unbelief, and by nature and habit they are kinder to the Muslim stranger. Their manners, in other words, are gentler. Their dwellings are larger and more spacious. The state of the Muslims in this city is easier and more peaceful.[150]

Cultivation in the valley below the fortress of Banyas was an interesting example of Muslim–Frankish co-operation. According to Ibn Jubayr, who passed by the area in 580/1184,

> The cultivation of the vale is divided between the Franks and the Muslims, and in it there is a boundary known as 'The Boundary of Dividing'. They apportion the crops equally, and their animals are mingled together, yet no wrong takes place between them because of it.[151]

A well-known passage in Ibn Jubayr's account speaks of good relations between Franks and the Muslims under their rule in the area between Tibnin and Acre. It is worth quoting at length:

> Our way lay through continuous farms and ordered settlements, whose inhabitants were all Muslims, living comfortably with the Franks. God protect us from such temptation. They surrender half their crops to the Franks at harvest time, and pay as well a poll-tax of one dinar and five qirat for each person. Other than that, they

are not interfered with, save for a light tax on the fruits of trees. Their houses and all their effects are left to their full possession. All the coastal cities occupied by the Franks are managed in this fashion, their rural districts, the villages and farms, belonging to the Muslims.[152]

Ibn Jubayr goes on to reflect that it is very unfortunate that these Muslims are receiving better treatment under Frankish rule than others who are governed by their co-religionists:

They observe how unlike them in ease and comfort are their brethren in the Muslim regions under their (Muslim) governors. This is one of the misfortunes afflicting the Muslims. The Muslim community bewails the injustice of a landlord of its own faith, and applauds the conduct of its opponent and enemy, the Frankish landlord, and is accustomed to justice from him.[153]

According to Ibn Jubayr, in that same area near Acre the Franks had appointed a Muslim headman to oversee Muslim workers.[154]

Another extract, this time from 'Imad al-Din al-Isfahani, corroborates the view of Ibn Jubayr who might otherwise be criticised for having the superficial view of a tourist:

As for Nablus, the inhabitants of its villages and most of its people were Muslims and were threaded on the thread of the subject people of the Franks (i.e. lived as subjects of the Franks) who annually collected from them a tax and did not change any law or cult of theirs.[155]

This suggests that the Franks were levying something similar to the Islamic poll-tax (*jizya*) from their Muslim subjects.

Frankish Justice

Usama relates two stories in this connection. The first one is about a duel in Nablus between two Franks, a healthy young blacksmith and a strong-willed old man. It is a bloody and protracted struggle, supervised by the lord of the town and watched by the people in a circle. In the end, the old man is killed, dragged away and hanged. Usama comments wryly: 'This case illustrates the kind of jurisprudence and legal decisions the Franks have – may Allah's curse be upon them!'[156]

Usama's second story concerns a Frankish ordeal by water, the victim being a Muslim man accused with his mother of assassinating Frankish pilgrims:

They installed a huge cask and filled it with water. Across it they

Figure 6.34 *Terracotta figurine of a dancer, thirteenth century, Wasit, Iraq*

set a board of wood. They then bound the arms of the man charged
with the act, tied a rope around his shoulders and dropped him
into the cask, their idea being that in case he was innocent, he
would sink in the water and they would then lift him up with the
rope so that he might not die in the water; and in case he was
guilty, he would not sink in the water. This man did his best to
sink when they dropped him into the water, but he could not do
it. So he had to submit to their sentence against him–may Allah's
curse be upon them! They pierced his eyeballs with red-hot awls.[157]

Travel

Travel in medieval times was difficult, dangerous and slow. Nevertheless, many a trip was undertaken, for reasons of administration,
war, commerce, piety and the search for knowledge. According to
Goitein's analysis of the Geniza documents, a collection of medieval
documents found in Fustat (Old Cairo), people preferred to travel by
water rather than overland, even for short distances.[158] The Islamic
sources do not conceal the fact that Christian travellers from Europe
often perished at Muslim hands. Frankish ships carrying pilgrims or
Frankish pilgrims (*hujjaj al-afranj*) travelling on land did not always
reach their destinations. Ibn Muyassar mentions the slaughter of an
entire group of pilgrims in or near Tripoli in 546/1151.[159] In 551/1157
ships carrying Christian pilgrims were wrecked in the port of Alexandria: the pilgrims were captured and sent to Cairo.[160] For security
reasons it was customary for land journeys to join caravans, which
came into special prominence in the winter months when it was
not possible to travel by sea. Overland travel was especially slow,
expensive and hazardous. Wheeled transport was very rare.[161]

Travel on land was facilitated by the vast network of caravansarais
(also called *khan*s) where the traveller, merchant or pilgrim could put

Figure 6.35 *A messenger,
painting on paper, twelfth
century, Egypt*

Figure 6.36 *Lady travelling
in a litter on a camel, Blacas
ewer, 629/1232, Mosul, Iraq*

up under the same roof as his beast and his belongings. Ibn Jubayr's account is sprinkled with references to the *khan*s where he stayed during his trip. When located in remote places, the *khan*s were vulnerable to attack and had to be well fortified. One such place was the Khan of the Turcomans in Baqidin in Syria, south of Aleppo. As Ibn Jubayr remarks: 'The khans on this road are like fortresses in their unassailableness and their fortifications. Their doors are of iron, and they present the utmost strength.'[162] The *khan*s were not just well defended. Ibn Jubayr describes the Khan of the Sultan on the road from Hims to Damascus as having 'running water which flows through underground conduits to a fountain in the middle'.[163]

However, there were obvious dangers. Being attacked by highwaymen was common.[164] Usama describes how he protected money with which he had been entrusted. When the caravan stopped he would put the bags containing the money in the centre of a rug, fold its ends around them, spread another rug on top and sleep on top of the bags.[165]

Corrupt officials were a hazard, especially in Upper Egypt, according to Ibn Jubayr, who complains bitterly about the humiliation experienced by pilgrims to Mecca, such as he was:

> The stopping of travellers' ships and their search and examination, the plunging of hands into the clothing of the merchants in search of what dirhams and dinars they might have under their arm-pits or in their bosoms, is abominable to hear, and hateful to relate . . . amongst these tax-receivers the pilgrims stand in shame and abasement . . . There was no bundle or sack into which they did not drive those accursed staves . . .[166]

Figure 6.37 Camel rider on a glazed ceramic vase, twelfth century, Iran

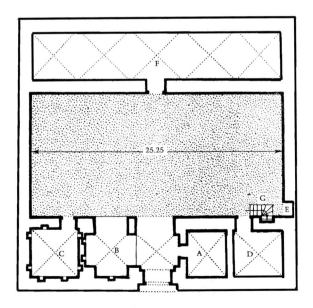

Figure 6.38 Staging post near al-Qutayfa, plan, thirteenth century, Syria

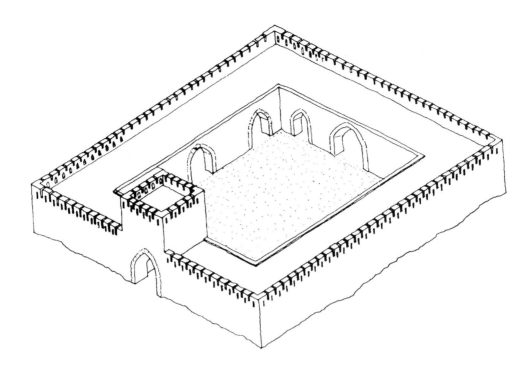

Figure 6.39 Khan al-'Arus,
staging post/caravansarai built
by Saladin, 587/1191–2, Syria

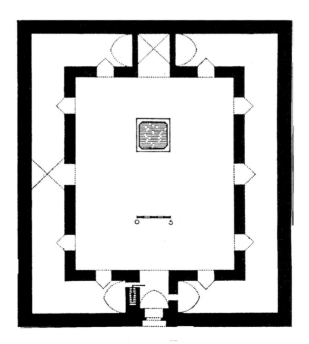

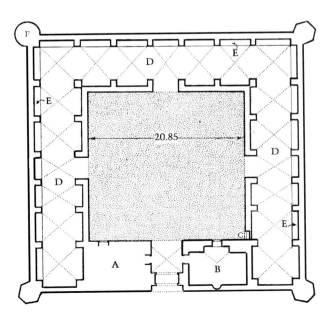

Figure 6.40 *Khan al-Inqirata, staging post/caravansarai, plan and perspectival view, 773/1371–2, Syria*

In the twelfth century it was common for people from the Islamic countries to travel on Genoese, Pisan and other European ships, as the Geniza documents testify.[167] It is not clear whether it was always possible for Muslims to secure separate accommodation from Christians when travelling by sea. Certainly there is no mention of such an arrangement when Ibn Jubayr set out from Spain eastwards in 578/1183. However, on his return journey he states specifically: 'The Muslims secured places apart from the Franks.'[168]

The traveller by sea was totally dependent on the winds. If they did not blow, the ship could be delayed for a considerable time, as was the fate of Ibn Jubayr in the ship at Acre. In Rajab 580/October 1184 he was obliged to wait twelve days for a favourable wind to sail westwards. As he rightly puts it: 'Voyagers to the Maghrib, to Sicily, or to the lands of the Rum, await this east wind in these two seasons as they would await (the fulfilment of) an honest pledge.'[169] Later, as a result of a long buffeting in the ocean, he reflects: 'All (modes of) travel have their (proper) season, and travel by sea should be at the propitious time and the recognised period.'[170]

A wind from the west could sabotage the journey westwards. Thanks to the skill of Genoese sailors, although the ship on which Ibn Jubayr was travelling lost half its mast and the attaching sails, the situation was rectified.[171] A little later, the ship was becalmed when the sea became like 'a palace made smooth with glass'.[172]

Ships carried a wide variety of food products for sale to the passengers, if Ibn Jubayr's experience is typical; he mentions pomegranate, quince, water-melon, pear, chestnut, walnut, chick-pea, broad bean, onion, garlic, fig, cheese and fish.[173] This would be supplemented by fresh produce, such as bread, meat and oil, which would be sold by local people to the ship as it passed by an island or a piece of mainland.[174] However, after a long time at sea, the food supplies inevitably petered out; most travellers brought enough food for fifteen or twenty days.[175]

The Conduct of Religious Worship: The Appropriation of the Religious Monuments of 'the Other Side'

Since the days of the Islamic conquests in the seventh century the Muslims had on occasion taken over existing Christian places of worship or built on sites that other faiths had held to be holy. During the period of the Crusades, both Franks and Muslims generally tended to retain the function of religious buildings when they appropriated them from the enemy and to respect their sanctity, although they adapted them to the rites of their own faith.

How the Franks Treated Islamic Monuments

Despite the Franks' initial brutality, their bestial qualities which were condemned in the Muslim sources, and the conviction that the

Dome of the Rock had been 'polluted', its fabric was not damaged and its inscriptions were not destroyed. In the early period of Crusader occupation, the same process was repeated outside Jerusalem. For example, in Ascalon the Green Mosque became the church of Sancta Maria Viridis.[176] As Ibn Jubayr sadly laments in the case of Acre: 'Mosques became churches and minarets bell-towers'.[177]

Yet it is important to point out that despite the sense of Islamic public outrage and humiliation, certain Muslim observers were able to comment on the fact that the Franks had sometimes behaved with commendable restraint towards Muslim religious monuments. Al-Harawi mentions, for example, that in the Aqsa mosque, the *mihrab* of the second caliph 'Umar had been left untouched by the Franks. He then speaks of an inscription on the ceiling of the mosque in the name of the Fatimid caliph al-Zahir dated 426/1035: 'This whole inscription, the gold mosaic foliages as well as the Qur'anic

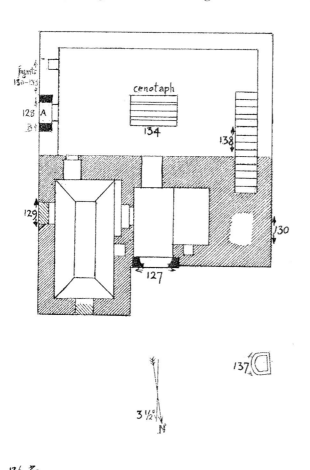

Figure 6.41 *Turbat 'Ali al-Harawi, plan, 602/1206, Aleppo, Syria*

verses and the caliphs' names above the doors have been left intact by the Franks.'[178] According to al-Harawi, the Franks had also not touched the *mihrab* of 'Umar in Bethlehem.[179]

When Saladin's men entered the Dome of the Rock in 1187, they found that although an altar had been placed on the rock, it was shielded by a fine iron grille. Some damage had been caused, however, by Christian pilgrims, who had broken off small pieces of rock to take home as pious souvenirs.[180] One may tentatively suggest on the basis of these details that the Franks seem to have been interested in superimposing large public symbols of Christian domination on key Muslim monuments – the cross on the Dome of the Rock and pictures of Christ and so on – rather than in altering the basic fabric of the buildings.

Sometimes financial gain could come to the Christians from the use of a Muslim religious monument. 'Imad al-Din mentions under the year 583/1187–8 that at Sebastiyya (Sivas) the tomb of Zakariyya (Zechariah), the father of John the Baptist,[181] had been made into a church by priests:

> It was their venerated place of worship and revered shrine. They had covered it with screens and decorated it with silver and gold. They appointed for it set times for visitors and a community of monks were living in it. Only those who had a present of value with them were allowed to visit.[182]

Muslim Treatment of Christian Religious Buildings

The process of appropriation worked both ways. There were clearly no religious scruples felt by the Muslims about taking over what had

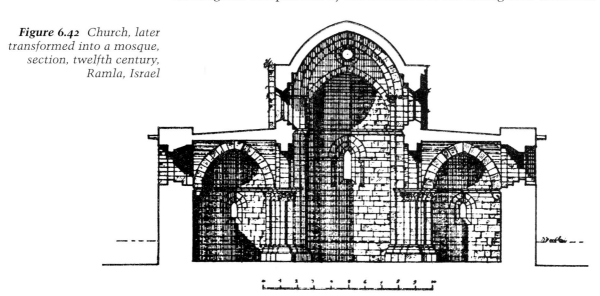

Figure 6.42 *Church, later transformed into a mosque, section, twelfth century, Ramla, Israel*

been Crusader religious buildings and consecrating them for an Islamic purpose. An early instance of churches being converted into Islamic religious buildings is reported for Aleppo in 518/1124–5 by the local chronicler Ibn al-'Adim.

Yet, despite local anger at the Frankish raiding of the Aleppan area, the Muslims kept these churches as religious monuments, converting some of them into mosques (figures 6.42 and 6.43) and others, somewhat later, into religious colleges (plates 6.1 and 6.2; cf. plate 6.3).

Another example of this process was the Salahiyya *madrasa*, a college founded in 588/1192 by Saladin – as a surviving inscription above the door indicates – for the teaching of Islamic law according to the Shafi'ite *madhhab*. Ibn Shaddad was appointed as its first *shaykh*.[183] In Crusader times this had been the fine Romanesque church of St Anne's, and few architectural changes were deemed necessary for its transformation into a *madrasa*.[184] Saladin also dedicated the patriarch's palace to the Sufis and established a large bequest (*waqf*) for it.[185] A church once belonging to the Hospitallers was made into a hospital.[186] Money was allocated to it and rare drugs brought to it.

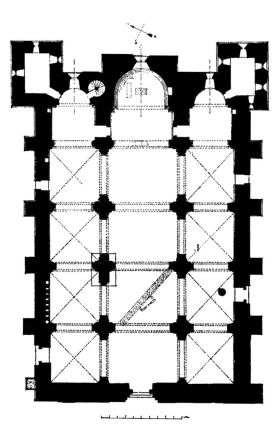

Figure 6.43 Cathedral (later turned into a mosque), plan, twelfth century, Tartus (Tortosa), Syria

Plate 6.1 *Madrasa al-Halawiyya (a church converted into a* madrasa *in 543/1148–9), courtyard, Aleppo, Syria*

(Creswell Photographic Archive, Ashmolean Museum, Oxford, neg. C. 5658)

The Frankish churches built in the Levant were extremely Western in design and decoration. Indeed, they would not have looked at all out of place back in Europe.[187] Despite their strangeness in a Muslim context, however, some of them were transformed into mosques, as for example at Ramla, Hebron and Tarsus.[188] The remains of the Frankish cathedral at Tripoli are now part of the town's main mosque which boasts a bulky, rectangular tower with twin and triple arches and shafted openings and stands four storeys high, an unusual sight in a Muslim townscape. The Great Mosque in Beirut, a striking example of Romanesque architecture, was formerly the cathedral church of St John the Baptist.[189]

Another interesting example of the wholesale take-over of an existing Crusader monument for an Islamic purpose is the outer cell of the Chapel of the Repose of Christ overlooking the Haram. This became a tomb for a Kurdish Ayyubid amir and was then known as the tomb (*madfan*) of Shaykh Darbas al-Kurdi al-Hakkari, who died around the beginning of the thirteenth century.[190] The particular sanctity of this site to Christians – it was where Jesus was said to have rested after his capture in the Garden of Gethsemane – did not inhibit its subsequent use as a Muslim burial place.

374

It should be pointed out that a similar fate awaited some of the Crusader churches outside Jerusalem which were converted into Muslim monuments. A typical example is the Crusader church at Gaza which is now the Great Mosque.[191]

The Incidence of Conversion amongst Muslims and Franks

Instances of Crusaders and Muslims changing faith are reported occasionally in the Islamic sources, although such a process must have

Plate 6.2 *Madrasa al-Halawiyya, prayer hall (note typical Byzantine pendentives), 543/1148–9 and earlier, Aleppo, Syria*

(Creswell Photographic Archive, Ashmolean Museum, Oxford, neg. C. 5657)

375

Plate 6.3 *Madrasa al-Halawiyya, wooden* mihrab *dated 643/1245, Aleppo, Syria*

(Creswell Photographic Archive, Ashmolean Museum, Oxford, neg. C5659)

occurred frequently as a result of the exigencies of war and survival. How lasting such conversions were is generally not discussed in the sources. Ibn al-Athir mentions one Muslim apostate who was mayor (*ra'is*) of Saruj in 502/1108–9:

> The mayor of Saruj was a Muslim who had apostacised. Jawali's associates heard him denigrating Islam and they beat him. There ensued a dispute between them and the Franks because of him. That was mentioned to the count [Baldwin] and he said: 'This [kind of person] is not suitable either for us or the Muslims'. So they killed him.[192]

Ibn Jubayr rises to heights of invective against a former Maghribi prisoner who was now in the employ of a Syrian merchant:

> In one of his patron's caravans he had come to Acre, where he had mixed with the Christians, and taken on much of their character. The devil increasingly seduced and incited him until he renounced the faith of Islam, turned unbeliever, and became a Christian.[193]

Worse was to come, however: 'We left to Acre, but received news of him. He had been baptised and become unclean, and had put on the girdle of a monk, thereby hastening for himself the flames of hell.'[194]

Usama tells the story of a man called 'Ali 'Abd b. Abi'l-Rayda' who fell into the hands of a Frank called Theophile, the lord of Kafartab. Under his new master, 'Ali led the Franks against the Muslims. His wife who was with him in Kafartab objected to his behaviour, but to no avail. So she arranged to secrete one of her relatives in the house and at night they both killed her husband. She ran away with all her possessions to Shayzar; there she said: 'I was angered on behalf of the Muslims at what this infidel perpetrated against them.'[195] It is not clear from this story whether 'Ali had converted to Christianity but it seems likely.

We have already mentioned the young Frankish woman captive who married Malik b. Salim, the lord of Qal'at Ja'bar. She bore Malik a son called Badran, who later succeeded his father. At that point his mother escaped from the castle by a rope and went to Frankish-held Saruj: 'there she married a Frankish shoemaker, while her son was the lord of Qal'at Ja'bar'.[196] Usama comments at the beginning of this story that 'The Franks (may Allah's curse be upon them!) are an accursed race, the members of which do not assimilate except with their own kin'.[197]

Usama gives another example of the tenacity of the Christian faith. He tells the story of a young Frankish prisoner 'who accepted Islam, and his conversion was genuine, judging by what he showed in the practice of prayer and fasting'. He learned the craft of working marble from a stonecutter and was married off by Usama's father to a pious young Muslim woman – Usama's father paid for the wedding.

holy monuments of Islam and worship therein were guaranteed in the agreement:

> The Haram, and the Dome of the Rock and the Aqsa mosque which lay therein, should also remain to the Muslims, with no Franks allowed to enter save as visitors, while its custodians should be Muslims. All the practices of Islam, with the call to prayer and the prayers themselves, should continue to be observed within the sacred area.[210]

The Destruction of Religious Monuments

It is of course understandable that sometimes feelings of anger and vengeance should prevail. Perhaps it is surprising that more religious buildings were not destroyed in the long conflict between Franks and Muslims. But both sides in the conflict were guilty on occasion.

A key moment had been the destruction of the Church of the Holy Sepulcre by al-Hakim – an aberrant and disgraceful act which his successor al-Zahir had attempted to rectify by agreeing that the monument should be rebuilt. Although the Franks massacred the inhabitants, Muslim and Jew, in Jerusalem in 492/1099, and although they pillaged the portable contents of the Dome of the Rock and the Aqsa mosque, they did not destroy the monuments themselves. This was probably out of respect for the Holy City and its *haram* area and because they could see the propagandistic value of appropriating these monuments for Christian use. Nevertheless, some Islamic sources report without comment that the Franks burned down the Jerusalem synagogue with the Jews inside it, and that they also burned other important shrines.[211]

Similar destructive acts are reported for the Muslim side. In 517/1123–4 the zealous Artuqid warrior Balak destroyed Christian shrines at Khartpert in retaliation for an uprising of Frankish prisoners.[212] In Jumada I 584/July 1188 Saladin destroyed the church at Antarsus (Tortosa) which was 'one of the largest of its kind'. In 587/1191 he demolished the church at Lydda.[213] Saladin's biographers draw a discreet veil over this information; but al-Maqrizi, who lived in a more overtly 'fanatical' age, has no inhibitions about mentioning this in the same way as he recounts the similar activities of Baybars.

The Ayyubid period witnessed dreadful destruction in Jerusalem: the Khwarazmians – at least nominally Muslims – sacked Jerusalem in 642/1244–5, destroying structures in the Church of the Holy Sepulcre and pillaging Christian graves.[214] In 661/1263 Baybars took the lead personally in ordering that the Church of the Annunciation in Nazareth should be razed to the ground.[215] The church was destroyed so systematically that its original ground plan can be discerned only through the results of archaeological excavation. Five Romanesque capitals, probably the finest sculptures emanating from Palestine under Frankish occupation, have survived; their carvings of

Figure 6.45 *Courtiers by a fountain, Cappella Palatina, ceiling, c. 1140, Palermo, Sicily*

human figures portray scenes from the lives of the Apostles.[216] Perhaps it was this very representation of the human form in a religious context that inflamed Baybars into destroying the church. He is reported to have known the importance of the church for the Christians: 'the most famous of their holy places, where in their view the Christian religion had its origin'.[217] In 666/1267–8 Baybars also demolished churches in al-Hadath.[218]

Cultural Exchanges between Muslims and Franks – the Evidence of Islamic Art and Architecture

It is very difficult to pinpoint the direction of the flow of artistic influences between Muslims and Crusaders and vice versa, and to establish whether a motif or a style was borrowed at the time or reused later. Hence it is important to establish at the outset that the Islamic perspectives which form the focus of this book do not necessarily fit neatly into the art-historical sphere, where it is not always possible to say firmly that Muslims borrowed from Crusaders or Crusaders from Muslims. Nevertheless, some very interesting insights into cultural borrowings and how and why they occurred can be made by analysing the surviving artistic and architectural material from the Crusading period.

As already mentioned, the major architectural achievements of the Crusaders were in fortresses and churches, and the physical evidence of the Crusader presence in the Levant must have been striking. They built great castles and fortified existing towns. They brought with them a deep knowledge of military technology and the science of masonry. They also built numerous churches both inside and outside Jerusalem.

Architecture

It is difficult to assess the impact of the Crusader presence on the building activities of the Muslims. One might have expected that in response to the Crusaders' attacks and to their network of castles and fortifications the Muslims might have responded by building similar structures to defend themselves. This issue will be examined in Chapter 7.

Here, however, we will look at the question of whether Crusaders and Muslims 'borrowed' from each other's architectural repertoires in religious buildings (e.g. figure 6.46). A few warning notes should be sounded first. It is perhaps misleading to attempt to assess cross-cultural influences on the basis of what has chanced to survive until the present day. After all, the twelfth and thirteenth centuries witnessed prolonged warfare and a number of serious earthquakes, notably in 1157 and 1170, and the all-important city of Jerusalem was sacked in 1244 by the Khwarizmians and much valuable evidence has been destroyed. It is also important to stress that it is often difficult to assess both the direction and the chronology of architectural borrowings between two traditions. An obvious meeting point for artistic cross-fertilisation in the Crusading period is the city of Jerusalem itself, which was held successively by the Franks and the Muslims between 1099 and 1291. The evidence for mutual artistic influences is, however, sparse since most of Ayyubid Jerusalem has not been preserved.

The reusing of Crusader Handiwork in Muslim Monuments

It was quite common for parts of a Crusader building to be reused in an Islamic setting. It is often difficult to disentangle what are Crusader and what are Islamic remains, what is Crusader handiwork in its original site and what has been reworked. What is clear, however, is that Muslim masons were not averse to reusing fragments of Crusader stonework in Islamic religious monuments. And they probably had a variety of motives for doing so.

In the Aqsa mosque, for example, some of the second-hand material used in the arches of the facade includes sculpted ornament taken from Crusader structures of the twelfth century (plate 6.4).[219] One of the inscriptions on the porch records that the facade of the portico was constructed by the Ayyubid prince al-Mu'azzam 'Isa in c. 609/1217–18.[220]

The entrance of the monument known as the *Qubbat al-mi'raj* on

Figure 6.46 White Mosque, minaret (note European elements), 718/1318, Ramla, Israel

(Creswell Photographic Archive, Ashmolean Museum, Oxford, neg. C. 4996)

Plate 6.4 *Aqsa Mosque, Ayyubid porch (note incorporation of Frankish elements, perhaps as references to Muslim victory), 615/1218–19, Jerusalem*

383

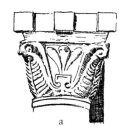

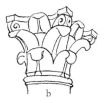

Figure 6.47 *Romanesque capitals reused in Muslim buildings (a: Mashhad al-Husayn, Aleppo; b: Madrasa al-Zahiriyya, Aleppo; c: Citadel, Damascus); twelfth–thirteenth centuries, Syria*

Figure 6.48 *Frankish capitals reused in the Jami' al-Hanabila, 599/1202–3, Damascus, Syria*

the upper platform of the so-called Temple Mount, dated 592/1200–1, is very similar to the Chapel of the Ascension on the Mount of Olives and the Muslim monument has a number of Crusader *spolia*.[221] Other examples of the reuse of Crusader sculpture in Islamic monuments include the upper part of the *Bab al-silsila*, where the pendentives of the domes are probably an Ayyubid reconstruction of Crusader pieces (dated by Burgoyne to between 1187 and 1199), and the Nahwiyya *madrasa*, founded by the Ayyubid ruler al-Mu'azzam 'Isa, which has a facade in a hybrid style, reusing Crusader *spolia*.[222]

What motivated Muslim craftsmen to reuse Crusader architectural fragments in their construction of new Islamic monuments and to incorporate Crusader *spolia* into existing Islamic monuments? There were often practical reasons for this. Crusader prisoners of war who had skills as masons would be employed in building new Islamic monuments.[223] Material from ruined buildings could be used in constructing new ones nearby and thus save costs. This was especially the case when the *spolia* bore vegetal or abstract decoration which would not offend Muslim susceptibilities.

Figure 6.49 *Crusader capital reused deliberately upside down as a trophy of victory,* mihrab *of Abu'l-Fida, Jami' al-Nuri, early fourteenth century, Hama, Syria*

Aesthetic considerations could also have played a part in the selection of which *spolia* or motifs would be reused in Muslim buildings (plate 6.5; cf. also plates 2.9 and 5.4). And no doubt, above all, there was the wish on the part of the triumphant Muslim conquerors to display the spoils of their victory.

A key moment was 1291. The beautiful doorway of the church at St Jean d'Acre was brought from Acre in 1291 and incorporated in the mosque of al-Nasir in Cairo (plate 6.6). This was, of course, no mere borrowing of an architectural feature just because the architect,

Plate 6.5 *Great Mosque, treasury (1923 photograph), perhaps seventh century, Hama, Syria*

(Creswell Photographic Archive, Ashmolean Museum, Oxford, neg. C. 6071)

385

Plate 6.6 *Madrasa-Mausoleum of Sultan al-Nasir Muhammad, Gothic doorway from Acre reused as a trophy, 695–703/1295–1304, Cairo, Egypt*

(Creswell Photographic Archive, Ashmolean Museum, Oxford, after K. A. C. Creswell, *The Muslim Architecture of Egypt* II, 1959. pl. 85a)

mason or patron liked it. The propagandistic value of the door was enormous. Here a fine but portable artefact was carried away to be displayed in the centre of the Mamluk empire as a permanent testimony of a glorious victory, the definitive defeat of the Crusaders in the Levant, the inevitable victory of Islam over Christianity.

The Evidence of the Architecture of Nur al-Din

Antique patinas (sigma-shaped tables) were reused in Syrian mosques. One such table was the object of much admiration in the Hanafi Madrasat al-Halawiyya in Aleppo (the former Christian cathedral).[224] Ibn al-Shihna, quoting Ibn al-ʿAdim, reports:

> They show in the Madrasat al-Halawiyya an altar on which the Christians used to sacrifice, of royal transparent marble, a stone of exquisite beauty: when a candle is placed under it, one sees its light shining through. We were told that Nur al-Din had it brought from Apamea in 544.[225]

386

Figure 6.50 Mosque lamps, Fatimid manuscript, twelfth century, Egypt

Ibn al-Shihna also mentions that the sigma-shaped sacramental table also had a Greek inscription which perhaps bore Diocletian's name (Herzfeld comments that this 'good piece of medieval criticism' was correct).[226]

The prominent displaying of this patina in the Madrasat al-Halawiyya epitomises the reasons why Muslim conquerors and religious leaders, such as Nur al-Din, were keen to reuse objects that had previously been part of Christian worship. It was also clearly an artefact of great beauty. Its translucent quality fitted well into the context of Islamic worship where God's light is such a powerful symbol, epitomised by mosque lamps (figures 6.50 and 6.51) and windows (figure 6.52). The Qur'an itself declares in the Light verse: 'Allah is the Light of the Heavens and the earth.'[227]

This patina was thus not only a constant and splendid reminder of Islam's victory over Christianity, but in its new context acquired distinctively Muslim connotations.

Figure 6.51 Inscription in the form of a lamp carved in a mihrab, *stone, Mosque of Qusun, 730/1329–30, Cairo, Egypt*

Figure 6.52 Mamluk stained-glass windows, fifteenth century, Cairo, Egypt

Ayyubid Metalwork with Christian Imagery

Compelling evidence survives to indicate that the Crusader knightly and mercantile classes acquired a taste for the luxury goods of the Near East. Indeed, the interiors of their houses must have been sumptuous, judging by the precious enamel-painted glass beakers and glazed pottery fragments excavated at Crusader sites.[228] The Ayyubid period is noted for the production of many fine Islamic artefacts – silver inland brasses, underglaze-painted ceramics and tiles and enamel-painted glass. This flourishing of the so-called 'minor' arts owed much to the refined taste and sponsorship of the Turkish and Kurdish rulers who commissioned such works and whose names – such as the Turkish atabeg Badr al-Din Lu'lu' and the Ayyubid sultan al-Malik al-Salih Najm al-Din Ayyub – figure on the pieces. The examples of such artefacts which have survived testify to the tastes of the Islamic upper classes but also, it is important to add, to the tastes of the Christians, both Oriental and Crusader.

Figure 6.53 The Virgin and Child, inlaid metal pyxis, early thirteenth century, Syria

It is noteworthy that although Christian imagery can be found sporadically in Islamic art which pre-dates the Crusades, it is during the thirteenth century that it becomes a salient feature in the Islamic decorative repertoire. Baer has studied eighteen surviving Ayyubid inlaid brasses with very elaborate workmanship and shown how Christian themes and motifs were adopted and absorbed by Islamic craftsmen on a large scale in thirteenth-century Syria (figures 6.53, 6.54–6.56). These brasses depict Gospel scenes, images of the Madonna and Child, and friezes of Christian saints and clerics alongside traditional Islamic themes such as the standard cycle of princely amusements. This representation of Christian motifs in Islamic art was unprecedented. Amongst the various questions raised by these artefacts – which include incense burners, trays, caskets, ewers, candlesticks – the most relevant in the context of this chapter is why they were produced in thirteenth-century Muslim society.[229]

A particularly interesting example is a large canteen which demonstrates refined workmanship and a profusion of visual imagery in which Christian themes predominate.[230] The obverse shows the enthroned Virgin and Child, surrounded by three panels with scenes from the life of Jesus (plate 6.7). Baer describes them as strikingly un-Islamic and inspired by Byzantine models.[231] Following Islamic decorative conventions, however, the Christian scenes are separated by roundels with birds and imaginary creatures in them. Two Kufic inscription bands contain traditional formulae of blessing. Although there are Syriac Christian, Coptic and Byzantine precedents for much of the iconography on these brasses, other visual elements – such as the Islamic imagery of the secular ruler – also play a part in some of the scenes.[232] Baer suggests that some of the brasses which are inlaid with Christian figures symbolise political power.[233] Other brasses, however, which are almost exclusively decorated with motifs and figures that had little significance for Muslims, may well have

Figure 6.54 Christian figures, tray, inlaid metal, early thirteenth century, Syria

Figure 6.55 Christian figures, tray, inlaid metal, early thirteenth century, Syria

reflected the taste of the Crusader nobility who had settled in Palestine and Syria and who – like the Normans in Sicily – may well have liked what they saw of Islamic art around them. These brasses include the Freer canteen and the Leningrad tray. They are luxury objects and may well have been designed for the wealthy Crusader class who would prefer to use local craftsmen to furnish their houses and emulate their Muslim counterparts in some of the appurtenances of elegant living. It was not important that Crusader customers were probably unable to read the Arabic inscriptions that adorned their metal objects made and acquired in the Levant. A candlestick now in Paris, inscribed with the maker's name, Da'ud b. Salama al-Mawsili, and decorated with Christian religious subjects and other similar artefacts, seems likely to have been made by Muslim craftsmen for Crusader consumption.[234] Such objects were probably prized for their 'exotic' value in much the same way as Oriental carpets are treasured today by their Western owners.

Muslim and Crusader rulers exchanged luxury gifts as part of political life and there is little doubt that brasses given to or bought by the Crusader aristocracy would have pleased them, just as gifts of exotic animals (such as giraffes and elephants), mechanical contraptions and Oriental textiles titillated their tastes.[235] In the case of the brasses, they were portable and could have been displayed in the lavishly furnished homes of the Crusader knights in the Levant or even brought back to Europe as a memento of their stay in the Holy Land. The more exotic the artefact the better, since quite apart from their obvious Christian allusions these works pandered to the medieval Western taste for marvels of the East. It is well known that the Arabic script appeared on many medieval European works of art often without any knowledge on the part of its users that it enshrined Islamic political messages.

To sum up the significance of these brasses, it is clear that they were made for both Muslims and Crusaders for a short while in the

Figure 6.56 Christian figures, tray, inlaid metal, early thirteenth century, Syria

Plate 6.7 *Ayyubid canteen with Christian scenes, front, inlaid brass, c. 1250, Syria*

390

thirteenth century. Baer concludes that for the Muslims who owned some of these objects the Christian scenes and figures depicted on them reminded them of their authority over the Christians.[236] The Crusader nobles in their turn admired and possessed some of these brasses because of their delicate decoration and exotic aspect, including Arabic inscriptions.

This discussion of a small group of brass artefacts, far from being abstruse and esoteric, has shed an unexpected sidelight on the interplay between Crusaders and Muslims on an everyday level in Ayyubid Syria. The Crusaders were well ensconced in the Levant in a period in which, as already mentioned, they came to form part of the political fabric of Near Eastern life. There is clear evidence that Crusaders shared Muslim artistic tastes and that Muslim craftsmen tailored their artefacts to please a Crusader clientele.

The Long-Term Effects of Crusader–Muslim Contact

Scholars have alleged that there were two major effects of the Crusades on the Muslim world: first the opening up or enhancement of East–West trade and secondly a growth of discrimination by Muslims against Oriental Christians. We shall now look at these two broad areas.

Realpolitik – *Diplomacy and Trade between Muslims and Franks*

Side by side with the ideological divisions which separated Muslim and Crusader and the crescendo of *jihad* activity that punctuated the years 1099–1291, both protagonists saw the need for periods of respite from war, in order to protect property and land and – perhaps even more importantly – to facilitate travel and trade. Köhler's book, based on a careful reading of the sources, is an important contribution to our knowledge of the *modus vivendi* which developed between Muslims and Franks.[237] Concentrating on the incidence of co-operation between the two sides, especially in the first half of the twelfth century, Köhler demonstrates that many contracts and treaties were signed, which suggests that co-existence and compromise were often deemed to be preferable to confrontation and warfare. Such arrangements were often interconfessional – Muslims and Franks aligning themselves against other Muslims and Franks – and were motivated, as we saw in Chapter 2, by shared local territorial interests and by the need for military help against political rivals. For the Muslims, they were also necessary for obtaining access to the Levantine ports, many of which remained in Frankish hands for considerable periods of time. The importance of sea-borne trade in this period guaranteed that the Muslims would try to reach some compromise with the Franks in order to protect and foster their mercantile interests.

Similar pragmatism lay at the heart of the policies of co-operation

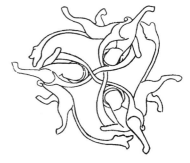

Figure 6.57 Sphinxes in wheel formation, inlaid metal trays made for Badr al-Din Lu'lu', first half of thirteenth century, Mosul, Iraq

Figure 6.58 Musicians,
Cappella Palatina, ceiling,
c. 1140, Palermo, Sicily

promoted by the Ayyubid princes, and despite the hard-line stance of the Mamluk sultans they too pursued realistic commercial and economic goals which involved collaborating with the Franks. Treaties were signed, inaugurating periods of truce and often stipulating precise arrangements for trade and commercial and pilgrim travel.

A number of treaties were signed by Mamluk sultans with western European states, such as Genoa and Aragon.[238] The actual treaties were preceded by a flurry of reciprocal diplomatic missions to Europe and the Levant. The treaty signed by the Mamluk sultan Qalawun with Genoa in 1290 is a typical example and indicates some of the practical motives on the Muslim side for making trade agreements with the enemy: 'In the end, for the sake of the prosperity of the ports, and because of the wealth brought in by this nation, and the large sums accruing to the customs from them, a truce was drafted for them.'[239]

The treaty assured the personal security of Genoese merchants and of their possessions throughout the Mamluk empire. It also granted the Genoese bringing merchandise, gold or silver to Alexandria or elsewhere the right to sell without coercion, and it established procedures for customs administration. A far cry then from the high-flown anti-infidel rhetoric of the writings of the *ulama* and the bellicose posturings shown in exchanges of letters between Mamluk sultans and European sovereigns.

According to Holt, there are seven treaties drawn up between the Mamluk sultans and the Frankish states whose wording has been preserved in historical works of the period. These treaties are bilateral and reciprocal in their provisions. One such treaty is the one

Figure 6.59 Dancer, Cappella Palatina, ceiling, c. 1140, Palermo, Sicily

concluded by Baybars with Isabella of Ibelin, the Lady of Beirut in 667/1269. It opens as follows:

> The blessed truce is established between the Sultan al-Malik al-Zahir Rukn al-Din Baybars and the exalted, virtuous and glorious Lady N, the daughter of N, the Lady of Beirut and of all its mountains and lowlands, for the period of ten successive years beginning on Thursday, 6 Ramadan 667.[240]

This treaty is typical in that it is precisely dated and it gives the duration of the truce and the names of the contracting parties. The treaty guarantees security for travellers coming and going to and from the sultan's lands and it guarantees similar security for Isabella's subjects too. Details are given on the compensation to be made for a homicide; this takes the form of the release of a captive of equal status, with four grades being given – knight, Turcopole, foot-soldier and peasant. As with other such treaties, the final provision requires Isabella not to afford any help to the enemies of the sultan and more especially 'any Franks of any kind'. As Holt says in his analysis of this treaty, it may be in the form of a truce but its real purpose was to agree to maintain normal political and diplomatic relations.[241]

This book will not dwell at any length on the important topic of trade between Europe and the Middle East during the Crusading period. Much work has already been done in this area, notably by Heyd, Ashtor, Abulafia, Udovitch and others.[242] Such scholars as these, drawing on extensive documentation from western European sources, have presented very detailed accounts of European–Levantine trade in the twelfth and thirteenth centuries and beyond. There is, of course, evidence from the Islamic side, which these scholars have also used in drawing up their corpus of information on the minutiae of trade – ships, merchandise, customs duties, commercial agreements – and their broad theories on the nature and importance of this trade. Readers who wish to deepen their knowledge of this facet of the Crusading phenomenon and medieval Islamic and western European economic history generally should consult these works and the vast array of scholarly articles which chronicle individual aspects of this subject in greater detail.[243]

Until the early eleventh century the main commercial centre of the Islamic world had been Baghdad. Thereafter, with the commercial expansion of western Europe and its renewed trade links with the Islamic lands that bordered on the Mediterranean, the centre of Muslim commercial gravity shifted to Egypt.

In the early eleventh century a small group of merchant cities such as Naples, Marseilles, Venice and Amalfi traded directly with the Levant.[244] Towards the end of the century the building of larger ships enabled more distant countries such as Spain or France to sail to Egypt or the Levant directly.[245]

It is no easy task to reconstruct the development of Muslim–Frankish trading relations, either locally or internationally. The French scholar Claude Cahen writes: 'Economic and social history is written above all with the help of archival documents. For the Muslim world, apart from Egypt, we do not have any.'[246] In making an exception of Egypt, Cahen is referring to what can only be described as the phenomenon of the Geniza.

Scholars of medieval Islamic economic history have made great use of a vast cache of documents known as the Geniza (Hebrew: 'a hiding place') which was found in the eighteenth and nineteenth centuries in a synagogue in Fustat (Old Cairo). They date mostly from the tenth to the fourteenth centuries and include valuable first-hand documentary evidence in the form of some 10,000 private and business letters and deeds of sale. Written for the most part in Judaeo-Arabic (Arabic in Hebrew script), the Geniza documents cast important light on the everyday life of Jews (and Muslims) in the medieval Islamic world and in particular on the realities of Mediterranean trade.[247] The brilliant synthesis of the Jewish scholar Goitein reveals that before the Crusades the Italians already had the largest share of Mediterranean trade. The Geniza documents show that there was lively interaction before the Crusades between East and West in

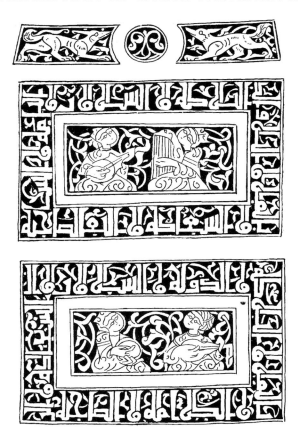

Figure 6.60 Brass casket with benedictory Kufic inscriptions and musicians, c. 1200, Iraq or Iran

the Mediterranean and that merchants from Pisa and Genoa traded actively in North Africa before 1100 and occasionally reached Alexandria.[248]

On the specific issue of trade in Syria and Palestine, detailed knowledge from Arabic sources is lacking. Ashtor claims that in the second half of the eleventh century the rich merchants in the Syrian ports, such as Tripoli and Tyre, wanted to take advantage of trading opportunities with the Italian mercantile republics. These ports shook off the yoke of Fatimid control from the 1070s onwards and set up independent city-states.[249] Whatever the situation may have been before 1099, what is clear is that once the Franks had seized the ports of the Syro-Palestinian littoral the Muslim hinterland needed to come to a commercial accommodation with them.[250] Reciprocal arrangements were also needed for the transportation of goods by land through each other's territory. With Frankish ships in the waters off the Levantine coasts and in possession of the Syrian ports, the local Muslim merchants must have feared for their livelihood.

Not surprisingly, therefore, the immediate result of this new situation was that some of the Muslims in authority along the Levantine coast sought to protect these interests. Speaking of Shams al-Khilafa, the governor of Ascalon in 504/1111, Ibn al-Qalanisi mentions that he made a truce with Baldwin, since he preferred trade to battles. 'Now Shams al-Khilafa was more desirous of trading than of fighting, and inclined to peaceful and friendly relations and the securing of the safety of travellers.'[251] Pressures from commercial inactivity could make traders foolhardy. Ibn al-Qalanisi reports for the year 504/1110–11 that 'a company of travelling merchants, chafing at their prolonged inaction, lost patience and set out from Tinnis, Damietta

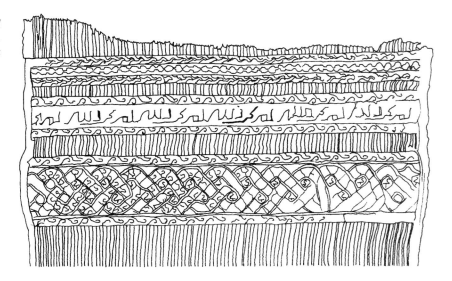

Figure 6.61 Border of Fatimid tiraz *textile, twelfth century, Egypt*

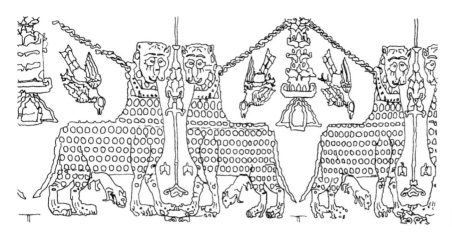

Figure 6.62 *Fatimid textile with repeat patterns of lionesses attacked by birds, eleventh century, Egypt*

and Misr [= Fustat] with a great quantity of merchandise and moneys'. They and their goods were, however, soon seized by Frankish vessels.[252]

It is significant that merchants as well as religious leaders figured prominently in the various delegations that made their way to Baghdad in the first decade of the twelfth century to protest and ask for help against the Franks from the caliph and the sultan.[253] Usama writes in one of his stories that the word *burjasi* means merchant and that such a person does not fight.[254] Nevertheless their livelihood depended on the military classes to create the right conditions for trade.

The basis of international trade between Europe and the Levant was mutual need, and increased contact at the time of the early Crusades brought an expansion of European–Levantine trade. The Europeans wanted Oriental spices, especially pepper and ginger, which came to the Near East via both land and sea routes, and alum (a fixative) used by Western cloth manufacturers.[255] They also imported perfumes, cloth and gold. Conversely, the Muslim world needed timber and iron for constructing ships and weapons of war, such as battering rams and other siege machines, and armaments. They were also keen to acquire linen, silks and woollens from Europe,[256] especially in the thirteenth century and thereafter.

Lasting evidence of trading links between the Muslim world and Europe is found in the words of Arabic (or Persian) origin which have become embedded in European languages – financial terms such as cheque, tariff, douane and the names of textiles such as damask, fustian, taffeta, cashmere, samite, organdy and muslin. The profusion of these names is a clear enough indication of the key importance of the textile trade.[257] The word *fondaco* (from the Arabic *funduq* – inn) denotes an inn with ample storage space which the Italian 'merchant nations' were allowed to have in certain Muslim cities.[258] The so-called Arabic numerals were first used in Europe around 1200 by notaries charged with drawing up commercial contracts for use in the Islamic world.[259] Certain terms of key importance in navigation, such as zenith, azimuth and astrolabe, also betray the European debt to Arabic technology in this field.

Trade in the Period 492–690/1099–1291 – the Evidence of the Islamic Sources

It is fortunate that transcriptions of the texts of the actual commercial/ diplomatic treaties drawn up between Muslims and Franks have survived. They give a precise flavour to the actualities of such links, and their details reveal an array of practical needs and considerations. On the other hand, the Islamic chronicles are disappointingly meagre in their information on this topic. Even within the usual rigid limits of Islamic historiography, the chroniclers reveal little about trade. Perhaps this deficiency is caused by the fact that trade was such an integral part of daily life that it occasioned little comment, just as so many other aspects of the social relations between Muslim and Frank remain unmentioned in the sources.

It is true, however, that some chroniclers had become aware that the Franks had not just come out of religious zeal and desire for military conquests. Ibn al-Furat, for example, mentions in his account of the arrival of Franks in the 1120s those who had come by sea 'for trade and visitation'.[260] Having obtained possession of the Syrian ports, the Franks continued to strike and circulate coins (*bezants*) in imitation of Muslim dinars. The Muslim biographer Ibn Khallikan notes that when the Franks took Tyre in 518/1124 they continued for three years to strike coins in the name of the Fatimid caliph al-Amir.[261] Such a procedure no doubt was based on the practicalities of trade; indeed, with their so-called 'Tyre dinars' the Crusaders imitated Muslim coinage from the middle of the twelfth century for over a hundred years.[262]

Trade had always been an honourable activity within the Islamic context: after all, the Prophet himself had engaged in commerce. Merchants were respected members of the community. Their

Figure 6.63 *Crusader gold coin imitating Ayyubid issues. Inscribed in Arabic on the obverse: 'Struck at Acre in the year 1251 of the Incarnation of the Messiah' and on the reverse 'We take pride in the Cross of our Lord Jesus the Messiah. In Him is our salvation, our life and our resurrection, in Him our safety and redemption'*

honoured status is confirmed in the Crusading period by the scholar 'Ali al-Harawi who counsels Saladin's son, al-Malik al-Zahir, to give special consideration to merchants who are 'the providers of everything useful and the scouts of the world'.[263]

It is clear that on an everyday level the Muslims and the Franks engaged in trade with each other throughout the period of Crusader occupation and beyond it. The trade was both local and international. The Spanish Muslim traveller Ibn Jubayr observes in 580/1184:

> One of the astonishing things that is talked of is that though the fires of discord burn between the two parties, Muslim and Christian, two armies of them may meet and dispose themselves in battle array, and yet Muslim and Christian travellers will come and go between them without interference.[264]

Clearly, then, the theatre of war did not extend into civilian life at this time. There are good reasons for this. Muslim–Western Christian trade was of enormous benefit to both sides, even in times of heightened military hostility. Saladin's attitude towards the Crusader mercantile communities, as expressed in a letter written to the caliph in Baghdad in 1174, shows a clear grasp of the economic advantages to be gained from trading with the enemy:

> The Venetians, the Pisans and the Genoese all used to come, sometimes as raiders, the voracity of whose harm could not be contained . . ., sometimes as travellers trying to prevail over Islam with the goods they bring, and our fearsome decrees could not cope with them . . . and now there is not one of them that does not bring to our lands his weapons of war and battle and bestows upon us the choicest of what he makes and inherits.[265]

This comment further suggests that there was no effective military or political control imposed by the Western powers as to what should and should not be traded with the other side. Accordingly, Muslims and Franks traded with each other, crossed each other's territories and imposed taxes on each other's merchants. Whilst Saladin was conducting the siege of Karak in 580/1184 the caravans still continued to pass from Egypt to Damascus, 'going through the lands of the Franks without impediment from them'.[266] Even during Saladin's vigorous siege of Karak, it is noteworthy, according to Ibn Jubayr, that business continued as usual: 'One of the strangest things in the world is that Muslim caravans go forth to Frankish lands, while Frankish captives enter Muslim lands.'[267]

According to Ibn Jubayr, Muslim merchants journeyed from Damascus to Acre (also through Frankish lands) and similarly Christian merchants were not hindered in Muslim territory. Both sides imposed a tax on the goods of the other in return for 'full security'.[268] Ibn Jubayr goes so far as to say that the ordinary people and

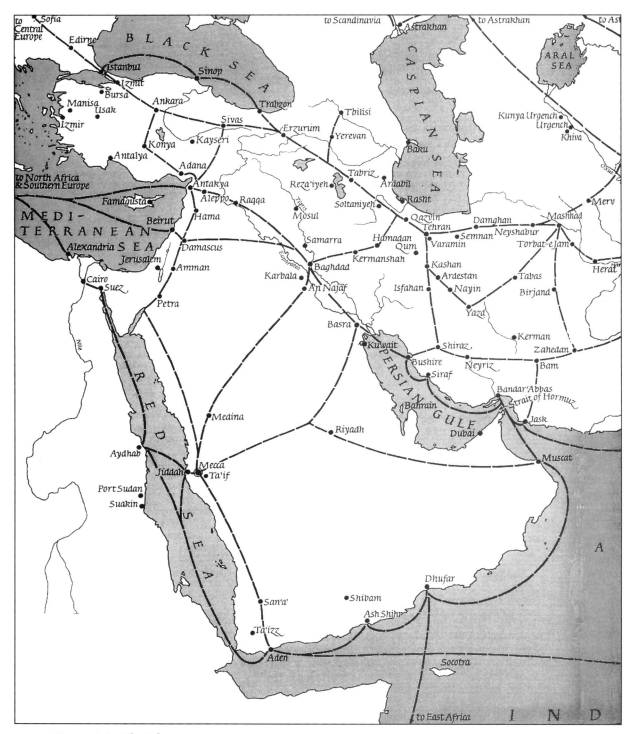

Figure 6.64 *The Islamic heartlands showing the main trade and* hajj *routes*

the merchants are not involved in the disputes of kings: 'Security never leaves them in any circumstances, neither in peace nor in war. The state of these countries in this regard is truly more astonishing than our story can fully convey.'[269]

Despite Ibn Jubayr's positive evidence, there were infringements of the agreements allowing merchants safe-conduct through enemy territory. Saladin's scribe discusses the problem of Muslim trade going through Frankish territory. Writing to Baghdad, he says in 1177:

> No reply has come to our letter about the need to stop the passage of the Muslim caravans . . . These merchants are risking their lives, reputations and goods and they also take the risk of strengthening the enemy.[270]

What he does not say is that these merchants took such risks in the hope of considerable profit. A letter from Saladin to 'Adud al-Din, the caliph's vizier, dated the same year, notes that Saladin had escorted a large number of Muslim merchants, thereby preventing them from having to pay the heavy taxes which their goods would have incurred if they had gone through Frankish territory.[271]

How much attention do the Islamic sources give to the phenomenon of what Heyd describes as soaring European trade with the Levant?[272] What was carried in Frankish ships? Usama's memoirs contain an anecdote which mentions how Baldwin III sent out some men to break up and pillage a Frankish ship near Acre bearing Usama's family. The ship was loaded with 'women's trinkets, clothes, jewels, swords and other arms, and gold and silver to the value of about 30,000 dinars'.[273]

Figure 6.65 *Lutanist, Seljuq stone sculpture, thirteenth century, Turkey*

The fall of Acre to the Muslims under Saladin in 583/1187 offers Muslim chroniclers the opportunity to reflect on its role as a trading entrepôt under Crusader rule. Ibn Shaddad reports that Saladin at Acre 'took possession of what was in it in the way of riches, treasures and merchandise because it was the location of trade'.[274] Ibn al-Athir gives more precise detail:

> The Muslims plundered what remained of what the Franks had not been able to carry. The vast amount of it cannot be counted. They saw there a lot of gold, jewels, silk stitched with gold (*siqlat*), Venetian sequin (*al-bunduqi*), sugar, weapons and other kinds of commodities, for it was a destination for Frankish and Byzantine traders and others from lands near and far.[275]

This is a very useful indication of the range of goods in which the Franks of Acre had traded – Ibn al-Athir explicitly mentions *al-bunduqi*. He also makes it clear that Acre was an international entrepôt.

Ibn Jubayr had been in no doubt about the commercial importance of Acre when he visited it in 1184. Prefacing his description with a pious imprecation – 'may God exterminate (the Christians in) it and restore it (to the Muslims)'[276] – he continues as follows:

> Acre is the capital of the Frankish cities in Syria, the unloading place of 'ships reared aloft in the seas like mountains'[277] and a port of call for all ships. In its greatness it resembles Constantinople. It is the focus of ships and caravans, and the meeting-place of Muslim and Christian merchants from all regions.[278]

Ibn Jubayr is impressed by the Crusader custom-house at Acre and the way in which its officials conducted their business:

> We were taken to the custom-house which is a khan prepared to accommodate the caravan. Before the door are stone benches, spread with carpets, where are the Christian clerks of the Customs with their ebony ink-stands ornamented with gold. They write Arabic, which they also speak.[279]

The examination of the merchandise and baggage was obviously thorough and it was not only the merchants whose belongings were searched:

> The baggage of any who had no merchandise was also examined in case it contained concealed [and dutiable] merchandise, after which the owner was permitted to go his way and seek lodging where he would. All this was done with civility and respect, and without harshness and unfairness.[280]

This is high praise for the Crusader port administration.

In sharp contrast is Ibn Jubayr's description of the chaotic and corrupt customs administration in Muslim Alexandria which he encountered first-hand in the spring of 1183. He describes the treatment received by the Muslim travellers and merchants as follows:

> The Customs was packed to choking. All their goods, great and small, were searched and confusedly thrown together, while hands were thrust into their waistbands in search of what might be within . . . During all this, because of the confusion of hands and the excessive throng, many possessions disappeared.[281]

Ibn Jubayr is at pains to point out that this disgraceful business is the only flaw that he encountered in Saladin's Egypt and he places the blame squarely on the customs officials.[282]

Evidence of the spice trade is given by Ibn Jubayr, who met caravans bearing merchandise from India through Yemen to 'Aydhab on the shores of the Red Sea: 'The greater part of this was the loads of pepper, so numerous as to seem to our fancy to equal in quantity only the dust.'[283]

Figure 6.66 *Seljuq silk chasuble with lions in roundels, thirteenth century, Turkey*

Trade in the Ayyubid and Mamluk Periods

Figure 6.67 Urban khans, *al-Hariri*, al-Maqamat *('The Assemblies'), 634/1237, and c. 1230, probably Baghdad, Iraq*

According to Cahen, Acre did not rival Constantinople or Alexandria for most of the twelfth century. The real surge in Levantine trade seems to have begun in the 1180s and continued until the late 1250s.[284] The Ayyubid princes promoted commercial links with the Italian maritime cities and maintained as much as possible peaceful relations with the Crusader states of Syria. Despite their militant ideological stance, the Mamluks encouraged trade with the Christian powers of Europe and this trade was an integral part of Mamluk success. Reference has already been made to the treaties signed by the Mamluk sultans and European powers. At a practical level, the demands of commerce outweighed ideological scruples. In Baybars' time, for example, the majority of *mamluk*s came from the Qipchaq steppe. The greatest part of this slave-trade between the Crimea and Egypt was carried out by Genoese vessels.[285]

The important trading links forged during the period of military confrontation between Europe and the Muslim world were to outlast the fall of Acre and to have significant repercussions on Mamluk Egypt in the fourteenth and fifteenth centuries. It is difficult to say whether such trading links would have been fostered without the impetus provided by the Crusades; what is certain is that waves of Crusaders were brought to the Levant in the ships of the Italian maritime republics and that the mercantile colonies set up in the Crusader Levantine ports survived long after 1291. Since by this date the entire Levant was under the political suzerainty of the Mamluk sultans of Egypt, whose capital was Cairo, it is not surprising that Egypt itself, which was the entrepôt for the lucrative Indian Ocean

Figure 6.68 *Shop front, with details of its woodwork, fifteenth century, Cairo, Egypt*

trade, was involved in this enterprise. It is also not surprising that after the fall of Acre in 1291, the Mamluk sultans decided not to uproot the European trading communities in the Levant, preferring instead to encourage trade with Europe.

Of course, from the European side, there were ideological inhibitions and strong hostility in some quarters to the continuance of commercial relations with the enemy; indeed, successive popes tried hard to terminate trade between the Italian maritime republics and the Muslim Levant. But papal pronouncements were powerless to prevent this mutually beneficial trade from continuing.[286] In Alexandria, for example, the hostels of the European trading communities

poll-tax (*jizya*) and to observe certain restrictions in dress and social conduct.[291]

Discriminatory measures against Christians and Jews had certainly become enshrined in the legal books by the eleventh century. This is clear from the work entitled the *Kitab al-tanbih* composed in Baghdad between 452/1060 and 453/1061 by the Shafiʿite legal scholar al-Shirazi.[292]

Al-Shirazi writes: 'It is necessary that *dhimmis* should distinguish themselves from Muslims in dress.'[293] He goes on to stipulate that male *dhimmis* should wear a lead or copper ring or a little bell around their necks when they go into the baths.[294] As for the *dhimmi* woman: 'She will wear a ring around her neck to go into the public baths; one of her shoes will be black and the other white.'[295]

Similar restrictions should be imposed in other spheres of activity. Al-Shirazi points out that the *dhimmi*s should not ride horses but only mules or asses and that they should hold back from any form of public display:

> They will not occupy the first place in an assembly and they will not be greeted first and they will move to the side of the road to give way [to Muslims]. They will be forbidden from raising structures higher than those of the Muslims but they will not be forbidden from raising them to the same height ... They will be forbidden the public use of what displeases God, such as wine, pork, the clapper for the call to prayer and the reciting of the Old and New Testament.[296]

Thus we see that social contacts between Muslims and *dhimmi*s were not encouraged. The great medieval Muslim thinker al-Ghazali speaks in similar vein, and enjoins his fellow-believers not to take Christians as friends. Muslims should not make way for Christians, greet them first, follow their customs or engage in business with them.[297] A century later Nasir al-Din Qunawi, writing about the essential teachings of Islam, urges the seeker after truth to remember prophets and saints who tread the path to God and to seek 'refuge from the companionship of the outsiders who were deprived of this blessing – like Jews, Christians and other truth-concealers'.[298]

Such strictures were the result of the evolution of the *Shariʿa*, an ideal code based on the sacred Islamic texts, the Qurʾan and the *hadith*, as interpreted by successive generations of Islamic legists. Although such legists might urge Muslims to stay away from the People of the Book, it is nonetheless important to stress that there is not a single religious injunction which urges or indeed permits Muslims to persecute Christians and Jews. On the contrary, the Qurʾan lays down that once such groups have entered into a covenant with the Muslims, they should be given a clearly defined status within the Islamic community, tolerated with justice and given protection. Whilst later scholars may have wished to place Christians and Jews

Figure 6.73 *Leisure pursuits,*
inlaid metal basin made by
Da'ud ibn Salama al-Mawsili,
650/1252, probably
Damascus, Syria

in an inferior position within Muslim society, it is difficult to determine to what extent in any one particular time or place such measures were implemented in reality. The occasional instance of religious persecution launched by Muslim rulers, such as the ninth-century 'Abbasid caliph al-Mutawakkil,[299] or the Fatimid caliph al-Hakim (ruled 996–1021), who passed some highly eccentric and discriminatory laws against his Christian and Jewish subjects, plainly flouted the dictates of the Islamic faith.[300]

In general, then, the medieval Muslim sources themselves confirm that there *were* isolated cases of religious persecution of *dhimmi*s in certain periods of Islamic history and in various areas of the Muslim world. But it can be argued overall that there must have been broad tolerance and a measure of autonomy for the indigenous communities in Egypt, Syria and Palestine. Indeed, the very longevity of such groups as the Copts in Egypt suggests strongly that they must have been allowed freedom of worship under Muslim rule. In other words, it is justifiable to say that before the coming of the Crusaders the 'House of Islam' within certain limits treated its Christian and Jewish communities well.

The modern writer who uses the Hebrew pseudonym 'Daughter of the Nile' (Bat Ye'or) goes so far as to suggest that Islamic society has not been tolerant towards *dhimmi*s – Christians or Jews – in any period of its history.[301] Another Jewish scholar, Goitein, however, drawing upon his vast knowledge of the Geniza documents and the history of Islam, concludes that in the Near East in the eleventh and the major part of the twelfth century 'a spirit of tolerance and liberalism prevailed, in particular in the Fatimid empire'.[302]

Did the Crusaders Trigger Muslim Discriminatory Measures against the Oriental Christians?

Certainly it would not have been surprising if lessons learned from Crusader fanaticism engendered a more zealous attitude amongst those Muslims most directly in contact and conflict with them, and thus that the Crusades sharpened religious differences between Islam and Christianity. From the Western side, Runciman says with his customary eloquence à propos the fall of Jerusalem and the ensuing bloodbath of Muslim and Jewish inhabitants: 'It was this bloodthirsty proof of Christian fanaticism that recreated the fanaticism of Islam.'[303]

However, this whole issue is more complex than it seems and should be discussed with historical sensitivity and without the retrospective imposition of any modern political or religious agenda.[304] In particular, the question of how the Oriental Christians within the House of Islam were treated during the period of Crusader occupation of parts of the Near East and after their departure needs to be analysed.

Modern scholarship has produced a wide spectrum of opinion on these issues. Claude Cahen, for example, insists that the concept of *jihad* was unaffected by contact with the idea of the Crusade and by response to it and that the treatment of the local Christians living under Muslim protection did not change.[305] Edward Atiya, on the other hand, argues that the lot of the Oriental Christians worsened after the coming of the Crusades: 'The most enduring result of the crusades was the vehement reaction of the Islamic polity to the continued aggression of Western Christendom against Moslem territory for three centuries.'[306] It will be convenient to treat this issue in chronological sequence rather than trying to impose generalities on the entire period.

The Period 492–583/1099–1187

Sivan argues that the revitalised *jihad* movement which arose in reaction to the Frankish presence did not have any impact in the twelfth century on the People of the Book (that is, the local Christians and Jews) under Muslim rule.[307]

Certainly, it must have taken the Muslims some time to differentiate and compare the Franks and the Oriental Christians and to become aware of the more fanatical stance and alien ways of the newcomers in contradistinction to the local Christians with whom they had been in contact all their lives. The situation was by no means clear-cut, however. Ibn al-Qalanisi mentions an instance when the Armenians who were in the castle of Artah in 498/1104–5 surrendered to the Muslims under Ridwan 'because of the injustice and grievous tyranny which they suffered from the Franks'.[308] Sometimes local Christian forces fought alongside the Franks, as in 510/1116–17.[309]

Yet even in the early days of the Frankish occupation there was a tendency, according to the chroniclers, to use the Oriental Christians

Figure 6.74 *Virgin and Child, Gospel book, 1216–20, Mosul, Iraq*

Figure 6.75 *Bust of Christ, lustre ceramic fragment, eleventh–twelfth century, Fustat, Egypt*

(Kufic inscription illustration)

Figure 6.76 *'Blessing from Allah, the Merciful, the Compassionate': Kufic inscription on a metal lamp, c. 900, perhaps from Iran*

as scapegoats for Muslim defeat. Whether this is just a device imposed by later Muslim writers for their own motives or a reflection of genuine collusion between Franks and Oriental Christians is impossible to say. It is intrinsically likely that the Oriental Christians might have seen their best interests as often residing in collaborating with their fellow Christians, the Franks. The fall of Antioch in 491/1098 is blamed, for example, on 'the devices of the armourer who was an Armenian named Firuz'.[310]

One episode in the year 518/1124–5 is worthy of mention in this context. The Frankish leader Joscelin had been conducting devastating raids in northern Syria. The geographer Ibn Shaddad writes that:

> When the Franks besieged Aleppo in the year 518 and they disturbed the graves which were outside it and burned what was in them, they [the people of Aleppo] went to four of the churches that were there and made them into mosques.[311]

Ibn al-ʿAdim, the chronicler of Aleppo, is even more explicit:

> With the agreement of the leaders of Aleppo the qadi Ibn al-Khashshab ordered that the altars (*maharib*) of the churches belonging to the Christians in Aleppo should be destroyed and *mihrab*s should be made for them towards the direction of the *qibla* and their doors should be altered and they should be made into mosques. That was done in their great church and it was called the mosque of the saddlers (*masjid al-sarrajin*) and it is the college of the candy sellers (*madrasat al-halawiyyin*) now. The church of the ironsmiths (*kanisat al-haddadin*) is now the college of the ironsmiths (*madrasat al-haddadin*) . . . He left only two churches, no more, for the Christians in Aleppo and that is still the case.[312]

Figure 6.77 *Coptic priest swinging a censer, lustre bowl, after c. 1050, Egypt*

The Copts are not only blamed for undermining the Egyptian administration but they are also accused of collaborating with their co-religionists, the Crusaders:

I have heard that they [the Christians of Egypt] wrote to the Frankish kings of the Sahil [the Levantine coastline] and the islands, saying to them: 'Do not fight the Muslims. We ourselves are fighting them night and day, we are taking their possessions and attacking their women, we are ruining their country and weakening their soldiers. Come, take possession of it! There is no obstacle left for you!'

The enemy is near you, in your state; it is the Christians. Do not trust those who convert to Islam . . . Even if they do so, it is for another reason. Their faith is hidden in their heart like fire in ashes.[336]

This hostility is reiterated in the accusations made by al-Maqrizi, who attacks the Copts for sabotaging the Egyptian land tenure system (*iqta'*) on which the military depended:

The Copts practised every kind of deceit and they started to weaken the Egyptian army. They scattered a single *iqta'* in different places so that some of the collection took place in Upper Egypt, some in al-Sharqiyya province and some in al-Gharbiyya province, in order to exhaust the soldiery and increase expense.[337]

Al-Maqrizi is also hostile to the Christian clergy. He describes one Jacobite patriarch as being 'fond of power and the amassing of wealth . . . given to simony, exacting ordination fees from those whom he ordained'.[338] This anti-Christian sentiment was enforced and intensified in the circles of the religious scholars and above all, in the Mamluk period, in the polemical writings and *fatwa*s of Ibn Taymiyya, who harboured no tenderness towards Christians either outside or inside the 'House of Islam'.

The Intervention of Europe

Thus we see that in a range of Islamic sources there is evidence for a backlash against the Oriental Christians. But its impact clearly varied according to geographical and political circumstances.[339] Such a backlash targeted Oriental Christians both inside and outside the Mamluk empire, and was often triggered by external acts of aggression on the part of western Europe, either in the form of individual acts of piracy or larger-scale campaigns. Occasionally, too, there were reprisals by western Christians triggered by anti-Christian measures being taken by the Mamluks. The capture and sack of Alexandria by Pierre I of Lusignan, the Crusader ruler of Cyprus, in 1365 is a good example of this process. The Muslim writer al-Nuwayri (Muhammad

417

al-Iskandarani) was in Alexandria at the time and gives a graphic account of the calamity of Muharram 765/October 1365,[340] when Pierre and his army sacked Alexandria for a week. This was, he says, 'the greatest catastrophe in the annals of Alexandria'. Al-Nuwayri himself attributes this attack, amongst other reasons, to the perse-cution suffered by the Oriental Christians who had been dismissed from their jobs and forced to wear distinctive clothing.[341] Other Muslim chroniclers make it clear that the Copts continued to be subjected to persecution at regular intervals throughout the fourteenth century and beyond.[342]

General Reflections

But how much of all this hardening of Muslim attitudes can be blamed on the effects of the Crusades? Certainly, to attribute it all to the fanaticism of Crusaders from Europe is too facile, although there must have been some cause and effect. On the other hand, it must be emphasised that Islamic society always had the ability to reform itself from within, to renew and redefine itself, to purify itself of unwanted innovations and pernicious influences. One has only to recall the rise of the two militant Berber dynasties in the eleventh- and twelfth-century Maghrib, the Almoravids and the Almohads, who had no need of Crusader attacks to feel the overpowering urge to impose their vibrant reformist Islam on the cities of North Africa and Spain. Such movements of reform (*islah*) have punctuated Islamic history in many parts of the world until the end of the twentieth century. Thus it could be argued that the renewed religious zeal of the Sunni Muslims in Syria, Palestine and Egypt from the twelfth century onwards did not spring predominantly from the bitter tribu-lations they had suffered at the hands of the Crusaders. Instead, this renewed spirit of *jihad* and internal hardening would have happened anyway, as an integral part of the nature of the Islamic community.

The sultans of Mamluk Egypt, whose rule extended well beyond the time when the Crusaders left the Levant, and indeed lasted until the early sixteenth century, constitute a special case. They were ethnic outsiders, recently converted to Sunni Islam, hard-headed military men with simple, uncompromising beliefs, who infused new life into the Muslim community. It could thus be argued – in theory – that the Mamluk rulers did not need the example of the Crusaders to pursue fanatical policies against religious minorities within their territories. The Mamluks, as newcomers to the Near East, did not understand or see the need to come to terms with the long-standing Christian pres-ence in the Levant and were not interested in drawing distinctions between different Christian groups. Nor for that matter would they tolerate the existence of 'heretical' groups of Muslims, such as Isma'ilis, Druzes or other bodies of Shi'ite believers in the Near East. The Islamic community had to purge itself from within against all contamination, innovation and heresy, and the Mamluks were the ideal warriors to defend Sunni Islam. They formed an alliance with the *'ulama'* who

Figure 6.83
(above and opposite)
Scenes of work, leisure and animals, Fatimid carved ivory plaques, eleventh–twelfth centuries, Egypt

were only too eager to instruct and reinforce their rulers in the latter's consolidation of the True Faith.

General Remarks on Muslim–Christian Relations after 690/1291

The preceding discussion has attempted to highlight the important but ultimately unanswerable issue of the effect of the Crusades on the attitude of the Muslims in Mamluk times towards Christianity and especially towards Near Eastern Christians. Whilst it is clear that Muslim society always had the inherent ability to redefine and renew its faith, the timing of the upsurge of Muslim religious zeal in the Mamluk period, after centuries of general tolerance towards the 'People of the Book' within the 'House of Islam', would seem on balance to suggest some connection with the Muslims' experience of the Crusades. Hence it can be argued that the coming of the Crusaders with their 'new brand' of fanatical Christianity acted as a catalyst, or even a direct agent, in the process of hardening Sunni Muslim hearts against people of other faiths, and indeed against any kind of religious deviancy within the ranks of the Muslims themselves.

The fanaticism of the newly arrived Crusaders shocked the Muslim world in 1099 and continued to do so. The so-called Counter-Crusade did not begin in the thirteenth century with Mamluk successes. Muslim reaction had been born in the twelfth century with Zengi or even earlier and had risen steadily to a crescendo first under Nur al-Din and Saladin and then later under the reinvigorated power of the Mamluks. After 1291 the Muslim response did not cease once their territories were purged of the Crusader presence. In addition to defending their own territories, they could now also launch counter-attacks against neighbouring eastern Christian states – Cilician Armenia, which was conquered by the Mamluk sultan al-Ashraf Sha'ban in 1375; the Latin Kingdom of Cyprus, which was made a tributary of Mamluk Egypt under Sultan Barsbay in 1427; Constantinople, which fell to the Ottomans in 1453; and the Knights Hospitaller in Rhodes, who held out until the Ottomans finally took the island in 1522. These events belong together.

Indeed, the Ottomans also harboured bellicose intentions towards Christian Europe, and as early as the fourteenth century Sultan Murad I (d. 1389) had announced that 'he would come to France when he had finished with Austria'.[343] This swell of reaction to the Crusades on the part of the Ottomans reached its climax in the sixteenth century. They conquered the Balkans, then Hungary, and moved ever deeper into the heart of Europe, to the very gates of Vienna. Indeed, the shadow of the Turkish threat hung like a black cloud over much of continental Europe throughout the sixteenth century. Thus the Muslim revanche lasted a very long time.

Conclusions

It is not surprising that the cultural interplay between Muslim and

Frank should have been almost entirely in one direction. A number of factors played a part. As already mentioned, the Muslims felt that they had little to learn from Europe in the religious, social and cultural spheres. The Franks, on the other hand, had much to learn from the lifestyle of the Muslims who had lived in the Near East for many centuries and were fully adapted to the climate and the terrain. Predictably it was in everyday life that the Franks were probably most influenced by Islamic mores, such as bathing and diet, and they came to identify themselves over generations as Levantines.

Yet in spite of evidence that the two sides, Crusaders and Muslims, could draw closer together, this process of *rapprochement* should not be exaggerated. Commercial and political alliances between Crusader and Muslim notwithstanding, the ideological divide remained. It is of course much easier to grasp the chronological framework of a period rather than its *Zeitgeist*. How can we ever know what ordinary Muslims really felt about the Crusades?[344]

The preceding discussion has shown that there were considerable points of contact and influence between Muslims and Franks at many levels over more than two centuries. But it is still difficult to generalise about how the Muslims really felt about the Franks. The existence of treaties and the reality of regular contact do not in any way imply that the Muslims respected or liked them, either individually or as a group.

Notes

1. Gabrieli, xvi.
2. Bernard Lewis is very negative about Muslim knowledge of the Franks: 'We still cannot be but astonished at how little they did know, even more at how little they cared.' Cf. *The Muslim Discovery of Europe*, 146.
3. *Fath*, 50.
4. Cf. Chapter 5.
5. Usama, Hitti, 95.
6. Arabic text, 140. The verb used for 'prattle' is *barbara*, which is linked to the word for 'Berber'. It has a negative connotation.
7. Al-Maqrizi, Broadhurst, 287. Richard the Lionheart is called *Malik al-Inkitar* (King of England); cf. Ibn al-Furat, Lyons, 107.
8. Usama, Hitti, 130.
9. Cf. Ibn Shaddad and 'Imad al-Din, quoted by Lyons and Jackson, *Saladin*, 341.
10. Ibn al-Furat, Lyons, 110.
11. *Manaqib Rashid al-Din*, quoted by Gabrieli, 242.
12. Ibn Jubayr, Broadhurst, 317.
13. Usama, Hitti, 163; Arabic text, 134.
14. Arabic text, 134–5; Usama, Hitti, 164.
15. Cf., for example, V. G. Berry, 'The Second Crusade', in K. M. Setton and M. W. Baldwin, *A History of the Crusades*, I, Madison, Milwaukee and London, 1969, 509; W. B. Stevenson, *The Crusaders in the East*, Cambridge, 1907, 163; M. W. Baldwin, 'The Latin states under Baldwin

III and Amalric I 1143–74', in Setton and Baldwin, *A History*, I, 530.

16. Ibn al-Athir, *Kamil*, XI, 86; cf. also Ibn al-Athir, *Atabegs*, *RHC*, II, 161; Ibn al-Furat, Shayyal, 517.

17. Ibn al-Athir, *Kamil*, XI, 86.

18. Ibn Nazif al-Hamawi, *Al-tarikh al-Mansuri*, ed. A. Darwish, Damascus, 1981, under the year 625, cited by Atrache, *Die Politik*, 229.

19. Derived from the Latin *hospitalis* – lodging place for travellers – cf. *EI²*, Supplement: art. *Dawiyya and Isbitariyya*.

20. Probably derived from Latin *devotus*, 'one devoted to God's service'.

21. Usama, Hitti, 164. Hitti puts the date at around 1140 and Humphreys suggests between the years 532/1138 and 538/1144. (*EI²*, Supplement: art. *Dawiyya and Isbitariyya*).

22. Ibn al-Qalanisi, Gibb, 330.

23. Ibn Shaddad, *RHC*, III, 97–8; Ibn al-Athir, *RHC*, I, 688.

24. Ibn al-Athir, *Kamil*, XII, 304.

25. Quoted by Abu Shama, *RHC*, IV, 273. Lit.: 'the heads were beneath the soles of the feet'.

26. Ibid. Cf. also 'Imad al-Din, *Fath*, trans. Massé, 30–1.

27. Ibn Wasil, III, 146, 148.

28. Ibn Wasil, II, 149.

29. *EI²*, Supplement: art. *Dawiyya and Isbitariyya*. This article is a detailed, scholarly treatment of this topic; cf. for the Crusader side, J. Riley-Smith, *The Knights of St. John in Jerusalem and Cyprus, c. 1050–1310*, London, 1967.

30. Ibn al-Qalanisi, Gibb, 208.

31. Ibn al-Athir, *Kamil*, XII, 42.

32. Ibn Shaddad, *RHC*, III, 220.

33. Ibn al-Furat, Lyons, 14.

34. Michaud, *Histoire*, II, 548, quoting Ibn Wasil.

35. Michaud, *Histoire*, IV, 449; C. Cahen, 'St. Louis et l'Islam', *JA*, 258 (1970), 6.

36. *Mémoires*, 475.

37. Ibid.

38. Ibid.

39. Ibn al-Furat, Lyons, 35.

40. Eddé, 'Saint Louis', 90–1.

41. Al-Idrisi praises his patron Roger of Sicily (trans. Jaubert, xvi–xviii) and Ibn Jubayr waxes lyrical about King William (Broadhurst, 340–3).

42. Ibn Wasil, IV, 234.

43. Ibn Wasil, IV, 242.

44. *Kitab al-Suluk*, I, 232.

45. Ibn al-Furat, Lyons, 9.

46. Ibn al-Furat, Lyons, 39.

47. Cf. the discussion in Chapter 5.

48. Of course the Muslim view of Frederick should be weighed against other opinions. Abulafia concludes, for example, that he lived 'less like an oriental prince than is easily assumed' (D. Abulafia, *Frederick II: A Medieval Emperor*, London, 1988, 439).

49. Ibn Wasil, IV, 248.

50. Ibn Wasil, IV, 248.

51. Ibn Wasil, IV, 248.

52. Ibn Wasil, IV, 248.

53. Al-Maqrizi, *Kitab al-muqaffa'*, ed. M. al-Yalawi, Beirut, 1991, biography no. 930, 440. The account is based on the earlier one of Ibn Zafir, 90.

54. Al-Yunini, III, 92–3.
55. Al-Yunini, III, 92–3.
56. This is typical of the inconsequentiality of al-Yunini's obituaries.
57. Ibn Shaddad, *RHC*, III, 94–5; cf. also Ibn al-Athir, *Kamil*, *RHC*, I, 674.
58. Abu Shama, *RHC*, IV, 257–8.
59. Ibn Jubayr, Broadhurst, 324.
60. Ibn Jubayr, Broadhurst, 324.
61. Quoted by Michaud, *Histoire*, II, 482.
62. Abu Shama, *RHC*, IV, 396–8; cf. al-'Umari, Lundquist, 33; Ibn Khallikan, de Slane, IV, 534; Ibn Shaddad, *RHC*, IV, 121, 130.
63. Ibn al-Athir, *Kamil*, XI, 366.
64. Ibn Shaddad, *RHC*, III, 284.
65. Abu Shama, *RHC*, IV, 310.
66. Ibn Shaddad, *RHC*, IV, 39.
67. Ibn al-Athir, *Kamil*, XI, 310.
68. Ibn Shaddad, *RHC*, III, 39–40.
69. Al-Maqrizi, *Kitab al-Suluk* I, 78–9; Ibn al-Athir, *Kamil*, XI, 323–4; Abu Shama, *RHC*, IV, 230–4.
70. Ibn al-Athir, *Kamil*, XI, 323–4.
71. Ibn al-Athir, *Kamil*, XI, 323–4.
72. Ibn al-Athir, *Kamil*, XI, 354–5. For other accounts of the killing, cf. Abu Shama, *RHC*, IV, 284; Ibn Shaddad, *RHC*, III, 39–40.
73. Abu Shama, *RHC*, IV, 97.
74. Abu Shama, *RHC*, IV, 299.
75. Ibn Shaddad, *RHC*, III, 252.
76. Ibn al-Athir, *Atabegs*, *RHC*, II, 278.
77. Lit.: 'rising in the east'.
78. 'Imad al-Din, *Kharida*, I, 99.
79. Abu Shama, *RHC*, IV, 433; cf. also 'Imad al-Din, *Fath*, 230.
80. Usama, Hitti, 164–5.
81. Thorau, *The Lion*, 96.
82. Ibid., 96. Thorau thinks they were there for the benefit of Western seamen.
83. Ibid., 196, citing Ibn 'Abd al-Zahir, *Rawd*, 350.
84. According to Abu Shama, *RHC*, IV, 434.
85. According to Abu Shama, *RHC*, IV, 434.
86. Ibn al-Athir, *Kamil*, *RHC*, I, 726.
87. Ibn Shaddad, *RHC*, III, 231–2.
88. Abu Shama, *RHC*, IV, 468. Usama tells the story of a Muslim woman wearing a coat of mail and helmet and carrying a sword and shield and of an old woman who rushed into battle, sword in hand (cf. colour plate 8) (Usama, Hitti, 154).
89. Ruled 551/1156–c. 581/1185.
90. Ibn Jubayr, Broadhurst, 189–90, 207.
91. Usama, Hitti, 152, 156.
92. According to Abu Shama, *RHC*, IV, 434.
93. Usama, Hitti, 167.
94. Ibn Shaddad, *Al-a'laq al-khatira*, Bodleian ms. Marsh 333, fol. 34a; Usama, Hitti, 159–60.
95. Usama, Hitti, 168.
96. Ibn Jubayr, Broadhurst, 320.
97. Ibn Jubayr, Broadhurst, 320.
98. Ibn Jubayr, Broadhurst, 320.
99. Ibn Jubayr, Broadhurst, 320.
100. Usama, Hitti, 161.

101. Usama, Hitti, 144.
102. Usama, Hitti, 106.
103. Usama, Hitti, 80.
104. Usama, Hitti, 175.
105. Usama, Hitti, 213 ff.
106. *Nushaf/nishaf*: Gabrieli's translator gives 'consumption'.
107. Usama, Hitti, 162; Arabic text, 133.
108. Usama, Hitti, 162–3; Arabic text, 133–4.
109. Usama, Hitti, 163; Arabic text, 134.
110. Cahen, 'Indigènes', 352.
111. Ibid., 352–3.
112. Arabic text, 140.
113. Arabic text, 140.
114. Al-Maqrizi, Broadhurst, 188.
115. Ibn al-Athir, *Kamil*, X, 322–3. For a more extended discussion of the treatment of prisoners on both sides, cf. Chapter 8, 549–56.
116. 'Imad al-Din, *Fath*, 56.
117. Usama, Hitti, 164.
118. Arabic text, 132.
119. Usama, Hitti, 93.
120. Usama, Hitti, 93–4.
121. Usama, Hitti, 97.
122. Arabic text, 141.
123. Usama, Hitti, 94.
124. Usama, Hitti, 95.
125. Usama, Hitti, 141.
126. Usama, Hitti, 140.
127. Quoted by Abu Shama, *RHC*, iv, 458.
128. For a recent discussion of this topic, cf. Mouton, *Damas*, 302–3.
129. Ibn al-Qalanisi, quoted by Mouton, *Damas*, 305.
130. Ibn al-Qalanisi, Le Tourneau, 54, 86, 128.
131. Sivan, 'Réfugiés', 141.
132. According to Kedar, 'The subjected Muslims', 150.
133. Abu Shama, *RHC*, IV, 409.
134. Ibn al-Qalanisi, Gibb, 129; cf. also a similar statement in Usama, Hitti, 111.
135. Cahen, 'Indigènes', 358.
136. Ibn Tulun, *Al-qala'id al-jawhariyya*, ed. M. A. Duhman, Damascus, 1949, vol I, 26–39.
137. Ibn Tulun, *Qala'id*, 26.
138. Ibid., 27; Kedar, 'The subjected Muslims', 170.
139. Ibn Tulun, *Qala'id*, 27.
140. Ibid., 28.
141. Abu Shama, *RHC*, IV, 301–2.
142. According to Kedar, 'The subjected Muslims', 150.
143. Al-Harawi, trans. Sourdel-Thomine, 68.
144. B. Lewis, *The Political Language of Islam*, Chicago and London, 1991, 104.
145. Ibid., 105.
146. Ibn al-'Adim, *Zubda*, *RHC*, III, 597–8; Kedar, 'The subjected Muslims', 147; Cahen, *La Syrie du Nord*, 343.
147. Kedar, 'The subjected Muslims', 138.
148. Ibn Jubayr, Broadhurst, 321.
149. Ibn Jubayr, Broadhurst, 321–2.
150. Ibn Jubayr, Broadhurst, 319.

151. Ibn Jubayr, Broadhurst, 315.
152. Ibn Jubayr, Broadhurst, 316.
153. Ibn Jubayr, Broadhurst, 317.
154. Ibn Jubayr, Broadhurst, 317.
155. According to Abu Shama, *RHC*, IV, 301; cf. also D. Richards, 'A text of 'Imad al-Din on 12th century Frankish–Muslims relations', *Arabica*, 25 (1978), 203.
156. Usama, Hitti, 168. For the full story, cf. Usama, Hitti, 167–8.
157. Usama, Hitti, 168.
158. For a longer discussion of the Geniza, cf. p. 395.
159. Ibn Muyassar, *RHC*, III, 470.
160. Ibn Muyassar, *RHC*, III, 471.
161. S. D. Goitein, *A Mediterranean Society*, Berkeley and Los Angeles, 1967, vol. I, 275; R. Bulliet, *The Camel and the Wheel*, Cambridge, Mass., and London, 1975.
162. Ibn Jubayr, Broadhurst, 264; cf. also 269.
163. Ibn Jubayr, Broadhurst, 264.
164. Ibn Jubayr, Broadhurst, 249.
165. Usama, Hitti, 38.
166. Ibn Jubayr, Broadhurst, 55–6.
167. Goitein, *Mediterranean Society*, I, 40; Ibn Jubayr, Broadhurst, 313.
168. Ibn Jubayr, Broadhurst, 325.
169. Ibn Jubayr, Broadhurst, 326.
170. Ibn Jubayr, Broadhurst, 332.
171. Ibn Jubayr, Broadhurst, 327.
172. Ibn Jubayr, Broadhurst, 328.
173. Ibn Jubayr, Broadhurst, 329.
174. Ibn Jubayr, Broadhurst, 330, 333.
175. Ibn Jubayr, Broadhurst, 335.
176. Kedar, 'The subjected Muslims', 161–2.
177. Ibn Jubayr, Broadhurst, 318.
178. Al-Harawi, trans. Sourdel-Thomine, 65.
179. Al-Harawi, trans. Sourdel-Thomine, 70.
180. 'Imad al-Din, *Fath*, quoted by Gabrieli, 170–1.
181. Cf. Qur'an, 19:2.
182. According to Abu Shama, *RHC*, IV, 302.
183. Cf. Gabrieli, 174.
184. M. Rosen-Ayalon, 'Art and architecture in Ayyubid Jerusalem', *Israel Exploration Journal*, 40/1 (1990), 307.
185. K. al-'Asali, *Watha'iq maqdisiyya tarikhiyya*, Amman, 1983, vol. I, 91 ff.
186. Cf. pp. 334–6.
187. R. C. Smail, *The Crusaders in Syria and the Holy Land*, London, 1973, 187.
188. Ibid., 136.
189. Ibid., 137.
190. M. Burgoyne, *Mamluk Jerusalem*, London, 1987, 48 and 204–5.
191. Creswell, *Muslim Architecture of Egypt*, II, 199, n. 1.
192. Ibn al-Athir, *RHC*, I, 263.
193. Ibn Jubayr, Broadhurst, 323.
194. Ibn Jubayr, Broadhurst, 323.
195. Usama, Hitti, 157–8.
196. Usama, Hitti, 159–60.
197. Usama, Hitti, 159.
198. Usama, Hitti, 159–60.

199. 'Imad al-Din quoted by Abu Shama, *RHC*, IV, 278.
200. Quatremère, 30. The other prisoner was released in order that he might inform the Franks of what had happened.
201. 'Ifrir Liyun'. Ibn al-Furat, Lyons, 95–6.
202. Thorau, *The Lion*, 222, quoting *Rawd*, 401.
203. For a general discussion of this topic, cf. Kedar, 'The subjected Muslims', 135–74.
204. J. Drory, 'Hanbalis of the Nablus region in the eleventh and twelfth centuries', in *The Medieval Levant*, ed. B. Z. Kedar and A. L. Udovitch, Haifa, 1988, 95–112.
205. Arabic text, 134–5; Usama, Hitti, 163–4.
206. Ibn Jubayr, Broadhurst, 300.
207. Ibn Jubayr, Broadhurst, 318.
208. Ibn Jubayr, Broadhurst, 321.
209. Ibn Jubayr, Broadhurst, 318–19.
210. Al-Maqrizi, trans. Broadhurst, 206; cf. also Holt, *Age*, 64–5.
211. Cf. al-'Azimi, 373; Ibn al-Qalanisi, Gibb, 48; Ibn Taghribirdi, *Nujum*, V, 150.
212. Al-'Azimi, 332.
213. Al-Maqrizi, trans. Broadhurst, 88, 94.
214. Al-Maqrizi, trans. Broadhurst, 273.
215. Ibn al-Furat, Lyons, 56; al-Maqrizi, Quatremère, 200.
216. Cf. Smail, *Crusaders*, 158.
217. Cf. Thorau, *The Lion*, 147.
218. Ibn al-Furat, Lyons, 115.
219. Hamilton concludes that since the porch was remodelled at a point when second-hand twelfth-century material was available, this work was probably done after Saladin's reconquest of Jerusalem in 1187. Cf. R. W. Hamilton, *The Structural History of the Aqsa Mosque*, London, 1949, 43–4 and plates xxv: 4–5; Rosen-Ayalon, 'Art and architecture', 310.
220. Further confirmation of the use of Crusader material is by the zigzag moulding which was found carved on the backs of twelfth-century architectural fragments. Cf. Hamilton, *loc. cit.*
221. Rosen-Ayalon, 'Art and architecture', 308. Burgoyne concludes that this is probably an Ayyubid construction composed mainly of Crusader *spolia*, *Mamluk Jerusalem*, 38.
222. Rosen-Ayalon, 'Art and architecture', 308–9. The twisted Crusader columns of this portal are locally known to this day as 'the testicles of the unbelievers' (*baydat al-kuffar*). Cf. 386 above, plate 6.6.
223. M. S. Briggs, *Muhammadan Architecture in Egypt and Palestine*, Oxford, 1924, 81.
224. I am very grateful to Dr Barry Flood for generously allowing me access to his ongoing research on this topic.
225. Quoted by Herzfeld, *Damascus: Studies in architecture*, 4–5; cf. Ibn al-'Adim, *Bughya*, Zakkar, III, 340; D. Morray, *An Ayyubid Notable and His World*, Leiden, 1994, 42.
226. *Damascus*, 4.
227. Sura 24: 35.
228. Cf. E. Baer, *Ayyubid Metalwork with Christian Images*, Leiden, 1989, 4.
229. Ibid., 7.
230. Ibid., 19, and pls 73–4.
231. Ibid., 20.
232. Ibid., 32.
233. Ibid., 42.

234. Ibid.

235. Ibid., 44.

236. Ibid., 48.

237. Köhler, *Allianzen*.

238. Cf. P. M. Holt, 'Al-Nasir Muhammad's letter to a Spanish ruler in 699/1300', *Al-Masaq*, 3 (1990), 23–9. There had been two earlier diplomatic missions to Aragon in 1290 and 1293 (al-Qalqashandi, *Subh*, XIV, 63–70). As Holt suggests, the letter of al-Nasir Muhammad b. Qalawun may well have been sent as an interim confirmation of privileges already granted to Aragonese merchants and pilgrims in Mamluk Egypt.

239. Ibn 'Abd al-Zahir, *Tashrif al-ayyam*, ed. M. Kamil and M. A. al-Najjar, Cairo, 1961, 161, as cited by Holt, *Early Mamluk Diplomacy*, Leiden, 1995, 142.

240. Cf. P. M. Holt, 'Baybars' treaty with the Lady of Beirut in 667/1269', in *Crusade and Settlement*, ed. P. W. Edbury, Cardiff, 1985, 244, quoting al-Qalqashandi, *Subh*, XIV, 40–2.

241. 'Baybars' treaty', 242–4.

242. Cf. U. Heyd, *Histoire du commerce du Levant au Moyen Âge*, Paris, 1885; E. Ashtor, *A Social and Economic History of the Near East in the Middle Ages*, London, 1976; D. Abulafia, 'The role of trade in Muslim–Christian contact during the Middle Ages', in *The Arab Influence in Medieval Europe*, ed. D. A. Agius and R. Hitchcock, Reading, 1994, 1–24; A. Udovitch, art.: Trade, Islamic in *Dictionary of the Middle Ages*, New York, 1989, XII, 105–8.

243. The scattered information found in the medieval Islamic sources on trade makes it difficult to construct a convincing set of general propositions about specifically Muslim, as distinct from Jewish and Jewish–Muslim, trade; there is no Muslim equivalent of the Cairo Geniza which allows such a detailed picture of the minutiae of the trading activities of Jewish merchants to be constructed. But the Islamic literary evidence can often corroborate interpretations of East–West trade which are based on the extensive medieval European sources.

244. Abulafia, 'The role of trade', 4.

245. Goitein, *Mediterranean Society*, I, 32.

246. C. Cahen, 'L'histoire économique et sociale de l'Orient musulman mediéval', *Studia Islamica*, 3 (1955), 58.

247. Goitein, *Mediterranean Society*; for an excellent summary of research on the Geniza, cf. R. S. Humphreys, *Islamic History: A Framework for Inquiry*, Princeton, 1991, 261–72.

248. Abulafia, 'The role of trade', 5.

249. Ashtor does not, however, provide evidence from the primary sources that such trading links were set up (*A Social and Economic History*, 226).

250. Cf. J. Riley-Smith, 'Government in Latin Syria and the commercial privileges of foreign merchants', in *Relations between East and West in the Middle Ages*, ed. D. Baker, Edinburgh, 1973, 109.

251. Ibn al-Qalanisi, Gibb, 109; Köhler, 107.

252. Ibn al-Qalanisi, Gibb, 108.

253. E.g. the delegation of 504/1110–11. Cf. Ibn al-Jawzi, IX, 163.

254. Arabic text, 141.

255. Ashtor, *A Social and Economic History*, 4; Heyd, *Histoire*, 373; Abulafia, 'The role of trade', 5.

256. Ashtor, *A Social and Economic History*, 5, 8, 246; Heyd, *Histoire*, 378;

Abulafia, 'The role of trade', 5.

257. Abulafia, 'The role of trade', 1; A. S. Atiyah, *Crusade, Commerce and Culture*, Bloomington and Oxford, 1962, 240–1.

258. Abulafia, 'The role of trade', 10; Ashtor, *A Social and Economic History*, 240.

259. Abulafia, 'The role of trade', 1.

260. Ibn al-Furat, Shayyal, 18.

261. Ibn Khallikan, de Slane, IV, 456.

262. M. Bates and D. M. Metcalf, 'Crusader coinage with Arabic inscriptions', in *A History of the Crusades*, ed. H. W. Hazard and N. P. Zacour, Madison, 1989, vol. VI, 439–40.

263. Quoted by S. D. Goitein, 'Changes in the Middle East (950–1150) as illustrated by the documents of the Cairo Geniza', in *Islamic Civilisation 950–1150*, ed. D. S. Richards, Oxford, 1973, 19.

264. Ibn Jubayr, Broadhurst, 300.

265. Cited in Lewis, *The Muslim Discovery of Europe*, 26.

266. Ibn Jubayr, Broadhurst, 301.

267. Ibn Jubayr, Broadhurst, 313.

268. Ibn Jubayr, Broadhurst, 301.

269. Ibn Jubayr, Broadhurst, 301.

270. Quoted by Lyons and Jackson, *Saladin*, 115.

271. Quoted by Lyons and Jackson, *Saladin*, 113.

272. Heyd, *Histoire*, 163.

273. Usama, Hitti, 25–6.

274. Ibn Shaddad, *RHC*, III, 98.

275. Ibn al-Athir, *Kamil*, XI, 356.

276. Ibn Jubayr, Broadhurst, 318.

277. Qur'an 55: 24.

278. Ibn Jubayr, Broadhurst, 318.

279. Ibn Jubayr, Broadhurst, 317.

280. Ibn Jubayr, Broadhurst, 317–18.

281. Ibn Jubayr, Broadhurst, 31–2.

282. Ibn Jubayr, Broadhurst, 32.

283. Ibn Jubayr, Broadhurst, 61: he also mentions cinnamon.

284. See generally C. Cahen, 'Notes sur l'histoire des croisades et de l'Orient latin. 3: Orient latin et commerce du Levant', *Bulletin de la Faculté des Lettres de l'Université de Strasbourg*, 29 (1950–1), 328–416.

285. Thorau, *The Lion*, 120.

286. P. M. Holt, *Early Mamluk Diplomacy*, 25; cf. also Heyd, *Histoire*, I, 386–7.

287. Cf. Holt, *Early Mamluk Diplomacy*, 25.

288. S. J. Auld, 'Kuficising inscriptions in the work of Gentile da Fabriano', *Oriental Art*, 32/3 (Autumn 1986), 246–65.

289. Ashtor, *A Social and Economic History*, 298.

290. Sura 3: 118.

291. For a recent discussion on this issue, cf. D. S. Richards, 'Dhimmi problems in fifteenth century Cairo: reconsideration of a court document', in *Studies in Muslim–Jewish Relations*, ed. R. L. Nettler, Chur, 1993, vol. I, 128.

292. Al-Shirazi, *Kitab al-tanbih*, trans. G. H. Bousquet, Algiers, 1949, vol. IV. This book was still on the *madrasa* curriculum in Baghdad a century or so later and probably remained so for much longer.

293. Ibid., 46.

294. Ibid.

295. Ibid.
296. Ibid., 47.
297. Quoted in H. Lazarus Yaleh, *Studies in al-Ghazzali*, Jerusalem, 1975, 442.
298. W. C. Chittick, *Faith and Practice in Islam*, Albany, 1992, 142.
299. Al-Mutawakkil's decree was promulgated in 235/850.
300. Al-Hakim's aberrant conduct is chronicled in full by al-Maqrizi, no doubt exploiting his opportunity to linger on the unacceptable behaviour of 'heretical' Shi'ites. Cf. al-Maqrizi, *Khitat*, II, 285–9, quoted by Lewis, *Islam*, I, 55–7.
301. Cf. Richards, 'Dhimmi problems'.
302. Goitein, *Mediterranean Society*, I, 29.
303. Runciman, I, 287.
304. Cf. E. Ashtor, 'The social isolation of *ahl adh-dhimma*', in *Pal Hirschler Memorial Book*, Budapest, 1949, 73–93.
305. Cahen argues that Oriental Christians were maltreated only on rare occasions, when action was taken by the Muslims in direct reprisal for specific Crusader attacks. Cf. C. Cahen, 'L'Islam et la Croisade', in *Turcobyzantina et Oriens Christianus*, London, 1974, 633–4.
306. A. S. Atiyah, 'The aftermath of the Crusades', in *A History of the Crusades*, 3: *The Fourteenth and Fifteenth Centuries*, ed. H. W. Hazard, Madison, Wis., 1975, 662. This view is shared by Hitti. Cf. P. K. Hitti, 'The impact of the Crusades on eastern Christianity', in *Medieval and Middle Eastern Studies in Honor of Aziz Suryal Atiya*, ed. S. A. Hanna, Leiden, 1972, 211–18.
307. Sivan, *L'Islam*, 180.
308. Ibn al-Qalanisi, Gibb, 69; Ibn Shaddad, Eddé, 270.
309. Ibn al-Qalanisi, Gibb, 155; cf. also other instances of Frankish–Armenian co-operation: 267, 274.
310. Al-'Azimi 373; Ibn al-Qalanisi, Gibb, 45.
311. Ibn Shaddad, *Al-a'laq al-khatira*, quoted in Ibn al-'Adim, *Zubda*, Dahan, II, 214–15, n. 2.
312. Ibn al-'Adim, *Zubda*, Dahan, II, 214–15.
313. Cahen, 'L'idée de Croisade', 634.
314. Morray, *An Ayyubid Notable*, 72; Ibn al-'Adim, *Bughya*, Zakkar, 5/659.
315. Ibn al-Shihna, trans. Sauvaget, 48 and 76–7.
316. Ibn Jubayr, Broadhurst, 296.
317. Ibn Jubayr, Broadhurst, 53.
318. Lewis comments on 'the often well-grounded suspicion that they [the Oriental Christians] were collaborating with the enemies of Islam' (*Islam*, II, 217).
319. Sivan, *L'Islam*, 180.
320. *EI²*. s.v. Kibt (A. S. Atiya).
321. Al-Maqrizi, trans. Broadhurst, 120.
322. Ibn Abi Usaybi'a, *Uyun al-anba' fi tabaqat al-atibba'*, Beirut, 1957.
323. There is even the example of the Jewish doctor Yusuf b. Yahya al-Sabli (d. 1226) who was originally from Morocco and fled persecution there to take refuge in Aleppo around the turn of the twelfth century. This indicates that the situation in Aleppo must have been tolerable for *dhimmi*s – A. -M. Eddé, 'Les médicins dans la société syrienne du VIIᵉ/XIIIᵉ siècle', *Annales Islamologiques*, 29 (1995), 93–4.
324. According to al-Maqrizi, a version of the Covenant of 'Umar was issued in 700/1300: *Suluk*, II, 922–4.
325. Al-Maqrizi, according to Ashtor, 'Social isolation', 76.

326. Ibid., 80.
327. Ibid., 81.
328. Al-Nawawi, *Al-masa'il al-manthura*, Damascus, 1348, 16.
329. Al-Qalqashandi, *Subh*, XIII, 378.
330. *EI²*: s.v. Kibt.
331. Cf. L. Pouzet, 'Hadir ibn Abi Bakr, al-Mihrani', *BEO*, 30 (1978), 173–83.
332. Al-'Ayni, *'Iqd al-juman, RHC*, II, 215–16.
333. Al-Maqrizi, *Suluk*, quoted by Lewis, *Islam*, I, 89.
334. Al-Qalqashandi, *Subh*, VIII, 36–8; Lewis, *Islam*, I, 99.
335. C. Cahen and I. Chabbouh, 'Le testament d'al-Malik as-Salih Ayyub', *Mélanges Laoust, BEO*, 29 (1977), 97–114.
336. Ibid.
337. Al-Maqrizi, *Khitat*, I, 90.
338. Al-Maqrizi, trans. Broadhurst, 223.
339. A. S. Atiya, *The Crusade in the Later Middle Ages*, London, 1938, 260.
340. This author should not be confused with another better-known scholar of the same name, al-Nuwayri.
341. Atiya, *Crusade*, 365.
342. Ibid., 272.
343. Atiya, *Crusade*, 11.
344. Lyons, 'The Crusading stratum', 148.

ages. Two works in particular are important in the context of Crusader–Muslim warfare: R. C. Smail, *Crusader Warfare 1097–1193*;[2] and C. Marshall, *Warfare in the Latin East, 1192–1291*.[3] Using the wealth of Western medieval source material and such Islamic sources as have been translated into European languages, these two books cover in a very clear and comprehensive manner many aspects of this subject. In particular, they point to the vital importance of castles and strong points in the military history of the twelfth and thirteenth centuries;[4] the archaeological and architectural research of D. Pringle has highlighted this point very persuasively.[5]

Important work has also been carried out by specialists on arms and armour who have used Islamic sources to elucidate certain aspects of Islamic warfare, and the results have appeared in scholarly monographs and articles.[6] But broader interpretations of Islamic warfare in the particular context of the Crusades have not generally been undertaken by specialists in Islamic history either in the Middle East or in the West.[7]

Figure 7.2 *Officer, Dioscorides,* De Materia Medica, *619/1222, Iraq*

The Aims of this Chapter

True to the avowed focus of the present book, this chapter will highlight only those military themes which emerge from the Islamic sources, and will show how medieval Muslim writers themselves viewed the Crusader–Muslim conflict. A second aim will be to test this evidence against the theories of modern military historians.

The Problem of the Medieval Islamic Sources

The information provided by Muslim historians of the Middle Ages does not permit a clear or systematic description of Muslim or Frankish military tactics in battle, or of the course of individual battles and sieges during the Crusading period, or of the actual weapons used. Individual snippets of interest to historians of war may be gleaned from a laborious trawl through hundreds of pages of medieval chronicles; but even when they are pieced together they do not constitute a corpus of data on which confident generalisations can be based.

Part of the problem lies in the very nature of Muslim historical writing itself and in the milieu of those who composed the medieval chronicles. Muslim chroniclers of the Middle Ages were decidedly not professional military historians and it is therefore not appropriate to expect them to display any specialised military insight in their work. Sometimes, and especially in the Mamluk period, they were essentially administrators. More often they were, first and foremost, religious scholars who moved laterally into writing history from a deep study of the Qur'an, the *hadith* and the Shari'a. This was the background, for example, of arguably the greatest Muslim historian of the Crusading period, Ibn al-Athir,[8] and of many others.

Such scholars came to historiography with a clear aim: to record the victories of the Muslims as a reflection of God's will for the world, and to chart the immutable Divine design which was the triumph of Islam, God's final and complete Revelation. Usama, although a soldier himself and very much a man of the world, also shares this view-point, declaring: 'Victory in warfare is from Allah and is not due to organisation and planning, nor to the number of troops and supporters.'[9] The parallel with the 'Deus vult' mantra of the First Crusade leaps to the eye.

With such an overall religious purpose firmly fixed in their minds, Muslim chroniclers tend to stress the propagandistic aspects of the events they record. They skate over the practicalities of war – the details of the sequence of battles and sieges, the terrain, the weapons – and dwell instead on the glory (or occasionally humiliation) which ensued from military engagements with the Franks. The numbers of troops present at a certain battle are sometimes given in the Muslim chronicles, but these 'facts' are vague and unreliable. Even successful skirmishes against the Franks can be transformed into great victories by the simple device of grossly inflating the size of the enemy army and emphasising a brilliant performance on the battlefield by the greatly outnumbered but valiant Muslim soldiers, aided by God.

Another problem with many of the Muslim accounts of military engagements between Muslim and Frank is that the chroniclers were not present at the event and often record it after one or more genera-tions have passed. They do not understand the practicalities of warfare and prefer to describe the build-up and outcomes of military engage-ments rather than what happened in the thick of the fighting. They rarely reveal a sensitivity to the details and implications of terrain.

The Evidence of Works of Art

Military historians who wish to use the evidence of surviving works of art encounter particular difficulties. Even if architecture, miniature painting, metalwork and pottery from the period of the Crusades can be dated accurately – not always an easy task – such visual evidence is not always entirely reliable as a guide to actual military practice. Artistic time and chronological time are not necessarily synchronic, and allowance has to be made for the imaginative creativity of the artist. What did the Muslim and Frankish armies look like? The simplest way to describe their appearance at the time of the Crusades – their armour, horses, weapons, battle formations – would be to look closely at contemporary depictions in miniature painting, ivories, pottery, metalwork, sculpture and other artefacts made in the Levant during the twelfth and thirteenth centuries. Unfortunately, for the key area of Palestine there is virtually no securely dated contemporary evidence of this kind and there is not much more in the case of Syria. It is tempting, therefore, to use works of art from neighbouring areas – such as Egypt, Anatolia, Iraq and even Iran – or which may date to just before and just after the Crusading periods. By this means

Figure 7.3 *Foot soldier,* Varqa va Gulshah *('Varqa and Gulshah'), c. 1250, Turkey*

Figure 7.4 *Spear, Nasir al-Din,* Anthology, *671/1272–3, Turkey*

it is possible to assemble a critical mass of information. This is precisely the aim of the illustrations (particularly the drawings) in this book, which are intended to evoke in general fashion the ambience of life in the Middle East between the eleventh and the fourteenth centuries. At the same time, it is not the intention to force this visual material to fill gaps in the record. There are obvious limits to its reliability. In the specific field of armour and weapons, for example, it is tempting to select works which pre-date or post-date the Crusading period and to argue from them that, given the slow pace of change in military practice and technology in the medieval period, it is likely that in the twelfth and thirteenth centuries the Muslim armies must have shared the same characteristics as those in the periods immediately preceding and thereafter. This is not good scholarship, however, and is a dangerous path to follow. Evidence for Muslim weapons in Palestine and Syria during the twelfth and thirteenth centuries has to be taken either from specific detailed descriptions in literary sources – and, as noted above, these scarcely exist – or from the few surviving works of art produced in that area in that very period. Very often those works of art will prove to be too general in their depiction of the relevant details to be of much use. But they suffice to give the flavour of the times and of contemporary material culture.

There are also significant problems in relating the evidence of works of art to the information found in written sources. It is again very tempting for scholars with a specific interest in costume, weapons, armour and the like to use the sources to develop categories of these objects and to propose a detailed evolution for some of them, or to suggest patterns of change in their typology or use. The difficulty with such procedures is that it is all too easy to read more into the sources than they actually say and to attribute to them fine distinctions which are simply not there in the original Arabic.

Thus – to take a single example – the carefully fashioned prose of 'Imad al-Din al-Isfahani with its balanced repetitions and antitheses, and with its carefully constructed climaxes, cannot be used as a concrete source for military technology. To put it more succinctly, if 'Imad al-Din gives us several different words for 'sword' it does not necessarily mean that all these words refer to different *kinds* of sword used in the Crusader–Muslim conflict. Indeed, quite often he is just showing us his vast repertoire of learned Arabic vocabulary. There is no point in modern scholars using such quotations to embroider a preconceived theory of how weapons of a specific type were used (or evolved) in a particular place or period.

The obvious conclusion is that the Arabic chronicles are an unsatisfactory source for such information whereas works of art, if interpreted judiciously, are a still under-exploited mine of information for widening our knowledge of military aspects of the Crusades. This is especially true when they are used carefully in conjunction with the evidence of written sources. Such artefacts include coins, metalwork and pottery as well as arms and armour.

Architectural and archaeological evidence, especially castles and citadels, is vital, but again it has to be evaluated in combination with a careful study of the topography of the area in question and of the relevant texts. One also has to remain aware of the problems posed by epigraphically unidentified later rebuildings and restorations.

The Military Manuals of the Muslims

Introduction

From an early stage the Muslims wrote treatises on the arts of war. As well as the genre of books of *jihad* already mentioned, which bore such titles as *The Book of Horsemanship in the Conduct of Jihad in the Path of God*, others dealt with horsemanship in a more practical way, with archery or with military tactics. In his valuable book *The Catalogue* (*Al-Fihrist*) Ibn al-Nadim (d. between 380/990–1 and 388/998), a Baghdad bookseller and bibliophile, lists all the books in Arabic known to him. He includes a whole section outlining 'the books composed about horsemanship, bearing of arms, the implements of war, and the management and usage of these things among all nations'.[10] According to him, this genre dated back to pre-Islamic Persia, and a number of these works were written for the 'Abbasid caliphs, for example al-Mansur and al-Ma'mun. Such treatises reflect not only the influence of pre-Islamic Persia but also that of Byzantine (and even ancient Greek) theory, and all of these elements enriched the Islamic military tradition.[11]

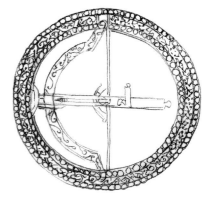

Figure 7.5 *A combination of shield and bow,* Tabsirat arbab al-albab *('The Perception of Those with Understanding'), written by al-Tarsusi for Saladin, c. 583/1187, probably Syria*

A significant number of Muslim military manuals date to the Ayyubid period and their production increased markedly under the Mamluks.[12] A greater interest in writing these kinds of books and presenting them to sultans and commanders characterised the increasingly militarised society of Syria and Egypt and had much to do with the irruption of the Mongols and Franks into the Islamic world.

A general note of caution should be sounded here. Despite their detailed presentations, the evidence of these works (cf. figures 7.10 and 8.8) should be treated with caution, since it is impossible to say with certainty whether they reflect actual military practice or merely an ideal. Reference will, however, be made to them at different points in this chapter and their evidence will be evaluated in combination with what the chronicles say.

A Survey of the Military Manuals of the Muslims from the Crusading Period

Al-Tarsusi

A military manual from Saladin's time has survived.[13] It was written by al-Tarsusi around the year 570/1174 especially for Saladin, because of his 'exploits in the *jihad* against the infidels'.[14] This work is of particular value precisely because it dates from Saladin's time.

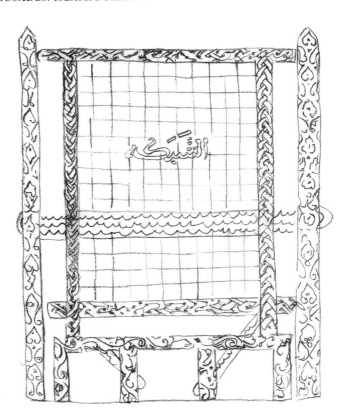

Figure 7.6 *Protective shelter for manœuvring a piece of siege machinery into position,* Tabsirat arbab al-albab *('The Perception of Those with Understanding'), written by al-Tarsusi for Saladin, c. 583/1187, probably Syria*

Al-Tarsusi, who was incidentally of Armenian extraction but wrote in Arabic, is at pains in his book to emphasise that he has relied for much of his information on the expertise of an arms maker from Alexandria called Ibn al-Abraqi. His manual lays particular emphasis on the bow but it also gives a thorough survey of a range of weapons, how they are made, what they looked like and how they were used. He also discusses war machines – mangonels, battering-rams, towers – and the use of Greek fire (*naft*), the disposition of armies on the battlefield, and how to make armour. Of course, it is very difficult to know how closely the arms and tactics which al-Tarsusi describes in his manual correspond to actual military practice in Saladin's time. But there is certainly a practical tone to his statements, and an array of technical details, which together lend some credibility to his work.

Al-Harawi

A work written by 'Ali b. Abi Bakr al-Harawi (d. 611/1214) gives comprehensive coverage of tactics and military organisation and discusses such topics as the conduct of sieges and battle formations.[15] Scanlon describes it as 'a very thorough study of the Muslim army in the field and under siege'.[16]

436

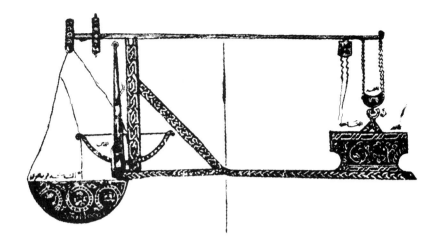

Figure 7.7 *Catapult with counter-weight,* Tabsirat arbab al-albab *('The Perception of Those with Understanding'), written by al-Tarsusi for Saladin, c. 583/1187, probably Syria*

The Military Manuals of the Mamluks

The Mamluk military environment produced a large number of works of *furusiyya* ('horsemanship'). The term *furusiyya* means much more than equestrian skills: it involved a whole range of expertise including the training of both horse and rider, the way in which the knight should use his weapons and how the cavalry as a whole should conduct itself.[17] A noted scholar of the Mamluks, David Ayalon takes the definition of *furusiyya* even further, describing it as embracing 'all that the horseman had to master by systematic training in order to become an accomplished knight'.[18]

Some of these *furusiyya* manuals are still extant in manuscript form, lavishly illustrated with vignettes of the life of the horse and its rider, together with the military uniforms and weapons of the period.[19] Such practical manuals need to be assessed within a wider and not exclusively military context, namely the development of what might be termed 'Islamic chivalry'. This set of ideals found expression particularly in the reign of the vigorous 'Abbasid caliph al-Nasir (1175–1225). The concept of *futuwwa* (roughly translatable as 'youthful manliness') encouraged by al-Nasir seems to have involved formal ceremonies calculated to foster personal loyalty to the caliph, and rites of investiture such as girding with trousers. There are parallels here with the ceremonies of knighthood in Europe. In the Islamic world, there was the further dimension of links with guilds, Sufi brotherhoods and all four Sunni legal schools. Thus, as in European knighthood, the religious element was well to the fore. The exact role of *futuwwa* beliefs and ceremonies amongst the Muslims of Syria and Palestine up to 1291 has yet to be explored in detail.

Al-Aqsara'i

A typical example of a *furusiyya* manual is the work of al-Aqsara'i (d. 749/1348) entitled *An End to Questioning and Desiring [Further*

Figure 7.8 *Prince in majesty,*
Seljuq stone relief on city wall,
c. 1220, Konya, Turkey

Knowledge] Concerning the Science of Horsemanship.[20] Although this treatise with its typically pompous title dates from a period a little after the disappearance of the Franks from the Near East, its contents can reasonably be taken as typical of other such manuals of a slightly earlier date which have not survived or which have not yet been published.

The work covers the following topics: an introduction which extols the virtues of *jihad* and of martyrdom in the path of God, followed by sections on archery, the lance, the shield, the mace, the 'art of soldiers and cavalrymen', weapons, conscription and assembling troops, battle lines (cf. figure 8.8), incendiaries and smoke devices, the division of spoils and a final discussion with useful hints to the soldier.

Al-Aqsara'i claims to be giving the sum of knowledge of the military art in his own time. It is a model work of *furusiyya*, outlining the qualities and skills which should be possessed by an accomplished cavalryman. Yet, as Tantum suggests,[21] it is hazardous to argue that this manual necessarily reflects actual fighting methods in the writer's own time. Al-Aqsara'i borrows material and quotes verbatim from earlier military manuals, including a work by al-Kindi (d. c. 235/850) on swords and a treatise on the lance by Najm al-Din al-Rammah (d. 694/1294), whose name means 'the manufacturer of lances'. In fact al-Aqsara'i goes even further back in time for his source material; he uses about a third of the *Tactica* of Aelian, written in Greek during the reign of the Roman emperor Hadrian around 106 AD.[22]

438

The 'Mirrors for Princes' Literature

This genre was widespread in the medieval Islamic world. Such works gave advice to kings, princes and governors on how to rule, and they often included whole chapters on military matters. Again it is prudent to remember that they reflect model rather than actual practice, advice rather than information. They too have their roots in the pre-Islamic period, especially in Sasanian Iran.

The Book of Government by Nizam al-Mulk [23]

Nizam al-Mulk (d. 485/1092) wrote this work for the Seljuq sultan Malikshah. In it he includes chapters on spies, couriers, the ethnic composition of the army, hostages and the preparation of arms and equipment for war.

The Wisdom of Royal Glory by Yusuf Khass Hajib

Written in 1069 in Kashgar in Central Asia under the Karakhanid dynasty by Yusuf Khass Hajib, the *Wisdom of Royal Glory* is the oldest surviving monument of Islamic literature in a Turkic language. It is a work in the Mirrors for Princes genre and advises the ruler on how to govern. Apart from the language in which it is written, this work, despite its distant origin, is very similar to other works of this kind written in Arabic or Persian. These two examples of the Mirrors for Princes literature have been selected as useful source material for this chapter because they deal respectively with the Seljuq armies (which operated not just in Iran but also in Iraq and Syria) and with the Turkish military tradition (and of course Turks provided much of the manpower of the Muslim armies in the Levant).[24]

Figure 7.9 *Seated ruler,* Kitab al-Diryaq (*'The Book of Antidotes'*), c. 1250, Mosul, Iraq

The Composition of the Muslim Armies at the Time of the Crusades

Introduction

The composition of most medieval Muslim armies had long been mixed, embracing varying combinations of tribal warriors, compulsory levies and irregular volunteers, as well as paid professional troops, who were often slaves. From the middle of the ninth century, there was an increased tendency on the part of Muslim rulers to rely on the services of professional armies rather than tribal contingents, Bedouin, Berber or Turcoman, which had often brought them to power and from which they soon wished to distance themselves. These professional armies were not drawn from one area or ethnic group and were based on the acquisition of military slaves (*mamluk*s). Such slave troops were bought in the markets of Central Asia, or obtained as prisoners of war or as gifts from other potentates; at all events, they came from outside the Muslim world (the *dar al-harb*).

They were brought to the court of their new masters, housed nearby in barracks and given a military training plus instruction in the Islamic faith. Rulers believed that such troops, without any tribal bias or previous affiliations in the Islamic world, would give total loyalty to their masters. Turkish knights had acquired a high reputation in horse archery and formed an important part of the contingents of professional soldiers used by the 'Abbasid caliphs from the ninth century onwards.[25]

Smail rightly stresses the composite nature of those Muslim armies which were mustered for large military enterprises, and this is clearly revealed in the Islamic chronicles. A sultan or commander would call on the provincial governors with their contingents and other auxiliaries, including urban militia forces and Turcoman or Kurdish tribal contingents.[26] For smaller engagements a standing force (*'askar*) was usually enough. Before the emergence of the great military commanders of the twelfth century – Zengi, Nur al-Din and Saladin – the Muslim armies lacked effective leadership against the Franks and were prone to disorder and dispute. They lacked staying power and quarrelled over the spoils of war. A notorious example was the conduct of Il-Ghazi, the Artuqid ruler of Mardin (and for a short time Aleppo), who celebrated his victory over Roger of Antioch at Balat in 513/1119 by indulging in excessive bouts of drinking.[27] Instead of following up his success by moving immediately on Antioch, Il-Ghazi allowed his troops to disperse with their booty.[28]

Figure 7.10 *Plans for mobilising troops in battle,* furusiyya *manuscript, c. 1500, Egypt*

The Turkish Heritage: The Seljuq Armies

Whilst it is clear, as we saw in Chapter 2, that the Seljuq sultans in the eastern Islamic world exerted very little effort to fight the Franks,

the influence of the Seljuq empire and of the Turks generally on the military heritage of the Levant in the twelfth and thirteenth centuries was very strong. Nur al-Din and Saladin stood firmly in military traditions which came from the Eastern Islamic world.

The Role of the Turcomans

Since their irruption into the Islamic world in the first half of the eleventh century, the Turcomans had proved to be something of a loose cannon. They were an unavoidable fact of life; they could not be dislodged and, as time went on, they continued to move into and across the Islamic world from its eastern perimeter to the western-most parts of Asia Minor, and it became increasingly clear that they were inside the Islamic world for good. Their relationship with the Seljuq sultans and military commanders was complex and often turbulent. In the Crusader context they were often an important element in the Muslim military machine.

In Iran in the eleventh century the Turcoman tribesmen had paved the way for the eventual seizure of the eastern Islamic world by the Seljuqs, a family which indeed came from their ranks. Soon, however, a rift seems to have developed between the Turcomans, who retained their perennial nomadic way of life, and their Seljuq overlords, who were tempted to adopt concepts of power and government alien to the traditions of the steppe. The presence of large groups of lightly Islamicised and even marauding nomads was often inimical to the security of both city and countryside and the Seljuq sultans encour-aged the Turcomans to move to the borders of Seljuq territory, towards the Caucasus and Asia Minor and away from the centres of Seljuq power in Iran. There, on the periphery of the Islamic world, they functioned, according to the Muslim sources, as warriors for the faith (*ghazis*). They are often mentioned in the sources as being called on to provide troops if there was a concerted Muslim effort against the Franks.

In the Islamic sources the activities of the Turcomans are por-trayed as *jihad*. But this high-sounding title cannot be taken at face value. It is even debatable whether they were at this point more than superficially Islamicised. Their piecemeal but persistent erosion of infidel territory seems rather to have been the continuation of their time-honoured means of survival, the opportunistic raid. They led a precarious and hard life and were always prone to the lure of booty. This motive led them on many occasions to accept the call from the leaders of the Muslim Counter-Crusade as part of the Islamic con-tingents in engagements against the Crusaders. But it was precisely their lack of deep religious commitment, or of any supra-tribal loyalty, that made them so unreliable in the early Muslim military encounters with the Franks.

Despite their very different lifestyle, the Turkish nomads were admired by Muslim writers of the Middle Ages for their military prowess and qualities of endurance. Sharaf al-Zaman Tahir Marvazi,

Figure 7.11 Enthroned ruler and attendants, underglaze painted ceramic dish, early thirteenth century, Kashan, Iran

Nizam al-Mulk, it was, however, necessary, in addition to cavalry, that 'the names of four thousand unmounted men of all races should always be kept on the rolls'. Of these one thousand were for the exclusive use of the sultan and three thousand were for the retinues of governors and commanders 'so as to be ready for any emergency'.[35]

It is important to remember that many of the Turkish military commanders in Syria and Palestine in the early twelfth century – men such as Il-Ghazi, Tughtegin and Zengi – had come to prominence in the military service of the Seljuq sultans, and they must have passed on many of the features of the Seljuq military system to the independent rulers of the Levant. So the blueprint of Nizam al-Mulk may well have been followed there, to some extent at least.

The Fatimid Armies

The Fatimid armies were made up of very disparate elements. Just as the Seljuqs had come to power on the basis of nomadic Turcoman military support but had rapidly distanced themselves from this often precarious assistance in favour of a paid standing army, so too the Fatimids had relied initially on Berber military strength but had soon seen the wisdom of diversifying the composition of their army. Various ethnic groups are mentioned as having formed part of the Fatimid armies: these include Berbers, Armenians, Sudanese and Turks, as well as Arab Bedouins (cf. colour plate 3).

The Fatimids used troops from a variety of sources: the easterners (*mashariqa*) who came from the countries east of Egypt, the westerners (*maghariba*) from North Africa, and the blacks (*sudanis*) from sub-Saharan Africa. Such diversity could on occasion prevent one group from gaining too great an influence in the armies as a whole, but it also aroused factional strife in times of political weakness. The Fatimid armies contained both professional troops and irregular militia. In the latter category were the Bedouins from Egypt and southern Palestine, as well as Turkish and other mercenaries.[36]

Hamblin describes the Fatimid army in the three battles of Ramla (1101–5) as being 'a medium-sized but well-developed fighting machine composed of various ethnic units and arms'. It lacked leadership and motivation.[37] The Fatimid army in the field, as Hamblin and Brett contend on the basis of the Arabic sources, numbered between 5,000 and 10,000 men.

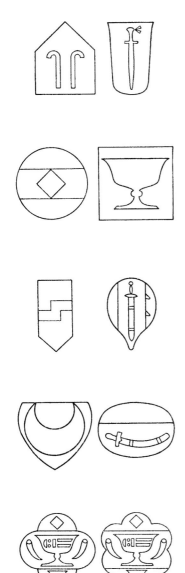

Figure 7.14 *Standard Mamluk blazons of office showing the types of shield employed, thirteenth–fifteenth centuries, Egypt and Syria*

The Armies of Saladin and His Successors, the Ayyubids

Like those of his predecessors, Zengi and Nur al-Din, Saladin's army was made up to a large extent of Kurdish and Turkish professional fighting men. Saladin also had an elite corps which was composed of slave soldiers (*mamluk*s). Apart from this bodyguard of his who were attached to him by bonds of personal loyalty, he relied for military support on the power of blood links between himself and his sons,

444

Figure 7.15 *Two warriors, ink drawing on paper, eleventh century, Egypt*

nephews, brothers, cousins and other relatives whom he had established in provincial posts throughout his territories. In other areas he hoped for the honouring of alliances made through the usual mixture of coercion and inducements.

On occasion he also used the services of mercenaries of various ethnic origins as well as tribal troops, whether Turcomans or Arab Bedouin. Despite the Kurdish origins of Saladin and his descendants, the Ayyubids, their armies contained more Turks than Kurds.[38] At the battle of Hattin Saladin also had in his ranks volunteer *jihad* fighters (*al-mutatawwi'a*) who are described as being ascetics and Sufis. Each of them asked Saladin's permission to execute one of the Templars and Hospitallers who had been captured during the battle.[39]

The Mamluk Armies

There is considerably more information in the sources on the Mamluk armies than on those of earlier periods and extensive research has been done in this area, notably by Ayalon. The Mamluk military was characterised by unusual cohesion and unity. Based as it was in Cairo, which was the cynosure of all Mamluk eyes, its formalised structures were repeated in microcosm in the provinces and were the

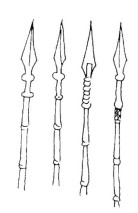

Figure 7.16 *Bedouin lances, al-Hariri, al-Maqamat ('The Assemblies'), c. 1230, Iraq*

445

main factor contributing to the longevity of the dynasty. Sultans and governors could come and go, sometimes with remarkable speed, but the firm foundation of this remarkable political state was its military organisation and the loyalty it engendered amongst those who belonged to its military elite. Baybars relied on a caste of commanders who were, like him, Mamluks. These commanders were assigned the revenues from pieces of land or other endowments (*iqta*'s) a portion of which was distributed to the commanders' own *mamluk*s. Everybody within the elite had a stake in its continuing stability. The Mamluk army had three principal units: the sultan's *mamluk*s, the *mamluk*s of the commanders, and the *halqa* troops, a corps of freeborn cavalry. The Mamluk sultans were able to replenish their supplies of troops by the import of new Turkish slaves from the Caucasus and Central Asia along the trade routes through Anatolia. The Mamluk state could draw on far more troops than the Franks were ever able to do. Moreover, when the time came to embark on the systematic destruction of Frankish castles, settlements and ports in Syria, the Mamluks could draw on tens of thousands of auxiliary troops – Turkish, Kurdish and Mongol – to help in the carrying out of this task.

Military Education and Equestrian Exercises
in the Mamluk Period

A great deal of scholarly work has been produced on the military education of the Mamluks.[40] When the *mamluk* arrived as a young boy from the steppes of southern Russia or the Caucasus, he was housed in barracks in Cairo and given a rigorous education; his curriculum included the study of the Qur'an and the *hadith*, but, not surprisingly, the emphasis was also on the arts of war and especially equestrian skills. But the religious dimension of the military education of the *mamluk* was crucial. His identification with his new faith of Islam complemented his superb skills in the arts of war.[41]

Figure 7.17 *Polo players, enamelled and gilded glass beaker, c. 1260–70, Damascus, Syria*

Figure 7.18 Horseman, al-Aqsara'i, Nihayat al-Su'l ('An End to Questioning'), 767/1366, Egypt

The Role of the maydan

From the Umayyad period onwards, horse-racing was a popular sport among the Muslim elite, and one in which the caliphs themselves participated.[42] At the ʿAbbasid caliphal capital of Samarra there survives a clover-leaf racing track. The chronicles suggest that the role of the hippodrome (*maydan*) was particularly important in the time of Nur al-Din. He encouraged the construction of hippodromes in Aleppo, for example, so that his troops could be drilled there. In the new quarter of the city known as the 'Turcomans' quarter', the Turcoman troops carried out their exercise drills on a nearby *maydan*.[43]

This custom of drilling the troops on *maydan*s was elaborated by the Mamluk rulers of Egypt into a major spectator sport. They took the training of their troops very seriously. Many of the *maydan*s mentioned in the chronicles were constructed under the Mamluks, and Sultan Baybars, in particular, was keen to build *maydan*s and to attend performances by the cavalry as an enthusiastic spectator. Special equestrian exercises were devised to produce the best possible

Figure 7.19 Knight with a deliberately ignited shield, al-Aqsara'i, Nihayat al-Su'l ('An End to Questioning'), 767/1366, Egypt

cavalry troops. The *maydan*s formed the focal point for the carrying out of these exercises as well as for playing sports such as polo or *qabaq* – a game which came originally from the steppes of Central Asia and involved shooting arrows from a moving horse at a gourd placed at the top of a high pole – and *birjas*, in which mounted horsemen threw palm staves. Other games were played with a mace and javelin. The importance of the *maydan* and its central role as a public manifestation of military strength and artistry are attested by the frequent presence of the sultan and his court in specially constructed pavilions around the *maydan*.[44] From these pavilions the sultan could watch the entertainment and to them he could bring foreign dignitaries whom he wished to impress and intimidate. He could then show off his horses, a most prestigious possession, in the nearby stables.

Figure 7.20 Mounted warrior, painted ivory box, twelfth century, Sicily

Mamluk Military Arts

Mamluk troops were trained to use two swords, one in each hand.[45] The level of skill with the sword was very high; the Mamluk knight was trained to know exactly how much or how little harm to inflict on his enemy. The high level of sophistication of movements and skills achieved by Mamluk troops is demonstrated in several illustrated thirteenth-century manuscripts of the work of al-Aqsara'i (see figures on pp. 447, 449–51, 453, 455).[46] The paintings which accompany these manuals show a wide range of equestrian and military expertise. One illustration depicts two riders bearing lances in a jousting exercise, passing at the gallop. Another painting shows an elaborate equestrian exercise in which four riders canter clockwise round the pool of the *maydan* in a formalised manner reminiscent of today's synchronised swimming exercises (figure 7.24). Yet another drawing shows the riders cantering anti-clockwise round a circular pool in the *maydan*. There is a total symmetry in the spacing of the riders and their horses and even in the flowers and the ripples of the water. The illustrations show the riders performing exercises with

Figure 7.21 Combat scene, manuscript painting, seventeenth century, Iran

One of the most poignant tales related by Usama concerns a Muslim warrior, a Kurd named Mayyah who had just got married and went out to fight against the Franks:

> with full armor but wearing over his coat of mail a red garment of his bridal clothes, making himself especially conspicuous. A Frankish knight smote him with a lance and killed him (may Allah's mercy rest upon his soul!).[61]

The lance in general was not just used against a human enemy, of course. Usama gives a lively account of how he killed a lion by rushing at it with his lance.[62]

In the Mamluk period, there might have been changes in the way in which the lance was deployed, but its popularity was uncontested,[63] and training in its use was very important. The lance figures very prominently in the manual of al-Aqsara'i; perhaps the popularity of the lance is a reflection of the dramatic way in which it had to be used, its status as a 'virile', heroic weapon, as well as its key place in the tournaments and equestrian exercises in the *maydan*.[64] In the popular imagination the lance could grow to gargantuan proportions. In one medieval epic, the amazon Fatima Dhat al-Himma points out that the lances of the Franks could 'swell to monstrous size, with composite shafts built up of eighteen iron tubes'.[65] One is reminded of Goliath, with his spear like a weaver's beam, though Freudian interpretations also come to mind.

Swords and Daggers

Although the lance and the bow were probably the most effective weapons for an individual warrior, the sword enjoyed a high status in the Islamic world. As early as the ninth century, the Islamic philosopher

Figure 7.27 Mamluk targets (casks) for lance and archery practice, furusiyya manuscript, c. 1500, Egypt

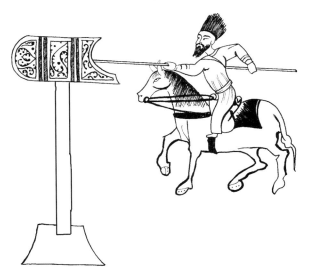

453

al-Kindi (d. after 252/865) wrote two works on swords: one entitled *Kinds of Swords and Iron* and the other *That with which Swords and Iron Are Treated so that the Edges Are Not Blunted and They Are Not Dulled*.[66] A copy of the first of these was apparently in Saladin's possession.[67]

There is frequent reference in the sources to the sword of 'Ali, the Prophet's cousin and son-in-law, which was called Dhu'l-Fiqar. The sword is the weapon *par excellence* that is mentioned metaphorically in the religious honorific titulature of Islam – titles such as 'The Sword of the Faith (*Sayf al-din*) and 'The Sword of the State' (*Sayf al-dawla*) were bestowed by the caliph on military and political leaders and were very highly valued by the recipients. Not surprisingly, the sword was the proudest possession of a Muslim warrior. Usually, the sword used by Muslim warriors in the Crusading period was straight and made of iron or iron with a steel edge.[68] Swords were identified

Plate 7.1 Islamic swords, iron and steel, undated but late medieval, Egypt and Syria

454

Figure 7.28 Sword play,
al-Aqsara'i, Nihayat al-Su'l
('An End to Questioning'),
773/1371, Egypt

by their place of origin, and those with blades that came from China
and India were especially sought after. The famous Baptistère of St
Louis depicts a number of different kinds of swords which were all,
it seems, in use in Mamluk Egypt in the thirteenth century. The
sheaths were also greatly praised; they were made of wood and
covered with materials as diverse as velvet, damask, metal or fine
shagreen. Abu Shama relates that the Muslims wore their swords at
their waist but that Nur al-Din, having heard that the Prophet used
to hang his sword from his shoulder with a baldric, adopted this
custom for himself and for his army.[69] This statement may well be
part of the chronicler's desire to highlight the piety of Nur al-Din;
certainly the practice did not become widespread.

Usama relates a number of instances of blows administered by
sharp swords and daggers. An extraordinary tale is that of Usama's
father who in anger struck his groom with his sword still in its
sheath: 'The sword cut through the outfit, the silver sandal, a mantle
and a woolen shawl which the groom had on, and then cut through
the bone of his elbow. The whole forearm fell off.'[70]

Al-Qazwini, however, praises Frankish swords made in Europe:
'They forge very sharp swords there, and the swords of Frank-land are
keener than the swords of India.'[71]

Figure 7.29 Sword of Badr
al-Din Lu'lu', Kitab al-Aghani
('The Book of Songs'),
614/1217–18, Mosul, Iraq

Figure 7.30 Horseman with
sword, al-Aqsara'i, Nihayat
al-Su'l ('An End to
Questioning'), 773/1371, Egypt

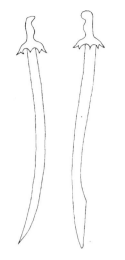

Maces, Axes and Other Heavy Striking Instruments

There was a range of heavy weapons which were designed for smiting the enemy in close combat. As al-Tarsusi so graphically puts it, they can be used in any way which 'brings death and destruction'.[72] He goes on to say that some such instruments are made exclusively of iron, others have an iron head and a wooden handle, while still others have a round head covered with large or small iron teeth.[73] Two terms usually denoted the mace: *dabbus* and *'amud*. Al-Tarsusi describes the *dabbus* as being made entirely of iron – 'It will immediately break every body it encounters, making clear the coming of death'[74] – whilst the *'amud* had an iron head and a wooden handle. At the battle of Mansura in 1250, Ibn Wasil reports that 'the Franks were massacred one and all with sword and club'.[75]

The weapon known as the *tabar* was a large axe with a semicircular blade and a wooden or metal handle. In Mamluk times it was carried by a special corps, the *tabardariyya* (plate 7.2). The dagger (*khanjar*) was also used in hand-to-hand fighting.

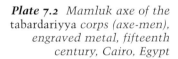

Figure 7.31 Seljuq swords, probably thirteenth century, Turkey

Bows

Al-Tarsusi covers the terminology for different kinds of bows in some detail and he also describes how bows should be made.[76] He

Plate 7.2 Mamluk axe of the tabardariyya corps (axe-men), engraved metal, fifteenth century, Cairo, Egypt

Figure 7.32 *Mace* (jukan) *of the Mamluk sultan Tuman Ba'i, early sixteenth century, Cairo, Egypt*

mentions the leg bow (*qaws al-rijl*) which was the smallest and could be loaded by standing on the bow. Another larger portable bow was called the *'aqqar*. A third type was known as the grasshopper (*husban*); it had a tube through which short arrows, stones and bottles or breakable capsules (literally 'eggs') containing Greek fire (*naft*) were shot: 'The bottle departs like an arrow with the force of propulsion and reaches its desired goal; its encounter with bodies breaks it and it sets alight everything with which it comes into contact.'[77]

There was also a mechanical crossbow, the *qaws al-ziyar*, which was mounted on supports and was used in sieges. According to al-Tarsusi, the *ziyar* 'needs a number of men to pull its string . . . it is placed up against towers and similar obstacles and nobody can withstand it'.[78]

Al-Tarsusi gives a clear picture of the intricacies of carrying several weapons at a time, and especially on horseback. He suggests that the archer should have two bows with him.[79]

The composite bow, constructed in three to five sections of alternating stiff and flexible elements, with a strongly double-curved outline, reached its most sophisticated form with the medieval Turks and Mongols.[80] Such bows had a maximum range of more than 800 yards, though it seems that they were truly effective at distances of some 300 yards or less. Although the arrows shot from these bows could cover such great distances, they were exceptionally penetrating at shorter range. Those defending a fortress or a city would shoot

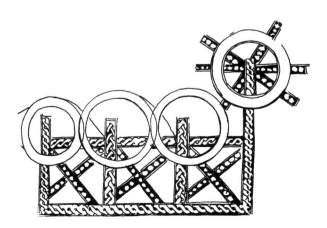

Figure 7.33 *Mechanism for a triple bow from a treatise on war,* Tabsirat arbab al-albab *('The Perception of Those with Understanding'), written by al-Tarsusi for Saladin, c. 583/1187, probably Syria*

Figure 7.34 Cross-bow training, Kitab al-makhzun ('Book of Treasure'), 875/1470, probably Egypt

arrows at the besiegers from oversize crossbows mounted on the walls.

Although in Crusader times it was the horse archers who had most prominence and were justifiably feared and admired by the Franks, it should not be forgotten that there was a long tradition of infantry archers in the Islamic world. The Fatimid army contained Sudanese infantry archers,[81] and Usama mentions 'about twenty footmen of Armenian troops who were good archers'.[82]

Figure 7.35 Archer, glazed ceramic bowl, twelfth–thirteenth centuries, Shirvan, southern Caucasus

Shields

Al-Tarsusi mentions a variety of shields: 'Each nation has its own technique for the manufacture of them.'[83]

The round shield is called *turs* and was made of wood, metal or hide.[84] The kite-shaped shield, known in the Muslim world as the *tariqa*, is, according to al-Tarsusi, used by the Franks and the Byzantines: 'It is a long shield made in such a way as to hide the knight and the foot soldier. It is rounded at the top and narrows down into a point.'[85]

A third type of shield is the *januwiyya* which is like the *tariqa* but is made so that it can be held on the ground. It is used by foot soldiers and 'in a row it forms a fortress which resists archers'.[86]

The Bab al-Nasr (Gate of Victory) in Cairo was built in 1087 by the Fatimid vizier Badr al-Jamali.[87] One of the outstanding features of this gate are the shields that decorate it (plates 7.3–7.4). Shalem argues convincingly that shields were an important symbol of Fatimid hegemony:[88] the Gate of Victory depicts circular and kite-shaped shields, thus showing that both kinds were known and probably used by the Fatimids.

Figure 7.36 Helmeted soldier holding shield with multiple bosses, glazed ceramic statuette, late twelfth century, Raqqa, Syria

Although the primary purpose of the shield was the protection of as much of the body as possible, it was also an object of display, a Levantine tradition that goes back for millennia. The shield could be made of a variety of materials, including polished wood, wood covered with shagreen, untanned leather, horse, ass, camel or giraffe skin or varnished or painted leather.

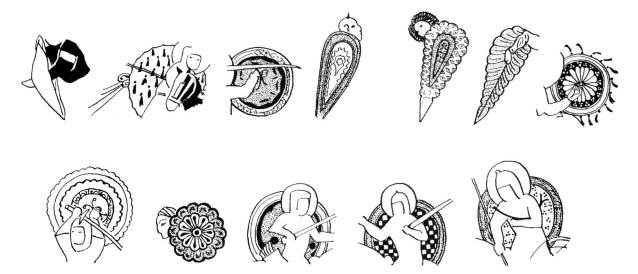

The implication of Usama's story about Tancred's putting out the right eye of a Muslim warrior, Hasanun, is that the shield was held high up and that the lance was held in the right hand. As Tancred allegedly said: 'Rather put out his right eye, so that when he carries his shield his left eye will be covered, and he will be no more able to see anything.'[89]

Figure 7.37 Shield types, Varqa va Gulshah ('*Varqa and Gulshah'*), c. 1250, Turkey

Armour

Armour was certainly not for everybody. According to Usama, whose evidence is supported by roughly contemporary works of art, the common foot soldier usually went without mail. Armour remained the prerogative of a small, rich elite, even in the highly militarised society of Mamluk Egypt; the horses of such warriors also had protective armour. Even when it was worn, it may not have been put on until the going became hard, probably because of the sheer discomfort of wearing it in the intense Levantine heat.

Usama's memoirs mention various types of armour. He remarks on one occasion that his quilted jerkin or brigandine (*kazaghand*) was 'furnished with two coats of mail, one on top of the other'.[90]

Later on, he describes this protective armour in greater detail:

> The jerkin enclosed a Frankish coat of mail extending to the bottom of it, with another coat of mail on top of it reaching as far as the middle. Both were equipped with the proper linings, felt pads, rough silk and rabbit's hair.[91]

Figure 7.38 Kite-shaped shield, glazed ceramic bowl, late twelfth century, Raqqa, Syria

Whether the 'Frankish coat of mail' was an item which he had acquired through the spoils of war, or as a gift from one of his Frankish friends, is not clear. Yet another possibility is that the

Plate 7.3 *Bab al-Nasr, 480/1087,*
Cairo, Egypt

(Creswell Photographic Archive, Ashmolean Museum, Oxford, neg. C. 3433)

Plate 7.4 *Bab al-Nasr, detail showing shields, 480/1087, Cairo, Egypt*

(Creswell Photographic Archive, Ashmolean Museum, Oxford, neg. C. 3431)

Plate 7.5 *Turkish foot-soldiers wearing splint armour, thirteenth century, Turkey*

Figure 7.39 *Warrior in mail armour, glazed ceramic cup, c. 1200, al-Mina, Syria*

Figure 7.40 *Soldier in mail hauberk, inlaid metal pen-case, early thirteenth century, probably Iraq*

Muslims called a particular type of coat of mail 'Frankish', just as they referred to – and often used – 'Frankish mangonels'.

Coats of mail were worn under other clothes; Usama cites an example of a Frankish horseman wearing a green and yellow silk tunic; he smote the Frank with his lance but as the latter had linked mail under his tunic, Usama's lance did not wound him.[92] On another occasion, Usama tells the story of how his father was wounded by a pike because his servant had not fastened the hooks on the side of his long mail.[93]

Allowing for exaggeration, Usama suggests that coats of mail were extremely resistant to the lance's thrust. He tells the story of his paternal cousin, Khitam, who made a charge single-handed against the Franks. They let him into their midst and then set about him with their lances, overthrowing him and striking his horse: 'Reversing their lances, they then began to dig into him with them. But Khitam was wearing a coat of mail, the links of which were so strong that their lances could have no effect upon it.'[94]

Figure 7.41 *Warrior wearing a 'corset cuirass' with lamellar and laminated armour, Firdawsi,* Shahnama *('Book of Kings' – the Great Mongol* Shahnama)*, c. 1330, Tabriz, Iran*

462

The Franks, too, were equipped, according to Usama, with very effective armour. He tells the story of a Frank 'wearing double-linked mail and carrying a spear in his hand, but not equipped with a shield'. In spite of various blows administered to him by a Turk with a sword he escaped totally unscathed, presumably because of the effectiveness of his armour.[95]

But perhaps the most revealing episode concerns Saladin himself and one of the attempts on his life which occurred in 571/1175. Ibn al-Athir provides considerable detail:

Figure 7.42 Foot soldier, inlaid bronze bowl of Aybak, c. 1250, Damascus, Syria

> An assassin attacked him and struck him with a knife on his head and wounded him. Were it not for the fact that the chain skullcap (*al-mighfar al-zarad*) was under his pointed bonnet (*qalansuwa*) he would have killed him. Saladin seized the assassin's hand with his own hand. Although he could not prevent him from striking altogether he only struck weakly. The assassin kept on striking him in his neck with the knife. He had on a quilted jerkin (*kazaghand*)[96] and the blows were falling on the collar of the jerkin and cutting through it and the chain mail was preventing them (the blows) from reaching his neck . . . Saladin rode to his tent, like one terrified, hardly believing his escape.[97]

Here, then, is a clear illustration of the protection which coats of mail and helmets could give. Body armour and the shirts worn under it were often covered with Qur'anic inscriptions and indeed these were believed to have a protective power.[98]

The importance of an efficacious helmet is emphasised. Speaking of a knight called Rafi' al-Kilabi, Usama writes:

> He had on his head a helmet without a visor. He looked back in order to see whether he had a chance to halt and attack his pursuers. As he turned aside, a jagged arrow hit him and gashed his throat, thus slaying him.[99]

But Usama also mentions that his own father wore on his head a helmet with a nasal protection. When a javelin hit the nasal protection, it made his nose bleed but otherwise he was unhurt.[100] A fourteenth-century Mamluk military manual written by Ibn Mangli offers the following counsel on putting on a helmet:

Figure 7.43 Helmet of the Mamluk sultan Barsbay (reigned 825–41/1422–38), Egypt

> It is necessary that the buttons of the skull cap of the helmet on the inner side of the lining of the helmet are passed through loops so that the helmet is not detached from the cap . . . The interlining of the helmets should be made of fine holes. This will protect against the impact which a heavy blow would make on the helmet . . . And the point of the device is that the numerous holes in the fibre will diffuse the substance of the blow.[101]

Figure 7.44 Helmet types, Varqa va Gulshah (*'Varqa and Gulshah'*), c. 1250, Turkey

It is interesting to note that when a person was wearing armour it was not easy to recognise them. This could lead to some unusual disclosures; according to Usama, there were women fighting (cf. colour plate 8) during the siege by the Isma'ilis of his home citadel of Shayzar, but as they were wearing full armour the sex of these warriors was not known until after the fighting.[102] In his important article on Muslim arms and armour, Mayer sums up as follows what the typical Muslim commander of the Ayyubid period must have worn: as armour, a helmet, a shirt of mail, leggings and boots with spurs; and as arms, a sword, a dagger or knife, a lance, a javelin and a shield.[103]

The Views of Nizam al-Mulk on the Ceremonial Role of Arms and Armour

Nizam al-Mulk was well aware of the ceremonial importance of arms and armour and of their role in the life of the court as well as the battlefield. He suggests that the ruler's bodyguard should have two hundred sets of weapons kept in readiness for them, of which: 'Twenty sword-belts and twenty shields should be (decorated) with gold, and one hundred and eighty belts and shields with silver, together with pikestaffs.'[104]

Figure 7.45 Armour types, Varqa va Gulshah (*'Varqa and Gulshah'*), c. 1250, Turkey

Of course, these were troops who had an important role on special occasions. Weapons excited awe and wonder, especially decorated

Figure 7.46 *Helmet of the Mamluk sultan Tuman Ba'i, early sixteenth century, Cairo, Egypt*

ones, 'studded with gold, jewels and other ornaments', and they were brought out at state ceremonies to impress visiting dignitaries.[105]

> There should be at least fifty mace-bearers constantly at court, twenty with golden maces, twenty with silver ones and ten with large clubs. The equipment and outfit of the guard must be of the finest and he must be surrounded with the utmost possible pomp.[106]

Some faint reflection of this splendid kind of spectacle survives in the fragmentary frescoes which were found in the royal throne-room at the Ghaznavid site of Lashkar-i Bazar in south-western Afghanistan, datable to c.1020 (figure 7.47).[107] The same theme occurs, this time in sculpture, in the roughly contemporary palace at Ghazna, in southern Afghanistan.[108] This iconography was also known in the lands bordering the Islamic world; the Armenian historian Thomas Artsruni describes frescoes of the bodyguard of King Gagik of Vaspurakan adorning the throne-room of the royal palace at Aght'amar in eastern Anatolia in the early tenth century.[109]

The Social Role of Arms and Armour

Arms and armour were much prized in a militarised society such as that of the Muslim states of the Levant in the twelfth and thirteenth centuries. They were an obvious target of looters after battle. They were part of the currency of luxury goods offered and accepted by rulers and commanders and were used to demonstrate prestige. In 610/1214 the Ayyubid ruler al-Zafir celebrated the birth of his son and heir, offering the new-born child amongst other gifts two coats of mail, two helmets and a decorated harness all encrusted with precious stones, and similarly ornate lances.[110] Saddles were often very

Figure 7.47 Turkish bodyguard, fresco in palace, eleventh century, Lashkar-i Bazar, Afghanistan

ornate and were offered as gifts. Usama describes an exceptionally fine saddle which had been made in Ghazza: 'This saddle was brought with me from Syria on one of the extra horses led by my side. It was quilted, had black stripes and was of extraordinarily beautiful effect.'[111]

466

At festival times the army was very much in evidence. In Ayyubid and Mamluk times troops would don their best costumes and parade in the hippodrome (*maydan*) of the town. Games of polo, jousts and simulated combats would be organised in the cities of Ayyubid Syria and in Mamluk Cairo, as part of the celebrations.[112]

Fortifications in the Levant in the Twelfth and Thirteenth Centuries

General Introductory Remarks

It should be stressed at the outset that there are significant differences between town fortifications and castles in the medieval Islamic period. In the case of towns, the fortifications consisted of a long wall around the area of settlement. This wall was made as tall and thick as resources allowed; and its role was purely defensive. The principal technology of a city wall lay in its gates: for example in the approach to the gate, sometimes by a drawbridge as at Aleppo, and in the use of successive supplementary gates, bent entrances or machicolation.

As for the castle, its purpose could be offensive as well as defensive, and this was especially true of Crusader castles which were placed in positions where they could do the most harm to the Muslims, denying them entry to important areas (they were often placed at the head of a valley), preventing Muslims from moving freely and threatening their lines of communication. Crusader castles were, moreover, garrisoned by very few people – the Crusaders were, after all, always a beleaguered minority – and, to offset this disadvantage, the defences of their castles had to be much more subtle and multi-layered than those of a city wall.

With the notable exception of the castles of another beleaguered minority, the Assassins, whose castles, often intervisible, clustered in northern Syria, Muslim castles do not generally serve the same functions. The indigenous Armenian Christians, however, who were also a minority, faced the self-same problem and concentrated their strength in castles. Structures in Cilicia such as Sis and Gökvelioğlu were built to last and Armenian craftsmen were often employed by the Muslims in the construction of city walls, as in Cairo. The city walls of Edessa, which had a large Armenian population, bear lengthy medieval Armenian inscriptions;[113] they are of excellent quality and are technologically superior to most of the Muslim castles in Syria.

Almost all Crusader castles were built to withstand siege; Muslim castles were not – the Crusaders were always too few to inflict significant harm on them. A few men had to do the work of many on the Crusader side, whilst the Muslims were always plentiful in number. Given this fundamental difference of approach and function between Crusader and Muslim castles, it is unlikely that the Muslims would feel the need to make significant borrowings in the art of castle fortification from the Crusaders, even though the Crusader

Figure 7.48 *Iranian warrior,* Kitab-i Samak 'Ayyar *('Book of Samak the Adventurer'), c. 1330, Shiraz, Iran*

Figure 7.49 *Iranian warrior,* Firdawsi, Shahnama *('Book of Kings'), c. 1320, Iran*

castles were manifestly superior in design and execution.

The Mamluk sultan Baybars razed many of the Crusader castles to the ground since he had learned the hard way that a small number of men in such castles could inflict a disproportionate amount of damage on the Muslims. The Crusader castle phenomenon in the Levant was linked to very specific circumstances which did not recur – a conquering minority attempted to maximise its resources and utilised its superior technological skills in building castles – and this phenomenon resulted in inventions and devices which were tailored to those circumstances.

As for the Muslims, they certainly learned to besiege the Crusader castles, but once the Crusaders had departed from the Levant the Muslims did not build castles like these. There was no need. Quite apart from the very specific circumstances and the special European background which had engendered Crusader castles, they had been extremely expensive to build. Indeed they had been made possible only by an enormous economic input from western Europe and by desperate necessity. The Crusaders built and rebuilt steadily throughout the period of their occupation and vastly exceeded the output of labour that might have been expected from their limited manpower.

Crusader castles have survived because of their magnificent building techniques. Muslim castles have not fared so well. The Crusaders did not build on poor existing foundations, preferring instead to construct *de novo*. They took few short cuts, realising that there was no substitute for massive squared masonry, although it was so expensive and above all time-consuming to produce. Large blocks of stone were used to construct thick walls of ashlar masonry; this task required a large body of skilled craftsmen and thus an enormous financial input from western Europe.

Muslim castles, on the other hand, have tended not to survive because their handiwork was of significantly lower quality. The Muslims constructed castles made of brick or of rubble masonry, not of large blocks of squared stone carefully fitted together. Their castles were too big and were built too quickly and unimaginatively. This is not to say that Muslim architects and masons were unskilled in the art of fortification. On the contrary, they could on occasion emulate the Crusader achievement; but their finest work is found in city fortifications, such as Damascus, or Diyarbakr, whose mile upon mile of multi-towered black basalt walls are among the most impressive medieval fortifications in the whole world. Conversely no Crusader walled city has survived. If the Muslims had wanted to borrow from Crusader skills in building castles they would have needed to be erecting the same kind of structure. Elaborate castles with concentric defences, moats, inner and outer wards, a glacis and other defensive features were not necessary for a Muslim castle in which often a simple keep sufficed. Such Muslim castles – Shayzar, for example (figures 7.50 and 7.51) – were little more than strong points and places of temporary refuge; they acted mainly as the seat of the local princeling.

Frankish Castles and Strong Points

A vast amount of scholarship exists on Crusader castles.[114] The focus here will be on how the medieval Muslims viewed them. The most visible reminder of the Franks' presence in the Muslim Near East is the string of castles which they built or rebuilt in the twelfth and thirteenth centuries in Palestine and Syria. When they arrived in Syria they found that many fortifications already existed; these they took and strengthened, as for example in the area of Tripoli and Antioch. They also built a network of new castles and towers. With their perennial problem of manpower, their strategy of erecting castles and towers along key routes was an appropriate and effective tactic for them to attempt to defend themselves. Pringle has pointed out that the most common type of rural building erected by the Franks was the tower, of which more than eighty have been recorded.[115]

The function of the castle or tower was, of course, to provide shelter as well as to offer a good defensive and attacking position. A high place was useful because of the greater visibility it afforded over the surrounding countryside (with the possibility of communication by flares or heliograph with other such fortresses). An elevated position also increased the speed and range of missiles and their eventual impact and impeded access by medieval artillery and sapping on the part of an enemy. The Frankish practice of building fortresses in the sea – Sidon (Château de Mer), Maraqiyya, Ladhiqiyya and Ayas,

Figure 7.50 *Castle, aerial view from the north, twelfth–thirteenth centuries, Shayzar, Syria*

469

Figure 7.51 *Castle,*
twelfth–thirteenth centuries,
Shayzar, Syria

to cite but a few examples – was an added problem for the Muslims
with their traditional distrust of maritime warfare. The Franks also
fortified the island of Arwad, north-west of Tripoli.

The Frankish castles were not just defensive structures, of course.
They were centres of power and symbols of the occupation of an
area; they were also residential centres where it was customary to
store arms, water and provisions. When, for example, Saladin took
the citadel of Sahyun in 584/1188, he found cows, beasts of burden,
provisions and other items.[116] In the case of Shaqif (Beaufort), al-Maqrizi
records, no doubt with gross exaggeration, that Saladin took away
20,000 sheep.[117]

Muslim Views of Frankish Castles and Fortifications

Medieval Muslim chroniclers are well informed about Frankish castles
and often mention them. Ibn al-Furat, for example, gives a detailed
list of Frankish fortresses and castle towns before undertaking individual accounts of how they were captured by the Muslims.[118]

The Franks were competent in building fortifications both inland
and on the coast. Ibn Jubayr dwells for example, on the formidable
defences of Tyre:

> It has only two gates, one landwards, and the other on the sea,
> which encompasses the city save on one side. The landward gate
> is reached only after passing through three or four posterns in the
> strongly-fortified outer walls that enclose it. The seaward gate is
> flanked by two strong towers and leads into a harbour whose

remarkable situation is unique among maritime cities. The walls of the city enclose it on three sides, and the fourth is confined by a mole bound with cement. Ships enter below the walls and there anchor. Between the two towers stretches a great chain which, when raised, prevents any coming in or going forth, and no ships may pass save when it is lowered.[119]

Small wonder that on several occasions it proved so hard to take.

Muslim writers were also aware of the strategic position of the Frankish castles and why they were placed in particular locations. For example, the castle of Karak, a few miles from the Dead Sea, was built by the Crusader Pagan the Butler in 1142. Ibn Shaddad comments on the harm caused to the Muslims by this castle which blocked the route to Egypt, so that caravans could only set out escorted by large quantities of troops.[120] Since the terrain in this part of Jordan is so forbidding, the principal arterial route has a disproportionate significance, and Karak was ideally placed for the Crusaders to prey on the Muslim traffic along it and to threaten the traditional way to Mecca for the pilgrimage, as already mentioned.

The importance of the network of Frankish castles for the survival of the Franks was fully recognised in the Muslim military strategy against them, especially in the thirteenth century under the determined leadership of Baybars and his successors, whose major military efforts were directed at them. In the twelfth century, however, the Muslims had not yet achieved a decisive superiority over the Crusaders in the open field, and were therefore not yet in a position to embark on a campaign of reducing their fortresses.

Individual Crusader Castles – How the Muslims Saw Them

Sahyun

This castle is now called Qal'at Salah al-Din (Saladin's Castle) and was known to the Crusaders as Saone. Situated in the mountains north-east of Latakia, and set on a ridge between two spectacular ravines, it was described by T. E. Lawrence in a letter to his mother in 1909 as the 'most sensational thing in castle-building I have seen'.[121]

The Muslims at the time of the Crusades shared this admiration for the structure and position of Sahyun. 'Imad al-Din al-Isfahani stresses with his usual literary flourishes how difficult it was to reach the castle when Saladin attacked it in 584/1188–9: 'The way to Sahyun was through valleys and mountain paths, difficult openings, soft flat ground and rough terrain, highlands and low-lying areas.'[122]

Describing the castle itself he writes:

It is a castle on the summit of a mountain between two deep valleys which converge on it and encircle it. The mountain side [of the citadel] is cut off from it by a great deep ditch and a firm wall to which there is no access except by fate and divine decree. The castle is possessed of five walls as if they were five flattened hills, filled with hungry wolves and angry lions.[123]

Ibn Shaddad also writes about Sahyun in some detail on the occasion of Saladin's seizure of it in 584/1188–9. He stresses the castle's inaccessibility, impregnability and careful construction. His undoubted admiration for its handiwork is, of course, a prelude to the main theme, Saladin's glorious victory in taking it by siege.[124]

One may, however, feel a nagging doubt as to whether 'Imad al-Din or Ibn Shaddad had actually seen this castle, for neither of them mention its most spectacular and awe-inspiring feature. To strengthen its defences the Franks had excavated a deep ravine on its most vulnerable east side, thus isolating it from the headland to which its site originally belonged. This task involved the removal of some 170,000 tons of solid rock to create a gorge 50–90 feet wide, 450 feet long and between 60 and 130 feet high. To help carry the drawbridge giving entry to the castle, they left a towering needle of rock in the middle of this man-made gorge. It is tempting to speculate that part of the work was done by conscripted Muslims. Similar rock-cut ditches are found at Karak, Shayzar, the Isma'ili castle of al-Mayniqa and the castle of Lampron in Armenian Cilicia.

It is worth noting that after its fall to Saladin in 1188 the Muslims built within the castle a mosque (with a tall square minaret, probably the work of Qalawun in the 1280s), a small palace, a bath and a cistern, which probably date to the late twelfth or thirteenth century.

Bayt al-ahzan (Known to the Crusaders as Le Chastelet)

This was a castle built by the Templars by 1178 at the latest, close to the west bank of the Jordan. The Muslim chronicler Ibn Abi Tayyi' mentions the enormous costs involved in building it and records that Saladin tried in vain to bribe the Crusaders into demolishing it.[125] The castle was well equipped with provisions and, like Karak, was positioned in a good place to hold up Muslim caravans.[126] No wonder the Muslims dubbed it 'The Abode of Miseries'.

In Rabi' I 575/August-September 1179 – only a year or so after the castle had been built – Saladin managed to capture the castle and to demolish it. A letter from the Qadi al-Fadil to Baghdad gives a detailed description of this imposing edifice:

> The width of the wall exceeded ten cubits: it was cut out of enormous dressed stone slabs, each block of which was seven cubits, more or less. Their number exceeded 20,000 stones. Every stone was secured in its position and fixed in its place for four dinars or more than that.[127]

Lime sealed the stone making it stronger and firmer, 'harder than iron'.[128] Such a description shows an eye for detail combined with undisguised admiration for the building techniques of the Franks – and thus for the Muslim commander who succeeded in capturing such a castle.

Muslim Fortifications

The Muslim approach to defence was somewhat different. Of course, strongholds – many of which were inherited from the network of frontier fortresses of the Byzantine–Sasanian confrontation – had always existed on the borders of Islam, both for purposes of defence and also to house warriors engaged in extending Muslim territory. But within the House of Islam itself, the Muslims preferred to shelter behind walled cities and to build strong citadels within such cities. Possession of the citadel in any town denoted sovereignty over it. Aleppo, Damascus, Cairo and Jerusalem (plate 7.6) – the prime targets of concern to the Franks – were walled and possessed citadels within those walls. The population sheltered there and defended themselves from within. The Syrian geographer Ibn Shaddad gives a detailed description of one of the most redoubtable citadels of the Islamic world, Hisn Kayfa, in the far-away Jazira, an area which often supplied troops for the Muslim armies in the twelfth and thirteenth centuries. This citadel was clearly not just a fortification but also the epicentre of the life of the town and its environs. Other such contemporary citadels included that of Mardin on its precipitous rock, Kharput and Mayyafariqin; Ibn Shaddad lists many more.[129]

It is significant that the major construction work on the citadels of Cairo (plates 7.7 and 7.8), Damascus and Aleppo occurred in the Crusading period. All of these cities were, of course, prime targets for

Figure 7.52 *Citadel, mainly twelfth century, Bosra, Syria. Note that the citadel hugs the perimeter of the Roman theatre*

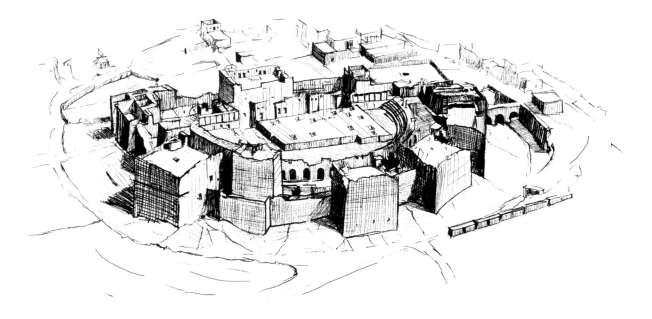

Figure 7.55 Fortifications expanded by 'Ala' al-Din Kayqubad, 623–9/1226–31, Alanya, Turkey

arises at this point: what motivated this sudden burst of activity in the construction of fortifications? A brief glance at the history of Muslim fortification in the Levant before and after the Crusades reveals no precedent for this trend. It seems likely, therefore, that the Muslims found themselves caught up in a kind of arms race, and the flurry of military building activity in the twelfth century was a powerful reaction triggered by the rapid and disturbing proliferation of Crusader castles. These changed the landscape of the Levant permanently and remained as a visible reminder of the Crusaders even when they had long departed. The irony is that after the First Crusade, when Crusader manpower and morale alike were at their peak, the Franks rarely undertook sieges of large inland cities (a notable exception being the siege of Damascus in the Second Crusade); they simply lacked the numbers to do so. The major sieges of the twelfth century typically involved naval operations, in which the shortage of manpower counted for less. Meanwhile, the Muslims undertook expensive restoration and extension of inland cities and strongholds. After the Third Crusade Muslim fortifications continued to be built apace, but as much as ever – or even more – in order to guard against attacks from rival Muslim armies, and against the real or perceived threat of the Isma'ilis, as against the Crusaders. Nevertheless it was the Crusaders who gave the initial impetus.

After his conquest of Jerusalem, Saladin set about fortifying it. He took a personal interest in the city. Complete sections of the walls were rebuilt and strengthened with towers. Saladin himself helped in the rebuilding.[132] Al-'Umari records that in 587/1191, Saladin went to Jerusalem: 'He began rebuilding and fortifying Jerusalem and he

476

Plate **7.6** *City walls, exterior, various periods from antiquity onwards, but largely early sixteenth century, Jerusalem*

(Creswell Photographic Archive, Ashmolean Museum, Oxford, neg. C. 4953)

ordered the troops to carry stones. The sultan himself was carrying stones on his horse in order to give an example thereby to the troops.'[133] In 588/1192, Saladin went back to Jerusalem: 'He examined its conditions and ordered that its walls should be strengthened.'[134] He feared a further Frankish attack on Jerusalem and used Frankish prisoners to dig a deep ditch and to work on the walls and towers.[135]

Individual Muslim Citadels

The Citadel of Cairo

The citadel of Cairo was constructed on Saladin's orders after he had formally terminated the Fatimid caliphate (plate 7.9).[136] In the typical

Plate 7.7 *Citadel, eleventh century onwards, Cairo, Egypt*

(Creswell Photographic Archive, Ashmolean Museum, Oxford, neg. C. 4202)

fashion of the founder of a new dynasty and the reinstater of Sunni Islam in Egypt, Saladin did not wish to live in the palaces which had been erected by the 'heretical' Fatimids; he chose instead to dismantle their buildings and to construct a new citadel both as a fortification for the city and as the sultan's residence,[137] with accommodation for the military elite and its troops.

Saladin began work on the citadel in 1176; his aim was to construct defensive works which would encircle al-Qahira, the Fatimid capital, and al-Fustat, the economic centre, within a single wall. Ibn Jubayr describes the construction work taking place on the citadel in Cairo – sawing marble, cutting huge stones and digging the fosse – and mentions that Saladin was thinking of taking up residence in it.[138] The chronicler al-Nuwayri gives a detailed description of the building of the citadel and includes measurements.[139]

An inscription over the Bab al-Mudarraj, dated 579/1183–4, reveals

*Plate **7.8*** *Citadel, bastions, undated, Cairo, Egypt*

(Creswell Photographic Archive, Ashmolean Museum, Oxford, neg. C. 4257)

much about the intentions of its founder, who 'has ordered the construction of this magnificent Citadel, near the God-protected city of Cairo, on a strong mound, which (the citadel) combines utility and embellishment, and comfort and shield'.[140]

The citadel was built on a promontory 75 metres high which extends westwards from the cliffs of the Muqattam hills towards the Nile, almost midway between al-Qahira and al-Fustat. Saladin selected the site himself, primarily for its strategic position.[141] Security was a prime consideration in Saladin's mind, as well as the desire to build a structure worthy of his prestige. The citadel also housed an impressive library, inherited in part from the Fatimids and enlarged by Saladin's own patronage of writers.

The work which Saladin began on the fortifications was completed by his brother, al-Malik al-'Adil (1218–38). Saladin had built two towers, but al-'Adil enclosed them with much larger round towers. Such activity clearly indicates the need to maintain and improve the city's defences at regular intervals.[142] Two Mamluk sultans, Baybars and al-Nasir Muhammad (d. 1341), added palaces and other structures. This citadel, the so-called Citadel of the Mountain (Qal'at al-jabal) is the only urban citadel in Egypt. In time it became both the focus and the symbol of Ayyubid and Mamluk power.

479

Plate 7.9 *Citadel, northern enclosure, largely by Saladin 572/1176, Cairo, Egypt*

(Creswell Photographic Archive, Ashmolean Museum, Oxford, neg. C. 4249)

The Citadel of Damascus

The citadel of Damascus is one of the best preserved of the great Syrian fortresses of the Crusading period.[143] It is unusual in its location on flat ground, on the same level as the rest of the city, instead of being placed like nearly all the medieval military fortifications of Syria on top of a hill. Information on the citadel in the twelfth century is incomplete, but it must have played an important role in the life of the city and its rulers. Tughtegin and his descendants lived in the citadel and probably Nur al-Din did too. There is an inscription dating from the time of Saladin which commemorates the restoration of a tower of the citadel in 574/1178–9. Saladin was very attached to the citadel; indeed, in spite of his burning desire to conquer Jerusalem, he was in the event buried in the garden of the citadel of Damascus.[144]

It was in the Ayyubid period that the citadel was developed more fully as a defensive precinct of superlative quality. It was extensively reconstructed under the Ayyubid ruler al-Malik al-'Adil, Saladin's brother, who had good reason to fear attacks from his own relations more than from the Franks. The structure possessed a total of ten towers which probably accommodated troops to protect the safety of the ruler, and as Sauvaget describes it, the Ayyubid citadel is a 'perfectly homogeneous ensemble'.[145] The citadel's history can be traced by the inscriptions that it bears; from them it is clear that in the Mamluk period the citadel continued to play an important role in the

Plate 7.10 Citadel with Ayyubid inscription, early thirteenth century, Damascus, Syria

Plate 7.11 Citadel, mainly
thirteenth century,
Damascus, Syria

Plate 7.12 Citadel, inscription, thirteenth century, Damascus, Syria

defence of the city. Baybars, fearing a return of the Mongols, strengthened the citadel against possible siege and his name appears on an inscription on the northern tower. Qalawun also undertook restoration work on the citadel, and eight inscriptions bear his name.[146]

The Citadel of Aleppo

The citadel of Aleppo (often known in Arabic as al-Shahba' – 'the grey-coloured')[147] is a magnificent example of Muslim military architecture at the time of the Crusades (plates 7.14–7.17) and was the subject of extensive study by the great French scholar Sauvaget.[148] It was also described very elegantly by Rogers.[149] It stands, enclosed by its surrounding walls, atop a dramatically steep glacis, brooding over the city from a height of fifty metres.[150] The Aleppo citadel played an important role in the military and political life of the twelfth and thirteenth centuries. The wall of the citadel was rebuilt by none other than Nur al-Din himself, who erected his 'golden palace' there.[151] As Sauvaget remarks, the citadel, which also contained the arsenal and the treasury, thereafter possessed what was necessary to govern and to stage public ceremonies.[152] As Ibn Jubayr passed through Syria, he described the awe-inspiring spectacle of its citadel:

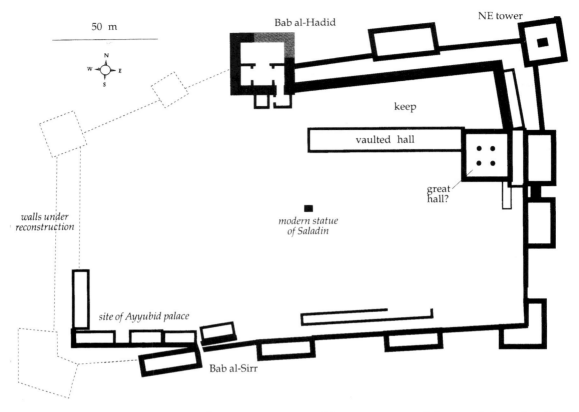

50 m

N
W ✦ E
S

Bab al-Hadid

NE tower

keep

vaulted hall

great
hall?

walls under
reconstruction

modern statue
of Saladin

site of Ayyubid palace

Bab al-Sirr

Figure 7.56 *Citadel, plan,
mainly twelfth century,
Damascus, Syria*

Its fortress is renowned for its impregnability and, from far distance
seen for its great height, is without like or match among castles . . .
It is a massy pile, like a round table rising from the ground, with
sides of hewn stone and erected with true and symmetrical proportions. Glory to Him who planned its design and arrangement,
and conceived its shape and outline.[153]

After Nur al-Din the citadel of Aleppo was closely associated with
the family of Saladin, whose brother al-Malik al-'Adil lived there
for a while. Major construction work was undertaken by Saladin's
descendant, the Ayyubid ruler al-Zahir Ghazi who, although Nur
al-Din had renewed the citadel only forty years earlier, felt the need
to adapt it further to the needs of his court, as well as to improve its
defences. As defensive measures, al-Zahir Ghazi built the massive
bridge, moat, talus and glacis.[154] Instead of the two old fortress gates,
he constructed a new single entrance, 'perhaps the most inspiring of
all Muslim fortifications',[155] protected by two powerful protecting
towers (figure 7.60). Any would-be attacker was confronted with a
ramp with no less than five right-angled bends, each provided with
arrow slits. Elaborate steps were taken to collect water for the use of
those in the citadel; a deep well was constructed in 1209 and there

484

Figure 7.57 Citadel tower, 606/1209, Damascus, Syria

Figure 7.58 Citadel tower, 606/1209, Damascus, Syria

Plate 7.13 *Citadel, tower, thirteenth century, Damascus, Syria*

(Creswell Photographic Archive, Ashmolean Museum, Oxford, neg. C. 933)

(Creswell Photographic Archive, Ashmolean Museum, Oxford, neg. C. 5682)

Plate 7.14 Citadel, mainly late twelfth to early thirteenth century, Aleppo, Syria

Figure 7.59 Citadel, mainly thirteenth century, Aleppo, Syria

487

Plate 7.15 *Citadel, outer gateway, erected 606/1210, rebuilt 913/1507, Aleppo, Syria*

(Creswell Photographic Archive, Ashmolean Museum, Oxford, neg. C. 5690)

Plate **7.16** *Citadel, bridge over the moat, 606/1209–10, Aleppo, Syria*

(Creswell Photographic Archive, Ashmolean Museum, Oxford, neg. C. 5692)

were also numerous cisterns, thus helping the citadel in time of siege. The upper storey of the citadel was also supplied with arrow slits, arranged differently from those at the level of the bridge to ensure maximum scope for the shooting of arrows. At the foot of the mound a ditch was dug which was straddled by a bridge, barred by an iron gate. The glacis, its surface paved with ashlar masonry, stretched from the ditch to the bottom of the rampart, and virtually excluded any attempt at mining the citadel or climbing up to it. The citadel contained two secret passages, 'the secret door' and 'the mountain door', which allowed communication with those outside the city.

Other measures taken by al-Zahir Ghazi were aimed at transforming the citadel into a royal residence. He built more palaces, a bath, and a garden with trees and flowers in it. He undertook work on the House of Justice and joined it to the citadel by a passage reserved for the ruler alone. He built a Great Mosque which also served as an observation post. It was to this mosque, and not to the city's Friday mosque, that

Plate 7.17 Citadel, inner
gateway, 606/1209–10,
Aleppo, Syria

the sultan went to perform the prayer, no doubt in part for security reasons. The memory of this prince is perpetuated by three iron-plated doors studded with nails which are disposed in the form of a rectangular grid, containing motifs and inscriptions bearing his name. In 1212 when he married Dayfa Khatun, the arsenal and the palace caught fire, and one of his successors, al-Malik al-'Aziz, rebuilt them, the arsenal in 1228 and the palace three years later (figures 7.62 and 7.63). The account provided by Sauvaget of the extensions and innovations made to the Aleppo citadel is drawn from the detailed descriptions of two contemporary writers, Ibn Shihna and Ibn Shaddad, who were justifiably impressed by the achievements of this Ayyubid ruler. The citadel in Ayyubid times must have been an awe-inspiring sight as it towered like a colossus above the city, with its impressive foundation inscription carved in enormous black basalt letters halfway up the white limestone glacis.[156] Under the Mamluks the citadel was the residence of the governor and his state officials.

As Sauvaget so eloquently expressed it: 'This ensemble certainly

Figure 7.60 Citadel, plan, mainly thirteenth century, Aleppo, Syria

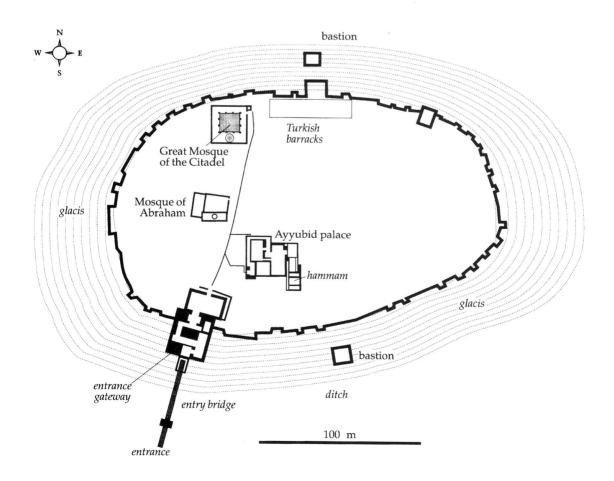

Figure 7.61 *Citadel, outer and inner gateway, mainly thirteenth century, Aleppo, Syria*

constitutes the most prodigious fortification work left to us by the military architecture of the Middle Ages.'[157] Yet even this masterpiece of Muslim military engineering was not proof against really determined sapping. The chronicler Qirtay al-'Izzi al-Khaznadari (d. 734/1333) relates an absorbing eyewitness account of the siege of Aleppo by the Mongol ruler Hülegü. Several mines were dug; Hülegü gave orders that one of them, already wide enough to hold 6,000 men, should be enlarged to hold 10,000;[158] and the citadel duly fell, after only a few days of siege, on 27 January 1260.[159]

The Citadel of Hims

The citadel of Hims in the thirteenth century must have looked very similar to the citadel of Aleppo, especially with the slope below the citadel proper accentuated by a paving of stone slabs. Built – like the somewhat less well-preserved citadel of Hama – atop an ancient tell in the middle of the town, the citadel possessed a huge glacis built by Baybars. Its walls formed, like those of Cairo, Damascus, Aleppo and Hama, a single continuous enceinte. Unfortunately this important monument was blown up by Ibrahim Pasha in the 1830s, but much of its encircling walls with their inscriptions datable before 1239 remains (plates 7.18–7.19).[160]

492

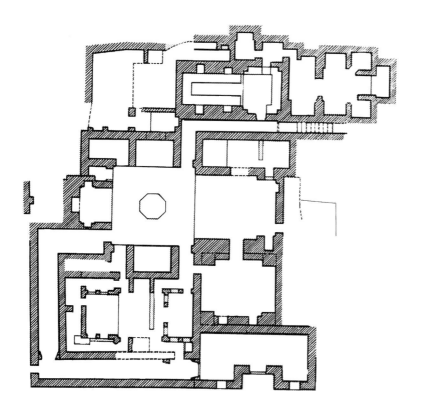

Figure 7.62 *Citadel, palace of al-Malik al-ʿAziz, plan, 628/1230–1, Aleppo, Syria*

Muslim Castles

ʿAjlun

This Muslim castle was built in 580/1184–5 by ʿIzz al-Din Usama, one of Saladin's commanders, on a hilltop opposite the Crusader castle of Belvoir, overlooking the Jordan Valley (figure 7.64).[161] It was quadrilateral with four square corner towers. Johns, who published this site, concludes that those few Frankish features which the castle has were the result of local tradition and common experience.[162] In an attempt to improve the site's defences, which were compromised by the rather too gentle slope on which the castle stood, the Muslims – perhaps following the Frankish example of Sahyun – deepened the rock ditch around it, leaving a stumpy pillar for the drawbridge. Otherwise the castle is notable for its small size and the plethora of towers crammed into it.

Some thirty years later Aybak, a close associate of the Ayyubid sultan al-ʿAdil, enlarged ʿAjlun's outer defences. According to al-ʿUmari, ʿAjlun was a link in a chain of beacons and pigeon stations by which alarm signals could be conveyed to the sultan in Cairo.[163] It served as an arsenal and housed supplies for the relief of Damietta.[164]

493

Figure 7.63 *Citadel, palace of al-Malik al-'Aziz, portal elevation (note the apotropaic knots flanking the doorway), 628/1230–1, Aleppo, Syria*

494

Qal'at Najm

Qal'at Najm on the right bank of the Euphrates near Manbij is 'a remarkable Arab castle of the thirteenth century'.[165] Enough remains, together with reconstructed elements, to give a clearer idea of Muslim fortification techniques than anywhere apart from the citadels of Damascus, Cairo and Aleppo (plate 7.20). Nur al-Din had reconstructed an existing fortress which was in turn rebuilt by al-Malik al-Zahir Ghazi from 1208 to 1215. The castle is on the river and has a cladding of dressed stone which acts as an effective glacis, plus two towers which defend the entrance gateway.[166]

Ibn Jubayr describes Qal'at Najm on the Euphrates as a newly built fortress.[167]

Qal'at Ja'bar

This castle, whose lower parts are built of rubble while its upper parts are of baked brick, follows the standard pattern of medieval

Plate 7.18 *Citadel, various periods from antiquity onwards, Hims, Syria*

(Creswell Photographic Archive, Ashmolean Museum, Oxford, neg. C. 5910)

495

Syrian Arab fortresses in that it occupies a high mound (in this case a bluff overlooking the Euphrates) surrounded by a defensive wall and ditch and punctuated by towers, with an entrance gateway and ramp. Originally built by the Banu Numayr, a local Arab tribe, it was extensively remodelled – after a spell of Crusader occupation – by Nur al-Din from 1168 onwards (plates 7.21–7.22), and contains a mosque with minaret and palace.[168]

Qal'at Subayba

This castle, dated to 1228–30, stands on the southern slopes of Mount Hermon (north-east of Banyas). It is the largest and best-preserved medieval fortress in Palestine.[169] It was built by one of the sons of al-ʿAdil, al-ʿAziz ʿUthman (d. 630/1232).[170] The castle was built in great haste on the eve of Frederick II's Crusade.[171] Placed on the main trade route between the Huleh Valley and Damascus, it was intended as an obstacle to anyone approaching the city from Frankish territory.[172]

It was built economically and quickly – it has simple vaults, almost no ornamentation, and not all the stones were perfectly dressed.[173] After Frederick II had left the Holy Land, al-ʿAziz ʿUthman

Figure 7.64 Castle,
580/1184–5, 'Ajlun, Jordan

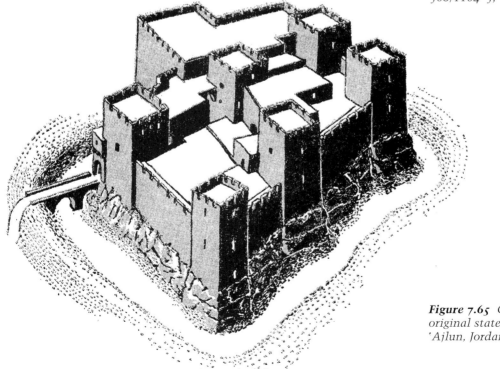

Figure 7.65 Castle, proposed
original state, 580/1184–5,
'Ajlun, Jordan

Plate 7.20 *Qal'at al-Najm, exterior, mainly twelfth–thirteenth centuries, Syria*

(Creswell Photographic Archive, Ashmolean Museum, Oxford, neg. C. 6096)

invested much effort in completing his castle. When Baybars took it he decided to fortify it (rather than destroy it). He built six new towers and made other sophisticated improvements.[174] Several inscriptions document these works.[175]

Muslim Additions to Crusader Castles

The fortunes of war sometimes allowed the Muslims to capture Frankish castles and to make significant additions to them. Mention has already been made of the mosque, minaret, palace and bath erected at Sahyun by the Muslims between 1188 and 1290. The Frankish castle at Bira was largely rebuilt by al-Zahir Ghazi;[176] the south-west tower at Beaufort exhibits the distinctive type of boss associated with al-Malik al-'Adil;[177] at Karak al-'Adil added the great south keep;[178] even Krak des Chevaliers reveals much Arab workmanship on its south enceinte,[179] while the square tower at its centre bears both the panther of Baybars and an inscription of Qalawun dated 1285.[180] The Isma'ilis too took over existing castles, whether they were of Byzantine, Fatimid or local Arab foundation.

Conversely, the Crusaders themselves sometimes built on and

Plate 7.21 Qal'at Ja'bar, exterior, mainly from 564/1168–9 onwards (rebuilding of Nur al-Din) and 736/1335–6 (rebuilding of the Mamluk governor of Damascus, Tengiz), Syria

Plate 7.22 *Qal'at Ja'bar,*
exterior, general view, mainly
from 564/1168–9 onwards
(rebuilding of Nur al-Din) and
736/1335–6 (rebuilding of the
Mamluk governor of
Damascus, Tengiz), Syria

(Creswell Photographic Archive,
Ashmolean Museum, Oxford,
neg. C. 6658)

extended earlier Muslim fortifications, as at Marqab.[181] And the
Muslims themselves on occasion adapted pre-Islamic structures for
their own fortifications. Thus al-Malik al-'Adil made the Roman
theatre of Busra the nucleus for the city's citadel, adding concentric
walls to it between 1202 and 1218.[182]

The Castles of the Assassins

A notable exception to the Muslims' general preference for seeking
to protect and defend themselves in walled towns rather than isolated
fortresses and castles was the castles of the Assassins, whose sites
were especially chosen for their remote location and impregnable
position. This much-feared Isma'ili group had acquired a reputation
for building inaccessible and impregnable strongholds in Iran in the
early 1100s.[183] They also acquired and built a string of fortresses in
Syria in the Crusading period,[184] where they adopted the same
approach of choosing inaccessible mountainous areas. These Syrian
castles are listed by various Muslim chroniclers, including Ibn

Muyassar.[185] He relates that by the death of the first leader of the Assassins, Hasan-i Sabbah, in 518/1124, this group – who, he says, are called the Hashishiyya (the 'eaters of hashish') in Syria – had taken, usually by ruse or bribery, a number of mountain citadels in Syria, eight of which they retained until Baybars took them in 1270–3.[186] They were careful to select areas in which they could call on a local civilian population susceptible to the Isma'ili form of Islam.

Perhaps the most famous Syrian Assassin castle is Masyaf, with its double concentric fortified walls (figures 7.66 and 7.67). It was positioned carefully to the west of Hama in the Jabal Ansariyya where the road turns north towards the Orontes Valley.

Al-Dimishqi describes Masyaf as the 'mother of the frontier fortresses built by the Assassins to propagate their missionary message (*da'wa*) and to house missionaries "to kill kings and notables"'.[187] Boase dismisses it (and other Assassin strongholds in Syria) as being 'roughly built, generally on earlier foundation' and having 'little architectural interest'.[188] What is most striking about the Assassin castles is their dramatic locations.[189] Like the Crusaders, the Isma'ilis were an embattled minority in the Levant, and like the Crusaders they sought to offset their disadvantage in sheer numbers by building castles at strategic points, castles that were often interdependent and intervisible. Unlike the castles of the Crusaders, the Isma'ili castles housed a whole community of 'heretical' believers within the shelter of their walls. Yet this was no substitute for a trained and disciplined army ready for instant action. A further significant distinction is that while many Crusader castles had a marked offensive role – for example

Figure 7.66 Castle, Masyaf, *mainly twelfth century, Syria*

501

Karak – the Isma'ili castles were conceived essentially in a defensive spirit.[190]

Similarities between Muslim and Crusader Military Architecture

Perhaps not surprisingly, given their proximity to each other and the fact that they sometimes shared workmen, there are a number of similarities which can on occasion make it hard on stylistic grounds to tell Crusader from Muslim work – bigger towers, box machicolations of almost identical design at Krak des Chevaliers, Aleppo and Damascus, and other architectural features such as pointed arches and vaults. It is also very difficult to establish who influenced whom.[191] But the likelihood is that the Franks were the dominant element here, not only because they arrived in the Levant possessed of a markedly superior technology in military architecture, but also because their perilous situation in hostile territory made them much

Figure 7.67 *Castle, Masyaf, proposed original state, mainly twelfth century, Syria*

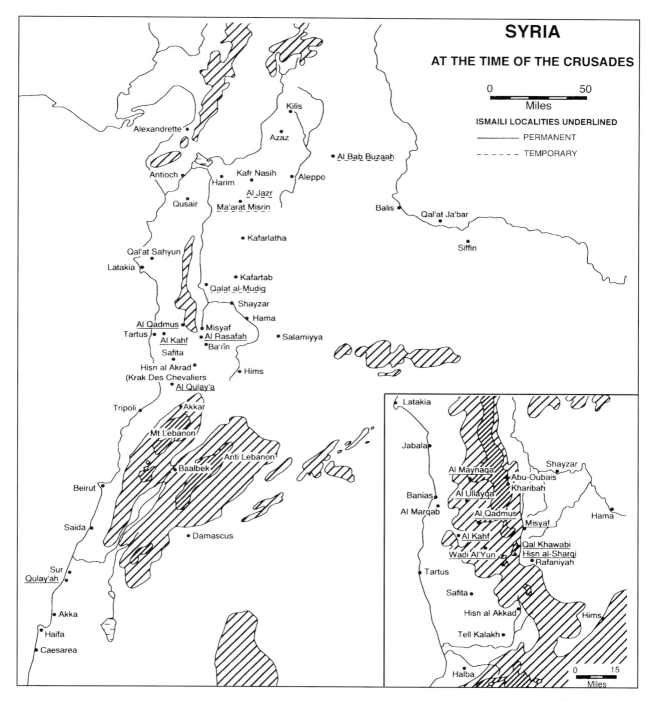

Figure 7.68 *Map of the Syrian Isma'ili Amirate at the time of the Crusades*

more inventive. There is moreover the possibility that the Franks may have adopted techniques from what they saw of Byzantine and Islamic defensive structures;[192] but the extent to which this occurred is a matter of ongoing scholarly debate.

Recent work on Muslim castles

The last couple of decades or so have seen a dramatic increase in survey and excavation work on medieval Muslim castles in the Levant. While some of these buildings have attracted full-scale publications, like the Ayyubid castle, Qal'at al-Tur, excavated on Mount Tabor,[193] and the Damascus citadel – especially the Ayyubid towers,[194] whose modules and unit of measurement suggest the work of Armenian craftsmen[195] – the majority of these buildings await systematic examination.[196] The sequence begins with small coastal defensive forts built in 'Abbasid times, like Kefor Lam, Ashdod Yam and the tower at Mikhmoret; these probably supplemented the major fortifications round such ports as Caesarea, Acre, Jaffa, Ascalon and Gaza. Among pre-Crusader fortifications inland, Baysan with its flimsy walls and single gate was clearly not built to withstand a determined siege. Recent research suggests that several castles have been misattributed to the Crusaders, such as Qaqun (mainly Mamluk), Jazirat Fira'un in the Gulf of 'Aqaba and Banyas north of Lake Hula (both Ayyubid structures with Mamluk additions), Qal'at Safuriya and Afula (both in Galilee). The Muslim castle of Abu'l-Hasan near Sidon predates 1128; it has features in common with Qasr Zuwayra at the south end of the Dead Sea. Qal'at ibn Ma'an or Qal'at Salah al-Din, in Galilee, a well-nigh impregnable eyrie set in a high cliff with numerous caves behind, uses two-tone masonry of Mamluk type. Other Muslim rock-cut fortresses include al-Wu'ayra in Petra, captured by the Crusaders in 1107; al-Habis, another rock-cut castle in Petra, may also be Muslim. Further castles of probably Mamluk date include that of Jiza/Ziza and Qasr Shabib in Zirka, both in Jordan. Lebanon too attests several rock-cut castles which have strong claims to be regarded as Muslim, like Magharat Fakhr al-Din and Qal'at al-Dubba; a related structure is Khirbat al-Sila near Tafila in Jordan. The time is ripe for a full-scale co-ordinated study of all these buildings.

Notes

1. Qur'an, 8: 60.
2. Cambridge, 1967.
3. Cambridge, 1992.
4. Marshall, *Warfare*, 6.
5. D. Pringle, *The Red Tower*, London, 1986.
6. Cf., for example, D. Alexander, *The Arts of War*, London, 1992; D. Ayalon, *Gunpowder and Firearms in the Mamluk Kingdom*, London, 1956; R. Elgood (ed.), *Islamic Arms and Armour*, London, 1979; D. Nicolle, *Early Medieval Islamic Arms and Armour*, Madrid, 1976.

7. An interesting collection of articles is found in *War, Technology and Society in the Middle East*, ed. V. J. Parry and M. E. Yapp, London, 1975; and there is an important contribution made by C. E. Bosworth, 'The armies of the Prophet', in B. Lewis, *The World of Islam*, London, 1976, 201–24.

8. Thus Ibn al-Athir wrote a biographical dictionary of the Prophet's Companions: '*Usd al-ghaba fi ma'rifat al-sahaba*, Beirut, 1994.

9. Usama, Hitti, 177.

10. Ibn al-Nadim, *Al-fihrist*, trans. B. Dodge, New York, 1972, vol. II, 737–8.

11. Cf. the discussion of al-Aqsara'i on pp. 437–8.

12. Ritter lists 38 such treatises. Cf. H. Ritter, '"La parure des cavaliers" und die Litteratur über die ritterlichen Künste', *Der Islam*, 18 (1929), 116–54.

13. The work was partially translated and analysed by C. Cahen, 'Un traité d'armurie composé pour Saladin', *BEO*, 12 (1947–8), 1–61. More recently, it has been edited and translated by A. Boudot-Lamotte, *Contribution à l'étude de l'archerie musulmane*, Damascus, 1968.

14. Cahen, 'Un traité', 1.

15. It is entitled *Al-tadhkirat al-harawiyya fi'l-hiyal al-harbiyya*, trans. J. Sourdel-Thomine, *BEO*, 17 (1962), 105–268. Cf. also the discussion of it in G. Scanlon, *A Muslim Manual of War*, Cairo, 1961, 14; H. Ritter, 'La parure', 144–6.

16. Scanlon, *A Muslim Manual*, 14.

17. Ibid., 6–7.

18. D. Ayalon, 'Notes on the Furusiyya exercises and games in the Mamluk sultanate', *Scripta Hierosolymitana*, 9 (1961), 34.

19. Cf. R. Smith, *Medieval Muslim Horsemanship*, London, 1979.

20. Ritter considers it to be the most important work of its kind ('La parure', 125). This work has been extensively analysed, with accompanying illustrations, by two scholars; cf. R. Smith, *Medieval Muslim Horsemanship* and G. Tantum, 'Muslim warfare: a study of a medieval Muslim treatise on the art of war', in Elgood, *Islamic Arms and Armour*, 187–201.

21. Ibid., 190.

22. Ibid., 194.

23. Nizam al-Mulk, *The Book of Government or Rules for Kings*, trans. H. Darke, London, 1978.

24. Other eleventh- and twelfth-century Mirrors for Princes either deal with other military traditions connected only distantly with the theatre of war in the Levant (such as the *Qabusnama*) or do not mention military matters at all (such as the *Bahr al-fawa'id*, already mentioned, and the *Nasihat al-muluk*, normally attributed to al-Ghazali).

25. Cf. Bosworth, 'Armies of the Prophet', 204–6.

26. For a discussion of the Muslim armies at the time of the Crusades, cf. Smail, *Crusading Warfare*, 66 ff.

27. Usama, Hitti, 149.

28. Cf. C. Hillenbrand, 'The career of Najm al-Din Il-Ghazi', 276–7.

29. V. Minorsky, *Sharaf al-Zaman Tahir Marvazi on China, the Turks and India*, London, 1942, 38.

30. J. Sauvaget, *Alep*, Paris, 1941, 118.

31. *The Book of Government*, 100.

32. Ibid., 102.

33. Ibid., 99.

34. Ibid., 93.

35. Ibid., 93.

36. These remarks are based on the scholarly research of Y. Lev in a number of articles and books.
37. Cf. W. J. Hamblin, *The Fatimid Army during the Early Crusades*, Ph.D. thesis, Michigan, 1985, 294–301; analysed by M. Brett, 'The battles of Ramla (1099–1105)', in *Orientalia Lovaniensia Analecta: Egypt and Syria in the Fatimid, Ayyubid and Mamluk Eras*, ed. U. Vermeulen and D. de Smet, Louvain, 1995, 17–38.
38. Cf. Gibb, 'The armies of Saladin', 138–57.
39. Abu Shama, *RHC*, IV, 277.
40. Cf. the many articles and books by D. Ayalon.
41. A point made by Ayalon in many of his articles about the Mamluks. The information here is based on his work.
42. Such as al-Walid II.
43. Ibn Shaddad, Eddé, 74; Sauvaget, *Alep*, 118.
44. Similarly, in the 'Abbasid clover-leaf race-course at Samarra there was a central grandstand.
45. H. Rabie, 'The training of the Mamluk Faris', in Parry and Yapp, *War, Technology and Society*, 162.
46. Illustrated in Smith's book (see note 19).
47. Smith, illustration 14.
48. For specialist work on this topic, cf. the various works of D. Nicolle cited in the Bibliography; J. D. Latham and W. F. Paterson, *Saracen Archery*, London, 1970; D. Alexander, *The Arts of War*.
49. Mayer, 'Saracenic arms and armor', 10.
50. Usama, Hitti, 78, 87, 90, 114, 125–6, 151.
51. Al-Jahiz, *Manaqib al-turk*, trans. C. T. Harley-Walker, 671.
52. Quoted by Gabrieli, 173.
53. Trans. Cahen, 'Un traité', 32.
54. Usama, Hitti, 68.
55. Cf. the evidence of the floor fresco at Qasr al-Hayr al-Gharbi, east of Damascus. Cf. B. Spuler and J. Sourdel-Thomine, *Die Kunst des Islam*, Berlin, 1973, pl. XLII (in colour).
56. Usama, Hitti, 68.
57. Usama, Hitti, 70.
58. Usama, Hitti, 66.
59. Usama, Hitti, 131.
60. Usama, Hitti, 76.
61. Usama, Hitti, 76.
62. Usama, Hitti, 155.
63. Ayalon, 'Furusiyya', 47–8.
64. Smith, *Medieval Muslim Horsemanship*, 8.
65. Lyons, *The Arabian Epic*, I, 55.
66. Cf. Ibn al-Nadim, *Fihrist*, trans. Dodge, II, 625.
67. Cf. Cahen, 'Un traité', n. 1.
68. Mayer, 'Saracenic arms and armor', 8.
69. Abu Shama, I, 11; Mayer, 'Saracenic arms and armor', 9.
70. Usama, Hitti, 147.
71. Quoted by Lewis, *Islam*, II, 123.
72. Al-Tarsusi, trans. Cahen, 'Un traité', 37.
73. Ibid.
74. Ibid. Cf. also al-Qalqashandi, II, 135.
75. According to Gabrieli, 290.
76. Al-Tarsusi, trans. Cahen, 'Un traité', 27–32; Arabic text, 6–10.
77. Ibid., 31.
78. Ibid., 27.

79. Ibid., 34 and 45. See p. 541 below.
80. *Dictionary of the Middle Ages*, s.v. 'bow', 2/351.
81. Smail, *Crusading Warfare*, 85.
82. Usama, Hitti, 136.
83. Al-Tarsusi, trans. Cahen, 'Un traité', 34.
84. If made of hide, it was called a *daraqa*. Cf. al-Qalqashandi, II, 138; Mayer, 'Saracenic arms and armor', 12.
85. Ibid., 35.
86. Ibid., 35.
87. Illustrated in Creswell, *Muslim Architecture of Egypt*, I, plates 49 and 50, and p. 168.
88. A. Shalem, 'A note on the shield-shaped ornamental bosses on the facade of Bab al-Nasr in Cairo', *Ars Orientalis*, 26 (1996), 58.
89. Usama, Hitti, 95.
90. Usama, Hitti, 129.
91. Usama, Hitti, 130.
92. Usama, Hitti, 90.
93. Usama, Hitti, 80.
94. Usama, Hitti, 88.
95. Usama, Hitti, 104.
96. Protective padded clothing.
97. Ibn al-Athir, *Kamil*, XI, 285.
98. Alexander, *The Arts of War*, 20. Alexander unfortunately gives no reference or date for this information. The most famous example of the talismanic use of the Qur'an in a military context are the shirts of the Ottoman sultans which bear large portions of the Qur'an (J. M. Rogers and R. Ward, *Suleyman the Magnificent*, London, 1988, 175–6).
99. Usama, Hitti, 74.
100. Usama, Hitti, 79–80.
101. A translation amended from Mayer, 'Saracenic arms and armor', 7, quoting Ibn Mangli, *Al-tadbirat al-sultaniyya*, B.M. Or. 3734, fol. 14v.
102. Usama, Hitti, 153.
103. Mayer, 'Saracenic arms and armor', 2.
104. *The Book of Government*, 93.
105. Ibid., 94.
106. Ibid., 131.
107. D. Schlumberger, 'Le palais ghaznévide de Lashkari Bazar', *Syria*, 29 (1952), 261–7.
108. U. Scerrato, 'The first two excavation campaigns at Ghazni 1957–1958', *East and West*, N.S. 10 (1959), 23–55.
109. Thomas Artsruni, *History of the House of the Artsrunik'*, trans. R. W. Thomson, Detroit, 1985, 357.
110. A.-M. Eddé, 'Villes en fête en Proche Orient', in *Villes et sociétés urbaines au Moyen Âge*, Paris, 1996, 76, quoting Ibn Wasil, III, 220–2.
111. Usama, Hitti, 54.
112. Eddé, 'Villes', 78; quoting Ibn al-'Adim, *Zubda*, Dahan, III, 155.
113. Cf. C. J. F. Dowsett, 'A twelfth-century Armenian inscription at Edessa', in *Iran and Islam*, ed. C. E. Bosworth, Edinburgh, 1971, 197–228.
114. A good starting point is R. Fedden and J. Thomson, *Crusader Castles*, London, 1957, and H. Kennedy, *Crusader Castles*, Cambridge, 1994.
115. D. Pringle, 'The state of research: the archaeology of the Crusade Kingdom of Jerusalem: a review of work 1947–1972', *Journal of Medieval History*, 23/4 (1997), 398.
116. Ibn al-Athir, *Kamil*, XII, 5–6.

117. Al-Maqrizi, trans. Broadhurst, 68.
118. Ibn al-Furat, Lyons, 47–8.
119. Ibn Jubayr, Broadhurst, 319–20.
120. Ibn Shaddad, *RHC*, III, 358.
121. Quoted by Boase, *Castles*, 49.
122. For a recent discussion of Sahyun, cf. Kennedy, *Crusader Castles*, 84 ff.
123. Abu Shama, *RHC*, IV, 364–7.
124. Ibn Shaddad, *RHC*, III, 111–12; cf. also al-Dimishqi, *Kitab nukhbat al-dahr*, 208.
125. Abu Shama, *RHC*, IV, 197.
126. Abu Shama, *RHC*, IV, 197.
127. Abu Shama, *RHC*, IV, 206.
128. Abu Shama, *RHC*, IV, 206.
129. Cf. *EI²*: Hisn Kayfa; 'Izz al-Din Ibn Shaddad, *Al–a'laq al-khatira*, Bodleian ms., Marsh 333.
130. Rabbat, 'The ideological significance', 15.
131. Ibid.; cf. also Elisséeff, *Nur al-Din*, III, 705–20.
132. 'Imad al-Din, *Fath*, 562, 565, 582, 610.
133. Lundquist, Arabic text, VII, 53; cf. also Chapter 4, 192.
134. Lundquist, Arabic text, VII, 53.
135. Little, 'Jerusalem', 179.
136. The citadel of Cairo has recently received detailed treatment in an excellent scholarly monograph. Cf. N. O. Rabbat, *The Citadel of Cairo*, Leiden, 1995.
137. D. Behrens-Abouseif, 'The citadel of Cairo: stage for Mamluk ceremonial', *Annales Islamologiques*, 24 (1988), 25–6.
138. Ibn Jubayr, Broadhurst, 43.
139. Al-Nuwayri, 365–6.
140. Rabbat, *The Citadel of Cairo*, 69.
141. Ibid., 51.
142. Cf. Kennedy, *Crusader Castles*, 183.
143. Cf. J. Sauvaget, 'La citadelle de Damas', *Syria*, XI (1930), 60.
144. Ibid., 62–3.
145. Ibid., 221.
146. Ibid., 227–9.
147. Al-Dimishqi, *Kitab nukhbat al-dahr*, 202.
148. J. Sauvaget, *Alep*, Paris, 1941.
149. J. M. Rogers, *The Spread of Islam*, Oxford, 1972, 43–8.
150. Sauvaget, *Alep*, 145.
151. Sauvaget, *Alep*, 116; *RCEA*, IX, inscription no. 3275, 52.
152. Sauvaget, *Alep*, 116.
153. Ibn Jubayr, Broadhurst, 260.
154. Rogers, *The Spread of Islam*, 43–6.
155. Ibid., 45.
156. For a drawing of part of this inscription, see Sauvaget, *Alep*, 146, fig. 35.
157. Ibid., 145.
158. Lewis, *Islam*, I, 92.
159. Sauvaget, *Alep*, 156 and 159.
160. This information is based on a conference paper given by G. King at *The Art of the Zengids and the Ayyubids* Conference held at the School of Oriental and African Studies, University of London, on 18 November 1998. The inscriptions in the name of Shirkuh II were read by M. van Berchem.
161. Cf. Boase, *Castles*, 71. Cf. al-Qalqashandi, *Subh*, IV, 105; Abu'l-Fida, *RHC*, I, 70, 86, 143.

162. He cites one or two stones with characteristic diagonal chisel-dressing. Cf. C. N. Johns, 'Medieval 'Ajlun', *Quarterly of the Department of Antiquities in Palestine*, 1 (1931), 29.
163. Ibid., 31.
164. Ibid., 30.
165. Burns, *Monuments of Syria*, 183; Boase, *Castles*, 82.
166. Ibid.
167. Ibn Jubayr, Broadhurst, 258.
168. See now C. Tonghini, *Qal'at Ja'bar*, London, 1998.
169. R. Ellenblum, 'Who built Qal'at al-Subayba?', *Dumbarton Oaks Papers*, 43 (1989), 103–12.
170. Sibt, Jewett, 392–3.
171. Ellenblum, 'Who built . . .?', 112.
172. Kennedy, *Crusader Castles*, 184.
173. Ellenblum, 'Who built . . .?', 111.
174. Al-Yunini, III, 259–60.
175. Boase, *Castles*, 68.
176. Ibid., 82.
177. Ibid., 67.
178. Ibid., 70.
179. Ibid., 53–4.
180. Ibid., 54.
181. Ibid., 59.
182. Creswell, 'Fortifications', 123.
183. Cf. M. Situdeh, *Qila' Isma'iliyya*, Tehran, 1983.
184. Cf. the map of these citadels on p. 503. Cf. also N. A. Mirza, *Syrian Isma'ilism*, London, 1997. These castles were al-Qadmus, al-Kahf, al-Khariba, Masyaf, al-Khawabi, al-Qulay'a, al-Mayniqa and al-Rusafa. Other castles built or used by the Isma'ilis include Qamugh, al-'Ullayqa and Qal'at al-Qahir near Masyaf.
185. Ibn Muyassar, 68.
186. Ibn Muyassar, 68; cf. also al-Dimishqi, *Kitab nukhbat al-dahr*, 208.
187. Ibid.
188. Boase, *Castles*, 82. Some were probably Byzantine in origin and others were Fatimid constructions or built by local rulers.
189. Burns, *Monuments of Syria*, 152, 176–7.
190. For a brief guide to the Isma'ili castles, see R. Boulanger, trans. J. S. Hardman, *The Middle East*, Paris, 1966, 443–4 and especially 448–51.
191. Cf. Kennedy, *Crusader Castles*, 154–5.
192. Cf. Smail, *Crusading Warfare*, 214–44.
193. A. Battista and B. Bagatti, *La fortezza saracena del Monte Tabor (A.H. 609–15: A.D. 1212–18)*, Studia Biblica Franciscana, col. min., 18, Jerusalem.
194. H. Hanisch, *Die ayyubidischen Toranlagen der Zitadelle von Damaskus*, Wiesbaden, 1996; *idem*, 'Masssystem und Massordnung der ayyubidischen Bauten der Zitadelle von Damaskus', *Ordo et Mensura* IV–V (1998), 341–50.
195. H. Hanisch, personal communication. Similar work is to be found in the citadel of Harran.
196. What follows summarises information most generously provided by Andrew Petersen, and partly delivered by him in a lecture entitled 'Qal'at ibn Ma'an and Qasr Zuweira. Two medieval castles and their position in the military architecture of Muslim Palestine' delivered at the *8th Colloquium on Egypt and Syria in Fatimid, Ayyubid and Mamluk Times* (University of Leuven, May 1999).

CHAPTER EIGHT

The Conduct of War

Victory in warfare is from Allah and is not due to organisation and planning, nor to the number of troops and supporters.[1] (Usama)

Muslim Military Strategy

The Tactics of the Fatimid Armies

IN THE PAST, military historians spoke of the vast size and resources of the Fatimid army.[2] Smail, in particular, attributed Fatimid failure in the early Crusading period to the fact that their army was old-fashioned. Its 'mass of bowmen on foot, and horsemen who were capable of awaiting attack' were an ideal target for the Franks' most powerful weapon – 'the charge of the mailed and mounted knights'.[3] Smail argues that the mounted archers of the Turkish armies were a far more dangerous foe to the Crusaders. However, more recent research has modified this view. Brett argues convincingly that the Bedouin Arab cavalry may well have played a more significant part in the Fatimid army than has been thought hitherto.[4]

Lev attacks the rather simplistic assumption that the Fatimids fielded enormous armies of low quality. Although it has often been alleged that the Frankish knights were more heavily armed than their Muslim counterparts, Brett stresses that by the end of the tenth century the Fatimid cavalry wore armour in battle.[5] They were therefore as heavily armoured as the Franks. It should also be remembered that the effectiveness of the Frankish cavalry depended not only on the amount of armour worn by the horse and rider but on the strength and size (not necessarily the speed) of the Frankish horses. As for the Fatimid infantry, it contained troops armed with pikes, maces, javelins and crossbows;[6] clearly this too was a well-equipped fighting force.

The arrangement of the Fatimid armies in combat was clearly laid down, with each unit having defined tactical responsibilities. As Lev points out, the infantry was organised in tightly packed ranks with heavy pike-armed infantry in the front, supported by missile troops behind.[7] The cavalry performed diverse tasks – assault,

Figure 8.1 *Warrior wearing traditional Iranian armour,* Kitab-i Samak ʿAyyar *('Book of Samak the Adventurer'), c. 1330, Shiraz, Iran*

scouting, raiding, pursuit and other activities. Lev also stresses the high level of Fatimid siegecraft. Given all this, why were the Fatimids so unsuccessful against the Crusaders? The failure of the Fatimid armies in Palestine was due much more to problems of leadership and finance than to military weaknesses in the army.[8] Nor should it be forgotten that the Fatimids were facing a foe not hitherto encountered in the warfare of the Levant, a foe accustomed to a style of combat for which the Fatimids were unprepared and actuated by a militant religious faith which energised the morale of the entire Crusader army.

The Role of the Turkish Horsemen

Figure 8.2 *Turkish horse-archer, Pseudo-Galen, Kitab al-Diryaq ('The Book of Antidotes'), c. 1250, Iraq*

It is worth remembering that it was Central Asia – the launching pad for the Turkish invasions of the Islamic world – which was the source for the 'celestial' or 'blood-sweating' horses so prized in China from the second century BC onwards.[9] As al-Jahiz (d. 255/868–9) mentions long before the coming of the Franks, the Turks were accustomed to fighting on horseback. The nomadic invasions of the eleventh century did, however, bring the Turkish horse archers into greater prominence and their astonishing success came, as Boudot-Lamotte puts it, from the 'union of horse and bow'.[10] Their extraordinary mobility formed a sharp contrast with the heavily mailed and armed knights of western Europe.

The Turks were famed for the so-called 'Scythian' method of shooting, also called the 'Parthian shot' (figure 8.3),[11] which was of very ancient origin. They would come charging at full speed towards the enemy and then at the last moment wheel round and shoot as they retreated. According to al-Tarsusi, the Turks 'all pull the arrows right back as far as their chests'.[12] Such tactics as these were ideal for disconcerting the Frankish cavalry. The last thing the Turks were ready to do was to 'stand and fight'. It is important to note that Turkish horsemen such as these performed a key role in the armies of Nur al-Din, Saladin and their successors.

The reputation of the Turcomans and of other Turkish troops as mounted archers was legendary. Over millennia the Turks in their

Figure 8.3 *Turco-Mongol mounted archer, painting, sixteenth century, Iran*

nomadic milieu had learned speed and mobility on horseback; these were characteristics of Turkish warfare even before the arrival of the stirrup.[13] They would appear and disappear, lay ambushes, harass their foes, choose their own time and location for fighting and then move away when the enemy had barely had the time to react. According to al-Jahiz in his well-known treatise on the merits of the Turks, their ability with the bow and arrow was remarkable:

> If a thousand Turkish horsemen charge and discharge a thousand arrows all at once, they prostrate a thousand men; and there is no other army that can charge as well . . . Their arrows hit the mark as much when they are retreating as when they are advancing.[14]

Even when the impact of their bows did diminish in accuracy, they could still shoot and injure horses at a considerable distance.

It would be misleading to assume that the Turks were archers alone; in the context of a pitched battle rather than a harassing pursuit of an enemy convoy, the Turcomans could and did engage in hand-to-hand fighting with lance or sword, having disencumbered themselves of their bows by hanging them over their shoulders. Although the Turks kept a range of animals other than horses, it was the horses that were used in raids and other military encounters. It is noted in the sources that the Turcomans often had not just one horse but several, which enabled them to keep up the harassment in a raid by recourse to fresh horses when needed.

The remarks of al-Jahiz, although made during the ninth century with special reference to the Turks used by the 'Abbasid caliphs as their bodyguards and crack troops, hold good too for the twelfth-century Turks in both their nomadic environment and as slave soldiers of medieval Muslim rulers. Al-Jahiz is quick to point out the equestrian skills of the Turks, their resilience and sheer gritty determination in the face of adversity:

Figure 8.4 *Horseman, fresco, tenth century, Nishapur, Iran*

> His patience for continuing in the saddle and for going on without stopping and for long night journeys and for crossing a country is remarkable . . . and supposing at the end of a Turk's life one were to number his days, it would be found that he had spent longer time sitting upon his beast than he had spent sitting upon the earth.[15]

The Turks had a great capacity to disconcert their enemy by grouping and regrouping and returning repeatedly to the fray. Unlike the more formally disposed order of their enemies, such as the armies of settled Muslim rulers, the Turks were not organised into three main divisions, the right and left flanks and the centre; instead, they were in many small groups which tried to encircle the enemy. Although these groups were separate, they were able to reinforce each other when required and kept up the relentless pressure on the enemy.

513

Following their time-honoured lifestyle, the Turks fought for plunder, and this was often criticised by medieval writers who came from sedentary backgrounds:

> The Turk does not fight for religion nor for interpretation of Scripture nor for sovereignty nor for taxes nor for patriotism nor for jealousy ... nor for defence of the home nor for wealth, but only for plunder.[16]

Al-Tarsusi gives some insight into the tactics of medieval Muslim mounted archers in Saladin's army. If the enemy is positioned far away but within striking distance of arrows, al-Tarsusi advises the archers to disperse and to shoot at them separately. He counsels the archers to join up together if the enemy comes closer. If the enemy has dismounted, al-Tarsusi tells the Muslims to hasten to position themselves in such a way that the enemy is between water and marshy ground. If this is impossible, he concludes: 'Precipitate yourselves upon them, shooting at their riding animals, and shoot again and again, for that will be the cause of their being defeated.'[17]

At the battle of Balat in 513/1119 the devastating effects of the hail of Turkish arrows is graphically described by the Aleppan chronicler Ibn al-'Adim. Noting that all the Turks attacked as one from all directions, he comments: 'The arrows were like locusts because of the vast quantity of the arrows which fell onto the horses and men ...'[18]

In his description of the battle of Balat, Ibn al-Qalanisi also stresses the importance of the archers in bringing about this victory: 'They [eyewitnesses] saw some of the horses stretched out on the ground like hedgehogs because of the quantity of arrows sticking into them.'[19]

A key factor in Turkish military strength lay in their horses. For centuries they had been justifiably famed in the caliphal and other Muslim armies for their ability with the bow whilst on horseback. But the exact role played by their horses remains tantalisingly obscure. The bonds between men and horses must have been very strong but we do not know, for example, how the Turkish nomads tended their steeds or how they deployed them in raids and battles. Slow, heavy horses were probably used to carry weapons and supplies; once arrived near the battle front, these would be corralled and lighter, faster horses would be mounted for the actual fray.

Figure 8.5
(above, opposite and overleaf)
*Coins of various Turcoman
principalities,
twelfth–thirteenth centuries,
Turkey and Iraq*

The Avoidance of Military Engagement and the Use of Stratagems

The Muslim military manuals devote considerable space to the strategy of war, although their instructions are rather unspecific and vague.

The importance of conserving manpower and deploying stratagems to avoid military engagement is emphasised. Al-Ansari says rather cryptically: 'Victories which have occurred through excellence of stratagem and grace of ingenuity, with the self safe and the armies preserved and with no expenditure of effort, are the best.'[20] Battle with the enemy is emphatically the last resort, undertaken only when all other stratagems have failed. As al-Ansari points out:

> In general, the one seeking to do battle against the enemy should not move to engage him, but should accept safety and peace as long as they are granted to one . . . One does not seek victory by engaging him so long as victory can be attained through stratagems.[21]

In his Mirror for Princes work, Yusuf Khass Hajib also points out the importance of using guile and cunning with which 'you make the enemy's face yellow'.[22]

The evidence in the Muslim chronicles confirms that the model advice in the military manuals was carried out in practice by rulers and commanders. Al-Maqrizi remarks in his obituary of the Ayyubid sultan al-'Adil, Saladin's brother (d. 615/1218): 'Al-'Adil did not see it as wise to engage his enemy openly, preferring rather in his designs to use guile and deception.'[23]

The Importance of Good Leadership

The fate of the army general was crucial to the eventual outcome of the battle. If he fell, the morale of the whole army was affected. This was the case in the battle of Marj al-Suffar in 520/1127 when Tughtegin fell from his horse and, thinking that he had been killed, his companions fled.[24]

Such an incident explains why Muslim military manuals stress the importance of good leadership in the army. Al-Ansari, for example, writes:

> The general of the army must be perfect of intelligence, strong of heart, full of courage, greatly vigilant, very cautious, strong in resolution; perceptive about the rules of wars . . . aware of stratagems . . . informed about the management of armies and the organisation of troops . . . painstaking about the maintenance of morale among his soldiers; disinclined to give battle through favouring stratagems whenever possible . . .[25]

The importance of charismatic leadership is also stressed by the chroniclers. Saladin's presence could snatch victory from the jaws of defeat. As Ibn Shaddad records:

> On the day of the great battle on the plain of Acre the centre of the Muslim ranks was broken, drums and flags fell to the ground, but he stood firm with a handful of men until he was able to withdraw

all his men to the hill and then lead them down into battle again, *shaming them* into turning and fighting.[26]

Ultimately the victory was given by God to the Muslims.[27]

Even allowing for the panegyrics showered on Baybars in the sources, he emerges beyond dispute as an outstanding general, towering over Nur al-Din and Saladin in his grasp of the practicalities of war. He ruled his territories with an iron hand and controlled his army with similar austerity and discipline. According to Ibn Shaddad, Baybars forbade all gatherings, had everyone watched, and kept the spies in their turn under surveillance. Even at home, people feared that the walls had ears. Those who disregarded his prohibitions were hanged, drowned, crucified, imprisoned, banished and blinded at the sultan's orders.[28] His recent biographer, the German scholar Thorau, remarks that he consistently distinguished himself as a military commander.[29]

Yet even a first-class general could not achieve much without good troops and weapons. Like the Persian vizier Nizam al-Mulk, the Central Asian Turk Yusuf Khass Hajib, writing in Chagatay, is interested in military strategy. He stresses that it is not the size of an army that matters but the quality of its troops and weapons:

> Look not for numbers in your troops
> But soldiers choice and weapons sure.
> Few and disciplined are the best:
> Many a large troop did not endure.[30]

A Muslim Army on the Move

During the period of the Crusades the chief theatre of war was Syria. Certain predictable patterns can be discerned in the Muslim war effort against the Franks. Campaigns were usually undertaken in the spring. The preparations for important campaigns were prolonged and complicated; an army on the move over long distances and for several months at a time needed a vast amount of provisions, equipment and camp followers. Small wonder that there was little attempt to conceal the progress of a large expeditionary force.

The observance of the faith of Islam was an essential aspect of the life of an army on the move, not only for purposes of ideology and morale but also for the reinforcement of corporate discipline. This was particularly the case from the time of Nur al-Din onwards and was certainly a vital part of Mamluk military life. Prayers were probably conducted in the open by the army on campaign, although it is interesting to note that in 661/1262-3 Baybars ordered the manufacture of a tented mosque (*jami' kham*). This structure contained a *mihrab* and a *maqsura* and was pitched to the right of the royal tent.[31] Whether this practice harked back to his own steppe heritage or had some other source is not clear.

Amongst the personnel escorting the Mamluk army were doctors, including surgeons and pharmacists, as well as those who tended to the spiritual needs of the army, such as Qur'an readers, preachers, religious lawyers and Sufi *shaykh*s. Women often went with the army. The military expedition would be accompanied by a large baggage train transported by carts which were drawn by oxen or other beasts of burden. Food and arms were transported with the army. In Mamluk times, camels were used when possible. The different sections

Figure 8.6 *Horsemen waiting to participate in a parade, al-Hariri, al-Maqamat ('The Assemblies'), 634/1237, probably Baghdad, Iraq*

Figure 8.7 *A drum in use during an attack on a city, fragment of Rashid al-Din, Jami' al-Tawarikh ('World History'), early fourteenth century, Tabriz, Iran*

of the army were recognised by their banners (*raya*) (plates 8.1 and 8.2; cf. figure 8.6). The commander-in-chief had his own standard (*liwa'*). The army would also be accompanied by drummers (cf. figures 8.7 and 8.9) and trumpeters. Usama mentions an incident when trumpeters were used to instil order and discipline into the army during a dangerous march through enemy territory.[32]

Battles

Introduction

Despite the genuine reluctance on both sides in the conflict to engage in open battles, with their high risk factor, a number of key battles did take place and they are recorded in the Islamic sources. Their propaganda value, if the Muslims were victorious, was enormous, but the surviving accounts of them are virtually useless for anyone seeking to gain an overview of Muslim battle strategy or to find the cause of individual victories on either side. Nearly two centuries of Crusader occupation saw surprisingly few battles, however, and yet they have been given a disproportionate amount of attention in accounts of the Crusades.

The Battle Formation of the Muslim Armies

Lo! Allah loveth those who battle for His cause in ranks, as if they were a solid structure.[33]

Plate 8.1 *Mamluk banner, openwork steel, fifteenth century, Egypt*

In view of this Qur'anic injunction it is not surprising that the faithful believed in the efficacy and necessity of fighting on the battlefield in even and closely serried ranks like rows of worshippers at prayer. The Muslim military manuals, too, have something to say about the disposition of troops. Indeed, al-Tarsusi devotes a special section in his manual to the disposition (*tartib*) of the Muslim armies.[34] The details he provides correspond to the references to battle formations in the Islamic chronicles, although there must have been some variations between armies in different periods and areas during the Crusades.

He writes that: 'Amongst the principles are that the army should have a centre, a right wing and a left wing.'[35] The battle order of the troops should be as follows:

> The foot soldier is placed in front of the knight in order to be as it were a fortress for him. A fence or cuirass or parapet should be placed in front of each foot soldier in order to fend off from him the harm of those who would attack him with sword or lance or piercing arrow. Between every two of these men an archer ... should be positioned in order that he may shoot if an opportunity presents itself.[36]

These preliminary measures are clearly designed to protect the cavalry and to choose the ideal moment for the charge. As al-Tarsusi explains: 'The cavalry and the champions behind them should stand aside from the danger from which these archers protect them.' Eventually a 'door is opened' for them through which to charge.[37]

Al-Tarsusi seems to be well aware of enemy tactics:

> It is necessary when arranging the battlefield to organise the contingents (*ajnad*), one by one, and to arrange the cavalry flag by flag, portion (*khamis*) by portion, since the custom of the enemy is to attack in their entirety ... as do the accursed Franks and neighbours like them.[38]

Without describing any specific battles, al-Ansari speaks at considerable length about the desirable conduct of the army in battle.[39] The army should have its back against a mountain, river or hill. Alternatively, the commander should build trenches or set up ambushes.[40] The sun and wind should be behind the rear of his army, to dazzle and blow dust into the enemy's eyes.[41] He outlines how to set up ambushes.[42] When in battle formation, the army should have a centre and a left and right flank (figures 7.10 and 8.8). The infantry is to be positioned in front of the cavalry.[43] The different parts of the army should attempt to hold their positions.

Yusuf Khass Hajib offers the following counsel in his book:

> Put trusty men in the van and the rear, and some also in the wings, both left and right. Then, as they approach the opposing force, let them meet them head on and raise a shout. They should let fly their arrows while yet at some distance; as they draw closer, attack with their spears; and when they engage in the fray, use sword and battle-axe, grab hold the collar, fight tooth and nail.[44]

Thus we see at least three stages of fighting: cavalry arrows, closer encounters with spears and then bitter hand-to-hand fighting.

These model instructions appear to correspond to the actual formations of the battles themselves. When the Franks came to the Levant

Plate 8.2 *Mamluk banner, openwork steel, fifteenth century, Egypt*

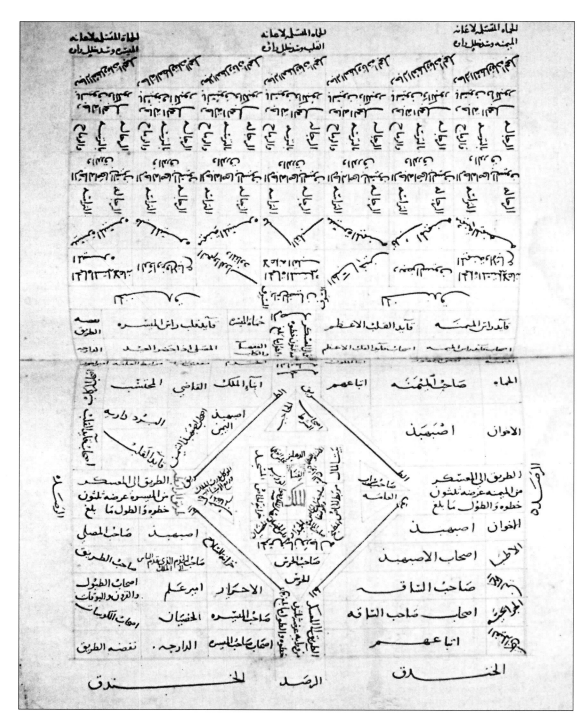

Figure 8.8 *Page explaining battle tactics in diagrammatic form, al-Aqsara'i,* Nihayat al-Su'l *('An End to Questioning'), 773/1371, Egypt*

they brought with them a military tradition which relied heavily on frontal cavalry charges. These had a massive impact, but they went in one direction only and could be reversed only with great difficulty once they had begun. The Frankish cavalry was often very effective against the Fatimid armies but had problems dealing with the light Muslim cavalry of the Turks.

In battle the Franks were famous for their cavalry charges with lances. These were not conducted *en masse* but were aimed by chosen units at chosen targets.[45] A number of instances of Frankish cavalry charges are cited in the Muslim sources. Such charges were very effective if used at the right moment and on suitable terrain. The Frankish cavalry were very heavy and were capable of decimating their enemy if the latter was unhorsed and in disarray.

Clearly, the Muslims were obliged to develop strategies to deal with the initially awesome Frankish cavalry. If the Muslims managed to get out of the way of the cavalry charge, hamper the pace of their horses and engage them in fighting in disorganised and static formations, then the Franks were no longer necessarily at an advantage. The way to success for the Muslims lay in trying to prevent the Frankish lancer – an indubitably strong but inflexible opponent – from using his advantage in the cavalry charge. The mounted archers of the Muslims, arranged in small groups, would try to envelop the flank or rear of their enemies. There was danger if the Franks were allowed to deliver a cavalry charge.[46] In open country the main task for the mounted archers was to break the enemy charge by shooting from a distance. The battle order in almost every important battle of the Mamluk period was the familiar tripartite arrangement of the centre (*qalb*), and the right (*maymana*) and left (*maysara*) wings. The crack troops were placed in the centre; they fought under the personal command of the sultan and under his royal banner. It was very common that the wings of the army would be defeated first and that the centre would hold out longer. Not infrequently, the wings of both armies could become detached from the centre and remain cut off from the course of the ensuing battle. It was also not unknown for the wing of the ultimately losing side in a battle to enjoy success in earlier stages of the conflict in routing the wing of the opposing side.[47]

As with the crucial moment just before capturing a citadel under siege, it was customary at the beginning of a battle to make a great din to terrify the enemy, using trumpets, drums (figures 8.7 and 8.9) and cymbals.[48] A herald would give the order to attack and could also intervene in the heat of the battle to call for a regrouping of troops.[49]

Figure 8.9 *Mamluk brass drum inlaid with silver and gold and inscribed with the name of al-Malik al-Ashraf, late fifteenth century, Egypt*

Siege Warfare

Introduction

The importance of siege warfare in the Crusader–Muslim conflict cannot be over-emphasised. Pitched battles were, after all, as already

Plate 8.3 *Qal'at al-Najm,
exterior fortifications in
dressed stone, mainly
twelfth–thirteenth centuries,
Syria*

(Creswell Photographic Archive,
Ashmolean Museum, Oxford,
neg. C. 6101)

noted, rare. Recent scholarly studies have indeed underlined the fact that well-planned siege warfare held the key to Muslim victory. This interpretation is upheld by the evidence of the Islamic chronicles, which are full of accounts of individual sieges, and it is confirmed by the importance attached to siege warfare by the Islamic military manuals. There is, of course, no overall analysis or reflection in the chronicles about why Muslim siege warfare was so successful, but the medieval historians do proudly record, with a vivid sense of occasion, the individual sieges in the careers of Nur al-Din and Saladin and the wave of victorious sieges undertaken by the Mamluks between 1260 and 1291. The Muslim sources are well aware of the difficulty of capturing Crusader strongholds, whose size and impregnability are emphasised.[50]

The Franks were anxious to avoid pitched battles and to conserve their resources. Given the nature of Frankish settlement in the Levant and the concentration of their manpower within fortified places, an obvious way for the Muslims to get rid of them was to besiege their strongholds and to gain possession of them, one by one. Quite often the Muslims thereupon razed them. Even if there were not sufficient resources to effect a total siege of a fortress, other strategies could be

Plate 8.4 Qal'at al-Najm, interior, mainly twelfth–thirteenth centuries, Syria

(Creswell Photographic Archive, Ashmolean Museum, Oxford, neg. C. 6111)

adopted, for example to block access, thereby preventing supplies of food and water from reaching the garrison, and thus to force it to surrender. The Muslim sources speak with greater precision about sieges than they do about battles. This is scarcely surprising, perhaps, since the details of the successive stages of a siege could be grasped and understood more easily than battles, which by their very nature were more fluid and amorphous and which were impossible to follow in every corner of the field. Even an eyewitness was liable to grasp only part of the entire action.

Siege Weapons

Both sides in the conflict used much the same basic equipment and machines for defence and attack in sieges.[51] Some siege machines were transported ready-made, whilst others were assembled on site. The siege weapons for attacking Safad in 1266 were made in the area of Acre and Damascus and then borne by camel to Safad. They were so heavy that men had to help to carry them.[52] These devices for throwing missiles varied in the method of propulsion used.

The Mangonel (Manjaniq)

The siege engine known in Arabic as the *manjaniq* was a swing-beam machine, which unleashed stones or other projectiles by rocking a giant arm. The mangonel had long been in use in the Islamic world. Until the twelfth century manpower had been used to pull down the short end of the beam, but certainly by Saladin's time a new swing-beam machine which used a heavy counterweight had been introduced. Such machines are illustrated by al-Tarsusi, who identifies three kinds of mangonels – Arab, Turkish and Frankish.[53] According to the same source, the maximum range of such machines was around 120 metres, but it was probably longer.[54] The ammunition comprised either specially rounded stones (these have been found on the sites of many Crusader castles in the Levant) or Greek fire.

Usama mentions the Byzantines using mangonels in 532/1138; they were capable of throwing 'a stone to a distance farther than the distance covered by the arrow, their stone being twenty to twenty-five ratls[55] in weight' (that is, c. 64–80 kilos).[56] There were machines in the thirteenth century capable of hurling much heavier missiles than this (cf. figures 8.15 and 8.18).

A counterweight mangonel was used in the siege of Hims in 646/1248–9. It could throw a stone weighing 140 Syrian *ratls* (c. 448 kilos).[57] Mangonels were also used by Baybars at Arsuf, Safad, Beaufort, Krak des Chevaliers and Gibelacar. He was able to supervise their use, and he had the resources to erect them quickly *in situ* and to operate them effectively.[58] These devices were not used with uniform frequency throughout the period of Frankish occupation. The mangonel remained the main machine for throwing heavy missiles in the sieges of both the twelfth and thirteenth centuries; but as a weapon of war it faded out after the removal of the Franks from the Near East.[59] This presumably has much to do with the distinctly lower quality of the Muslim fortifications (plates 8.5 and 8.6). Muslim castles could therefore be reduced by simpler and quicker means.

Ayalon and others have already emphasised the paramount importance of the siege warfare of the Mamluks; indeed, siege warfare was the decisive, almost the only, factor which brought about the final removal of the Franks from Muslim soil. There were many more sieges under the Mamluks than their predecessors, the Ayyubids, and the seriousness of their endeavours can be gauged by their increased investment in mangonels. Ayalon has made a revealing comparison between the number of mangonels used by the Ayyubid sultans, including Saladin (who used a maximum of ten mangonels and often many fewer), and those deployed in Mamluk sieges.[60] Even allowing for exaggerations, all records were broken at the siege of Acre where some sources say the mangonels numbered 92 and others 72. It is thus a telling symbol of Muslim desire to rid the Near East of the Franks that at this siege – usually taken as the last major decisive action against the Franks in the Levant – al-Ashraf Khalil used so many mangonels. This was the testimony of the chronicler Abu'l-Fida, who was present at the siege.[61] A massive mangonel called al-Mansuri (possibly named after Baybars himself) was used: it had to be dismantled to be transported, an operation that required a number of wagons.[62] The types of mangonels at Acre, like others in earlier sieges, had nicknames: Frankish (*ifranji*), devilish (*shaytani*), black bull-like (*qarabugha*) and playful (*la'ib*).[63]

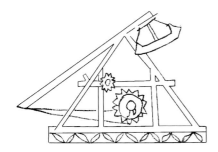

Figure 8.10 *Mangonel, furusiyya (military horsemanship) manuscript, thirteenth century, perhaps Egypt*

Plate 8.5 *Qal'at Ja'bar, exterior, mainly from 564/1168–9 onwards (rebuilding of Nur al-Din) and 736/1335–6 (rebuilding of the Mamluk governor of Damascus, Tengiz), Syria*

(Creswell Photographic Archive, Ashmolean Museum, Oxford, neg. C. 6660)

The Ballista ('arrada)

For a less heavy projectile a ballista ('*arrada*) was used. This device achieved the same effect as the mangonel by twisting a cord. It is not always possible to distinguish in the sources between a mangonel and a ballista. It seems that the ballista was lighter and could be moved around relatively easily, whilst the mangonel once assembled was too bulky to transport.

Plate 8.6 *Qal'at Ja'bar, exterior, mainly from 564/1168–9 onwards (rebuilding of Nur al-Din) and 736/1335–6 (rebuilding of the Mamluk governor of Damascus, Tengiz), Syria*

(Creswell Photographic Archive, Ashmolean Museum, Oxford, neg. C. 6661)

The Wheel Crossbow

A third machine was the wheel crossbow (*qaws al-ziyar*); it was operated like an ordinary crossbow but required several men to operate it. A contemporary drawing of it exists but the sources do not appear to discuss such key elements as the type of missile used, its range and its penetrative power.

Siege Towers and Penthouses

On flat terrain, both Frankish and Muslim attackers would use the tower (*burj*) or the penthouse or covered shelter (*dabbaba*) which was mounted on wheels and pushed to the bottom of the fortifications. When close to the walls, those ramming them or sapping beneath them would be protected by these machines.

The term *dabbaba* (penthouse) is an especially evocative one: the Arabic root *dabba* has a range of meanings including to crawl (like an insect or reptile) and to move slowly. The Roman *testudo* readily comes to mind. Nowadays, the word *dabbaba* means an armoured tank. In Crusader times it signified a kind of tower housing soldiers whose task it was to attack the walls of a citadel or town. Sometimes the penthouse had four storeys, one of wood, one of lead, one of iron and one of copper.[64] From a contraption such as this the besiegers could fight the defenders on the walls and then jump across to continue the struggle.

Ibn Shaddad describes a special Frankish tower (*burj*) which had been made at sea aboard a 'frightening ship' (*butsa*):

> In it [the ship] they had constructed a tower (*burj*) with a trunk. If they wanted to turn it against the wall it would turn with amazing movements and would make a path to the place against which it was directed: on it [the path] the warriors would walk.[65]

So the machine seems to have been a kind of elaborate gangplank or portable drawbridge.

Battering Rams

Once the Frankish attackers were close to the walls of a fortified place the battering ram, known in Arabic as *kabsh* or *sinnawr* (cat), would be used against the ramparts.

The 'King of the Germans' (Frederick of Swabia) produced some remarkable machines in 586/1190–1. Ibn Shaddad writes:

> He made use of amazing machines and strange contrivances that terrified the viewer. The people of the town were frightened of those machines and fearful of them. Amongst the items they had created was a vast war machine beneath which a great number of warriors could enter; it was covered with plates of iron. Underneath it, it had carts to drag it along. It had a large head with which to butt the wall. It is called a ram (*kabsh*) with which to butt the wall with great force because many people drag it along and it causes it [the wall] to collapse through repeated butts.[66]

Ibn Shaddad also mentions a machine known as the 'cat' (*sinnawr*): '[There is] another machine which is a vault (*qabu*) under which are a number of men. But its head is sharpened [to a point] in the shape of a ploughshare.'

Comparing the ram and the cat, Ibn Shaddad concludes that the former destroys by its sheer weight alone whereas the latter does so both by its sharpness and its weight.[67]

After Baybars' use of siege machines, the Muslim chroniclers fall silent about the use of such devices and although the encyclopaedists al-'Umari (d. 749/1349) and al-Qalqashandi (d. 821/1418) write chapters on siege machines, they do not refer to either the *burj* or the *dabbaba*.[68]

Greek Fire (Naft)

The term *naft* is used in the medieval Islamic sources to denote an incendiary device, capable of spontaneous combustion.[69] The use of such a weapon dates back to ancient times but the Byzantines exploited it to great advantage against the Arabs in the early Islamic period with a newly improved version of Greek fire allegedly devised by a man from Syria called Kallinikos in 673.

Ships were equipped with catapults, which as well as holding stones and arrows were also loaded with clay jars filled with *naft*. On impact the jars broke into pieces and their contents ignited. Ships also carried incendiary rockets together with a mechanism for launching them.[70] By the middle of the seventh century the Muslims were also throwing Greek fire.

Sea battles were rather rare, however; few examples stand out between the battles of Actium in 31 BC and Lepanto in 1571 and certainly no major military encounter at sea occurred in the Crusading period. But Greek fire was used to great effect by the Muslims on land, in attacking and defending citadels and walled towns.[71] *Naft* was thrown in bottles by means of catapults and slings at towers and penthouses which were working above ground.

Al-Tarsusi describes various 'recipes' for making Greek fire.[72] One of the 'recipes' given by al-Tarsusi is as follows:

Figure 8.11 *Specialists in Greek fire* (naffatin); *rockets known as 'Chinese arrows' and using saltpetre ('Chinese snow') are mentioned by al-Hasan al-Rammah in the late thirteenth century. Furusiyya (military horsemanship) manuscript, fourteenth century, Egypt*

> *How to make an excellent naphtha to be thrown*
> *with the mangonel*
>
> Take 10 pounds of tar, 3 pounds of resin, 1½ pounds each of sandarac and lac, 3 pounds of pure, good quality sulphur, free from all soil, 5 pounds of melted dolphin fat, the same quantity of liquefied, clarified fat from goats' kidneys. Melt the tar, add the fats, then throw in the resin after having melted it separately. Then grind the other ingredients, each one separately, add them to the mixture, put fire under it, and let it cook until all is thoroughly mixed. If you wish to use it in time of war, take one part, add about a tenth part of the mineral sulphur called naphtha, which is greenish and looks like old oil, place the whole in a skillet and boil until it is about to burn. Take the pot, which should be earthenware, and a piece of felt. Then throw it with a mangonel against whatever you wish to burn. It will never be extinguished.[73]

At Kafartab one of the Muslim soldiers, a Turk, approached the tower and threw a bottle of naphtha at the Franks on the top of it: 'The naphtha flashed like a meteor falling upon those hard stones, while the men who were there threw themselves on the ground for fear of being burnt.'[74]

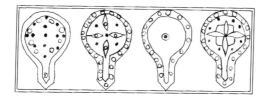

Figure 8.12 Glass projectiles containing white naphtha, Kitab al-makhzun *('Book of Treasure'), 875/1470, probably Egypt*

The development of *naft* as a vital aspect of siege warfare seems to have been the favoured Muslim response to the problem of dealing with the Frankish siege machines, namely the *burj* and the *dabbaba*. *Naft* proved effective against the wooden siege machines of the Franks but was of little use against their castles and fortifications which were generally made of stone. It is worth citing the example of the Muslim use of *naft* in 587/1191–2 against a Frankish *dabbaba*, as related by Ibn Shaddad:

> The enemy had constructed a large terrifying *dabbaba* of four storeys. The first storey was of wood, the second one of lead, the third of iron, and the fourth of copper. It was higher than the wall and warriors rode inside it. The inhabitants of the town were very afraid of it and resolved to ask the enemy for safe-conduct. They [the Franks] had brought it [the *dabbaba*] near the wall so that there was at a glance a distance of only five cubits between it and the wall. The people began to throw *naft* at it continuously by night and by day until Almighty God decreed that it should be burnt.[75]

The Conduct of Sieges

Preparations for Sieges

Both sides undertook careful and lengthy preparations before beginning a siege. Both sides used the same basic weapons for defence and attack,[76] although, as Marshall points out, the Muslims seem to have been the only ones to use naphtha and hand-held slings for hurling stones.[77]

Baybars is reported on several occasions, such as at Arsuf in 663/1265, to have inspected the mangonels himself.[78] Careful preparations were also made before the siege of Acre in 1291. The Muslims spent several days preparing trenches and palisades and placing their machines around the walls.[79]

Strategies for Capturing Citadels

There were various strategies by which to gain possession of a castle, tower or walled city. Sometimes it was possible to batter the fortifications in such a devastating fashion that the besiegers could enter. Alternatively, negotiations would take place, after a protracted siege, and the fortified place would surrender on agreed terms. Some of the most impregnable fortresses in the Levant changed hands through ruse, duplicity and bribes. This approach was, of course, preferable, since it prevented the subsequent expense of rebuilding the fortress after it had been captured – if, indeed, that was to be done.

There were, however, other factors which played a part in the successful prosecution of a siege; above all, much depended on the morale of the troops in the garrison inside. As Smail so aptly puts it, 'men, not walls, made the city'.[80] For example, in the period immediately following Saladin's great victory at Hattin, his prestige was so high that the fortresses he went on to besiege surrendered within three days and Acre after only one. Two years later, however, the garrison at Acre resisted capture by siege for almost two years against the Franks, in part at least because they knew that Saladin's army was in the field helping them.

Procedures in Conducting Sieges

Certain general procedures were usually followed in a siege and have been well described by Cahen and Ayalon.[81] Part of the moat was filled in, so that the attackers could move across it. At night there would be attempts to scale the walls using ladders and ropes and open one of the gates (cf. plate 4.24) to the besiegers.

Another important aspect of most sieges was the breaching of the ramparts and walls. If successful, this procedure effected openings in the walls or, better still, made them collapse. Breaching was performed by making tunnels or by using siege machines. The sappers

Figure 8.13 *Siege of fortress by mailed cavalrymen, silver dish, perhaps tenth century, Central Asia*

would dig a tunnel and support it with wooden props; they would then extend it gradually until they ended up underneath the walls or ramparts. At that point they would set fire to wood in the tunnel and this would cause the ground and the edifice above it to subside. When digging a tunnel (*naqb*), it was essential to remain out of sight of the besieged, since if they became aware of the tunnel they would attempt to destroy it by making their own tunnel to intercept it. Such a counter-tunnel aimed at digging into the enemy's tunnel, killing the sappers – or smoking them out – and then destroying the tunnel.

The art of sapping in the Muslim world reached its peak in the twelfth and thirteenth centuries, no doubt as a result of the necessity of applying and refining it against a new foe, the Franks, whose renowned expertise in building castles and towers now required on the Muslim side a technique capable of undermining them. It was certainly preferable to use sapping wherever possible since the sappers would work underground out of the firing range of the missiles.

The length of time taken by Muslim attackers to capture Frankish castles became shorter in the Mamluk period as the Muslims became more and more competent in the use of artillery. As Kennedy says, 'castles fell within a few weeks or not at all'.[82] A spate of Crusader citadels which were besieged by the Mamluks in the second half of the thirteenth century – including Arsuf (1266), Krak des Chevaliers (1271), Margat (1285) and Acre (1291) – each took only six weeks to capitulate.[83]

Whilst, as already mentioned, the mangonel remained a very significant siege weapon, the other pieces of equipment – the tower, penthouse and Greek fire – were less significant in the Mamluk period than they had been in the earlier confrontations with the Franks. But as mentioned already, the technique of sapping fortifications was regularly used.

Sapping

Sapping was a technique used more by the Muslims than the Franks.[84] Instances of its effectiveness are recorded from the earliest period of the Crusader presence. It was dangerous and time-consuming, however, and required great skill.[85]

In 509/1115–16 Bursuq was commissioned by sultan Muhammad to lead an expedition against the Franks. Usama and his father joined him. They encamped before Kafartab, which was in the possession of the Franks. The Muslims built an underground tunnel which Usama inspected. He describes it in some detail:

I was struck with the great wisdom with which the tunnel was executed. The tunnel was dug from the trench to the barbican (*bashura*). On the sides of the tunnel were set up two pillars, across which stretched a plank to prevent the earth above it from falling down. The whole tunnel had such a framework of wood that extended as far as the foundation of the barbican. Then the assailants dug under the walls of the barbican, supported it in its place, and went as far as the foundation of the tower. . . .

Having stuffed the tunnel with dry wood, the sappers set fire to it. The layers of mortar between the stones of the wall began to fall out, a crack appeared and the tower collapsed.[86]

Usama points out in this account that the miners came from distant Khurasan (in north-eastern Iran).[87] Possibly, as Kennedy has suggested, this might indicate that the technology described here was novel and had been introduced in the wake of the Seljuq conquests.

The use of sapping increased greatly in the Mamluk period as the Muslims intensified their efforts to get rid of the last Crusader strongholds.[88] As Ayalon rightly points out, one factor in the Mamluks' success in their sapping operations was that in their besieging of the Frankish coastal fortresses they could act with fewer inhibitions than usual, since they were aiming at razing them to the ground and abandoning the area. These sapping techniques were often enough to force the capitulation of a fortress, but on occasion they were supplemented by frontal attacks on city walls,[89] as for example at Caesarea in 1265.

The Defenders in a Siege

The defenders of a citadel or walled city could adopt various strategies against their attackers.[90] The Franks would sally out against the Muslims, would hurl missiles at them or dig counter-mines. The Franks were particularly successful at Arsuf in 663/1265, where they dug tunnels below the Muslim trenches. Ibn al-Furat writes:

> The Franks cunningly drove a tunnel from within the citadel until they got to a point beneath the blockage. They then cut through the earth until they reached the wood. They had made barrels full of grease and fat and they lit fires, having constructed bellows in the tunnels. The Muslim army knew nothing of this stratagem until the flames had taken hold. This happened at night and the Sultan himself came in the dark; people threw themselves at the fire to extinguish it, and water was poured from water skins, but it was of no use. All the wood in the moat blazed up and scattered into ash and the Franks' stratagem was complete.[91]

Figure 8.14
(above, opposite and overleaf)
Blazons on Mamluk coins,
thirteenth–fifteenth centuries,
Egypt and Syria

The Muslim defenders of a citadel or town showered arrows on the men operating the siege machines, who were protected by huge shields. The defenders also attempted to set fire to the machines by throwing *naft* at them; it was not too difficult to hit such a huge target but as a precautionary measure the siege machines and towers were often covered with hides doused with vinegar to make them fire-proof.

Other Aspects of Siegecraft

It was usual in the conduct of a siege to make a very loud noise to frighten the enemy. During the final attack on a town, the Mamluks would beat many drums (*kusat*) carried on the backs of 'three hundred' camels; this produced a noise like a terrible thunder which turned the world 'upside down'.[92] The depictions of sieges in illustrated manuscripts of the *Jami' al-Tawarikh* ('Compendium of Histories') of Rashid al-Din dating to the early fourteenth century include scenes of such huge drums being beaten (figure 8.7).[93] Ropes are fastened to them, each grasped by a man in such a way as to hold the drum aloft and to ensure maximum tension, while the drummer himself strikes the drum with a stick. The drum was not the only instrument of psychological warfare. Baybars forged letters to weaken enemy morale.

The Aftermath of Sieges

After the completion of a siege and the conquest of a citadel or walled city, there remained for the victorious conqueror the important decision of whether to destroy it or refortify it.

After conquering the citadel of al-Atharib in 524/1130, Zengi, with his legendary ferocity, destroyed it and razed it to the ground. The chronicler Ibn al-Furat remarks that it has remained in ruins until his own time.[94]

Baybars could show similar severity. Jaffa fell to him on 20 Jumada II 666/7 March 1268. The fortifications of this citadel had been improved by Louis IX but Baybars destroyed the edifice and its timber and marble were put on ships and used to build the sultan's mosque in Cairo. This use of spolia no doubt had psychological and propaganda undertones and made this a victory mosque.

In 668/1270 Baybars destroyed the fortifications at Ascalon and made the harbour unusable by submerging tree-trunks and rocks in it.[95]

However, when Baybars acquired the mighty fortress of Safad in Shawwal 664/July 1266, he did not follow his usual practice with captured castles and destroy it, but instead made it into a Mamluk fortress.[96]

Muslim Accounts of Individual Sieges

The military historian Marshall is wary of attaching too much importance to individual accounts of particular sieges, since the format of such accounts may be stereotyped rather than specific.[97] In part this view is surely correct. But it remains true that the Islamic perspective is sometimes highlighted in an unexpected way in the medieval Muslim accounts of individual sieges, especially those of eyewitnesses. Even though such eyewitnesses are inevitably biased, particular snippets of information and the evocation of an atmosphere combine to reveal fresh aspects of the siege phenomenon in the Crusading period.

Many chronicles give descriptions of sieges which took place during the Frankish occupation of the Near East. Those that concern Saladin are particularly detailed; his two major biographers, Ibn Shaddad and 'Imad al-Din, are obviously interested in describing in some detail the sieges in which their hero was involved. A few examples will give the flavour of these accounts.

The Siege of Alexandria by the Sicilian Fleet in 570/1174–1175

'Imad al-Din quotes a letter from Saladin which describes the arrival of the Sicilian fleet in Alexandria in 570/1174–5. Six ships carried 'machines of war and siege made of large pieces of wood and other things'.[98] Other ships transported those who constructed ships, 'crawling' towers,[99] penthouses (*dabbaba*) and mangonels. The attack began the morning after the fleet's arrival:

> In the morning they advanced, harassed and laid siege. They set up three penthouses (*dabbaba*) with their rams and three mangonels, great in size which hurled black stones which they had brought along from Sicily. Our companions were amazed by the violence of their impact and the size of their stones. As for the *dabbabas*, they were like towers in the heaviness of their pieces of wood, their elevation, the number of their warriors and their range [of fire]. They advanced with them until they [the machines] came close to the wall. They [the Sicilians] persevered in fighting for the whole of the above-mentioned day.[100]

Despite the awesome sight of these monstrous enemy machines of war, the letter declares that God gave the Muslims the eventual victory. They fought valiantly and overturned the *dabbabas* which were set up against the walls.

The Siege of Karak in 580/1184–1185

The Muslim sources are explicit about the difficulties of taking the citadel of Karak in 580/1184–5. 'Imad al-Din al-Isfahani gives the following account of the siege:

> He [Saladin] encamped in the valley of Karak and set up nine mangonels against it [the citadel] in a row in front of the gate. They destroyed the wall opposite them. The only obstacle remaining was the wide, deep moat. It is a frightening ravine, an obstructing chasm and a low-lying place of danger. There was only one course of action: choke it up, block it with everything possible and fill it with earth; that was considered a most difficult exercise. Digging tunnels was impracticable because of the ruggedness and rocky nature of the ground. So the sultan gave orders for bricks to be

made, for pieces of wood to be collected and for walls to be built, leading from the suburb to the ditch and that they [the walls] should be roofed and that their [wooden] palisades should be pieced together and smoothly joined.

Once this extensive shield against hostile fire from the walls of the citadel had been constructed, the way was clear to begin filling the moat. Saladin's followers now flocked to carry whatever they could find with which to fill it. The enterprise was also facilitated by *dabbaba*s and tunnels. Because of all these careful preparations, the people were in no danger, according to the chronicler:

> The people found a broad road to the moat and they flocked [there], safe from being wounded, working joyfully. The people below the citadel on the edge of the moat did not feel the need to act cautiously nor did they fear arrow or stone. The moat had been filled [so well] that a prisoner in fetters could have thrown himself into it and escaped after a succession of stones had been thrown at him by the Franks.[101]

Behind the obvious bias and emotional intensity of this account, the author nevertheless provides valuable details of the practicalities of embarking on the early stages of a siege. An account like this shows the problematic nature of sapping in certain kinds of terrain. When performed successfully, however, sapping could bring the attackers right up to the ramparts with the besieged still remaining unaware of the exact location of the tunnel.

The Siege of Sahyun in 584/1188

The siege of the citadel of Sahyun by Saladin in 584/1188 proved notoriously difficult. All the medieval geographical descriptions of this citadel stress its impregnability.[102] It is worth while quoting the account of Saladin's siege of it, as given by Ibn al-Athir, since his narrative reveals some of the general problems facing the besiegers of Frankish castles in the Levant:

> Then Saladin left Ladhiqiyya on 27 Jumada II (584 AH/24 July 1188) and he made for the citadel of Sahyun which is a well-fortified citadel towering in the air, difficult to climb, on a salient of a mountain, surrounded by a deep valley, where some places were narrow enough to allow the stones of a mangonel to reach the citadel from them. However, the mountain was joined to it [the citadel] from the northern side. They [the Franks] had constructed for it [the citadel] a deep moat, the bottom of which could not be seen, and five well-fortified walls. Saladin made camp on that mountain next to it. Mangonels were set up and he launched [projectiles] with them. He gave orders to his son, al-Zahir, lord of

Aleppo, and he went down into the narrow part of the valley and also set up mangonels there. He threw projectiles at the citadel from there. He had with him many Aleppan infantrymen whose level of courage was legendary.

Eventually, the Muslims found a vulnerable point by which to gain access to the citadel wall: 'They attached ladders[103] to a salient of the mountain which the Franks had neglected to fortify and they scaled up from there between the rocks until they reached the first wall.'[104]

It is interesting to note that this account does not mention the principal feature of Sahyun, and one unique in its scale and ambition in the whole Middle East (though more recent versions of this concept are known at 'Ajlun and Shayzar) – the gorge cut by the Franks through the rock to separate the castle's promontory from the rest of the mountain, leaving only a towering needle of rock in the middle on to which a drawbridge could be set. One is tempted to conclude that Ibn al-Athir (or his source) had not actually been at Sahyun.

The Siege of Acre in 586/1190–1191

There are two powerful Muslim accounts of this siege written by Ibn Shaddad and 'Imad al-Din. The latter describes Frankish preparations for the siege of Acre in 586/1190–1 as follows:

> They [the Franks] began to build great high towers (*abraj*). They had transported by sea their machines and heavy timbers and pieces of iron. They built three high towers in three places in the environs of the town. They laboured seven months in [building] them and they did not finish them until Rabi' I [April–May]. They were made as if they were three towering mountains; their storeys were filled with instruments and troops.

> Each tower without fail had in its corners four high, thick, heavy columns. The length of each one was 50 cubits in order to tower over the height of the town walls. They spread them out on wheeled carts. Then they covered them, after a coating of iron and strong bonds, with the hides of cows and [animal] skins. Each day, they would bring them closer, even if [only] by a cubit, as much as was possible, and they would pour vinegar and wine over them.[105]

The town was on the verge of collapse when the tide was turned in an amazing way and the siege towers were burned and collapsed as a 'sign of the power of God'. A young man from Damascus called 'Ali, the son of an expert coppersmith, came forward with an offer to make a mangonel which would burn the towers. According to Ibn Shaddad:

> He said that he had a skill in burning them [the towers] and that, if he could enter Acre and obtain remedies which he knew, he

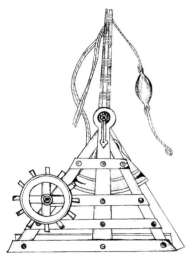

Figure 8.15
Mangonel, Rashid al-Din,
Jami' al-Tawarikh ('World
History'), 714/1314, Tabriz,
Iran

Figure 8.16 *Mounted huntsman with spear, inlaid brass basin known as the 'Baptistère de St Louis', c. 1300 or earlier, Syria*

could set fire to them. Everything he sought was provided for him and he entered Acre, cooked the remedies with the *naft* and put it into copper pots until the whole [concoction] became like a live coal.[106]

The mixture proved efficacious against the Frankish attacks: 'He struck one tower with a pot and it immediately ignited and became like a vast mountain of fire.'[107] The same process occurred with the second and third towers.

Useful information about the aftermath of the burning of the machines is also provided by 'Imad al-Din's narrative. He reports that seventy knights with arms and baggage perished in the first tower. Pieces of iron and metal coats of mail (*zardiyyat*) were unearthed from the ashes.[108]

Even allowing for the usual exaggerations and bias of both these authors, there is here a lively picture of the strategies of attack and defence used in an important siege.

The Siege of Caesarea in 663/1265

In 663/1264–5 Baybars began his first major attacks on the Frankish strongholds in Syria. During this campaign he reduced the key Frankish possession of Caesarea. This was a very difficult citadel to storm. As al-Maqrizi points out:

The Franks had taken there blocks of granite which they had placed horizontally in the body of the walls, in such a way that they would have nothing to fear from sapping, and so that they [the walls] would not fall when they were mined. The attacks and assaults followed one another uninterruptedly. The fortress was continually hit by the impact of machines, ballistas and a hail of arrows.[109]

Baybars had five catapults of Maghribi construction. Additional siege equipment, stonemasons and carpenters were summoned from surrounding fortresses and soldiers set about making scaling ladders.[110] On 9 Jumada I 663/26–27 February 1265 he encircled and stormed Caesarea. The struggle then began for the citadel. It lay on a peninsula which, with naval help, could be attacked from the town, but from one side only. Louis IX had fortified it very well. He had reinforced its walls by classical granite pillars secured crosswise with one another. They could not be mined, as Arabic chroniclers themselves point out. The citadel became the target of stones and Greek fire from catapults and the defenders were overwhelmed with arrows from siege towers. Baybars himself shot arrows continuously from a nearby church tower. When a siege tower was successfully brought up to the wall, Baybars himself participated in the fighting. On 15 Jumada I/5 March the defenders surrendered the citadel and embarked for Acre.

Baybars ordered the town and the citadel to be razed to the ground, probably in order to prevent once and for all Caesarea ever being used again as the bridgehead for a Crusading army.[111]

Figure 8.17 *Foot-soldiers in combat, Blacas ewer, inlaid brass, 629/1232, Mosul, Iraq*

The Siege of Krak des Chevaliers in 669/1270–1271

The sources give plentiful details of the siege of Krak des Chevaliers (*Hisn al-akrad*).[112] In Safar 669/Sept.–Oct. 1270, Baybars, feeling no longer threatened by a Frankish attack launched from overseas, for he had heard of the death of St Louis, led a powerful force into Syria and laid siege to Krak. There were various stages to the siege which are recorded in the sources; first, on 19 Rajab 669/3 March 1271, Baybars occupied the front defences and battered the outer enceinte. Two days later, he captured the first barbican (*bashura*); on 1 Sha'ban/15 March he took the second barbican, at the elbow of the access ramp. Lastly, on 15 Sha'ban/29 March he forced an entry into the central courtyard and the defenders fled into the keep. Baybars launched further attacks with ballistas and on 25 Sha'ban/8 April the keep was surrendered to him and the knights in it were allowed to leave under safe-conduct to take refuge in Tripoli. This citadel was clearly a vital fortification for the Muslims to retain and Baybars personally supervised the necessary repair work to restore it to its former state before leaving on 15 Ramadan/27 April. The short period needed for these repairs indicates clearly enough that the damage inflicted on the fortress was limited – but it must have been at absolutely key areas of the defence.

The Siege of Marqab in 683/1285

Ibn 'Abd al-Zahir gives a detailed account of the siege of Marqab by the Mamluk sultan Qalawun in 683/1285.[113] His account shows the careful preparations which preceded the actual siege. He begins by stressing the difficulties of taking the citadel: 'It is a great forbidding citadel which our master Sultan al-Malik al-Mansur – may God grant him victory – continually persevered to command and tried to take for Islam.'

Yet the taking of it eluded him, although he tried on more than one occasion to do so. The Hospitallers in it had waxed very proud and powerful and had held other nearby citadels in thrall. Indeed, the Franks believed that Marqab could never be taken.[114]

Qalawun equipped mangonels from Damascus: 'Weapons of iron and *naft*, the like of which were only to be found in his store houses and arsenals, were prepared.'

This was all done in advance and the expertise of those who knew about sieges was utilised: 'The mangonels and weapons were carried on necks and heads.'[115] The Muslims used three so-called 'Frankish' mangonels, three 'black bull' mangonels, and four 'devilish' mangonels.[116]

After taking the citadel and deliberating whether to destroy it or not, Qalawun decided to keep it and to reinforce it. He placed in it

Figure 8.18 Mangonel, Rashid al-Din, Jami' al-Tawarikh ('World History'), 714/1314, Tabriz, Iran

warriors, 400 artisans, mangonels, weapons, blocks of wood, firewood, arrows, arsenals, Greek fire and other items of siege warfare.[117]

General Remarks

It is clear from the Islamic sources that the most common form of Crusader–Muslim confrontation was the siege. These sources corroborate Marshall's conclusion that sieges decided the fate of the Crusaders and that 'other forms of military activity were largely incidental'.[118] What the Islamic sources do not reveal – perhaps because it was so self-evident to them or because such a truth would have undermined the glory of their victory – is the overwhelming fact of the Muslim numerical superiority over the Franks.[119]

The Evidence of Three Islamic Works of Art

The Fustat Drawing

The twelfth century is almost entirely devoid of Islamic painting on paper. There is, however, one surviving piece of artistic evidence from the twelfth century which because of its rarity is of great value; it is a much damaged Fatimid drawing found in the rubbish heaps of Fustat, the old Islamic capital of Egypt before the building of Cairo,[120] and is probably datable to some time between 1150 and 1180 (colour plate 13). This tinted drawing shows us a first-hand illustration of weapons used in the twelfth century (figure 8.16). In particular, it depicts the kite-shaped shield which had been known in Egypt at least since the erection of the Bab al-Nasr (Gate of Victory) in Cairo, where it is depicted in monumental form. It also depicts a round shield.

It is difficult to ascertain what actual historical event, if any, this painting is commemorating. As already mentioned, the Franks fought against the Fatimids at various points in the twelfth century, and these clashes included the initiatives of al-Afdal in the early stages of the Crusader presence and the involvement of the Franks in Egyptian affairs during the 1160s. It is possible, therefore, that this picture records a real military encounter between Fatimids and Franks, even one involving the Syrian troops sent out by Nur al-Din. A significant date to be remembered here is 1168, when the Fatimid wazir burned down Fustat. Probably the picture dates from before that time since it was found in the debris there.

The painting depicts some kind of military encounter which is being enacted just beneath the walls of a town or fortified place. The seven warriors illustrated all carry shields and at least four of them are wearing mail. The warriors' headgear is carefully shown: one is wearing a conical Norman helmet with a short nose-piece whilst others have what appear to be turbans on their heads. The two

Figure 8.19 *Foot-soldier, drawing with added colour, twelfth century, Fustat, Egypt*

mounted warriors are wearing long mail hauberks. One of the infantry-men wears baggy knee-length pantaloons.

The Baptistère of St. Louis

The Baptistère of St Louis is an acknowledged masterpiece of Islamic metalwork. It was the subject of a masterly study by Storm Rice accompanied by a series of beautiful drawings and photographs (cf. figures 8.17–8.18, 6.44, 1.7, 8.24, 1.20, 1.9, 9.2, 3.15, 1.8, 8.14, 3.16, 6.72, 1.16 and colour plate 9).[121] This brass basin, now in the Louvre, is signed by a Muslim artist, Muhammad b. al-Zayn, and the consensus of scholarly opinion dates it to the period 1290–1310, though other datings have been suggested. The whole surface of the basin is covered with engraved designs inlaid with silver and gold, and since most of them depict figural scenes, they are a remarkable visual historical document. They show the Mamluk court, battles and hunting expeditions. The details of the costumes are striking. One amir is heavily armed,[122] carrying a sword, mace and bow. Two others are armed with axes.[123]

The battle scenes depicted on the 'Baptistère' are especially interesting (figure 8.18). In one such scene a central figure is wearing splint armour worn over a quilted garment.[124] He is shown having just shot an arrow from his bow. The arrow is lodged in his enemy's neck.[125] A second battle scene shows three horsemen equipped with lance, bow and sword respectively.[126] The dismembered parts of an enemy soldier lie at their horses' feet. The artist has powerfully evoked the danger and ferocity of the battlefield. The basin, which presumably formed part of the table service of a high-ranking Mamluk notable, brings to life the dry, somewhat lifeless instructions of the military manuals.[127] It corroborates their information and adds much vivid detail of its own. We also have here first-hand evidence of the

Figure 8.20 Battle scene, inlaid brass basin known as the 'Baptistère de St Louis', c. 1300 or earlier, Syria

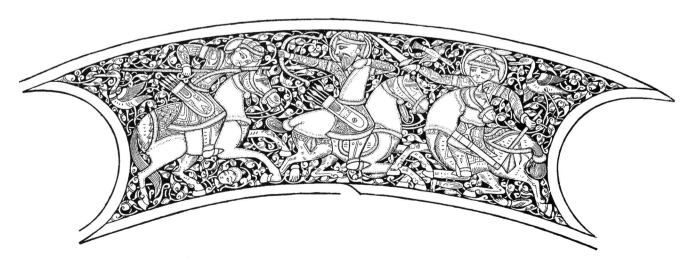

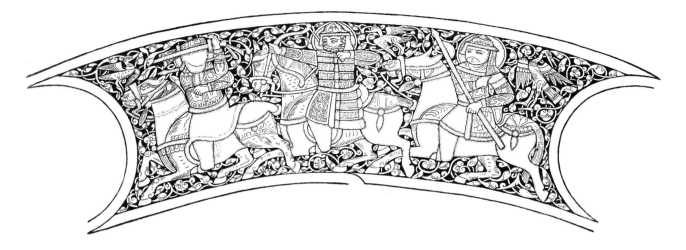

Figure 8.21 *Battle scene, inlaid brass basin known as the 'Baptistère de St Louis', c. 1300 or earlier, Syria*

Mamluk obsession with adding blazons (marks of rank) to the various objects used in an *amir*'s service, such as clothing and weapons. The basin depicts a wide variety of weapons – axes, maces, daggers – in precise detail. It is also an excellent source for contemporary military costume, from headgear to boots, and for the details of horse harness and accoutrements.

A Seljuq Bowl

A surviving early thirteenth-century polychrome *mina'i* Seljuq bowl in the Freer Gallery in Washington is a unique piece of material evidence about the conduct of war in the Crusading period (colour plate 12).[128] Although it comes from Iran and not from the areas under attack from the Franks, it is highly relevant to Crusading warfare because it depicts Turkish warriors attacking a fortress. There was, as already mentioned, a heavy preponderance of Turkish *mamluk* forces and Turcoman auxiliaries in the armies of Zengi, Nur al-Din, Saladin and later commanders. There were probably no great differences in military practice between the Turks in Iran and those in Syria. The dish is therefore of obvious relevance to that military environment. Although some of the warriors depicted here are named on the bowl – most of them bearing Turkish names – the actual event which this bowl commemorates has not been identified in print. It may, however, depict Turkish warriors attacking an Assassin fortress in western Iran. The assailants are in mid-action; the battle has not yet been won. This is not a slow, painstaking siege but a fierce cavalry attack on the fortress. Perhaps it is even the climax of the battle if the figure falling from the battlements is indeed the leader of the defenders.

The mounted attackers rush towards the fortress in parallel rows: their leaders are dressed in greyish-purple, those immediately behind them in green. Perhaps this denotes that only the leaders are wearing

Figure 8.22 Horsemen, mina'i dish, c. 1240, probably Kashan, Iran

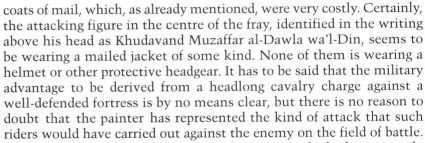

Figure 8.23 Armour types, mina'i *dish, c. 1240, probably Kashan, Iran*

coats of mail, which, as already mentioned, were very costly. Certainly, the attacking figure in the centre of the fray, identified in the writing above his head as Khudavand Muzaffar al-Dawla wa'l-Din, seems to be wearing a mailed jacket of some kind. None of them is wearing a helmet or other protective headgear. It has to be said that the military advantage to be derived from a headlong cavalry charge against a well-defended fortress is by no means clear, but there is no reason to doubt that the painter has represented the kind of attack that such riders would have carried out against the enemy on the field of battle.

The defenders in the fortress, the lower part of which is ornately tiled, are firing arrows through openings in the ramparts. They are also using a catapult which is mounted at the highest point in the fortress and is discharging stones on to the attackers. In the foreground, some of the defenders have come out of the fortress on foot, bearing either sword, spear or bow, in a counter-attack which seems doomed to failure, in view of the dead bodies which lie, already stripped of armour or clothing, on the ground. Some aspects of the depiction of the fortress remain rather enigmatic – perhaps the empty suits of armour and weapons strewn along the ramparts are intended to make the attackers believe that the fortress has more defenders than there really are, or perhaps this section depicts an arsenal.

Although the bowl incorporates many stylised and symbolic elements, it exudes the atmosphere of a real battle and manages to portray the very heat of war, its bloody chaos, panic, confusion and terror; the attacking warriors spill over on to the sides of the bowl and suggest the still invisible menace of many more to come.

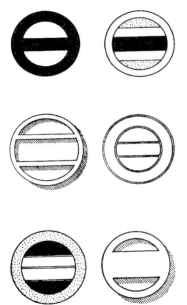

Figure 8.24
(above and opposite)
Mamluk blazons for the barid
*(postal service) couriers,
thirteenth–fifteenth centuries,
Egypt and Syria*

Other Aspects of the Conduct of War

Raids and Ambushes

Much of the fighting between Muslim and Frank was more desultory and mundane than pitched battles with all their attendant pomp, bloodshed and expense. A raid had limited objectives like seizing a caravan and its merchandise, or helping to capture a castle; or it formed part of larger offensives. Sometimes a raid was undertaken to exact vengeance and as a show of strength. Marshall's book outlines in detail the importance of raids in Crusader–Muslim military encounters.[129] In the Islamic sources it is sometimes difficult to distinguish between fully-fledged battles and small-scale engagements, although many encounters probably fall into the latter category.

Typical of a small-scale engagement was the so-called 'battle' of al-Quhwana (al-Uqhuwana) on the shores of Lake Tiberias in Muharram 507/June 1113. An advanced Turkish foraging party from the combined forces of Mawdud of Mosul and Tughtegin of Damascus encamped at al-Quhwana only to find that the Franks under Baldwin and Roger of Antioch had already pitched their tents there:

> battle was joined on both sides without any preparations for an engagement, pitching of tents, settling down in camps, or preliminary skirmishing. Both sides engaged in a hand-to-hand fight, and God the Bountiful, to Him be praise, gave victory to the Muslims, after three charges.[130]

A typical example of a minor military engagement was an ambush laid by Saladin against a Frankish contingent near Ramla in 1192. For this engagement Saladin employed Bedouin Arab troops[131] who fought with lances made of reeds. He had chosen them because of their speed and agility. In the ambush a number of Frankish cavalry were unseated by the attack of the Bedouin. Thereafter, some Turkish troops joined in and inflicted serious injuries on the Frankish knights by throwing javelins at them. No doubt a very useful outcome of this encounter would have been the capture of enemy horses.

Raids had a number of other benefits. They could weaken the enemy and undermine their morale.[132] They were conducted against villages, churches and mosques and often damaged agricultural land. Al-Aqsara'i's manual contains an interesting section on surprise attacks and ambushes. Tantum concludes that here the author is describing the actual practice of his own time. The value of ambushes is clearly underlined: 'Ambushing is necessary for the army and the safeguarding of it . . . Men of perception judge ambushes by their effectiveness; they are a principle laid down for an army as a mighty source of strength.'[133]

Al-Aqsara'i explains, but in no great detail, how to mount an ambush:

> Now it is better if the ambush party is divided into two groups because of the likelihood that if the enemy sees them to be few in number they will seek to attack them and when the Muslim force is routed will give chase and then the second group will break out upon them.[134]

He emphasises the importance of choosing a good site near water for the ambush, in case the Muslims have to wait to attack, and the need for maintaining silence whilst in hiding.

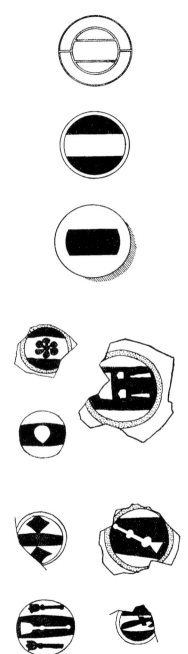

Communications

During the Crusading period, the simplest way to transmit messages of military import was to send messengers on fast horses or camels. But flares were also used to communicate news from one high place to another over considerable distances.[135] Even swimmers were charged with the task of transmitting important messages. A swimmer notified Saladin of the situation in Acre in 586/1190–1.[136] The Egyptian postal service (which had an intelligence arm) used mules and swift camels.[137] Baybars reorganised his postal service, which eventually extended as far as the Syrian coast and the Taurus fortresses, and he established special staging posts on the routes for changing horses and housing riders.[138]

Figure 8.25 Tents in an early fourteenth-century album painting, probably Tabriz, Iran

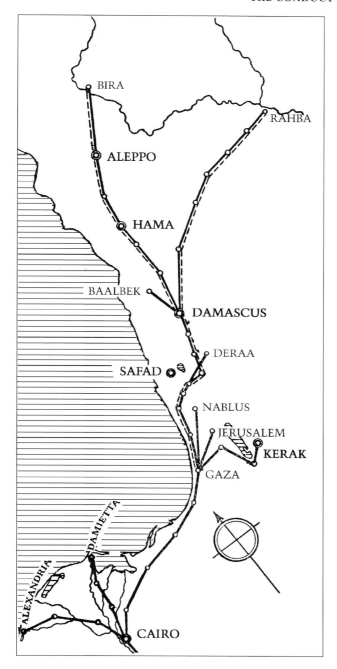

Figure 8.26 The state of the postal routes at the time of Baybars' death, 676/1277. The network of pigeon-houses is marked by a strong black line, and signal towers by a dotted line

Pigeons were used to send messages too (figure 8.27). In his military manual, al-Ansari says: 'It is obvious that pigeons are among the fastest means of communication because the pigeon covers the distance of twenty days' walking in less than a day.'[139] According to al-Ansari, Egypt had a whole network of pigeon towers.[140] As for Syria, Ibn al-Athir

547

gives a detailed account of the way in which Nur al-Din set up a system of pigeon post within his territories there:

> In the year 567 [1171–2] al-Malik al-ʿAdil Nur al-Din gave orders to use carrier pigeons. These are the messenger birds which fly back to their lofts from distant lands. They were adopted in all his territories.
>
> The reason for this is that his territories had become so extensive and his realm so great that it reached from the border of Nubia to the gate of Hamadan, with only the land of the Franks intervening. The Franks, may God curse them, sometimes attacked some of the border areas, but by the time news of this reached him and he was able to set out against them, they had already in part achieved their purpose. He therefore issued orders concerning this matter and sent them in writing to all his territories. He authorized rations for the pigeons and for their breeders. They gave him great satisfaction. News reached him at once in this way. On every border he had men on duty with pigeons from the neighboring city. When they saw or heard anything, they at once wrote it down, attached it to the bird, and sped it without delay to the city from which it came. There the message was transferred to another bird, which came from the next city on the way to Nur al-Din, and so on until the report reached him. In this way the borders were protected, and when a band of Franks attacked one of them, news reached him on the same day. Then he wrote to the troops nearest to that border, ordering them to muster and march with dispatch and take the enemy by surprise. They did so and were victorious, while the Franks were lulled in the belief that Nur al-Din was far away from them. May God have mercy on Nur al-Din and be pleased with him. How great was his concern for his subjects and his realms![141]

At the siege of Alexandria in 570/1174–5 news came to the Muslim camp by pigeon ('on the wing of the bird').[142]

Spies

We may assume that a network of spies existed on both sides; they provided information on local conditions. Such a network may well have included ex-prisoners, converts to the faith of the other side, who, faced with the stark choice of death or conversion, preferred to embrace a new religion and live.

Nizam al-Mulk mentions the necessity for spies in his *Book of Government*.[143] Spies must constantly go out to the limits of the kingdom in the guise of merchants, travellers, Sufis, pedlars and mendicants, and bring back reports of everything they hear, so that no matters of any kind remain concealed. Nizam al-Mulk is suspicious of formal ambassadors, pointing out that there is often a secret purpose to their visit: 'In fact they want to know about the state of

Figure 8.27 *The Pisa Griffin, cartouche with pigeon, cast and engraved bronze, eleventh century, Egypt(?)*

the roads, mountain-passes and rivers, to see whether an army can pass or not.' He then goes on to mention a host of other items of information an ambassador may wish to acquire in addition to the overt purpose of his embassy.[144]

Al-Ansari also devotes considerable space in his military manual to spies, couriers and informers.[145] Spies, in his, view, should be trustworthy, possessed of excellent insight and sound judgement, shrewd and crafty, well travelled and fully conversant with the language of the enemy.[146]

A typical example of a possible spy was William the Frank, a Genoese merchant, who appeared in Cairo in 607/1210–11, bringing gifts for al-'Adil. The sultan asked him to live in his entourage and to accompany him to Syria. In reality, so al-Maqrizi says, he was a Frankish spy. Nevertheless, when al-'Adil took up residence in Cairo four years later, William was requested to live with him.[147]

The Treatment of Prisoners

Muslim Prisoners in Frankish Captivity

There is no doubt that Muslim prisoners languished in Frankish prisons but their numbers cannot be assessed. There is, for example, little credibility in the statement by Ibn Shaddad that 3,000 Muslim prisoners were held in Jerusalem in 1187.[148] Even more grossly exaggerated is the suggestion made by Saladin's enthusiastic biographer, 'Imad al-Din, that Saladin freed 20,000 Muslim prisoners in his campaign of reconquest.[149]

Despite these understandable inaccuracies, it does seem clear that Muslim prisoners in Crusader hands must have been quite numerous, especially in the period of the greatest Crusader military and territorial successes. Kedar argues that Muslim prisoners must have contributed significantly to the Frankish economy.[150] According to Ibn al-Furat, a thousand Muslim prisoners were involved in the building of Safad.[151] The relentless programme of castle-building which took up so much of Frankish energies during the twelfth century must have created a well-nigh inexhaustible demand for manpower – for the quarrying of stone, the transport of materials, the construction of ramps and the digging of moats. Muslim prisoners were an essential element in this endless and ambitious enterprise.

In 661/1263 Sultan Baybars castigated the Crusaders for not keeping to the terms of an agreement and for holding on to Muslim prisoners to use them as forced labour rather than exchanging them for their counterparts languishing in Muslim jails:

We have sent the prisoners to Nablus and thence to Damascus; you have sent nobody . . . You have not taken pity on the prisoners who have professed the same religion (*milla*) as you and who had already arrived at the doors of your house. All that was in order that your jobs undertaken by Muslim prisoners should not be discontinued.[152]

Usama admits that he used to visit the king of the Franks (Fulk V) often in times of truce. He writes that the queen's father, King Baldwin, 'was under obligation to my father'. During such visits the Franks used to allow Usama to buy off some of their Muslim captives.[153] Usama also talks about a 'devil of a Frank called William Jiba' who captured around 400 Maghribi pilgrims. Some of these were brought to Usama by their owners and he would buy those of them that he could.[154] Later, Usama reports that some of these captives actually escaped and were hidden away by the inhabitants of the villages of 'Akka: 'Being all Muslims, whenever a captive came to them they would hide him and see that he got into Muslim territory.'[155]

Isolated anecdotal references, such as the testimony of Ibn Jubayr, should be treated with caution, since they cannot be taken as broad generalisations about the way in which the Crusaders treated Muslim prisoners. Clearly, both sides handled their captives with varying degrees of severity depending on particular circumstances. Ibn Jubayr rises to great heights of emotion when describing the plight of Muslim prisoners:

> Among the misfortunes that one who visits their land will see are the Muslim prisoners walking in shackles and put to painful labour like slaves. In like condition are the Muslim women prisoners, their legs in iron rings. Hearts are rent for them, but compassion avails them nothing.[156]

Richard the Lionheart, otherwise noted for his chivalrous conduct, was nonetheless capable on occasion of extreme severity towards prisoners. In 587/1191, according to al-'Umari, he had many Muslim prisoners killed at Acre.[157] Ibn Shaddad does not mince his words in his account:[158]

> They were in his custody and he behaved treacherously towards them . . . Then they summoned from amongst the Muslim prisoners those whose martyrdom God had written down that day. They numbered around 3,000 in ropes. They [the Franks] attacked them to a man and killed them all in cold blood by sword and lance.[159]

There may well have been coercive measures applied by Frankish captors towards those Muslim prisoners in their hands. This is certainly the implication of a letter written by Ibn Taymiyya to a 'king' in Cyprus around the year 703/1304. Ibn Taymiyya requests that the king should show kindness towards some of his Muslim prisoners and he invites him to release them. They were probably the victims of a raid by Frankish pirates off the Levantine coast and had little hope of finding ransom money. At the end of the letter he asks the

Frankish king to refrain from changing the religion of the prisoners: 'I will seal up this letter by recommending (to the King) to treat with indulgence those people of the Qur'an . . . and to refrain from changing the religion of a single one of them.'[160]

A relevant contemporary document is an Arabic inscription on a block of basalt preserved in the mosque known as Dayr al-Muslimin (or Dayr al-Muslim) at Busra in southern Syria. It records an endowment of an oven and a mill by the atabeg Mu'in al-Din Unur, and states that their revenue is to be used for 'the liberation of Muslims from infidel prisons', and specifically 'those who are without family and cannot free themselves. They must be Sunnis, must not distance themselves from the community and must know the Qur'an by heart'. In addition to this endowment, the inscription mentions a certain Surkhak who had set aside one-sixth of the revenue of a little village called Marj Harasa for the same purpose. This inscription, securely datable on historical grounds to the year that Unur died, that is 544/1149,[161] is larded with Qur'anic quotations (2: 177, 229 and 231), and the titles of Unur stress his piety.[162] It offers valuable insights into the mechanics and conditions of ransoming Muslim prisoners. Another (now lost) inscription from Busra also dealt with the ransom of prisoners;[163] this custom was widespread at the time,[164] and indeed continued well into the Mamluk period. In the reign of Baybars a governor of Damascus set up a special foundation for this purpose,[165] and as late as the fourteenth century Muslims were ransoming their co-religionists from the Franks of Cyprus.[166] Finally, it is worth noting that, as Usama's *Memoirs* make clear, he and his friend Unur

Figure 8.28 Prisoners wearing the yoke or cangue, early fourteenth-century album painting, probably Tabriz, Iran

competed with each other in the pious task of ransoming Muslim pilgrims captured by the Franks.[167]

Frankish Prisoners in Muslim Captivity

The number of Frankish prisoners in Muslim hands was probably significantly smaller given that the Franks were always a minority in the Levant. Moreover, the Muslims would have less need for forced labour than the Franks, with their huge and urgent building enterprises – though the citadel at Cairo was built with the help of large contingents of Frankish prisoners of war.

The Islamic sources are full of stories about the fate of famous Crusader prisoners who fell into Muslim hands; these accounts testify sometimes to cruelty and sometimes to chivalry. The early twelfth-century Turkish ruler of Damascus, Tughtegin, who was involved in the first tentative Islamic military responses to the Crusaders, was tough and uncompromising in his treatment of important Crusader captives who had the misfortune to fall into his hands.

In 502/1108–9, he took captive the nephew of Baldwin of Jerusalem. As Ibn al-Athir relates:

> Tughtegin offered Islam but he refused, offering as a ransom for himself thirty thousand dinars and the release of five hundred prisoners. But Tughtegin was not satisfied with that without Islam and when he did not respond he killed him with his own hand and he sent the prisoners to the caliph and the sultan.[168]

The passage could be interpreted to mean that he was offering the release of 500 Muslims in Frankish captivity, but it seems more likely that he was proposing that Tughtegin should release not only himself but also 500 Frankish prisoners for a total of 30,000 dinars.

This story has implications that extend beyond the treatment of prisoners. It indicates that, whether for political or religious reasons, Tughtegin was set upon making the nephew of the Frankish King of Jerusalem apostasise, and that in pursuit of this aim he was prepared to forego the huge fortune of 30,000 gold coins. It is possible, of course, that for military reasons alone he was not prepared to release 500 Frankish prisoners. But the episode is perhaps an indication of the power of piety on both sides at this time.

Robert, son of Fulk, the lord of Sahyun, was a valiant warrior and on good terms with Tughtegin. Nevertheless, neither this previous friendly relationship nor the fact that Robert was a leper (*abras*) occasioned any soft treatment on the part of Tughtegin. Robert fell from his horse in battle in 1119 and was taken prisoner by Tughtegin, who executed him personally.[169]

Tughtegin captured Count Gervase of Basoches, the Lord of Tiberias, in Shawwal 501/14 May–11 June 1108: 'He hollowed out his skull while he was still alive and drank wine from it with the count watching him. He lived for an hour and then died.'[170]

Figure 8.29 Warrior wearing the khayagh or 'cut coat' in lamellar armour, Rashid al-Din, Jami' al-Tawarikh ('World History'), 714/1314, Tabriz, Iran

Such gruesome and in this case medically nonsensical episodes as this were often laid at the door of Turkish commanders in the twelfth and thirteenth centuries. These Turkish notables are often mentioned as indulging in drunkenness and their conduct is viewed by Muslim, especially Arab, chroniclers as unacceptable. Such writers relate stories involving Turkish rulers cutting prisoners in half and the inflicting of hideous punishments on captives. A particular villain was Salah al-Din al-Yaghi-Siyani. The Arab aristocrat Usama describes this Turkish *amir* who feared neither God nor Zengi as possessing unusual ferocity and cruelty.[171] Ibn al-Azraq, the town chronicler of Mayyafariqin, records that in 528/1133–4 al-Yaghi-Siyani punished an employee of his by tying him to a dog and then putting both of them into a sack. The resourceful official managed to trap the dog's neck between his thighs inside the sack, strangle the animal and escape.[172] Such stories as these, apocryphal as they probably are for the most part, are a reflection of the strong resentment felt by the Arabs at being ruled by the Turks. Usama asks God to overlook the excesses of al-Yaghi-Siyani and speaks of tales which would 'make the hair of the newborn turn white'.[173]

Baybars seems to have exacted unusually severe punishments even by the standards of the time. All but two of the defenders of Safad in 664/1266 were killed and about 1,500 men were beheaded on a nearby hill.[174]

High-ranking Frankish captives would usually be kept until they could purchase their liberty. Usama writes: 'Allah decreed that the Frankish captives who were taken in Kafartab be set free, since the amirs divided them among themselves and kept them under their charge until they could buy themselves off.'[175]

It could take years for the ransom to be paid, during which time the captive would languish and perhaps even die in a dungeon. Alternatively, a high-ranking – and especially – royal captive might be given special treatment befitting his status. Thus in 648/1250–1 St Louis, the French king, was taken to al-Mansura; he was fettered by the leg and confined in a house which had belonged to a high-ranking chancery official. He was allotted a special person to look after him and bring him food. The ordinary Frankish prisoners, however, were killed in batches each night and their bodies thrown into the Nile.[176]

Protracted and intricate negotiations which might boil down to direct bargaining were apt to occur between captor and captive. A typical example is the episode of the Muslim ruler of Mosul, Jawali, and his Frankish prisoner, referred to by Ibn al-Athir as the 'Frankish count' (Baldwin). Under the year 502/1108–9, he writes:

When he [Jawali] came to Maskin he released the Frankish count who was a prisoner in Mosul. He had taken him with him. His name was Baldwin and he was the lord of Edessa and Saruj and other places. He had remained in custody until then and had spent much money but had not been released. At the appropriate moment

Figure 8.30 Warrior, album, early fourteenth century, Tabriz, Iran

Jawali released him and put ceremonial garments on him. His stay in prison was nearly five years. Jawali had stipulated with him that he should ransom himself with money and that he should release the Muslim prisoners who were in his prison and that he should support him personally and with his troops and money whenever he wanted.[177]

This was not, however, the end of the story for Baldwin was sent to Qal'at Ja'bar and was not released until Joscelin, the lord of Tell Bashir, became a hostage in place of Baldwin. Jawali then released Joscelin, replacing him with his brother-in-law and Baldwin's brother-in-law.[178]

Hostages were part of everyday life: they were offered as a pledge of good faith in a deal between Frank and Muslim. Usama gives a number of examples of this practice. In Shayzar, on one occasion, Baldwin II had sent hostages – Frankish and Armenian knights – as security for a debt he owed to the Muslim Artuqid ruler of Mardin, Timurtash. When the amount was paid, the hostages could go home.[179] It is worth pointing out that such was the sense of family honour that Usama's father insisted on rescuing these selfsame Frankish hostages when they were captured by Muslims from Hama on their way home.[180]

The Islamic sources do not describe the unusual appearance of the Knights Templar (in their garb of white cloaks and red crosses) and the Hospitallers (with their black robes and white crosses) but such alien groups must have stood out prominently and struck the Muslims who saw them. Saladin, fabled in both East and West for his chivalry, singled out these military orders for ruthless treatment, killing all those who would not convert to Islam after the battle of Hattin in 1187. The mood of the massacre is one of high religious exultation. Volunteer warriors, religious scholars, Sufis and ascetics who were in Saladin's company were each asked to kill one of the prisoners: 'The sultan was sitting with his face delighted and the infidels were glowering.'[181] No reason is given for this severity but it may be assumed with confidence that these easily identifiable warriors particularly symbolised Western Christian fanaticism as well as arousing the ancient Islamic dislike of monkery. Hence the deep hatred and resentment which the narrative exudes.

On an earlier occasion, in 575/1179, Saladin had inspected a large group of prisoners, 'all enchained'.[182] Amongst the prisoners was Baldwin II of Ibelin who was ransomed after a year. Al-Maqrizi also records that Odo, the Grand Master of the Templars, was one of these prisoners, but he died in custody.[183]

It was occasionally possible to escape from prison, whether by bribe, ruse or ingenuity. The vizier al-Afdal Ridwan al-Walakhshi was imprisoned in a building on one side of the palace in Cairo but he escaped by digging a hole fourteen cubits long with an iron nail.[184] The chronicler al-'Azimi records that the Artuqid prince Balak took

Figure 8.31 *Warrior wearing the* khayagh *or 'cut coat' in lamellar armour, Firdawsi,* Shahnama *('Book of Kings' – the Great Mongol* Shahnama*), c. 1330, Tabriz, Iran*

Baldwin king of Antioch captive in 517/1123–4 and threw him into the pit (*jubb*) of Khartpert with Joscelin. Joscelin managed to escape from there in disguise.[185] Since Khartpert (modern Harput) is in eastern Turkey, not far from Hisn Kayfa, he was a long way from Crusader territory, and it would have been no easy matter for him to regain it.

How were captives treated? As noted above, the Muslim captives who awoke the pity of Ibn Jubayr were shackled and, in the case of the women, had leg rings. According to Usama, on one occasion – at the surrender of Kafartab in 509/1115 – the Christian captives were chained in twos to one captor:

> We were bringing out the captives, each two chained to one man from Shayzar. Some of them had half of their bodies burned and their legs remained. Others were dead by fire. I saw in what befell them a great object lesson.[186]

Those who were incarcerated in Muslim prisons, whether they were Crusader prisoners-of-war or Muslims – miscreants, or *amir*s and high officials who had fallen foul of individual rulers – often suffered a terrible ordeal. Ibn Wasil describes the fate of one such unfortunate, a Muslim military commander who had been thrown into the pit (*jubb*) at Ba'lbakk: 'It was dark and there was no difference between night and day there. Each day the prisoner was given a little bread and salad.'[187]

The great Muslim thinker and reformer Ibn Taymiyya, who was at times a thorn in the side of the Mamluk ruling elite, was put with his two brothers in the worst prison of the Cairo citadel, the *jubb* (cistern or pit), a stinking dungeon full of bats. He records his feelings in one of his letters dated 706/1307, comparing his fate with that of other prisoners who are Christians: 'The Christians are in a good prison . . . If only our prison was the same kind as the Christians'.'[188]

These Christians were probably Crusaders, since it would be highly unlikely that ordinary Copts or other Oriental Christians would have been so well treated in the prisons of Cairo. Numerous Christian prisoners were held in Cairo after the fall of Acre in 1291 and if they were to be ransomed it is understandable that their Muslim captors should choose to treat them more leniently than a so-called dissident and 'trouble-maker' like Ibn Taymiyya who was the self-appointed conscience of the Mamluk regime.

There is interesting evidence on the way in which Frankish prisoners were treated in the Mamluk period. It is to be found in a legal document composed in 679/1280 by one Ibn al-Mukarram during the reign of Sultan Qalawun. The document gives practical advice on a number of legal topics and includes the following section on prisons: 'Prisons should be guarded and protected during the day and at night. The beards of all prisoners of war – Franks and Antiochans, or others – must be shaved, and make sure they do so whenever their

Figure 8.32 *Warrior wearing the* khayagh *or 'cut coat' in lamellar armour, Firdawsi,* Shahnama *('Book of Kings' – the Great Mongol* Shahnama*), c. 1330, Tabriz, Iran*

beard grows back.'[189] What probably lay behind these measures was a desire to be able to distinguish clearly between bearded Muslim and beardless non-Muslim prisoners.

There are suggestions of previous laxity in the Muslim treatment of Frankish prisoners in the rather strict counsels offered by Ibn al-Mukarram. Indeed, he suggests that some prisoners in the past may even have been granted certain privileges which will now no longer apply: 'Prisoners of war who are employed (in public works) must not spend the night outside the jail. None of them is to be allowed to go to the bathhouse or to any church or any attraction.'[190]

Ibn al-Mukarram then goes on to stress the need for the prisoners' chains to be checked and secured at all times. He urges that the security around and in the prisons in which the Franks reside must be doubled during the night. He mentions specifically a prison known as the *khizanat al-bunud* which was used to detain Frankish princes and their families.[191]

As already noted, it is clear from the sources that Frankish prisoners were used as forced labour, especially in building projects. The huge undertaking of constructing the Cairo citadel would not have been possible without a labour force comprising huge numbers of Frankish prisoners. According to al-Maqrizi, quoting Ibn 'Abd al-Zahir, 50,000 Frankish prisoners were used to build the Cairo citadel.[192] This is, of course, a suspiciously round figure; nevertheless it indicates that the numbers must have been unusually high. This information is corroborated by Ibn Jubayr who saw the citadel being built in 1183.[193]

Saladin again used prisoners when he was rebuilding the fortifications of Acre in 1187, 'bringing his tools, animals and prisoners'.[194] Najm al-Din Ayyub employed Frankish prisoners to work on the building of his new citadel on Rawda Island. The Ayyubid sultan al-Malik al-Salih, in his dying advice to his son, suggests that the strengthening of the defences of Damietta should be carried out by Frankish prisoners.[195]

Figure 8.33 *Ocean-going ship, al-Hariri,* al-Maqamat *('The Assemblies'), c. 1230, probably Baghdad, Iraq*

The Naval Dimension

A neglected area of the narrowly military aspect of the Crusader–Muslim conflict is the maritime dimension. Most scholarly studies pay scarcely any attention to this question, although the weakness of the Levantine Muslims in naval matters at the time of the Crusades was clearly a major factor in the longevity of Frankish rule in the region. It is true that as early as 1848 Reinaud remarked on the fact that the Muslims were inferior in matters maritime. But his important statement was not taken up by scholars until the 1970s, when the researches of Ayalon[196] and Ehrenkreutz[197] confirmed the truth of his generalisation.

There is an evocative saying attributed to the Prophet Muhammad himself: 'A campaign by sea is like ten campaigns by land'.[198] And certainly non-seafaring Arabs – those who lived in the desert or towns far away from the coasts – seem to have been afraid of the sea. According to Muslim tradition, there was an alleged Arab aversion to the sea which went back to the time of the second caliph of Islam, ʿUmar (d. 644), and his request to his great general ʿAmr b. al-ʿAs, the conqueror of Egypt, to describe the sea to him. ʿAmr responded thus:

> The sea is a boundless expanse, whereon great ships look tiny specks; nought but the heavens above and waters beneath; when calm, the sailor's heart is broken; when tempestuous, his senses reel. Trust it little, fear it much. Man at sea is an insect on a splinter, now engulfed, now scared to death.[199]

It comes as no surprise that ʿUmar forthwith recommended that Muslims should avoid seafaring. If they did venture forth on the sea, they did so without his knowledge and were punished for it. Where did this alleged fear of the sea come from? Of course, at one level, it may be seen as a reflection of the deep-rooted unease of desert peoples more used to manipulating vast land expanses than the unfamiliar dangers of the ocean. The Arab proverb 'It is preferable to hear the flatulences of camels than the prayers of fishes' expresses this prejudice.[200] Moreover, most of the territories of the eastern Islamic world did not have access to major sea waterways and were also not acquainted with seafaring and military engagements at sea. Indeed, the story of ʿUmar suggests a woeful lack of naval experience on the part of the early Muslims.

Yet the hypothesis that navigation is alien to the Islamic world is clearly simplistic. Those peoples of the Arabian peninsula itself who lived on the coasts had long been familiar not just with local fishing but also with long-distance maritime trade. Indeed, they were the dominant mercantile force in the waters between India and the Persian Gulf from the third millennium BC onwards, and knew the secrets of the monsoon winds.[201] As early as the eighth century there were Arab trading settlements as far east as Canton. Moreover, when the Arab conquerors took over Egypt, Syria and Palestine, they inherited a time-honoured Mediterranean maritime tradition which went back to Phoenician times, and they began to challenge the Byzantines at sea.[202] Further east, the Muslim rulers also became heirs to the expertise possessed by their newly conquered coastal subjects who plied their trade along the traditional sea lanes of the Red Sea, the Persian Gulf and, as noted above, beyond. Indeed, the ʿAbbasids built on this firm foundation and Baghdad, an inland port thanks to the navigability of the Tigris and the Euphrates, looked out on vast horizons – the Mediterranean, Africa, India, Indonesia and China.

The long-lived Mediterranean maritime tradition had not died with the advent of Muslim rule. There were dockyards in Alexandria, al-Fustat, Damietta and other Egyptian ports, and the islands of Crete and Sicily were conquered for Islam in ships built in Egypt. Muslim

Figure 8.34 Boat, al-Hariri, al-Maqamat ('The Assemblies'), 634/1237, probably Baghdad, Iraq

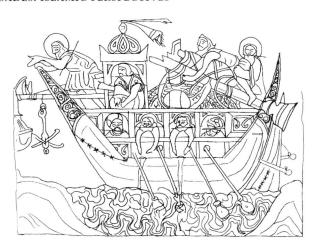

Figure 8.35 Broken-masted dhow, al-Hariri, al-Maqamat ('The Assemblies'), c. 1230 (note the single cabin for the captain on the main deck, the high prow, anchor and hinged rudder), probably Baghdad, Iraq

naval power flourished under the early Fatimids, and Alexandria, Damietta and Fustat were major centres for shipbuilding after the Fatimids had moved to Egypt from North Africa in 969. Alexandria was an ideal naval base, possessing a superb harbour, large shipyard and Coptic builders.[203] Both riverine and oceangoing ships were made. The only commodity lacking in Egypt was good timber; this had to be imported. The extent of the trade in wood in the early Islamic period may be judged by the fact that the pulpit (*minbar*) in the Great Mosque of Qayrawan in Tunisia, dated 862, is made of Burmese teak.

Although Ibn Khaldun is carried away by his own rhetoric in his assessment of Muslim supremacy at sea in the heyday of the Fatimids of Egypt and the Umayyads of Spain, he nevertheless points to a robust Muslim naval tradition in parts of the Mediterranean and to the Muslims' ability to fight at sea and to launch campaigns of conquest by sea aimed at the islands of the Mediterranean:

> During the time of the Muslim dynasty, the Muslims gained control over the whole Mediterranean. Their power and domination over it was vast. The Christian nations could do nothing against the Muslim fleets, anywhere in the Mediterranean . . . They (the Muslims) covered most of the surface of the Mediterranean with their equipment and numbers and travelled its lanes on missions both peaceful and warlike. Not a single Christian board floated upon it.[204]

Muslim Attitudes to the Sea in the Crusading Period

Many Muslims were terrified of the sea. Travelling, let alone fighting, at sea was a very hazardous affair and must have daunted all but the most stout-hearted. Transporting troops and horses was also dangerous and potentially expensive. A little-known testimony to the problems of sea travel is the account of Ibn al-'Arabi in the 1090s. He and his father were unfortunate enough to be shipwrecked off the North

African coast. Ibn al-'Arabi writes as follows: 'We emerged from the sea like the dead man from the grave . . . We were starving from the shipwreck and in a foul state of nakedness. The sea had (even) ripped open the receptacles containing oil.'[205]

Apart from the problems of the weather, these overcrowded ships were often in difficulties, as Ibn Jubayr points out: 'Sometimes the ship's hull struck one of the corals during its passage among them, and we heard a crashing sound which caused us to despair; and sometimes we did not know whether we should live or die.'[206]

The experiences of Ibn Jubayr on his journey east reveal the typical fears of the twelfth-century traveller. Even more momentous were journeys undertaken on campaign in ships bearing valuable arms, machines of war and fighting men. In 1189 Saladin travelled along the coast to Acre. Ibn Shaddad records his own grave anxiety about the sea:

It was the deepest winter, the sea was very rough 'with waves like mountains' as God says in the Qur'an. I had little experience of the sea and it made a deep impression on me; in fact I thought that if anyone had said to me that if I spent a whole day sailing on the sea he would make me master of the whole world I could not have done it. I thought that anyone who earned his living from the sea must be mad . . . All these thoughts were caused by the sight of the tempestuous sea.[207]

Similar prejudices against the sea are expressed a century later in an alleged conversation, reported by Ibn Wasil, between the captured French king, St Louis, and the Muslim amir Husam al-Din, who had been deputed to guard him. Husam al-Din said to his royal prisoner:[208]

How could it have come into the mind of a man as perspicacious and judicious as the King to entrust himself thus to the sea on a fragile piece of wood, to launch (himself) into a Muslim country defended by numerous armies and to expose himself and his troops to an almost certain death? At these words the King smiled and said nothing. So the amir went on as follows:

'One of our religious scholars thinks that anyone who exposes himself and his belongings twice to the sea must be considered as mad and that his testimony can no longer be accepted in law.' Thereupon the King smiled again and said: 'He who said that was right'.[209]

However apocryphal or stereotyped this conversation may be, it is yet another piece of evidence of Muslim antipathy to the sea.

Types of Ships

Our knowledge of types of medieval Muslim ships comes partly from works of art (plate 8.7), notably thirteenth-century book painting, and also from numerous, disparate references in Islamic geographical and travel literature and historical chronicles. These literary texts are the principal source of information for vessels before the thirteenth century. However, a major problem is that many writers often assume that their readers know what particular terms mean and do not define them or differentiate between warships and trading vessels or between oceangoing and riverine boats.

The tenth-century Muslim geographer al-Muqaddasi (d. 378/988–9) lists 36 types of ship which according to his testimony existed in his lifetime.[210] Of these 36, ten are mentioned in a Mediterranean context.

As Agius points out,[211] in the time of al-Muqaddasi, there were two broad categories of ships: the sewn type (*khaytiyya*), which 'were stitched together with coconut cord by the shell-first method (i.e. the hull first, then the ribs inserted later)', and the nail type, in which

Plate 8.7 Lateen-rigged boat, Almohad glazed ceramic dish, twelfth century, Spain

Figure 8.36 *Fatimid galley, lustre dish, tenth century, Bahnassa, Egypt*

ships 'were nailed together with ribs first and then the planks attached to them' (the so-called skeleton method). The galleys were constructed by the second method, which was more expensive. Sewn hulls were, according to Ibn Jubayr and Ibn Battuta, flexible and more resilient against high waves and the dangers of shipwreck.[212] Goitein found evidence in the Geniza documents that Muslim ships carrying up to 500 passengers were not unusual in Cairo in the late eleventh century. Travellers and merchandise were carried in light galleys (*ghurab*) powered by oars. Writing around 1190, Ibn Mammati mentions that a *ghurab* had 140 oars.[213]

The Importance of the Frankish Fleets in the Early Crusading Period and the Muslim Neglect of Naval Matters

As already mentioned, the disunity and weakness of the Muslims made them powerless to prevent the seizure of the Levantine ports by the Crusaders in the first decades of the twelfth century. The Crusaders' successes were due in no small measure to the support of the Italian fleets.[214] The city-states of Venice, Genoa and Pisa participated from the outset in the sea offensive from Europe; crews from Genoa helped to lay siege to Antioch and Jerusalem, and in 1099 a large fleet from Pisa arrived in the seas off Syria, supported in the following year by a fleet from Venice. Ships from the Italian maritime cities were used to supply armies, rescue trapped forces and keep up communications with western Europe. The dispatch of these Italian fleets was at least in part motivated by the desire for commercial gain but, be that as it may, they were invaluable in the establishment of the Frankish states in the Levant from 1100. They also helped considerably during that period in the capture of the remaining ports;[215] al-Sulami had alerted his fellow Muslims to this imminent danger in his prophetic book, the *Kitab al-jihad*. In fact, in spite of the solemn warnings by al-Sulami of the dire consequences to the Muslims of the loss of the Syrian ports, the Crusaders rapidly seized nearly all of them.

Furthermore, even the waves of newcomers who continued to arrive by sea from western Europe did not arouse a response from the Muslims on land or at sea and the Crusaders, having captured the Levantine ports, were able to fortify them, thus defending themselves from the Muslims and providing themselves with bases to which further reinforcements of troops, arms and supplies could come, unimpeded, from Europe. The Crusaders learned from the bitter and gruelling experiences of the First Crusade that the land routes to the Levant were not the best way to approach their goal. Thereafter, they came predominantly by sea. When subsequent Crusades were launched, the warriors from Europe took the sea routes to Syria and Palestine. Moreover, the influx of Franks, both soldiers for the faith and pilgrims, who flowed in a steady stream into the Levant in the periods in between the formal Crusades also arrived by sea. Access to the coast was crucial to continuing Crusader survival. The extraordinary nature of the Syrian coastline – one of the straightest in the world, with few natural harbours – made possession of those ports which did exist, such as Tyre, Sidon, Beirut and others, all the more precious (colour plate 5).

With the benefit of hindsight, it seems remarkable that no Muslim leader until Saladin saw the need to make a priority of the ports rather than of the cities inland, such as Damascus, Aleppo and Jerusalem. After all, it was through the ports that reinforcements of men, arms and provisions kept on arriving and at this early juncture the Muslims were unable to do anything about it. Ideally, joint operations by sea and land would have been best, but even concerted attacks on the ports from inland would have been within the reach of Muslim military leaders in the period 1100–60, had they made those targets their priority. They did not.

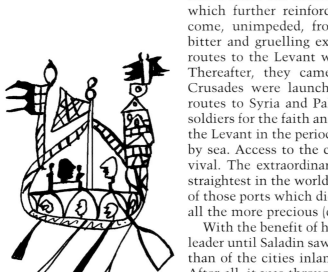

Figure 8.37 *Probably a Fatimid* shalandi, *of the kind described by Ibn Mammati: a 'decked ship on which soldiers fought while rowers plied their oars beneath'; c. twelfth century, Fustat, Egypt*

The Fatimids and the Navy

Since the Muslims possessed so few of the coastal towns of Syria and Palestine, it was an inevitable consequence that they would find it difficult to build up a fleet and put it to sea to confront the Franks in that part of the Mediterranean. Of the Muslim territories with easy access to the eastern Mediterranean after 1110, there remained only the Fatimid empire, which retained the Egyptian ports. Further to the west, Tunisia had been the springboard for the conquest of Sicily and could have been used again to establish Muslim outposts on various islands to counter growing western European power in the Mediterranean. But here again nothing materialised at the key moment of Crusader expansion. It is hard to resist the conclusion that the Muslims tamely let the Crusaders secure a massive strategic advantage, and it took the Muslims the best part of two centuries to make good that initial loss.

Some time in the eleventh century, Egyptian naval power declined and from the end of the first decade of the twelfth century, the

Fatimids seem to have withdrawn into their shell after a series of military failures against the Franks. The loss of supply bases, such as Acre and Tyre, had a serious impact on the Fatimid navy and disturbed the naval alarm systems protecting the security of the Egyptian coast.

Some sporadic activity by the Fatimid fleet is reported in 496/1103,[216] and again in 516/1122. In the latter case, a convoy of forty galleys built in the arsenal at Cairo made for Jaffa in response to an appeal for help from the Muslims of Syria, and on its way back was destroyed by the Franks.[217] The Egyptian historian Ibn Muyassar mentions that Fatimid fleets continued to operate in the mid-twelfth century. A naval expedition was launched in 546/1151 by the Fatimid vizier al-'Adil ibn al-Sallar against the Levantine ports, apparently in retaliation for the Franks' destruction of al-Farama the previous year.[218] But this initiative seems to have been a rare instance of Fatimid naval success. The fleet is described by the contemporary chronicler Ibn al-Qalanisi as a fleet of 'exceeding strength and plenitude of number and equipment'. The fleet numbered seventy warships and was 'such a fleet as had never come forth in previous years'.[219] It seized many Byzantine and Frankish ships at Jaffa and wrought havoc at Acre, Tyre, Beirut and Tripoli. But the possibility of a joint Muslim attack by land and sea against the Franks was lost because of Nur al-Din's unwillingness to fulfil his promise of help.[220] So these efforts seem to have made little impact.[221]

After the fall of Ascalon, the last of the Syrian coastal towns still in Muslim hands, in 1153, Egypt lost its last bastion through which

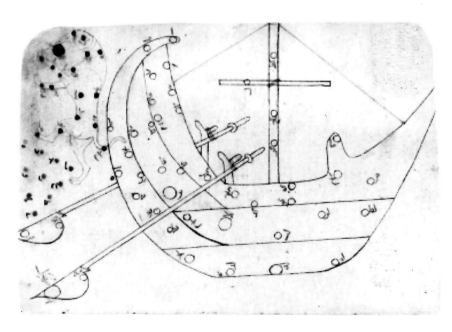

Figure 8.38 *The constellation Argo Navis, al-Sufi,* Kitab suwar al-kawakib *('Book of Fixed Stars'), 519/1125, Baghdad, Iraq*

the rest of the country could be warned of the coming of enemy ships. The loss of Ascalon ushered in a period of great pressure on Egypt from the Crusaders, described in some detail by Ehrenkreutz.[222] Combined sea and land offensives then followed, culminating in 1168 with Amalric's all-out attack on Cairo. The Egyptian fleet had fewer ships than the Crusaders (in 1152 the Fatimids had a raiding fleet of seventy ships), and even those ships they did possess in 1168 were burned in the conflagration at Fustat in an attempt to impede the Crusader advance. Thus Saladin would have to start more or less from scratch in trying to build a fleet.

It may well be possible, too, that the Egyptian navy declined because the Fatimids experienced difficulty in acquiring the raw materials necessary for building new ships in the twelfth century. After all, timber from the cheapest source, namely the European countries to the north, became part of the sinews of war from the moment that the Crusaders arrived in Fatimid Syria. No doubt trade did not grind to a halt once war had broken out, but it is only to be expected that key military supplies (including timber for ship-building) would now be somewhat harder to obtain from European sources. The enthusiastic papal support for the Crusades was also a potential deterrent for European Christian traders contemplating commercial undertakings with Fatimid merchants.[223]

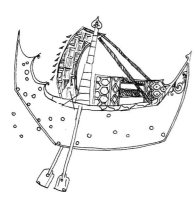

Figure 8.39 The constellation Argo Navis from a brass celestial globe dated 674/1275–6, Iraq (?)

The Naval Policies of Muslim Leaders in the Period 1100–1174

Why did the Syrian Sunni Muslim forces under Zengi and Nur al-Din not attempt to take the coastal towns and to confront the Franks at sea? It would seem that they were too involved in the difficult tasks of carving out a realm for themselves against their many political rivals and of beginning to reunite the various post-Seljuq successor states, whose genesis had been occasioned by Seljuq weakness and fragmentation. Besides, all the early Muslim Counter-Crusade leaders – Il-Ghazi, Mawdud, Tughtegin, Zengi and even Nur al-Din – were psychologically land-locked. They all came originally from lands east of the Euphrates and did not have a mind-set that thought with ease about naval matters. This deficiency seems also to have afflicted the Mamluks later on.

The task of retaking the Syrian ports was, in any case, a difficult one, requiring commitment and resources and, ideally, simultaneous attacks by land and sea. Characteristically, the Franks had taken good care to bolster the defences of the coastal towns as soon as they had taken them in the early years of the twelfth century. So it fell to Saladin to perceive the importance of building up the Muslim navies once he had acquired access to the sea with his conquest of Egypt in 1171. But his success in this enterprise was only limited and transient.

Muslim Views of Crusader Fleets

The Muslim chroniclers were clearly awe-struck and impressed by the Crusader naval war effort. Muslim strength on land was constantly threatened by Frankish power on the high seas; a typically audacious and offensive demonstration of this fact was the raid by Reynald of Chatillon on the Red Sea in 1191. Indeed, the venom with which this expedition is described in the Muslim sources – due of course to its avowed aim of attacking the holiest shrines of Islam – may also owe something to the fact that it was a maritime expedition and totally unexpected. The whole episode for the Muslims is not just another Crusader military strike; it is sinister, criminal and depraved.

'Imad al-Din gives a detailed description of the Sicilian fleet which attacked Alexandria in 569/1174: 'The beginning of the fleet arrived at noon and kept coming fast and furious[224] until the late afternoon.'

This was a famous Frankish fleet which, according to 'Imad al-Din, had threatened the islands belonging to Byzantium. He then lists the number and kinds of ships:

> They disembarked their horses from the transport ships and their infantry from the vessels. The horses numbered 1,500 and the warriors, including cavalry and infantry, were 30,000. The transport ships carrying the horses numbered 36. They had with them 200 galleys, each containing 150 infantrymen. There were six ships carrying weapons of war and siege, made of large pieces of wood and other materials. The number of ships carrying provisions and men was 40; in them were royal horse guards, grooms for the horses, builders of ships, towers, siege machines and mangonels, numbering 50,000 men.[225]

The total number of ships of various kinds listed for this Sicilian fleet by Abu Shama is 282. Even if this number is exaggerated, his evidence is a clear indication of the sophistication of this fleet, the grandiose nature of its operations and the range of ships used.

Nor do the Islamic sources shirk the task of chronicling dire Muslim losses at sea because of superior Frankish maritime expertise. Ibn Shaddad describes the sinking of a Muslim ship after the arrival of Richard from England in 587/1191. He mentions that Richard came accompanied by twenty-five galleys, full of men, weapons and provisions. He then gives details of the incident, which involved a naval battle, though sadly he does not discuss the actual fighting techniques used at sea. There is in his account no awareness of the practicalities of war at sea – how the ships were actually propelled by sail or oarsmen – and there are no details of ramming or climbing aboard the enemy's vessels and of the ensuing hand-to-hand fighting.

> On 16 Jumada I a great ship (*busta*) arrived from Beirut laden with war machines, weapons, provisions, foot-soldiers and fighting

men. The sultan [Saladin] had ordered that it should be loaded and sent from Beirut and he had placed in it a great number of warriors in order that it should be able to enter the town [Acre] in spite of the enemy. The number of fighting men was 650. [The king of] England intercepted it with a number of ships, numbering, it was said, forty sails. They surrounded it on all sides and launched a fierce attack on it. Fate decreed that the wind stopped. They fought hard and a great number of the enemy were killed. Then the enemy galleys multiplied their attacks on the people in the ship. Their leader [on the ship] was an excellent man, courageous and experienced in war, called Ya'qub, a native of Aleppo. When he saw the signs of [Frankish] victory, he made an opening in the ship and all those in it were drowned, together with all the war machines, provisions and other items and the enemy did not obtain any of it at all.[226]

It is interesting to note that although Ibn Shaddad records this disaster at some length, albeit with gritted teeth, he softens the blow somewhat by pointing out that at least the Franks did not succeed in enriching themselves with the spoils of the ship. He follows up this story with a description of the Muslims' triumphal burning of the Frankish *dabbaba*, the implication being that what the Franks can do well at sea the Muslims can do just as well on land, an attitude fully shared by the Mamluks later on. The advent of the awe-inspiring fleets of the Franks must have provoked defensive measures on the part of the Muslims to protect the Levantine parts, although precise details are rare in the sources. Early in the thirteenth century the Seljuq sultan 'Ala al-Din Kayqubad built a naval installation for constructing ships in the lee of the massive fortifications which he erected in the port of Alanya on the south-west coast of Turkey. It was the practice for important Muslim harbours to be protected at their entrance by an iron chain. The port of Damietta was defended

Figure 8.40 Tershane *(ship-building installation) and citadel walls, elevation, shortly before 634/1237, Alanya, Turkey*

SEA ELEVATION

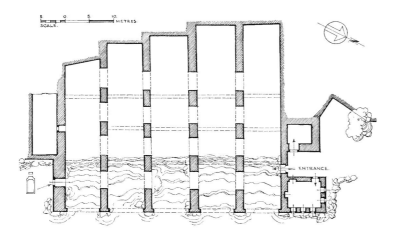

Figure 8.41 Tershane
(ship-building installation),
plan, shortly before 634/1237,
Alanya, Turkey

against attack by sea in the 1180s by two towers and a chain (*silsila*).[227] In the fourteenth century al-Dimishqi mentions that an iron chain defended Ladhaqiya, a 'marvellous and extensive harbour' against enemy ships.[228]

Saladin and the Navy

In 1955 Ehrenkreutz wrote a very detailed article on Saladin and the navy in which he chronicled the phases by which Saladin tried to take on the Crusaders at sea. Ehrenkreutz rightly pointed to Saladin's role in the naval history of Egypt since, after all, nearly all accounts of his exploits emphasise what he did on land.

It should be stressed that Saladin was the first Muslim leader of the Counter-Crusade to tackle the sea. But given the seemingly impossible task in the period c. 1130–60 of recapturing the Syrian ports in view of the land-locked internal power struggles of Muslim leaders, and given Fatimid inertia and impotence, it was only Saladin's seizure of Egypt that empowered him to be the first Muslim leader of the Counter-Crusade actually able to launch naval offensives against the Crusaders. Egypt, as already noted, was the key to the development of a Muslim fleet, given the continuing entrenched occupation of the Syrian coastline by the Crusaders.

In 1169, when Saladin took power in Egypt, there were few naval resources. But his earlier experiences in Egypt had made it clear to him that the Crusaders had to be tackled at sea as well as on land. He began well. In a visit to Alexandria in March 1177 he ordered the construction of a fleet. He revived the arsenal[229] at Alexandria and he raised sailors' pay by 20 per cent, probably to encourage recruitment into this unpopular job. According to Ibn Abi Tayyi', the Egyptian ships were in a poor state of repair. Saladin began therefore to acquire the material and craftsmen necessary for rebuilding a fleet.[230] With this in mind, he concluded commercial treaties with the Italian maritime city-states and they undertook to supply him with timber, iron and wax. Although these were the very cities which were launching Crusader fleets against the Muslims, the Italian merchants were clearly not inhibited by religious scruples from selling munitions of war to the Muslim enemy. Business is business.

The importance of the navy for Saladin is emphasised in the so-called testament of the Ayyubid sultan al-Malik al-Salih Ayyub, as recorded by al-Nuwayri. In a letter 'written in his own hand' – this detail invests the advice contained in the letter with a particular solemnity and force – Saladin recommends that the tax (*kharaj*) of al-Fayyum, Samannud and the Sahil should be allocated to the fleet: 'For the fleet is one of the wings of Islam. Therefore the sailors must be well fed.'[231]

The letter goes on to say that if the sailors are paid a fixed sum regularly, they will enrol. Properly qualified men who know how to shoot and fight will come from all directions. This testimony indicates clearly that sailors had not been fed or paid regularly in the past and that only men of indifferent fighting skills had enlisted in the Egyptian navy, at least in the period immediately preceding Saladin's time in power.

By the spring of 1179, the Egyptian fleet numbered eighty ships – sixty were galleys and twenty were transport vessels – and thus the fleet was restored to the level it had enjoyed in the heyday of the Fatimids. Nevertheless, this was small in comparison with the Frankish Sicilian fleet already described. Fifty of Saladin's ships were to protect the coast of Egypt and the remaining thirty were to attack the Crusaders. In 1179 the Egyptian fleet attacked Acre, taking all the enemy ships, and the Muslims seemed poised at last to challenge the Crusaders at sea. As Abu Shama said: 'Our fleet, once destroyed, became in turn the destroyer of the enemy . . . Never was a similar victory achieved by a Muslim fleet.'[232] In the following year, 1180, Saladin established the *diwan al-ustul*, a separate department to finance the navy.

Saladin's inexperience at handling military operations at sea began, however, to show in 578/1182 in the fiasco against Beirut. On this occasion he tried out the navy in a combined land and sea operation against Beirut. He blockaded the port for a month, but when 33 Crusader galleys appeared he lifted the siege and returned to Damascus. The operation was a failure because he had failed to synchronise his fleet with his land forces – indeed, instead of making a simultaneous attack by land and sea, he had sent the navy ahead. Above all, however, this enterprise against Beirut failed because of an inability or unwillingness on the part of Saladin's navy to take on the Crusader fleet. Saladin's naval commanders lacked the courage and skills necessary to embark on a sea battle even on this occasion when the balance of power between the two naval forces was roughly equal.[233] Perhaps they were daunted by the psychological pressure exerted by

Figure 8.42 Warship, furusiyya (military horsemanship) manuscript, thirteenth century, perhaps Egypt

the Crusaders with their history of almost a century of unchallenged superiority at sea.

In 1187, Saladin's greatest year, he launched major attacks against the Levantine ports held by the Franks. In that year the Franks held around 350 miles of coastline, including Ascalon, Jaffa, Acre, Tyre, Sidon, Beirut, Jubayl and Latakia. After his victory at Hattin that same year, Saladin and his commanders retook a good number of the ports, from Ascalon to Jubayl. But his performance at Tyre, a most crucial Crusader base, proved disastrous. At the end of 1187, he besieged it on land and he ordered his fleet in Acre to leave the harbour and establish a naval blockade, thus depriving the Crusader defenders at Tyre of any relief at sea. But the Muslim ships were taken by surprise on 30 December by Crusader raiding parties; five ships were seized. Saladin immediately ordered the remaining five ships to lift the blockade and to make for Beirut. Worse was to follow. Some Crusader galleys followed the five retreating Muslim vessels; the Muslim crews abandoned the ships and swam to the shore.

This was an ignominious episode and a serious blow to Saladin's prestige. The loss of the first five ships had come about through lack of vigilance, the second five through the pusillanimous conduct of the sailors. As 'Imad al-Din said:

> This incident showed that the naval administration of Egypt . . . could not muster suitable manpower. Instead, it had to reassemble ignorant men, without skill or experience, or any fighting tradition, so that whenever these men were faced by danger, they were terrified, and whenever it was imperative to obey, they disobeyed.[234]

The Muslim land forces at Tyre became totally demoralised by the defeat at sea, and Saladin's army retreated.

Subsequently Saladin seems to have continued to underestimate the naval strength of the Crusaders. This was particularly apparent at Acre during the years 1189–91 before it fell to Richard the Lionheart and Philip II of France in July 1191. With the coming of the Third Crusade there were at least 552 ships at the initial blockade of Acre – 'Imad al-Din wrote that they transformed the coast 'into a forest of masts'.[235] Their arrival in such strength ruined Saladin's ambitions at sea. Indeed, by the end of the Third Crusade the Franks had secured their hold over the Levantine ports from Tyre to Jaffa.

An Assessment of Saladin's Naval Strategy

In sum, Saladin had made a valiant but ultimately unsuccessful attempt to enter the maritime fray against much more seasoned opponents. When under real pressure at Tyre, he demonstrated a disturbing lack of naval tactical skills. His earlier maritime successes were those of a promising debutant, but in the real test of the Third Crusade he could not cope. However much the Muslim chroniclers tried to dress up his naval achievements, they were only brief moments of Muslim success in an otherwise uniform picture of Crusader maritime superiority.

Saladin's efforts in matters maritime are reminiscent of those of Napoleon whose activity at sea was so much less effective than on land. Saladin saw the need to deal with the Crusaders at sea and to plan concerted land and sea attacks on the Muslim side; but he was inexperienced, lacked skilled naval advisers and worked only fitfully at naval matters. Faced with the accumulated naval knowledge and resources of the European maritime states, their numerically much greater naval forces and their more intrepid attitude to the sea, Saladin was bound to lose.

Ibn Khaldun is well aware of Crusader naval superiority in Saladin's time:

> When Salah al-Din [Saladin] Yusuf b. Ayyub, the ruler of Egypt and Syria at this time, set out to recover the ports of Syria from the Christian nations . . . one fleet of unbelievers after another came to the relief of the ports, from all the regions near Jerusalem which they controlled. They supported them with equipment and food. The fleet of Alexandria could not stand up against them.[236]

This comment makes it clear that the various Crusader principalities maintained naval forces which they used to reinforce each other in times of crisis. It was therefore not simply a question of Muslim fleets being overwhelmed by much larger forces arriving directly from Europe. The early loss of the Levantine ports to the Crusaders meant that the leaders of the various Muslim forces could not offer each other mutual support at sea.

With the benefit of hindsight, one may ask what Saladin should have done to counter the Crusaders at sea. Certainly, for the coastal towns of Syria, so well fortified by the Crusaders from the beginning of the twelfth century, he would have done well to have pursued the same policy as that adopted a hundred years or so later by the Mamluks, and to have tried to invest the Syrian ports one by one and in turn raze them to the ground. In Saladin's defence, however, it should be pointed out that in his time the Crusaders and the Muslims were often evenly balanced, as demonstrated by his only narrowly failing to eradicate the Crusader presence altogether after Hattin. In Mamluk times the Muslims held the balance of power.

Ehrenkreutz describes Saladin as the last medieval ruler of Egypt to try to revive its naval power.[237] Under him, the Egyptian fleets made a last attempt to compete for domination of the eastern Mediterranean. As al-Maqrizi writes: 'After the death of Saladin the affairs of the fleet were given little attention . . . Service in the navy was considered to be a disgrace to such an extent that to call out to an Egyptian "O sailor" was treated as an insult.'[238]

Figure 8.43 Graffiti of ships, Ehmedek section of citadel walls, undated but post-Seljuq, Alanya, Turkey

The Navy in the Mamluk Period

The Mamluks in Egypt certainly knew how to build ships and al-Maqrizi points to continuing activity in this domain. This knowledge was not, however, exploited to best advantage in their military efforts against the Franks. The status and efficiency of the Mamluk navy as a fighting force were undermined by the use of convicts and prisoners of war to man the fleet. Not one Mamluk biographical dictionary contains an entry for a naval man.[239] The chronicler Ibn ʿAbd al-Zahir rebukes Sultan al-Muʿazzam Turanshah because during the crisis provoked by St Louis's campaign, Turanshah did not ride a horse into battle but 'sailed in a boat like a spectator'.[240] It was perhaps predictable in a militarised society, where the horse reigned supreme, that the Mamluks should have held strong prejudices against the sea.

Baybars and the Navy

By omission Ehrenkreutz seems to bypass completely the contribution of Sultan Baybars at sea; this is certainly one conclusion to be drawn from his statement that under Saladin the Egyptian fleets made their last efforts at dominance in the Mediterranean.[241] Baybars also shared the Mamluks' distrust and dislike of the sea, but he was too shrewd a strategist to neglect the Mamluk navy altogether. Indeed, in his reign, the Mamluk navy is at least mentioned as playing some role in military events, although how important it was in reality remains unclear. One wonders how large the fleet actually was, how much financial investment Baybars really made in it and how he expected it to function properly without qualified mariners and marines. Probably, in fact, naval matters had not improved since the time of Saladin.

In 668/1270 Baybars heard of an impending Crusade led by Louis IX, and directly put the coastal cities and his fleet on the alert. It is widely reported that Baybars ordered his fleet to attack Cyprus in 669/1271. According to the Arabic sources, this was a diversionary tactic intended to lure Hugh of Lusignan away from Acre. To deceive the enemy, the Mamluk galleys were painted black like Crusader ships and displayed flags bearing the cross. The whole enterprise was a complete disaster. During the night most of Baybars' ships were blown by a strong wind on to reefs off Limassol and were stranded. Around 1,800 crew and soldiers were taken prisoner.[242]

After this destruction of Baybars' fleet, Hugh wrote a triumphantly snide letter to the sultan telling him about the disaster. Baybars' alleged response is recorded by al-ʿAyni, quoting Baybars al-Mansuri:

> It is remarkable that you [Hugh] should prize the seizing of iron and wood more than the seizing of fortified citadels. Victory given by the wind is not beautiful. Only victory by the sword is beautiful. We can erect a number of ships in a single day whilst not a piece of a citadel could be erected for you. We can prepare a

Figure 8.44 *'Hugh de Lusignan [transcribed ʿUk de Lazinyan'], may his power endure': Arabic inscription on a brass basin made for Hugh de Lusignan, King of Jerusalem and Cyprus (1324–59); probably Egypt or Syria*

Figure 8.45 *Noah's ark,*
Rashid al-Din, Jami'
al-Tawarikh *('World History'),*
714/1314, Tabriz, Iran

hundred sails, whilst not a single citadel could be made ready for you in a hundred years. Anyone who is given an oar can row but not everyone who is given a sword can cut and thrust extremely well with it.[243]

Such nonchalance towards shipbuilding skills is a probable reason why the Mamluk ships sank. Baybars goes on to make his famous distinction between the power of the Islamic world and that of the Franks: 'For you, your horses are ships; for us, our ships are horses.'[244]

Baybars was immersed in a society which emphasised equestrian skills above all. This scornful attitude on the part of Baybars, provoked as it was by Hugh and by the need to retaliate appropriately in the epistolary war of words, is nevertheless revealing of the mind-set of Baybars and indeed of the Mamluks. At one level, the letter reveals a complete lack of realism about the time needed to build sturdy and secure ships – never mind manning them – as well as a marked prejudice against maritime warfare and for conventional fighting on land and seizing land-based citadels. The episode in Cyprus demonstrated too that Baybars did not have naval experts on whom to rely.

The sources relate that on hearing the news of the disaster, Baybars thanked God for giving him such a light punishment; his ships were, after all, manned only by peasants and the common folk.[245]

The Final Mamluk Offensive against the Crusaders

Predictably, in the end the Mamluks did not eradicate the last Crusader presence in the Levant by fighting them even partly at sea. Instead, they destroyed the Crusader fortifications along the coastline of Syria and Palestine. Saladin had begun this policy by destroying Ascalon in 587/1191. The Mamluks followed suit by demolishing one after another of the ports and fortifications of the Syro-Palestinian littoral. The resultant devastation was particularly marked in the region

between Sidon and al-'Arish. Thereafter, the Syro–Palestinian coastline was abandoned. Henceforth, the Mamluks would concentrate on the fortifying of the Nile delta only; the Egyptian ports and coastal fortifications were retained both to defend Cairo with its major concentration of Mamluk forces and also to encourage the continuation of trade with the outside world.[246]

Figure 8.46 Mamluk river boat with archers, painted leather (used in shadow plays), fifteenth century, Egypt

The Link between the Navy and Siege Warfare in the Mamluk Period

An important dimension of the Mamluk neglect of the sea was the resultant impact on their siege warfare. In all their offensives against the Franks, there is not one example of a siege conducted simultaneously by land and by sea. As Ayalon points out, all the Mamluk sieges along the coast were carried out 'almost as if the Mamluk navy did not exist at all'.[247] This crucial strategic flaw on the part of the Mamluks meant that they could undertake only partial investment of the fortresses which overlooked the sea, and – still worse – that they allowed the besieged the possibility of being reinforced and indeed rescued by sea. Such was the case in the siege of Acre in 690/1291, when an especially fireproof Frankish warship was on hand to attack the Muslims.[248] Even the presence of a Mamluk warship was not enough to stop the Franks evacuating refugees and taking them to harbours still under Frankish control and bringing

573

Saladin and Baybars tried to reverse Muslim misfortunes at sea but their efforts were neither consistent nor sustained and were not followed up by their successors. Indeed, in sum, the Muslim naval effort against the Crusaders was a fiasco.

To what can this fiasco be attributed? Certainly economic factors played a significant part; there was already a chronic shortage of funds to pay the land troops, so how could the sailors, an inferior and supplementary resource, be paid too? It was as expensive to keep a fleet at sea as to man it. One of the causes of the decline of ship-building in the Near East during the twelfth century may have been an increasing shortage of timber. Moreover, once the Muslims had lost the Levantine ports they also lost the facilities for building ships there.

The main initiative on the Muslim side had to come from Egypt. The Mamluks held the upper hand in military matters generally and they faced a weaker Crusader enemy; yet they too, like the Fatimids and Ayyubids before them, could not cope with naval strategy.

As Marshall rightly notes: 'The Muslim fleet was not normally used against Christian targets, either generally to threaten the shipping routes or, more specifically, to support a Muslim land-based assault against a strongpoint.'[262]

The Mamluks had no geographical barriers to prevent their building up fleets against the Franks. They were very probably aware of the sophisticated docking facilities (the *tershane*) developed by the Seljuqs of Rum in the thirteenth century at Alanya on the southern coast of Anatolia (figures 8.32–8.33), since Alanya was a crucial transit port for the shipment of slaves from the Black Sea marts to Egypt. Yet they seem to have built no similar facility themselves. So what was their excuse? It is usually argued – and very convincingly by Ayalon – that their stress on horsemanship and equestrian fighting skills was inevitably land-based. Their society was permanently geared for war, but – as noted above – the idea of fighting at sea was envisaged only sporadically and undertaken only tentatively. Thus Mamluk failures against the superior expertise of western Europe in matters maritime are not surprising. Mamluk myopia and fear of the sea played a part in their general failure to fight their enemies at sea but this still does not fully explain this important gap in their otherwise formidable armoury of military skills.

Economic factors should therefore be examined in any investigation of the Muslims' failure to build up a navy comparable to those of the Crusaders. Just as there was a constant problem of paying troops fighting on land, so too it was expensive to hire people to man the ships, while a wood shortage and the need to import it from Europe or Anatolia (via Alanya?) hindered the construction of ships. Even when the Mamluks decided to confront the problem of the Syrian ports which were still in Frankish hands, their final solution was not to capture them, with some inevitable destruction of fortifications, in order to rebuild and use them as part of their own defence system.

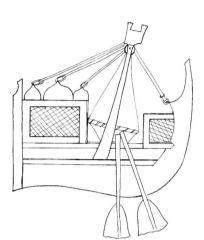

Figure 8.49 *The constellation Argo Navis, al-Sufi,* Kitab suwar al-kawakib *('Book of Fixed Stars'), 400/1009, Iraq (?)*

Instead, they deliberately eradicated the ports along the Syrian littoral and concentrated on the maritime defence of Egypt itself.

Ibn Khaldun, with his usual insight, declares: 'The Byzantines, the European Christians, and the Goths lived on the northern shore of the Mediterranean. Most of their wars and most of their commerce was by sea. They were skilled in navigating and in naval war.'[263]

The Views of Military Historians

According to the famous military historian Oman, military aspects of the Crusades comprise 'a subject sufficiently vast and varied to fill many volumes'.[264] As early as 1848 the French Orientalist Reinaud observed that the military arts of the Muslims must have been effective in order for them to have managed to chase the Franks out of the Holy Land.[265] A counter-argument to this statement might well be the question: why did it take the Muslims so long to do this? Reinaud was right, however, to stress that experience of the military tactics of the two major foreign groups that assailed the Muslim world – the Franks and the Mongols – may well have improved the fighting methods of the Muslims and helped them in their task of removing these unwanted intruders.[266]

More recently, Scanlon argues that the coming of the Franks emphasised to the Muslims their own vulnerability and the need to improve their weaponry and military tactics 'in the face of the heavier European cavalry and more complicated siege machines and weapons'.[267] Lynn White agrees with this view, stating that the Franks came to the Near East with the advantage of superior arms. The Muslims imitated Frankish military techniques and this helped them to defeat the Franks in the end.[268]

Other scholars, however, believe that while the Muslims adopted individual weapons arms and fighting techniques from the Franks and refined their tactics in response to how the Franks fought, the impact of Frankish military methods on the Muslims should not be overplayed. After all, the Muslims had their own widely varying range of military traditions on which to draw, as well as the experience of facing the terrifyingly lethal military methods of the Mongols.

Historians of military tactics, such as Oman, have concentrated on what actually happened in the battlefield. Smail and Marshall take a broader view, examining the diverse kinds of military encounter which occurred during the Crusades. They argue persuasively that it was the capture of fortresses and castles, not victory in battle, which proved the key to the military history of the Crusades in the twelfth and thirteenth centuries.[269] Marshall argues that, by the thirteenth century, the Muslims were superior in most types of military encounter.[270]

Marshall also emphasises that low-level warfare was a regular feature of the Crusading period and he stresses the importance of raids, both in their own right and as an integral part of a wider strategy, for

Figure 8.50 Brass box with blazon of 'Izz al-Din Aydemir al-Ashrafi al-Dawadar, Governor of Aleppo (whose citizens nicknamed him 'Salam 'Alaykum' because of his propensity to hail people before they had a chance to greet him), 773/1371, Syria

instance when they acted as the prelude to a siege.[271] The series of raids conducted in the thirteenth century against Acre were in his view part of the Muslims' overall military strategy. They deployed their resources carefully and cumulatively built up the pressure on Christian targets. The aim of most warfare in this period was the capture or defence of territory by taking or keeping fortresses.[272] The obsessive castle-building programme of the Franks in the twelfth-century Levant was conceived in the same spirit.

A number of military historians point out that both sides in the Crusading period, although they had a small standing army ready, would avoid pitched battles until the very last moment.[273] As Scanlon aptly puts it: 'Battle, then, was the very last recourse.'[274] Keegan points out that the Franks' weakness in battle lay in their undue dependence on the armoured charge when their Muslim enemy was not prepared to stand and receive it. The Muslims were quite prepared to fight at a distance and to retreat so as to avoid the critical blow.[275]

An Overview of the Value of the Islamic Sources on the Conduct of War

An analysis of the Islamic sources, both chronicles and military manuals, leaves many large questions unanswered. Although there are scattered references in the Islamic sources which shed light on aspects of warfare, they do not provide sufficient basis on which to build firm hypotheses. Ibn al-Qalanisi, for example, speaks of 'the [cavalry] charges for which they [the Franks] are famous',[276] but there are few concrete details in his chronicle, or any other for that matter, about the nature and sequence of individual cavalry charges in important battles between Franks and Muslims. A statement of 'Imad al-Din describing a Frankish cavalry charge as 'the passing of mountain winds' is powerful but imprecise.[277] The Islamic sources do not give a clear picture of the Frankish armies, of how they fought and the degree, if any, to which they adapted to local challenges and military methods as time went on. The Islamic sources do not give us any idea of how Muslim armies really functioned,[278] or of the actual sequence of particular battles or of whether Muslims in their turn were influenced by Frankish military methods and technology.

The use of military terminology by these sources is vague and unexplained. Their statements about the size of the Muslim and Frankish armies cannot be taken seriously. All that can be deduced about the numbers of troops is a rather vague order of magnitude.[279] There is no explicit emphasis in the Islamic sources on the fact that the Muslims were able to call on vast resources of manpower, although that was clearly the case. The Muslim rulers of Syria, such as Nur al-Din and Saladin, would often summon military help from their vassals in distant Jazira, for example, and considerable reinforcements would be sent to them. The Franks, on the other hand, often did not have sufficient men to defend their citadels and field an

Figure 8.51 *Centrifugal group of riders on a cast brass bowl, probably first half of thirteenth century, Mosul, Iraq*

army in battle, unless they received reinforcements in the form of a new Crusade from Europe. The numerical superiority of the Muslims was obviously a key factor in their eventual (and inevitable) success.

The Islamic sources leave on one side the important issue of Muslim maritime weakness and choose to ignore the fact that it was a very significant factor in the Franks' continuing presence in Muslim territory. Had the Muslims been masters of the sea as well as the land, the whole conflict could – as argued above – have been terminated much more quickly.

What *do* the Islamic sources say? They give a clear impression of the sheer number of small-scale engagements – raids, skirmishes, ambushes – as well as short and long sieges throughout the Crusading period. They also point to the comparative rarity of pitched battles. There was certainly no major naval battle. The sources underline clearly that in the end the Muslims defeated the Franks through a steady and systematic campaign of sieges of individual Crusader strongholds and ports.

The Islamic sources do not hide the fact that Crusaders and Muslims often fought on the same side against other confederations of Crusaders and Muslim troops. Such expediency sits ill with the exalted concepts of Crusade and *jihad*. Clearly such ideals were apt to be jettisoned in favour of a cold-eyed *Realpolitik* whenever occasion served. Such a reality, highlighted as it is in both the twelfth and thirteenth centuries, suggests that their fighting methods must have been quite similar or at least mutually compatible.

The extensive and spectacular network of castles and towers built by the Franks had a deep impact on the way in which the Muslims dealt with the problem of ousting them. Whatever the efficacity of battles and raids may have been in reducing Frankish forces and equipment and lowering the enemy's morale, there remained the obstacle of the Frankish monuments – castles and fortresses – to which the depleted Frankish forces could retreat, recover their strength and await reinforcements from Europe. Whilst the string of castles remained occupied by the Franks there was always the chance of Frankish revival and counter-attacks. It follows from this state of affairs that the only sure way to defeat the Franks was to conduct a remorseless series of sieges and to capture and destroy these Frankish implants, one by one. In this procedure lay the key to Muslim success far more than in any number of pitched battles.

If the Muslims had followed this course of action sooner, the Franks would not have survived as long as they did. The fact that it took so long is testimony to the lack of concerted will on the part of the Muslims to get rid of the Franks. It argues, indeed, that the Muslims did, for protracted periods of time, get accustomed to the Frankish presence in the Near East and treated them almost as just another group of 'indigenous' elements in the political jigsaw of the time. The word 'Crusade' signals to a Western sensibility something special about these warriors, but it awakened no answering resonance

Figure 8.52 *Mounted warrior, glazed ceramic figurine, twelfth century, Raqqa, Syria*

in the accounts of the medieval Muslim chroniclers, to whom these Franks were adventurers, polluters and infidels but absolutely not the vanguard of long-term Christian expansion into the Levant.

Eventually, it was the Mamluks who had the expertise, resources and will to conduct such a series of sieges and to uproot the Franks definitively. Had the Muslims also developed a more effective navy, had they blockaded and taken all the Levantine ports and thus prevented the Franks from continuing to land more troops and resources, the Muslims would have managed to strangle the power of the Franks much more quickly. The words of al-Sulami after the coming of the First Crusade ring prophetically true, for at that stage he had already foreseen that the Franks would seize the Syrian ports if the Muslims did not act quickly. However, such a far-sighted strategy would have required overall Muslim unity, powerful, astute military leadership and, above all, overcoming the strongly ingrained Muslim prejudice against maritime warfare. After Hattin, the Muslims were poised to win but they lost their advantage, arguably because of their lack of means of dealing with the Franks' maritime superiority. There was no permanent Muslim navy in Ayyubid or Mamluk times, and no experienced naval personnel. Fleets were constructed from time to time in response to external aggression from the Franks but they usually had to be built from scratch. It is not surprising that the Franks ruled the waves, harried the coasts of the Levant and went unchallenged at sea, landing men and equipment at will as reinforcements for their beleaguered co-religionists on land.

As already mentioned, it appears that the Franks were not always perceived to be an enemy by the Muslims. They may have been regarded as an irritant, even a menace, but not to a degree sufficient to mobilise united and reiterated campaigns against them. The Franks must have become part of the fabric of Levantine society. This speaks volumes for their capacity to accommodate to an initially unfamiliar lifestyle and incidentally gives the lie to the familiar, indeed hackneyed, image of fanatical Western Christians dedicated to the extermination of the Muslim presence in the Holy Land. So what motivated the Muslims in the end to launch the final offensives against the Franks in the Mamluk period? It would seem that a key factor, a catalyst in the deteriorating relationship between Muslim and Frank, was the Mongol onslaught. This series of attacks on the Muslim world from a second and much more lethal foe than the Franks must have hardened the Muslim resolve to rid the *Dar al-Islam* of outsiders of any kind. Xenophobia increased as the Muslim world was assailed from both East and West; both these enemies, the Western Christians and the pagan Mongols, had to be excised from Muslim territory once and for all. Moreover, the perception that western Europe and the Mongols were moving towards an alliance against the Muslims, a pincer movement, would have strengthened the determination of the Mamluks to move definitively against them. The fall in rapid succession of Muslim Central Asia, Iran and Iraq, culminating

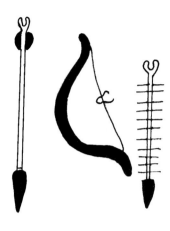

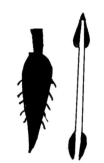

Figure 8.53 Spear-head, bow and arrows, furusiyya manuscript, c. 1500, Egypt

in the sack of Baghdad in 1258, constituted an unprecedented series of disasters for the Muslim world at large at the hands of the Mongols; indeed, taken collectively, this was the worst catastrophe that the Islamic world had ever suffered. The destruction of Baghdad, the ancient seat of the caliphate, placed the leadership of central Islamic lands squarely on the shoulders of the Mamluks. It was they who, at the battle of Goliath's Spring in 1260, inflicted the first serious reverse on the hitherto invincible Mongol hordes. The boost to Muslim morale was incalculable, and within a generation or so the Crusaders had reaped the bitter harvest of that victory.

The Muslim sources do not apparently evince any surprise that the Franks should have proved so tenacious, although from the fall of Edessa in 1144 they were restricted to the area between the Mediterranean Sea and the Syrian desert. The Muslim sources do not, of course, praise the infidel Franks for their achievement in hanging on for so long, with ever-diminishing resources, to any territory at all in the Levant, although this was ample evidence of military skills of an unusually high order. The Franks were, however, despite the traditional curses which usually accompanied any reference to them in the Muslim sources, deemed to be redoubtable foes possessed of great cunning and ingenuity in war.

Notes

1. Usama, Hitti, 177.
2. R. Grousset, *Histoire des Croisades*, Paris, 1934, vol. I, 224–45; Runciman, I, 295–7; Runciman, II, 74–91. These sources are analysed by M. Brett, 'Ramla', 18.
3. Ibid.
4. Ibid., 19.
5. M. Brett, 'The battle of Haydaran', in Parry and Yapp, *War, Technology and Society*, 85.
6. Ibid., 298.
7. For the important research by Lev on the Fatimid army, cf. Y. Lev, 'Army, regime and society in Fatimid Egypt, 358–487/968–1094', *IJMES*, 19/3 (1987), 337–66; Y. Lev, ed., 'Regime, army and society in medieval Egypt, 9th–12th centuries', in *War and Society in the eastern Mediterranean, 7th–15th centuries*, Leiden, 1997, 115–52.
8. The decline of Fatimid power in the twelfth century still awaits thorough scholarly analysis.
9. W. Watson, *The Genius of China*, London, 1973, 110.
10. *EI²: kaws.*
11. This technique is depicted in Han dynasty art in China.
12. Boudot-Lamotte, *Contribution*, 121.
13. C. Cahen, 'Les changements techniques militaires dans le Moyen Orient médiéval et leur importance historique', in Parry and Yapp, *War, Technology and Society*, 116.
14. *Manaqib al-turk*, trans. Harley-Walker, 666.
15. Ibid., 667.
16. Ibid., 670.

17. Boudot-Lamotte, *Contribution*, 148–9.
18. Ibn al-'Adim, *Zubda*, Dahan, II, 189.
19. Ibn al-Qalanisi, Gibb, 160.
20. Trans. Scanlon, 59.
21. Trans. Scanlon, 78.
22. *Wisdom*, 117.
23. Al-Maqrizi, trans. Broadhurst, 170.
24. Ibn al-Athir, *Kamil*, X, 451. Cf. also Mouton, *Damas*, 75.
25. Trans. Scanlon, 70–1.
26. Gabrieli, 99 (my italics).
27. Ibid.
28. Ibn Shaddad, *Tarikh al-Malik al-Zahir*, ed. A. Hutait, Wiesbaden, 1983, 214.
29. Thorau, *The Lion*, 251.
30. *Wisdom*, 116.
31. Ibn 'Abd al-Zahir, trans. Sadeque, 89–90.
32. Usama, Hitti, 39. For a general discussion of Muslim armies, cf. *EI²*: *harb*; *EI²*: *djaysh*.
33. Qur'an, 61: 4.
34. 'Traité', 46.
35. Ibid., 23–4.
36. Ibid.
37. Ibid., 24.
38. Ibid., 24.
39. Trans. Scanlon, 95–111.
40. Ibid., 95.
41. Ibid., 95–6.
42. Ibid., 97–8.
43. Ibid., 104.
44. Yusuf Khass Hajib, *Wisdom*, 117.
45. Smail, *Crusading Warfare*, 210.
46. Unfortunately, the battle of Dorylaeum (1097) is not recorded in Muslim sources but it is known from Crusader sources that the Franks won this battle through a decisive cavalry charge by a relief force.
47. Cf. Ayalon in *EI²*: *harb*: *the Mamluk sultanate*.
48. Mouton, *Damas*, 75, citing Sibt, 80.
49. Ibid., 75, citing Ibn al-Qalanisi, Le Tourneau, 123.
50. For example, Shaqif which could not be worn down by any mangonel. Cf. al-Dimishqi, *Kitab nukhbat al-dahr*, 211.
51. Marshall, *Warfare*, 212–13.
52. Ibid., 229.
53. According to Kennedy, *Crusader Castles*, 108.
54. Al-Tarsusi, 'Traité', 39.
55. A *ratl* is a measure of weight which in Syria corresponds to around 3.202 kilos.
56. Usama, Hitti, 143.
57. D. Hill, *Islamic Science and Engineering*, Edinburgh, 1993, 120.
58. Kennedy, *Crusader Castles*, 109.
59. Ayalon in *EI²*: *hisar*.
60. Ibid.
61. Abu'l-Fida, *RHC*, IV, 24.
62. Abu'l-Fida, *RHC*, IV, 24; Gabrieli, 344–5.
63. Little, ''Akka', 171.
64. Dozy, *Supplément*, I, 421.
65. Ibn Shaddad, *RHC*, III, 188.

66. Ibn Shaddad, *RHC*, III, 187.
67. Ibn Shaddad, *RHC*, III, 187.
68. Cf. Ayalon in *EI²: hisar*; al-Qalqashandi, *Subh*, II, 136–8.
69. Cf. *EI²: naft*; L. Casson, *The Ancient Mariners*, Princeton, 1991, 214–15.
70. Ibid., 215.
71. *EI²: naft*.
72. Al-Tarsusi, 'Traité', 43.
73. Lewis, *Islam*, II, 223; al-Tarsusi, 20–1.
74. Usama, Hitti, 104.
75. Ibn Shaddad, *RHC*, III, 221–2.
76. Marshall, *Warfare*, 212.
77. Ibid., 214.
78. Ibn al-Furat, Lyons, 76.
79. Quatremère, II, 125; Marshall, *Warfare*, 224.
80. R. C. Smail, *The Crusaders in Syria and the Holy Land*, London, 1973, 120.
81. *EI²: hisar*.
82. *Crusader Castles*, 100. Cf. also Marshall, *Warfare*, 247.
83. Ayalon in *EI²: hisar*.
84. Ayalon in *EI²: hisar*; C. W. C. Oman, *A History of the Art of War in the Middle Ages*, London, 1924, vol. I, 134.
85. Kennedy, *Crusader Castles*, 105.
86. Usama, Hitti, 102–3.
87. *Crusader Castles*, 104. Perhaps, too, these sappers were *muqannis* – specialists in digging underground water-channels.
88. Ayalon in *EI²: hisar*; Oman, *War in the Middle Ages*, I, 134.
89. Marshall, *Warfare*, 232.
90. Cf. ibid., 237–8.
91. Ibn al-Furat, Lyons, 73–4.
92. Ibn Kathir, *Bidaya*, XIII, 321; Ibn Taghribirdi, *Nujum*, VII, 6.
93. M. S. Ipşiroğlu, *Das Bild im Islam. Ein Verbot und seine Folgen*, Vienna and Munich, 1971, pl. 36 (colour).
94. Ibn al-Furat, Shayyal, 30.
95. Ibn 'Abd al-Zahir, *Rawd*, 292–4; al-Yunini, II, 374–5; Thorau, *The Lion*, 204.
96. Ibid., 171; cf. R. D. Pringle, *Secular Buildings in the Crusader Kingdom of Jerusalem*, Cambridge, 1997, 91–2.
97. *Warfare*, 211–12.
98. According to Abu Shama, *RHC*, IV, 165.
99. *Abraj al-zuhaf*: towers in which there were soldiers armed with arbalests and war machines. Such a tower was transported on a cart which was pushed against the walls of a fortress under siege. Dozy, *Supplément*, I, 581–2.
100. This passage is translated particularly badly in the *Recueil*, with whole phrases omitted or misunderstood. Abu Shama, *RHC*, IV, 165–6.
101. Abu Shama, *RHC*, IV, 254–5.
102. G. Le Strange, *Palestine under the Moslems*, Beirut, 1965, 526–7.
103. *Ta'allaqa*.
104. Ibn al-Athir, *Kamil*, XII, 5–6.
105. Abu Shama, *RHC*, IV, 447–8.
106. Ibn Shaddad, *RHC*, IV, 155.
107. Ibn Shaddad, *RHC*, IV, 156.
108. Abu Shama, *RHC*, IV, 449.
109. Quatremère, I, 7.

110. Thorau, *The Lion*, 160.
111. Ibn 'Abd al-Zahir, *Rawd*, 231; Quatremère, I, 7; al-Yunini, II, 318; Thorau, *The Lion*, 161.
112. Cf., for example, Ibn al-Furat, Lyons, 144–6.
113. Ibn 'Abd al-Zahir, *Tashrif*, 77–86.
114. Ibn 'Abd al-Zahir, *Tashrif*, 77.
115. Ibn 'Abd al-Zahir, *Tashrif*, 78.
116. Ibn 'Abd al-Zahir, *Tashrif*, 78.
117. Ibn 'Abd al-Zahir, *Tashrif*, 78.
118. *Warfare*, 210.
119. Ibid.
120. B. Gray, 'A Fatimid drawing', in *Studies in Chinese and Islamic Art*, ed. B. Gray, London, 1987, vol. II, 193–9.
121. D. Storm-Rice, *Le baptistère de St. Louis*, Paris, 1953.
122. Ibid., plate IX.
123. Ibid., plates XII, XV.
124. Ibid., plate XXXIII.
125. Ibid., plate XXXIV.
126. Ibid., plates XXVI, VII and VIII.
127. Storm-Rice, *Le baptistère*, 22–3.
128. E. Atil, *Ceramics from the World of Islam*, Washington, 1973, 112–15.
129. *Warfare*, 183–209.
130. Ibn al-Qalanisi, Gibb, 134–5.
131. Cf. p. 445.
132. Marshall, *Warfare*, 209.
133. Al-Aqsara'i, trans. Tantum, 196–8.
134. Al-Aqsara'i, trans. Tantum, 199.
135. Al-Ansari, trans. Scanlon, 47.
136. Abu Shama, *RHC*, IV, 448.
137. Al-Ansari, trans. Scanlon, 49.
138. Cf. J. Sauvaget, *La poste aux chevaux dans l'empire des Mamelouks*, Paris, 1941; *EI²: barid*.
139. Al-Ansari, trans. Scanlon, 48.
140. Al-Ansari, trans. Scanlon, 49.
141. Lewis, *Islam*, I, 223–4; Ibn al-Athir quoted in Abu Shama, I/2, 520–1.
142. Abu Shama, *RHC*, IV, 166.
143. Trans. Darke, 74–5.
144. Ibid., 95.
145. Trans. Scanlon, 51–8.
146. Al-Ansari, trans. Scanlon, 51.
147. Al-Maqrizi, trans. Broadhurst, 154–5, 159.
148. Quoted by Abu Shama, *RHC*, IV, 319.
149. Abu Shama, *RHC*, IV, 328.
150. Kedar, 'The subjected Muslims', 152–4.
151. Ibn al-Furat, Lyons, II, 88–9.
152. Al-Maqrizi, *Suluk*, I, 485.
153. Usama, Hitti, 110.
154. Usama, Hitti, 111.
155. Usama, Hitti, 111.
156. Ibn Jubayr, Broadhurst, 322.
157. Ibn Shaddad, *RHC*, III, 242–3; cf. also al-'Umari, trans. Lundquist, 50.
158. Ibn Shaddad, *RHC*, III, 243.
159. Lit. 'in custody by striking and stabbing'.
160. Ibn Taymiyya, *Lettre à un roi Croisé*, trans. J. R. Michot, Louvain, 1995, 74.

161. M. van Berchem, 'Inscriptions arabes de Syrie', *Mémoires de l'Institut Egyptien*, III (1897), offprint 32 (repr. in *Opera Minora*, 380).
162. RCEA, VIII, inscription no. 3146, 254–6.
163. Van Berchem, 'Inscriptions arabes', offprint 23, *Opera Minora*, 371.
164. Ibid.
165. Ibid., offprint 24, *Opera Minora*, 372.
166. M. van Berchem, 'Notes sur les Croisades', *Journal Asiatique*, 9th series, 19 (1902), 422.
167. Usama, Hitti, 111.
168. Ibn al-Athir, *Kamil*, X, 327.
169. Ibn al-'Adim, *Zubda*, Dahan, II, 192–3.
170. Ibn al-Furat, Lyons, 45–6.
171. Usama, Hitti, 187–9.
172. Ibn al-Azraq, *A Muslim Principality*, 65.
173. Usama, Hitti, 190.
174. Thorau, *The Lion*, 170.
175. Usama, Hitti, 106.
176. Ibn al-Furat, Lyons, 28. According to al-Maqrizi (trans. Broadhurst, 308), the figure was 300–400 prisoners beheaded a night.
177. Ibn al-Athir, *Kamil*, X, 321–2.
178. Ibn al-Athir, *Kamil*, X, 322.
179. Usama, Hitti, 133.
180. Usama, Hitti, 133.
181. Abu Shama, *RHC*, IV, 277.
182. Al-Maqrizi, trans. Broadhurst, 60.
183. Al-Maqrizi, trans. Broadhurst, 60.
184. Usama, Hitti, 58.
185. Al-'Azimi, 391.
186. Usama, Hitti, 105.
187. Ibn Wasil, V, 328–9.
188. Ibn Taymiyya, *Croisé*, 73.
189. L. Fernandes, 'On conducting the affairs of state', *Annales Islamologiques*, 24 (1988), 84.
190. Ibid.
191. Al-Qalqashandi, *Subh*, III, 354.
192. Rabbat, *The Citadel of Cairo*, 55.
193. Ibn Jubayr, Broadhurst, 43.
194. Al-Maqrizi, trans. Broadhurst.
195. Cahen and Chabbouh, 'Le testament', 110.
196. *EI²*: bahriyya.
197. Cf. p. 567 below.
198. Quoted by Lewis, *Islam*, I, 211, from al-Muttaqi, *Kanz al-'ummal*.
199. W. Muir, *The Caliphate: Its Rise, Decline and Fall*, Edinburgh, 1915, 205.
200. J. L. Burckhardt, *Arabic Proverbs*, London, 1972, 120.
201. Casson, *The Ancient Mariners*, 167.
202. A key moment was the battle of Dhat al-Sawari in 34/655 in which the Byzantine fleet was defeated. *EI²*, Supplement, art.: Dhat al-Sawari.
203. G. Hourani, *Arab Seafaring in the Indian Ocean in Ancient and Medieval Times*, Beirut, 1963, 57.
204. Ibn Khaldun, *The Muqaddima*, 210.
205. Ibn al-'Arabi, 77. The evidence of underwater archaeology reveals that many Byzantine and Muslim ships are lying on the seabed. The incidence of shipwreck is confirmed by the written sources.
206. Ibn Jubayr, Broadhurst.

207. Ibn Shaddad, *RHC*, III.
208. Michaud, *Histoire des Croisades*, IV, 449.
209. Cahen, 'St. Louis et l'Islam', 6–7, quoting Ibn Wasil.
210. D. A. Agius, 'Historical-linguistic reliability of Muqaddasi's informa-tion on types of ships', in *Across the Mediterranean Frontiers: Trade, Politics and Religion* (650–1450), eds D. A. Agius and I. R. Netton, Brepols, 1997, 303–32; cf. also Goitein, *Mediterranean Society*, I, 305 ff.
211. Agius, *loc. cit.*
212. Hourani, *Arab Seafaring*, 96.
213. Quoted by Goitein, *Mediterranean Society*, I, 305. Acacia and sycamore wood was used for the building of the *ghurab*. Possibly such wood came from Malabar (this information came from a personal com-munication from Dr. Agius).
214. Heyd, *Histoire*, I, 131–2.
215. Ibn al-Qalanisi refers to the help of the Genoese in the capture of Haifa in 494/1100–1, and at al-Suwaydiyya in 503/1109–10. Cf. Ibn al-Qalanisi, Gibb, 51 and 100.
216. Ibn Muyassar, 40.
217. Ibn Muyassar, 63. The Fatimid ships left Jaffa after six days, having been left in the lurch by the Muslims of Syria.
218. Ibn Muyassar, 91.
219. Ibn al-Qalanisi, Gibb, 307–8. Cf. also Abu Shama, *RHC*, IV, 72.
220. Ibn al-Qalanisi, Gibb, 308.
221. Further Fatimid naval raids occurred in 550/1155–6, 551/1156–7 and 553/1158. Cf. Ibn Muyassar, 92, 95–6.
222. A Ehrenkreutz, 'The place of Saladin in the naval history of the Mediterranean Sea in the Middle Ages', *JAOS*, 75 (1955), 100–16.
223. Cf., however, the discussion on p. 568 below.
224. Lit.: continuously and completely.
225. Abu Shama, *RHC*, IV, 164–5.
226. Ibn Shaddad, *RHC*, IV, 220–1. Cf. also Ibn al-Athir, *Kamil*, XII, 42; he writes that the number of warriors on the ship was 700 and that the Muslim leader went by night to the bottom of the boat and pierced a wide hole in it.
227. Al-Maqrizi, *Suluk*, I, 72.
228. Al-Dimishqi, *Kitab nukhbat al-dahr*, 209.
229. *Dar al-sina'a*, the term most frequently used to denote a place where warships were built and equipped.
230. Quoted by Lyons and Jackson, *Saladin*, 114.
231. Cf. Cahen and Chabbouh, 'Le testament', 102 and 112.
232. Abu Shama, *RHC*, IV, 211.
233. Abu Shama, *RHC*, IV, 223; Ibn al-Athir, *Kamil*, XI, 317.
234. Quoted by Ehrenkrentz, 'The place of Saladin', 111.
235. Abu Shama, *RHC*, IV, 413.
236. Ibn Khaldun, trans. Rosenthal, abridged Dawood, 211–12.
237. Ehrenkreutz, 'The place of Saladin', 116.
238. *Khitat*, II, 194.
239. *EI²*: bahriyya.
240. *Rawd*, 49; Holt, 'Ideal', 49.
241. In his thorough analysis of Baybars' career, covering 300 pages, Thorau devotes only four to Baybars' involvement in naval matters. Cf. Thorau, *The Lion*, 203–7.
242. Ibn 'Abd al-Zahir, *Rawd*, 386–7; al-Yunini, II, 453–4; Thorau, *The Lion*, 207.

243. Al-'Ayni, *RHC*, II, 241.
244. Al-Maqrizi, *Suluk*, I, 594, quoted by Ayalon in *EI²: bahriyya*.
245. Ibid.
246. Ibn Taghribirdi, *Nujum*, VI, 590 ff.; VII, 122 ff.
247. *EI²: hisar*.
248. Abu'l-Fida', *RHC*, I, 164.
249. Ibn Kathir, *Bidaya*, XIII, 321; al-Maqrizi, *Suluk*, I, 747, 764–5; Ibn Taghribirdi, *Nujum*, VIII, 8, 11; Stevenson, *The Crusaders*, 385.
250. Ibn 'Abd al-Zahir, *Sirat al-Malik al-Mansur*, Cairo, 1961, 88.
251. *EI²: hisar*.
252. Ibid.
253. Ibn Taghribirdi, *Nujum*, VIII, 154–7.
254. Lyons, *The Arabian Epic*, I, 60–1.
255. Ibid.
256. Ibid., 61.
257. Ibid.
258. Ibid., 62.
259. Ibid., 63–4.
260. Goitein, *Mediterranean Society*, I, 37.
261. Marshall, *Warfare*, 120.
262. Marshall, *Warfare*, 214.
263. Ibn Khaldun, *Muqaddima*, 208.
264. Oman, *War in the Middle Ages*, I, 232–3.
265. 'De l'art militaire', 194.
266. Ibid.
267. Al-Ansari, trans. Scanlon, 4–5.
268. Lynn White, jun., 'The Crusades and the technological thrust of the West', in Parry and Yapp, *War, Technology and Society*, 100–1.
269. R. C. Smail, *Crusading Warfare 1097–1193*, Cambridge, 1967, 83; Marshall, *Warfare*, 5–6.
270. Ibid., 257–61.
271. Ibid., 183ff.
272. Ibid., 17.
273. Smail, *Crusading Warfare*, 83.
274. Al-Ansari, trans. Scanlon, 29.
275. J. D. P. Keegan, *A History of Warfare*, London, 1993, 294.
276. Quoted by Gabrieli, 58.
277. Abu Shama, *RHC*, IV, 425.
278. Al-Aqsara'i, trans. Tantum, 188.
279. Cf. Mouton, *Damas*, 72.

CHAPTER NINE

Epilogue
The Heritage of the Crusades

With such glorious civilisations and military achievements behind them, the Arabs cannot stop brooding over the comparison between their present and their past. That history was constantly bedevilled with the conflict with Europe, which made them look all the time over their shoulder, check and compare.[1] (Kishtainy)

Introduction

THIS BOOK has highlighted some of the Islamic perspectives of the phenomenon known in the West as the Crusades and has attempted to show how medieval Muslims were affected by this unheralded invasion from Christian Europe.

It is of course true that the Crusading phenomenon did not stop abruptly with the fall of Acre in 1291. Offensives on both sides, European and Muslim, were repeatedly launched in subsequent centuries. These could be, and often were, labelled as Crusade or *jihad* and were conducted in the same spirit as similar undertakings which had taken place in the twelfth and thirteenth centuries. So there was no sudden or decisive end to the Crusades, whose reverberations continued to echo long after the withdrawal of the European military presence from the Levant.

The story of the confrontation of the Muslim world with the Crusaders who lingered in the Mediterranean after 1291 is beyond the remit of this book.[2] Nor is it the aim here to discuss the Ottoman offensives in Europe which many have seen as an Islamic revanche for the Crusades.[3] The psychological scars left by the Crusades on the Islamic world and the way in which the experience of the Crusades has moulded the Muslim corporate psyche will, however, be discussed here. These factors are, after all, of direct relevance to a clearer understanding of the long-term Muslim perception of the Crusades and they also shed light on twentieth-century relationships between the Islamic world and the West.

Such an enormous topic as modern Islamic perceptions of the Crusades should really be the subject of several other books; so what is offered here are only a few general thoughts and brief glimpses into

Figure 9.1 *Sphinx, glazed ceramic bowl, late twelfth–early thirteenth centuries, Raqqa, Syria*

Figure 9.2
(above, below and opposite)
*Animal friezes, inlaid brass
basin known as the
'Baptistère de St Louis',
c. 1300 or earlier, Syria*

a vast and multifaceted phenomenon. The 'idea' of the Crusades quietly permeates many aspects of modern life in the Arab and the wider Islamic world. For some, the concept of the Crusades is seen as a manifestation of the continuing struggle between Islam and Christianity, of which the chain reaction began with the Islamic conquests, produced a Christian counter-response in the Crusades themselves, an Ottoman revanche notably in the fifteenth and sixteenth centuries and Western colonialising interference in the last two hundred years. Others see the Crusades as the first stage of European colonialism (*isti'mar mubakkar* – 'premature imperialism') or as a combination of the effects of religious zeal and political intervention. Whatever their interpretation of the Crusading phenomenon may be, there is no doubt that it affects political rhetoric, *jihad* literature and, more pervasively but intangibly, the way in which many Muslims view western Europe, and by extension, the United States. It is no exaggeration to say that international understanding and world peace would benefit significantly from a better understanding of this issue.

As Akbar Ahmed, a prominent Islamic writer who lives in the West, remarks:

> The memory of the Crusades lingers in the Middle East and colours Muslim perceptions of Europe. It is the memory of an aggressive, backward and religiously fanatic Europe. This historical memory would be reinforced in the nineteenth and twentieth centuries as imperial Europeans once again arrived to subjugate and colonize territories in the Middle East. Unfortunately this legacy of bitterness is overlooked by most Europeans when thinking of the Crusades.[4]

The Development of Muslim Interest in the Crusading Phenomenon

It is difficult to assess the validity of drawing parallels between the past and the present. Of course, the past is often a live issue. On 10

Muharram each year Shi'ite Muslims solemnly re-enact in deeply emotional ceremonies the battle at Karbala' in 680 and the martyrdom there of the Prophet's grandson, al-Husayn. The past can live on in different ways. It can be a source of pride – the Palestinians invoke the three glorious military victories of Yarmuk, Qadisiyya and Hattin and their hopes of present victory over Israel are sustained. On the other hand, the past can fester. It is a strange irony that western Europe lost the Crusades militarily but went on to 'win the world', whilst the Muslims won the Crusades but subsequently viewed themselves as being trapped in a subordinate position to the West: as the Tunisian scholar Matwi writes: 'All the profit (*ghunm*) of those wars fell to the lot of the Crusaders, all the damage (*ghurm*) was the share of the Muslims.'[5]

The Islamic world was slow to draw lessons from the Crusades, their first experience of European interventionism. Nor did the Muslims tap the propagandistic potential of the Crusades until relatively recent times. Occasionally, within the context of Turkish military defeats at the hands of Russia or Austria, the Ottoman imperial historiographer Na'ima (d. 1716) would draw parallels between past and present, between the Crusades and his own time. As Bernard Lewis points out,[6] Na'ima was not just a chronicler of events; he also reflected on the philosophy of history. He describes how the Crusaders established themselves along the coasts of Syria and Palestine where they remained until Saladin restricted their power and his successors finally drove them out. Na'ima suggests that the leaders of his own time should model themselves on the example of the Ayyubid and Mamluk sultans. When in defeat, the Muslim rulers at the time of the Crusades had seen the wisdom of making truces with the Crusaders – after all, one of the sultans had even signed a treaty handing Jerusalem over to them. So, Na'ima argues, the Ottomans who have been heavily defeated should be ready to make peace in order to build up their resources for an eventual victory.[7]

The Muslims showed little interest in the Crusades as a discrete entity, as a phenomenon of world history; the Arabic terms *al-hurub al-salibiyya* (the 'Cross' wars) or *harb al-salib* (the war of the 'Cross'),

which are used nowadays to signify the Crusades, were introduced as late as the middle of the nineteenth century. It is important to stress that these terms are European borrowings, although they have been embraced wholeheartedly into modern Arab and Muslim culture and indeed have acquired their own emotive force in Arabic in recent years. The Middle East learned to use these terms after Christian Arab authors began to translate the history of the Crusades from European sources. It is an ironically roundabout route for Muslims to take in search of their own past.

A history of the Crusading wars appeared in Arabic in Jerusalem in 1865: entitled *History of the Holy Wars in the East, Called the Wars of the Cross*, it was a translation by Muhammad Mazlum from a French work by Monrond, but it bore the imprimatur of the Patriarch of Jerusalem himself.[8] The first work on the Crusading phenomenon by a Muslim, written in 1899, was the *Splendid Accounts in the Crusading Wars* (*Al-akhbar al-saniyya fi'l-hurub al-salibiyya*) of the Egyptian scholar Sayyid 'Ali al-Hariri.[9] This book is a pioneering landmark in Islamic historiography since it drew extensively on medieval Islamic sources which the author quotes at length. Even at this early stage, however, al-Hariri is well aware of the relevance of the Crusades to his own time. He writes in the introduction to this work: 'Our most glorious sultan, Abdülhamid II has rightly remarked that Europe is now carrying out a Crusade against us in the form of a political campaign.'[10] Yet al-Hariri's book was not followed up very energetically by other similar works.[11]

The Evolution of the Saladin Myth

Surprising as it may seem, Saladin, who was soon eulogised in medieval Europe in the centuries after the Crusades and then eagerly

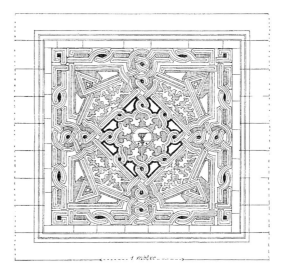

Figure 9.3 *Marble panel, Mosque of al-Rifa'i, fifteenth century, Damascus, Syria*

Figure 9.4 Hunting scenes, inlaid metal basin by Da'ud ibn Salama al-Mawsili, 650/1252, probably Damascus, Syria

cast in heroic mould by the European Enlightenment – one has only to think of how G. E. Lessing or Sir Walter Scott portrayed him[12] – was ignored for centuries in the Middle East. In the period immediately after the Crusades, it was two other Muslim rulers who spoke more directly to their people as foes of the Crusaders. Nur al-Din earned the accolades of the Muslim religious classes as the model *mujahid*, combining personal piety with public service to the Islamic cause, while Baybars became the intrepid hero of Arabic folk literature.

The first biography of Saladin to be written in relatively modern times by a Muslim was that of Namik Kemal, which was published in 1872. Kemal was one of the luminaries of the Young Ottoman movement.[13] He was anxious to write a work which would be firmly based on Muslim sources contemporary with Saladin and to respond to what he perceived to be a highly tendentious and misleading European work on the Crusades – Michaud's *Histoire des Croisades*, published in Paris between 1812 and 1822 – which had been translated into Turkish. Significantly, Kemal placed his work on Saladin in the same volume as the biographies of two great heroes of Ottoman history, Mehmet the Conqueror and Selim the Grim.[14]

Gradually, the idea of parallels between European policies past and present crystallised in the Muslim consciousness. These parallels appeared increasingly apt as the nineteenth century progressed and the wave of European imperialism swept through the Middle East. A key voice was that of the Ottoman sultan Abdülhamid II (ruled 1876–1909), who announced repeatedly that Europe was conducting a 'Crusade' against the Ottoman empire. This idea of his was embraced and disseminated by the pan-Islamic press. 'Ali al-Hariri refers to the words of Abdülhamid II, as already mentioned, in the introduction to his book on the Crusades.[15]

Saladin's fame grew greater as the news of his glowing reputation in Europe percolated into the Middle East. Kaiser Wilhelm II, who made the effort to visit Saladin's tomb in Damascus in 1898, publicly proclaimed Saladin's heroic status in Europe, eulogising him as 'a knight without fear or blame, who often had to teach his opponents the right way to practise chivalry'.[16] The following year, the famous Egyptian poet Ahmad Shawqi responded enthusiastically with an ode (*qasida*) eulogising Saladin's achievements.[17] In an article in a pan-Islamic journal written at the same time, Shawqi declared that of all the great

Muslims of the past none, after the first four Rightly Guided caliphs, had been more meritorious than Saladin and Mehmet the Conqueror. He then poses a rhetorical question: how could Muslim writers have been so slow to awaken the memory of these two great heroes of Islam?[18]

It has already been pointed out that Saladin was ethnically a Kurd, that he was brought up in a Turkish military milieu and that he came to rule the traditionally Arab lands of Syria, Palestine and Egypt. As a leader of the non-Arab Muslim military elite class he was also at the forefront of a movement of reinvigorated *jihad* which united the Sunni Muslim world of the Near East under his banner. He was therefore well placed to become a hero to many different groups in the Middle East in modern times.

Saladin is probably the most famous Kurd of all time. Though without a homeland of their own, nowadays the Kurds comprise sizeable sections of the populations of Iran, Iraq and Turkey and nurture powerful nationalist ambitions. They are well aware of Saladin's exploits and take pride in the fact that he is of their race. The Kurdish poet Shaykh Rida Talabani (d. 1910) speaks nostalgically of brief periods of an independent Kurdish past, and in particular of the Baban Kurdish dynasty which flourished on the western slopes of the Zagros mountains in the late eighteenth century. He writes: 'Arabs! I do not deny your excellence; you are the most excellent; but Saladin who took the world was of Baban-Kurdish stock.'[19]

However, the perception that Saladin waged a monumental struggle against the western European Crusaders was applicable not only to his own 'people', the Kurds. He was also eagerly embraced as a role model by Arabs, and also Turks, in their fight for nationhood and freedom from European interference. Despite his Kurdish origins, Saladin is viewed as leading the *jihad* of the Arabs and is an exemplar for all Muslims to follow. Though he was Kurdish, it is often argued that Saladin was immersed in Arabic culture and was the embodiment of Arabic chivalry.[20]

Even before the First World War, an Arab author gave himself the pseudonym of Salah al-Din (Saladin) and warned against the Zionist threat in Palestine.[21] A new university named after Salah al-Din Ayyubi was opened in Jerusalem in 1915. During the period of the British Mandate after the First World War, Saladin's victory over the Crusaders at Hattin became a central theme in the Palestinians' political struggle against the Zionists.[22]

During the twentieth century the didactic value of the Crusade experience became fully recognised in the Arab world, especially after the establishment of the state of Israel. In general, it is Saladin who receives most attention as the heroic ancestor, the prototypical religio-political fighter against foreign oppression, rather than Nur al-Din or Baybars, both of whom made as great a contribution as he did to the Muslims' ultimate victory over the Crusaders. Saladin's special place in the affection and admiration of Muslims springs from the fact that it was he who recaptured Jerusalem in 1187; and his adulation in Europe in the Middle Ages as the epitome of chivalry and later as the model of Enlightenment virtue also helps.

In the Arab world the usual perspective on Saladin nowadays is that of a great fighter for Islam against external aggression from the West, and Arab political leaders vie to become the 'Second Saladin'. A notable example is Saddam Husayn, who, like Saladin, hails from Tikrit (plate 9.1). When the story of Saladin and the Crusades is told in Arab schools it is told in bold, heroic strokes, with no shades of grey.[23] There is little reference to the pragmatic realities of Crusader history, such as the Muslim–Crusader alliances which punctuated the period 1099–1291, to the long periods of truce and *détente*, to trading links between East and West, to Saladin's personal and family ambitions. Not surprisingly, the Crusades are seen through an anti-imperialist prism and the Islamic response in the twelfth and thirteenth centuries is viewed as the blueprint for modern Arab and Islamic struggles for independence from Western colonialist aggression, above all from Israel and the United States.

The abiding memory of the Crusades to this very day finds striking visual expression in an ambitious and over life-size sculptural group erected in Damascus at municipal expense in 1992 (plate 9.2). It also figures prominently in the design of the current Syrian 200-*dirham* banknote. While statues of modern political leaders are not rare in

Plate 9.1 *Saddam Husayn as the heir of Saladin, propaganda picture, probably 1980s*

Plate 9.2 *Statue of Saladin,*
1992, Damascus, Syria

Islamic countries – and indeed Syria is full of statues of President
Hafez Asad – there is no indigenous tradition of public sculptures of
historical subjects. For this reason alone the Damascus group sculpture
is noteworthy. But it is the choice and the treatment of the subject
that is particularly remarkable here. Its central focus is an equestrian
portrait of Saladin. Flanked on one side by a Sufi in simple clothing
(plate 9.3) and on the other by a spear-wielding infantryman, he urges

596

Plate 9.3 *Statue of Saladin,*
foot soldier and Sufi, 1992,
Damascus, Syria

his horse forward. Behind the horse two Crusaders slump listlessly on a rock (plate 9.4). One, who grabs the bag of money containing his ransom, is King Guy of Jerusalem. The other, his eyes fixed on the ground, his bowed posture betraying perhaps his certainty that he will not be spared, is Reynald de Chatillon. The Muslims all look ahead; the Christians are turned in the opposite direction. Significantly enough, the group is placed right in front of the Damascus citadel, a military ambience that matches its rousing message of protecting Islam from the infidel. The creator of the sculpture, ʿAbdallah al-Sayed

Plate 9.4 Statue of Saladin, Reynald de Chatillon (left) and King Guy of Jerusalem (right), 1992, Damascus, Syria

598

Plate 9.5 *Statue of Saladin, members of his army and Crusaders, with the sculptor, ʿAbdallah al-Sayed, Damascus, Syria*

(plate 9.5) explains that the group represents Saladin not as an individual warlord but as a leader who embodies a wave of popular feeling against the Franks.[24] Hence the emphasis on the Sufi, representing the down-to-earth religion of the people, and the simple foot soldier. Together they express a unity of purpose under the banner of Islam. Not a hundred metres away, the gate of the medieval citadel is hung with a massive portrait of the President of Syria, Hafez Asad (colour plate 15). The parallelism between the ancient and the modern defender of Islam and its territories against foreign infidel encroachment is plain to see. Saladin's subjugation of the Franks depicted here is a powerful symbol which is easily understood by the man in the street – Israel is the new Crusader state of the Middle East, which will be brought to heel in the same way as the medieval Frankish Kingdom of Jerusalem.

Modern Manifestations of the Islamic 'Counter-Crusade': A Few Case Studies

The following discussion deliberately uses borrowed terminology – 'Counter-Crusade' – since it seeks to restrict itself to modern movements, ideologies and political rhetoric which target the West and which are seen in the Muslim world as direct extensions of the Crusading phenomenon itself. Although much of what is labelled *jihad* is indeed directed against the West and can of course be seen as a continuation of the Islamic response to the Crusades, it should be stressed that the term *jihad* in the Muslim consciousness has associations more profound and subtle than mere military or propaganda movements directed at Europe and America.

Ayatollah Khumayni wrote extensively on *jihad*, stressing that man must wage the 'greater *jihad*' within his soul before fighting against injustice, corruption and tyranny in this world.[25]

In these statements Khumayni is drawing on the centuries-old tradition of *jihad* interpretation within Islamic legal circles, but his views are interpreted by Western observers – not without some justification – as a *jihad* against Western civilisation.

The concept of the Crusades is widespread and deep-rooted in modern Islamic political ideologies.

The Writings of Sayyid Qutb

Sayyid Qutb, the Egyptian 'fundamentalist' writer, the principal spokesman for the Muslim Brothers movement in Egypt after its dissolution in 1954, was eventually executed for treason in 1966. In his most famous work entitled *In the Shade of the Qur'an* he speaks of a confrontation between Muslims and polytheists which has gone on for fourteen centuries; within this struggle he mentions specifically two key periods, the early Islamic conquests and the Crusades.[26]

Figure 9.5 Hunting scenes, Blacas ewer, inlaid brass, 629/1232, Mosul, Iraq

Figure 9.6 *Cartoon of the Gulf War (adaptation of a medieval stained-glass window, St-Denis, Paris), Jack Sherman,* Newsday, *6 September 1990*

In his rhetorical outbursts Qutb argues that Crusade should be interpreted to mean all Christian attacks on Islam from its earliest days. Crusade even embraces Christian military opposition to the first Islamic conquerors in Syria and Palestine in the seventh century. Crusade encompasses Christians fighting Muslims in medieval Spain, just as it includes the twentieth-century persecution of Muslims in parts of Africa – Zanzibar, Ethiopia, Kenya and southern Sudan – in recent times. The battle of Christianity against Islam may be conducted in the name of 'land, of economics, of politics, of military bases . . . whatever' but its secret purpose is about doctrine – 'international Zionism, international Crusaderism – in addition to international Communism'.[27]

For the Muslim Brothers after 1947, the activities of the United Nations in Palestine were viewed as 'a new declaration of Zionist–Crusading war against the Arab and Islamic peoples'. Zionism was fully identified with Crusading Western imperialism and the terms 'European Crusading' (*al-salibiyya al-urubbiyya*) and 'Jewish Crusading' were interchangeable.[28] Qutb describes Crusading as being against 'the spirit of Islam': Crusading concerns the retreat of Muslim civilisation in the face of Western civilisation. Rising to heights of anti-Western invective he declares:

Crusading was not confined to the clangor of arms, but was, before and above all else, an intellectual enmity. European imperial interests can never forget that the spirit of Islam is firmly opposed to the spirit of Imperialism . . .

There are those who hold that it is the financial influence of the Jews of the United States and elsewhere which has governed the policy of the West. There are those who say that it is English

ambition and Anglo-Saxon guile which are responsible . . . And there are those who believe that it is the antipathy between East and West . . . All these opinions overlook one vital element in the question . . . the Crusader spirit which runs in the blood of all Westerners.[29]

Hizb Allah *and Other Radical Groups*

For the even better-known *Hizb Allah* in the modern Middle East, the Crusades have never ended. Khumayni spoke of the need to fight the 'last stage of the historical Crusades'.[30] Moreover, some Muslim radical groups believe that the Crusades have not ended for Christians either; in their view, the 'Christian powers' of the West remain determined to destroy Islam. Mehmet Ali Agha, the Turk who made an attempt on the Pope's life in 1981, wrote in a letter: 'I have decided to kill John Paul II, the supreme commander of the Crusades.'[31] Eighteen years later, on 9 June 1997, two hijackers held up an Air Malta Boeing plane *en route* to Istanbul and diverted it to Cologne/Bonn airport; they were demanding the release of Mehmet Agha.

The year 1998 saw the rise to prominence in the world media of an umbrella organisation of Islamic groups led by Usama bin Laden, described as 'America's most wanted man'[32] – it is called The World Islamic Front for Crusade against Jews and Crusaders.[33]

Hamas

Hamas, which is an acronym of *harakat al-muqawama al-Islamiyya* ('movements of Islamic resistance') was founded in the Israeli Occupied Territories in 1967 and has been mentioned regularly in the media ever since. The goal of *Hamas* is to liberate Palestine from occupation by the 'Zionist enemy' and to re-establish an Islamic state.[34]

According to *Hamas* ideology, Palestine has a special position in Islam because Jerusalem was the first *qibla* (direction of prayer) for Muslims and the Aqsa mosque is revered as the third most holy place in Islam.[35] Given the central importance of Jerusalem and Palestine to Islam, it is not surprising that throughout history enemies have sought to regain Palestine from the Muslims.[36] The Crusaders fought in and for Palestine for two hundred years during the Crusades, and the attempts by the West to take it in the First World War were only yet another example in a long line of Western incursions into Palestine.[37] The fight for Palestine can be won only under the banner of God – this fact has been proved in history by Muslim victories over the Crusaders and the Tartars (Mongols).[38]

Figure 9.7 *Blazons on Mamluk coins, thirteenth–fifteenth centuries, Egypt and Syria*

The Islamic Liberation Party (the Hizb al-tahrir al-islami)

The ideals and activities of the Islamic Liberation Party (ILB) have been studied very thoroughly in the recent research of Suha Taji-Farouki.

602

Figure 9.8 *Marble intarsia work,* sabil *(fountain), fifteenth century, Cairo, Egypt*

Her scholarly findings reveal once again the omnipresent memory of the Crusades in modern Islamic political thinking.[39] The ILB was established in Jerusalem in 1952 by Shaykh Taqi al-Din al-Nabhani, who had broken away from the Muslim Brotherhood. The group presented itself as a political party with Islam as its ideology; its goal was the revival of the Islamic *umma*, purged of the contamination of colonialism.[40] The Islamic character of the party was stressed by its choice of Jerusalem as its headquarters.

The party claims to be active in a wide range of Middle Eastern countries as well as in parts of Europe.[41] The Palestine question is not central to the main thrust of the ILP's efforts but the party certainly has strong views on this issue.[42] Israel is seen as a colonialist bridge-head through which America and Europe perpetuate their control and their economic exploitation of the Muslim world. Israel is 'a poisoned dagger plunged deep into its breast'.[43] The creation of the state of Israel, according to ILP thinking, was inspired by the Crusades. They view Saladin's reconquest of Jerusalem on behalf of the Muslims as a momentous psychological blow to the world of the unbelievers. Ever since that time, the West has been obsessed with the desire for revenge: the history of the last eight centuries consists of a reaction to the battle of Hattin and its immediate consequences:

The Crusaders' malice remained concealed in their hearts, till they disclosed it when they succeeded in doing away with the Ottoman Caliphal state and then establishing a Jewish state in Palestine.

This they deemed a two-fold revenge for their defeat at the hands of the heroic Muslim leader Salah al-Din.[44]

Links between the Crusades and European colonialism are also highlighted. Colonialism is seen as a strategy to exploit the Muslim world in vengeance for the failure of the Crusades. There is, according to the ILP perspective, evidence of a continuing Crusader mentality among Westerners, as evidenced by the remark allegedly made at the time of the First World War by General Allenby on his occupation of Jerusalem in December 1917: 'only now have the Crusades come to an end'.[45]

It is not significant in the war of propaganda that Allenby did not actually make his famous 'remark'. Indeed, it seems clear that the British government wished to be respectful to Islam. Allenby in fact wanted to enter Jerusalem in a more culturally sensitive way than the German emperor Wilhelm II, who twenty years earlier had arrived on horseback dressed as a medieval Crusader.[46] Nevertheless, Allenby's alleged remark was propagated by Sayyid Qutb and other Muslim writers and it epitomises the way in which the modern Islamic world views the spectre of the Crusades.

Figure 9.9 *Page of Qur'an made for the Mamluk sultan al-Mu'ayyad, early fifteenth century, Cairo, Egypt*

Figure 9.10 *Kufic inscription forming an architectural silhouette and spelling the* shahada *or Muslim creed, manuscript frontispiece, fifteenth century, Egypt*

The response to the neo-Crusaders must be the Islamic solution of *jihad*: Muslims must fight until the last invader has been expelled, however many martyrs fall, however much time it takes. Again the model of the Crusader is used – Muslims are reminded that their predecessors fought for almost two centuries until the Crusaders were ousted and Muslim territorial integrity was restored.[47] The destruction of Israel and the restoration of Palestine must be achieved through *jihad*, just as the Muslims had regained Palestine through *jihad* at the time of the Crusades. Victory will come, if not today, then in the future: 'An *umma* that fought against the Crusaders and the Tartars [Mongols] for more than two hundred years . . . until it did away with them and expelled them, is capable of fighting and defeating its enemy . . . if not today, then tomorrow.'[48]

Parallels between the Crusader Kingdom of Jerusalem and the Modern State of Israel

It is a deep-rooted characteristic of Muslim historiography to draw moral lessons from the study of the past. The didactic value of the Crusade experience has been fully recognised in the Arab world since the Second World War and the establishment of the state of Israel. In October 1948 'Abd al-Latif Hamza wrote: 'The struggle against Zionists has reawakened in our hearts the memory of the Crusades.'[49]

Parallels are frequently drawn in the Arabic media, works of literature and academic books between the rise and fall of the Kingdom of Jerusalem and the current situation in the state of Israel.[50] Some Arabs speak of the need for patience. Is it not true, they say, that the Crusader Kingdom of Jerusalem lasted 88 years (1099–1187) whilst the state of Israel has been in existence only since 1948? The fact that the Palestinian nationalist struggle focuses so closely on the status of Jerusalem and that modern Islamic movements also stress the sanctity of the city as the third holiest in Islam, after Mecca and Medina, only enhances the potency of such parallels.

A very powerful medium for expression of Arab and Muslim longing for Jerusalem is poetry. As the Palestinian critic Jabra I. Jabra writes:

> Poetry might be condemned as too weak a toy against guns, but in actual fact it was often as good as dynamite. It gave point to a whole nation's suffering and wrath. It crystallised political positions in telling lines which, memorised by old and young, stiffened popular resistance and provided rallying slogans.[51]

An interesting example is the work of the Iraqi woman poet and essayist Nazik al-Malaika. Writing in the 1970s, she gives the Arab nationalist struggle a distinctively religious interpretation and focuses on Palestine, and especially Jerusalem. Once again, familiar symbols from the Arabic poetry and prose of the Crusading period re-emerge and are given new significance and poignancy in the contemporary political situation. The Dome of the Rock (cf. plate 9.6) occupies a central place as a powerful spiritual and political image:

> [You are] a mosque thirsty for their Qur'an and their prayers . . .
> When man achieves victory, the call to prayer will rise,
> Announcing the prayer, the call to Holy War and
>   the Revolution.[52]

In another poem, emotively entitled 'Migration to God' (al-hijra ila Allah), she speaks of her grief for Jerusalem and for the degradation suffered by the Aqsa mosque when it lacked defenders of the calibre of the 'Abbasid caliph al-Mu'tasim, and Saladin.[53] Thus, once again, as in the Crusading period, the two sacred Islamic monuments in occupied Jerusalem, the Dome of the Rock and the Aqsa mosque, are personified, thirsting for the Qur'an and the prayers of the faithful, and suffering under the yoke of alien oppression.

The Dome of the Rock in particular, with its compact, immediately recognisable exterior, has become a potent symbol, almost a logo, in much of the Arab world (plate 9.7). Images of it decorate the exterior walls of ordinary houses to celebrate the fact that the occupants have made a visitation there. It is employed in all kinds of contexts from letterheads to tea-trays, and is a centre-piece of revolutionary and poster art in such overtly Islamic states as Iran, always with the message of resurgent Islam and Palestinian identity. Hence the immediate and violent reaction to any action, political or otherwise, that might conceivably threaten the monuments of al-Haram al-Sharif, such as the opening of the tunnel in late 1996 in the vicinity of the

Plate 9.6 *Dome of the Rock, interior, 72/691–2 onwards, Jerusalem*

(Creswell Photographic Archive, Ashmolean Museum, Oxford, neg. C. 180)

Aqsa mosque. The incendiary bomb detonated by an Australian zealot in the Aqsa mosque in 1969 – which reduced to ashes the celebrated twelfth-century wooden *minbar* of Nur al-Din, made in anticipation of his planned capture of Jerusalem – shows that such fears are not without foundation.

Despite the pull of the modern political agenda and the emotions aroused by the Holy City of Jerusalem, however, it is unwise to draw simplistic parallels between the Crusader Kingdom of Jerusalem and the modern state of Israel. It is true enough that modern Muslim heads of state see this danger all too clearly. Nevertheless, as long as Israel, a state with a Western orientation and a militarised society,

607

Plate 9.7 Dome of the Rock, exterior, 72/691–2 onwards, Jerusalem

(Creswell Photographic Archive, Ashmolean Museum, Oxford, neg. C. 1272)

continues to occupy the same geographical space as the Crusader Kingdom of Jerusalem did in the twelfth and thirteenth centuries, it is all too easy for such parallels to be made.

Of course, it is also possible to draw rather different parallels from the historical evidence. One might, for example, compare the Ayyubid ruler al-Kamil, who bowed to political exigencies and ceded Jerusalem to the Crusaders again, with those modern Arab leaders who have concluded treaties with Israel. The Crusader states, as has been shown in this book and in many others, owed their longevity (almost two centuries) to their military expertise in defence, to their regular reinforcements from the West, and to their ability to make alliances with neighbouring Muslim states. In short, as has been discussed elsewhere in this book, for a while – at least in the thirteenth century – the Crusaders became almost an integral part of the Middle Eastern political landscape, before the Mamluks unified Egypt and Syria and raised the banner of *jihad* and Muslims once again felt the over-powering urge to remove the Crusaders from Islamic territory. It remains to be seen which scenario will prevail in the present-day context. But it should not be forgotten that there is always a yawning gap between rhetoric and reality, between public posturings and private negotiations.

Libyan anti-Western Propaganda

In addition to making military and political parallels between the medieval Crusades and the current situation in the Middle East, contemporary Muslim leaders and thinkers draw on deeply held views about Crusader/Western pollution and their defiling of Muslim sacred space.

Colonel Qaddafi's regime in Libya was officially inaugurated on 1 September 1969. During a period of maximum hostility on the part of the West towards his government in the early 1980s a spate of defensive pamphlets were produced in Libya. Their tone is virulently anti-imperialist, anti-Christian, anti-Western; the imagery and rhetoric are strongly reminiscent of the Muslim response at the time of the Crusades. The strength of feeling is apparent in the title of one such green-coloured booklet entitled *Nationalist Documents to Confront the Crusader Attack on the Arab Homeland*.[54] The enemy is different from the twelfth- and thirteenth-century Crusaders who originated from western Europe: the United States of America have now assumed the mantle of the Crusaders (the writer speaks of the 'filth of the American Christians'),[55] and it is the Jews who have occupied Jerusalem. But, otherwise, the tone and content are very familiar:

> Yesterday we were summoning Muslims to conduct a mass Muslim holy march to liberate Jerusalem, the first of the two *qibla*s, but today we are surprised that, after the Jews have occupied Jerusalem, the Christians have occupied the sky [airspace] of Mecca, Medina and the mountain of Arafat.[56]

Figure 9.11 Marble intarsia work, sabil *(fountain), fifteenth century, Cairo, Egypt*

The task of the writers of Qaddafi's leaflets is made easier by the fact that they can fan the flames of already deeply felt prejudices on the part of Muslims: Christians are 'dirty' and they pollute the Muslim environment.

The Western infidels are seen as violating the most sacred places in Islam and the imagery used of 'these filthy American pigs' reminds one of the impressions of the Crusaders of Acre recorded by Ibn Jubayr in 1184.[57] The leaflet pronounces: 'While hundreds of thousands of Muslims of various colours and languages and races were standing on Mount Arafat, the American Crusader Christians threw their garbage and defilement from their planes on to Mount Arafat.'[58]

The battlelines are drawn up between 'Islam and the Christians, between East and West', and between on the one hand 'the Arab nation, the Islamic nation' and the 'foreigners' (*ifranj*) on the other.[59] The Americans are viewed as having launched the 'offensive of the Cross against Islam'; they are 'the leaders of the modern Crusader offensive'.[60]

Colonel Qaddafi, the leader of the Libyan people, himself a military figure like the Muslim heroes of the Counter-Crusade, is described in the following rousing terms: 'It is he who has uncovered the conspirators, exposed the fascist reactionary rulers and made a true summons to the holy *jihad*.'[61] The message of this booklet is uncompromising and crystal clear, and is a powerful reminder of the spectre of the Crusades in modern Arab consciousness.

Figure 9.12 *Amirs and servants, inlaid brass basin known as the 'Baptistère de St Louis', c. 1300 or earlier, Syria*

Figure 9.13 *Panel, Mosque of Barquq, 786–8/1384–6, Cairo, Egypt*

The analogy with Crusader times made in these pamphlets is of course striking. The propagandists here are using the same theme as the Muslim Brothers, and they link 'Christian' Americans on the one hand and Zionist Israelis on the other. The rhetoric is meaningful because the conflict is polarised as a political and military one between East and West, as once again the West attempts to interfere, as in Crusading times, in the affairs of the Middle East.

Some General Reflections

To sum up modern Muslim opinion on the Crusades is a difficult task. At first glance there would appear to be grounds for pride and triumph in modern Muslim hearts; after all, it was Islam that had the ultimate victory, both politically and culturally. The Crusaders were uprooted after two centuries of interference and proto-colonialism. Contact with the Crusaders had, moreover, shown very clearly that the Islamic world was at that time superior in cultural terms to western Europe.

Yet this whole episode in the long relationship between Islam and Christianity is etched deeply into the modern Islamic consciousness, and the Crusades are viewed more frequently by Muslims as having exerted a negative and deleterious influence on the Islamic world. The Crusades are seen as a movement of imperialism, the first in a long series of territorial rapes of the Muslim homelands.

It is certainly indisputable that since the Crusades the political and cultural hegemony and prestige of the Muslim world have waned, just as the power and the political and cultural imperialism of the West have increased. Speaking of the undermining of the Muslim self-image, the American scholar Hodgson writes with appropriate force:

Not Muslims but the despised Christians of the far north-west, long since written off as too cold and fog-bound to produce anything more intelligent than the unpolished Crusaders that had already come from there, now suddenly had the mastery in the world's affairs.[62]

After the Crusaders departed, the Muslim world turned in on itself, going on the defensive, feeling excluded and viewing modern technological developments as a manifestation of 'the other'.[63] Modernism was synonymous with the West, whence had come the Crusades. After the Crusades, then, the Muslim world which had defeated the western Europeans faced the undeniable and bewildering truth that these same defeated enemies were enjoying genuine economic, technological and cultural growth and had gone on to rule the world.

Of course, the decline of the great medieval Islamic civilisation cannot be laid exclusively at the door of the Crusades. But Islam cannot and will not forget the Crusades, especially as its territorial space continues to be the focus for Western intervention and Arabs and above all Palestinians are obliged to react to the existence of the state of Israel. Muslims seek now to embrace ideologies which are true to their own self-image and not contaminated by Western imperialism and secularism. It is an unpalatable fact that, just as many deep-seated Western prejudices about Muslims can be traced back to attitudes moulded in the period of the Crusades, so too Muslim opinion about the West has been profoundly influenced by Islam's encounter with western Europe in the twelfth and thirteenth centuries. In the final years of the twentieth century it is common for political leaders in the Muslim world to speak of Saladin and to view Israel as a latter-day Crusader state. The fact that this is not a parallel that naturally recommends itself to the Western world, with its traditional culture based on Christianity rather than Judaism, is neither here nor there.

Figure 9.14 *Carved stone frieze, modern, outside the Officers' Club, Cairo, Egypt*

Mahmud Darwish: *Memory for Forgetfulness*

A recent masterpiece of Arabic literature is the moving and evocative work of Mahmud Darwish on the Israeli invasion of Lebanon. Entitled *Memory for Forgetfulness*,[64] it is an extended elegy on this deeply tragic event. In it the writer moves seamlessly between present and past catastrophe, between the bombed city of Beirut and the Crusader occupation of the Holy Land. In a poetic meditation on water, Darwish declares: 'Our water has been cut off by those acting on behalf of leftover Crusaders, yet Saladin used to send ice and fruits to the enemy in the hope that "their hearts would melt", as he used to say.'[65]

Jerusalem was and is the cynosure of all eyes, the cherished object of all hearts: 'I love Jerusalem. The Israelis love Jerusalem and sing for it. You love Jerusalem. Feiruz sings for Jerusalem. And Richard the Lion-Hearted loved Jerusalem.'[66] Interspersing his own reflections on the current tragedy with direct quotations from the memoirs of Usama and the chronicle of Ibn Kathir (d. 1373), Darwish is not crudely didactic: the mere juxtaposition of the medieval passages with his own contemporary voice is telling enough. This whole work is permeated with the memory of the Crusades. The term 'Frank' can be seen as an extended metaphor for the occupation of Arab lands by foreign intruders. The Islamic historical heritage continues to provide potent symbols for contemporary situations.

Figure 9.15 Radiating inscription on candlestick of Muhammad b. Qalawun, early fourteenth century, Egypt

Concluding Remarks

This book has deliberately presented a one-sided view of the Crusades, a view from the Muslim side alone. Clearly, such an approach is as biased and incomplete as one which studies the Crusades from an exclusively European standpoint. Yet it has to be said that the overpowering weight of Crusading historiography and secondary literature over the past century has tended towards the latter approach, with a perfunctory nod at some Muslim sources. It seemed high time to attempt to redress the balance a little. The task for modern historians of the Crusades is, of course, to weigh up the evidence from all sides – western European, Byzantine, Jewish, Oriental Christian and Islamic – in order to gain a more holistic view of the Crusades, that brief but momentous period of conflict and co-existence between Islam and European Christianity in the twelfth and thirteenth centuries. Brief it may have been in actual chronological terms; but its impact, against all the odds, has lasted and has resulted in battle lines of misunderstanding and hostility being drawn up between East and West. Many a lesson derived from an analysis of Islamic perspectives on the Crusades will help towards better understanding between the West and those lands where Islam is still very much a political rallying-cry and a predominant religious ideology. In 1999, the year of the 900th anniversary of the Crusader capture of Jerusalem and the approach of a new Christian millennium, efforts towards a lasting peace, focused on the Holy City, must be continued: as Walid Khalidi so eloquently puts it: 'A viable solution for Jerusalem must steal the thunder of all irredentists – of Crusades and proxy-Crusades, of jihads and counter-jihads.'[67]

Whilst there are many interpretations of the phenomenon of the Crusades, reflecting both medieval Christian and modern Western attitudes, this book has attempted to show how *Muslims* felt about the Crusades. It seems indisputable that the Crusades brought little benefit to the Islamic world. On the contrary, in the religious sphere and all that pertains to it, they caused Muslims great offence and inflicted on them profound and lasting psychological scars. It is my view that the modern Western views of the Crusades take far too little account of this. Those who support the present 'demonisation' of Islam in the Western media would thus do well to bear in mind this history of psychological damage and religious affront. Many Muslims today still remember with pain – centuries later though it may be – what was done in the name of the Cross. As so often in the Islamic world, the events of the distant past have a sharp contemporary relevance.

Notes

1. K. Kishtainy, *Arab Political Humour*, London, 1985, 198.
2. For a detailed account of the later Crusades, cf. A. S. Atiya, *The Crusade in the Later Middle Ages*, London, 1938; *A History of the Crusades*, vol. 3: *The Fourteenth and Fifteenth Centuries*, ed. H. W. Hazard, Madison, Wis., 1975.
3. This whole issue is discussed in B. Lewis, *The Muslim Discovery of Europe*, London, 1982.
4. A. S. Ahmed, *Living Islam*, London, 1995, 76.
5. M. Al-Matwi, *Al-hurub al-salibiyya*, Tunis, 1954, 121; quoted by Sivan, 'Modern Arab historiography', 141.
6. Lewis, *The Muslim Discovery of Europe*, 164–5.
7. Ibid., 166.
8. M. Monrond, *Tarikh al-hurub al-muqaddasa*, trans. Muhammad Mazlum, Jerusalem, 1865. Cf. Sivan, 'Modern Arab historiography', 110.
9. Cairo, 1899.
10. Sivan, 'Modern Arab historiography', 112, quoting al-Hariri, *Al-akhbar al-saniyya*, 6.
11. Sivan, 'Modern Arab historiography', 110.
12. Cf. Lessing's highly favourable portrayal of Saladin in his play *Nathan der Weise* and Sir Walter Scott's romantic views of him in *The Talisman*.
13. *EI²*: Namik Kemal.
14. W. Ende, 'Wer ist ein Glaubensheld, wer ist ein Ketzer?', *Die Welt des Islams*, N.S. 23 (1984), 81.
15. Ibid.
16. Ibid., 83, n. 37.
17. S. J. al-Tu'ma, *Salah al-Din fi'l-shi'r al-'arabi*, Riyadh, 1979, 20–2.

18. Ende, 'Wer ist ein Glaubensheld', 84.
19. C. J. Edmonds, *Kurds, Turks and Arabs*, London, 1957, 57–8; *Kurdish Culture and Identity*, ed. P. Keyenbrock and C. Allison, London, 1996, 22.
20. S. 'Ashur, *Al-harakat al-salibiyya*, Cairo, 1963, 583.
21. Ende, 'Wer ist ein Glaubensheld', 86; N. J. Mandel, *The Arabs and Zionism before World War I*, Berkeley, 1976, 84 and 88.
22. The speeches of Isaf al-Nashashibi and Muhammad Rashid Rida on the anniversary of the battle of Hattin in 1932 reveal such sentiments. Cf. Ende, 'Wer ist ein Glaubensheld', 86.
23. Cf. the fascinating analysis of Saladin as role model for Saddam Husayn in O. Bengio, *Saddam's word. Political discourse in Iraq*, New York and Oxford, 1998, 82–4. Occasionally, a dissenting voice protests against the untarnishable image of Saladin. Hasan al-Amir, a Shi'ite writer, portrays Saladin as a power-hungry, unscrupulous opportunist and criticises him for anti-Shi'ite activities, for collaborating with the Crusaders and for aiming at family aggrandisement; Hasan al-Amin, 'Haqiqat Salah al-Din al-Ayyubi', *Irfan* 55 (1967), 95–9; Ende, 'Wer ist ein Glaubensheld', 91.
24. In a personal conversation in Damascus in December 1998.
25. Cf. Ayatallah Khumayni, *Al-jihad al-akbar*, trans. H. Kurani, Tehran, 1979, 57–9, 80–2. According to Khumayni, the truth is hidden from man by a succession of veils, which are his mortal sins. The believer must strive to remove these veils so that God's light may shine within his soul; it is this striving to remove the veils which is called the 'greater *jihad*'. Once this has been accomplished, man should wage the 'lesser *jihad*'. Cf. also al-Buti, *Jihad in Islam*.
26. Sayyid Qutb, *Fi zilal al-Qur'an*, Cairo and Beirut, 1992, vol. III, 1593.
27. Ibid., I, 108.
28. *Al-Shihab*, 14 November 1947, 86–8; quoted and analysed by Mitchell. Cf. R. P. Mitchell, *The Society of the Muslim Brothers*, Oxford, 1993, 229.
29. S. Qutb, *Al-'adalat al-ijtima'iyya fi'l-Islam*, trans. J. B. Hardie as *Social justice in Islam*, Washington, 1955, 235; Mitchell, *Muslim Brothers*, 230.
30. A. Taheri, *Holy Terror*, London, 1987, 111.
31. Maalouf, *The Crusaders*, 265.
32. *Newsweek*, 11 January 1999, 12.
33. *Newsweek*, 17 August 1998, 20.
34. A Nüsse, 'The ideology of Hamas: Palestinian Islamic fundamentalist thought on the Jews, Israel and Islam', in Nettler, *Muslim–Jewish Relations*, 108.
35. Ibid., 107.
36. Ibid.
37. Ibid.
38. Ibid., 110.
39. Cf. S. Taji-Farouki, 'A case in contemporary political Islam and the Palestine question: the perspective of Hizb al-tahrir al-islami'; and S. Taji-Farouki, *A Fundamental Question: Hizb al-tahrir and the Search for the Islamic Caliphate*, London, 1996.
40. Taji-Farouki, 'A case', 35.
41. Ibid., 36.
42. Ibid., 38.
43. Ibid., 40.
44. Ibid., 41.
45. Similar analogies have been made in more recent times. President Bush's speech to the American troops before they departed for the Gulf was compared by the ILP with Pope Urban II's call for Crusade at Clermont in 1095.

46. Cf. P. Partner, *God of Battles*, London, 1997, 241–2, citing L. James, *Imperial Warrior: The Life and Times of Field Marshal Viscount Allenby 1861–1936*, London, 1993, 143 ff.
47. Ibid., 47.
48. Ibid., 52.
49. 'Abd al-Latif Hamza, *Adab al-hurub al-salibiyya*, Cairo, 1949, 304, quoted by Sivan, 'Modern Arab historiography', 113.
50. E.g. 'Ashur, *Al-harakat al-salibiyya*, 6; W. Talhuq, *Al-salibiyya al-jadida fi Filastin*, Damascus, 1948, 4–5.
51. J. I. Jabra, 'The rebels, the committed and the others: transitions in modern Arabic poetry today', *Middle East Forum*, 43/1 (1967), 20.
52. Y. Suleiman, 'Nationalist concerns in the poetry of Nazik al-Malaika', *Brismes Journal*, 22/1–2 (1995), 103.
53. Ibid., 104.
54. The booklet is produced in both English and Arabic. The quotations which follow refer to the Arabic text. It has no date.
55. *Nationalist Documents*, 35.
56. Ibid., 34.
57. The idea of pollution as an insult is very prevalent. When Netanyahu visited Cairo in 1997, an Arabic newspaper commented that the air of the city had become polluted.
58. *Nationalist Documents*, 32.
59. The term *ifranj* has the double meaning of 'Franks' and now in modern Arabic 'foreigners'.
60. *Nationalist Documents*, 35.
61. Ibid., 37.
62. M. G. S. Hodgson, *Rethinking World History*, ed. E. Burke III, Cambridge, 1993, 224.
63. Maalouf, *The Crusades*, 264.
64. M. Darwish, *Memory for Forgetfulness*, trans. I. Muhawi, Berkeley, 1995.
65. Ibid., 33–4.
66. Ibid., 41.
67. W. Khalidi, *Islam, the West and Jerusalem*, Washington, 1996, 20.

Bibliography

Primary Sources

Abiwardi, al-, *Diwan*, ed. U. al-As'ad, Damascus, 1974–5.

Abu Shama, *Kitab al-rawdatayn*, ed. M. H. M. Ahmad, 2 vols, Cairo, 1954.

Abu'l-Fida, *Al-Mukhtasar fi tarikh al-bashar*, Cairo, 1907.

Anon., *Khizanat al-silah*, ed. N. M. 'Abd al-'Aziz, Cairo, 1978.

'Azimi, al-, 'La chronique abrégée d'al-'Azimi', ed. C. Cahen, *JA*, 230 (1938), 353–448; new edn as *Tarikh halab*, ed. I. Za'rur, Damascus, 1984.

Baybars al-Mansuri, *Kitab al-tuhfa al-mulukiyya fi'l-dawla al-turkiyya*, ed. A. S. Hamdan, Cairo, 1987.

Baybars al-Mansuri, *Zubdat al-fikra fi tarikh al-hijra*, ed. D. S. Richards, Beirut, 1998.

Bundari, al-, *Sana al-barq al-shami*, ed. R. Seşen, Beirut, 1971; ed. F. al-Nabarawi, Cairo, 1979.

Bundari, al-, *Zubdat al-nusra*, ed. M. T. Houtsma, Leiden, 1889.

Dimishqi, al-, *Nukhbat al-dahr fi 'aja'ib al-barr wa'l-bahr*, ed. A. F. Mehren, St Petersburg, 1866.

Ghazali, al-, *Kitab al-Mustazhiri*, partial ed. by I. Goldziher in *Streitschrift des Gazali gegen die Batinijje-Sekte*, Leiden, 1916.

Harawi, al-, *Kitab al-isharat ila ma'rifat al-ziyarat*, ed. J. Sourdel-Thomine, Damascus, 1953.

Husayni, al-, *Akhbar al-dawla al-saljuqiyya*, ed. M. Iqbal, Lahore, 1933.

Ibn 'Abd al-Zahir, *Al-rawd al-zahir*, ed. A. A. al-Khuwaytir, Riyadh, 1976.

Ibn 'Abd al-Zahir, *Sirat al-Malik al-Mansur*, Cairo, 1961.

Ibn 'Abd al-Zahir, *Tashrif al-ayyam wa'l-'usur*, ed. M. Kamil and M. A. al-Najjar, Cairo, 1961.

Ibn Abi'l-Ash'ath, *Kitab al-hayawan*, Ms. Bodleian I, 456, 6 (Hunt. 534).

Ibn al-'Adim, *Bughyat al-talab*, ed. S. Zakkar, Damascus, 1988; partial ed. A. Sevim, Ankara, 1976.

Ibn al-'Adim, *Zubdat al-halab*, ed. S. Dahan, Damascus, 1954; ed. S. Zakkar, Damascus, 1997.

Ibn al-Athir, *Al-Kamil fi'l-tarikh*, 12 vols, ed. C. J. Tornberg, Leiden and Uppsala, 1851–76.

Ibn al-Athir, *Al-tarikh al-bahir fi'l-dawlat al-atabakiyya*, ed. A. A. Tulaymat, Cairo, 1963.

Ibn al-Dawadari, *Kanz al-durar*, VI, ed. S. al-Munajjid, Cairo, 1961.

Ibn al-Faqih, *Kitab al-buldan*, ed. M. J. de Goeje, Leiden, 1885.

Ibn al-Furat, 'Tarikh al-duwal wa'l-muluk', ed. M. F. El-Shayyal, unpublished Ph.D., University of Edinburgh, 1986; IV, pts 1–2, ed. H. Al-Shamma, Basra, 1967–9.

Ibn al-Jawzi, *Al-muntazam fi tarikh al-muluk wa'l-umam*, X, Hyderabad, 1940.

Ibn al-Khayyat, *Diwan*, ed. H. Mardam Bek, Damascus, 1958.

Ibn al-Mubarak, *Kitab al-jihad*, ed. N. al-Hammad, Tunis, 1972.

Ibn al-Murajja al-Maqdisi, *Fada'il bayt al-maqdis*, ed. O. Livne-Kafri, Shfaram, 1995.

Ibn al-Nabih, *Diwan*, ed. 'U. M. As'ad, Damascus, 1969.

Ibn al-Qalanisi, *Dhayl tarikh Dimishq*, ed. H. F. Amedroz, Leiden, 1908.

Ibn Iyas, *Bada'i' al-zuhur*, 3 vols, ed. M. Mostafa, Wiesbaden, 1960–75.

Ibn Jubayr, *Rihlat Ibn Jubayr*, ed. W. Wright and M. J. de Goeje, Leiden and London, 1907.

Ibn Kathir, *Al-bidaya wa'l-nihaya*, Cairo, 1932–9.

Ibn Khallikan, *Wafayat al-a'yan*, ed. I. 'Abbas, Beirut, n.d.

Ibn Muyassar, *Akhbar Misr*, ed. H. Massé, Cairo, 1919.

Ibn Nazif al-Hamawi, *Al-tarikh al-Mansuri*, ed. A. Dudu, Damascus, 1982.

Ibn Nubata, *Diwan Khutab Ibn Nubata*, with commentary by T. al-Jaza'iri, Beirut, 1894.

Ibn Qudama, *Mughni*, ed. R. Rida, Cairo, 1947.

Ibn Shaddad, Baha' al-Din, *Al-nawadir al-sultaniyya*, ed. J. El-Shayyal, Cairo, 1964.

Ibn Shaddad, 'Izz al-Din, *Al-'alaq al-khatira*, Bodleian ms., Marsh 333.

Ibn Shaddad, 'Izz al-Din, *Tarikh al-Malik al-Zahir*, ed. A. Hutait, Wiesbaden, 1983.

Ibn Taghribirdi, *Nujum al-zahira*, Cairo, 1939.

Ibn Taymiyya, *Al-jawab al-sahih li-man baddala din al-Masih*, Cairo, 1322.

Ibn Taymiyya, *Majmu' fatawa Shaykh al-Islam Ahmad b. Taymiyya*, XXVIII, Riyadh, 1383.

Ibn Tulun, *Al-qala'id al-jawhariyya fi tar'ikh al-Salihiyya*, ed. M. A. Duhman, 2 vols, Damascus, 1980.

Ibn Wasil, *Mufarrij al-kurub*, ed. J. al-Shayyal, Cairo, 1953–7.

Ibn Zafir, *Akhbar al-duwal al-munqati'a*, ed. A. Ferré, Cairo, 1972.

'Imad al-Din, *Al-bustan al-jami*, part published by C. Cahen as 'Une chronique syrienne du VI/XIIe siècle', *BEO*, 7–8 (1937–8), 113–58.

'Imad al-Din al-Isfahani, *Al-barq al-shami*, III, ed. M. al–Hayyari, Amman, 1987; V, ed. R. Seşen, Istanbul, 1971, and M. al-Hayyari, Amman, 1987; I, unpublished edition by L. Richter-Bernburg.

'Imad al-Din al-Isfahani, *Kharidat al-qasr*, Cairo, 1951; Baghdad, 1955; Tunis, 1966.

'Imad al-Din al-Isfahani, *Kitab al-fath al-qussi fi'l-fath al-qudsi*, ed. C. Landberg, Leiden, 1888; ed. M. M. Subh, Cairo, 1965.

'Imad al-Din al-Isfahani, *Sana al-barq al-shami*, summarised by al-Bundari, ed. F. al-Nabarawi, Cairo, 1979.

Maqrizi, al-, *Itti'az al-hunafa'*, II and III, ed. M. H. M. Ahmad, Cairo, 1971 and 1973 respectively.

Maqrizi, al-, *Kitab al-suluk*, ed. M. M. Ziyada and S. 'A. 'Ashur, Cairo, 1934–9.

Maqrizi, al-, *Muqaffa'*, ed. M. al-Yalawi, Beirut, 1991.

Nationalist Documents to confront the Crusaders' campaign in the Arab world, People's Bureau, Socialist People's Libyan Arab Jamahiriyya, London, n.d.

Nuwayri, al-, *Nihayat al-arab fi funun al-adab*, XXVIII, ed. S. A. al-Nuri, Cairo, 1992.

Qalqashandi, al-, *Subh al-a'sha fi sina'at al-insha'*, ed. M. A. Ibrahim, Cairo, 1913–20.

Raba'i, al-, *Fada'il al-Sham wa Dimashq*, ed. S. al-Munajjid, Damascus, 1951.

Sayyid Qutb, *Fi zilal al-Qur'an*, I–VI, Cairo and Beirut, 1992.

Sibt b. al-Jawzi, *Mir'at al-zaman*, facsimile edn by J. R. Jewett, Chicago, 1907; ed. unidentified, Hyderabad, 1951.

Sulami, al-, *Kitab al-jihad*, Unpublished ms., Damascus.

Usama b. Munqidh, *Kitab al-manazil wa'l-diyar*, ed. S. Arna'ut, Damascus, 1965.

Usama b. Munqidh, *Kitab al-i'tibar*, ed. P. K. Hitti, Princeton, 1930; ed. Q. al-Samarra'i, Riyadh, 1987.

Wasiti, al-, *Fada'il al-bayt al-muqaddas*, ed. A. Hasson, Jerusalem, 1979.

Yunini, al-, *Dhayl mir'at al-zaman*, 4 vols, Hyderabad, 1954–61.

Primary Sources in Translation

'Abd al-Latif al-Baghdadi, *The Eastern Key*, trans. K. H. Zand and J. A. and I. E. Videan, London, 1965.

Abu Shama, *Kitab al-rawdatayn*, partial trans. E. P. Goergens as *Zur Geschichte Salahadins*, Berlin, 1879.

Abu'l-Fida, *Al-Mukhtasar fi akhbar al-bashar*, partial trans. P. M. Holt as *The Memoirs of a Syrian Prince – Abu'l-Fida, Sultan of Hama*, Wiesbaden, 1983.

'Ali M. M., *A Manual of Hadith*, London and Dublin, 1977.

Anon., *The Book of the Thousand Nights and One Night*, trans. J. C. Mardrus and P. Mathers, Norwich, 1980.

Anon., *The Sea of Precious Virtues*, trans. J. S. Meisami, Salt Lake City, 1991.

Ansari, al-, *Tafrij al-kurub fi tadbir al-hurub*, trans. G. T. Scanlon as *A Muslim Manual of War*, Cairo, 1961.

Aqsara'i, al-, *Nihayat al-su'l wa'l-umniyya fi ta'lim a'mal al-furusiyya*, trans. G. Tantum as 'Muslim warfare: a study of a medieval Muslim treatise on the art of war', in Elgood, *Islamic Arms and Armour*, 187–201.

Gabrieli, F., *Arab Historians of the Crusades*, London, 1969.

Ghazali, al-, *Al-munqidh min al-dalal*, trans. R. McCarthy, in *Freedom and Fulfillment*, Boston, 1980, 61–114.

Guillaume, A., *The Traditions of Islam*, Oxford, 1924.

Harawi, al-, *Al-tadhkira al-harawiyya fi'l-hiyal al-harbiyya*, trans. J. Sourdel-Thomine, *BEO*, 17 (1962), 105–268.

Harawi, al-, 'Ali, *Kitab al-ziyarat*, trans. J. Sourdel-Thomine as *Guide des lieux de pèlerinage*, Damascus, 1957.

Ibn 'Abd al-Zahir, *Al-Rawd al-zahir*, trans. S. F. Sadeque as *Baybars I of Egypt*, Dacca, 1956.

Ibn al-Azraq, *Tarikh Mayyafariqin*, partial trans. C. Hillenbrand as *A Muslim Principality in Crusader Times*, Leiden, 1990.

Ibn al-Dawadari, *Die Epitome der Universalchronik Ibn ad-Dawadaris*, partial trans. G. Graf, Berlin, 1990.

Ibn al-Firqa, *Kitab ba'ith al-nufus ila ziyarat al–Quds al-mahrus*, trans. C. D. Matthews as *Palestine-Mohammedan Holy Land*, New Haven, Conn., 1949.

Ibn al-Furat, *Tarikh al-duwal wa'l-muluk*, ed. and trans. U. and M. C. Lyons as *Ayyubids, Mamlukes and Crusaders*, 2 vols, Cambridge, 1971.

Ibn al-Nadim, *Al-fihrist*, trans. B. Dodge, New York, 1972.

Ibn al-Qalanisi, *Dhayl tarikh Dimishq*, trans. H. A. R. Gibb as *The Damascus Chronicle of the Crusades*, London, 1932.

Ibn al-Shihna, *Les perles choisies d'Ibn Ach-Chihna*, trans. J. Sauvaget, Damascus, 1933.

Ibn al-Suqa'i, *Tali wafayat al-a'yan*, ed. and trans. J. Sublet, Damascus, 1974.

Ibn Jubayr, *The Travels of Ibn Jubayr*, trans. R. J. C. Broadhurst, London, 1952.

Ibn Khaldun, *The Muqaddima*, trans. F. Rosenthal, abridged and edited by N. J. Dawood, London, 1967.

Ibn Khallikan, *Wafayat al-a'yan*, 4 vols, trans. W. M. de Slane as *Ibn Khallikan's Biographical Dictionary*, Paris, 1843–71.

Ibn Qudama, *Al-'Umda*, trans. H. Laoust as *Le précis de droit d'Ibn Qudama*, Beirut, 1950.

Ibn Shaddad, Baha' al-Din, *Al-nawadir al-sultaniyya*, trans. C. R. Conder and C. W. Wilson as *The Life of Saladin*, London, 1897.

Ibn Shaddad, 'Izz al-Din, *Description de la Syrie du Nord*, trans. A.-M. Eddé, Damascus, 1984.

Ibn Taymiyya, *A Muslim Theologian's Response to Christianity: Ibn Taimiyya's al-jawab al-sahih*, ed. and trans. T. F. Michel, Delmar, NJ, 1984.

Ibn Taymiyya, *Al-siyasa al-shar'iyya*, trans. H. Laoust as *Le traité de droit publique d'Ibn Taymiyya*, Beirut, 1948.

Ibn Taymiyya, *La profession de foi d'Ibn Taymiyya*, trans. H. Laoust, Paris, 1986.

Ibn Taymiyya, *Lettre à un roi croisé*, trans. J. R.Michot, Louvain, 1995.

Idrisi, al-, *Géographie d'Edrisi*, trans. P. A. Jaubert, Paris, 1836–40.

'Imad al-Din al-Isfahani, *Conquête de la Syrie*, trans. H. Massé, Paris, 1972.

Jahiz, al-, *Manaqib al-turk*, partial trans. C. T. Harley-Walker as 'Jahiz of Basra to al-Fath ibn Khaqan on the exploits of the Turks and the Army of the Khalifat in general', *JRAS* (1915), 631–99.

Khalil al-Zahiri, *La zubda*, trans. J. Gaulmier, Beirut, 1950.

Khumayni Ayatallah, *Al-jihad al-akbar*, trans. H. Kurani, Tehran, 1979.

Lewis, B., *Islam from the Prophet Muhammad to the Capture of Constantinople*, 2 vols, New York, 1974.

Maqrizi, al-, *Kitab al-suluk*, trans. R. J. C. Broadhurst as *History of Ayyubids and Mamluks*, Boston, 1980; trans. E. Quatremère as *Histoire des sultans mamlouks de l'Égypte*, Paris, 1837–45.

Mawardi, al-, *Ahkam al-sultaniyya*, trans. W. H. Wahba as *The Ordinances of Government*, Reading, 1996.

Muqaddasi, al-, *Ahsan al-taqasim*, trans. B. A. Collins as *The Best Divisions for Knowledge of the Regions*, Reading, 1994; partial trans. A. Miquel, Damascus, 1963.

Nasir-i Khusraw, *Safarnama*, trans. C. Schefer as *Sefernameh; relation du voyage de Nassiri Khosrau*, Paris, 1881; trans. W. N. Thackston, jun., as *Naser-e Khosraw's Book of Travels*, Albany, NY, 1986.

Nizam al-Mulk, *Siyasatnama*, trans. H. Darke as *The Book of Government or Rules for Kings*, London, 1978.

Nuwayri, al-, *Nihaya*, partly translated section by C. Cahen and I. Chabbouh in *Mélanges Laoust*, Damascus, 1978, 97–114.

Qur'an, trans. M. Pickthall, London, 1957.

Qutb Sayyib, *Al-'adalat al-ijtima'iyya fi'l-Islam*, trans. J. B. Hardie as *Social Justice in Islam*, Washington, 1955.

Recueil des historiens des Croisades: Historiens Orientaux, 5 vols, Paris, 1872–1902.

Répertoire chronologique d'épigraphie arabe, Cairo, 1931.

Sa'd al-Din b. Hamawiyya Juwayni, unnamed chronicle, trans. C. Cahen as 'Une source pour l'histoire ayyubide', in C. Cahen, *Les peuples musulmans*, Damascus, 1977, 457–82.

Shafi'i, al-, *Risala*, trans. M. Khadduri as *Islamic Jurisprudence*, Baltimore, 1961.

Sharaf al-Zaman Tahir Marvazi, *Kitab taba'i' al-hayawan*, trans. V. Minorsky as *Sharaf al-Zaman Tahir Marvazi on China, the Turks and India*, London, 1942.

Shirazi, al-, *Kitab al-tanbih*, trans. G. H. Bousquet, Algiers, 1949–52.

Tarsusi, al-, *Tabsirat arbab al-albab fi kayfiyyat al-najat fi'l-hurub*, partial trans. C. Cahen as 'Un traité d'armurie composé pour Saladin', *BEO*, 12 (1947–8), 1–61; trans. A. Boudot-Lamotte as *Contribution à l'étude de l'archerie musulmane*, Damascus, 1968.

Tibrizi, al-, *Mishkat al-masabih*, trans. J. Robson as *Mishkat*, Lahore, 1972.

'Umari, al-, *Masalik al-absar*, partial trans. E. R. Lundquist as *Saladin and Richard the Lionhearted*, Lund, 1996.

Usama b. Munqidh, *Kitab al-i'tibar*, trans. P.K. Hitti as *Memoirs of an Arab-Syrian Gentleman*, Beirut, 1964; trans. A. Miquel as *Des enseignements de la vie*, Paris, 1983; trans. H. Derenbourg as *Ousama Ibn Mounkidh, un émir syrien au premier siècle des Croisades*, Paris, 1889.

Yusuf Khass Hajib, *Wisdom of Royal Glory*, trans. R. Dankoff, Chicago, 1983.

Secondary Sources

'Abbadi, al-, A. M. and S. A. A. Salim, *Tarikh al-bahriyya al-Islamiyya fi Misr wa'l-Sham*, n.p., 1972.

'Abbas, I., 'Al-janib al-siyasi min rihlat Ibn al-'Arabi ila al-mashriq', *Al-Abhath*, 12/2 (1963), 217–36.

'Abbas, I., 'Rihlat Ibn al-'Arabi ila al-mashriq', *Al-Abhath*, 21/1 (1968), 59–92.

Abu Amr, Z., *Islamic Fundamentalism in the West Bank and Gaza*, Bloomington and Indianapolis, 1994.

Abulafia, D., 'The role of trade in Muslim–Christian contact during the Middle Ages', in *The Arab Influence in Medieval Europe*, ed. D. A. Agius and R. Hitchcock, Reading, 1994, 1–24.

Abulafia, D., *Frederick II: A Medieval Emperor*, London, 1988.

Agius, D. A., 'Historical-linguistic reliability of Muqaddasi's information on types of ships', in *Across the Mediterranean Frontiers: Trade, Politics and Religion (650–1450)*, ed. D. A. Agius and I. R. Netton, Brepols, 1997, 303–32.

Agius, D. A., 'Jerusalem in medieval fadail literature', *Melita Theologica*, 30 (1978–9), 14–31.

Ahmed, A. S., *Living Islam*, London, 1995.

Alexander, D., *The Arts of War*, London, 1992.

Allen, T., *A Classical Revival in Islamic Architecture*, Wiesbaden, 1986.

Altoma, S. J., 'The treatment of the Palestinian conflict in modern Arabic literature, 1917–70', *Middle East Forum*, 48 (1972), 7–26.

Amin, H. A., *Al-hurub al-salibiyya*, Cairo, 1983.

Amitai, R., 'Notes on the Ayyubid inscriptions at al-Subayba', *Dumbarton Oaks Papers*, 43 (1989), 113–20.

Amitai-Preiss, R., *Mongols and Mamluks: The Mamluk–Ilkanid War, 1260–1281*, Cambridge, 1995.

'Arif, al-, A., *Al-mufassal fi tarikh al-Quds*, Jerusalem, 1961.

Armstrong, K., *Holy War*, London, 1988.

Asali, K. J., *Jerusalem in History*, London, 1989.

Asali, K. J., *Ma'ahid al-'ilm fi Bayt al-Maqdis*, Amman, 1981.

Asali, K. J., *Makhtutat Fada'il Bayt al-Maqdis*, Amman, 1984.

Asali, K. J., *Watha'iq Maqdisiyya tarikhiyya*, I, Amman, 1983.

Ashtor, E., 'The social isolation of *ahl adh-dhimma*', in *Pal Hirschler Memorial Book*, Budapest, 1949, 73–93.

Ashtor, E., *A Social and Economic History of the Near East in the Middle Ages*, London, 1976.

'Ashur, F. H. M., *Al-jihad al-islami didd al-salibiyyin wa'l-Mughul fi'l-'asr al-mamluk*, Tripoli (Lebanon), 1995.

'Ashur, S. A., *Al-harakat al-salibiyya*, Cairo, 1993.

Athamina, K. and R. Heacock (eds), *The Frankish Wars and Their Influence on Palestine*, Birzeit, 1994.

Atil, E., *Ceramics from the World of Islam*, Washington, 1973.

Atiyah, A. S., 'A 14th century *fatwa* on the status of Christians in Mamluk Egypt', in S*tudien zur Geschichte des Nahen und Fernen Ostens, Festschrift Paul Kahle*, Leiden, 1935.

Atiyah, A. S., *A Fourteenth Century Encyclopedist from Alexandria*, Salt Lake City, 1977.

Atiyah, A. S., *Crusade, Commerce and Culture*, Bloomington and Oxford, 1962.

Atiyah, A. S., *History of Eastern Christianity*, London, 1967.

Atiyah, A. S., *The Crusades in the Later Middle Ages*, London, 1938.

Atrache, L., *Die Politik der Ayyubiden*, Münster, 1996.

Auld, S., 'Kuficising inscriptions in the work of Gentile da Fabriano', *Oriental Art*, 32/3 (Autumn 1986), 246–65.

Auld, S., 'The minbar of al-Aqsa', unpublished paper.

Ayalon, D., *Le phénomène mamelouk dans l'orient islamique*, Paris, 1996.

Ayalon, D., 'Le régiment Bahriyya dans l'armée mamelouke', *REI* (1952), 133–41.

Ayalon, D., 'Notes on the Furusiyya exercises and games in the Mamluk sultanate', *Scripta Hierosolymitana*, 9 (1961), 31–62.

Azhari, al-, T. K., *The Saljuqs of Syria during the Crusades, 463–549 AH*, Berlin, 1997.

Azmeh, al-, A., 'Barbarians in Arab eyes', *Past and Present*, 134 (Feb. 1992), 3–18.

Azmeh, al-, A., 'Islamic legal theory and the appropriation of reality', in id. (ed.), *Islamic Law: Social and Historical Contexts*, London, 1988.

Bacharach, J. L., 'African military slaves in the medieval Middle East', *IJMES*, 13 (1981) 471–95.

Badawi, A. A., *Al-hayat al-adabiyya fi ʻasr al-hurub al-salibiyya bi-Misr waʻl-Sham*, Cairo, 1954.

Badeen, E., 'Die sufik nach ʻAmmar al-Bidlisi', *Oriens*, 33 (1992), 86–93.

Baer, E., *Ayyubid Metalwork with Christian Images*, Leiden, 1989.

Baker, D. (ed.), *Relations between East and West in the Middle Ages*, Edinburgh, 1973.

Baldwin, M. W., 'The Latin states under Baldwin III and Amalric I 1143–74', in *A History of the Crusades*, ed. K. M. Setton and M. W. Baldwin, Madison, Wis., 1969, vol. I, 528–62.

Balog, P., *The Coinage of the Mamluk Sultans of Egypt and Syria*, New York, 1964.

Battista, A., and B. Bagatti, *La fortezza saracena del Monte Tabor (A.H. 609–15; A.D. 1212–18)*, Studia Biblica Franciscana, col. min. 18, Jerusalem.

Bat Yeʼor, *The Decline of Eastern Christianity in Islam: From Jihad to Dhimmitude*, London, 1996.

Baz al-Arini, *Muʻarrikhu al-hurub al-salibiyya*, Cairo, 1960.

Becker, C., *Beiträge zur Geschichte Ägyptens*, Strasbourg, 1903.

Beelaert, A. L. F. A., 'Mani ba ʻarus-i hagla-basta/dar hagla-yi car-su nisasta – The Kaʻba as a woman: a topos in classical Persian literature', *Persica*, 13 (1986–9), 107–23.

Behrens-Abouseif, D., 'The citadel of Cairo: stage for Mamluk ceremonial', *Annales Islamologiques*, 24 (1988), 25–79.

Bengio, O., *Saddam's word. Political discourse in Iraq*, New York and Oxford, 1998.

Berkey, J. P., 'The Mamluks as Muslims: the military elite and the construction of Islam in medieval Egypt', in *The Mamluks in Egyptian Politics and Society*, ed. T. Philipp and U. Haarmann, Cambridge, 1998, 163–73.

Berry, V. G., 'The Second Crusade', in *A History of the Crusades*, ed. K. M.

Setton and M. W. Baldwin, Madison, Wis., 1969, vol. I, 463–512.

Billings, M., *The Cross and the Crescent*, London, 1987.

Bloom, J., 'Jerusalem in medieval Islamic literature', in *City of the Great King*, ed. N. Rosovsky, Cambridge, Mass., and London, 1996, 205–17.

Bloom, J., 'The mosque of Baybars al-Bunduqdari in Cairo', *Annales Islamologiques*, 17 (1982), 45–78.

Boase, T. S. R., *Castles and Churches of the Crusading Kingdom*, Oxford, 1967.

Bosworth, C. E., 'The armies of the Prophet', in *The World of Islam*, ed. B. Lewis, London, 1976, 201–24.

Bosworth, C. E., 'The city of Tarsus and the Arab–Byzantine frontiers in early and middle 'Abbasid times', *Oriens*, 33 (1992), 268–86.

Bosworth, C. E., *The New Islamic Dynasties*, Edinburgh, 1996.

Bosworth, C. E. et al. (eds), *The Islamic World from Classical to Modern Times: Essays in Honor of Bernard Lewis*, Princeton, 1989.

Brett, M., 'The battles of Ramla (1099–1105)', in *Orientalia Lovaniensia Analecta: Egypt and Syria in the Fatimid, Ayyubid and Mamluk Eras*, eds U. Vermeulen and D. de Smet, Louvain, 1995, 17–38.

Brett, M., 'The origins of the Mamluk military systems in the Fatimid period', in *Orientalia Lovaniensia Analecta*, 39–52.

Briggs, M. S., *Muhammadan Architecture in Egypt and Palestine*, Oxford, 1924.

Bulliet, R., *The camel and the wheel*, Cambridge, Mass. and London, 1975.

Burgoyne, M., *Mamluk Jerusalem*, London, 1987.

Burns, R., *Monuments of Syria: An Historical Guide*, London and New York, 1992.

Buti, al-, *Jihad in Islam*, Damascus, 1995.

Cahen, C., 'An introduction to the First Crusade', *Past and Present*, 6 (1959), 6–29.

Cahen, C., 'Indigènes et croisés', *Syria*, 15 (1934), 351–60.

Cahen, C., 'La chronique de Kirtay et les Francs de Syrie', *JA*, 229 (1937), 140–5.

Cahen, C., 'Les changements techniques militaires dans le Proche Orient médiéval et leur importance historique', in *War, Technology and Society in the Middle East*, ed. V. J. Parry and M. E. Yapp, London, 1975, 113–24.

Cahen, C., 'Les mémoires de Sa'd al-Din Ibn Hamawiya Djuwayni', in C. Cahen, *Les peuples musulmans dans l'histoire médiévale*, Damascus, 1977, 457–82.

Cahen, C., 'L'histoire économique et sociale de l'Orient musulman médiéval', *SI*, 3 (1955), 93–115.

Cahen, C., 'Notes sur l'histoire des croisades et de l'Orient latin. 3: Orient latin et commerce du Levant', *Bulletin de la Faculté des Lettres de l'Université de Strasbourg* 29 (1951), 328–416.

Cahen, C., 'Quelques chroniques anciennes relatives aux derniers Fatimides', *BIFAO*, 37 (1937), 1–27.

Cahen, C., 'Some new editions of Oriental sources about Syria in the time of the Crusades', *Outremer Studies in the History of the Crusading Kingdom of Jerusalem*, Jerusalem, 1982, 323–31.

Cahen, C., 'St. Louis et l'Islam', *JA*, 258 (1970), 3–12.

Cahen, C., 'Un traité d'armurie composé pour Saladin', *BEO*, 12 (1947–8), 1–61.

Cahen, C., *La Syrie du Nord*, Paris, 1940.

Cahen, C., *Orient et Occident*, Paris, 1983.

Cahen, C., *Turcobyzantina et Oriens Christianus*, London, 1974.

Cahen, C. and I. Chabbouh, 'Le testament d'al-Malik as-Salih Ayyub', *Mélanges Laoust, BEO*, 29 (1977), 97–114.

Canard, M., 'La déstruction de l'église de la Resurrection', *Byzantion*, 35 (1965), 16–43.

Canard, M., 'La guerre sainte dans le monde islamique et le monde chrétien', *Revue Africaine*, 79 (1936), 605–23.

Canard, M., *Sayf al-Dawla*, Algiers, 1934.

Casson, L., *The Ancient Mariners*, Princeton, 1991.

Chamberlain, M., *Knowledge and Social Practice in Medieval Damascus, 1190–1350*, Cambridge, 1994.

Champdor, A., *Saladin*, Paris, 1956.

Chittick, W. C., *Faith and Practice of Islam*, Albany, 1992.

Chronicles of the Crusades, ed. E. Hallam, London, 1989.

Crawford, R. W., 'Ridwan the maligned', in *Studies in Honour of P. K. Hitti*, ed. A. S. Atiya, London, 1960, 135–44.

Creswell, K. A. C., 'Fortification in Islam before 1250', *Proceedings of the British Academy*, 38 (1952), 89–125.

Creswell, K. A. C., *The Muslim Architecture of Egypt*, 2 vols, Oxford, 1952, 1959.

Dahlmanns, F. J., *Al-Malik al-'Adil*, Giessen, 1975.

Daiber, H., 'Die Kreuzzüge im Licht islamischer Theologie', in A. Zimmermann and I. Craemer-Ruegensberg, *Orientalische Kultur und europäisches Mittelalter*, Berlin and New York, 1985, 77–85.

Dajani-Shakeel, H., 'A reassessment of some medieval and modern perceptions of the Counter-Crusade', in *The Jihad and Its Times*, ed. H. Dajani-Shakeel and R. A. Messier, Ann Arbor, 1991, 41–70.

Dajani-Shakeel, H., 'Al-Quds: Jerusalem in the consciousness of the Counter-Crusader', in *The Meeting of Two Worlds*, ed. V. P. Goss, Kalamazoo, 1986, 201–21.

Dajani-Shakeel, H., 'Jihad in twelfth-century Arabic poetry', *MW*, 66 (1976), 96–113.

Dajani-Shakeel, H. and R. A. Mossier (eds), *The Jihad and Its Times*, Ann Arbor, 1991.

Dictionary of the Middle Ages, New York, 1982.

Djait, H., *Europe and Islam*, London, 1985.

Douglas, M., *In the Wilderness: The Doctrine of Defilement in the Book of Numbers*, Sheffield, 1993.

Dowsett, C. J., 'A twelfth-century Armenian inscription at Edessa', in *Iran and Islam*, ed. C. E. Bosworth, Edinburgh, 1971, 197–228.

Dozy, R., *Supplément aux dictionnaires arabes*, Leiden, 1881.

Drory, J., 'Hanbalis of the Nablus region in the eleventh and twelfth centuries', in *The Medieval Levant*, ed. B. Z. Kedar and A. L. Udovitch, Haifa, 1988, 95–112.

Duri, A. A., 'Bait al-Maqdis in Islam', in *Studies in the History and Archaeology of Jordan*, I, ed. A. Hadidi, Amman, 1982, 351–5.

Edbury, P. W., *Crusade and Settlement*, Cardiff, 1985.

Eddé, A. M., 'Claude Cahen et les sources arabes des Croisades', *Arabica*, 43 (1996), 89–97.

Eddé, A. M., 'Les médécins dans la société syrienne du VIIe/XIIIe siècle', *Annales Islamologiques*, 29 (1995), 91–109.

Eddé, A. M., 'Ridwan, prince d'Alep de 1095 à 1113', *REI*, 54 (1986), 103–28.

Eddé, A. M., 'Saint Louis et la Septième Croisade vus par les auteurs arabes', in *Croisades et idée de croisade à la fin du Moyen Âge, Cahiers de Recherches Médiévales* (XIIIe–XVe s), 1 (1996), 65–92.

Eddé, A. M., 'Villes en fête au Proche Orient', in *Villes et sociétés urbaines au Moyen Âge*, Paris, 1994, 71–9.

Edmonds, C. J., *Kurds, Turks and Arabs*, London, 1957.

Ehrenkreutz, A., 'Arabic dinars struck by the Crusaders', *JESHO*, 5 (1964), 167–82.

Ehrenkreutz, A., 'The place of Saladin in the naval history of the Mediterranean

Sea in the Middle Ages', *JAOS*, 75 (1955), 100–16.

Ehrenkreutz, A., *Saladin*, Albany, 1972.

Elad, A., *Medieval Jerusalem and Islamic Worship*, Leiden, 1995.

Elgood, R. (ed.), *Islamic Arms and Armour*, London, 1979.

Elisséeff, N., 'La titulature de Nur al-Din d'après ses inscriptions', *BEO*, 14 (1952–4), 155–96.

Elisséeff, N., 'Les échanges culturels entre le monde musulman et les Croisés à l'époque de Nur al-Din b. Zanki', in *The Meeting of Two Worlds: Cultural Exchange between East and West during the Period of the Crusades*, ed. V. P. Goss, Kalamazoo, 1986, 39–52.

Elisséeff, N., 'Les monuments de Nur al-Din', *BEO*, 12 (1949–51), 5–43.

Elisséeff, N., *Nur al-Din: un grand prince musulman de Syrie au temps des Croisades*, Damascus, 1967.

Ellenblum, R., 'Who built Qal'at al-Subayba?' *Dumbarton Oaks Papers*, 43 (1989), 103–12.

Ende, W., 'Wer ist ein Glaubensheld, wer ist ein Ketzer?', *Die Welt des Islams*, NS 23 (1984), 70–94.

Esposito, J., *Voices of Resurgent Islam*, New York, 1983.

Fahmi, A. M., *Muslim Sea-Power in the Eastern Mediterranean from the Seventh to the Tenth Century AD*, Cairo, 1966.

Faris, N. A. and R. P. Elmer, *Arab Archery*, Princeton, 1945.

Fedden, R. and J. Thomson J, *Crusader Castles*, London, 1957.

Fernandes, L., 'On conducting the affairs of state', *Annales Islamologiques*, 24 (1988), 81–91.

Fierro, M., 'The treatises against innovations (*Kutub al-bida'*)', *Der Islam*, 69 (1992), 204–46.

Fink, H. S., 'Mawdud of Mosul, precursor of Saladin', *MW*, 43 (1953), 18–27.

Fink, H. S., 'The role of Damascus in the history of the Crusades', *MW*, 40 (1950), 41–53.

Finucane, R. C., *Soldiers of Faith*, London and Melbourne, 1983.

Fischel, W., 'The spice trade in Mamluk Egypt: a contribution to the economic history of medieval Islam', *JESHO*, 1 (1958), 157–74.

France, J., 'The First Crusade and Islam', *MW*, 67 (1977), 247–57.

France, J., *Victory in the East*, Cambridge, 1995.

Gabrieli, F., 'Frederick II and Muslim culture', *East and West* (1958), 53–61.

Gabrieli, F., 'The Arabic historiography of the Crusades', in *Historians of the Middle East*, ed. B. Lewis and P. M. Holt, London, 1962, 98–107.

Gaudefroy-Demombynes, M., *La Syrie à l'époque des Mamelouks*, Paris, 1923.

Gibb, H. A. R., 'Al-Barq al-Shami, the history of Saladin by the Katib 'Imad al-Din al-Isfahani', *WZKM*, 52 (1953), 93–115.

Gibb, H. A. R., 'The achievement of Saladin', in *Saladin: Studies in Islamic History*, ed. Y. Ibish, Beirut, 1972.

Gibb, H. A. R., 'The Arabic sources for the life of Saladin', *Speculum*, 25/1 (Jan. 1950), 58–74.

Gibb, H. A. R., 'The armies of Saladin', in *Saladin: Studies in Islamic History*, ed. Y. Ibish, Beirut, 1972, 138–57.

Gibb, H. A. R., *Studies on the Civilisation of Islam*, London, 1962.

Gibb, H. A. R., *The Life of Saladin*, Oxford, 1973.

Gil, M., *A History of Palestine, 634–1099*, Cambridge, 1992.

Goitein, S. D., 'Mediterranean trade in the eleventh century: some facts and problems', in *Studies in the Economic History of the Middle East*, ed. M. Cook, London, 1970, 51–63.

Goitein, S. D., 'The sanctity of Jerusalem and Palestine', in *Studies in Islamic History and Institutions*, ed. S. D. Goitein, Leiden, 1968, 135–48.

Goitein, S. D., *A Mediterranean Society*, Berkeley and Los Angeles, 1967.

Goss, V. P. (ed.), *The Meeting of Two Worlds: Cultural Exchange between East and West during the Period of the Crusades*, Kalamazoo, 1986.

Gottheil, R., 'An answer to the Dhimmis', *JAOS*, 41 (1921), 383–487.

Gottschalk, H. L., *Al-Malik al-Kamil von Ägypten und seine Zeit*, Wiesbaden, 1958.

Gray, B., 'A Fatimid drawing', in *Studies in Chinese and Islamic Art*, II, ed. B. Gray, London, 1987, 193–9.

Grousset, R., *Histoire des Croisades*, Paris, 1934.

Guillebaud, J. C., *Sur la route des Croisades*, Evreux, 1993.

Haarmann, U., *Quellenstudien zur frühen Mamlukenzeit*, Freiburg, 1970.

Haddad, W., 'The Crusaders through Muslim eyes', *MW*, 73 (1983), 234–52.

Hadidi, A. (ed.), *Studies in the History and Archaeology of Jordan*, I, Amman, 1982.

Hakim, H. and J. Jawish, *Saladin und seine Burg*, Damascus, 1998.

Hamblin, W. J., 'Saladin and Muslim military theory', in *The Horns of Hattin*, ed. B. Z. Kedar, Jerusalem, 1992, 228–38.

Hamblin, W. J., 'To wage jihad or not: Fatimid Egypt during the early Crusades', in Dajani-Shakeel and Mossier, *The Jihad and Its Times*, 31–40.

Hamblin, W. J., *The Fatimid Army during the Early Crusades*, Ph.D. thesis, Michigan, 1985.

Hamilton, R. W., *The Structural History of the Aqsa Mosque*, London, 1949.

Hamza, A., *Salah al-Din, batal Hattin*, Cairo, 1958.

Hanisch, H., *Die ayyubidischen Toranlagen der Zitadelle von Damaskus*, Wiesbaden, 1996.

Hanisch, H., 'Masssystem und Massordnung der ayyubidischen Bauten der Zitadelle von Damaskus', *Ordo et Mensura IV–V*, 1998, 341–50.

Hasan, H. I., *Al-Fatimiyyun fi Misr*, Cairo, 1932.

Hassan, I.Y. and D. R. Hill , *Islamic Technology*, Cambridge, 1986.

Hasson, I., 'Muslim literature in praise of Jerusalem: Fada'il Bayt al-Maqdis', in *The Jerusalem Cathedra*, Jerusalem, 1981, 168–84.

Hazard, H. W. (ed.), *A History of the Crusades*, 3: *The Fourteenth and Fifteenth Centuries*, Madison, Wis., 1975.

Heath, P., *The Thirsty Sword: Sirat 'Antar and the Arabic Popular Epic*, Salt Lake City, 1996.

Helbig, A. H., *Al-Qadi al-Fadil, der Wezir Saladins*, Leipzig, 1908.

Herzfeld, E., 'Damascus, studies in architecture', I–IV, *Ars Islamica*, 9 (1942), 1–53; 10 (1943), 13–70; 11–12 (1946), 1–71; 13–14 (1948), 118–38.

Herzfeld, E., *Matériaux pour un corpus inscriptionum arabicarum; Deuxième partie: Syrie du Nord*, I/1, Cairo, 1955.

Heyd, U., *Histoire du commerce du Levant au Moyen Âge*, Paris, 1885.

Hill, D., *Islamic Science and Engineering*, Edinburgh, 1993.

Hillenbrand, C., 'Jihad propaganda in Syria from the time of the First Crusade until the death of Zengi: the evidence of monumental inscriptions', in *The Frankish Wars and Their Influence on Palestine*, ed. K. Athamina and R. Heacock, Birzeit, 1994, 60–9.

Hillenbrand, C., 'The career of Najm al-Din Il-Ghazi', *Der Islam*, 58/2 (1981), 250–92.

Hillenbrand, R., *Islamic Architecture. Form, Function and Meaning*, Edinburgh, 1994.

Hitti, P. K., *History of Syria*, London, 1951.

Hitti, P. K., 'The impact of the Crusades on eastern Christianity', in *Medieval and Middle Eastern Studies in Honour of Aziz Suryal Atiya*, ed. S. A. Hanna, Leiden, 1972, 211–18.

Hiyari, M. A., 'Crusader Jerusalem 1099–1187 AD', in *Jerusalem in History*, ed. K. J. Asali, London, 1989, 130–76.

Hodgson, M. G. S., *Rethinking World History*, ed. E. Burke III, Cambridge, 1993.

Hodgson, M. G. S., *The Venture of Islam*, Chicago, 1973.

Holt, P. M., 'Al-Nasir Muhammad's letter to a Spanish ruler in 699/1300', *Al-Masaq*, 3 (1990), 23–9.

Holt, P. M., 'Baybars' treaty with the Lady of Beirut in 667/1269', in *Crusade and Settlement*, ed. P. W. Edbury, Cardiff, 1985, 242–5.

Holt, P. M., 'Mamluk–Frankish diplomatic relations in the reign of Baybars', *Nottingham Medieval Studies*, 32 (1988), 180–95.

Holt, P. M., 'Qalawun's treaty with the Latin kingdom (682/1283): negotiation and abrogation', in *Egypt and Syria in the Fatimid, Ayyubid and Mamluk Eras*, eds U. Vermeulen and D. de Smet, Leiden, 1995, 325–34.

Holt, P. M., 'Saladin and his admirers; a biographical reassessment', *BSOAS*, 46 (1983), 235–9.

Holt, P. M., 'Some observations on Shafi' b. 'Ali's biography of Baybars', *JSS*, 29 (1984), 123–30.

Holt, P. M., 'The presentation of Qalawun by Shafi' ibn 'Ali', in *The Islamic World from Classical to Modern Times: Essays in Honor of Bernard Lewis*, eds C. E. Bosworth, C. Issawi, R. Savory and A. L. Udovitch, Princeton, 1989, 141–50.

Holt, P. M., 'The sultan as ideal ruler: Ayyubid and Mamluk prototypes', in *Suleyman the Magnificent and His Age*, eds M. Kunt and C. Woodhead, Harrow, 1995, 122–37.

Holt, P. M., 'The treaties of the early Mamluk sultans with the Frankish states', *BSOAS*, 43 (1980), 67–76.

Holt, P. M., 'Three biographies of al-Zahir Baybars', in *Medieval Historical Writing in the Christian Worlds*, ed. D. Morgan, London, 1982, 19–29.

Holt, P. M., *Early Mamluk Diplomacy*, Leiden, 1995.

Holt, P. M., *The Age of the Crusades*, London, 1986.

Holt, P. M. (ed.), *The Eastern Mediterranean Lands in the Period of the Crusades*, Warminster, 1977.

Hourani, G. F., *Arab Seafaring in the Indian Ocean in Ancient and Medieval Times*, Beirut, 1963.

Housley, N., *The Later Crusades*, Oxford, 1992.

Humphreys, R. S., 'Ayyubids, Mamluks, and the Latin East in the thirteenth century', *Mamluk Studies Review*, 2 (1998), 1–18.

Humphreys, R. S., 'Legitimacy and instability in Islam', in *The Jihad and Its Times*, ed. H. Dajani-Shakeel and R. A. Messier, Ann Arbor, 1991, 10–11.

Humphreys, R. S., *From Saladin to the Mongols*, Albany, NY, 1977.

Humphreys, R. S., *Islamic History: A Framework for Inquiry*, Princeton, 1991.

Ibrahim, M., *Fada'il bayt al-muqaddas*, Kuwait, 1985.

Imber, C., *Ebu's Su'ud: The Islamic Legal Tradition*, Edinburgh, 1997.

Inan, M. A., *Mu'arrikhu Misr*, Cairo, 1969.

Irwin, R., 'Islam and the Crusades, 1096–1699', in *The Oxford History of the Crusades*, ed. J. Riley-Smith, Oxford and New York, 1955, 217–59.

Irwin, R., 'The image of the Byzantine and the Frank in Arab popular literature of the late Middle Ages', in *Latins and Greeks in the Eastern Mediterranean after 1204*, ed. B. Arbel, B. Hamilton and D. Jacoby, London, 1989, 226–42.

Irwin, R., *The Arabian Nights: A Companion*, London, 1994.

Irwin, R., *The Middle East in the Middle Ages*, London, 1986.

Islam Ansiklopedesi, art.: cihad.

Issawi, C., 'Crusades and current crises in the Near East', *International Affairs*, 33/3 (July 1957), 269–79.

Janabi, al-, T., *Studies in Medieval Iraqi Architecture*, Baghdad, 1983.

Jansen, G. H., *Militant Islam*, London, 1979.

Johns, C. N., 'Medieval 'Ajlun', *Quarterly of the Department of Antiquities in Palestine*, 1 (1931), 21–33.

Johnson, J. Turner and J. Kelsay (eds), *Cross, Crescent and Sword*, 1990.

Jones, T. and A. Ereira, *The Crusades*, Harmondsworth, 1994.

Jumayli, al-, R., *Dawlat al-atabaka fi'l-Mawsil*, Beirut, 1970.

Jurji, E. J., 'The Islamic theory of war', *MW*, 30 (1940), 332–42.

Juynboll, Th. W., *Handbuch des islamischen Gesetzes nach der Lehre der schafi'itischen Schule*, Leiden and Leipzig, 1910.

Katzir, Y., 'The conquests of Jerusalem, 1099 and 1187: historical memory and religious typology', in *The Meeting of Two Worlds*, ed. V. P. Goss, Kalamazoo, 1986, 103–13.

Kedar, B. (ed.), *The Horns of Hattin*, Jerusalem, 1992.

Kedar, B. Z., 'The subjected Muslims of the Levant', in *Muslims under Latin Rule, 1100–1300*, ed. J. M.Powell, Princeton, 1990, 135–74.

Kedar, B. Z., *Crusade and Mission*, Princeton, 1984.

Kedar, B. Z. and A. L. Udovitch (eds), *The Medieval Levant*, Haifa, 1988.

Keegan, J. D. P., *A History of Warfare*, London, 1993.

Keegan, J. D. P., *The Face of Battle*, London, 1976.

Kennedy, H., *Crusader Castles*, Cambridge, 1994.

Khadduri, M., *War and Peace in the Law of Islam*, Baltimore, 1955.

Khalidi, T., *Arabic Historical Thought in the Classical Period*, Cambridge, 1994.

Khalidi, W., *Islam, the West and Jerusalem*, Washington, DC, 1996.

Khattab, A., *Das Bild der Franken in der Litteratur des Mittelalters*, Göppingen, 1989.

Khowaiter, A. A., *Baybars the First*, London, 1978.

Kishtainy, K., *Arab Political Humour*, London, 1985.

Koch, Y., ''Izz al-Din ibn Shaddad and his biography of Baybars', *Annali dell'Istituto Universitario Orientale*, 43 (1983), 249–87.

Köhler, M. A., 'Al-Afdal und Jerusalem – was versprach sich Ägypten vom ersten Kreuzzug?', *Saeculum*, 37 (1986), 228–39.

Köhler, M. A., *Allianzen und Verträge zwischen frankischen und islamischen Herrschern im Vorderen Orient*, Berlin and New York, 1991.

Kreyenbrock, P. and C. Allison (eds), *Kurdish Culture and Identity*, London, 1996.

Krüger, H., *Fetwa und Siyar*, Wiesbaden, 1978.

Kruk, R., 'Back to the boudoir: Arabic versions of the Sirat al-amir Hamza, warrior princesses, and the Sira's literary unity', unpublished paper.

Kruk, R., 'The bold and the beautiful. Women and *fitna* in the Sirat Dhat al-Himma: the story of Nura', in *Women in the Medieval Islamic World: Power, Patronage, Piety*, ed. G. R. G. Hambly, New York, 1998, 99–116.

Lammens, H., 'Bilad Suriya fi'l-qarn aṱ-ṱani 'asar wifqan li-riwayat Ibn Gubair', *Al-Mashriq*, 10 (1907), 787–97.

Lane-Poole, S., *A History of Egypt in the Middle Ages*, Karachi, 1977.

Lane-Poole, S., *Saladin and the Fall of the Kingdom of Jerusalem*, London and New York, 1898.

Lane-Poole, S., *The Story of Cairo*, London, 1902.

Laoust, H., *Essai sur les doctrines sociales et politiques d'Ibn Taymiyya*, Cairo, 1939.

Laoust, H., *Le précis de droit d'Ibn Qudama*, Beirut, 1950.

Lapidus, I. M., *Muslim Cities in the Later Middle Ages*, Cambridge, Mass., 1967.

Latham, J. D. and W. F. Paterson, *Saracen Archery*, London, 1970.

Le Strange, G., *Palestine under the Moslems*, Beirut, 1965.

Lev, Y., 'Army, regime and society in Fatimid Egypt 358–487/968–1094', *IJMES*, 19 (1987), 337–66.

Lev, Y., *State and Society in Fatimid Egypt*, Leiden, 1991.

Lev, Y. (ed.), *War and Society in the Eastern Mediterranean, 7th–15th Centuries*, Leiden, 1997.

Lewis, A., 'Mediterranean Maritime Commerce, AD 300–1100', in A. Lewis, *The Sea and Medieval Civilisations*, London, 1978, 1–21.

Lewis, A., *Nomads and Crusaders*, Bloomington, 1991.

Lewis, B., 'The use by Muslim historians of non-Muslim sources', in *Historians of the Middle East*, ed. B. Lewis and P. M. Holt, London, 1962, 180–91.

Lewis, B., *Studies in Classical and Ottoman Islam (7th–16th Centuries)*, London, 1976.

Lewis, B., *The Middle East and the West*, New York, 1964.

Lewis, B., *The Muslim Discovery of Europe*, London, 1982.

Lewis, B., *The Political Language of Islam*, Chicago and London, 1991.

Lewis, B. and P. M. Holt, (eds), *Historians of the Middle East*, London, 1962.

Lindner, R., 'Nomadism, horses and Huns', *Past and Present*, 92 (1981), 3–19.

Little, D. P., 'Jerusalem under the Ayyubids and Mamluks 1197–1516 AD', in *Jerusalem in History*, ed. K. J. Asali, London, 1989, 177–200.

Little, D. P., 'The fall of 'Akka in 690/1291: the Muslim version', in *Studies in Islamic History and Civilisation in Honour of Professor David Ayalon*, ed. M. Sharon, Jerusalem, 1986, 159–82.

Little, D. P., *An Introduction to Mamluk Historiography*, Montreal, 1970.

Lutfi, H., *Al-Quds al-mamlukiyya*, Cairo, 1985.

Lyons, M. C., 'The Crusading stratum in the Arabic hero cycles', in Shatzmiller, *Crusaders and Muslims*, 147–61.

Lyons, M. C., *The Arabian Epic: Heroic and Oral Storytelling*, Cambridge, 1995.

Lyons, M. C. and D. E. P. Jackson, *Saladin: The Politics of the Holy War*, Cambridge, 1982.

Maalouf, A., *The Crusades through Arab Eyes*, London, 1984.

Mackenzie, N. D., 'The fortifications of al-Qahira (Cairo) under the Ayyubids', in *The Jihad and Its Times*, ed. H. Dajani-Shakeel and R. A. Messier, Ann Arbor, 1991, 71–94.

Mackenzie, N. D., *Ayyubid Cairo: A Topographical Study*, Cairo, 1992.

Marshall, C., *Warfare in the Latin East, 1192–1291*, Cambridge, 1992.

Matthews, C. D., 'A Muslim iconoclast (Ibn Taimiyya) on the "merits" of Jerusalem and Palestine', *JAOS*, 56 (1936), 1–21.

Matthews, C. D., *Palestine–Mohammedan Holy Land*, Yale Oriental Series, XXIV, New Haven, 1949.

Mattock, J., 'The travel writings of Ibn Jubair and Ibn Battuta', *Glasgow Oriental Society Transactions*, 16 (1965–6), 35–46.

Matwi, al-, M., *Al-hurub al-salibiyya*, Tunis, 1954.

Mayer, H. E., 'Latins, Muslims and Greeks in the Latin Kingdom of Jerusalem', *History*, 63 (1978), 175–92.

Mayer, H. E., *Bibliographie zur Geschichte der Kreuzzüge*, Hanover, 1960.

Mayer, H. E., *The Crusades*, Oxford, 1972.

Mayer, L. A., 'Saracenic arms and armor', *Ars Islamica*, 10 (1943), 1–12.

Mayer, L. A., *Islamic Armourers and Their Works*, Geneva, 1962.

Mayer, L. A., *Saracenic Heraldry*, Oxford, 1933.

Melville, C. P. and M. C. Lyons, 'Saladin's Hattin letter', in *The Horns of Hattin*, ed. B. Z. Kedar, Jerusalem and London, 1992, 208–12.

Michaud, M., *Histoire des Croisades*, Paris, 1829.

Michaud, M., *L'histoire des Croisades abrégée à l'usage de la jeunesse*, Tours, 1876.

Micheau, F., 'Croisades et croisés vus par les historiens arabes chrétiens d'Égypte', *Itinéraires d'Orient: Hommages à Claude Cahen, Res Orientales*, 6 (1994), 169–85.

Miquel, A., *La géographie humaine du monde musulman*, Paris and The Hague, 1967.

Mirza, N. A., *Syrian Isma'ilism*, London, 1997.

Mitchell, R. P., *The Society of the Muslim Brothers*, Oxford, 1993.

Möhring, H., 'Der andere Islam: Zum Bild vom toleranten Sultan Saladin', in *Die Begegnung des Westens mit dem Osten*, eds O. Engels and P. Schreiner, Sigmaringen, 1991, 131–56.

Möhring, H., 'Saladins Politik des Heiligen Krieges', *Der Islam*, 61 (1984), 322–6.

Möhring, H., *Saladin und der dritte Kreuzzug*, Wiesbaden, 1980.

Morabia, A., 'Ibn Taymiyya, dernier grand théoricien du jihad médiéval', *BEO*, 30/2 (1978), 85–99.

Morabia, A, *Le gihad dans l'islam médiéval*, Paris, 1993.

Morray, D., *An Ayyubid Notable and His World*, Leiden, 1994.

Morray, D., *The Genius of Usama ibn Munqidh*, Durham, 1987.

Mortimer, E., *Faith and Power: The Politics of Islam*, London, 1982.

Mouton, J.-M., *Damas et sa principauté sous les Saljoukides el les Bourides 468–549/1076–1154*, Cairo, 1994.

Muir, W., *The Mamelouke or Slave Dynasty of Egypt*, London, 1896.

Murphy, T. P. (ed.), *The Holy War*, Columbus, 1976.

Muslih, M., 'Palestinian images of Jerusalem' in *City of the Great King*, ed. N. Rosovsky, Cambridge, Mass., and London, 1996, 178–201.

Nasr, S. H., *Islamic Spirituality*, 2 vols, London, 1987.

Nasrallah, A., *The Enemy Perceived: Christian and Muslim Views of Each Other during the Crusades*, New York, 1980.

Netton, I. R., 'Ibn Jubayr: penitent pilgrim and observant traveller' in I. R. Netton, *Seek Knowledge: Thought and Travel in the House of Islam*, Richmond, 1996, 95–102.

Nicolle, D., 'An introduction to arms and warfare in classical Islam', in R. Elgood, *Islamic Arms and Armour*, London, 1979, 162–76.

Nicolle, D., 'Saljuq arms and armour in art and literature', in *The Art of the Saljuqs in Iran and Anatolia*, ed. R. Hillenbrand, Costa Mesa, 1994, 247–56.

Nicolle, D., 'The impact of the European couched lance on Muslim military tradition', *The Journal of the Arms and Armour Society* (June 1980), 6–40.

Nicolle, D., 'The reality of Mamluk warfare: weapons, armour and tactics', *Al-Masaq*, 7 (1994), 77–110.

Nicolle, D., *Early Medieval Islamic Arms and Armour*, Madrid, 1976.

Nicolle, D., *Islamische Waffen*, Graz, 1981.

Nicolle, D., *Saladin and the Saracens*, London, 1986.

Niermann, J. H., 'Levantine peace following the third Crusade: a new dimension in Frankish–Muslim relations', *MW*, 65 (1975), 107–18.

Norris, H. T., *The Adventures of Antar*, Warminster, 1980.

Noth, A., 'Heiliger Kampf (Gihad) gegen die "Franken": Zur Position der Kreuzzüge im Rahmen der Islamgeschichte', *Saeculum*, 37 (1986), 240–59.

Noth, A., *Heiliger Krieg und heiliger Kampf*, Bonn, 1986.

Nusse, A., 'The ideology of Hamas: Palestinian Islamic fundamentalist thought on the Jews, Israel and Islam', in *Studies in Muslim–Jewish Relations*, I, ed. R. L. Nettler, Chur, 1993, 97–127.

Ochsenwald, W. L., 'The Crusader kingdom of Jerusalem and Israel: an historical comparison', *Middle East Journal*, 30 (1976), 221–6.

Oman, C. W. C., *A History of the Art of War in the Middle Ages*, London, 1924.

Parry, V. J. and M. E. Yapp (eds), *War, Technology and Society in the Middle East*, London, 1975.

Partner, P., *God of Battles*, London, 1997.

Peters, R., *Jihad in Classical and modern Islam*, Princeton, 1996.

Peters, R., *Jihad in Medieval and Modern Islam*, Leiden, 1977.

Petersen, A., 'Two forts on the medieval Hajj route in Jordan', *Annual of the Department of Antiquities in Jordan*, 35 (1991), 347–59.

Philipp, T. and U. Haarmann (eds), *The Mamluks in Egyptian Politics and Society*, Cambridge, 1998.

Phillips, J. (ed.), *The First Crusade*, Manchester, 1997.

Picard, C., *La mer et les musulmans d'Occident au Moyen Âge*, Paris, 1997.

Pouzet, L., *Damas au VIIe/XIIIe siècle*, Beirut, 1988.

Powell, J. M. (ed.), *Muslims under Latin Rule, 1100–1300*, Princeton, 1990.

Prawer, J., *The Crusaders' Kingdom*, New York, 1972.

Prawer, J., *The Latin Kingdom of Jerusalem*, London, 1972.

Pringle, R. D., *Secular buildings in the Crusader Kingdom of Jerusalem. An archaeological gazeteer*, Cambridge, 1997.

Pringle, R. D., 'The state of research: the archaeology of the Crusader Kingdom of Jerusalem: a review of work 1947–97', *Journal of Medieval History*, 23/4 (1997), 389–408.

Pringle, R. D., *The Red Tower*, London, 1986.

Pryor, J. H., 'The transportation of horses by sea during the era of the Crusades', in J. H. Pryor, *Commerce, Shipping and Naval Warfare in the Medieval Mediterranean*, London, 1987, vol. V, 9–27, 103–25.

Rabbat, N. O., 'The ideological significance of the Dar al-'Adl in the medieval Islamic Orient', *IJMES*, 27 (1995), 3–28.

Rabbat, N. O., *The Citadel of Cairo*, Leiden, 1995.

Rabie, H., 'The training of the Mamluk Faris', in *War, Technology and Society in the Middle East*, eds V. J. Parry and M. E. Yapp, London, 1975, 153–63.

Reinaud, M., 'De l'art militaire chez les Arabes au Moyen Âge', *JA* (1848), 193–236.

Renard, J., *Islam and the Heroic Image*, Columbia, SC, 1993.

Richards, D. S., 'A consideration of two sources for the life of Saladin', *JSS*, 25/1 (1980), 46–65.

Richards, D. S., 'A text of 'Imad al-Din on 12th century Frankish–Muslim relations', *Arabica*, 25 (1978), 202–4.

Richards, D. S., 'Dhimmi problems in fifteenth century Cairo', in *Studies in Muslim–Jewish Relations*, I, ed. R. L. Nettler, Chur, 1993, 127–63.

Richards, D. S., 'Ibn al-Athir and the later parts of the *Kamil*', in *Medieval Historical Writing in the Christian and Islamic Worlds*, ed. D. O. Morgan, London, 1982, 76–108.

Richter-Bernburg, L., 'Funken aus dem alten Flint: 'Imad al-Din al-Katib al-Isfahani', *Die Welt des Orients*, 20–21 (1990), 121–66; 22 (1991), 15–41.

Rikabi, J., *La poésie profane sous les Ayyoubides*, Paris, 1949.

Riley-Smith, J., 'Government in Latin Syria and the commercial privileges of foreign merchants', in *Relations between East and West in the Middle Ages*, ed. D. Baker, Edinburgh, 1973, 109–32.

Riley-Smith, J., *The Atlas of the Crusades*, London, 1991.

Riley-Smith, J., *The Crusades: A Short History*, London and New Haven, 1987.

Riley-Smith, J., *The First Crusaders 1095–1131*, Cambridge, 1997.

Riley-Smith, J., *What Were the Crusades?*, London, 1992.

Riley-Smith, J. (ed.), *The Oxford Illustrated History of the Crusades*, Oxford, 1995.

Riley-Smith, L. and J., *The Crusades: Idea and Reality 1095–1274*, London, 1981.

Ritter, H., 'La parure des cavaliers', *Der Islam*, 18 (1929), 116–54.

Rogers, J. M., *The Spread of Islam*, Oxford, 1972.

Rogers, J. M. and R. Ward, *Süleyman the Magnificent*, London, 1998.

Röhricht, R., *Beiträge zur Geschichte der Kreuzzüge*, Berlin, 1874.

Rosen-Ayalon, M., 'Art and architecture in Ayyubid Jerusalem', *Israel Exploration Journal*, 40/1 (1990), 305–14.

Rosenthal, F., *A History of Muslim Historiography*, Leiden, 1968.

Runciman, S., 'Islam and Christendom in the Middle Ages – the need for restatement', *Islamic Studies*, 3 (1964), 193–8.

Runciman, S., *A History of the Crusades*, 3 vols, Cambridge, 1951–4.

Russell-Robinson, H., *Oriental Armour*, London, 1967.

Sa'dawi, N. H., *Al-mu'arrikhun al-mu'asirun li-Salah al-Din*, Cairo, 1962.

Sage, M. M., *Warfare in Ancient Greece*, London and New York, 1996.

Said, E., *Orientalism*, New York, 1979.

Salibi, K. S., *Syria under Islam*, Delmare, NY, 1977.

Salim, A. A., *Tarikh al-bahriyya al-islamiyya fi hawd al-bahr al-abyad al-mutawassit*, n.p., 1981.

Sauvaget, J., 'Decrets mamelouks', *BEO*, 2 (1932), 1–52; 3 (1933), 1–29.

Sauvaget, J., 'La tombe de l'Ortokide Balak', *Ars Islamica*, 5/2 (1938), 207–15.

Sauvaget, J., *Alep*, Paris, 1941.

Sauvaget, J., 'La citadelle de Damas', *Syria*, XI (1930), 59–90, 216–41.

Sayyid, A. F., 'Lumières nouvelles sur quelques sources de l'histoire fatimide en Egypte', *Annales Islamologiques*, 13 (1977), 1–41.

Sayyid, A. F., *Les Fatimides en Egypte*, Cairo, 1992.

Scerrato, U., 'The first two excavation campaigns at Ghazni, 1957–1958', *East and West* N.S. 10 (1959), 23–55.

Schimmel, A. M., *Deciphering the signs of God*, Edinburgh, 1994.

Schlumberger, D., 'Le palais ghaznévide de Lashkari Bazar', *Syria*, 29 (1952), 251–70.

Serjeant, R. B., 'Notices on the "Frankish chancre" (syphilis) in Yemen, Egypt and Syria', *JSS*, 10 (1965), 241–52.

Setton, K. M. and M. W. Baldwin (eds), *A History of the Crusades*, 6 vols, Madison, Wis., 1969–89.

Sevim, A., *Süriye-Filistin Selçuklu devleti tarihi*, Ankara, 1989.

Sezgin, F. (ed.), *Studies on Ibn Gubair*, Frankfurt, 1994.

Shalem, A., 'A note on the shield-shaped ornamental bosses on the facade of Bab al-Nasr in Cairo', *Ars Orientalis*, 26 (1996), 55–64.

Shatzmiller, M. (ed.), *Crusaders and Muslims in Twelfth-Century Syria*, Leiden, 1993.

Situdeh, M., *Qila' Isma'iliyya*, Tehran, 1983.

Sivan, E., 'La genèse de la contre-croisade', *JA*, 254 (1966), 197–224.

Sivan, E., 'Le caractère sacré de Jerusalem dans l'Islam aux XIIe–XIIIe siècles', *SI*, 27 (1967), 149–82.

Sivan, E., 'Notes sur la situation des chrétiens à l'époque ayyubide', *Revue de l'Histoire des Religions*, 172 (1967), 117–30.

Sivan, E., 'Réfugiés syro-palestiniens au temps des Croisades', *REI*, 25 (1965), 135–47.

Sivan, E., 'The beginnings of the Fada'il al-Quds literature', *Israel Oriental Studies*, 1 (1971), 263–72.

Sivan, E., 'The Crusaders described by modern Arab historiography', *Asian and African Studies*, 8 (1972), 104–49.

Sivan, E., *L'Islam et la Croisade*, Paris, 1968.

Sivan, E., *Radical Islam*, Newhaven, Conn., 1989.

Smail, R. C., *Crusading Warfare 1097–1193*, Cambridge, 1967.

Smail, R. C., *The Crusaders in Syria and the Holy Land*, London, 1973.

Smith, R., *Medieval Muslim Horsemanship*, London, 1979.

Sourdel, D. and J. Sourdel-Thomine, 'Un texte d'invocation en faveur de deux princes ayyoubides', in *Near Eastern Numismatics, Iconography, Epigraphy and History Studies in Honor of George C. Miles*, ed. D. K. Kouymjan, Beirut, 1974, 347–52.

Sourdel-Thomine, J., 'Les conseils du shaykh al-Harawi à un prince ayyoubide', *BEO*, 17 (1961–2), 205–66.

Spengler, W. F. and W. S. Sayles, *Turkoman Figural Bronze Coins and Their Iconography*, I, Lodi, 1996.

Stevenson, W. B., *The Crusaders in the East*, Cambridge, 1907.

Storm-Rice, D., *Le baptistère de St. Louis*, Paris, 1953.

Suleiman, K. A., *Palestine and Modern Arabic Poetry*, London, 1984.

Suleiman, Y., 'Nationalist concerns in the poetry of Nazik al-Mala'ika', *BRISMES Journal*, 22/1–2 (1995), 93–114.

Tabbaa, Y., 'Monuments with a message: Propagation of Jihad under Nur al-Din', in *The Meeting of Two Worlds*, ed. V. P. Goss, Kalamazoo, 1986, 223–40.

Taheri, A., *Holy Terror*, London, 1987.

Taheri, A., *The Spirit of Allah*, London, 1985.

Taji-Farouki, S., 'A case in contemporary political Islam and the Palestine question', in Nettler, *Studies*, II, 35–58.

Taji-Farouki, S., *A Fundamental Quest: Hizb al-tahrir and the Search for the Islamic Caliphate*, London, 1996.

Tamimi, al-, M. R., *Al-hurub al-salibiyya*, Jerusalem, 1945.

Tate, G., *The Crusades and the Holy Land*, London, 1996.

Thorau, P., *The Lion of Egypt*, trans. P. M. Holt, London, 1992.

Tu'ma, al-, S. J., *Salah al-Din fi'l-shi'r al-'arabi*, Riyadh, 1979.

Van Berchem, M., 'Eine arabische Inschrift aus dem Ostjordanlande', in M. van Berchem, *Opera Minora*, I, Geneva, 1978, 539–60.

Van Berchem, M., *Matériaux pour un corpus inscriptionum arabicarum*, II: *Jérusalem* [I: *Ville*] (Mémoires publiés par les membres de l'IFAO du Caire, XLIII/1–2), Cairo, 1922–3.

Viré, F., *Le traité de l'art de la volerie*, London, 1967.

Wansborough, J., 'Venice and Florence in the Mamluk commercial privileges', *BSOAS*, 28 (1965), 483–523.

Weber, E. and R. Reynaud, *Croisade d'hier, Djihad aujourd'hui*, Paris, 1989.

White, L., jun., 'The Crusades and the technological thrust of the west', in *War, Technology and Society in the Middle East*, ed. V. J. Parry and M. E. Yapp, London, 1975, 97–112.

Wiet, G., 'Les inscriptions de Saladin', *Syria*, 3 (1922), 307–28.

Wise, T., *Armies of the Crusades*, London, 1978.

Wright, R., *Sacred Rage: The Crusade of Modern Islam*, London, 1986.

Yared-Riachi, M., *La politique extérieure de la principauté de Damas, 468–549 H/1076–1154*, Damascus, 1997.

Zakkar, S., *Al-hurub al-salibiyya*, Damascus, 1984.

Zettersteen, K. V., *Beiträge zur Geschichte der Mamluksultane*, Leiden, 1919.

Author's note

Unfortunately the following books and articles were not available in time to be consulted:

Lev, Y., *Saladin in Egypt*, Leiden, 1999.

Khoury, N. N., 'Narratives of the Holy Land: memory, identity and inverted imagery in the Freer Basin and Canteen', *Orientations*, May 1998, 63–9.

Tabbaa,. Y., *Constructions of power and piety in medieval Aleppo*, College Park, 1997.

Index

647